Painting Trees

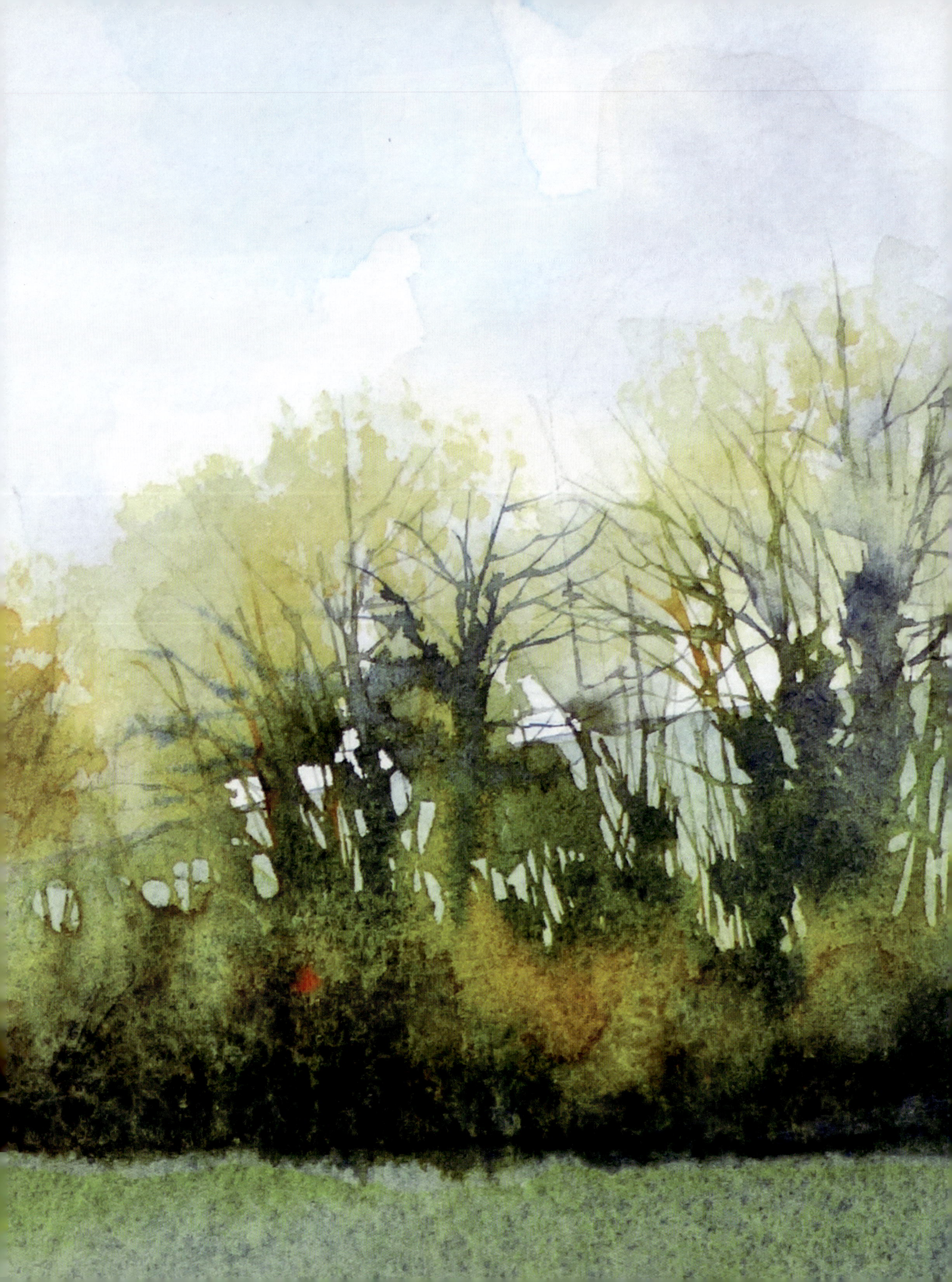

Painting Trees

Colour, Line and Texture through the Seasons

SIÂN AND ROB DUDLEY

THE CROWOOD PRESS

First published in 2019 by
The Crowood Press Ltd
Ramsbury, Marlborough
Wiltshire SN8 2HR

www.crowood.com

British Library Cataloguing-in-Publication Data
A catalogue record for this book is available from the British Library.

ISBN 978 1 78500 601 2

Frontispiece: *Tree Study, Modbury* (detail), watercolour, 10cm × 12cm (4in × 4¾in), Rob Dudley.

Dedication
For Huw, for quiet and steadfast support
and for helping us to stay rooted.
Thank you.

Graphic design and typesetting by Peggy & Co. Design Inc.
Printed and bound in India by Parksons Graphics

Contents

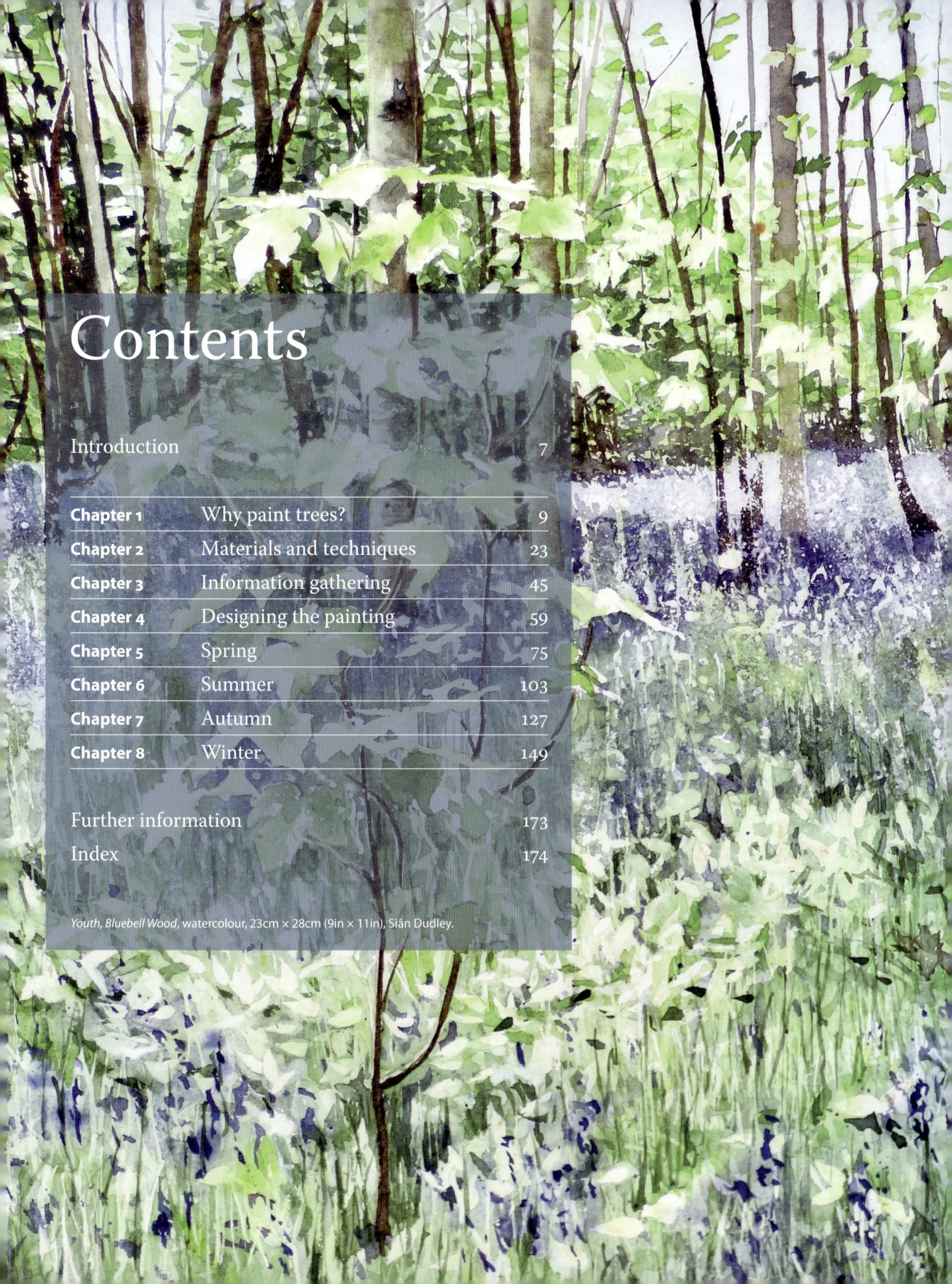

Youth, Bluebell Wood, watercolour, 23cm × 28cm (9in × 11in), Siân Dudley.

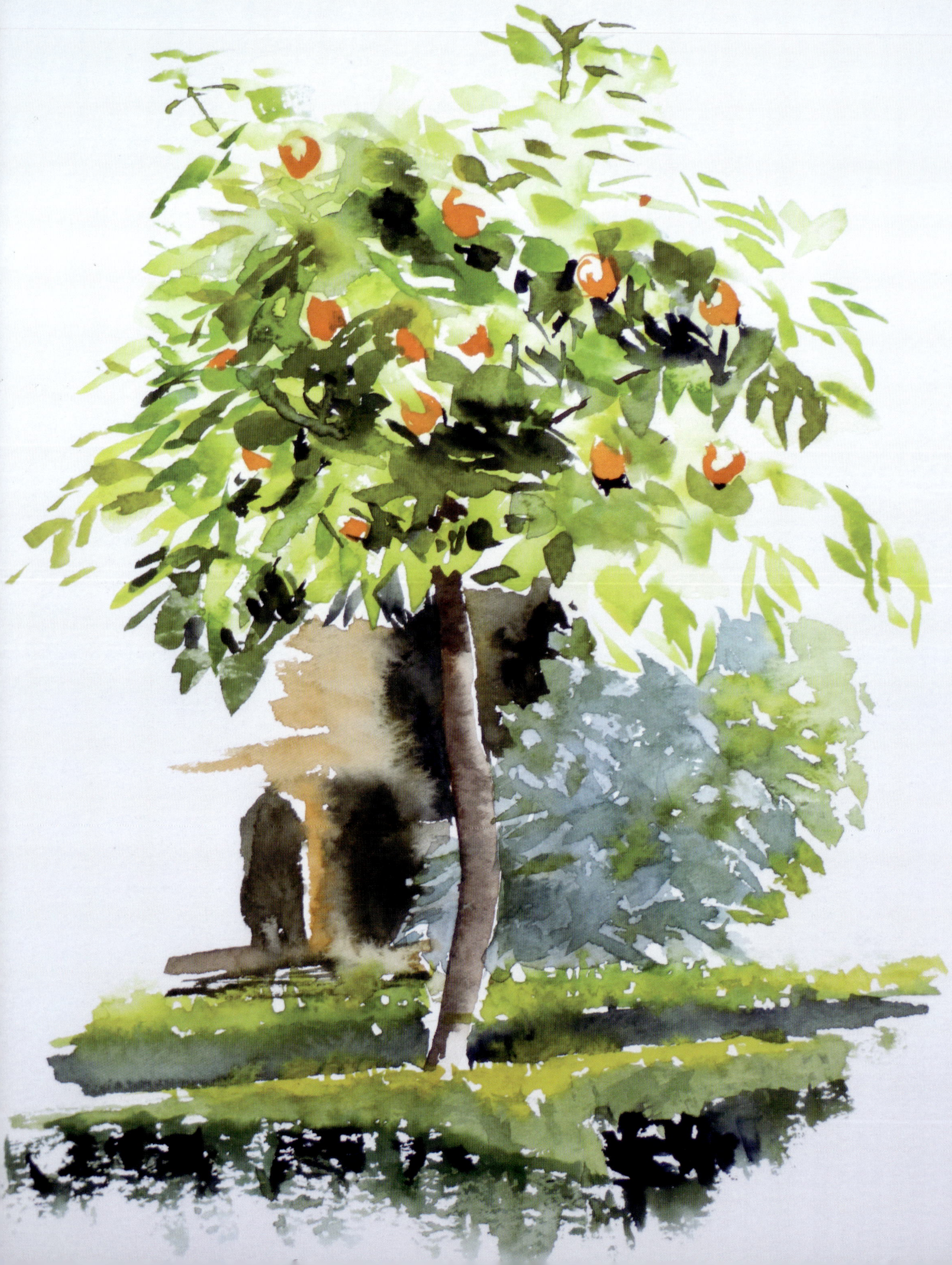

Introduction

As much as we love painting, and we really do love painting, we also enjoy watching other people delight in realizing that it is perfectly possible to learn how to do it. Achieving success in art is not magic, is not entirely due to innate talent and is rarely due to good luck. The one essential ingredient is having the desire to do it; as long as that is present, we believe that anyone can learn to paint.

Although a little bit of innate talent and an element of luck are undoubtedly helpful, continued success and progression result from the same attitudes that are important in every other part of life: endeavour, commitment and hard work. But do not let this put you off! As long as the desire to be creative is present, the effort that you put in will not seem at all like work.

As in other walks of life, when learning something new, it helps to have some sort of structure to guide you. In this book, we have tried to provide just that, by describing our working method. While, as artists, we have our own styles, we have worked and taught together for years and realized that our modi operandi are very similar. Through teaching together, we have developed a method of describing how we work that has enabled many, many students to get started, improve and progress to developing their own styles. Just as a modicum of talent can help, so does a modicum of discipline and, far from restricting creativity, it enhances it, freeing you up to enjoy painting *your* way, creating the art that *you* want to make.

Orange Tree, watercolour, 22cm × 28cm (8¾in × 11in), Siân Dudley. This sketch was made during a short visit to the Carmen de los Mártires gardens, Granada.

Trees are a versatile and fascinating subject matter as a basis for learning how to design and create a painting. Trees provide the most wonderful inspiration for us throughout the year, making crisp, winter sketching trips just as enjoyable as are those on warm, summer days.

The later chapters in this book comprise a series of step-by-step projects, organized according to the seasons. It is not just the quantity and colour of foliage that changes with the seasons, but the very character of trees and the impact this has on the mood of a painting change too. Similarly, the way that the trees are painted, the trees' placement on the page, the medium chosen and the techniques used to apply the paint have an impact on the way that a viewer responds to a painting. Within the step-by-step projects, you will find plenty of ideas and technical advice about how to make design decisions, so that you can paint trees expressively.

As we describe in Chapter 1, trees appear in paintings for different reasons and, in the step-by-step projects, we have attempted to cover a number of them. In some of these projects, the trees are the main subject of the painting; in others, they appear in the background or as the supporting act for the main subject.

The variety of ways in which trees are painted is so vast that one book simply could not cover it all. This book focuses on painterly, figurative styles, although we hope that the approach taken will encourage you to take this as a starting point and to develop your own way of working. You will be encouraged to think about what interests *you* and how *you* want to paint. In time, we hope that you will develop your own figurative way of working, or maybe even find yourself adopting a far more abstract style.

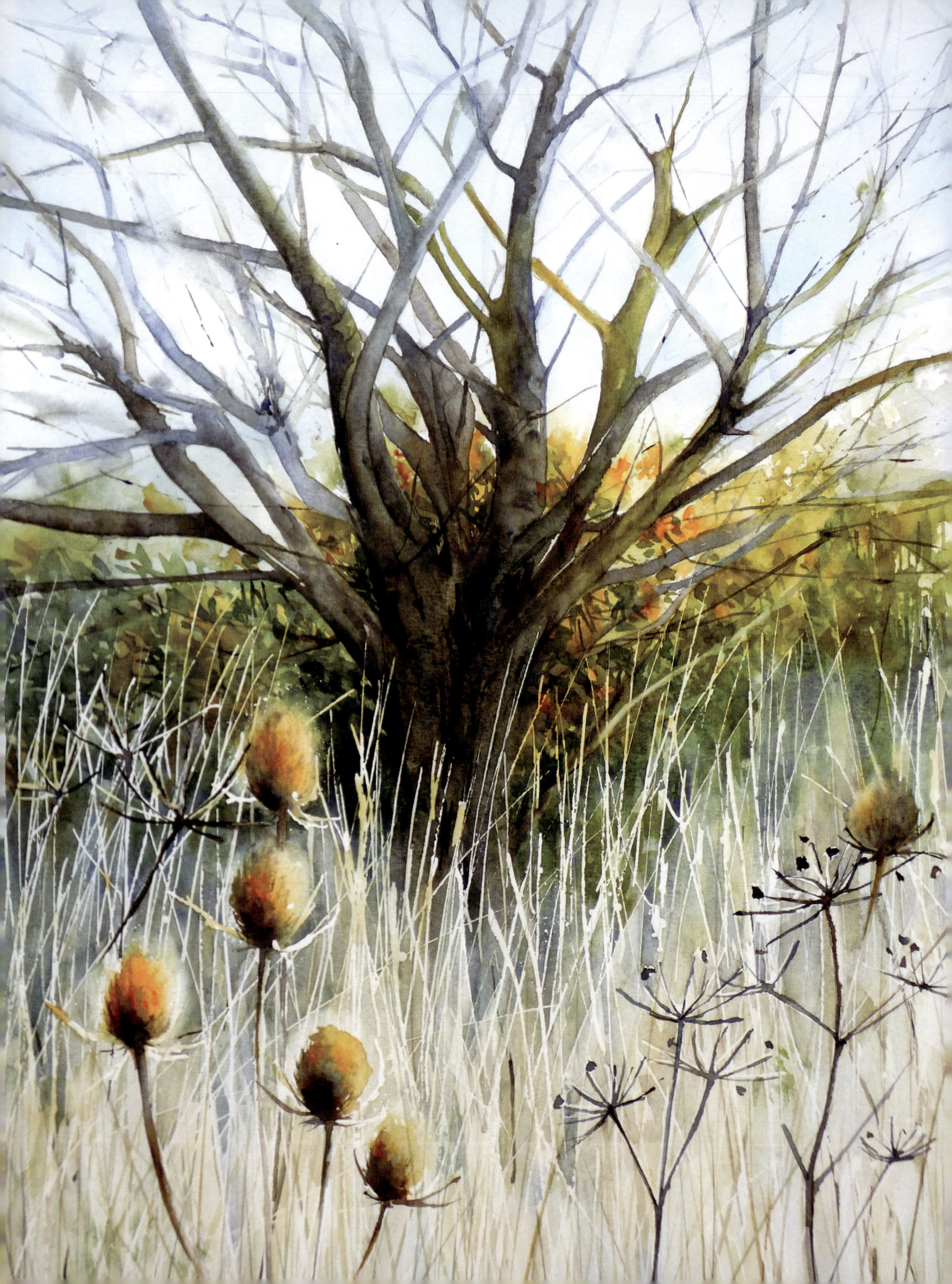

Chapter 1

Why paint trees?

Trees have captured the human imagination since the beginning of time. Through the ages, and in all corners of the globe, trees have played a prominent part in the lives of humans. Our relationship with them may have originated from an intuitive understanding of their significance to our physical well-being, dating back to our ancient ancestors. Trees meet our needs in so many different ways that our relationship with them goes beyond the purely physical, touching us at every level of human experience. It is perhaps not surprising that we feel an emotional bond with them and relate to them more closely than with almost any other plant. It is rare to find a person who does not like trees!

It is unsurprising then, that trees feature abundantly in the arts, inspiring poetry, literature, architecture and of course, painting. It is their place, or maybe their participation, in the latter with which we are concerned in this book.

Trees are so much part of our lives, so natural a choice of subject matter, that asking the question 'Why do you want to paint trees?' may seem superfluous. Yet, giving the question some serious thought might lead to some unexpected ideas and reveal exciting sources of inspiration that might otherwise have been lost in the mists of assumption. Having an awareness of *why* you want to paint trees will enable you to make informed decisions about *how* you will depict them in your paintings. As you consider this question, you will begin to discover what it is about trees that you personally find inspiring.

'Accidental' Inclusion!

It is very common for someone new to painting to begin by painting landscapes and notice, relatively quickly, that it is quite difficult to avoid trees! Faced with this realization, the novice painter recognizes that they have a challenge on their hands. At this stage, the artist is, appropriately, concerned with figurative representation of their subject matter, and the prospect of having to find ways to represent certain aspects of trees (for example, the character of a wooded hillside or a mass of leaves) can seem quite daunting. Do not be daunted! Throughout this book, there are many suggestions that will help you with these artistic problems.

As an artist gains more experience, techniques are learned and a personal style develops, and the inclusion of trees no longer is something forced upon the artist by the landscape in front of them but rather is something that they will seek out. Trees undeniably enhance a landscape, and being able to paint them convincingly and confidently can lead the artist to a point where the trees play a major role in the composition of the artist's images.

Teasels and Tree, watercolour, 32cm × 43cm (12½in × 17in), Siân Dudley. This painting was inspired by the way that the glowing autumnal light lit both the hedge behind the tree and the teasels in the foreground. As I was focused on the golden colours below, the uppermost branches of the tree seemed to melt into the bright, blue sky.

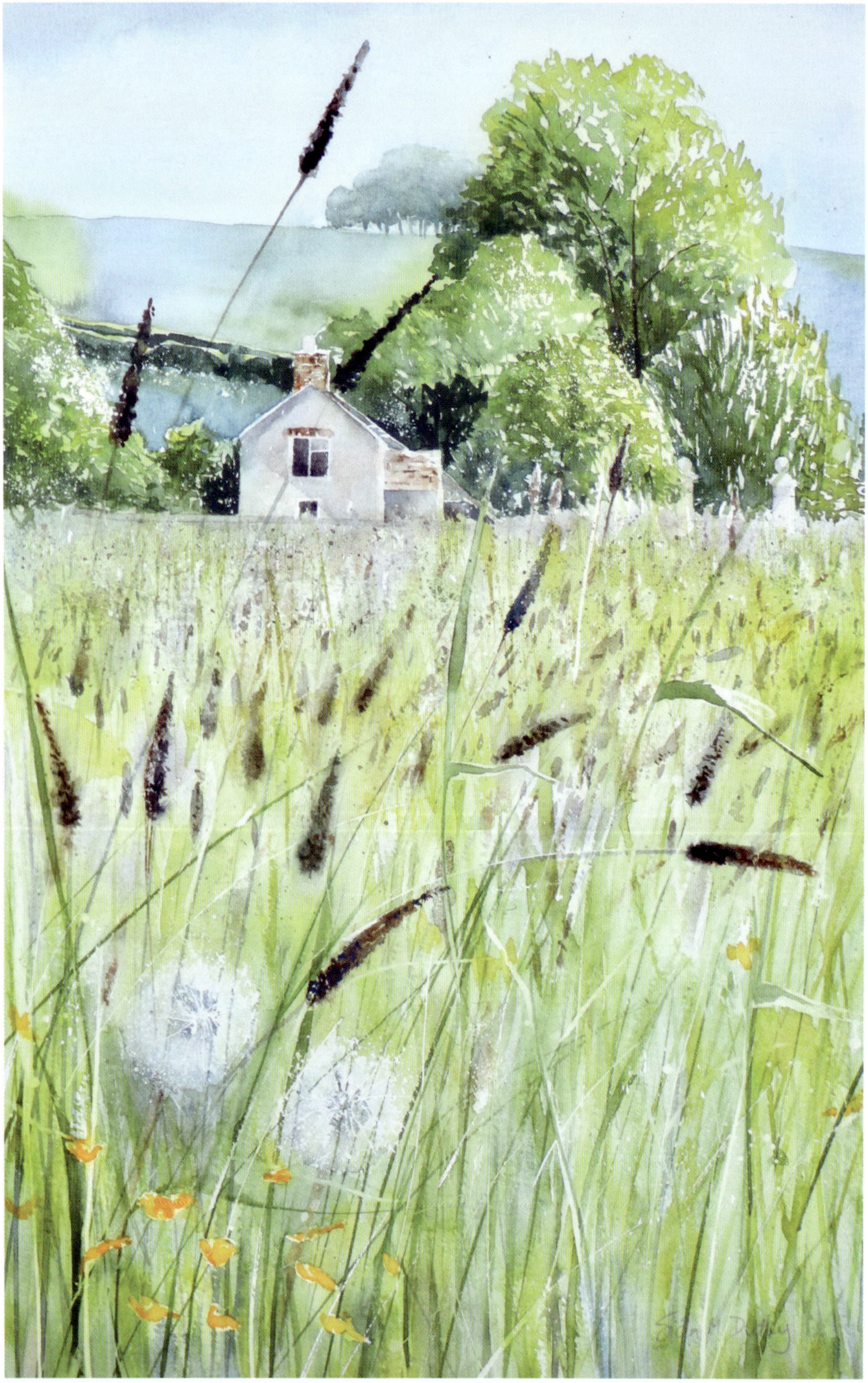

Home Through the Meadow, 29cm × 45cm (11½in × 17¾in), watercolour, Siân Dudley. In this painting, I wanted to capture the feeling of walking home through a summer meadow. The trees were an unavoidable part of the background to the cottage, but they served the useful purpose of providing darker tones against which to paint the light-toned cottage.

The Visual Beauty of Trees

It may be that, from the very beginning of your artistic journey, trees have been a major source of inspiration for you. Are you able to identify what it is that you find inspiring about them?

It may be tempting to state that you simply find them visually beautiful. This of course is indisputable; we all find trees beautiful, and you are more than entitled to your personal preferences. However, are you able to discern which physical characteristics you find especially appealing? Being able to identify *why* you find a particular tree or stand of trees visually beautiful will help you to make informed artistic decisions about how you paint the subject matter.

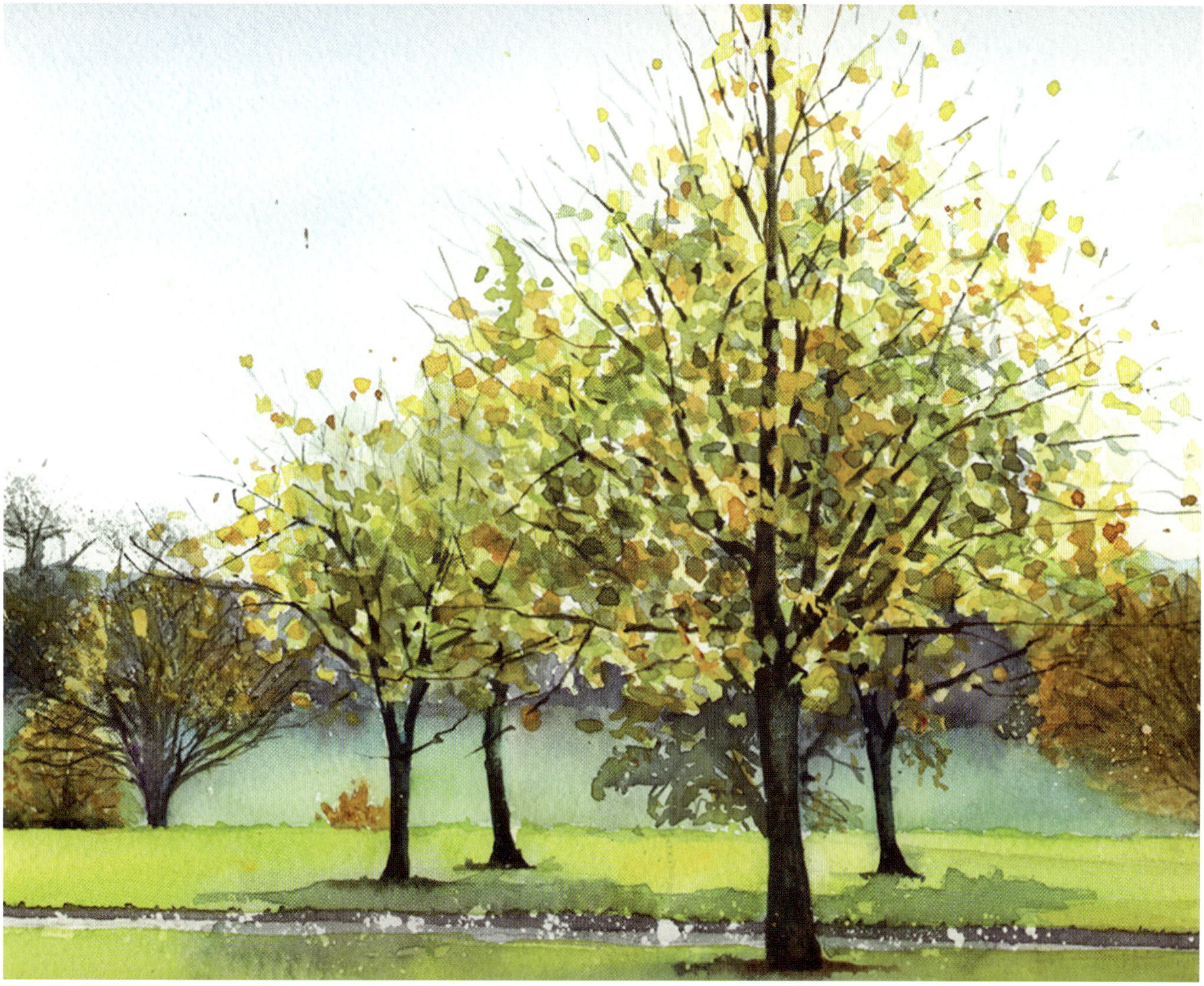

Autumnal Trees, watercolour, 29cm × 25cm (11½in × 9¾in), Siân Dudley. I found the light coming through these young trees, clothed in autumnal foliage, beautiful. That was reason enough to paint this scene.

For example, if what you love about a tree is its overall shape, describing the shape in a simple manner may take precedence over the careful depiction of the shape and distribution the tree's leaves. Think about images that you may have seen of the cypress trees so typical of Tuscany; paintings tend to focus on the trees' tall, slender shapes and on their position in the landscape, rather than on detailed descriptions of their leaves.

On the other hand, when we think about an apple tree or cherry tree in full blossom, we think about the flowers and their overall colour. This might inspire a painting that depicts just a few branches rather than the whole tree. Van Gogh took this approach when he painted *Almond Blossom*.

Contemplate the laciness of branches in winter, the autumnal colour of leaves, the texture of a trunk, the rich, dense foliage in summer and the bright, spring greens of newly opened leaves; all of these, and many, many more features of trees, are excellent starting points for paintings. Take time to ponder over what really excites you, and ask yourself how you can bring these qualities out in a painting.

For us, it is the play of light on and through trees that we both find particularly interesting. Strong sunlight accentuates the contrasts in tone of any subject; when it falls on a bare tree in winter, fascinating things happen. It is not always the outer branches that catch the sunlight but sometimes a branch in the middle of the tree, which

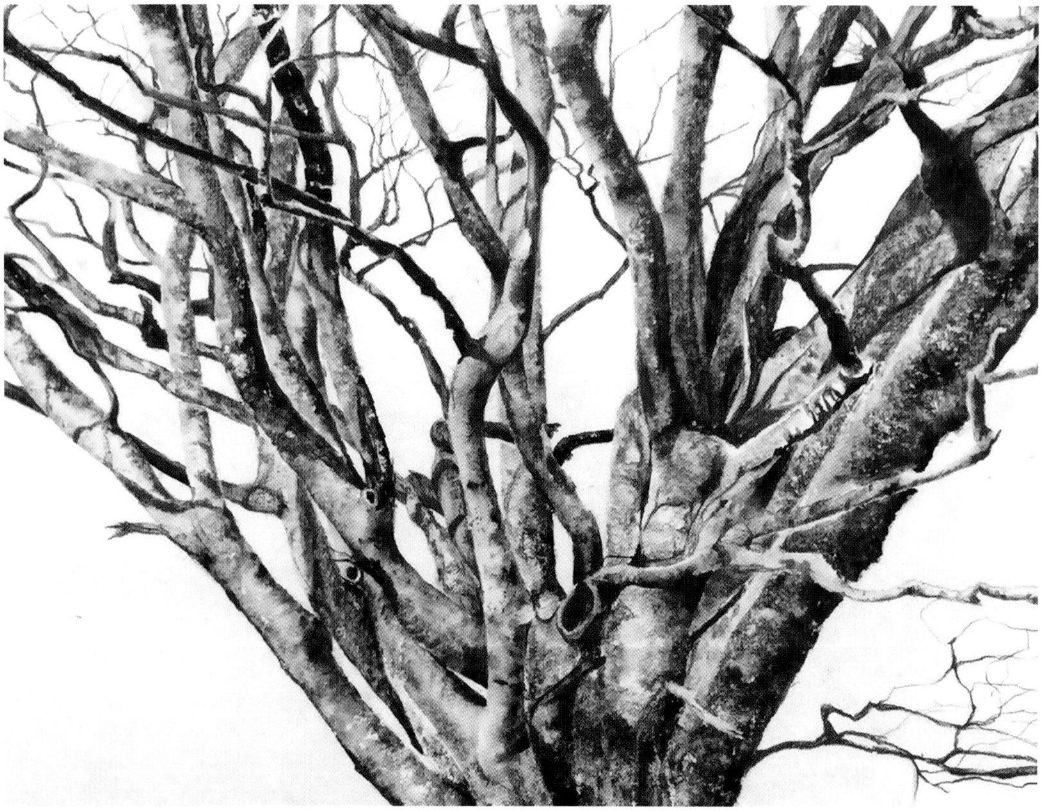

The Big Beech Tree: Winter (detail). The play of light amongst the branches, accentuating the branches' twisting shapes, inspired the making of this graphite image. The full image can be seen in Chapter 8.

gives a sense of intrigue due to its unexpectedness. At the same time, the tonal range from highlights on branches to the deep, dark shadows that the branches cast gives a real sense of the depth and shape, and it highlights textures of the bark. Similarly, in summer, a patch of sunlight may slip through an area of foliage, causing a group of leaves to positively glow against the rich, dark greens of an area more densely populated with leaves.

This book is about trees as the inspiration for painting. While we have a genuine interest in trees, and each of us has a favourite species, being able to identify a tree by name, or describe its growth pattern in botanical terms, is of little importance compared with the visual pleasure that the tree provides. Any information about the tree is interesting when developing your ideas of painting it, but care should be taken not to become embroiled in allowing what you know about the physicality of the tree to overly influence your design for your painting.

Focus your attention on what excites you about the tree that you see before you. This will free yourself up to create beautiful expressive paintings, rather than you expending any of your creative energy on things you may have learned from reading about the tree.

The Intangible Qualities of Trees

There are other aspects of trees that might inspire an artist to paint them or to include them in a painting. These qualities are more subjective, intangible qualities.

We describe trees as having strength, grandeur and elegance. We may say that they are ethereal or sinister. Many of the characteristics that we attribute to them could also be applied to ourselves, although, at this level, we are not anthropomorphizing trees but recognizing something about them with which we connect at a deep level. Our use of this type of language recognizes our emotional response to trees, and it is so ensconced in our daily language that we do this subconsciously.

As an artist, it might be useful to take some time to consider this aspect of trees and how it relates to the paintings that you make. Is this something that is important to you, in that recognizing your emotional response to trees is at the root of your inspiration? Or might it influence your work in another way, for example, in considering how your choice of tree might affect the narrative of a painting? If your intent in making the painting is to evoke a particular emotional response in the viewer, having an awareness of your own response to trees would be very useful.

To put some of this into context, consider the oak. The oak is considered to have the qualities of strength and endurance (its size and longevity obviously being the basis for this). It is often described as noble or majestic. It has a presence, an aura, that implies a history.

Imagine a painting of rural England, with a farm field taking centre stage. Placing an oak in the centre of the field immediately adds an element of history to the scene and, hence, depth to the narrative. If the oak is removed, or replaced with a different species, for example, a single apple tree, the painting acquires an entirely different feel and loses its sense of history.

Gainsborough used his understanding of this concept when he painted *Mr & Mrs Andrews* (*c.*1750). The featured couple sit under an oak tree, which was intended by Gainsborough to deliberately reflect Englishness, stability, continuity and a sense of successive generations managing the family estates.

TREES AND SYMBOLISM

Through the ages, trees have acquired symbolic meanings. These differ from culture to culture and between different mythologies and religions. Here are just a few…

Aspen: exploring, and spreading your wings
Birch: new beginnings
Cedar: healing, cleansing
Cherry (tree): love, romance and, when in flower, good fortune
Elm (old-growth): intuition, strength
Maple: balance, promise
Oak: stateliness, power and courage
Olive (branch): reconciliation
Palm: peace
Redwood: forever
Wisteria: romance

A Sense of Place

Trees stand tall, solid and strong, rooted in the earth. Unless moved by humans, they remain in that place where each tree's originating seed germinated, for their entire lives. They become an integral part of the place in which they live, contributing visually to the landscape and biologically to the local ecosystem. Since different species grow in different climates, it is easy to see how, on a global scale, trees can impart a sense of place.

At home in Devon, England, we are used to seeing hawthorn hedges, which are intended to keep farm animals enclosed within fields; these hedges are often wind pruned, indicating the direction of the prevailing wind. Many of the local farm fields have a large oak standing proud in their centre, under which cows and sheep shelter from the sun. Although relatively unfamiliar crops have invaded the landscape in recent years, the trees still tell us that we are at home in England. When on holiday in southern Spain, the local trees were olives and almonds, the surprising blackness of their trunks making a real and lasting impression on us of an unfamiliar landscape, which will forever remind us of the Alpujarras.

In paintings, trees can be used very effectively to convey a sense of place, simply by the artist's choice of species that are appropriate for a particular area. Close observation of *how* trees grow in a particular area will help you to describe that area. Conversely, a sense of mystery could be imparted to a painting by your deliberate choice of inclusion of an inappropriate species.

A single tree can also impart a strong sense of place. We become familiar with individual trees in the local area. Near our home is a wind-pruned hawthorn tree shaped just like a teapot; we call it The Teapot Tree. Another local tree, split by lightening, has earned the nickname The Tuning-Fork Tree. It is probable that every town, village and hamlet in the country has at least one tree known to all of the local residents, complete with nickname!

Single trees can make wonderful subject matter for artists. A popular project is to paint a particular tree throughout all of the seasons. The obvious thought here is to study a deciduous tree, which will have brilliant, bright, fresh growth in the spring, abundant summer foliage, rich autumn colour and open, lacy patterns in the branches in the winter. We have taken this approach with The Big Beech Tree, which we visit regularly, as we find it so inspirational. The paintings that we produce are intended not as a simple record of how the tree changes each time that we visit it but rather as a record of our response to it when we are in its vicinity. As a result, the paintings are varied in both style and the media that we chose to use for each painting. One of four different *The Big Beech Tree* paintings can be seen at the beginning of each of Chapters 5 to 8.

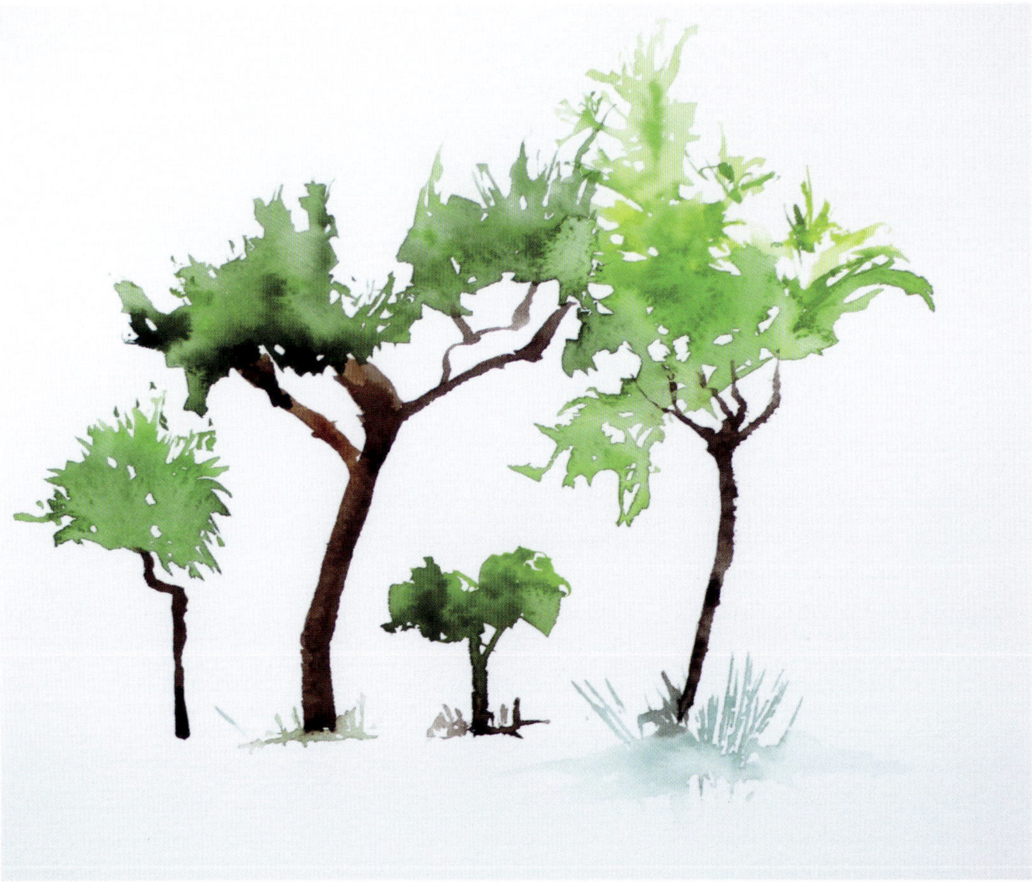

With just a few brushstrokes, this quick watercolour sketch captured the character of each tree that is so typical of the Alpujarras, Spain.

However, evergreen trees can also make marvellous subjects for such a project; since the changes in the tree are relatively small compared with those of a deciduous tree, the variations come from changes in light, weather and atmospheric conditions, and an evergreen tree can be every bit as inspiring as a deciduous tree. Other seasonal changes are recorded around the tree, and, as the project takes some time to complete, the artist will develop an affinity with the place too. The differences in the paintings made as the project progresses may be subtle, perhaps through more-confident mark-making or minor adjustments to the composition. All of this will add to the artist's sense of place and help to convey this to the viewer, so that they too feel the connection.

Environmental Advocacy Through Art

The obvious stature of trees in their environment belies the degree to which they are a part of a community of organisms. Underground, they are supported by mycorrhizal fungi, which help to bring water and nutrients close to the trees' roots. Above ground, there are a myriad of microcosms upon their trunks and within their branches, supporting all manner of life! Birds, fungi, mosses, frogs, mistletoe and ferns, and even other trees, can be seen growing amongst their branches. In addition to looking at how trees can help us to understand our geographical place on the planet, we have much to learn from trees about our place in the ecosystem.

In an era where science can often overshadow art, it is easy to focus on the ways in which trees can be of enormous benefit to both the planet and us as a species. The part trees play in maintaining the temperature of the planet is well-documented and reported frequently in the press, so that even those with little interest in global warming or science can hardly avoid gaining an understanding of the significance of trees. Many studies have been conducted on the ecosystem benefits provided by trees. Trees absorb carbon dioxide, release oxygen into the atmosphere, increase the stability of land and thus reduce erosion, cool water to a suitable temperature to support native fish, and much, much more.

Wanting to get the message across to those who have not yet heard it is inspiration enough for many artists! Art has, and has always had, the ability to reach those who are impervious to messages delivered by other means. TV and radio programmes end and are forgotten; a piece of artwork remains in place, always visible. Even for the viewers whose gazes are transient, the art sits there, subliminally entering their consciousnesses through the corners of their eyes.

Environmental advocacy is an excellent reason for painting images of trees! The message can be very deliberate, overtly causing the viewer to question, such as one might find in a surreal image of a dystopian future. But the message need not be so obvious. Beautiful images of trees can be enough to inspire the viewer to think about the planet. Painting something that inspires you may be enough to inspire your views to go out into the environment and make a similar connection with the viewer. Of course, if you can design an image with a narrative somewhere between these two extremes, you could successfully encourage people to take more action too.

Art has always been used to express messages and is perfectly valid as a reason for painting trees!

Trees and Health

Humans have always instinctively understood the value of trees to their own physical and mental health. The physical benefits are obvious. Trees provide shelter, oxygen, food, building materials, paper and so on. Medications can be made from various parts of a tree, including leaves, bark and roots.

Intuitively, we know we feel more relaxed and are more mentally alert if we spend time in natural surroundings. In an era where we are becoming increasingly urbanized, a number of studies have considered the link between trees and mental health. It is now well-documented that a short break during the working day that is spent outside amongst nature increases a person's ability to focus on their work, increases job satisfaction and reduces employee illness. Humans have a strong preference for landscapes with trees or woods; studies have shown that, in areas with more trees, house prices are higher, commercial regions attract more customers and employment rates are higher.

TREES

Joyce Kilmer

I think that I shall never see
A poem lovely as a tree.

A tree whose hungry mouth is prest
Against the earth's sweet flowing breast;

A tree that looks at God all day,
And lifts her leafy arms to pray;

A tree that may in Summer wear
A nest of robins in her hair;

Upon whose bosom snow has lain;
Who intimately lives with rain.

Poems are made by fools like me,
But only God can make a tree.

Joyce Kilmer makes his feelings about the beauty of trees quite clear in this short poem, 'Trees' (Kilmer, J., *Trees and Other Poems* [Doubleday Doran and Co., 1914]). While we cannot disagree with him on the beauty of trees, there is a feeling that he has slightly missed the point about art. Poems and paintings are not trees; they are about trees and can be beautiful in themselves. Artists are not making trees; they are making paintings – new entities in their own right. You will not be hanging a tree on your living-room wall but a painted image of one. And that can be a beautiful thing!

An artist has a huge advantage here! Since the time spent making a painting involves preparation in the form of information gathering, it is absolutely essential to spend time outdoors walking, looking, sketching and photographing. If the painting is completed *en plein air*, so much the better. Use your art to encourage others to do the same: organize sketching trips or paint images of places that people want to visit.

Painting trees has to be good for your heath!

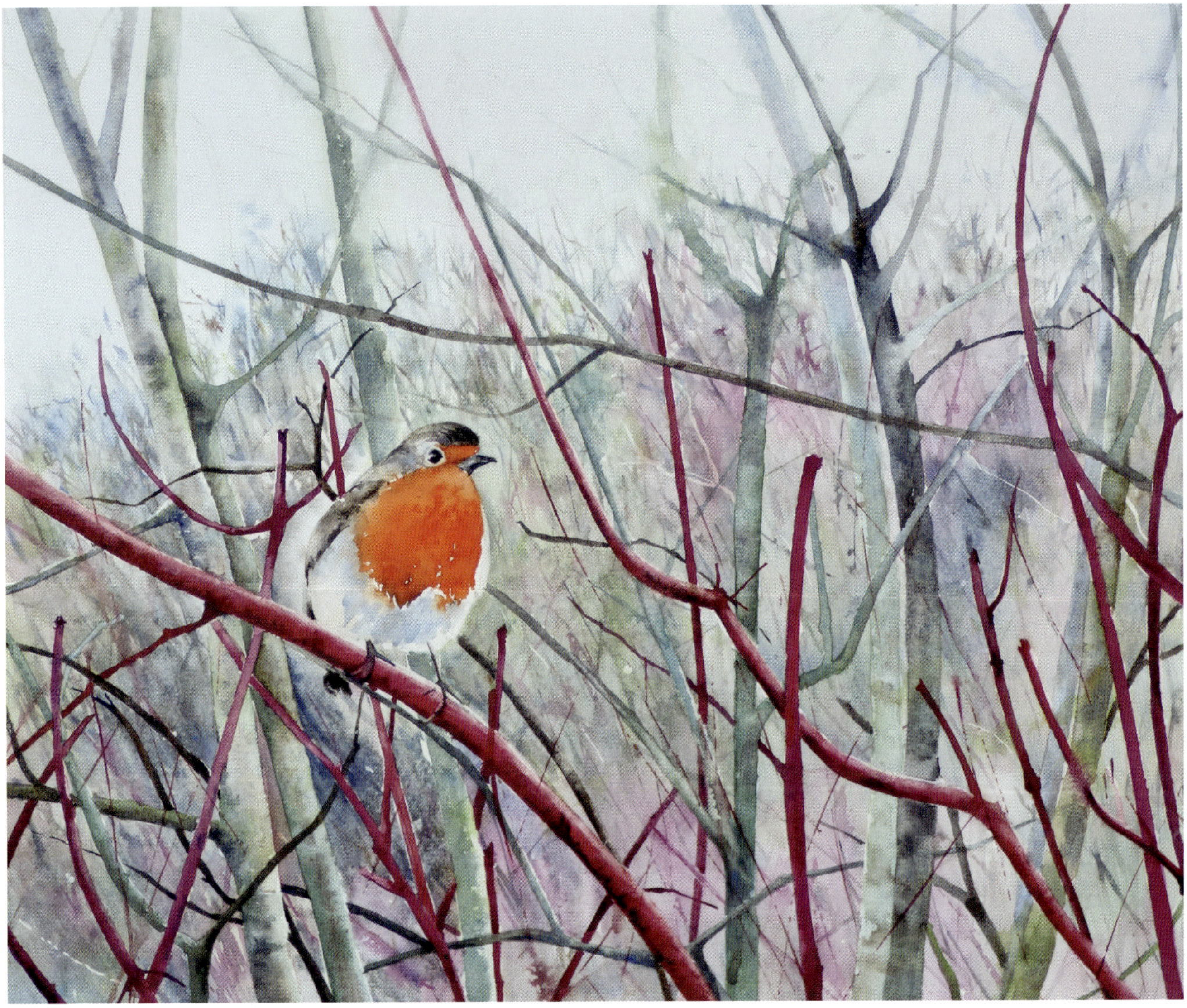

Lunch with Robin, watercolour, 37cm × 26cm (14½in × 10¼in), Siân Dudley. A short lunchtime walk amongst nature can be both refreshing and inspiring. After a tedious morning, just such a walk inspired the making of this cheerful watercolour painting.

PAINTING TREES: THE PRACTICALITIES

When it comes to how trees are portrayed in art, our emotional response to trees transcends our scientific understanding of our symbiotic relationship with them. Just as they are a staple part of our existence, they are a staple part of our artistic endeavours. It is no wonder that they have been the subject for painters for hundreds of years, either as elements within a painting or as the main subject of the artwork itself. The representation of trees in art can be as varied as the different trees themselves, transcending all styles and movements, from photorealist pixel-perfect representations to the often simplified colours, shapes and forms of abstract works.

Trees have been the inspiration, the focus, the background of countless artworks. They have been used as compositional devices, represented allegorical elements within narrative paintings, been pared down to abstracted simplicity or been examined in minute detail. The humble tree has done it all.

Considering two artists working with trees as their subject matter, compare the different interpretations by the English painter John Constable (1776–1837) with those of the Dutch painter Piet Mondrian (1872–1944). Constable's approach is very naturalistic, and his deft brushwork depicts the wind-lifted leaves along the banks

Glowing Teasels, watercolour, 23cm × 32cm (9in × 12½in), Rob Dudley. In this image, the trees are purely background. The viewer's eye is drawn first to the teasels and then to the grasses, the cottage and the sky. Finally, the viewer may notice the trees. Despite their seeming irrelevance to the subject matter, the trees perform an important role, in providing dark tones that highlight the glow on the teasels and in the sky, that frame the cottage and that act as stoppers, preventing the viewer's eye from leaving the scene and instead guiding it back to the teasels.

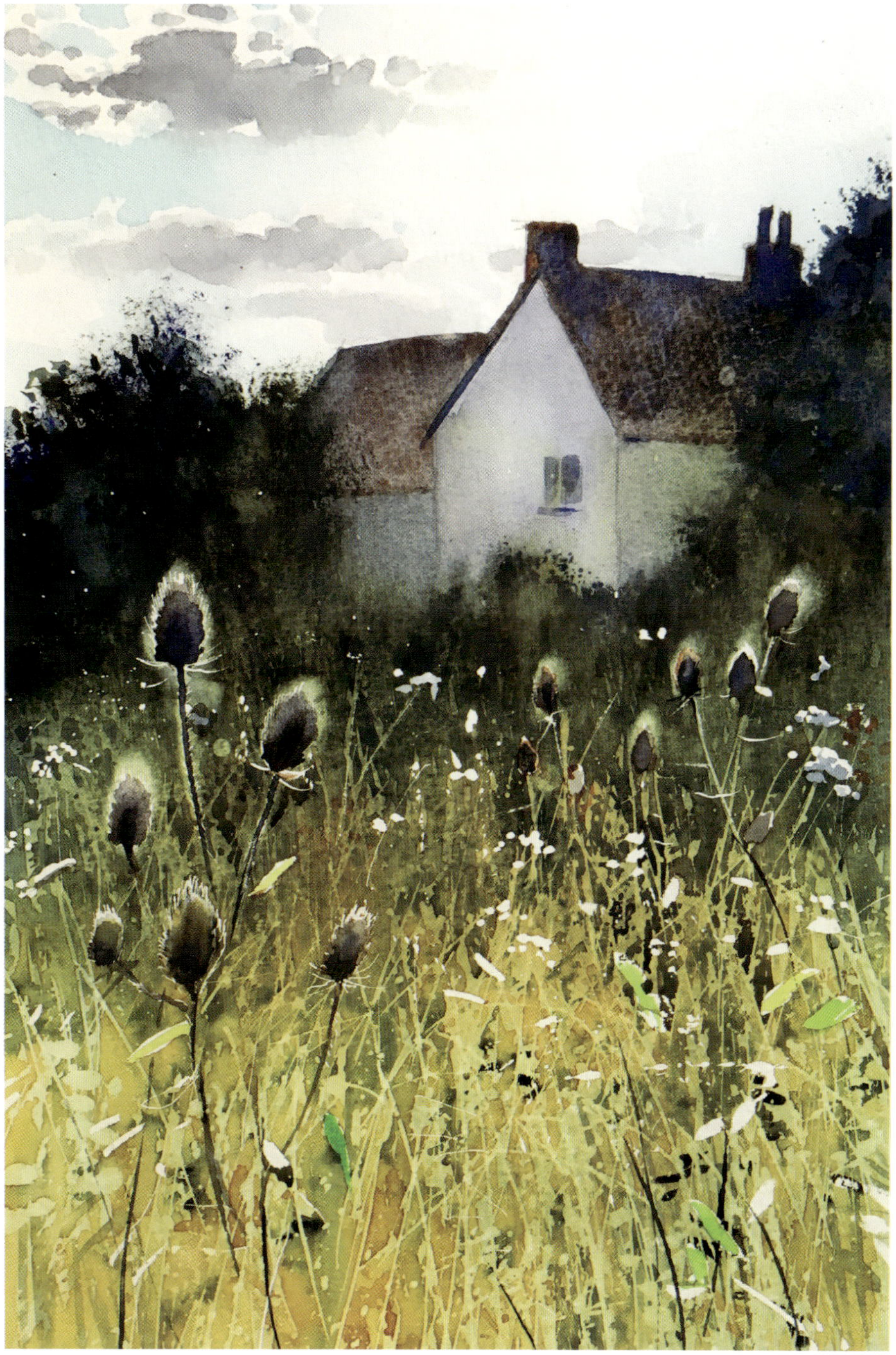

of the River Stour. Mondrian's far more abstract approach interprets leaves as geometric, interlocking, branch-like shapes. Using the same starting point, trees, both painters producing captivating, yet very different, images.

Painting Trees in the Landscape

One of the most popular painting genres found around the world is that of landscape painting. Within landscape painting itself there are numerous subgenres: towering snow-capped mountains, wide, expansive moorlands, flower-filled meadows and reed-filled marshlands. Whichever type of landscape is being portrayed in a painting, it is undeniable that trees play a prominent part. Indeed, for many a landscape painter, it is trees and the painting of them that fills their work. They are a staple of our lives; they are also a staple of our paintings. We cannot do without them.

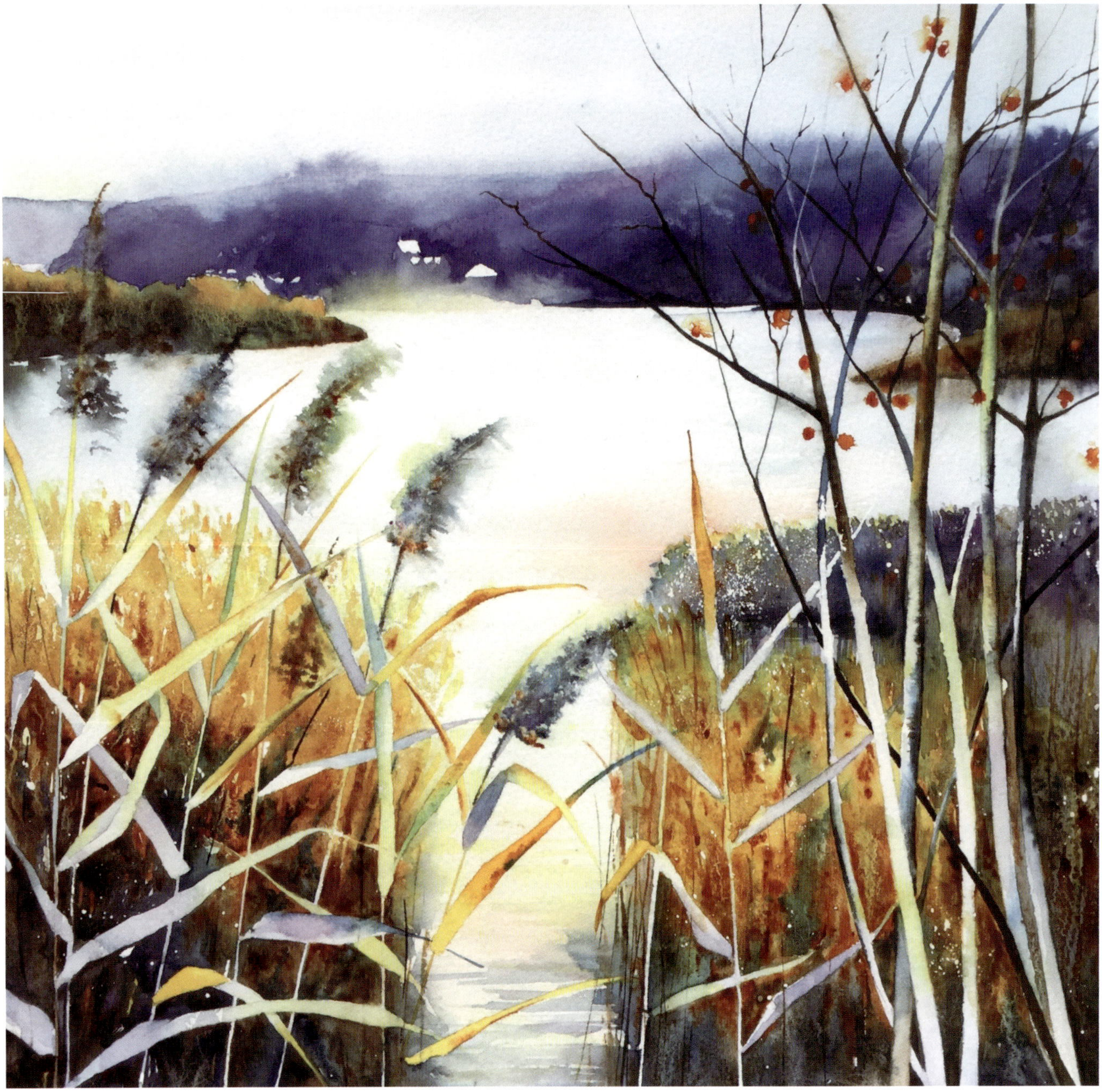

Slapton Ley, watercolour, 30cm × 30cm (11¾in × 11¾in), Siân Dudley. The trees (and the reeds) in the foreground of this painting are intended to attract attention, drawing the viewer's eye into the image, but they are not the focal point. The trees are designed, in particular by using specific shapes and tones, to lead the viewer's eye through them to the light on the water beyond. Once the viewer's eye arrives there, the trees recede in the viewer's mind, as they are subconsciously considered as being something to look through rather than at.

For generations trees have been the subject of, and are the indispensable elements within, landscape paintings and, for as long as trees grow on the planet, they are likely to be for generations to come. They might form only a small part of the artwork, but they can still have a dramatic impact on the overall mood or atmosphere of the painting. The colour of the foliage, or lack of it, can describe the season. Shadows within or cast from trees can suggest the time of day or even indicate the warmth of the day by implying the strength of the sunlight.

The careful inclusion of well-placed trees can add to the sense of space and distance within the artwork. Trees can

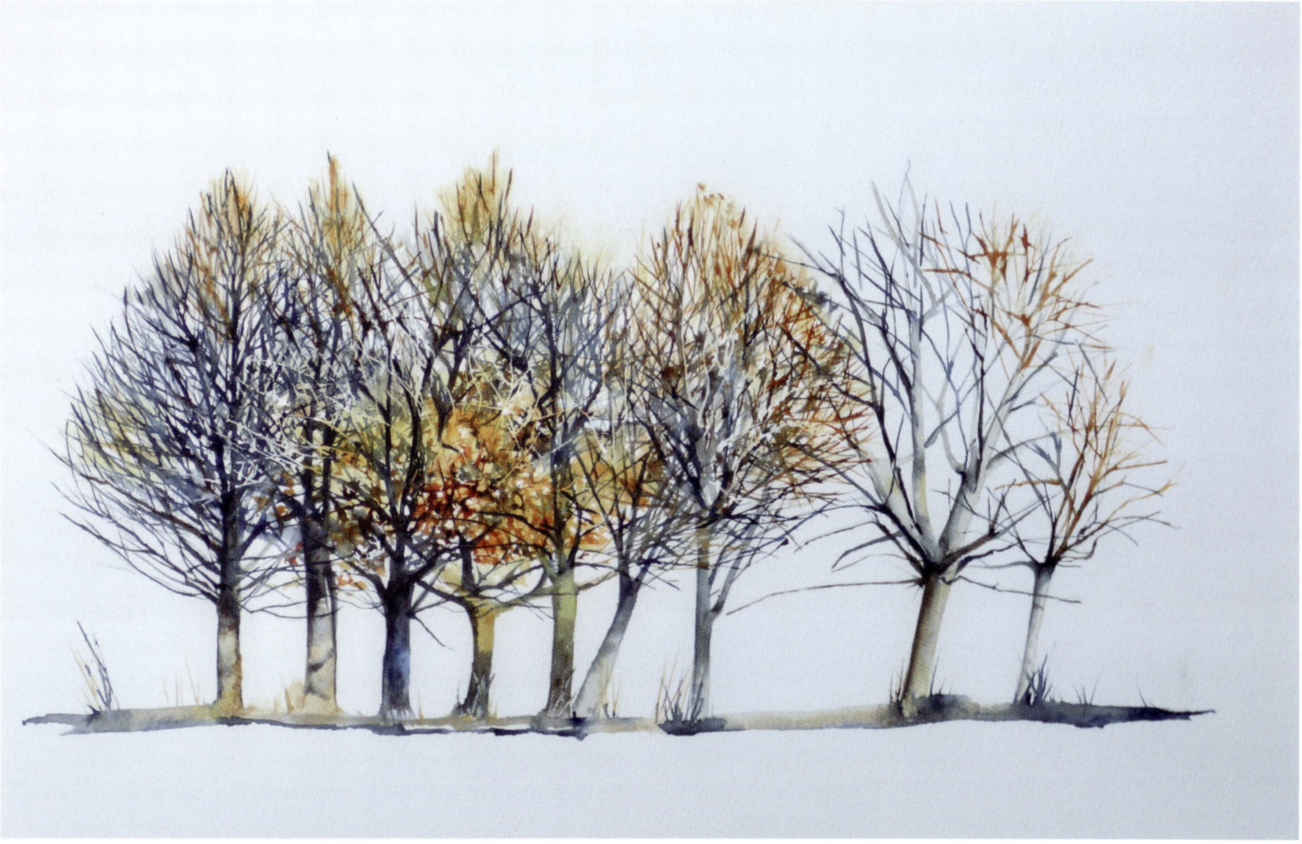

Untitled, watercolour, 50cm × 26cm (19¾in × 10¼in), Siân Dudley. This stand of trees was enchanting and needed no background or context within a painting. As the sun played on the bare branches, the trees' tips glowed, and the shadows deepened. Both of these effects were enhanced in the painting by the choice of complementary colours and exaggeration of the tones.

feature in the landscape in ones or twos or as vast woods and forests. In short, they are an essential component of the landscape-painter's art.

Within landscape paintings, trees can play different roles. They can be part of the background, be part of the supporting cast or be the focus of the painting. They can be used more overtly as compositional devices, playing a far more obvious role. They can be used as part of the narrative, having an essential role in the image.

Trees as a Background

Trees can be used as the background or as a backdrop to the action taking place in front of them. Used in this way, they are subtle compositional devices, used by the artist to lead the viewer's eye towards the main subject matter of the painting. They are painted in such a way that the viewer almost overlooks them, maybe coming back to reconsider them only after thoroughly examining the rest of the painting. Without wishing to imply a lack of importance to the overall image, in this sense, the trees are sometimes little more than fillers. If this is what you have intended from the start, this is no bad thing; it requires a degree of skill to paint the trees so convincingly that they perform this role!

Used in this manner, trees can be extremely useful. The tone and colour of these trees can be used to bring the focal point into sharp focus by, for example, ensuring that these trees are dark in tone if the focal point is light. They can be coloured to lead the viewer's eye around the painting, directing the viewer to the area that you wish their eye to rest on. Trees performing this role within a painting are usually en masse, such as you might see in a wooded hillside, a small copse or a hedge.

Trees as a Compositional Device

When designing a painting, it is not uncommon to rearrange, alter or even invent some of the elements that come together to make a successful painting. Moving a building here and adding a cloud there all add to making a stronger whole. Using trees in this way means placing them deliberately within an image, just where they are needed. For example, trees can be added to hillsides to balance compositional designs or be removed altogether, if it strengthens the overall image.

Used in this manner, the trees will claim some of the attention. They are a more obvious part of the composition than trees used as a background. Depending on how they are used, they may even be a part of the focal point, though not being the main subject matter of the painting.

The key, particularly when adding trees to the design, is to ensure that they look as if they could grow where they are positioned. Size, detail, texture, tone and colour must all be assessed correctly in relation to the rest of the painting, otherwise the arboreal addition will stand out like a sore thumb and likely unbalance the rest of the design.

Trees as the Subject

Trees are very beautiful and deserve to be the subject matter of paintings, where the artist invites you to examine the tree, or aspects of it, for what it is. These paintings can be pure, simple, descriptive and direct. Our love of trees is such that we can gaze at such paintings for hours, following the lines of the branches or enjoying the colour of the leaves, much as we would watch flames flickering in a fire.

Very descriptive, figurative paintings, verging on the diagrammatic, can be enjoyable and interesting. But trees inspire emotions, and the artist can evoke an emotional response to a painting of a single specimen, by carefully choosing the style in which it is painted. A tight, or detailed, descriptive rendition of the bark might evoke memories of the texture, while a loosely painted image might be more ethereal, evoking memories of long, summer days or of misty mornings.

Close inspection of trees can reveal whole new sets of subjects for the observant artist to consider. Deep fissures in the textured bark to the shapes, colours and patterns of leaves can all be starting points for exciting tree-based projects.

AN APPROACH TO PAINTING

Throughout this book, there will be plenty of practical advice on how to design paintings and to implement this advice to actually make a painting. Knowing why you are painting the image will help you to decide on your approach and which techniques to use.

The techniques demonstrated in this book are those used for the featured paintings or for the step-by-step projects in later chapters. There are many more techniques available to an artist than it is possible to include in one book! It is important to remember that our intention is not that you just learn how to paint each of the images provided in the later chapters but is that you absorb and develop the approach to painting. This allows you to extrapolate from the lessons in this book, to identify your own purposes for each painting that you make and to find the appropriate techniques to use; whether you discover those techniques through this book or by the attitude of experimentation that it promotes. Our intention is that you use this book as a springboard for your own work.

Choice of Media

This book features mainly watercolour, oil and pencil artwork. Painters using these media will find lots of techniques specific to these media.

However, much of the advice given applies across all media. All of the tips and techniques given for finding inspiration, developing your ideas, information gathering, layout, tone and colour are cross-media. *See* Chapter 2, Materials and Techniques, for ways to explore different media and apply them effectively to the realization of your ideas.

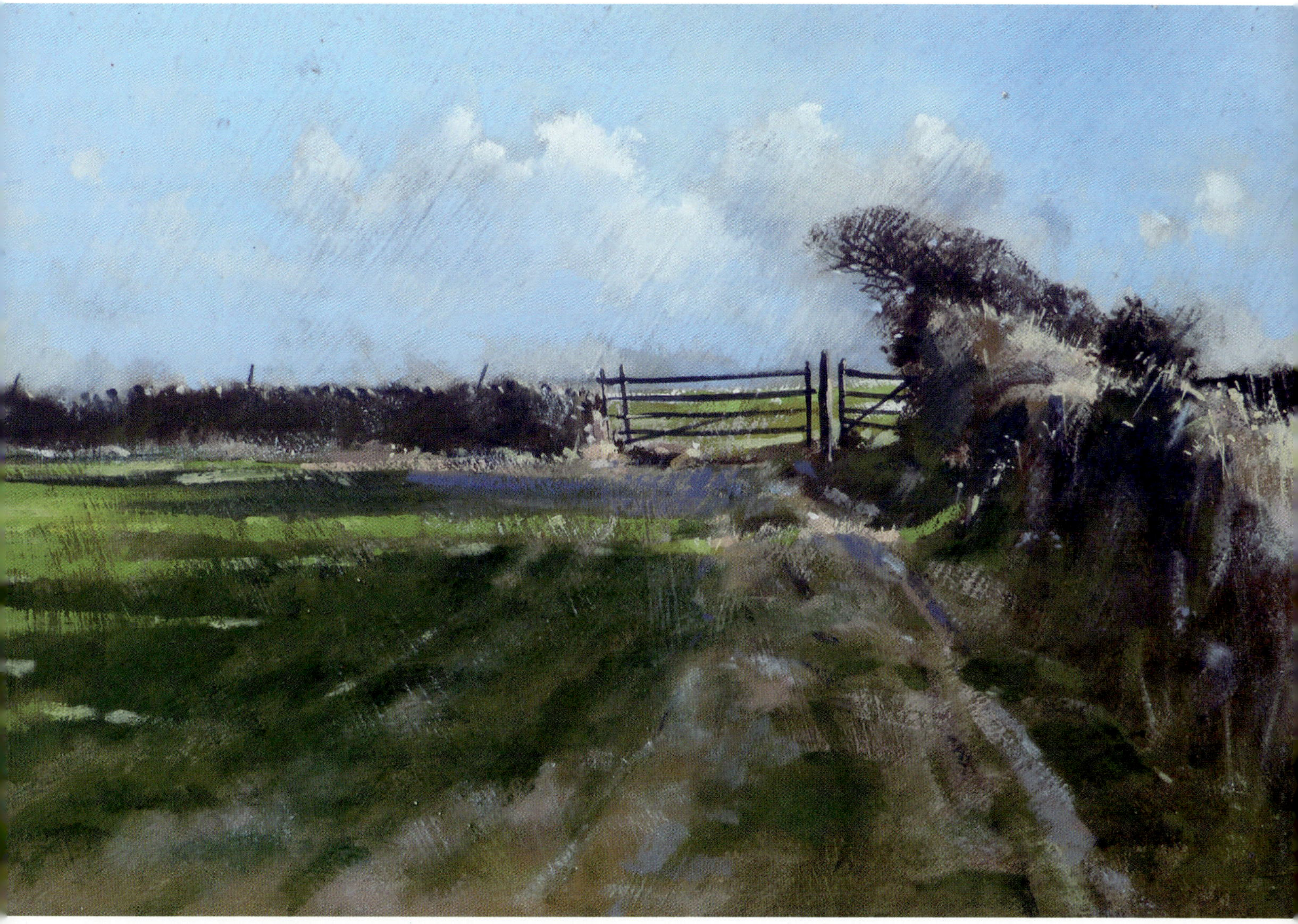

Trees Near Soar, water-mixable oils, 30cm × 20cm (11¾in × 8in), Rob Dudley. The wind had bent these trees into such an interesting shape and, with the low sun casting such long shadows from them, they just had to be painted!

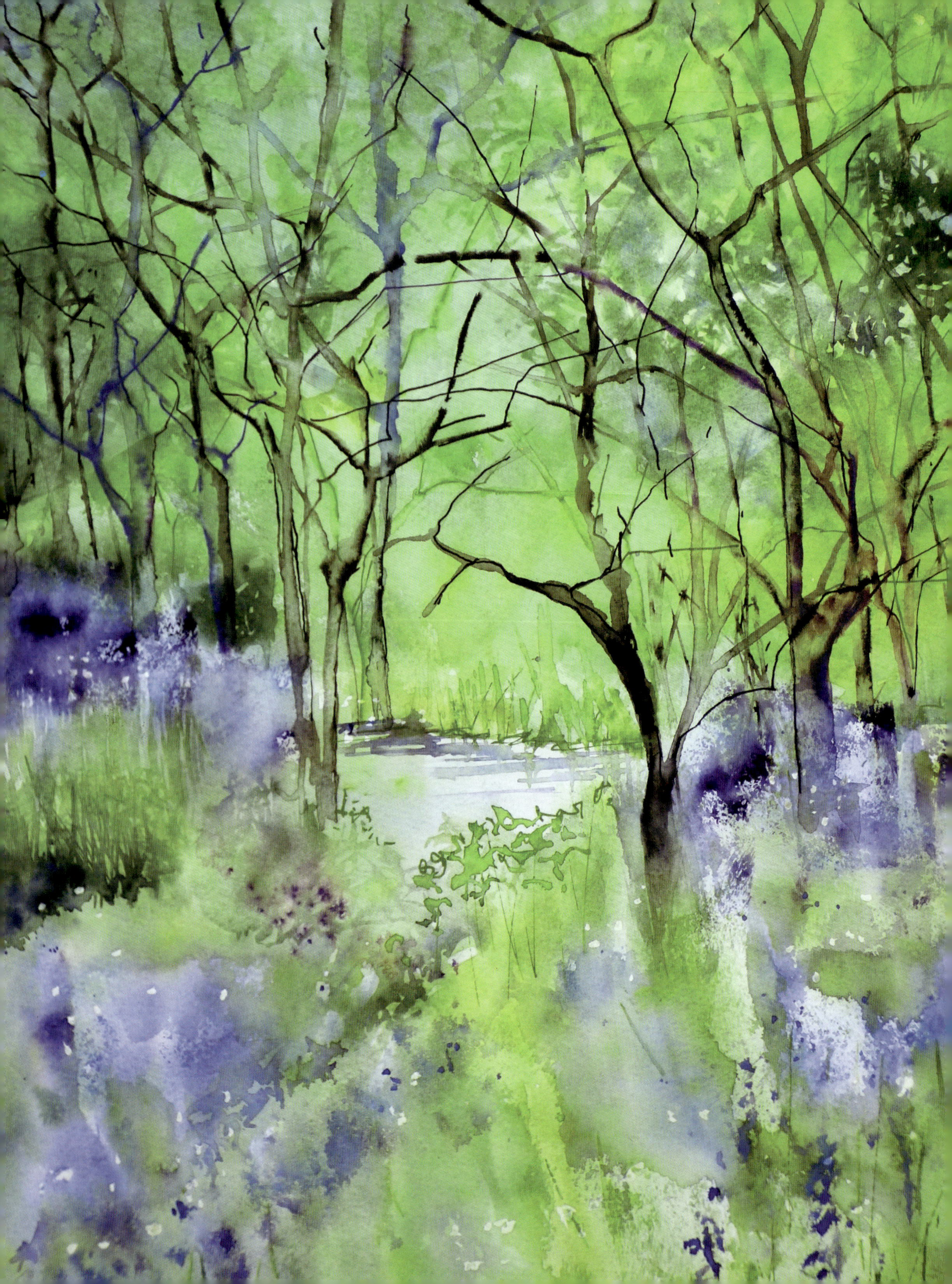

Chapter 2

Materials and techniques

Most books of this type have a chapter on materials and equipment, providing extremely useful hints and tips on what to use and how to use it to create beautiful works of art. This book is no exception. What follows in this chapter are many hints, tips and descriptions of techniques that can be used to create beautiful paintings. But, with all the best will in the world, this chapter will not be able to give you the vital ingredient that will enhance your painting.

The vital ingredient is you.

This chapter is not really about the art materials, equipment and techniques. This chapter is about *you*.

The vital piece of information that is often, perhaps strangely, overlooked is that the materials themselves are nothing without the hand that holds them. Art materials are inanimate. Left to their own devices, they will sit obediently wherever you left them, gathering dust rather than miraculously making paintings of their own accord. When you watch another artist painting, it is clearly important to take note of the tools that they are using, but never forget that it is not the tool that makes the mark, it is the artist's hand.

And, when it comes to making your own paintings, that hand is *yours*. No amount of watching or reading will enable *you* to make a painting. That will happen only when *you* pick up your materials and start using them. It follows that the best advice that you could receive would be to pick up those materials and try them out!

INVESTIGATING MATERIALS

In practice, the very best way to learn to paint is to pick up your materials and *play* with them. Children learn through play, but as adults we forget its value. In the context intended here, play means giving yourself permission to let go of the need to produce a painting. Instead, spend some time investigating what you are able to do with the materials that you have. There is an old adage that says that time in reconnaissance is never wasted; devoting time to simply playing with art materials will not only give you skills in handling them but enthuse you and inspire greater creativity. Adopting this approach can be as useful and inspiring for those with a little more experience as it is for beginners. Free yourself from the pressure of producing a great work of art, relax and relearn the art of experimental investigation. Play!

Experimenting with mark-making, Siân Dudley. In the initial stages, a watercolour painting went wrong. Having washed off the first washes and repeated them twice, I gave up. Rather than throw the failed painting away, I used it to give context to experiments with some water-based ink pens, experimenting with mark-making and observing how the two media worked together. This sheet will be kept for reference.

PROJECT

Learning through play

Time spent learning to use your materials is *invaluable*! It should *never* be underestimated.

Take time to get to understand how your materials work. How do your brushes respond to your hand movements? How do your paints respond to your supports? Are you easily able to find the exact colour or tone that you need?

Make time to experiment with your materials. Ask yourself these questions:

1 What can I do with…?

For example, what can you do with your brushes? Spend time playing with them, each in turn, to discover the different types of marks and effects that you can create with each one. Work on dry paper, wet paper, rough surfaces and smooth surfaces, change the angle of your hand and hold the handle in a different place. Try loading the brush fully and using it almost dry.

2 What will happen if…?

For example, try discarding the brush and picking up something else, *anything*, with which you think you could make a mark. Sticks, toothpicks, palette knives, feathers, string…

What happens if you use the 'wrong' hand, your non-dominant hand? What happens if you close your eyes and flick paint at the painting surface?

3 How did that happen?

Watch carefully what happens as you play. Remember to keep watching as the paint dries (over several days, if necessary).

Use any 'happy accidents' that occur as learning experiences. They need not be one-offs. Such an accident was happy because you liked the effect, so try to work out how it happened and then practise making it happen on purpose; with just a little practice, you *will* be able to do this.

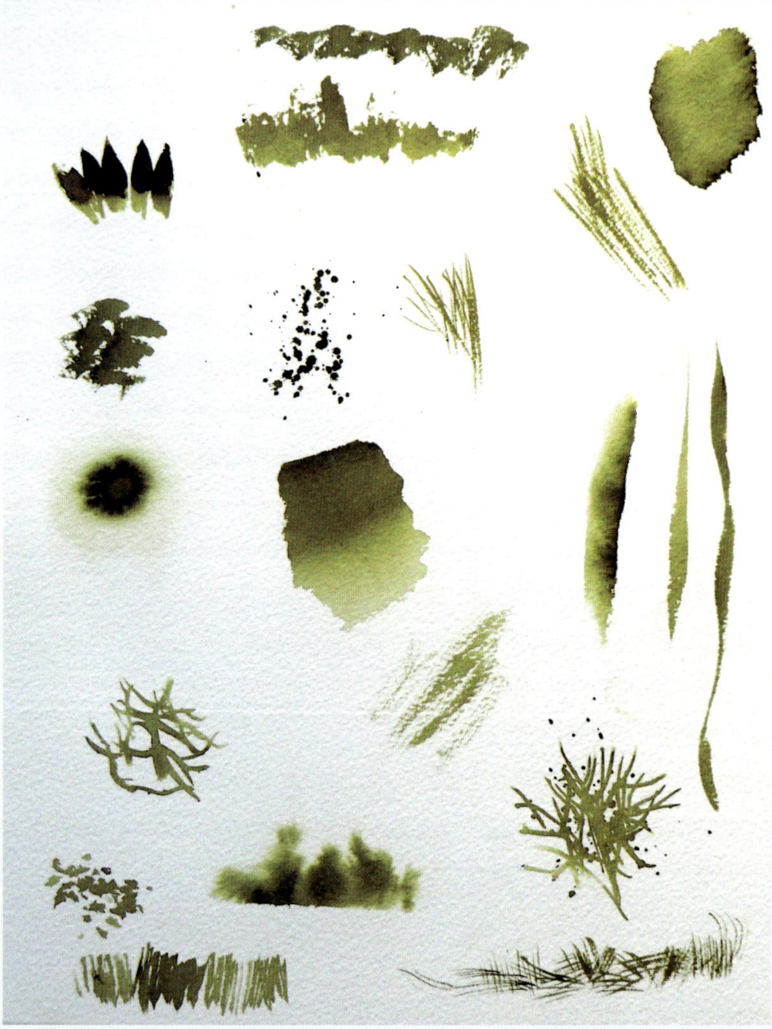

Experiment with mark making, play with your brushes, whatever the medium being used. Try to make as many different marks as you can with each of your brushes, for it is these marks that can lead to the creation of better paintings.

THE VARIETY OF MEDIA

The range of materials available to the artist is vast. In this book, we have used our preferred media, but this does not mean that what follows is a comprehensive list of materials suitable for painting trees. The quest for different experiences, to set new challenges, is what keeps the artist and their work fresh and exciting.

Try applying the approach to experimenting in the project 'Learning through play' to other media; try acrylics, charcoals, pastels or inks, and discover ways of using these media too. It is only the actual application of the medium that will differ. All the advice that you will find in the pages on finding inspiration, information gathering, composition, tone and colour will still apply!

Deciding which medium (or combination of media) to use for a particular painting is a very personal choice, and you will find more information on how to make this decision in Chapter 4, Designing the Painting. Of course, the decision will be much easier to make if you have a practical understanding of how each of these media works, and repeating the project 'Learning through play' with each medium will be very helpful in this respect.

This book focuses on our preferred media. You will find examples of paintings, sketches and projects where we have used watercolour, water-based oil, pencil and acrylic gouache. This chapter takes a look at each of these media, giving a few general points about each one and suggestions for materials and supports that are particularly useful for each. For some of the images in the book, we have given our reasons for making the choice of medium; as you become more familiar with the different media, you may be able to see for yourself why a particular choice was made.

As this is a book about painting trees, we have presented a selection of techniques and marks that are especially useful for the subject that we are studying, for example, tips on which marks might be a good way of painting branches or leaves. Please remember that these techniques and marks are just a selection; you will find more in the demonstrations included in the later chapters, and you will find out even more through your own experimentation!

WATERCOLOUR

Watercolour is an extremely popular medium. In truth, this is partly because it is so incredibly convenient. Watercolour materials do not take up much space and are light and therefore easy to transport. Watercolour is odourless, easy to clean up (which applies to spillages as well as the equipment) and relatively inexpensive. It is also extremely versatile and incredibly exciting to use!

The majority of modern watercolour paints are bright, vibrant and lightfast, so clarity of colour and brilliance of hue are no longer the problem that they were when Constable made his watercolour sketches of Flatford Mill. Delightful though they were, the colours available to him were dull by today's standard, with a tendency to fade. Known for his observational skills, it is doubtful that he thought trees were the dull grey-greens that we see in his sketchbooks today.

It is also a lively medium; as the paint is suspended in the water used to apply it, it moves. The mysterious marks and textures that appear as it dries can, with practice, be achieved deliberately, although many watercolourists prefer to allow the paint to do its own thing. In this way, the watercolour gives something back to the artist, playing its own part in the creation of the image.

Being such a versatile medium, it is supremely suitable for the painting of trees. It is possible to achieve rich, deeply toned washes that imply deep shadows within and under trees. Light, pale washes and soft, simple brushstrokes suggest trees on a distant hill. Broad washes laid in glazes are used to suggest a wooded area at a distance, while fine, delicate lines can be used to create twigs at the ends of branches. Layering splatters of wet paint not only builds up the impression of leaves but also implies movement and a slight breeze. And the infamous watercolour cauliflowers are superb for building up texture within foliage!

Although considered by some as a very difficult medium to perfect, there is no doubt that its layered washes of bright, translucent colours can result in brilliant, jewel-like paintings; this is a brilliance often difficult to recreate with other media. While suitable for creating meticulous, highly detailed paintings, rendered through thousands of tiny brushstrokes, it is equally suitable for creating spontaneous, sweeping, gestural works.

An Extremely Sensitive Medium

Watercolour is an extremely sensitive medium. It has been said that, when buying watercolour paints, price more accurately reflects quality than for any other medium, and we cannot disagree with this premise. However, it is not just the quality of the paint that is important; so too are the other two fundamental elements that come together to make a watercolour painting: brushes and paper. In watercolour painting, the quality of paint, of brushes and of paper each has a direct influence and effect on the outcome of the finished work.

One poor element will make a technically successful painting more difficult to achieve. We are not referring here to whether it is a 'good' painting or not but to the technical handling of the medium itself. Poorer paints will not flow as well or be as bright. Cheaper, thinner papers are often so absorbent that they make laying a wash almost impossible, and a brush that splays or sheds hairs when being used is almost worthless. In order to promote ease of technical handling, the three key elements – paint, brushes and paper – should each be of the highest quality that one can afford.

Watercolour Paints

Quality

Again, watercolour is an extremely sensitive medium, and it is undeniable that, the better the quality of the paint that you buy, the easier it will be to work with and the more satisfied you will be with the results. Most manufactures will produce two ranges of paints; one will be 'artist quality' and the other a cheaper student quality. Always buy the best you can afford, without exception. You will achieve greater success with a few tubes of artist-quality paints of primary colours than a large range of student-quality paints of an assortment of colours.

Tubes and pans

We both have a preference for tubes when working in the studio, because it is so much easier to make rich, dark tones. The larger quantities of darks required for landscapes and larger images are simply not possible to achieve with pan paints. Even apart from the creation of dark tones, it is easier to mix larger quantities of paint by using tubes; timing is important for watercolour, and the time taken to mix a quantity of paint by using pans may result in you missing the precise moment at which you needed to apply it to the painting.

However, when painting *en plein air*, pan paints can be extremely useful. They are easier to transport, and the box in which they come usually doubles as a portable palette. A good brand for *en plein air* work is St Petersburg White Nights; these paints give up plenty of colour as soon as they are wet.

An alternative would be to buy a folding palette with empty pans, which you can fill yourself from your tube paints.

Properties

Watercolour pigments have certain characteristics that are very useful to know about. These are granulation, opacity, staining and lightfastness. Understanding the effects of these characteristics will influence your choice of pigments to use in a painting.

A granulating pigment will dry to leave flocculation evident in the paint. This can be used to great effect when painting trees, as, by choosing a granulating pigment, you can encourage the formation of textures that represent foliage with relative ease.

Paints containing opaque pigments are very useful in landscapes, where the haziness caused by their opacity can be used effectively to suggest aerial perspective. For example, adding cobalt blue or cobalt violet to the green mix used for the depiction of trees in the distance will soften the colour and give the painting a greater sense of depth.

Due to their opacity, these pigments can be used over darker layers of paint, for example, to paint paler leaves over darker washes, although this can be of limited success and an alternative medium such as gouache or ink might be preferred.

Opaque pigments can be difficult to use as underwashes, as they have a tendency to move when re-wetted.

Some pigments stain the paper; this is very useful for underwashes and glazing techniques. Furthermore, glazing techniques are very useful when painting trees, wherever they appear in your composition, as the layers of colour add depth and texture to the foliage. Being aware that a pigment is of a staining character also means that you can avoid it if lifting-off techniques are to be used, such as when using a mask to lift off leaf-shaped patches of a glaze to reveal lighter 'leaves' in the lower glaze.

Get to know your paints. Ultramarine blue is a good example of a granulating colour that is also non-staining. These characteristics make it possible to lift dry paint of this colour with a damp brush. It is essential to understand how all of your watercolours perform, and tests such as this one should be employed for all of your watercolours.

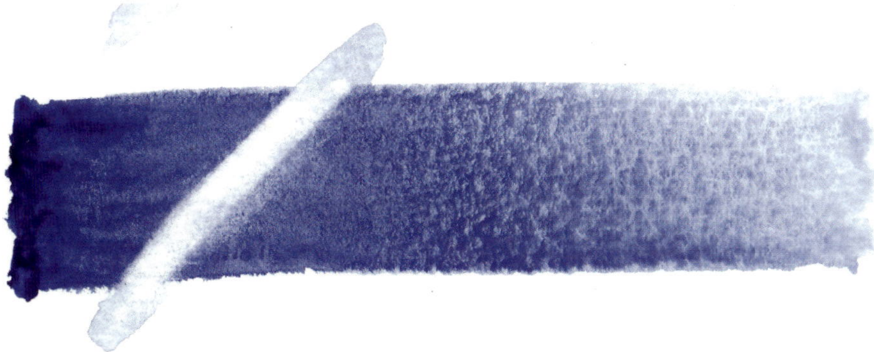

Useful paint colours (top to bottom):

Ultramarine blue

Cobalt blue

Winsor blue (green shade)

Permanent rose

Cadmium red

Sap green

Green gold

Burnt sienna

Raw sienna

New gamboge

Lemon yellow

Quinacridone gold

Permanent mauve

May green

Translucent orange

This is by no means a comprehensive list of colours; however, the listed paints will produce a wide range of useful mixes, particularly if the paints selected are of artist quality.

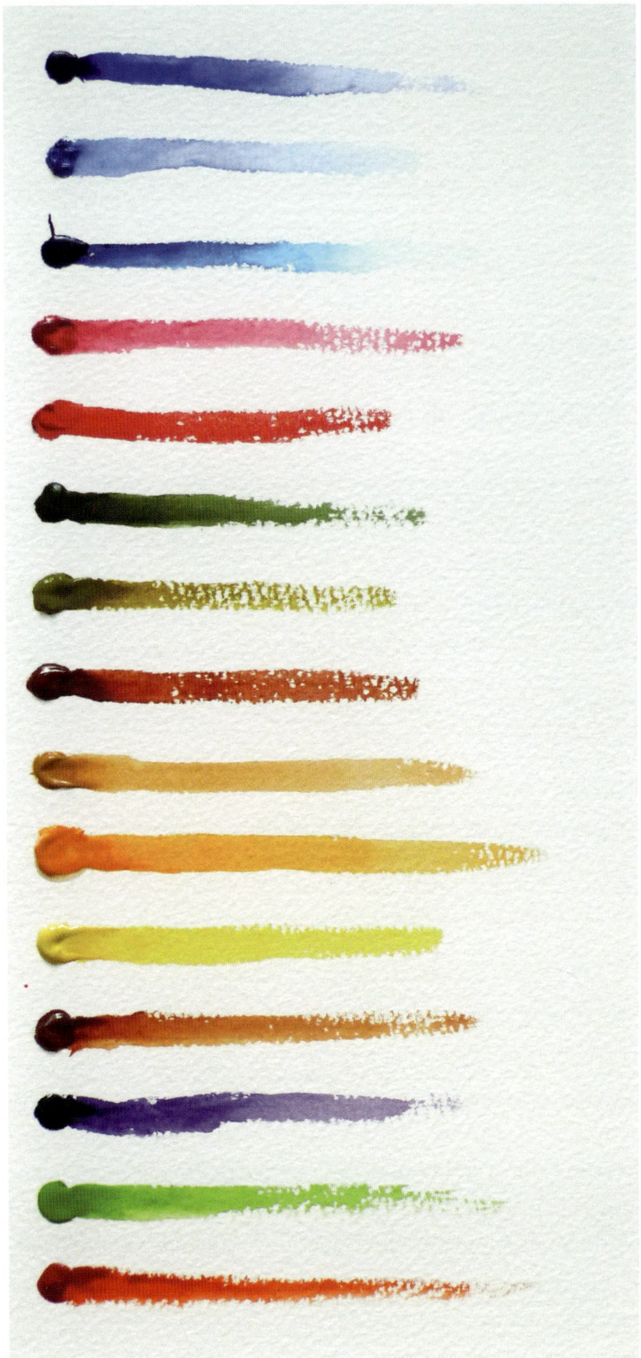

A WORD ON MIXING GREENS...

Amongst the art community, a long-running debate is over whether one should always mix a green or whether it is perfectly acceptable to work with a manufacturer's premixed green. When it comes to painting trees, at some stage, however much you might try to avoid it, you will have to work with a green and will also find yourself entering the debate. In our opinion, there is nothing wrong with using a prepared green.

One argument against manufactured greens is that they are often unnatural or too vibrant, having a very artificial appearance. But there is no rule that they should be used neat; after all, yellows and blues need to be mixed to produce a green! As with any other colour, if it is not exactly what you require, it is wise to add a touch of another colour to it, to achieve the desired hue

Another argument is that using too many pigments will cause the colours to become muddy. Note that not all manufactured greens are made by mixing numerous pigments; viridian, for example, is a single pigment, so this argument does not apply to its use. Many modern pigments remain bright and fresh even after mixing; alternatively, you may want muddied colours!

Used judiciously as one of the paints that you choose for the palette for an image, manufactured greens can provide a convenient and consistent base for the range of greens that you need.

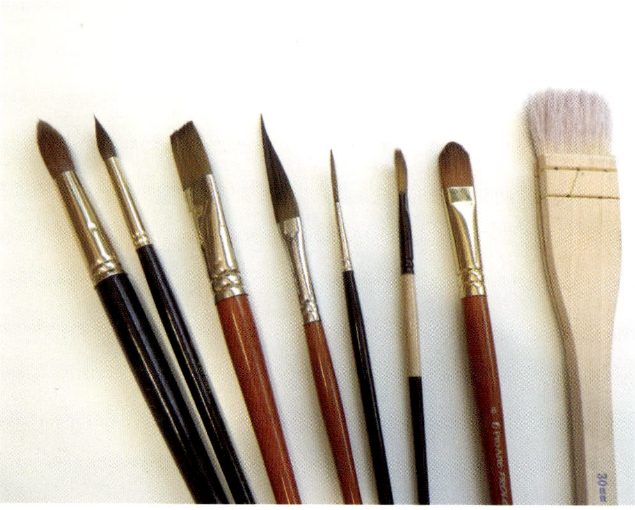

Watercolour brushes. Although it is not essential to have lots of watercolour brushes, it is essential to work with good-quality brushes. Illustrated are a selection of brushes: two rounds, a flat, a swordliner, a rigger, a dagger, a filbert and a hake.

Watercolour Brushes

Watercolour brushes come in a huge variety of sizes, shapes and qualities. Look for brushes that hold their shape when wet and spring back into shape when lifted from the paper, enabling you to make consistent marks.

Sable brushes are of an excellent quality, and it is worth investing in a few of your preferred shapes, but it is also true that you may find synthetic brushes very useful. Build up a selection of brushes with which you are able to make a wide range of marks; try rounds, flats, swordliners, riggers, daggers, filberts and hakes.

There will be brushes that will help you to create fine marks for twigs, for example, a rigger and a swordliner. Round brushes can make some interesting leaf shapes when used with a printing action, while a dagger brush can make superb leaf shapes when its tip is twisted as the brush is lifted from the paper as you apply the paint. A flat can be very helpful when laying down a base wash for tree trunks.

All brushes have been designed with particular purposes in mind, but through experimentation you may find that you are able to make many other marks that the original manufacturer had not thought of! Remember that the brush does not make the marks, you do. Try to complete the project 'Learning through play' each time that you acquire a new brush. Keep the result as a reference, a sort of dictionary of the marks that you can make with each brush (or other implement). You will soon have such a range of marks available to you for representing trunks, branches, leaves and whole trees that the question will not be 'How do I paint the...?' but 'Which way shall I choose to paint that ... in this image?'.

Watercolour Paper

The degree to which watercolour responds to the surface that it is painted on is remarkable. Watercolour papers have been very carefully designed so that the artist can use the surface of the paper to enhance or modify paint effects. The marks made using the same brush and hand movement will vary according to the texture and absorbency of the paper being used.

There are three types of surface texture available: rough, NOT (not hot pressed, or cold pressed) and HP (hot pressed).

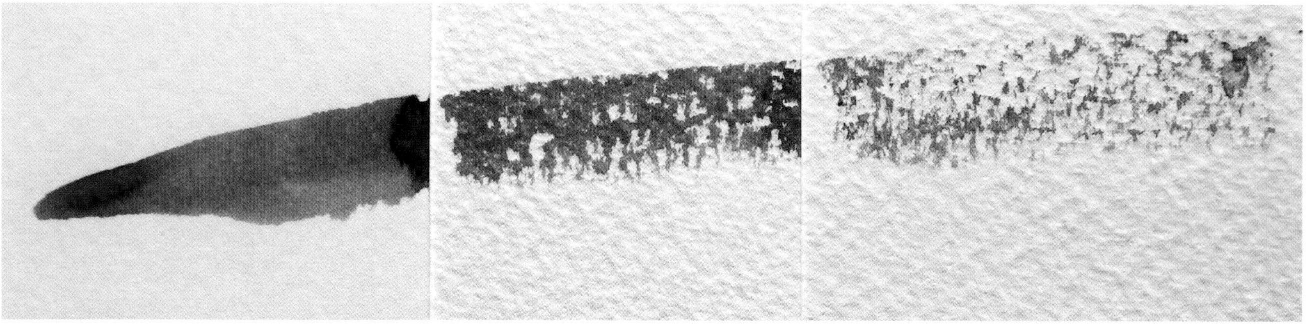

The single watercolour brushstrokes made on three different paper surfaces clearly show the different effects that each paper's texture has upon the brushstroke. Therefore, the choice of paper and the quality of brushstrokes wanted in the finished artwork must be carefully considered. The papers are, left to right, hot pressed (HP), cold pressed (NOT) and rough.

Rough and NOT papers have a textured surface so are the most suitable for paintings of trees. When using a dry brushstroke, paint can skim the surface of the bumps; this is an excellent way to paint leaves! When working with granulating paint, the pigment will gather in pools in the dips, the combination of the paint and the paper producing the effect of foliage with a variety of tones with little help from the artist.

Rough papers are more textured than NOT papers; this additional texture is an advantage when a great deal of painted texture or movement is required. NOT papers are more suitable if an image requires a degree of accuracy of line, which is harder to achieve on rough papers.

HP papers are very smooth; generally, they are used for careful, exact work. These papers might be suitable if you want to make a more precise study of a tree, such as *The Big Beech Tree: Winter* (*see* the beginning of Chapter 8), or a leaf.

While sketches and colour notes can be made on unstretched paper, it is advisable to stretch watercolour paper before attempting a painting. Neither of us would attempt making a painting on unstretched paper, as we do not like working with the inevitable cockles, or buckling and wrinkling (*see* the accompanying 'Stretching paper' box). For this reason, we tend to buy 300gsm (140lb) paper. Heavier papers do not cockle when wet, but manufacturers recommend stretching paper of up to about 600lb, at which point we find the price inhibits our creativity!

Always buy good-quality paper for watercolour painting. Watercolour paper has been designed to allow paint to sit on the surface and be moved around, adhering without being fully absorbed. All paper is delicate, but some papers have a harder surface than others, allowing reworking, washing off, the application of lifting techniques and the use of masking fluid. Your choice of paper will influence the techniques that you are able to use successfully.

For the watercolour step-by-step demonstration projects in this book, we have used Bockingford NOT paper (300gsm/140lb), because it fulfils the criteria mentioned previously. Its surface allows the use of masking fluid and gives the artist opportunities to lift off, wash off and rework paint, which are all useful attributes while experimenting and developing one's skills.

We have a few preferred papers, which include the just-mentioned Bockingford paper and papers from Two Rivers and Fabriano.

Two Rivers rag-based paper (300gsm/140lb) has a lovely, randomly textured surface, which contributes to some interesting granulation effects. It is a particularly useful paper when using lifting-off techniques.

The Fabriano papers Fabriano 5 and Fabriano Artistico are both very smooth papers with a lovely tooth that are excellent for very detailed work and a delight to work with when using graphite.

STRETCHING PAPER

Many artists stretch their watercolour paper before painting on it. Stretching is done to stop the paper from cockling when washes are applied; cockling can make painting very difficult, as the more washes that are applied, the greater the paper can buckle and warp.

1 Soak the paper in cold water for a couple of minutes, or longer if the paper is of a very heavy weight. If using the kitchen sink or bath, make certain that it is clear of any soap or cleaning residue, as any of this residue that is transferred to the paper can affect the paper's performance when it is being painted.
2 Carefully lift the sheet so as not to damage the paper's surface. Lay it carefully on to a wooden or plywood board, no less than 13mm (½in) in thickness, and leave it undisturbed for about one minute.
3 Cut four pieces of gum strip to appropriate sizes (each a little longer than the side of the paper to which the strip will be stuck, with one strip per side). One at a time, moisten each strip and stick it to the appropriate side of the paper, ensuring that it contacts both the paper and the board: make certain that at least a third of the gum strip is stuck to the watercolour paper and that the remainder of it is stuck to the board. Be careful not to moisten the gum strip too much, as this can weaken the strength of the adhesion. Masking tape will not do as a substitute for gum strip. If puddles of water have gathered on the paper's surface or the board, remove the water carefully with kitchen roll.
4 Avoiding direct heat, leave the paper to dry flat on the board, overnight if possible.

To check whether the paper is completely dry, use the back of your fingers or hand to test it. If it feels colder than the ambient temperature of the room, it is still damp and needs to be left longer to dry. Some artists will test the surface of the paper by drawing on it with a 2B pencil. If it makes a mark easily then it is likely to be dry enough to use.

Watercolour: Other Equipment

Palettes

Palettes with large, flat wells allow the paints to be mixed to show the full range of colours achievable with the pigments that you have chosen. A two-, three- or even four-way mix is possible. Given the accepted understanding amongst artists that the range of greens necessary when painting trees can be overwhelming, this method of mixing paint removes at least some of the difficulty.

Kitchen roll

This is an essential piece of equipment for watercolourists, and it is used to ensure the correct degree of wetness of the brush, by lightly touching the brush on to the kitchen roll to remove excess paint or water. It is also used to lift paint off of a painted image to create texture or reveal underwashes.

Masking fluid

Masking fluid is one of the most useful materials that a watercolourist can employ, especially when painting trees. Areas can be reserved for successive washes, so that it becomes easy to paint light, bright leaves against a darker background, or patches of sunlight hitting branches or trunks in shady areas.

This liquid rubber solution is applied either over paper to reserve its white surface or over washes to reserve colour. It can be applied with a colour shaper, ruling pen, dip pen, mapping pen, toothbrush or special masking-fluid brush; however, do not use it with good brushes, as it dries very quickly and is impossible to remove from the brushes' bristles or hairs. When applying it, think of it as paint and make similar marks as you would make with paint; this will ensure that the areas you reserve with it are correct for the image.

If you find the masking fluid a little too viscous to apply in fine lines, add a few drops of water to thin it. Fine lines and marks will be much easier to create with the freer-flowing formula, and the desired effect is therefore more likely to be achievable.

Apply it to dry paper, and wait for it to dry completely before continuing with the painting. Do not attempt to remove it until the paper is dry throughout (not just surface dry). Remove it by rubbing it gently with clean fingers, which releases the marking fluid from the surface of the paper.

Masking tape

This can be used to mask out areas of a painting, to hold paper to a board or to create a sharp, crisp edge to paint against. Whatever its role, make certain that you use the low-tack variety. If the tape is too sticky, it can damage the paper's surface when it is being removed, making further washes of colour difficult to apply.

Watercolour media

There is a good selection of watercolour media available, to assist the artist in creating a desired effect within a painting.

Gum arabic slows down the flow of paint; it can be useful, for example, when painting the reflections of trees in water.

Granulation medium increases the granulation effect of some pigments, which can really help with creating the texture of foliage.

Sponges

Sponges, both natural and synthetic, can be used for applying paint and for its removal. A painted natural sponge produces some interesting printed marks when it is dabbed on to paper; this technique is ideal for creating the foliage on distant trees. Clean, wet sponges can also be used to lift out watercolour, to soften areas of a watercolour painting, should they have become overworked, or to create particular effects.

Sandpaper

Scratching sandpaper over the surface of a watercolour painting executed on a rough, textured paper can produce some interesting effects. The scratching will remove the paint from the paper's highest points, thereby revealing the white of the paper, but it will leave the paint in the lowest points of the paper. Think of the paper as a series of hilltops and valleys. The paint is removed from the hilltops, but it will still remain in the valleys. This technique can be used to indicate sparkling, light leaves or to emphasize the rough texture of bark on a tree.

Watercolour: Tips and Techniques

Mixing colours

Mixing different colours of paints is an essential technique for every watercolour artist to master. The method described here avoids running out of a mixed colour, which is a common problem when simply adding paint colours to a palette and immediately making an homogenous mix.

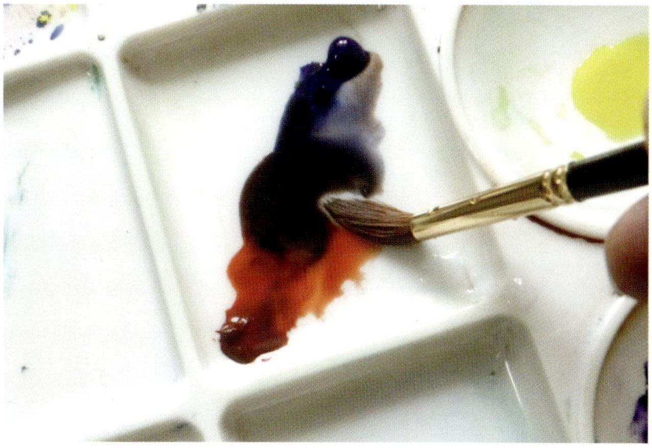

Two paint colours and water being mixed within a palette well.

For tube paints, squeeze out a pea-sized amount of each colour of paint required for a particular mix, placing the dispensed paint of each colour into opposite corners of a single palette well. With a brush loaded with water, pull the first colour towards the centre of the well. Rinse the brush. Using the wet brush, pull the second colour towards the first. Do not add more water than is necessary to move the paint, as too much water would allow the paint to mix in an uncontrolled way.

As the two paints meet, mix the colours together to produce a gradated strip that gradually blends from one paint to the other, giving you the full range of colours that can be made from the two starting colours.

Using this method makes it easy to see the colours as you mix them, taking the guesswork out of how much of each colour to add to achieve a particular hue. This means that, if you have not mixed enough of a particular colour, it is very easy to continue mixing it from your two original paints, quickly matching it to your original mix.

These mixes will be in the darkest tones possible to achieve from your two original paints. To create a lighter tone, make a puddle of water away from the gradated colour, and pull your chosen hue towards it. The tone can be adjusted by adding more water or pulling in more paint. If a large amount is needed, make the puddle of water in a second well, and use your brush to transfer your chosen mixed colour to that well. This ensures the gradated colours are undisturbed so that you can carry on using them.

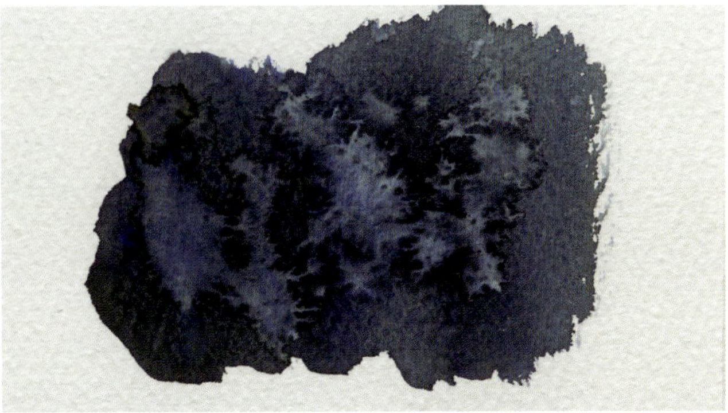

Multiple cauliflowers created throughout a wash covering a large area.

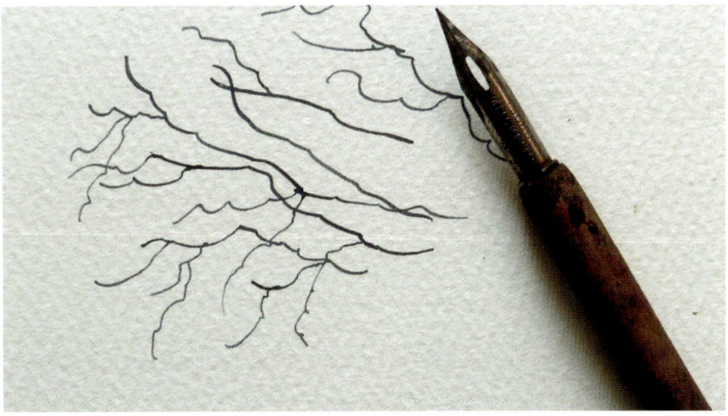

A selection of lines of different tones and thicknesses, drawn by using a dip pen and watercolour paint.

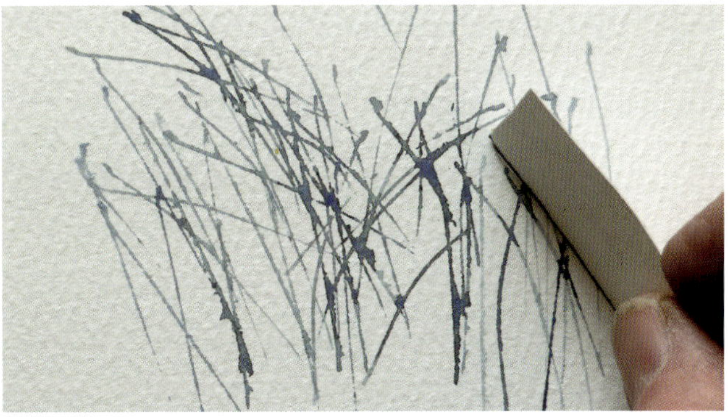

Watercolour paint can be applied by printing. Here, the edge of a piece of watercolour paper is being used.

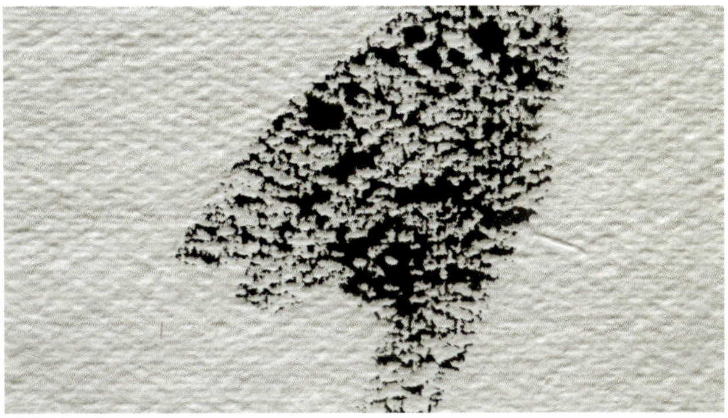

A dry brushstroke made on to a textured paper.

Creating cauliflowers

Cauliflowers, also known as back runs, are created when more paint or water is added to a previously applied wash before that wash is completely dry. Many painters work very hard to avoid creating them. However, they can be deliberately employed to create textures, particularly when depicting foliage and undergrowth.

Creating fine lines

It is often necessary to create fine lines within a painting. Although a fine rigger brush can be used to create fine lines in watercolour, an old-fashioned dip pen is sometimes more controllable and may be a better choice for depicting details such as twigs and branches. Often used with ink, these pens can work equally as well with watercolour paints.

Printing

Watercolour paint can be applied by printing using a variety of objects. One very simple method is to take a straight-edged piece of paper, dip it into a puddle of paint and use this edge to print marks. Since the paper can be held straight, held bent or held in a curved shape, it can be very useful for painting twigs, fine branches and even grasses. Similarly, the paper can be held straight, bent or curved to produce a variety of shapes.

Further variety can be achieved by using paper strips of different lengths. Variation in tone and colour can be created by working from mixed colours on the palette and by crossing printed marks while the paint is still wet, so that the colours run from one mark to another.

Using a dry brush

Another option available to the watercolourist is to use dry brushstrokes. Working with very little water in the brush is often referred to as working with a 'dry brush'. This creates a very broken brushmark. You can combine dry brushing with using a very rough paper; in this case, the resultant mark becomes very coarse indeed. This effect is wonderful when depicting the texture of a tree's bark.

Using masking fluid

Masking fluid is used to protect the colour – often white – of the paper, and it can be applied to suitable paper with a variety of implements. Suitable brushes, rubber-tipped colour shapers and dip pens are some of the most common types of equipment that are used for this purpose.

Dropping in and creating soft edges

For watercolour painting, 'dropping in' refers to paint being added to a still-wet wash. It is the basis for the wet-in-wet watercolour technique and can create some interesting colour mixes and effects.

Allowing the boundaries of two different regions of wet paint to touch before the paint dries can be used to create soft edges. Similarly, when applying paint with a brush to wet paper, a soft edge can deliberately be created, by stopping the brush short of where the edge is required; the water carries the paint beyond its region of application and causes the paint to diffuse slightly. It is important that the colour does not carry as far as the point where the wet area meets dry paper. The paint will flow where the paper is wet; if it meets the boundary of the wet area, it will form a hard line.

Another way to create a soft edge is to use a brush loaded with clean water to 'paint' along the edge of a region of dried paint, to disperse the paint a little where the water was applied. Again, it is important not to allow paint to flow to the boundary of the newly wetted area.

Alternatively, a brush holding some clean water can be used to lift some paint from a specific part of the painting, to produce a soft edge there.

Spattering

'Spattering' is the term given to flicking watercolour paint on to paper. It creates some wonderful foliage-like effects, particularly when built up gradually from light-toned colours to increasingly darker-toned ones. To work effectively, each stage must be allowed to dry before the application of the next.

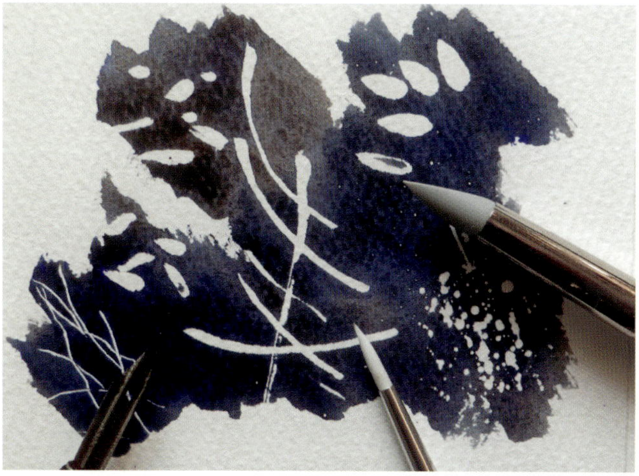

This example demonstrates the different types of marks that can be achieved when applying masking fluid with different artist's equipment.

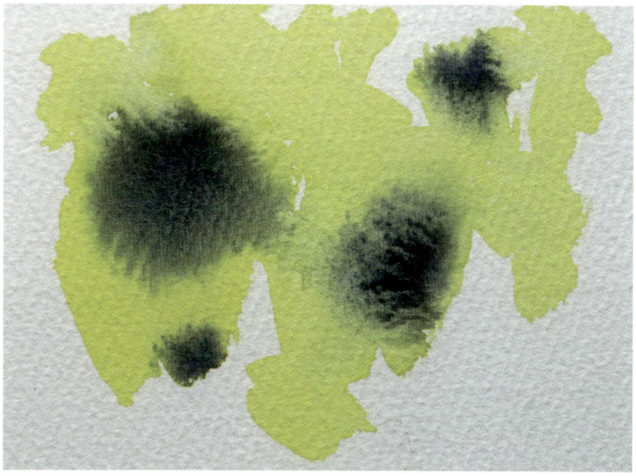

The still-wet yellow wash has had paint of a different colour dropped into it, resulting in various colours and tones.

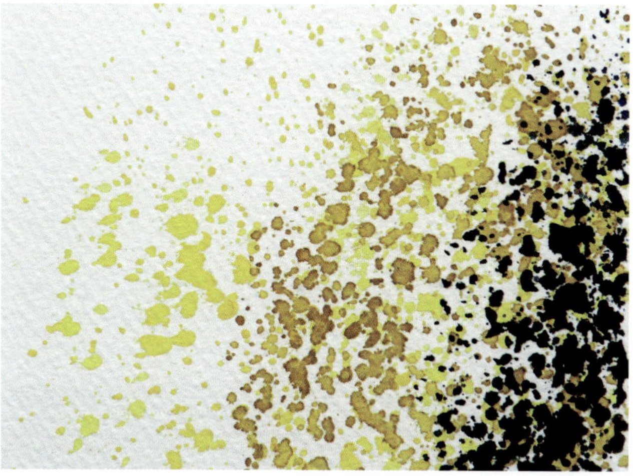

Spattering built up with three applications of paint of different colours and tones.

WATER-MIXABLE OILS

'Water-mixable oil paints' is a term that often raises an eyebrow; surely oil and water do not mix? Despite some initial reluctance to the very idea of them, the benefits they offer were tempting enough to overcome our reservations, and we both have been pleasantly surprised by their performance and outcomes.

Water-mixable oils (sometimes referred to as water-miscible or water-soluble oils) are genuine oil paints. Unlike their traditional counterparts, they do not require a range of solvents, such as turpentine and white spirit, for thinning and cleaning purposes. Instead, they can be thinned with water and are easily cleaned up with soap and water. While some may miss the aromas associated with traditional oils, water-mixable oils are odourless and are therefore much more convenient when working in a studio within a family home. Although they can be used with just water, there are ranges of speciality water-mixable media available to use with them. Used with water, they dry over just a few days, giving ample to time to continue working on a painting without having to wait too long for the layers of paint to dry.

As with any other medium, take time to familiarize yourself with water-mixable oils through experimentation. Given their name, it is tempting to simply compare them with traditional oils, but rather than do this, take time to also compare them with watercolours and acrylics, thinking of them as a medium in their own right and discovering what they are capable of.

There is a strong tradition of painting landscapes, which inevitably include trees, with oils. The choice of oil or watercolour is usually down to personal choice and may depend on the mood and atmosphere you intend to evoke in your painting. Having said that, there are some wonderful textural marks possible with oils, resulting from their consistency, that are not available to the watercolourist.

Of course, oil paints can be applied thinly and very smoothly, but when it comes to painting trees, it is the characteristics imparted by the consistency of the oil paints that should be used to advantage. Oil paints hold the shape of the brushmarks (or palette knife), which can be used to great effect when painting trees. A distant tree line can be implied in the texture of a sweeping brushstroke. The heavy solidity of a tree trunk is easily represented by oil paint applied thickly with a palette knife; a palette knife can also be used to scratch into the oil in order to depict branches. Leaves for which oil paint is applied with a dabbing action have a physical thickness that will cast shadows on the surface of the painting and add depth to the depicted foliage.

Note: All of the oil paintings in this book have been executed by using water-mixable oils.

Oil-Painting Brushes

It often appears that the oil painter has more brushes than does the watercolour painter. In part, this is because oil painting can be very hard on brushes; scuffing, dabbing and working on slightly abrasive surfaces all take their toll on the poor, old brush. Some artists refer to these actions on and changes to their brushes as 'breaking them in'; their brushes become like old friends, producing unique, telltale marks. Eventually, the brushes wear, and they have to be replaced; however, many artists find these brushes difficult to throw out, and they end up in pots dotted around the studio!

Brushes come in various shapes and styles. They can range from having natural or synthetic bristles, being soft or hard, or being short- or long-haired. They also span a range of prices.

A good place to start would be to gather a range of flats, rounds, filberts and riggers of varying sizes, as these will offer the painter a wide range of mark-making and painting opportunities.

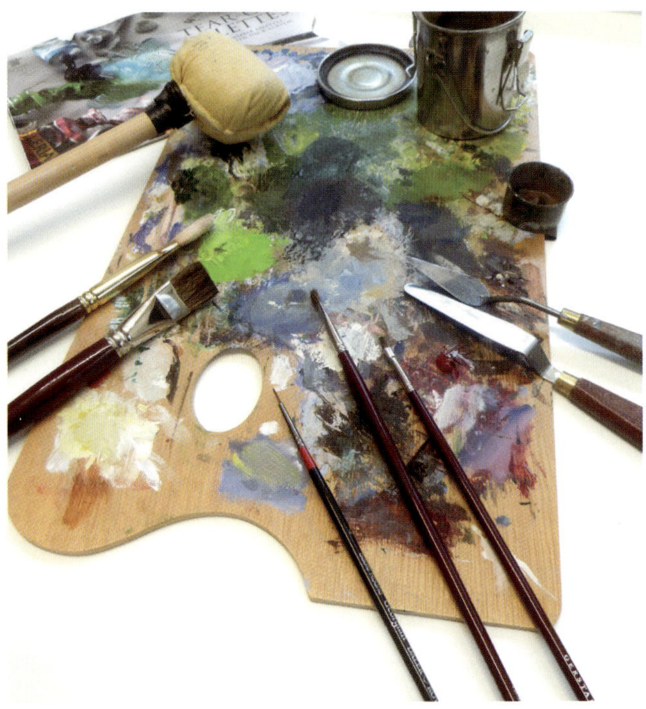

Clockwise from top left: a collection of palettes, a paint kettle, a dipper, palette knives, brushes and a mahl stick, used for oil painting.

The following list of oil colours will produce a wide range of mixes, from strong, interesting darks to bright lights, as well as a wonderful range of greens. Remember that colour is very much a matter of taste; take this list as suggestions of colours to use, and substitute other colours if those listed do not appeal to you.

Useful paint colours (top to bottom):

Alizarin crimson

Permanent rose

Cadmium red

French ultramarine blue

Cobalt blue

Lemon yellow

Cadmium yellow light

Sap green

Phthalo green (blue shade)

Olive green

Burnt sienna

Raw sienna

Titanium white

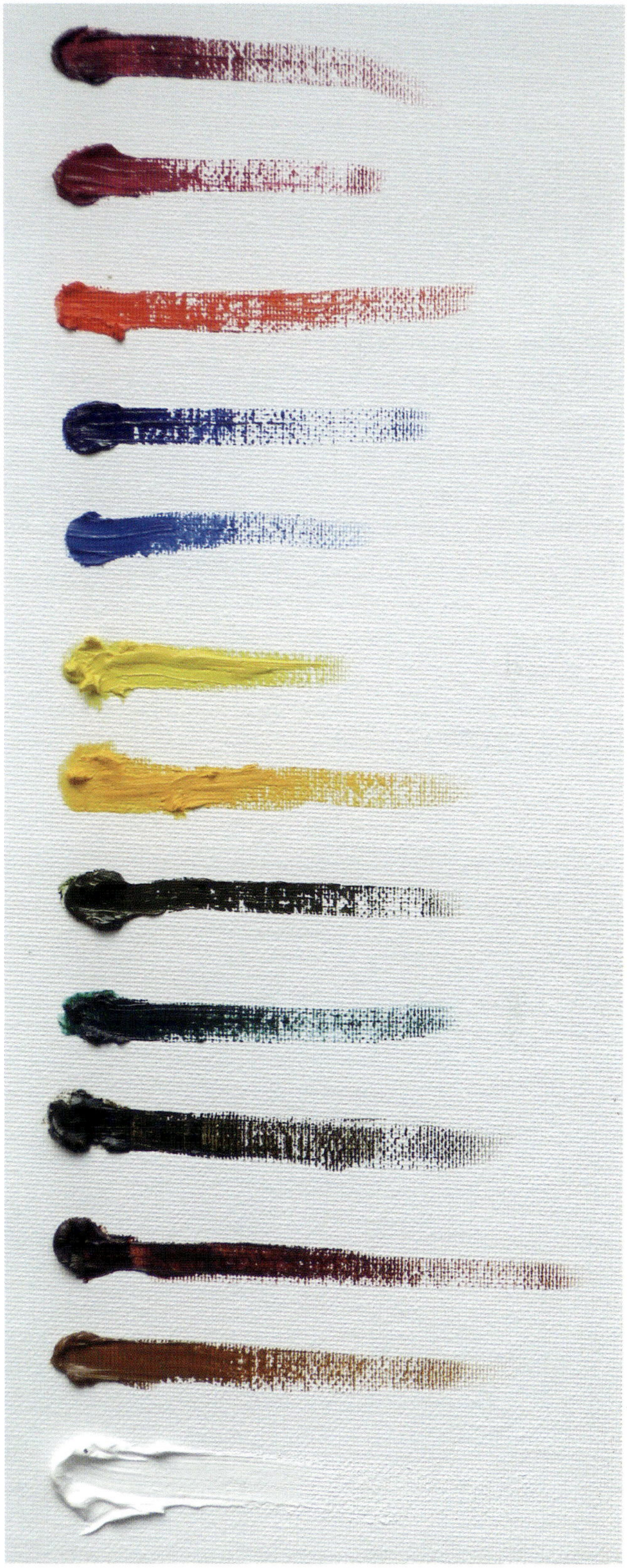

Palette Knives

Palette knives are used to mix paint on the palette or to scrape off areas of paint that haven't quite worked from the painting's surface. As mark-making tools, they are exciting. Palette knives are used to apply paint to the surface, and with skilful use, can produce an extraordinary range of marks, which in part accounts for the large range of sizes and shapes available. They can be used alongside brushes, although some artists chose to use them exclusively, because of the exciting marks that they can make with them. Although some plastic knives are now on the market, the traditional metal ones still seem to outperform their modern counterparts.

Water-Mixable Oils: Supports

There are many types of supports available for the oil painter. Stretched canvases, canvas boards, gessoed boards, wood, metal and even certain papers can be used to paint on. The surface to be painted on is usually primed with gesso, which is available as both traditional casein gesso and acrylic gesso. Ready-primed supports are also freely available from art suppliers.

The supports used in this book are home-made. For each support, a piece of MDF board is cut to size; this size is entirely subjective and dependent on factors such as having a particular image in mind or whether you need the board to fit neatly to a pochade box.

The board is then primed with a household acrylic primer that has been mixed with some powdered Polyfilla to the consistency of double cream. This surface works extremely well with the water-mixable oil paints. The acrylic primer supports the oil paint, preventing it from soaking into the board, while the addition of Polyfilla reduces the drying time. The Polyfilla also gives the surface a very nice 'tooth' to work upon. The addition of the Polyfilla means that a texture can be applied to the surface as it is primed. While it is a good idea to prepare boards in advance, having a particular image in mind before applying the priming coats means that you can make marks in the surface that are appropriate to the image, having the surface textured in some areas and smooth in others.

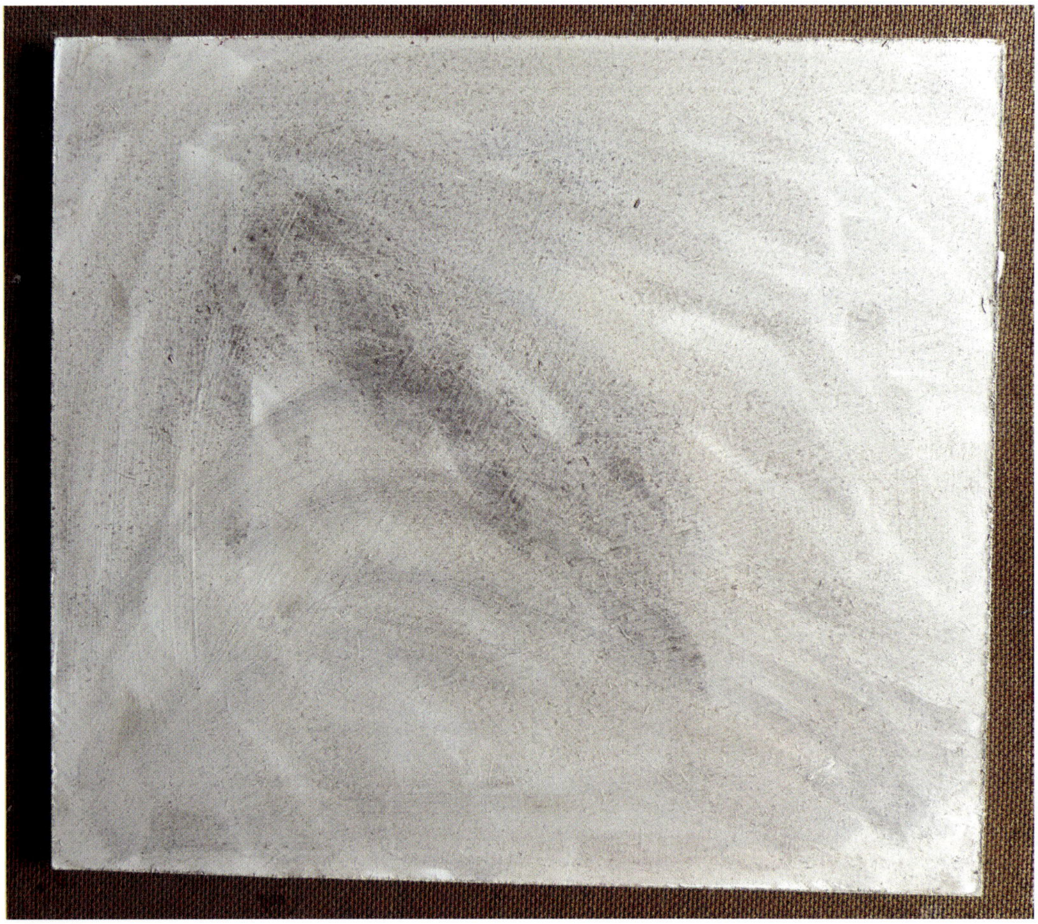

This board has been prepared by using an acrylic primer, over which a ground of a neutral grey has been applied.

The colour of the support is known as the ground. It is possible to work directly on to the white gesso ground; however, many artists prefer to tint the ground with a thin wash of midtone colour, making it somewhat easier to judge the lights and darks against. A coloured ground also has the added advantage that it pulls the painting together in its later stages. If small parts remain unpainted, the coloured ground peeps through, bringing more of a unity to the finished piece. These grounds tend to be neutral greys, commonly painted with mixes of French ultramarine blue, burnt sienna and raw sienna, although a ground can be of any colour.

When preparing a ground, mix the required colours into a very watery wash. Paint this on to the board with a brush, or wipe it on to the surface of the board with a rag, and leave the ground to dry.

Water-Mixable Oils: Other Equipment

Palettes

Many types of palettes are available; the decision of which to use is a matter of personal choice, and this will vary depending on where and when the palette is to be used.

In the studio, large, flat, rectangular palettes are often chosen, made from mahogany, glass or Perspex. Those with a thumb hole are easy to handle and hold and, being flat, allow for ease of mixing colours, especially if you will be mixing with a palette knife. Ceramic tiles make a good alternative, being flat and easy to wipe clean. For working on location, some portable easels and pochade boxes cleverly incorporate a glass palette within their overall design.

A very useful alternative is a tear-off palette. These come in the form of a pad consisting of tear-off sheets of greaseproof-like paper that is impervious to oil or acrylic. At the end of the painting session, the palette is simply folded and thrown away.

Tip: Whichever palette is chosen, it is useful to set out the colours in the same order every time that you paint. In the throes of painting, it is much easier to know where a colour is on the palette rather than having to hunt for it every time a mix with this colour is required.

Dippers and paint kettles

When you are in the studio, an old plastic pot or jam jar is ideal for keeping the water in that is used to thin the paint. However, when on location, a dipper or paint kettle is ideal to work with. The dipper clips to the side of the palette and is very easy to use. Being not too large, it doesn't get in the way when you are painting but carries enough liquid, reducing the need of constant refilling. The more expensive dippers have screw-on lids that make them perfect for carrying in a sketching bag, as the risk of leaking is greatly reduced.

A paint kettle, sometimes known as a brush washer, is much larger than a dipper and hangs from the easel when you are painting. Again, being leak-resistant, it is ideal for using when on location away from the studio.

Mahl sticks

This is a lightweight stick that allows the artist to rest their working hand on it, to steady the hand, thus avoiding touching of the wet paint of a painting that is under way. Traditionally, one end of the stick will have a ball made of cotton that is wrapped in soft or chamois leather, which is securely tied to the stick, and the stick will be about one metre (thirty-six inches) long. They are not overly expensive to buy.

A very simple home-made version can be easily assembled, consisting of a piece of thick dowel and a car-windscreen demister pad that is securely wrapped and attached to one end of the dowel. In practice, the mahl stick is obviously useful when resting your hand, but it is also handy when checking horizontals and verticals, or indeed anything that needs a straight edge.

Easels

It is difficult to picture an oil painter without seeing them in front of an easel although, of course, many prefer not to use one. For advice on choosing an easel, *see* the section 'General equipment' later in this chapter.

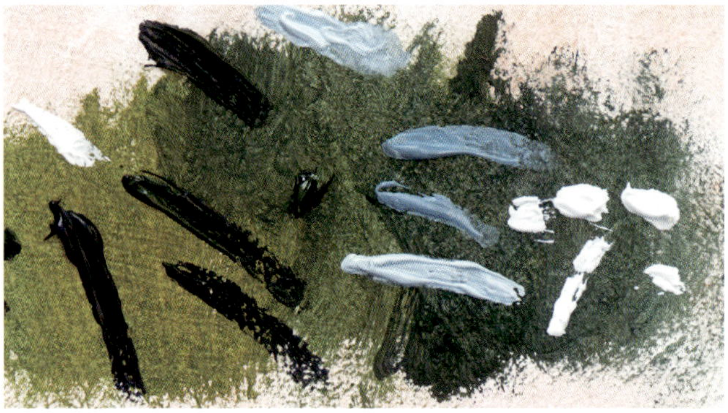

An example of the obvious, three-dimensional, textural effects achievable with the impasto technique.

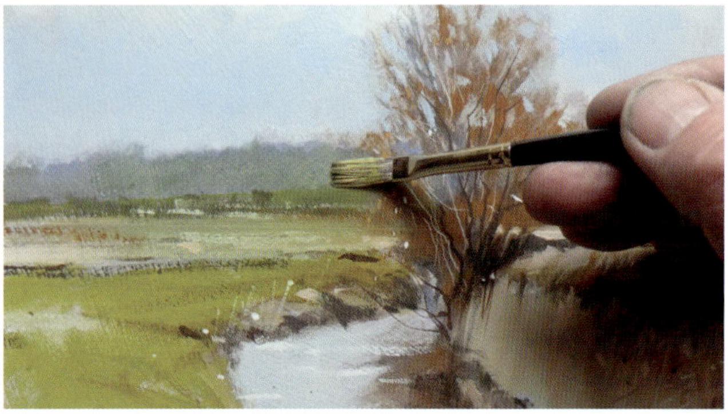

Applying a glaze to an underpainting.

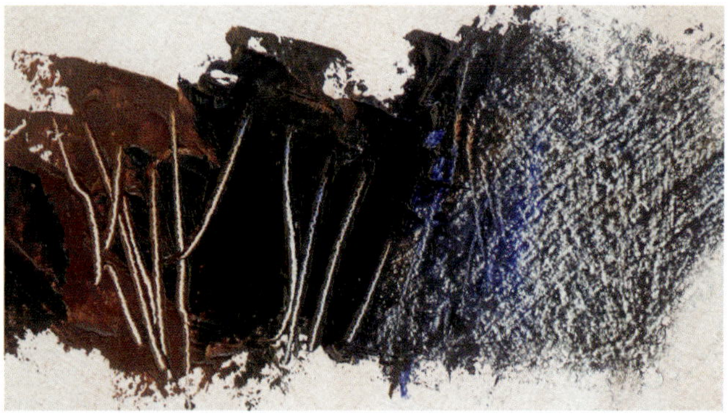

An example of some of the effects that can be achieved by scraping back and scratching out.

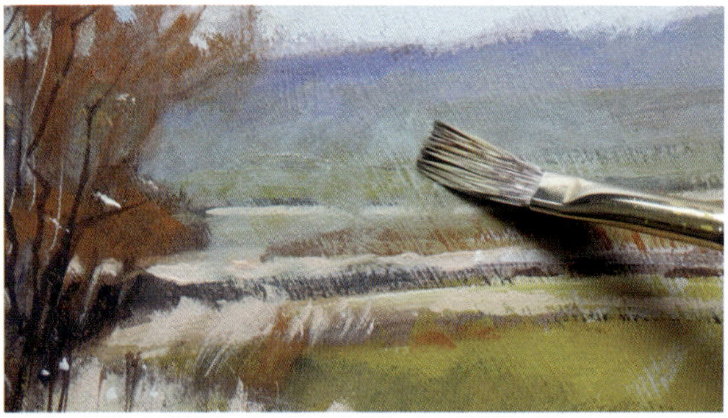

Using the scumbling technique.

Water-Mixable Oils: Tips and Techniques

Impasto

When paint is applied very thickly, creating obvious brushmarks and three-dimensional textures, it is referred to as 'impasto'. These bold, textural marks need to be applied confidently and with careful consideration, as their presence within a painting can command significant interest. The use of the impasto technique is ideal when painting the trunks or branches of trees, as the texture of the tree itself can be suggested by the form of the paint.

Glazing

A 'glaze' in oil painting, as the term might suggest, is a thin, transparent mix applied over a previously painted area that, although modifying the colours of the layers below it, allows for the colours to show through. It is important that the underpainting is touch-dry before adding the glaze, for the technique to work successfully. The colour used for the glazing needs to be thinned with a suitable medium; for this purpose, Winsor & Newton's artisan water-mixable stand oil works particularly well.

Scraping back and scratching out

This is not so much a technique – although it can produce some interesting effects – but a way of rescuing a painting! It would be a dishonest artist who would state that they never make a mistake when painting. Mistakes in oils can often be put right simply by scraping off the paint from the offending area with a palette knife and then repainting that area as required. The same palette knife can also be used to scratch out lines and other marks in painted areas, which is useful for creating the impression of fine branches and sunlit leaves.

Scumbling

Scumbling is similar to a glazing, but the scumbling mix has a little white paint mixed into it, making the scumbling semi-opaque rather than transparent. It is best applied over a previously dried area of the painting by using a dry-ish brush and a light, vigorous action. The scumbling mix's semi-opacity allows for some of the previously painted passages, or applications, of colour to show through the scumbling, creating interesting colour effects within the painting.

GOUACHE

Traditional Gouache

Gouache is similar to and behaves very much like watercolour. However, the significant difference between the two media is the high degree of opacity that is a characteristic of all gouache paints. It has been used by artists for hundreds of years and is sometimes referred to as body colour. The paint dries quickly to a chalky, matt finish and, when dry, can be re-wetted in much the same way that watercolours can be. Gouache lifts easily, so this re-wetting characteristic, although at times very useful, also means that any layering of paint must be handled very carefully, in order to prevent the previous layer from lifting. It will be noted that, when gouache dries, the colours seem to change; the darks tend to become slightly lighter and the lights a little darker: this is known as colour shift. Although this might sound rather worrying to the novice painter, with practice, one quickly compensates for this, adjusting mixes accordingly.

Although gouache can be used on its own to great effect, it is often used in combination with watercolour, its opacity allowing the painter to add lighter colours over darker ones within the painting. For artists who do not like using masking fluid, this can be useful for painting in lighter leaves over darker ones or highlights on a branch or trunk. The opacity of the body colour is also used effectively to imply aerial perspective, as the chalkiness adds to the hazy effect of a landscape being viewed at a distance. Gouache can also be used to increase the intensity and solidity of a deep shadow in a wood or under a tree depicted within a painting.

Traditional Gouache: Materials and Equipment

The materials and equipment (brushes, palettes, supports and so on) used for working with gouache are the same as those used for working with watercolour. However, because of the increased opacity of gouache compared to that of watercolour, many painters choose to keep the media apart when working with both, to prevent transparent watercolour washes from being clouded by traces of the opaque gouache. The same approach applies to water containers; it is a good idea to use one for watercolour and a separate one for gouache.

Acrylic Gouache

A relatively new medium addition to the art market in the last few years has been acrylic gouache. It is essentially an acrylic, matt, highly pigmented, opaque paint that, when dry, becomes waterproof. Unlike traditional gouache paint, which can be re-wetted once dry, the waterproof quality of acrylic gouache makes the building up of layers much easier to achieve and control, with the previous layers not being disturbed by the overpainting of the next layer. Unlike traditional gouache, where colours change upon drying, the dry colours are the same as those that were mixed in the palette, with negligible, if indeed any, colour shift. It is also more opaque than is traditional gouache, making it more useful for the painting of light colours over dark ones.

Within this book, this new medium has been used as an alternative to traditional gouache.

Acrylic Gouache: Materials and Equipment

As with traditional gouache, the materials and equipment used with acrylic gouache are the same as those used for watercolour painting. This includes the use of watercolour brushes. However, these paints include acrylic, which is quick-drying in nature and cannot be re-wetted. As a result, you will need to take care to keep the brushes wet as you work. Rinse them regularly, that is, every few minutes, even if that means reloading them with paint. Unlike acrylic brushes, watercolour brushes will become misshapen if left standing in a pot of water.

For these reasons, you may find that you prefer to use acrylic brushes, but be aware that some of the effects that you may wish to attempt will not be possible to achieve with acrylic brushes, although, of course, you may find it possible to create a whole range of marks that you prefer to include.

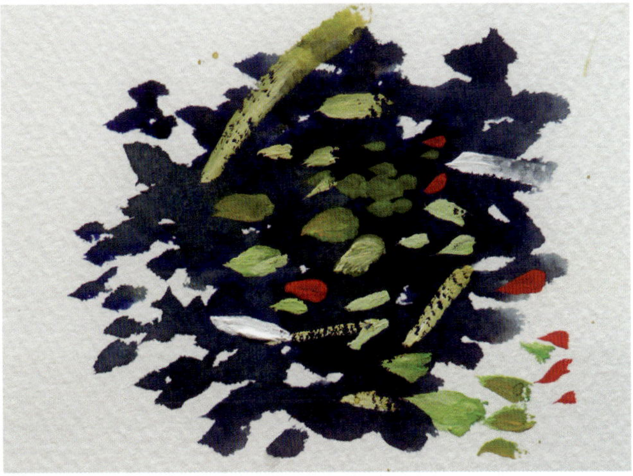

The opacity of acrylic gouache allows for a lighter colour to be successfully painted over a much darker one.

GRAPHITE

The pencil is such a commonplace household item, so humble and ordinary, that its capacity for artistic possibilities is often overlooked. It may be the first thing that you reach for when thinking about starting a drawing, but its potential as a medium in its own right remains unnoticed by many. Of course, it is usual to think of artists as owning and using pencils, and of course it is well known that a whole drawing can be made with them, but it is not the norm to consider them exciting.

And yet pencils can produce very exciting and extremely expressive marks! Available in a range of grades, they produce tones varying from light greys to rich, dark blacks.

Branching out into using graphite in its other forms, such as graphite sticks or powders, increases the possibilities of appealing and impressive mark-making. Graphite sticks, not having a wooden casing, allow the artist to make larger, more gestural marks. Graphite powders are useful for adding tone to large areas.

Graphite is usually thought of as a dry drawing medium, so it can be a delightful surprise to realize than it can be used wet.

AVOIDING MIXED-MEDIA MISHAPS

Working with mixed media can be exciting and invigorating, resulting in creative and interesting images. However, when you are lost in a flourish of creativity, the different properties of the media can result in some costly mistakes.

Watercolour is water-soluble and easily washes off of palettes, even after it has dried. On the other hand, acrylic media dry to an insoluble finish and have excellent properties of adherence. Palettes used for acrylic media quickly acquire layers of immovable dry paint, rendering them unsuitable for subsequent use with watercolours; note that it is difficult to mix transparent colours correctly if the palette is already coloured. It is advisable to keep separate palettes for watercolours and for acrylic media.

Similarly, brushes can quickly acquire dried acrylic paint or ink. If using both acrylic media and watercolour in the same painting, use separate jars of water; try labelling the water jars with masking tape or even placing them on different sides of the painting. Watercolourists, used to quickly rinsing and allowing their brushes to dry while they continue working, are particularly susceptible to this problem of appropriately managing and caring for their various brushes, so beware!

Graphite: Materials and Equipment

Pencils

Pencils are available in grades from 9H to H, in the HB grade and in grades from B to 9B. H stands for hard and produces soft greys. B stands for black, and the grades get progressively darker towards the darkest grade, 9B.

Novice artists are often surprised by the different qualities possessed by pencils made by different manufacturers. The difference really can be quite stunning. The technical specifications of pencils vary enormously. The binder used to hold the graphite particles together can affect the ease with which the pencil gives up its colour. The graphite itself can be smooth and silky, or gritty. The wood used can sharpen well or splinter and break the lead. The diameter and shape of the pencil will have to be considered, and some pencils will feel more comfortable to hold than others. Comfort should not be underestimated, since you will be holding a pencil for a considerable period, if you are intending to make a finished piece of artwork (as opposed to a quick sketch). Good-quality pencils are worth every penny spent on them.

Some pencils are designed to be water-soluble, which allows a different range of marks to be made with them.

Graphite sticks and blocks

These are often available in the same range of tones as are available for pencils. Graphite sticks and blocks will have a different quality to them, as the binder will have been adjusted compared to that used in pencils. The shape of the product will enable all sorts of marks to be made, as every surface can be used. Flat sides and corners can make wonderfully expressive marks, as the hand can change the angle of the stick or block throughout the making of a single stroke. Blocks can even be shaped to produce the required mark. Some, such as Derwent's Graphitint blocks, can be used in the same way as can a pan paint (although the result will be very different).

Graphite powders

These can be used dry, sprinkled on to paper and worked into the dry paper's surface by using a variety of tools (including your fingers). The powders can be used dissolved or suspended in water and applied with brushes. Alternatively, they can be sprinkled on to wet paper; allowing the water to move along the surface of the paper can produce some very interesting effects.

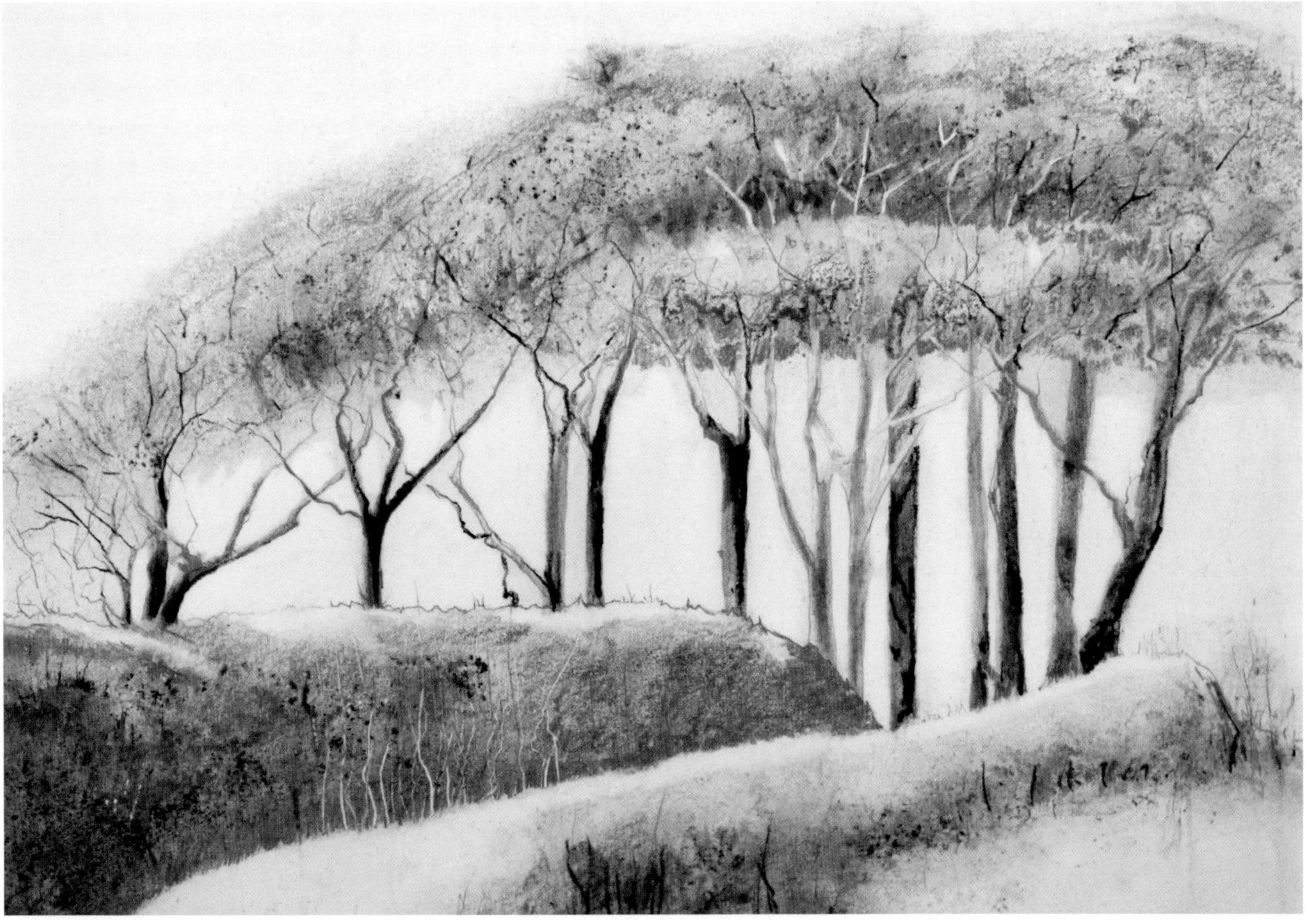

This graphite image was made by using a combination of wet and dry techniques. Traditional pencils were used to make a variety of expressive marks. Sandpaper was used to create a fine powder from graphite blocks that was then applied to the paper with fingers and colour shapers. The same powder was sprinkled on to damp paper, and it was also applied with a wet brush.

Erasers

Erasers vary hugely in the materials that they are made from. Some perform far better than others. In addition to their obvious use of removing mistakes, erasers make good drawing tools when used to remove tone, that is, when working from dark to light. They can be used to crisp up a soft edge or to soften a hard edge.

We both use Staedtler Mars plastic erasers for general purposes that remove graphite easily without damaging the paper. They can be cut to shape as required. Tombow MONO zero eraser pens are also excellent; shaped like a pen, they are brilliant for removing fine lines.

Although they are very popular, neither of us like putty erasers, as we find them too greasy and difficult to shape. As with all other art materials, experiment with different erasers until you find some that suit your purposes.

Pencil sharpeners

It is worth investing in a decent pencil sharpener. The Long Point pencil and lead sharpener by KUM gives a lovely, long point and a very sharp tip to pencils. This increases the range of marks that you can make with a sharpened pencil, as the pencil is easily used on its side. (This is not possible if there is a ridge where the wood and graphite of a pencil meet.)

Other equipment

Other tools, such as burnishing tools, stiff-staple brushes, colour shapers, masking tape, and stencils can all be employed to increase the ways in which graphite can be used.

Do not fall into the trap of neglecting graphite as an exciting medium in its own right!

GENERAL EQUIPMENT

A Place to Work

While it is an obvious advantage to have a dedicated place to paint, a designated studio is not essential. All that you need is a comfortable area to work in with good light, which you may find at the kitchen table or in a spare bedroom.

If it is possible to define an area within your home where you can keep your art materials handy, or better still laid out, then you will have more opportunity to take advantage of small slots of time; having to spend too much time gathering your materials and setting up can be restrictive.

The equipment that you acquire in your studio will appear over a number of years. An attitude of experimentation means that we have acquired a large range of different media, but we choose our basic equipment according to what makes working life in the studio more comfortable and accessible.

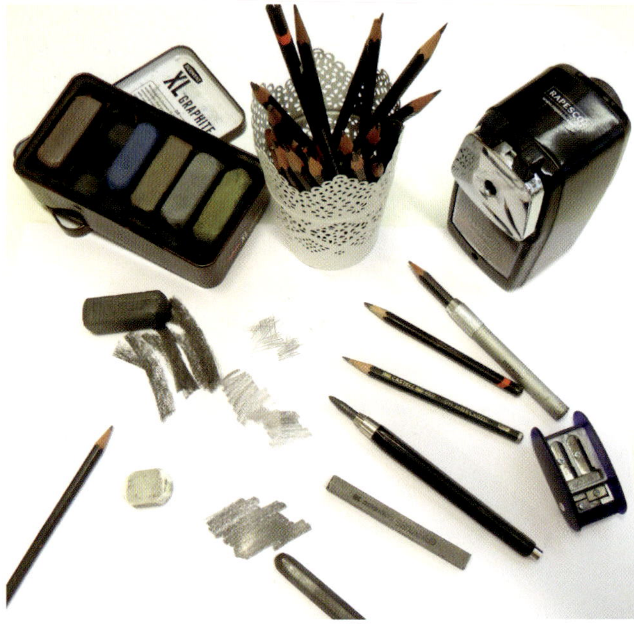

Many exciting forms of graphite and tools for working with it, some of which are shown here, are now available to the inquisitive artist.

Easels

If you look through any art-supply catalogue, you might be overwhelmed at the range of easels on offer: wooden studio easels and sketching easels, large freestanding easels, small tabletop easels and so on. It can be quite bewildering as to which one to buy. Many artists will have more than one easel: one for use when venturing outside and one or more for use back in the studio.

When choosing an easel to take on location, two requirements seem to be key to its suitability for the task at hand: weight and stability. The easel should be light enough to carry but firm enough to stand upright easily and reliably. The Frank Herring & Sons Versatile Easel is the choice of many artists. It is suitable for both watercolour and oil painting, particularly when painting *en plein air*. The clever, lightweight design makes it easy to fold away the easel when it is not in use, yet it is extremely stable when erected.

In the studio, where weight and size are often less of an issue, a heavier, wooden easel will prove useful. Some designs are now available that allow the artist to work with the paper oriented either vertically or, with a little adjustment, almost horizontally; this ability makes such easels ideal for both oil and watercolour work.

When choosing your own easel, or easels, consider the size that you prefer to work at; make sure that your easel will support your preferred size of paper or other surface to work on, and look at how it adjusts, for when you will feel that you would like a change. Consider how you like to sit, stand and move while you are painting, and think about the angle(s) that you like to work at. Make your choice based on what feels comfortable to you, rather than being led by tradition.

The choice of using a table or an easel will depend in part on the medium that you will be using. Watercolourists rarely work at an angle greater than 25 degrees; water runs downhill and takes the colour with it! The board that the paper is stretched on and a small block (for example, a house brick or thick book) to support it are sufficient.

Cameras, tablets and computers

Digital tools and equipment are now very much part of an art studio. Cameras play an important part in information gathering, as discussed in Chapter 3. Tablets are a convenient way to view a reference photograph and have the advantage over a printed copy for the option to manipulate the photograph as you work, for example, by viewing a monochrome version in order to assess tonal values. Taking a photograph of your painting during the painting process and viewing it in black and white can help you to assess tonal values in your work. A series of photographs, taken at different stages during the painting process, can help you to review the changes that you have made. It can also help you to learn when to answer that most difficult of questions: 'Have I finished?'. Looking back at the photographs of your work in progress will quickly help you to decide whether you should have stopped sooner!

Manipulating photographs digitally can also give some interesting effects and maybe inspire a new painting.

JUST A MOMENT …

Before leaving a chapter on equipment, let us take a moment to consider one of the most valuable assets in an artist's life: *time*.

It is rare to come across a creative person who feels that they have enough time to bring to fruition even a fraction of their ideas. It seems that we live in a world where there are so many calls on our time that it is all too easy to be pulled in other directions. There is no doubt that time is precious, and it must be used wisely.

It is obviously lovely to be able to set aside generous slots of time for creative activities. Feeling free from the guilty feeling that you should be doing something else can be very beneficial for one's creativity. Conversely, finding yourself with just half an hour, or even just a few minutes, here and there, can be very frustrating, especially when there are ideas in your head that are desperate to escape into the real world.

Consider how you might use small pieces of time to advantage. A fifteen-minute slot will not be enough time to make a whole drawing, but think instead about what might be useful to do in that time. Carry some pocket-size equipment with you at all times, so that you are ready to take advantage of these opportunities when they arise.

Here are a few suggestions:

- Begin a sketch of a small object or a small part of a scene. It is unlikely that you will finish it, but the fifteen minutes will have been spent observing a subject in more detail than you would have done otherwise, as well as allowing you to practise your eye–hand coordination.
- Devote the time to experimenting with mark-making; you can learn a lot about brushes, pencils or even ballpoint pens in fifteen minutes.
- Spend the time comparing the different marks that are possible to make on a selection of paper surfaces (smooth, NOT, rough).
- If paints are to hand, try a few new colour mixes. Keep the results for reference.
- Stretch watercolour paper, or prepare a board for oil painting.
- Nothing to hand? Stare hard at a subject, and imagine yourself drawing it; you will be surprised at how much more you will see, all of which will help you the next time that you have your materials with you.
- Jot down the ideas that have popped into your mind. It is sad how quickly they can evaporate, if left unattended to.

PURSUING PROGRESS

Over the many years as painters, both of us have worked with many media, enjoying some more than others. Each have their own characteristics, strengths and, if not quite weaknesses, then, some limitations. As for most professional artists, we each have a set of core materials that we couldn't live without. As we look around our studios, we see well-used boxes of watercolours and oil paints readily to hand.

On the shelves are boxes of pastels, acrylic inks, gouache, graphite in its many forms, coloured pencils and all sorts of things that we have experimented with, and although not used on a daily basis, can still prove useful, if only occasionally. Our point is that, after well over forty years of painting, we both still like to try new media and are still experimenting! Even within our preferred media, we both enjoy exploring new colours, trying paints from a manufacturer we haven't used before and experimenting with a new piece of equipment, such as a differently designed palette that might make life easier.

The important message is that we believe that, for an artist to maintain and even grow in creativity, they should remain open to new ideas. This extends beyond the academic application of ideas appertaining to the content of images to the exploration of and experimentation with materials for purely practical purposes. It is an enjoyable journey, not simply a means to an end.

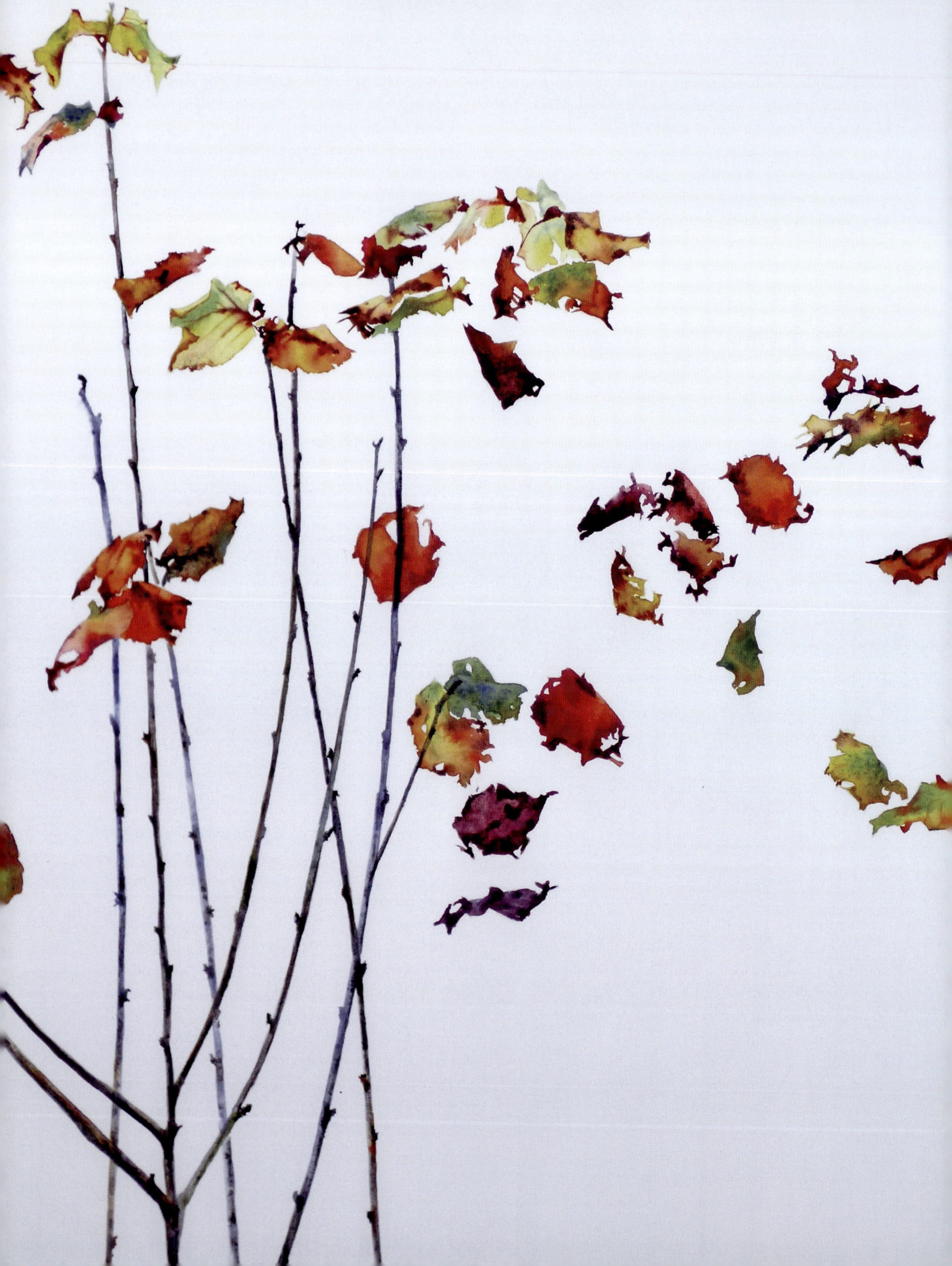

Chapter 3

Information gathering

Some reading this book might be surprised that this chapter is not entitled 'Learning to sketch' or 'How to draw before painting', or something very similar. They might be thinking that sketching is surely what an artist does. A rather idealized, romantic view is that the struggling artist scribbles a few sketchy lines on a restaurant napkin, rushing back to a freezing garret studio to paint a masterpiece that has buyers and dealers, offering both fame and fortune, flocking to the artist's door. Oh, that it were true! That little scrap of a sketch is meant to carry all of the information that the artist might need to paint a picture: information on scale, detail, tone, colour and texture, and the list could go on and on. The little sketch has such a pivotal role in the production of a painting – a lot rests on its shoulders – that it seems almost too much, and it likely is, to expect that one little sketch to do so much.

The wiser and more considered strategy is to use sketching as part of a broader approach to the gathering of information, using it in conjunction with other methods of recording that will prove to be of value to the process of making a painting. It is not uncommon for photographs to be taken, colour swatches made and notes written. Video clips might be useful in, for example, recording how leaves move in a breeze. Collecting twigs, leaves, flowers and fruits for reference will add more to the finished painting than merely visual information. Holding these items will inform the artist of their texture, maybe even suggesting ways in which the paint could be applied to represent them. Even their scent could be inspiring, reminding the artist of the weather when the items were collected, which might in turn affect their choice of colour for the painting.

Indeed, anything that would likely inform the painter when it comes to making the final artwork is worthy of consideration when gathering information.

Flying Leaves, watercolour, 35cm × 56cm (13¾in × 22in), Siân Dudley. This watercolour was intended as a study for the shapes and colours of autumnal leaves.

THE IMPORTANCE OF SKETCHING

One might think from previous paragraphs that the importance of sketching might be devalued, but you would be very wrong. Sketching is an essential part in the creative process, and its value to the artist cannot be underestimated. What is being suggested is to use sketching in addition to the other means of gathering information.

A camera is useful when trying to capture those fleeting, short-lived moments that the artist might come across when gathering information. A shaft of sunlight piercing the foliage of a tree, or a cloud's shadow moving across a tree-lined hillside, can be such a brief event that only a camera could capture the moment quickly enough before it passes forever; our hands just do not move fast enough!

But pointing a camera and clicking the button often means that we look for only a brief moment too. We rely on the camera to record the information, and we therefore do not take the time absorb the information contained within the scene in front of us.

SKETCHING ON LOCATION

When sketching on location, it is a good idea to study the scene first and then make a few very quick thumbnails before beginning the sketch. This gives you the opportunity to place the drawing on the page, avoiding that all-too-common problem of the drawing falling off the edge of the paper.

This making of thumbnails can also help you to decide on what to include in, and what to leave out of, the painting. Having decided on what you want to include, you do not waste precious time drawing things that you would later choose not to include. If leaving something out (for example, a car), you will be aware that there might be a hole in the painting and can gather some suitable information from the location, before you leave, to fill that hole.

The act of drawing enables us to 'see' more. Rather than passively glancing at the scene, we are actively engaged in recording it. Over time, we take in more of the scene than is recorded in the fraction of a second that the camera takes to record it. All of our senses are involved; we hear the sounds associated with the view, we feel the air quality and we respond to the weather conditions. In spite of our tendency to neglect our sense of smell, we are aware of the scents around us: the delicate, sweet aroma of apple blossom may subconsciously affect our choice of colour, as might the musty dampness of a woodland floor. By taking time to draw, we are giving ourselves opportunity to take in the depth and richness of the scene.

And, of course, we look harder at it, taking time to notice more details. We have to actively look at the scene, paying close attention to the things about it that we find interesting or important. The most useful sketches are made when some time is spent considering the scene before even picking up the sketchbook! We have time to make decisions about what to include and, just as importantly, what to leave out.

The act of drawing involves our memories. Between looking at the subject and committing a line to paper, we have to remember it. The physical act of making that line aids in committing it to memory. When we get the sketch back to the studio, we see far more in it than is recorded on the paper.

As we draw and sketch, over time, our visual knowledge will develop. The colour of a leaf or the texture of a branch that, at one time, might have been overlooked is now noticed and considered. Familiarity not just with a subject but also with the act of drawing will result in more-confident, authoritative artworks that will often engage more readily with the viewer.

An Important Point about Sketchbooks

Artists' sketchbooks are often wondrous things to behold. They come in all shapes and sizes, some with meticulous drawings, carefully annotated, and are things of beauty in their own right. Others are held together with bits of old masking tape, with pages falling out and filled with drawings that would make sense only to the artist. And that is the point.

Sketchbooks need to make sense only to the artist who owns them. They are generally not for public consumption. As long as the artist understands the sketches, they are useful sketches. Better a scruffy, useful sketch over a beautifully executed drawing with little meaning. The sketch pad is yours; you don't have to share it with anyone. The sketch, in paint or pencil, should be full of useful information. It could show where shadows fall or how tall a tree is compared to a figure and could even be accompanied by a selection of colour swatches. In short, anything that will be of benefit to the artist back in the studio when making the painting can be included.

PHOTOGRAPHY AND DIGITAL IMAGES

Cameras, smartphones and tablets have revolutionized the use of photography over the last decade or so. Gone are the days when films were sent off to the lab, for developing and printing, immediately followed by the anxious wait until the postman would pop an envelope through the letter box a few days later. Only then would the expectant photographer discover that, from a roll of thirty-six photographs, some images were out of focus, others were overexposed and others were underexposed, with just a few from the thirty-six proving to be useful. In today's digital world, images can be reviewed in seconds, zoomed in on screen, printed, if needed, and deleted easily, if not required. Some people turn their nose up to the use of photographs, but it is easy to believe that Da Vinci, Turner, Constable and all the other greats would have used and experimented with photography for their art, had it been available to them.

Photography should never be seen as a substitute for drawing to gather information but, instead, should be seen as a useful tool in its own right. The key to this usefulness is in the way that the photographs are taken.

The photographs that are useful to an artist preparing a painting are very different from the quick snapshots that we take as aides-memoires of a special moment. These latter photographs record an event; at the time of taking them, we are concerned with capturing the memory far more than we are concerned with capturing visual information. As a result, the quick snapshot is lacking in the type of detail needed for making a painting. We have seen many a disappointed student arriving back in class after a great holiday, wanting to paint the place that they have visited, only to find that there are gaps in the information provided in their snapshots. We hear 'The sea seemed bluer, and the trees seemed closer than that ... the photograph hasn't captured the details of the blossom...'

Sketch First, Photograph Second

The photographs that are useful to an artist should be taken with much more consideration than that for a quick snapshot. Just as with sketching, take time to consider the scene in front of you before picking up the camera. In fact, the photographs that are most useful when gathering information while preparing for making a painting are those that are taken after you have made the sketch. Cameras are non-selective, capturing all before them; they compress and flatten distance, average out tone and have a colour bias that can be quite skewed. Drawing first gives the artist a chance to get to know the subject really well. While drawing, you will have had time to refine and clarify some aspects of the scene and simplify and filter out others.

At this stage, you will know what extra information you need that might be difficult to include in the sketch. The photograph takes on the role of providing that extra information, backing up that which you have already recorded while drawing. You are now in the position to take numerous photographs, recording the overall scene, as well as zooming in on details or capturing any interesting textures that you see. By matching the photograph as nearly as possible to the same aspects of the subject that you drew, it is possible to take photographs that will be very useful back in the studio.

Capturing Light

Photography is particularly useful when it comes to recording the fleeting effect of light upon a scene or within the landscape.

A sudden change in the light alters the landscape; for example, a stand of trees can suddenly take centre stage as bright sunlight hits them, or a distant river can sparkle brightly as the sun pops out from behind a cloud. These short-lived occurrences are very difficult to get down in pencil or paint, time being very much against the artist.

At times like these, put down the sketchbook and reach for the camera. Take as many useful photographs as you can within the time that you have before the light changes again. As the light alters, so it is that you will return to sketching, safe in the knowledge that, between drawings and photographs, you have captured enough information to make a painting.

A note on colours in photographs and screenshots

'Cameras never lie' ... if they don't lie then at the very least they can often be a little economical with the truth!

We have already mentioned that cameras compress, flatten, and average out tones, but it is with colour that most novice painters have the biggest issues. Students often spend time struggling to mix the same colours as seen on screen or from photographs. But why try to match them? The colours in photographs are decided by the technical specifications of the camera, the computer, the printer, and finally the photographic paper that the photographs are printed on. If the photographs are to be viewed on a tablet, in addition to the specifications of the camera, there is the app through which the photographs will be viewed to consider and the fact that the digital photographs will be backlit. However, a photograph is taken and viewed, the colours that you see in it are arbitrary and, rarely, if ever, match the local colour present in the scene that you were inspired by.

There is great freedom in accepting this. The only colours that are correct are those that work together to produce a successful painting. You are free to choose them!

The colours in photographs can be useful as a guide, as something to consider, but they are not 'correct'. If the local colour is important to you, you can decide, while making the sketch, to make colour notes with the appropriate paints. Otherwise, have fun. Choose colours that you like for the painting.

360-DEGREE VIEW: SAME TREE, SAME DAY, SAME TIME...

When out sketching or drawing, it is worthwhile considering the same subject from a number of different viewpoints. If you will be painting a distant view, taking a few paces to the left or right is unlikely to have a huge impact on the overall scene. However, the closer that the subject is to you, the more influential any change of viewpoint is likely to be.

In the following series of photographs, note how different the same elements can appear when seen from four different viewpoints. Notice what happens to colour, tone, detail and texture. All of the photographs were taken on the same day within a period of under two minutes, the light remaining constant throughout.

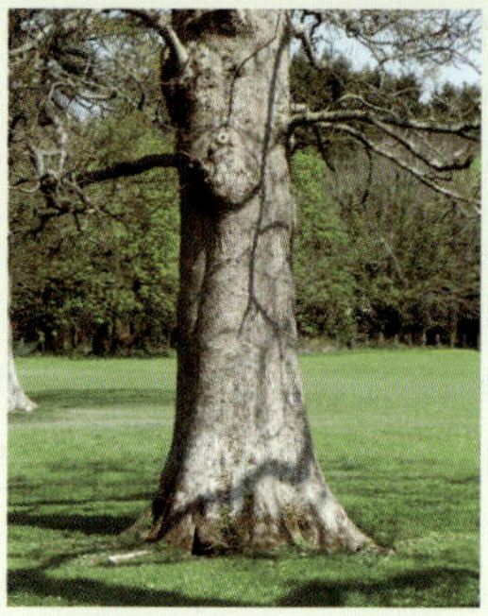

Photograph 1.

With the sun to the right, note how the bark is clearly visible; the shadows clearly express the bark's texture. Shadows also help to define the trunk's shape and its rotundity. The colours vary from green-greys through to soft browns. The overall tone of the tree is quite light, with the stronger tones to be found in the shadows.

The shape and form of an object is described by light and shadow. The greater the contrast, the more pronounced that the form becomes. But, if there is little variation between tones, the flatter the object will appear. With the sun directly facing the tree, fewer shadows will be cast within its bark, and the contrast between tones will be narrowed. This will result in an apparent smoothing of the tree's surface texture. However, we know that this cannot be. The bark has not changed; instead, only the direction that the light is coming from has changed.

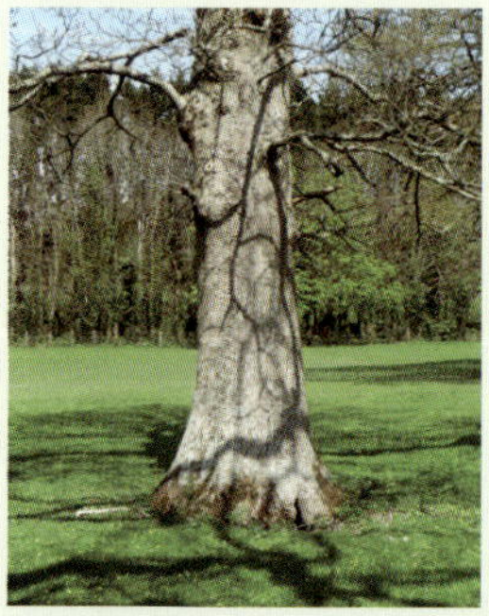

Photograph 2.

The lack of form-defining shadows will also appear to flatten the trunk, reducing its apparent roundness. Overall tones are slightly paler than in the first example, with the colours appearing slightly lighter.

We have moved further around the tree, so that the sun's position is now to the left of the tree. As in the first photograph, the sun's position creates shadows within the furrowed bark, the tonal contrast is broadened and the bark's texture seems restored.

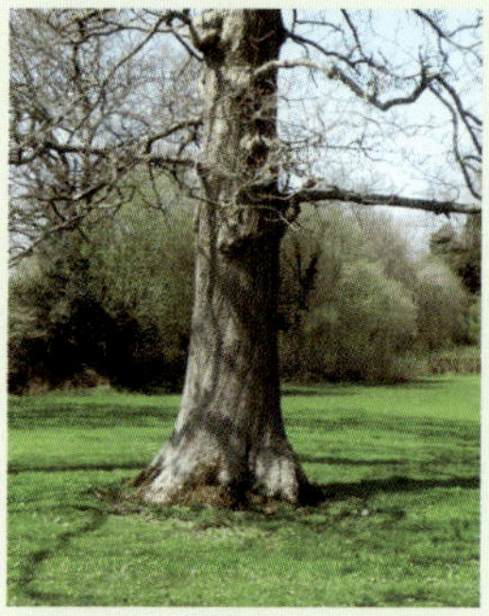

Photograph 3.

Again, similar to those of the first photograph, the overall tones are quite light, with only the stronger tones being found in the shadows, and the colours are once again the soft green-greys and browns. As we have moved further around the tree, now backlit by the sun, notice how the tones and colours within the trunk have dramatically changed and how much detail is now lost. Tonally, the trunk is now much darker, and branches have become lost as they pass in front of the trunk, to reappear only when crossing the paler sky. Colours have weakened, and the shadows are thrown forward. Texture and details within the trunk are barely visible; indeed, with so many dramatic changes, this tree could be mistaken for a different one.

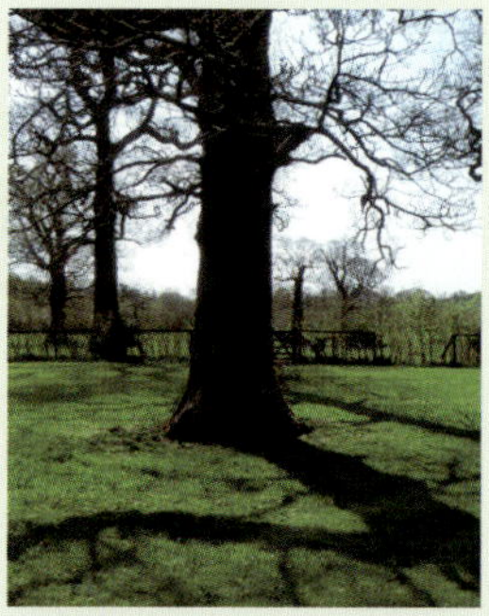

Photograph 4.

These dramatic backlit subjects have been a source of inspiration for many painters over the centuries and are just as popular today. For this type of painting – known as contre-jour, from the French, meaning 'against the day' – to be successful, the artist is required to pay close attention when assessing tonal values and to include the right level of detail. Pitch the tones incorrectly or include too much detail and the effect can be easily lost. As with so many things connected with painting and drawing, the ultimate success of the artwork usually starts with good observation, even before a brush or pencil touches paper or canvas!

INVESTIGATING TREES VISUALLY

Many a potentially good painting has been spoilt by the inclusion of such poorly observed and such badly depicted trees that they stand out like a sore thumb. On a daily basis, we come across stylized renditions of trees, perhaps so much so that some might consider that taking the time to properly observe trees is unnecessary. But, without knowing what makes a tree a tree, the unobservant artist is in danger of producing generic, characterless trees that are likely to add little to the painting and will probably take much away from it.

Any season of the year will provide useful information for the artist to work from. However, the bare deciduous trees of winter give a particularly useful insight into their skeletal structure, revealing how a tree is built and from what. This knowledge is useful when painting trees throughout the year, in that the artist will know what the leaves are hiding. Winter trees are therefore a good place to start.

THE SHAPES OF TREES

When planning a painting, one of the most important features of a tree will be the shape (and area) occupied by the depicted tree within the image. Getting to know the shapes of trees and their growing habits is a good place to start when sketching. The simplest way to get to know trees is to draw them, with paint, pen or pencil. Do it often, very often. The more that one draws, the more one sees.

Much like people, trees come in all sorts of different shapes and sizes and, just like people, they seem to possess different personalities. Some are tall and slender, others are fat and round, some are neat and tidy and others are in need of a trim. Note the direction in which the branches grow; some grow upwards, some hang downwards and some simply cannot make up their minds and wander around, looking for the sun, creating delightful, gnarly shapes.

These differences often escape the novice artist, who has a tendency (possibly influenced by stylized trees) to produce images where the trees are all very similar in height and shape and all growing in the same direction. This lack of variety makes boring paintings and should be avoided!

Try making some simple sketches. Begin by focusing on simplifying the overall shape of the tree. Don't get sidetracked into recording the smaller, more intricate details, concentrate instead on the form and shape. Half closing your eyes when drawing or painting will help in reducing the amount of detail that is observed, making it much easier to consider the tree's structure and shape. You might find it easier to think about geometric shapes. Trees refuse to be squashed neatly into spheres, oblongs, squares, triangles or a combination thereof (unless they are part of a topiary garden), but it might be helpful to think of them in terms of these shapes initially.

When a tree is backlit, it is often easier for the artist to see the outline of the tree's shape; the effect of the backlighting often renders the tree to being no more than a silhouette. Looking at the edges of the silhouette will give an indication of the direction in which the branches grow. Similarly, sketching trees on a misty day, when the mist cloaks the details, helps in focusing on the overall shapes of the trees.

There are many instances when all that is required in a painting are the overall shapes of trees, for example, when they are part of the background of the image. Understanding the overall shapes of trees will make it easier to place the trees within a composition in an interesting way.

Trees Are Round, Not Flat

Trees are not flat ... they are fat! They are round: fully three-dimensional. One can walk around them, birds can fly through them, and cats can get stuck in them; trees are most definitely fat!

Branches don't grow out from a single trunk in just one plane; they grow out in every direction: forward, backward, sideways, up and down. They grow from every point of the compass and in every direction! This pattern of growth is what creates trees' three-dimensionality.

Having observed the overall shape of the tree, begin looking for the tonal variation that will describe its form. Tone (or value) refers to lights and darks. Areas catching the light will be lightest in tone (that is, have a high value), whereas areas in shadow will be darkest (that is, have a low value). The contrast found between the light and shade clearly contributes to defining the roundness and overall mass of the tree.

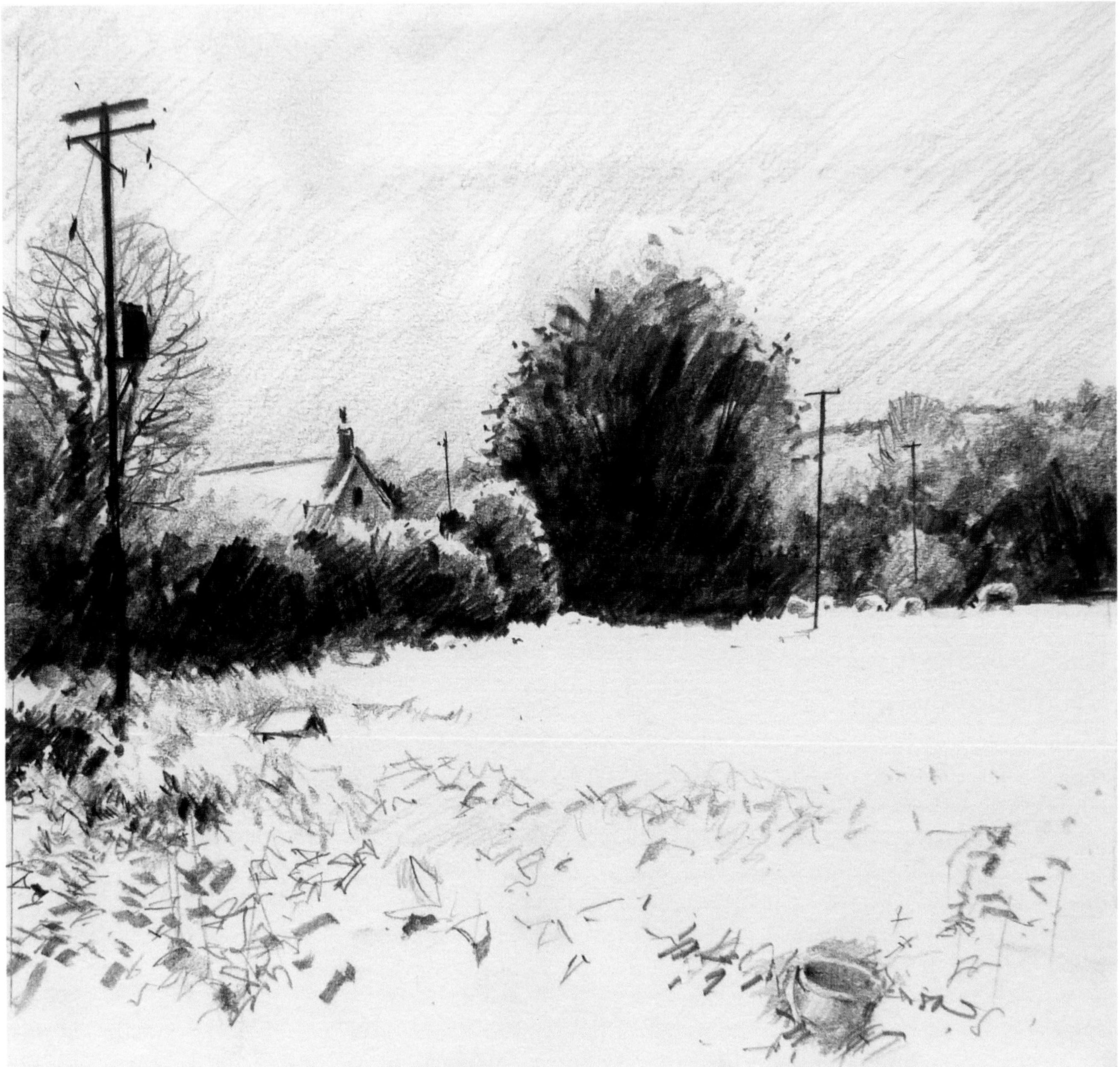

In this small pencil drawing of Harford Farm, note how the light regions and shadows of the trees help to emphasize the shape of the trees. Note also the interesting textures created with graphite in the foreground.

In the summer, trees are in full leaf and, treating the leaves as a mass (rather than as lots of individual leaves), the volume of the tree is easier to simplify. Additionally, bright, sunny days give rich contrasts between the lights and darks.

In the winter, the branches of deciduous trees are bare. Now, it is possible to directly observe branches growing in all directions out of the trunk. It is no longer possible to simplify the tree to a sphere-like shape, but the three-dimensionality of the tree comes into greater focus. On a bright winter's day, the shadows cast within the branches give a very real sense of depth, making interesting patterns. The range of lights and darks not only define the shapes of individual branches but work together to describe the form of the whole tree. For an example of this, *see The Big Beech Tree: Winter* at the beginning of Chapter 8.

In spring and autumn, the leaf distribution is fragmentary. This characteristic allows shafts of sunlight to peep through the gaps of foliage, giving some unexpected and

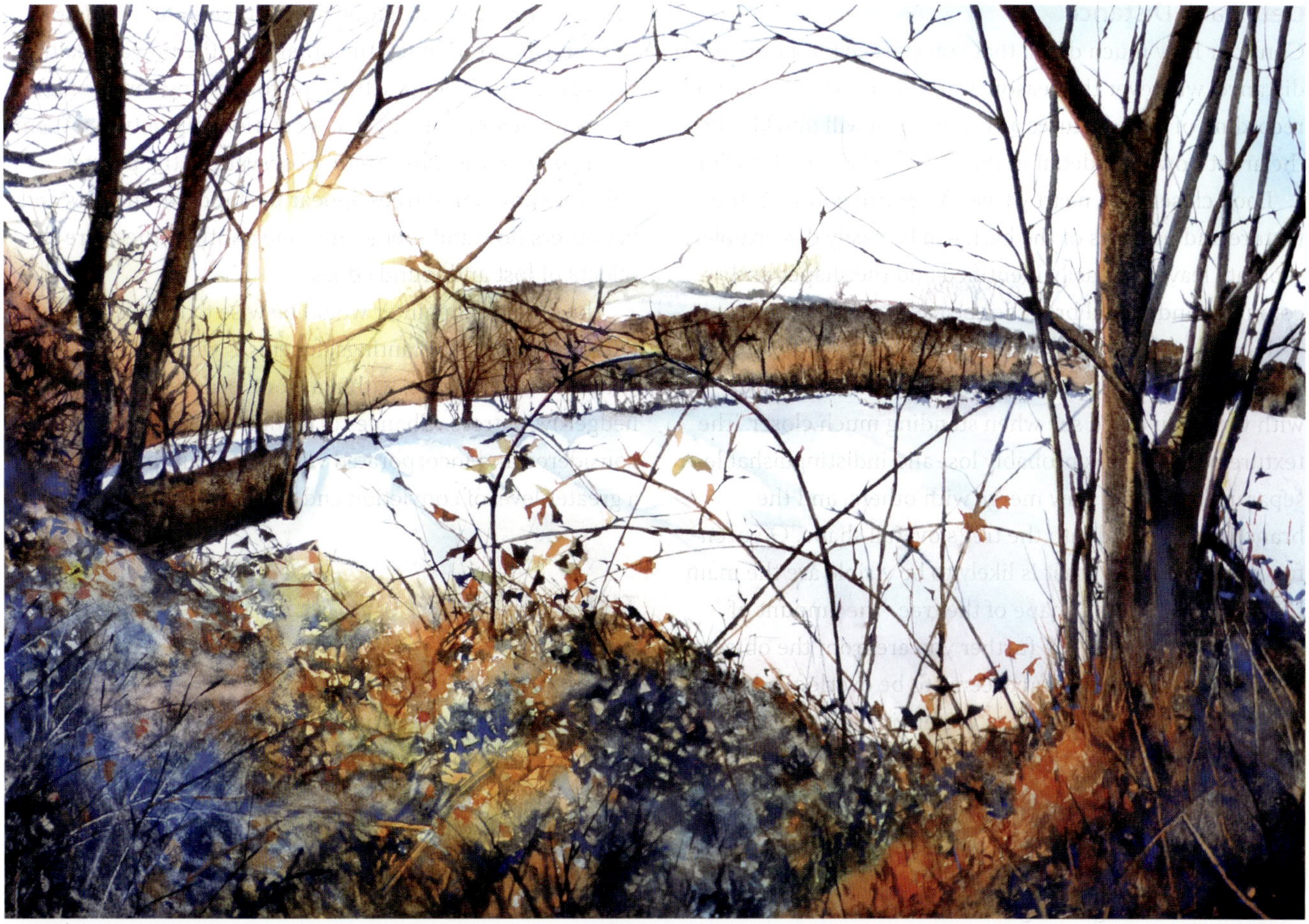

Close examination of this snowy scene will reveal that it includes a variety of elements that are based on the observation of nature and that make for an interesting painting. Note the loss of details in the trees in the distant hedge. There are lost and found edges within the foreground, seen clearly where the tree trunk on the right blends in to the ground. Where the sun shines through the branches, the bright light causes them to be lost from view; they appear to melt in the sunshine.

exciting light effects. Since most trees are lit by the sun, it is not unreasonable to make assumptions that, with such a unidirectional light source, you can anticipate where the lights and darks will be. However, it does not take long to realize that we cannot always tell how the path of light will travel through a tree. Some of the light effects within trees are simply delightful; do not miss out by making assumptions: go out to see for yourself.

Disappearing Branches and Melting Trees

This disappearing and melting might sound like something from a sci-fi story rather than a book about painting trees. However, it is real and does happen or, more accurately, it appears to happen.

With the tree in full summer foliage, trunks and branches often seem to disappear from view, their path and progress being hidden by the verdant leaf growth spreading across or hanging over sections of branches. Note how this effect appears to be adding to the tree's sense of depth, or its three-dimensionality, with branches being pushed back into the body of the tree as the leaves come forward. By including the same effect with paint or pencil, the artist can emphasize the sense of the tree's mass and volume, or its bulk.

Melting trees or melting branches is a visual phenomenon that takes place when a very bright light, usually the sun, shines from behind through trees or through branches. The sheer strength of the light seemingly melts the solid objects in its path to almost nothing.

It is a particularly beautiful effect and one that is worth recording; however, you must be careful not to look directly into the sun, as this can damage your vision.

Detail at a Distance

Consider how much detail that you can see for a tree in the distance, whatever the season. Careful observation and the recording of such features as can be seen will quickly show the artist how little detail in the distance is actually visible.

Look closely at a nearby tree. What can you see? The texture and patterns of the bark will be easily discernible, separate leaves be easily identified and the shapes and colours of individual branches be easy to distinguish.

However, walk one-hundred metres further away, and look again. Compare how much you can see now with what you could see when standing much closer. The texture of the bark is probably lost and indistinguishable, separate leaves will now merge with others, and the branches will blend into the tree's overall shape. Go even further away and all that is likely to be visible are the main trunk and the overall shape of the tree. The amount of visible detail reduces the further you are from the object.

And, yet, this simple fact seems to be overlooked by the student painter, who often prefers instead to paint what they know to be there rather than what can actually be seen.

Lost and Found Edges

'Lost and found edges' might not be an artistic term that you are familiar with, but you are certain to have seen these edges, even if you were unaware of the term being used to describe them.

Look at a group of trees against a skyline. It is likely that you can easily identify where the trees stop and the sky starts; the difference in colour and tone make the trees stand out from the sky quite distinctly. This is known as a found edge. But, returning to look at the trees, you are more than likely to have trouble in distinguishing where one tree stops and the next starts. They seem to flow one into another, the tones and colours being very similar, so creating a blending effect. This is a lost edge and, by their very definition, these edges are difficult to make out.

Painting Trees En Masse

When painting trees en masse, it is important to analyse what we are looking at, in order to paint convincing representations thereof. Essentially, we are looking at a collection of individual trees that, from a distance, appear to be as one. Therein lies the potential problem for the painter; to represent the mass of trees and also to indicate individual trees convincingly, so that neither mass nor individuality dominates. With too much of an emphasis on mass, the result can look like a green blob, with little or no form. If too much the other way, the unwary painter can seemingly end up with an unconvincing series of tree portraits that have little, if any, relationship between them.

Through close and careful observation, the painter will note how some trees appear to stand out in parts and yet others flow and merge into one another; these are the effects of lost and found edges.

The observant painter would be wise to include similar effects within their paintings, for this is what happens within a mass of trees, within a wood or forest or along a hedgerow of trees. Changes of colour or tone, if carefully considered and incorporated within the painting, will bring a greater level of conviction and authority to the work.

THE ELEMENTS OF TREES

Tree Trunks and Branches

What colours are tree trunks and branches? Many of us as children would have been encouraged to paint the trunks and branches of trees brown but, even on casual observation, it will be noted how few trunks and branches actually are of this colour. Yet, this idea that tree trunks and branches are brown is so ensconced in our cultural consciousness that it can be difficult for a novice painter to move past it.

Tree trunks and branches come in a huge variety of colours and are rarely a simple brown. For example, they may be brown and white (silver birch), black and white (aspen), grey (beech, oak), black (almond) or red (giant redwood). Of course, when covered in moss and ferns, they are bright green!

It is an interesting exercise to go out specifically to make colour swatches of tree trunks and branches. You will find a variety of trees in your local woods, but a visit to an arboretum will give you the opportunity to see a broader variety in one day.

Bark

As young children, many of us might have reproduced characteristics of the bark of trees by the process known as bark rubbing, similar to that of brass rubbing. The process involves taking a piece of thinnish paper, placing it over the bark of a tree and rubbing soft wax crayon or graphite over the paper, to record the texture of the bark. Working in this way, the huge variety of the textures of barks across different species of trees is very quickly apparent.

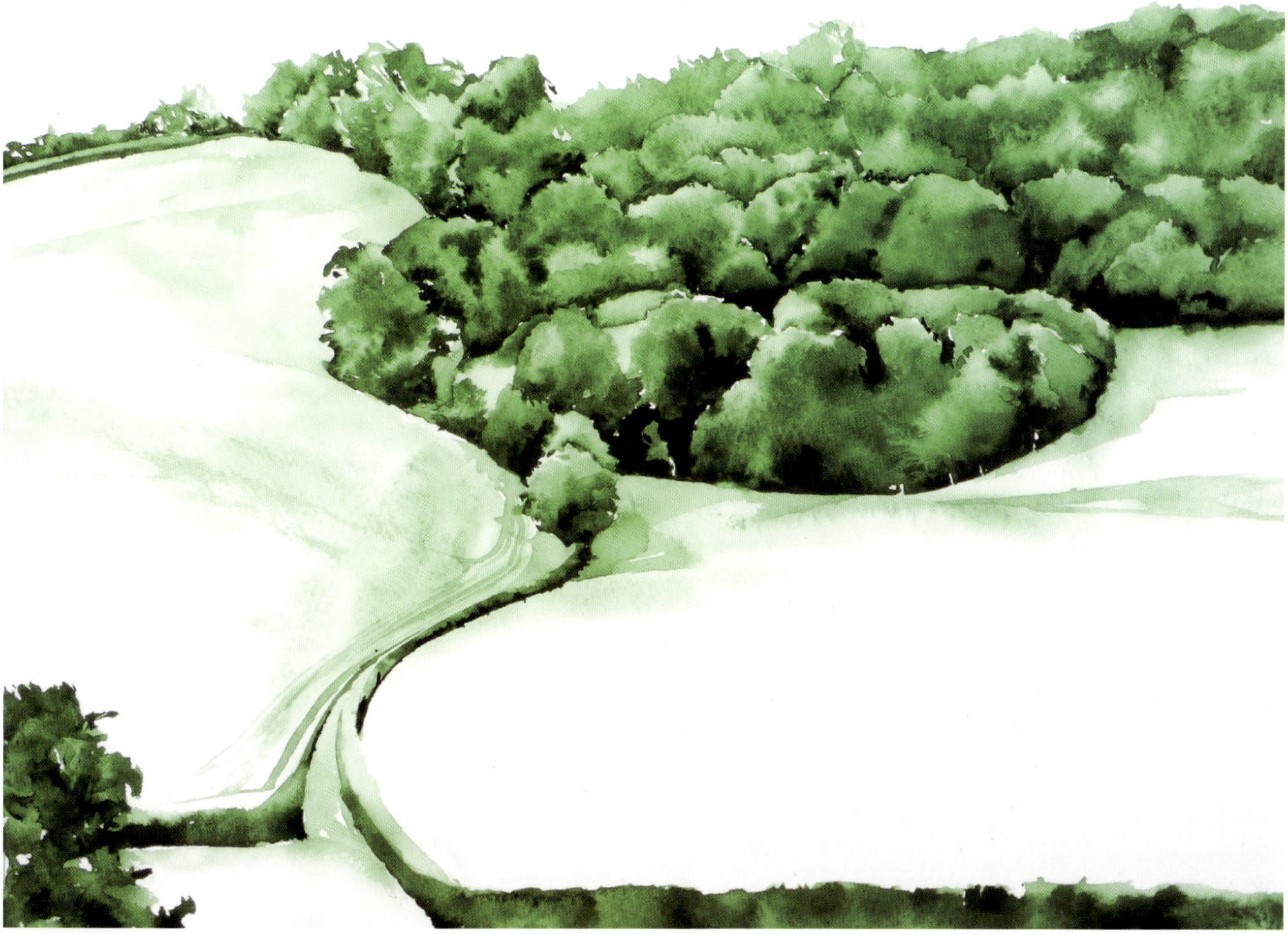

As light falls from above on to trees, the tree tops will appear lighter in tone and the trees will appear darker where the shadows are lower down and underneath these tree tops. A mix of hard and soft edges appear; some tree tops are well defined, while others, not catching as much light, seem to blend together.

The image above was created as follows. Begin by applying a layer of textured paint across the area where the wooded area is to be depicted (cauliflowers work well for this). Create the well-defined tree tops by applying dark tones to the lower edges of the trees above (or next) to them and blending away from the tree-top edges, leaving the light tones on the tree tops untouched (that is, painting them negatively). As you move away from the tree tops, manipulate the tones to form shadows within the trees above, being careful not to take the paint right to the top of the trees, where the tones need to remain light.

Do not look carefully at just the bark's colour but also examine its texture. Is it smooth and glossy or textured and matt? Some trunks are multicoloured, with the bark constantly breaking away in large flakes. The bark of the oak tree is smooth in its youth and yet becomes rugged with age, with deeply shadowed fissures. Trunks are as varied as the trees themselves and can make good subjects in their own right for the artist.

Take time to draw, paint and photograph the different types of tree trunks that you come across when gathering information; the results of these observations are useful for reference and will help inform your decisions when painting or drawing.

Leaves and Foliage

One of the most difficult aspects of painting a landscape is coming to terms with the huge variety of greens that are present. Trees are likely to be high on the list of culprits, with their leaves coming in so many different hues. While this is a delight to a gardener, it can be a nightmare for a landscape painter!

Trees produce leaves that range in colour; this range, broadly speaking, can include greens, yellows, browns, reds, purples, glaucous 'blues' (which are really the bluer end of the green spectrum), silvers and whites. We also describe leaves as being of rust and gold in colour. Is true blue the only colour in the spectrum that is not

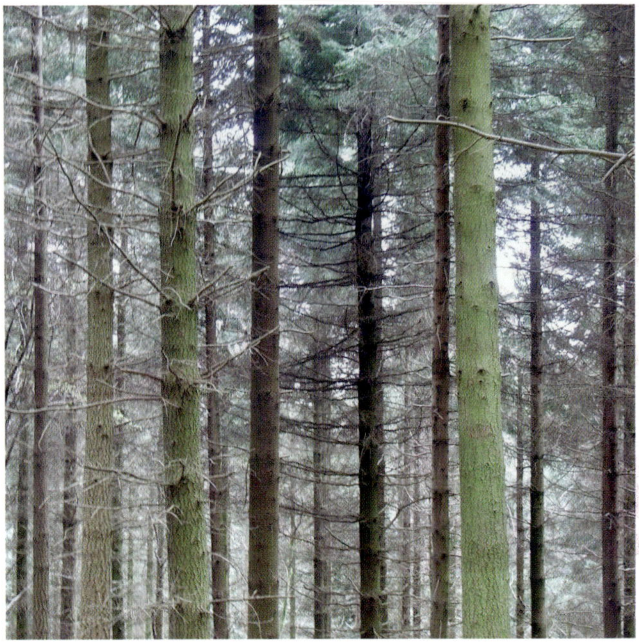

This photograph is a clear example of the range of colours present even in tree trunks.

represented? Bright purples are rare, but, if you have ever seen a *Jacaranda* tree in full bloom, you would be forgiven for thinking that it had bright purple leaves.

The seasons of the year greatly influence the colours of leaves. In the spring, leaves will often be a bright, yellowy green that seems to jump out at you excitedly. As the spring slips into summer, this vibrancy is often replaced with less-dramatic, softer greens. As the summer moves on, so too do the colours change again, with the greens appearing to be mixed with touches of brown. Autumn is the season of the most striking colours, with the collection of leaves being full of reds, golds, yellows, russets and warm browns. Yet, winter also has its own palette of colours, just as interesting and compelling to the artist as those of the other three seasons. The grey-green needle-shaped leaves of the conifer or the shining, dark, blue-green leaves of the red-berried holly contrasting with the white of the snow make for interesting winter paintings. Furthermore, whether the sunlight is falling on or through leaves can make a tremendous difference to their perceived colours.

Do not allow yourself to become overwhelmed by the enormous variety of colours. Banish a fear of greens in particular! There is a reasonably simple way of dealing with this variety, by choosing a limited palette for each image. This is described in more detail in Chapter 4, Designing the Painting, with examples of how to do it in the step-by-step projects in Chapters 5 to 8.

It is not just the colour of leaves that can motivate an artist to paint them, the variety in shape is enormous and equally as motivating. A quick glance at only one book on botanical illustration reveals sixteen different names for leaf shapes and twelve different names for leaf margins (edges), before even beginning to think about whether the leaves are simple or compound and considering how the leaves are attached to the branch!

Leaves can be very beautiful and inspirational, and are often all that is needed to motivate an artist to paint. They were all that was needed to inspire Siân to paint *Flying Leaves*, seen at the beginning of this chapter.

WORKING *EN PLEIN AIR*

In the studio, materials are readily to hand and the light is constant. The use of reference sketches and photographs allows the painter to spend as much time as they require in defining and refining parts of the painting in a comfortable, more relaxed situation.

Yet, it is undeniable that the vast majority of trees grow outdoors! This being the case, anyone who wants to paint trees must by necessity venture into the great outdoors at some point and attempt painting *en plein air*. This is one of the biggest challenges an artist can give themselves; yet, it is also one of the most enjoyable.

Painting on location is very different from painting in the studio. Materials should consist of what can be easily carried; easels must meet the same criterion, being sturdy enough to do their job but also being extremely portable. The constantly changing light and the vagaries of the weather are a continuous influence on the scene. There are frequent interruptions by passers-by, who pause to look and comment, seemingly all critics or knowing someone who is a 'brilliant' painter that, likely as not, you have never heard of! It can seem rather scary, and one might wonder who would possibly consider trying to paint under these circumstances. Nonetheless, an hour or two spent painting *en plein air* can be rewarding in so many ways that the rewards can outweigh the obstacles.

Discovering how to get down the essential elements of the scene swiftly and succinctly before the light alters and changes the appearance of the landscape completely is a worthwhile challenge. To assess both tone and colour, and to be able to make the relevant mixes quickly from just a few tubes of paint, is a skill that is worth developing. These decisions made at speed often produce dynamic, intense paintings that, although they might never be finished or suitable for framing, will nevertheless have an energy and immediacy that will be difficult to match in a studio painting. Responding to new environments can be testing, and exciting, as the burgeoning number of urban sketchers will be keen to tell you.

Materials for Working *En Plein Air*

Making the traditional sketch is a worthwhile occupation, because it requires the artist to intensely observe what is before them, in a way that just looking at the scene never could match.

Asking the question 'Why am I sketching?' and taking a few minutes to truly assess which type of information you are hoping to gather may change your approach. You may need to capture colour, or make expressive marks or capture delicate detail or a mood.... Think carefully about the type of information that you will need once you are back in the studio, and choose your sketching materials accordingly. Although the following is not an exhaustive list, you may find some of the items suit your purposes.

In truth, you can capture a scene, a mood or a moment with anything that will make a mark. At a lecture by Kurt Jackson, we heard Kurt describe how, if he has nothing else to hand, he will pick up a leaf or a blackberry and draw with the juice. Do not miss a magical moment that will lead to an inspired painting simply because you do not have traditional tools to hand!

It is a good tip to take as little as possible with you. Painting materials and equipment seem to become heavier as the day progresses. It is disappointing not to get to a potential painting spot because you have lumbered yourself with far more than you need.

Traditional sketch pads

The basic tools of a pencil or two and a sketchpad are quite adequate and surprisingly versatile. The size and shape of the sketchpad you choose, is your personal choice, as is the quality of the paper too.

After a little experimentation, you should choose both a grade of pencil and a size of sketchbook with which you are comfortable, paying no attention to advice that attempts to dictate either. The traditional advice that a pocket-size sketchbook is useful because of the ease of carrying it failed completely for Siân, who is incapable of drawing on anything smaller than A4. Size and quantity are limited by the amount of weight that you choose to carry.

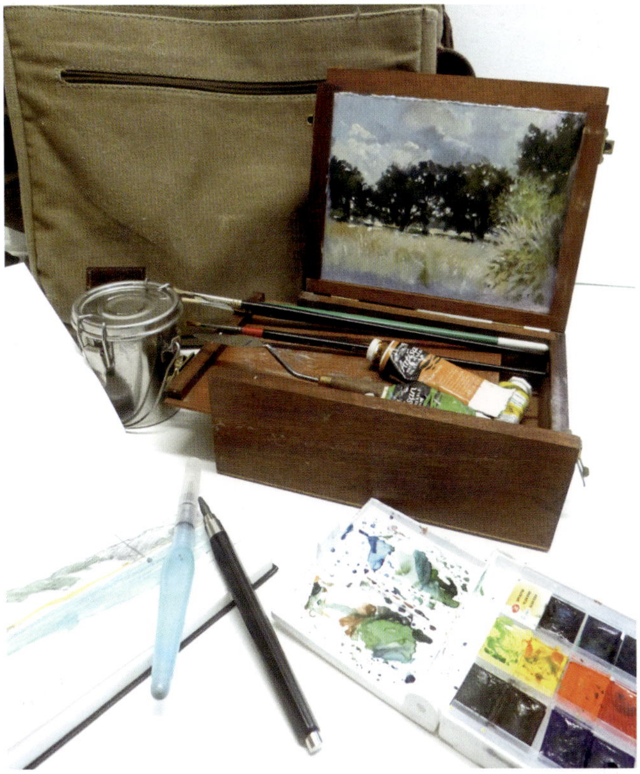

Don't forget that whatever you take when out sketching has to be carried! In a small bag, it is possible to take everything that the *en plein air* artist needs for a day's painting session. It is worth noting the small wooden thumb box in the illustration. This is a clever combination of palette, storage and easel in the form of a box that is smaller than a shoebox.

Brushes

Know what your brushes can do: what marks they can make and what effects can be created with them. Whichever medium you are working with, it is likely that you will need a range of flats, filberts and rounds. But remember, you will have to carry them. Use a brush roll or brush guards to protect the filaments of your brushes.

Pens and pencils

Graphite pencils

These can be of any grade; again, choose pencils that make marks that you like and that you find useful. Most artists prefer to sketch with soft pencils (the B grades) but, if your preference is for harder, crisper lines, you may find the H-grade pencils more to your liking.

Water-soluble pencils

Again, the range on the market is growing. The choice includes watercolour pencils, ink-based pencils (Derwent Inktense) and water-soluble, coloured graphite pencils.

Eraser
Erasers can be used for drawing with as well as removing mistakes, by lifting off graphite and pencil marks to leave lighter tones.

Pencil sharpener
Do not forget this piece of equipment if you are planning on using a pencil. Having a pencil blunted through use or by it being dropped is very frustrating to experience in the field!

Pens
The choice is vast. Consider whether you want waterproof or water-soluble pens, or a mixture of both. Black, or sepia, is a favourite choice for pen-and-wash techniques, but pens are available in a wide range of colours. Do not eschew the humble biro, or ballpoint pen. Henry Moore's *Sheep Sketchbook*, filled with biro-made sketches of sheep, is a joy to behold.

Watercolour
Watercolour is a very traditional medium for sketching, as the materials are lightweight and easy to carry. Additionally, the painted sketches dry very quickly, meaning that they are easy to transport back to the studio.

Watercolour paints
A small travel palette is excellent when working outdoors. These palettes are easy to carry and hold, and they can make the taking of colour notes very easy. These compact metal or plastic boxes open so that the lid serves as a palette for the mixing of the paints. Fill such a box with pan paints, or buy one with empty pans that you can fill from tubes of paint.

When you are painting *en plein air* with watercolours (and the same applies to oils), the choice of colours to be used should be a familiar one. This is not the time to experiment with unfamiliar colours. Time is limited, and it should be used wisely; the more one is accustomed to the colours chosen, the quicker the mixes will be achieved and the faster the painting will progress. Also, consider limiting your palette; fewer paints means less weight to carry.

Watercolour sketchbook
This is useful for any wet medium, as the paper will allow a greater range of mark-making than does traditional sketching paper, which is usually too absorbent. Watercolour sketchbooks are available with HP, NOT and rough surfaces and in a variety of weights. Choose heavier-weight paper if cockling annoys you.

Bulldog clips
When sketching or painting outside, a bulldog clip is useful to hold paper in place, especially on a blustery day. Working with paper flapping or lifting when you are attempting to lay a wash is almost impossible!

Water-filled brushes
Brushes that hold water in their handle are very useful in the field. The quantity of water that such brushes hold lasts longer than you would imagine, and the brush tips come in a variety of shapes and sizes.

Water pots
When working on location, something to carry and hold the all-important water in is essential. Some field boxes have a clever water-carrier-pot combination, which is very useful. The volume of water carried can be quite limited and, if painting for a full day, might prove insufficient. Instead, consider carrying water in a lightweight drinks bottle and using a collapsible water pot that can be hung on a field easel.

Oils
Sketching *en plein air* with oil paints requires a little more organization.

A pochade box will incorporate space for the paints, brushes, rags, solvents and so on and contain a carefully constructed slot for the board, so that the wet paint does not smudge on the return journey. It is, in fact, a small portable studio. Usually made from wood, they can sometimes be a little heavy, so choose one that you are comfortable carrying, especially when it is loaded with equipment. While this might seem irrelevant in the excitement of departure, it will make a difference later in the day, when you have wandered a half an hour's walk from your car.

Oil paints
The choice of paints should be carefully considered, as too many unused tubes all add to the physical and perceived weight of your load. It is not uncommon for the *en plein air* painter (whether working with watercolours or oils) to work with a limited number of colours: far fewer than they would use when working in the studio. However, the choice of colours made will be so familiar to the artist that they will be able to produce a surprising number of colours and tones from this limited selection of paints.

Panels

Whatever the choice of support, it is advisable to take boards of different sizes and formats, with differently coloured grounds, to have something appropriate available for whatever you might come across. However, you should take into account that a large panel will take much longer to paint than does a smaller one, and time is often the limiting factor when painting on location; there is a greater chance of finishing a smaller painting than a larger one.

Palettes

Choose one that allows for plenty of space on which to mix the paints but that is not so large that it becomes ungainly on breezy days. Many artists prefer to use a tear-off, disposable palette, particularly when it comes to cleaning up at the end of a painting session.

Dippers and pots

Whether working with traditional or water-mixable oils, you will need to carry turpentine, painting media, white spirit or water with you when out painting, and it is useful to have a variety of leakproof pots available to choose from for this purpose.

A dipper that clips to the side of the palette is an ideal way to hold the solvents or water needed to thin the oil paint while you are painting. They are inexpensive, and many are now available with leakproof, screw-top lids.

Remember to dispose of any used media according to the manufacturer's instructions, whether while you are at your painting location or once you have returned to your studio.

General equipment

Rags

Some old rags for wiping out palettes and containers or for cleaning brushes will be very useful, as will a plastic bag, for popping the dirty rags into at the end of a day's painting session.

Easels

An easel with adjustable legs that can be set at different lengths, to accommodate uneven ground, is extremely useful. Most of these easels can be set at heights that allow for you to paint standing up or sitting down. Many are adjustable for the angle of the support too, so that you can paint with the paper or board upright or at a much lower angle (such as a watercolourist might need).

Make sure that your easel is light enough to carry but sturdy enough not to blow over easily. Check the sizes of boards or canvases that the easel can hold and that you are comfortable working with panels of these sizes. (Also remember that the chosen panel, once set on to the easel, can act as a sail in the wind!)

Seating

Being comfortable will increase the amount of time for which you are able to paint outside. If you are happy to carry a lightweight chair or stool, there are many suitable ones available on the market. However, if you choose not to take a chair or stool with you, do think about taking something waterproof to sit on. Being wet is not conducive to an enjoyable painting session.

Clothing

When venturing out into the great outdoors for a day of painting, it is worth considering what to wear. Standing or sitting in one spot is not the same as going for a quiet stroll; take account of the fact that you might be so absorbed in what you are doing that you do not notice that you are either freezing or getting sunburnt.

A wide-brimmed hat is also useful when you are painting, for shading your eyes, making painting easier. Stout footwear is preferable when walking over rough terrain, and, particularly during the winter months, thick socks are a must. Standing in one spot on frozen ground in the middle of winter without decent footwear is likely to shorten any day's painting time.

Getting cold is no fun; a shaking, shivering hand makes the painting of straight lines almost impossible. During these cold spells, some gloves or fingerless mittens are essential and can prolong the time that you can spend painting and also help with the painting of straighter lines!

Responsible Painting

Whether working with oil or watercolour, it is important that the artist leaves nothing behind when they depart after a day of painting. Any litter or used media should be taken away and disposed of appropriately. An old plastic bag, kept in a rucksack pocket until needed, is an ideal item in which to gather up the surprising amount of rubbish that can be accumulated from a day's painting session.

Artists tend to go off the beaten track when looking for places to paint. Therefore, it is sensible to let someone know where you are likely to be painting and when you hope to be returning; if anything untoward should happen, it would be wise to have alerted others of your plans.

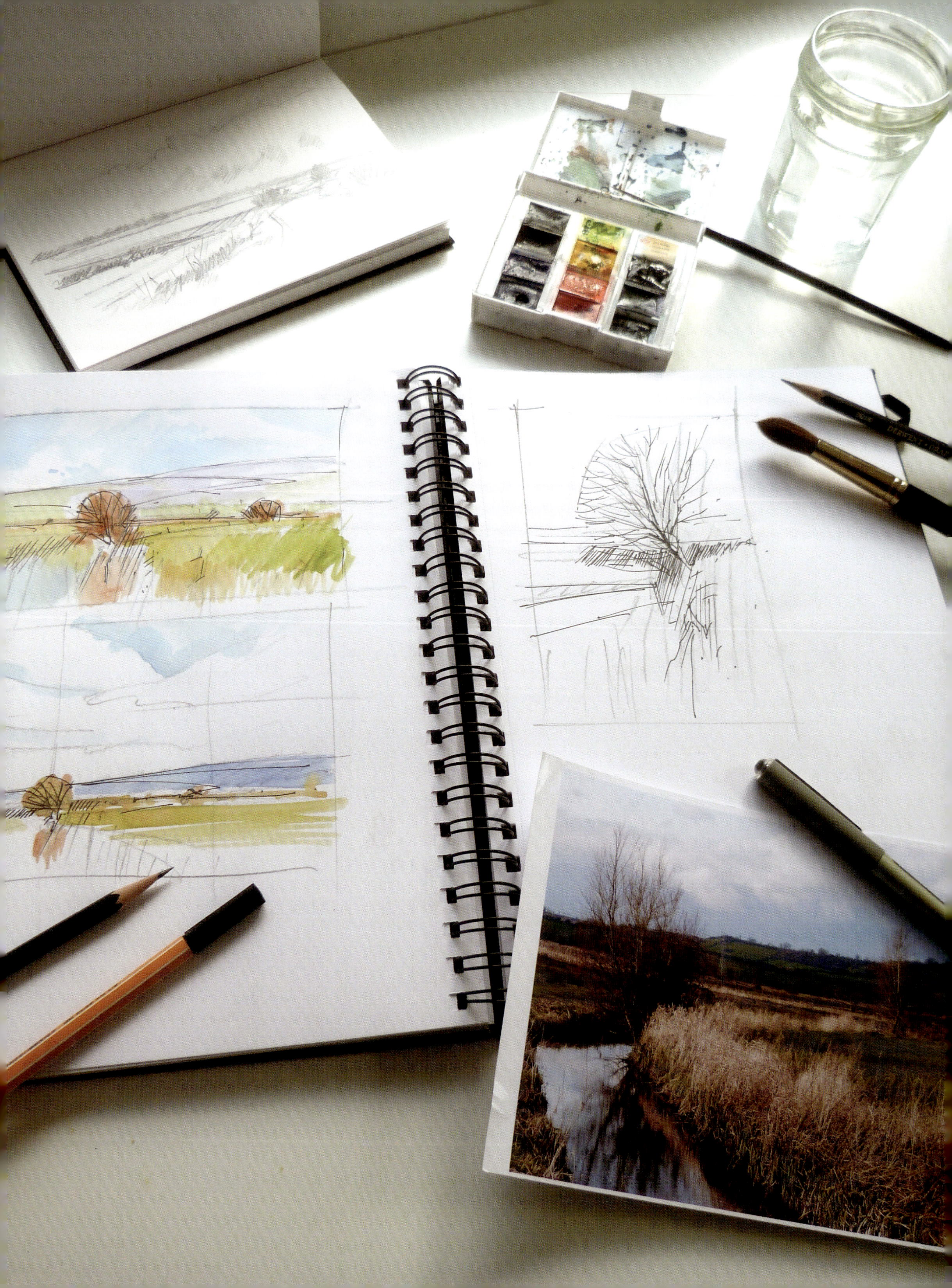

Chapter 4

Designing the painting

Moments of inspiration just happen. They usually appear unexpectedly, and suddenly. It can feel as though an idea has just popped into one's head. Sometimes, artists feel the need to create something, purely for the pleasure of making; this is when we actively look for an idea, seeking out inspiration, waiting for that magical eureka moment. If we do not find it, we can still paint something interesting, but these paintings never have quite the same life as those that are properly inspired. Whether your starting point is a eureka moment or the result of an active search for an engaging subject, one thing is true…

Paintings do not just happen – they have to be made.

Bringing an image into being means taking the inspiration and developing it into an idea, which can then be refined, before actually producing the painting. Questions need to be asked at every stage, and, more importantly, those questions have to be answered. Between the seemingly simple questions of 'What's the painting about?' and the old chestnut 'Is it finished?', there are many, many other questions.

For those who find the laying down of paint their main inspiration, the thought of delaying that moment may seem frustrating and tedious. Novice painters may find it a surprise, and also daunting, but there is no getting away from it: planning is the key to success!

The artist Brian Ryder put it perfectly when he wrote that one should 'Plan like a tortoise and paint like a hare' (Ryder, B., *Painting Watercolour Landscapes with Confidence* [David & Charles, 2005], p.6). Too often, the novice painter will do the complete opposite, spending far too little time planning the work, such is their rush to get painting. It is at this planning stage that much of the hard work towards realizing the final painting is done. Ideally, problems are resolved, and colours, tones and textures are decided upon at this point, not at the moment when a loaded brush is hovering almost expectantly over a pristine, white canvas.

Consider making a painting to be rather like following a recipe. There are ingredients to include and carefully measure out; too much of one ingredient and not enough of another can completely alter the end result. There are specific techniques to employ and timings to follow. A well-followed recipe results in a delicious meal. Not following the recipe often results in something unappetizing.

Although planning a painting thoroughly does not necessarily produce a masterpiece, it will mean that the finished artwork will be a considered piece, having more chance of success. Hope and luck are much less reliable!

Designing a painting, considering layout, tone, colour and texture.

Artists who are used to working in this way will enjoy asking and answering the relevant questions, seeing each stage as a valid part of the process of painting. This is, and should be, one of the most exciting parts in the process of making a painting, when some of the ideas are made real and begin to take shape. With time and experience, the process can become easier and faster. Just as an experienced cook can take a few risks and still produce something delicious, so too an experienced painter will be able to apparently dive in to making a painting and produce something delightful.

Until you have gained sufficient experience, following a methodical plan will be extremely helpful. The term 'methodical plan' does not sit easily in a book that extols the virtues of inspiration, but the apparent contradiction is false. Following a plan will teach you skills that will enable you to readily answer the questions that need asking, enabling you to be more creative and expressive.

A DESIGN APPROACH

Adopting a design approach to painting gives more opportunities for thorough planning than merely considering the composition. The term 'composition' is commonly thought of as just the placement of objects within the image and nothing more than that. 'Design' is all-encompassing, as it not just refers to the placement of the visual elements but also allows for developing an idea, deliberation of tonal values, and consideration of the choice of colours, the creation of texture, the format and the scale: in short, everything that goes together in making a painting.

The approach to painting advocated here involves spending some time planning. This planning stage should not be rushed; it takes as long as it takes. You will find that it will vary from one painting to the next. Sometimes, the process is almost instantaneous; at other times, it can take months!

Breaking down the development of a painting into four key stages is a useful approach and brings some order and structure to what, for some, might otherwise be a rather confusing process. The four stages are:

- Inspiration
- Developing the idea
- Information gathering
- Designing the painting

This to many might seem a somewhat formulaic approach to painting. However, it ensures that particular aspects of the planning process are not overlooked or underconsidered. In all of our years of painting and producing art, we both still follow this simple checklist. It has become so natural that it happens subconsciously, only coming to the foreground of our thoughts when we are asked to describe our working practice!

Inspiration

Most artists, indeed most people, when out for a walk will have come across a scene that was so beautiful or captivating that they have wanted to record it in some way. Some will have reached for a camera or smartphone and been happy with the subsequent snapshot, but for the artist this is where the fun starts! Something has caused them to stop and reach for a camera, sketchbook or canvas ... it might just be the start of a painting!

This moment of inspiration is an emotional response, but if you are inspired to reach for paint and brushes then a series of questions must be asked and answered, to discover what it is that has caused you to stop and to consider making a painting. This is developing a moment of inspiration into an objective idea for a painting.

Ask yourself why you have stopped to record the scene before you. Is it something specific, perhaps the texture of a tree's trunk, the way that the shadows fall across a furrowed field or simply the colour of a fresh spring leaf? Is it something more ethereal, such as the graceful dance of branches in a breeze or a mood evoked by a damp, dank wood? Being able to identify what is inspiring you is an important step, as it is at the core of your reason for wanting to paint the scene. Try to name it, as sometimes the language that we use helps us to decide on the response we are hoping to evoke in the viewer of our painting.

In Chapter 1, we asked the question 'Why paint trees?'. Revisiting this chapter may help you to become more aware of what inspires you, and why.

Developing the Idea

Once you have established what it was that inspired you, you can begin to work on translating that moment of inspiration into a more concrete idea. An emotional response to something that triggered your imagination then becomes more tangible.

Sometimes ideas are initially fleeting – jot them down quickly, before they evaporate! Good ideas can be elusive, and it is worth recording even a germ of an idea for future consideration. Keep a sketchbook just for ideas; such a book can be a good place to look, on days when inspiration itself is elusive.

Think about what first held your attention. From here, you can decide on what the focus of the painting is going to be, that is, what the painting is about. It may be an object, for example, a particular tree in a landscape, that will become the focal point of the painting. You can then design the painting in such a way that the viewer's eye is led around the painting, finally resting on that particular tree, perhaps by using lines and the relative positioning of other objects. Alternatively, thing of interest may have been shadows across branches, running through the tree and creating pathways for the eye to meander along, enjoying this journey. In this case, you might decide to make a very figurative painting, exaggerating tonal variations that lead the viewer's eye around.

At this point, you should consider the atmosphere that you would like to create. When painting trees, this is probably going to be related to weather conditions! Do you want to elicit thoughts of a bright, crisp, autumn day or a fresh, spring day, full of energy and promise? Were you attracted to trees peeping through soft mists; might you want to evoke an air of mystery?

Answers to these types of questions will give your painting purpose. They will guide you when making decisions on which medium to use, which textural marks you might use, whether you would like to use bright or muted colours and what the size and shape of the painting should be. Without deciding on your purpose for painting the image, the end result is more than likely to be a rather disappointing, aimless image, with little chance of engaging with others.

Information Gathering

Once you have decided on the purpose of your painting, you can ensure that you have all of the necessary information available. Sketches, photographs, actual objects ... anything that you might need for reference should be gathered together at this stage. Chapter 3, Information Gathering, covers ways of doing this in some detail.

Gathering together all of the reference material that you need before getting down to the nitty-gritty of planning the actual image will enable you to make more-informed decisions on layout, colour and mark-making.

Designing the Painting

The planning of the image can be broken down into the various elements of layout, tone, colour and texture. Decisions made about each one of these elements will affect all of the others, so it is an excellent idea to make decisions before committing paint to a surface.

Watercolourists are very good at this decision-making, since whites have to be reserved and light tones painted first as the painting progresses; for them, planning the order of execution of a painting is very important. While changes can be made during the course of painting, watercolours are noticeably fresher and brighter if corrections are not required.

Artists who use other media often feel that they have more opportunity to change things as the painting progresses but, by making decisions before beginning to paint, you are freer to enjoy the process. Familiar journeys are easier than travelling an unknown route and a new route is easier to travel if you have a good map!

Layout

By layout, we are referring to what is more traditionally known as composition. Many students of painting, when planning the composition, be it to be produced with oil, watercolour or pastel, will become preoccupied with the placement of objects: moving a tree here or a barn there. For them, it is something to do quickly, to be got out of the way, with as little fuss as possible, so that they can get on with the fun bit, the painting. Composition is indeed about the placement of objects, but it is also about so much more.

Altering the landscape

When we make a painting, we get to choose where to place the objects that we will include. Remember, we are not hanging the landscapes on our living-room walls, we are hanging paintings of the landscapes. We create these paintings and, yes, it gives us the ability to move mountains!

It is extremely unlikely that, when painting, drawing or photographing the landscape, you will find the picture-perfect scene laid out before you: a building will prove too intrusive, a single tree in the middle of a field will look out of place and detract from the focal point, or a distant hill will be too dominant. But, armed with the design checklist, we can bend the landscape before us to take into account these structural elements, with the aim of producing a more harmonious, balanced and pleasing

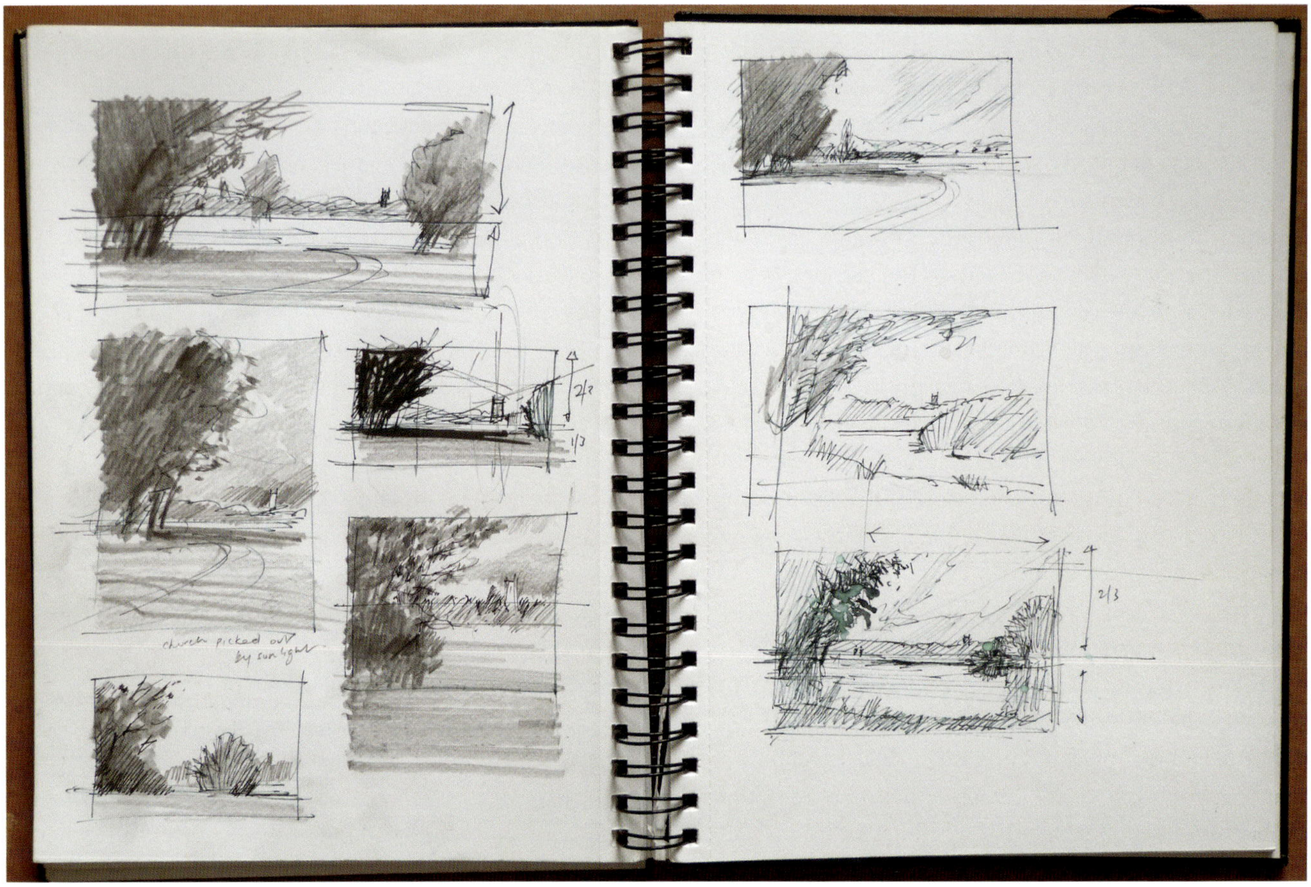

Once you have decided upon the satisfactory placement of objects within your painting, you can use the thumbnail sketch to add notes about tone and colour and even some written notes about the scene.

painting. Sometimes, it is not what you put into a painting but what you leave out that is more important.

Before making your first mark, revisit your original reason for making the painting: the inspiration. Ask the question 'Does putting X into the image add to the original idea, or does it take something away?'. If the inclusion of X dilutes the original idea then it might be wiser to leave it out; if it adds to or supports it, try to leave it in. For example, is it necessary to paint every tree in a forest? If you decide to leave a few out, will you still have a forest? Probably!

It is far better to move – or remove – things that damage the overall image than to include everything just because it was there. What works in nature does not always convert well into a two-dimensional image.

Thumbnail sketches

Thumbnail sketches are useful to the artist, as they are often small in scale, are executed rapidly and are the visual manifestations of the artist's thought process. Here, formats, tonal arrangements and alternative designs can be evaluated. Using a soft, black pencil, 4B or even 8B, allows you to cover the paper quickly. With little or no regard for detail at this stage, concentrate on the larger, broader masses that make up the painting's design.

When working on location, whether just sketching, gathering information or intending to paint *en plein air*, have a sketchbook close by, to try out and evaluate the proposed painting's design, whatever the medium, before making more-considered sketches and taking photographs. This will save a lot of time; why waste time drawing things that you will not need?

'If I do decide to leave something out, what do I put there instead?' is not an uncommon question, and it is one that seems to panic many a novice painter. For instance, removing a tree from a field or a distant wood from a hillside will leave a gap, but what goes into the gap to fill it? This genuine problem is more easily resolved than an inexperienced artist might think. By planning the layout of a painting, you can decide what is going to be on every part of the painting's surface. For example, it is often possible to extend the field or hillside from behind the tree or

DESIGN STUDY: *STARK SPRING TREES*

Rob Dudley

The format that the artist chooses for the painting of a particular scene can have a dramatic impact on design, composition and the response that the painting elicits within the viewer.

I find it rather odd, when asking some painters why they had chosen a particular size and format for a painting, to be told only that it was simply down to how big the available paper or board was! No thought, at any stage of the painting's development or design, seems to have been given to the effect that the format would have on the finished piece. This seems to be at the very least lazy, and this approach doesn't always result in the best outcomes.

Some paintings work within certain formats better than others. Some artists might suggest that landscape paintings work better within landscape formats or that maritime subjects seem to be more successful within letter-box formats. A wiser approach is to consider each subject independently and choose a format that complements the work, rather than trying to shoehorn the painting into the expected or traditional format.

A wide, letter-box format was the choice when planning this little watercolour of a landscape on the edge of Dartmoor on a rather chilly, spring day. The format was chosen to exaggerate the horizontal patterns of the field boundaries and to emphasize the trees of the title.

The three trees were carefully placed in the centre of the design, with little distracting detail or structure to the sides, and the narrow format concentrates and focuses attention towards the trees. Note how the limited sky and lack of detail in the foreground field keeps the viewer's eye returning to the trees. Many have been so surprised by this almost magnetic attraction towards the trees, created in part by both format and design, that they miss the two sheep to the right.

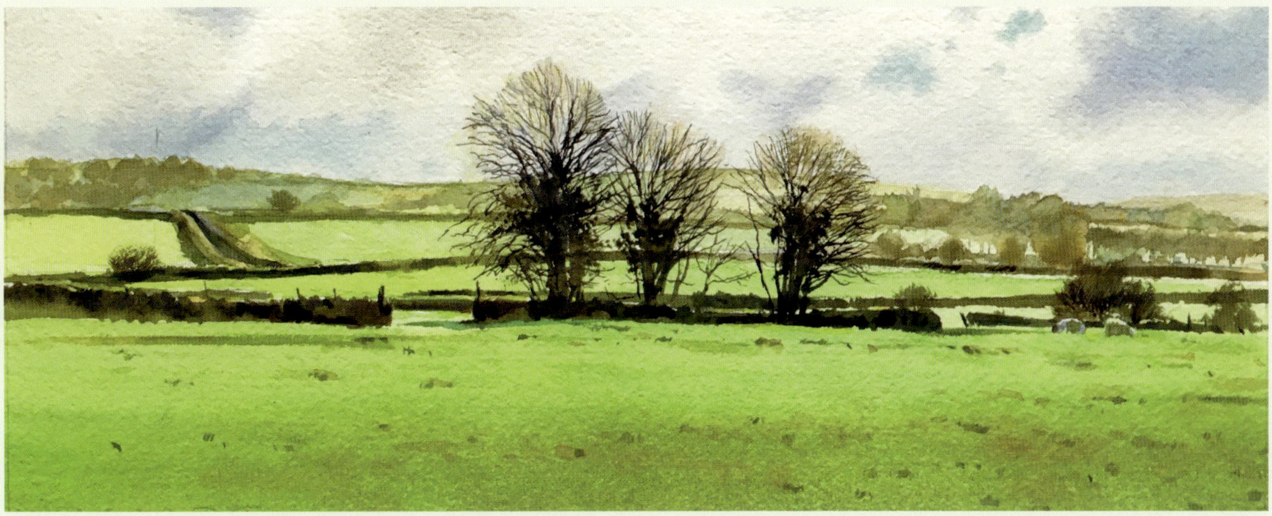

Stark Spring Trees, watercolour, 36cm × 14cm (14in × 5½in), Rob Dudley.

wood to fill the space. Use the same surrounding colours, tones, brushmarks and level of finish as used for the depictions of the actually present elements of the landscape for the extended filler, for it to blend seamlessly into the rest of the painting.

The time to make these decisions is while you are making your thumbnail sketches and gathering information. It is at this stage that you can collect more detail, if you need it.

Formats and focal points

The shape of a painting is known as its format. Paintings can be of any shape, but there are four commonly used formats with which we are all familiar: landscape, letter box, square and portrait.

The landscape format is a horizontal rectangle, wider than it is high, so named because it is a particularly suitable shape for painting landscapes.

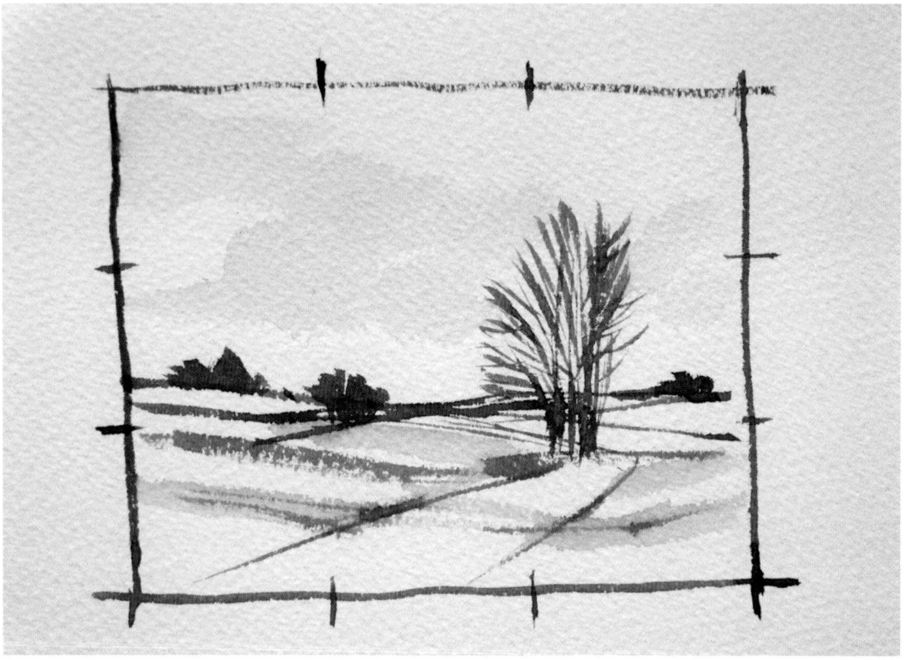

The rule of thirds involves breaking the painting down by adding two equally spaced lines on the horizontal and the vertical axes. Note how the horizon is placed slightly above the bottom-third line and the sweeping road leads the viewer's eye into the sketch and takes the viewer to the main group of trees – the painting's focal point – that are placed on a vertical third line. Placing the painting's focal point on to or close by the intersecting points of the horizontal and vertical lines is a useful device for the artist to call upon when designing the image.

An extra-wide version of the landscape format, known as 'letter box', has recently become more popular. It allows wider, more panoramic views to be painted, allowing the eye to roam freely across the painting's surface.

A landscape designed within the square format will impart a more compact feel to the painting.

Although the upright rectangle, taller than it is wide, is referred to as the portrait format, it can be very useful for painting landscapes. It is especially useful where you want to emphasize height, and it can therefore be an excellent choice for the painting of trees.

The focal point (or points, as there can be more than one within a painting) is an area of emphasis within the painting that the viewer is led to, and the viewer's eye will often come to rest upon this focal point, by the artist's skilful manipulation of the painting's design. Without a focal point, the viewer's eye can wander aimlessly around, almost as if lost. The placement of the focal points has a direct influence on the format used, so it will likely be a contributory factor in deciding on the format for the painting.

The rule of thirds

The rule of thirds is a simplified version of the golden ratio. The golden ratio is a mathematical formula that is commonly found in nature. When applied to design, it promotes natural-looking compositions that are aesthetically pleasing to the eye. We, being part of nature, are very attracted to images manifesting this ratio. Using this formula as a basis for our paintings makes perfect sense. Although referred to as a rule, it does not have to be strictly adhered to, but it is a very useful guide.

Many designers will base their work on the mathematical formula and ratio but, since the ratio is 1:1.618, most artists find it easier to use the simplified version, the rule of thirds. This is not as precise as the golden ratio, being 1:0.618:1, but it works well enough.

In fact, it works perfectly well for most artists to simplify it even further to a ratio of 1:1:1, literally dividing the image into equal thirds, horizontally and vertically, by adding four lines. It is a simple device that can really help in designing well-balanced, harmonious images.

The lines and their intersections are then used for placing elements within the image. In landscape paintings, placing the horizon line along or near one of the horizontal lines – sky above, land below – makes a very pleasing picture. Experiment yourself with moving this horizon line away from one of the two horizontal lines of thirds, and you will feel, rather than see, how the image becomes imbalanced; if you are wanting to evoke an unsettled feeling you could do this on purpose.

Similarly, placing elements of interest within the painting on or near the intersections of these lines draws a viewer's eye to them, making the intersections good locations for placing focal points.

When designing a painting, the artist should consider not only layout, tone, colour and texture but also how busy an image it is. If there is a lot of visual activity across the whole of the painting, the poor viewer might feel visually assailed by the level of liveliness. One approach in order to counteract creating a too-busy image is to divide the painting into four quarters and to have one less-busy quarter within the design. In the example shown, note how the top-left quadrant has very little visual activity within in it compared to that of the other quarters. This contrast allows the viewer to have visual rest, before their eye moves on to other parts of the painting.

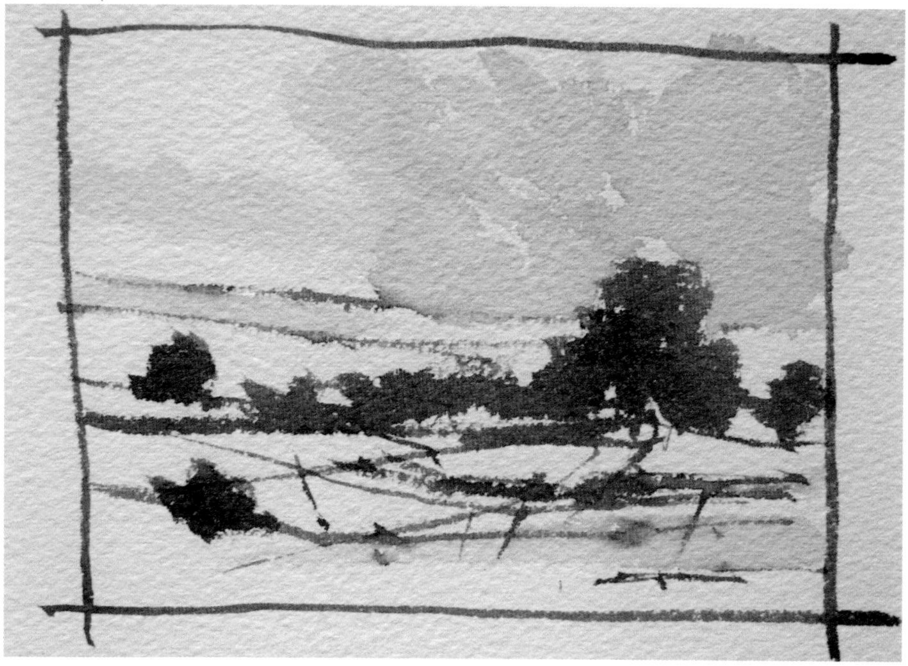

It is interesting, when analysing images that use other devices for organizing the elements within them, to find that they often also fit the rule of thirds, even if the artist had not given it much thought. This says something of the natural power of the golden ratio!

Busy, busy, busy, not so busy

There are several other formulas that make the basis of a good design for a painting. One such method is to divide the image into quarters, varying the amount of detail included in each one. It works well if one quarter is busy, including the most details and the focal point, two quarters have some detail and interest, and the final quarter is quiet and restful. This balance will lead the viewer's eye around the image, directing it towards the focal point, at the same time allowing a visual rest in the quiet quarter. Too busy a picture can often assail the visual senses, and the area of visual rest helps to balance this, by allowing the viewer to pause before moving on.

Horizontals, verticals and diagonal lines

When designing a painting, it is useful to give thought to the horizontal, vertical and diagonal lines within the painting and the role that they play in leading the viewer's eye around the image. These lines are not always apparent to the casual observer but, nevertheless, provide a solid foundation and make a vital contribution to the overall success, or otherwise, of the painting.

These hidden elements play an interesting role in an image. Used judiciously, they can lead the viewer's eye in the direction of our choosing, guiding them along the path that we want the viewer's eye to travel along. The lines do not have to be distinct objects but can be formed with tones, colours or brushmarks.

Strong horizontal lines lead the eye across the picture plane from side to side. These could be depicted clouds, fields and hedgerows, although a well-placed brushstroke can be a similar device.

Vertical elements within the painting's design tend to lead the viewer's eye upwards. In the landscape, trees are likely to be the most obvious of the present vertical elements, but don't overlook telegraph poles or buildings.

A diagonal aspect within the painting often leads the viewer's eye into the painting, creating the impression of depth and distance. Rivers and roads are often the most apparent examples of strong diagonals within landscape painting, but the branches of trees can be equally useful and significant as diagonals.

DESIGN STUDY: *WINTER ON THE MOOR*

Rob Dudley

I cannot think of an image that I have produced that more clearly demonstrates the use of horizontals, verticals and diagonals that underpin a painting's design than *Winter on the Moor*. Its simple geometric foundations are clearly on display: the distant moor, with strong horizontal features, and the commanding diagonal lines of the wall, leading the viewer's eye towards the trees, and these, in turn, direct the visual pathway upwards through the painting. This is a simple painting, with clear visual pathways, a broad range of tones and a limited palette. Yet, I think that it proves that it is often the simplest, most uncomplicated of images that often results in the most dramatic of paintings.

On this occasion, it might be noticed that the closest tree seems to be breaking one of the so-called rules of composition, with it being placed centrally within the design. Sometimes however, the breaking of rules, which are of course nothing more than words of guidance, can be just what the painting needs, bringing attention to a particular spot. In this case, the somewhat unconventional design is brought back into balance by the other elements within the painting.

Remembering once again the old adage that 'tone does all the hard work, yet colour gets all the praise', the importance of tone cannot be underestimated or indeed ignored in this watercolour painting.

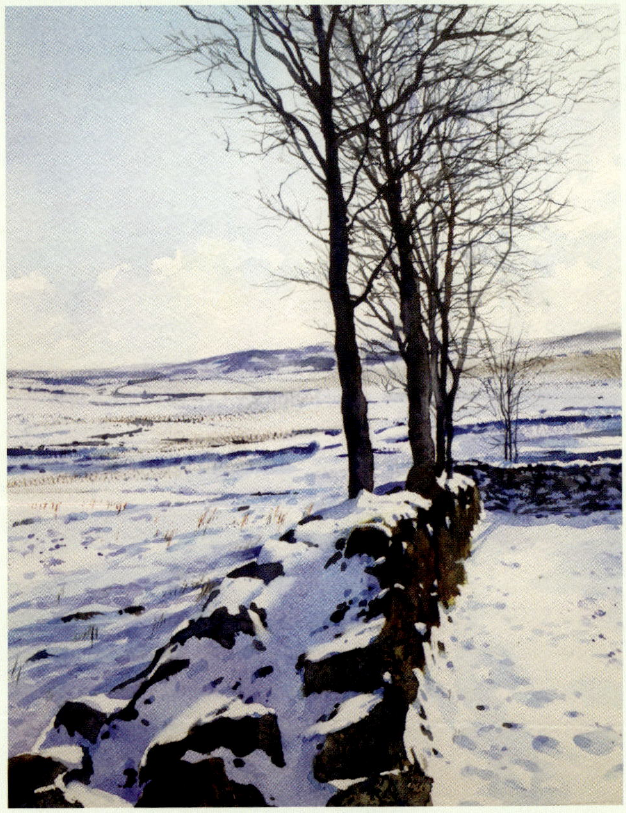

Winter on the Moor, watercolour, 28cm × 36cm (11in × 14¼in), Rob Dudley.

Essentially, the painting consists of no more than three or four key tones: the lightest tone being of the snow, the next of the shadows and moorland features, and through to the strong darks found in the wall and the all-important trees. The strength of the painting lies in the placement and the arrangement of these tones. I have deliberately placed some of the strongest, darkest tones alongside some of the lightest, of the white, unpainted paper. This juxtaposition of these light and dark tones brings a real kick and energy to the painting. As with all of my paintings, whatever the medium, the decisions regarding where to place the tones were made at the planning stage, worked out in small, tonal thumbnail sketches. I like to think of these sketches as little tonal maps, guiding me through the painting's journey, from start to finish.

I have heard it said that a winter palette consists of mainly blues and blue-greys. However, close observation will reveal a whole array of colours and shades that can bring interest to many a winter-themed painting. In this painting, the colours consist of mainly blues and blue-blacks, but hints of raw sienna and touches of green gold are also included, to warm up the sunlit side of the wall.

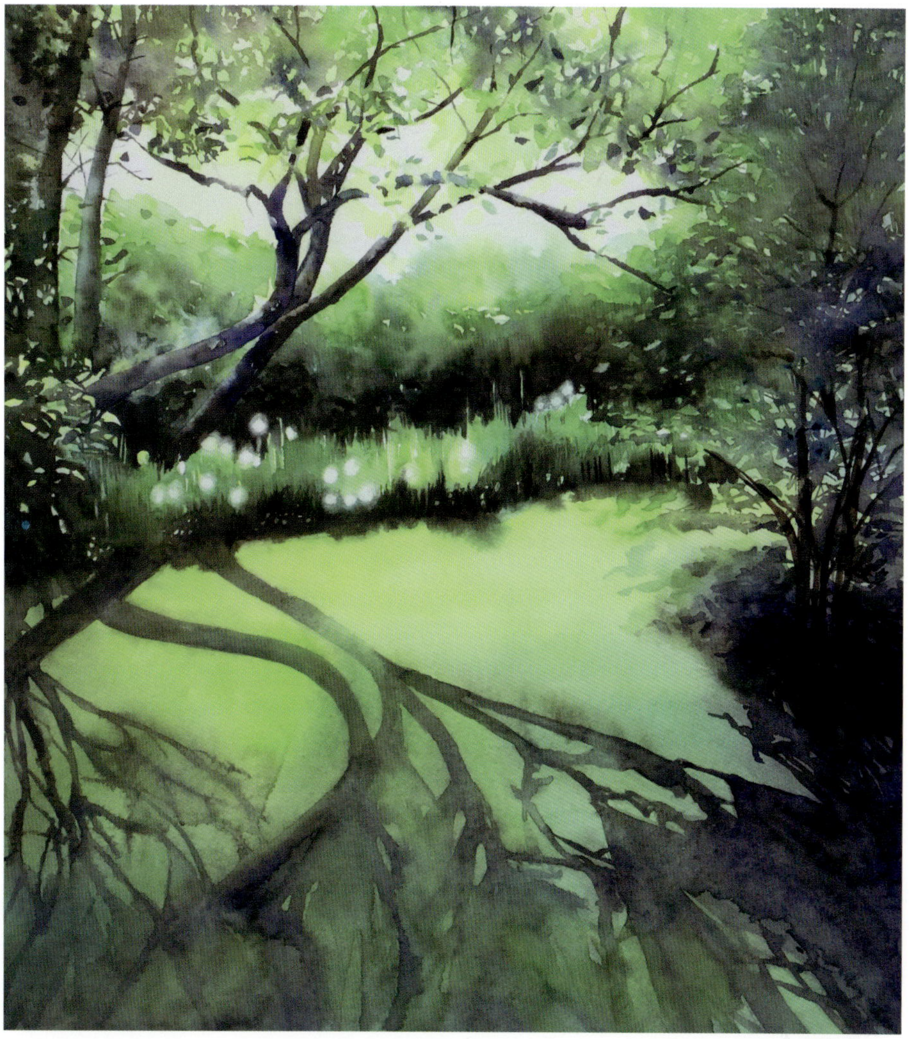

Springtime: Apple Trees and Dandelion Clocks, watercolour, 30cm × 34cm (11¾in × 13½in), Siân Dudley. In this painting, you can see examples of lost and found edges. Note that, where the main tree's trunk meets its shadow, the edges are well defined (found edges), but, as you follow both trunk and shadow outwards, both begin to blur into the background (lost edges). This image is painted for a low viewpoint, from which the viewer looks up to the underside of the main tree. On both sides of the image, there are vertical trunks and branches acting as stoppers; as the viewer's eye meets them, it moves along their length and is led back into the image, so the viewer's eye is effectively being stopped from moving out of the field of the painting.

Stoppers and signposts

When planning the painting's design, it will often become apparent that the viewer's eye might be in danger of falling off the edge of, or even being led out of, the composition. This may be planned and, if this is so, then all is well. However, if it is not intended then the artist must do something to prevent this and to guide the viewer's eye back into the painting. Using horizontal, vertical or even diagonal lines can be very useful here. Sometimes, the simple relocation of a tree or building, or perhaps the inclusion a group of people, or a strategically placed cloud, is all that is needed to prevent the viewer's gaze from wandering off.

But don't overlook the effectiveness of a simple, well-placed brushmark, a stronger tone or a splash of colour, all of which can have a similar effect to that of the placement of an object. We often refer to these points within the painting as stoppers; they stop the viewer's eye from leaving the painting and direct the viewer's attention back within the field of the painting.

High and low viewpoints

You might notice that, when drawing within the landscape, the view visible when you are sitting down is altered compared to that when you are standing. When you are in a standing position, the horizon will appear lower, the sky will be more dominant, and the sense of space and openness will appear to be increased from this higher viewpoint. Contrast this with the view that you get when you are in a sitting position. With this lower viewpoint, the horizon is lifted, the foreground takes on a more dominant role, and a more intimate feel to the design is created. Take some time to evaluate different viewpoints and the influence that they can have in creating the overall sense of space, openness and focus of the painting's design.

DESIGN STUDY: *SUMMER IN THE LANE*

Rob Dudley

Some paintings have trees in them; others are about the trees as subjects, as the focal point. *Summer in the Lane* was definitely about the tree; it was the subject and the reason for making the painting.

The painting was made back in the studio from references made on location: a couple of tonal sketches and photographs. The painting was designed to emphasize the magnificent oak, with the real landscape being changed to accommodate this. Compare the featured photograph to the finished painting. Note how elements within the landscape have been altered or rearranged to the benefit of the painting. The same elements are here in the painting as were present in the landscape on that particular afternoon, but they are not necessarily in the same order.

In reality, the lane curves slightly to the right, taking the viewer away from the tree. In the painting, the lane gently curves towards the tree, focusing and directing the viewer's attention towards this key point of interest. Think of these as visual pathways or signposts, leading the viewer's eye where you, the artist, want it to go.

Although it might appear insignificant compared to the oak, a small yet very important tree has been added to the right middle ground of the painting. Without its inclusion, the viewer's eye might have wandered out of the image. However, by including the tree, this is less likely to happen. The tree acts as a stopper, preventing the viewer's eye from leaving the image and directing it back into the painting.

There is quite a difference in tones between those in the photograph and those in the painting. In the reference photograph, the tones are much closer together from the foreground to the background. This narrowing of tones has the effect of reducing the feeling of distance. However, in the painting, I wanted to increase the sense of distance. To achieve this, I reduced the strength of the distant tones, while strengthening the tones found in some of the foreground elements. The contrast between the tones has the effect of pushing the paler tones into the distance, while bringing the darker tones forward.

It should be noted that over-reliance on the tonal values presented within a photograph, when using these tones as references for the painting, should be avoided. Often those tones recorded by a camera are very different to the actual tones present in the landscape; the camera is intended to record an average over a tonal range rather than to accurately assess the comparative relationships of each tone. If time and circumstances allow, a quick tonal sketch and a photograph produce the most useful information for the painter to work with.

Paintings don't just happen; they are made. As for any construction process, various parts come together to make the whole. Some parts are more obvious than others; in a painting, the colour and the tone, for example, are likely to be some of the first components to be seen by the viewer. But it is the underlying, structural elements, often hidden at first glance, that play a huge role in the overall success, or otherwise, of the painting. These structural elements are the foundation that other parts of the painting can be built on. And, much like architecture, wherein solid foundations make for stronger buildings, the same can be said for painting; the better the placement of the structural elements, the stronger the painting.

In *Summer in the Lane*, note how the hidden geometric elements, the horizontals, verticals and diagonals, have been used to underpin the painting's design and composition. Each is considered in its relationships to the others. If one of these geometric elements dominated then the painting would likely appear unbalanced.

The horizontal shadows falling across the lane link both sides of the painting together; the strong, dynamic verticals of the oak, telegraph pole and distant trees lead the eye upwards from the foreground and bring height to the design. The diagonals of the lane and hedgerow move the viewer's eye into the painting, towards the distant, sunlit corner.

Although *Summer in the Lane* is essentially a green painting, the touches of burnt sienna – a reddy brown – complement the greens and help to bring energy and life to this watercolour painting. Note how at the far end of the lane the juxtaposition of the red–green complementary pairing helps to draw the viewer's eye towards that point. A similar complementary device has been used with the purple shadows on the right foreground bank complementing the yellow-greens.

Lost and found edges
A good painting will have a balance between the inclusion of lost and found edges.

If the whole painting were to be painted in stark, pixel-perfect definition, with no lost or blurred edges, it would look rather unnatural, almost as if everything had been cut out and stuck on to the painting's surface.

Found edges will often be the ones that the eye goes to and rest on, so be careful not to have too many within the painting. Think of it, if you will, as a balance between areas in focus and other area slightly out of focus; you thereby create a far more natural visual experience for the viewer of the finished painting.

Lost and found edges can be built in to the design. Found edges can be used as directional lines to lead the viewer's eye around. Lost edges can provide moments of rest and also encourage the viewer to look for the next moment of clarity, encouraging their eye to return to the path leading them around the image. Because of this, lost and found edges should be placed carefully within an image.

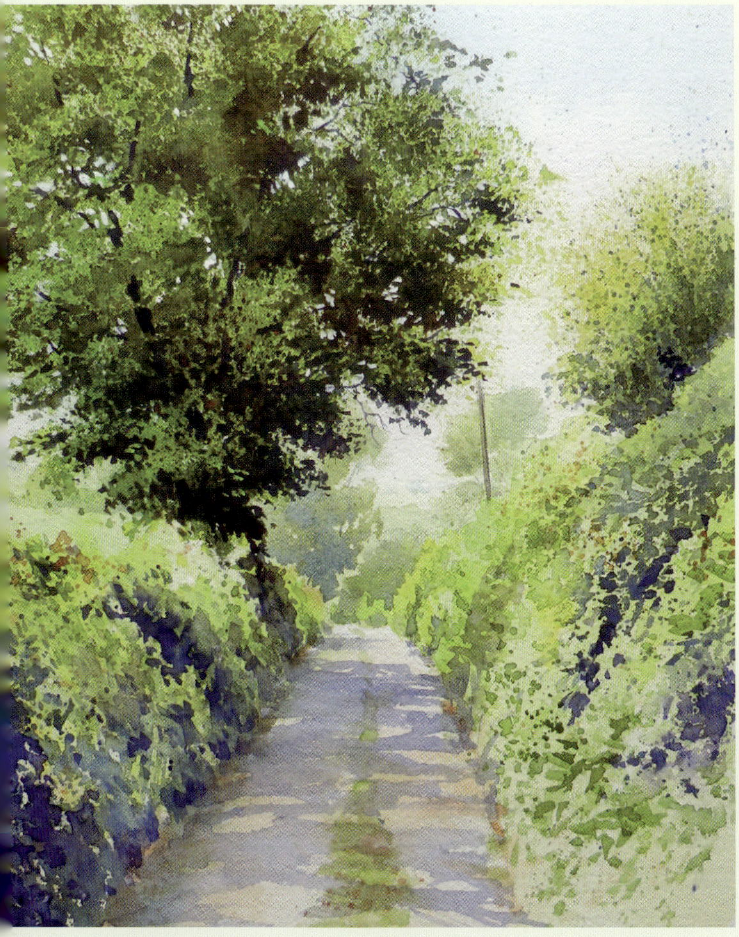

Summer in the Lane, watercolour, 30cm × 34cm (11¾in × 13½in), Rob Dudley.

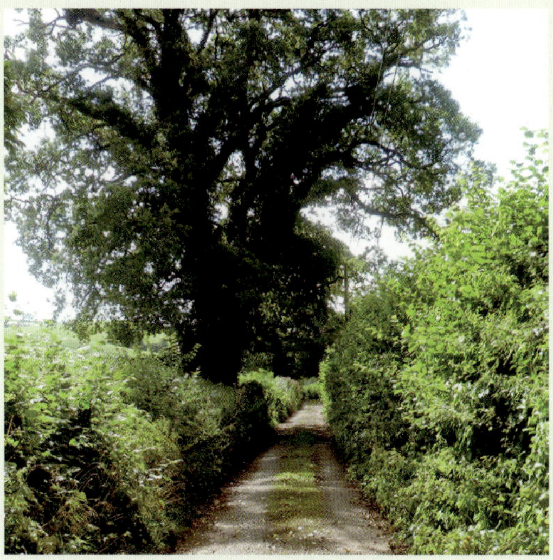

Reference photograph for *Summer in the Lane*.

Tone

Tone does all the hard work, yet colour gets all the praise

In a landscape painting, a viewer is likely to notice that trees on the horizon line are smaller and will probably notice that they are bluer. The majority of people are unlikely to notice that they are also of a lighter tone. Experienced artists know this, but it is not unusual for a novice painter to be unaware that this is the case.

The adage above contains one of the most important and fundamental tenets that we have ever heard relating to painting. People will notice the colour of a painting quickly and take on board the subject matter. But, unless one of the main reasons for making the painting was to emphasize the lights and darks, the tonal qualities of the work may go completely unnoticed.

And yet tone is far more important than colour! After all, an image will work in greyscale, where colour is absent. Remove tonal variation from an image and you are left with a flat block of colour.

'Tone' refers to the light and dark values that an artist uses when making a painting. These values are responsible for converting a flat shape into one that appears to have three-dimensional form. In paintings of trees, it is tone that will give the trunk its roundness, make the branches appear to curl and twine around each other, and define the overall shape of a tree in full leaf.

Do not make the mistake of confusing tone with colour. Unfortunately, colour is sometimes referred to as tone. Colour refers to hue, which is fundamentally different.

The local colour of tree trunk does not change. In bright sunlight, it may appear to be much paler than when in dark shadow. We may think of it as silvery grey in sunlight and charcoal grey in shadow, but the fundamental colour does not change, the tone does.

The pattern of and the balance between areas of light and dark are two of the most important aspects of a painting's design. Clear tonal differences are essential for describing found edges. The juxtaposition of lights and darks produces brighter, more energetic paintings. In describing a sunny day, or a shaft of sunlight shining through trees, strong tonal differences will be needed. The dark trunks of trees set against the light of the sky, or dark-toned branches placed through clusters of brightly lit leaves, can give real impact to parts of the painting and are often used to emphasize focal points.

Paintings where the tones are much closer together imply a more diffused, softer light. These paintings are calmer and more restful. Depicting a bank of trees on a hillside, representing soft foliage on a misty day and deliberately using lost edges all require a far smaller tonal range.

Planning tones by using thumbnail sketches

Producing a simple tonal thumbnail of the proposed painting in pencil or paint is useful, some might say essential, in discovering how the tones will work together. Think of it as a tonal map, using it to discover where the lights, darks and midtones will be placed in the finished work. The tonal thumbnail does not have to be full of detail; indeed, too much detail might make the thumbnail overly fussy and make it difficult to assess the tones successfully.

You can make a separate thumbnail sketch for experimenting with the placement of tone in the painting. At this stage in planning the painting, you should already have decided on the layout (placement of objects), so you could begin by adding tone to the thumbnail that you have already produced.

Use a soft, dark pencil or a single colour when working the thumbnail. Ultramarine blue is a useful colour to work with, as you can achieve a good range of tones with it, in

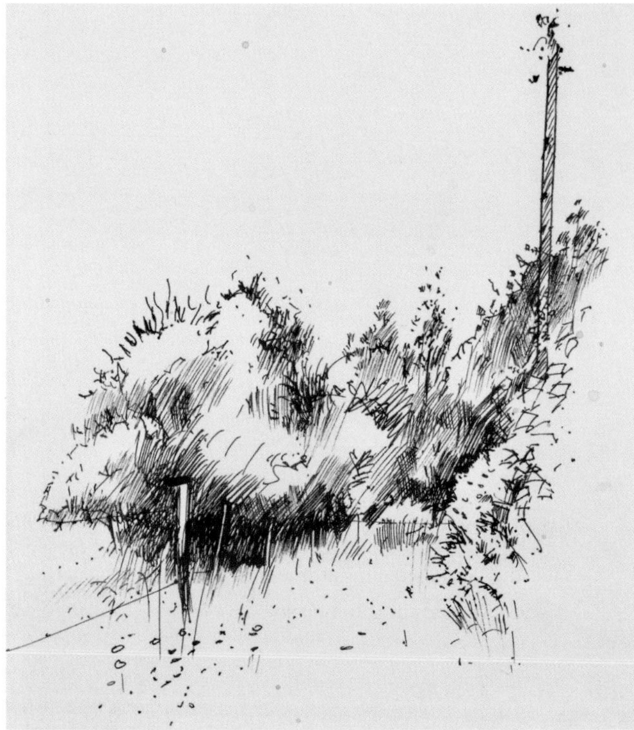

Note how the fence post is dark against the light grasses but appears light against the dark bushes. This is an example of counterchange.

both watercolour and oil. And, if you do need a strong dark, add a touch of burnt sienna to the mix.

Counterchange

Rather like lost and found edges, counterchange is likely something that you will definitely have seen even if you were unaware of it. We see objects as separate because they are either lighter or darker than what is behind them. 'Counterchange' is a term used by artists to describe what happens when you can follow an object along its height or length and the tonal values appear to change. It is seen under certain lighting conditions, where the object is viewed against different backgrounds.

Imagine a tree standing in front of a wall but being taller than the wall, so that, as you follow the tree to its tip, you are seeing the tree against the sky. At the base of the tree, the trunk is lighter in tone than is the wall. As your eyes move upwards, they reach a point where the trunk is darker than the sky behind it. At its base, it is light against dark; at its tip, it is dark against light. The point where the change occurs is often quite subtle. The overall effect is that the trunk itself changes in tone.

Counterchange can be used to great effect in paintings, to add interest to passages that might otherwise feel slightly flat or unexciting.

DESIGN STUDY: *SEASONS OF MISTS*

Rob Dudley

Even in front of nature one must compose.
– Edgar Degas

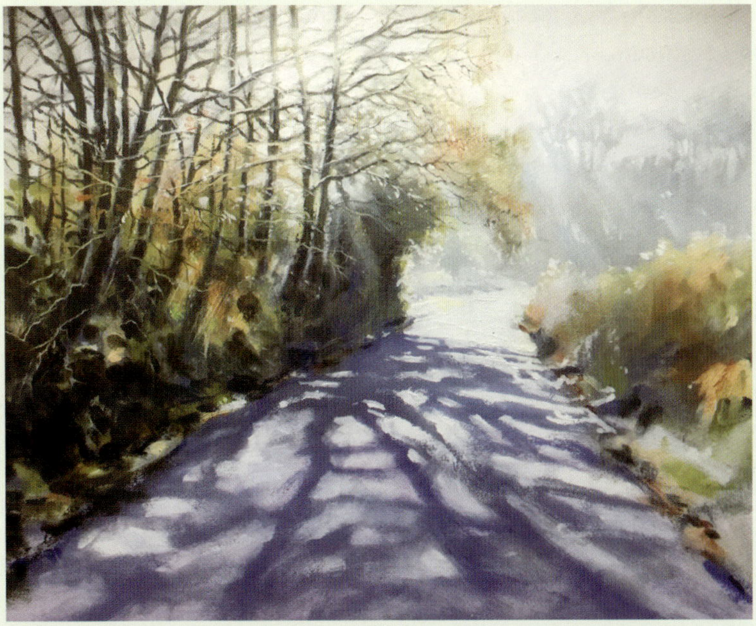

Seasons of Mists, water-mixable oils on board, 30cm × 25cm (11¾in × 9¾in), Rob Dudley.

This small oil study was not so much about the trees themselves but about the sunlight filtering through them and the shadows cast across the lane on this bright, autumn morning. Although bright in parts, along the lane, pockets of the early morning mist still lingered, streaked with shafts of sunlight, the mist shrouding the trees and turning them into ghostly silhouettes at the corner of the lane. Indeed, it was this that first caught my attention; it seemed to be the very essence of autumn laid out before me. It had to be painted.

It may seem odd to paint trees when so much detail is lost from view. But misty days are the perfect days in which to venture out and capture in paint or pencil the shapes of trees. With so much detail being lost, the artist can concentrate solely on shape without be sidetracked by all the fiddly bits!

Having the opportunity to study the shape of trees in this way is very useful to the artist, not simply in order to be able to successfully paint mist-filled landscapes but also because close observation makes the painting of trees so much easier, by facilitating the correct rendering of the shapes of the trees. The resultant images have a greater authenticity about them – more authority, even – whatever the weather conditions are that you choose to portray the trees in.

In *Seasons of Mists*, note how the distant trees are merely treelike shapes; most of the detail is lost, save for a few of the branches and touches of light shining through them. One tree flows into the next, and little if any indication of either foliage or three-dimensionality is present.

The painting's relatively simple design is built principally around the strong diagonals of the lane, hedged banks and shadows. These diagonals lead the viewer's eye into the painting, directing attention to the brightest part of the image, which is the sun-bleached corner of the lane. This is the focal point.

Note how the focal point of the painting is offset slightly to the right. To place it dead centre would have fixed the eye at that point, capturing the viewer's attention so keenly that it would make it difficult to lead the viewer's gaze towards other parts of the painting.

Once again, the use of tonal contrast as a design device is much in evidence here. The paler tones are used for the distant regions of the painting, and increasingly stronger tones are used for the foreground regions, causing the viewer's eye to move forward within the painting; this helps to create the sense of recession and distance and, in addition, the contrast is being employed to express the brightness of the sunshine. Notice how the lighter tones are juxtaposed against the darker ones. Notice how the viewer's eye is led to the focal point by both the arrangement of tones and the strong directional diagonals of the painting's design.

Although the painting took no more than a couple of hours to complete, the time spent making thumbnail sketches prior to painting was essential to ensure the overall success of the painting. In the sketches, I was able to consider the tonal values and their distribution within the image, the placement of the painting's underpinning geometry and the painting's format. Much better to make these decisions at the start rather than trying to decide halfway through the painting process.

Colour

Colour is often one of the first things that a viewer will notice about a painting. Colours can convey many moods and emotions, and the power of colours should not be underestimated. The choices made are critical to the overall success of the painting; therefore, colours should be chosen carefully.

Try to work from a limited palette per painting, as this will help you to produce a harmonious painting. Seven colours are usually adequate.

When choosing your colour palette for the painting, start with the features that are most important to you. This might be a particular tree, or a group of trees. Find the colours that you want to use for these features. Then consider other elements of the painting, trying to keep the number of different paint colours required to a minimum.

You might need to make compromises. For example, if you mix a delightful green for a specimen tree, but the paints you chose do not give you a dark enough tone for the shadowy areas, you might have to change your mix; tone outranks colour in defining form, so you might need to compromise on your original choices. Alternatively, you might need to change the blue that you wanted for the sky, in order to not have to compromise on your original green mix for the trees.

Choice of hue

The artist should consider how the colours behave and interact with one another. Use of contrasting colours, those that sit on opposite sides of the colour wheel, will result in lively paintings. Use of harmonizing colours, those that sit close together on the colour wheel, will produce calmer images. Using a wide colour range will produce a busier painting than that resulting from the use of a few different hues. Keep in mind that the choice and range of colours will be affected by the colours' tonal range and, in planning the choice of the colours, each paint's tone should be taken into account too.

When painting trees, especially trees in a landscape, there is a strong likelihood that you will be drawn towards a small colour range, given that so much of nature is green. To avoid producing a painting that has such a small colour range that it lacks excitement, consider ensuring that you have included other colours within the image. Turner famously advocated including a splash of red, which is guaranteed to enliven a landscape!

TAKING THE PAIN OUT OF GREENS

It is readily accepted amongst artists that the huge variety of greens in a landscape painting can cause immense problems. Trees are a major part of this problem, given that the huge variety of greens is caused in large part by the number of different species of trees that we see. Compromise is the answer, making a judgement call between accurate representation of local colour and deciding which greens you want to include in your artwork. Remember, when the finished painting is hanging on the wall, what is important is that the colours you used for the painting work together in the finished image.

When designing a painting, consider how closely you want to focus on the leaves. In close-up, the colour is much less likely to be a problem; it is probably one of the main reasons for wanting to paint the leaves. Matching local colour is a good starting point for deciding on the palette for a painting.

If individual leaves are a much less important feature in the image, just featuring as a mass of foliage, it is best to remember that they are just a part of your inspiration, so their local colour is much less important. Take colour notes from a distance, approximating the overall colour of the tree and ensuring that you are able to create a range of tones with the mix that you have chosen. This is likely to give a colour that is close enough for a particular type of tree to be recognized by your viewer. Given that you will have also observed the overall shape of the tree, you are directing your viewer to, for example, perceive a silver-green tree as a lime or an ochre-green tree as an oak. Limit your palette as far as possible to produce a coherent painting; if you do so, the enormous number of greens that we see in nature become far less of a problem.

Choice of pigment

Paints have different qualities according to the pigments that they contain. Some are transparent, some opaque, some granulate and some stain. Depending on the medium you are using, these factors might be quite important. Watercolourists will be aware that the features of pigments play an essential role in the order in which the painting is executed; for example, if glazing techniques are to be used then a staining colour might be chosen over an opaque colour, as the latter will lift when the glaze is applied, whereas the former will not. It makes sense to consider this while designing the painting.

Texture

Choice of medium

Each medium has its own particular strengths and characteristics, from the luminous transparent washes of watercolour and the rich strength of lush oils to the immediacy of pastel and variety of mixed-media pieces. The decision of which medium to use is often down to personal choice and familiarity but also to some extent to the subject being painted and the finished result that is desired.

For example, a dip pen or fine-nibbed marker might make it easier to render the delicate tracery of leafless branches that are seen in winter trees, but the same subject could be executed in charcoal or graphite. The result would be different but just as valid and interesting.

A valuable exercise that any painter would benefit from would be to paint the same subject in various media, to understand more readily the strengths and limitations of each. Some media will allow for the finest of lines to be made easily, whereas, for others, the production of a fine line will prove almost impossible. Some soft, crumbly pastels make it almost impossible to produce sharp, fine lines; however, they are ideal when trying to cover large, broad areas, when painting quickly and efficiently.

To extend their range of artistic skills and expression, artists should experiment with the media available. Taking a few steps beyond the comfort zone might at first be scary, but it can give you new insights to new media or offer new ways of using media that you might have thought held no further surprises or possibilities. Marks that you discover in one medium might affect the way that you use a different medium, causing you to find a whole new range of textural marks and exciting possibilities for the creation of expressive paintings.

Choice of support

The choice of support will be led by the choice of medium, but it should be taken into account at the design stage. With oils, the size and shape of the painting may influence the choice of support; for example, can you buy a prepared canvas off the shelf, or do you need to create a home-made support that is more readily adjusted to the format that you want?

With watercolour, the surface of the paper will have an impact on the painted textures and gestural marks that you can produce; therefore, a decision on whether to use HP, NOT or rough paper should be made now.

Mark-making

For examples of tips and techniques appropriate for the painting of trees, *see* Chapter 2, Materials and Techniques.

When choosing which medium to use, refer back to your original inspiration, consider the range of marks and overall effects possible to make with each medium and make your decision accordingly.

Before beginning to apply paint to your painting, whichever medium you are using, try out some marks first. Spend some time experimenting with different brushes, palette knives or other ways of applying paint, to make sure that the way you lay the paint down adds to the image in a painterly manner.

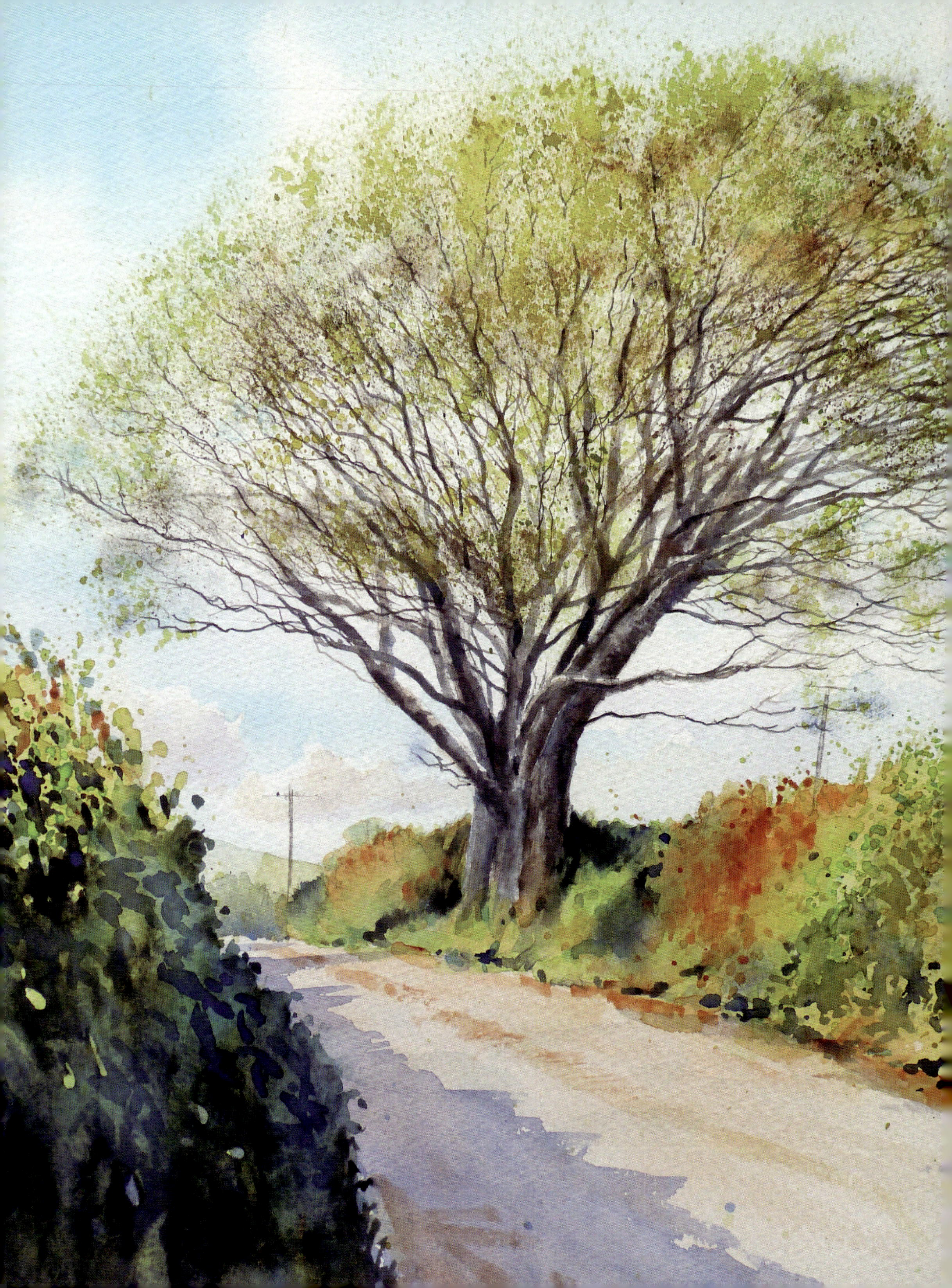

Chapter 5

Spring

After a long, dark, cold winter, the first signs of spring are always very welcome!

This is the time when a few brave flowers break free from winter's icy grip, insects take to the wing, birds are busy nesting and the world seems to be stirring into life. Trees begin to burst into leaf and blossom, with plenty to inspire the artist to reach for brush and paints…

Trees have a certain sort of magic about them at this time of year. Many trees blossom well before their first leaves appear, putting on wonderful displays of delightful colour and banishing thoughts of summer greenery to the backs of our minds. Delicate pinks, whites and yellows transform our countryside and gardens. Think of cherry trees, famous for their masses of pink flowers; as the petals fall, they drift over our gardens in a light, spring breeze, reminiscent of snow yet heralding the warmer weather that is on its way.

Trees in full flowers are an obvious source of inspiration for any artist and a welcome diversion for those who prefer not to paint with greens. But, for those who do like greens, springtime is exciting! As the new leaves open, we are presented with fresh, bright, vibrant colours, inspiring bright, lively, energetic paintings, as full of energy as are the leaves themselves. Choose palettes with crisp, clear, cool colours, ensuring that, as the paints mix, they retain their freshness and do not become muddy.

In spring, it feels as though our powers of observation wake up too, as we actively seek out signs of new life. Take care not to miss some of the other features of the season that can inspire and feed into the design of your paintings.

Unstable weather creates fascinating skies which, in turn, provide amazing backdrops for a stand of trees. Dark, rain-filled clouds can be seen set against clear, blue skies; placing the dark clouds behind the vibrant trees will accentuate the bright colours, while placing them predominantly within the bright, clear sky above will accentuate the freshness of the season.

In spring, shadows move quickly, not only under scudding clouds but also due to the relatively short length of the days compared with the length of the days in summer. You will need to take a camera on sketching trips to capture some of the light effects. Amongst all the energy, note the quieter subtleties. For example, hedge-maple leaves, green in summer, open with autumnal shades.

The Big Beech Tree: Spring, watercolour, 30cm × 37cm (11¾in × 14½in), Rob Dudley.

THE BIG BEECH TREE: SPRING

Rob Dudley

Spring can be one of the most colourful and brightest of seasons, and I wanted my painting to reflect this. When visiting the beech tree in early spring, I was struck by the vibrancy of the colours. They seemed so bright, almost unnatural in their intensity. I decided that I wanted to work with these colours, trying to capture the exhilaration that I felt when confronted by them. In order to do so, I decided to strengthen and brighten the palette of colours that I had initially chosen to work with, in order to emphasize my response to the scene.

The sky was a wonderful bright blue – pure, clean and crisp – and acted as the perfect backdrop to the beech. The strong sunlight provided some strong contrasts, which gave a real kick to the painting.

Working in watercolour allowed me to build up layers of bright colour, without the finished painting becoming heavy or overworked, and emphasized the light freshness of the season.

PROJECT

Spring Blackthorn

Siân Dudley

The Inspiration

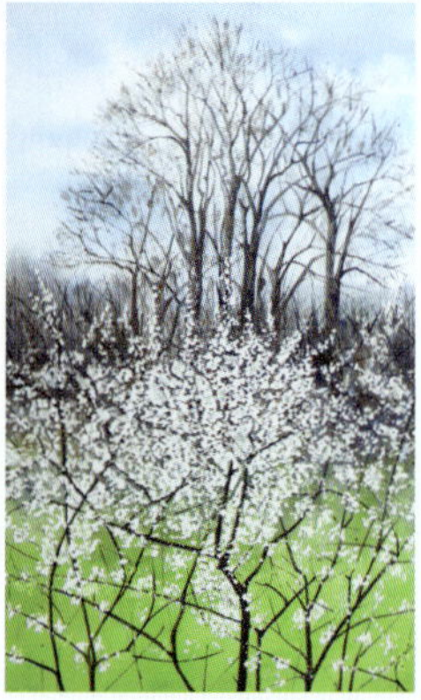

There is an excitement in the hedgerows in late winter, as spring approaches. The trees are losing their bareness, almost imperceptibly, as there are not yet any visible leaves, just swelling buds. For many species, it is the flower buds that pop open first, taking full advantage of the openness possible; unhindered by leaves and shade, the flowers can get on with the serious business of making new trees, early in the year.

Blackthorn (*Prunus spinosa*) is one of the earliest trees to flower, usually being covered with a mass of tiny, white flowers in early spring. Its early start is very useful for those who enjoy its fruit, sloes, which are best used to make sloe gin after the first frosts.

Blackthorn branches and trunks are a very dark brown, which in the low light of winter and early spring often appears to be a deep black. The colour stands out in hedgerows and is very likely to be the inspiration for this tree's common name. Blackthorn trees can be very sombre, the starkness of their dark branches eliciting memories of cold, unpleasant, winter weather and a sense of foreboding. In certain lights, they are almost threatening, especially for those who have picked sloes and are aware of the thorns! The flowers, on the other hand, are white, tiny and very delicate and, en masse, have a soft, ethereal quality, evoking the very different emotions of hope and cheery optimism for the brighter, sunnier days ahead.

Developing the Idea

With this painting, I wanted to emphasize the contrast of emotions that I experience when I see a blackthorn in flower. This painting is not of the blackthorn, it is about it. To be more precise, it is about the emotions it elicits.

Having said that, there is of course a visual element to this painting. The subject matter naturally includes strong tonal contrasts and, while these can obviously be used to accentuate the contrast in moods within the image, they are also interesting visually for the crisp patterns and shapes that they make, leading the viewer's eye around the painting.

The sharpness of these contrasts can be emphasized by the white flowers, of which there are so many that they are viewed en masse. The hedge itself should be indistinct, serving as a tonal backdrop to the blackthorn and providing a link between the soft and the stark areas within the image.

While the focus is on the black (or, rather, dark brown) and white, colour can also be introduced to put emphasis on the difference between winter and spring. The cold, dismal character of the colours in the hedge, placed in the background, can be contrasted with that of the fresher, brighter colours of spring in the foreground.

Information Gathering

This painting is based on a set of photographs that I have of blackthorn. This painting is about capturing certain qualities of the trees and flowers, rather than presenting a precise representation of them. While the painting will be reasonably figurative, it does not need accurate detail to achieve this effect. In fact, too much detail might be detrimental to the objective of the painting. The photographs provide enough information for the trees to be identifiable as blackthorn, without allowing access to too much information. As such, the photographs are being used as a method of simplifying the subject.

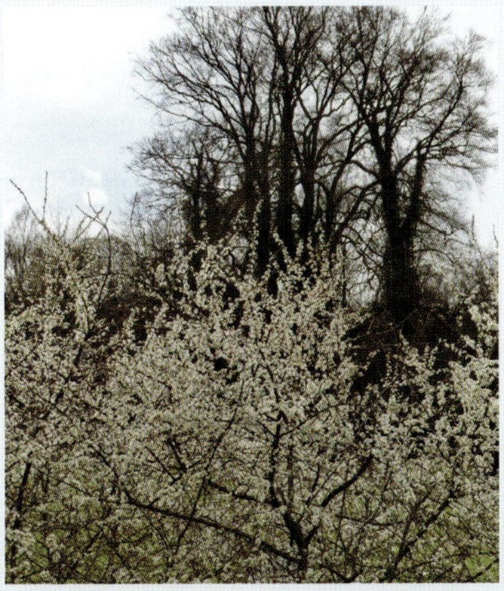

This photograph shows how the trees provide a dark background against which to place the very light blackthorn flowers within the painting of this scene.

The photograph shown here was particularly useful, as it demonstrated that the taller trees at the back of the hedge provided an extremely useful dark background against which to place the flowers. Their winter starkness emphasized the cold and wintry mood, while the flash of bright green provided in the foreground by the new growth in the grass introduced the cheerfulness of spring.

Designing the Painting

Layout

The image is about contrast, so the elements within it should be placed to emphasize that characteristic.

For the course of the viewer's eye to flow around the painting, the placement of the dark tones against the light tones should be considered carefully: *see* the section 'Tone' below.

However, for the painting to be viewed as a coherent whole, there also need to be links between the various elements. There are visual links between the structure of the mature trees in the background and the dark branches of the blackthorn, so care should be taken to place the branches to lead the viewer's eye from one section of the painting to another.

The shapes of the trees in the background can be based on the trees in the photograph, but the shapes of the trunks and branches of the blackthorn need to be 'designed'.

Spend some time making preliminary sketches in your sketchbook to ensure that you draw shapes that you like and that lead the viewer's eye towards the focal point. Include a few branches that stop the viewer's eye from falling off the bottom or out of the sides of the image.

The focal point of this painting is relatively subtle, since the idea is to encourage the viewer's eye to wander throughout the image. There is a subtle focal point, where the white tips of the blackthorn sit against the solid darks of the mature tree trunks. This point falls almost exactly in the centre of the painting, breaking conventional composition rules. Remember that these 'rules' are just guidelines; if the image is sitting comfortably without adhering to them, that is fine.

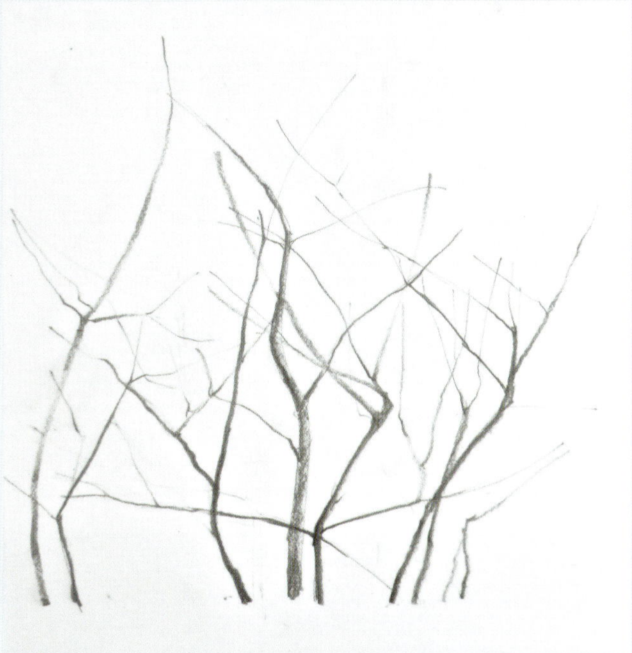

A page from my sketchbook, showing the mapped-out position of the main blackthorn branches.

Tone

Placing the flowers against dark tree trunks in the hedge behind is an obvious decision. There are practical reasons for doing this too. Painting white flowers on white paper is not easy; it is best to place them against a darker background. When applying paint to the areas of lighter tone, this difficulty should be kept in mind, to allow you to make the area behind the flowers dark enough for the flowers to show up.

A quieter area of less tonal contrast can be used as an area of transition between the bright foreground and the darker background, with branches judiciously placed across this area to lead the viewer's eye through the image. Lost edges in this area will enhance the feeling of airiness of the mass of flowers.

Keeping the tones at the bottom of the image no stronger than a midtone will make it possible to use the dark tones of the branches of the blackthorn in positions to lead the viewer's eye into the painting.

The mature trees in the hedge behind the blackthorn should be kept dark, emphasizing their leafless starkness against a pale, spring sky.

Colour

Black features strongly in this image, and it is tempting to use a black paint. However, black paints tend to dry flat and dead, which would not be suitable for a painting that looks towards the new life that spring brings. Using mixes of ultramarine blue and burnt sienna will give a very cold, dark mix but allow for a little variation, and therefore 'life', within it.

The softer greys can be made by using mixes of cerulean blue, cobalt blue and burnt sienna. Using these colours to make a slightly warmer, mink grey for the hedge will emphasize the relative blackness of the blackthorn.

The aptly named May green, by Schmincke, is the perfect base for the bright, spring grass; when mixed with tiny touches of the other colours, it also makes some interesting soft green-greys for the shadowy areas of the mass of flowers.

The colour of the depicted spring sky needs to be cool enough to imply spring but be warmer than that of a cold, winter sky. Adding a touch of cerulean blue to cobalt blue makes a suitable colour.

Techniques to practise

1 Applying masking fluid with different applicators, to develop different reserved shapes. *See* Chapter 2, Materials and Techniques, for more advice.
2 Drawing tree trunks and branches with paint. Experiment with different brushes or pens, to discover which suits your hand best. For the execution of this image, the paint will need to be quite thick to achieve the dark tones, which may alter the length of stroke that you can make. Also practise lifting the brush (or pen) towards the end of the stroke, to ensure there is a reduction of tone along the length of the depicted branch.

Painting the Image

Materials and equipment

- Watercolour paper:
  - Bockingford NOT 300gsm/140lb, stretched and taped to a board
- Watercolour brushes:
  - Da Vinci Series 35, size 4
  - St Petersburg round, size 10
  - Swordliners, large, medium and small
  - Rigger
- Artist-quality watercolours:
  - Burnt sienna (Daler Rowney)
  - Cerulean blue
  - Cobalt blue
  - May green (Schmincke)
  - Ultramarine blue
- Tracing paper
- Black pen
- 4B pencil
- Eraser
- Masking fluid
- Small masking-fluid brush
- Colour shaper
- Palette
- Kitchen roll
- Additional watercolour paper, for printing

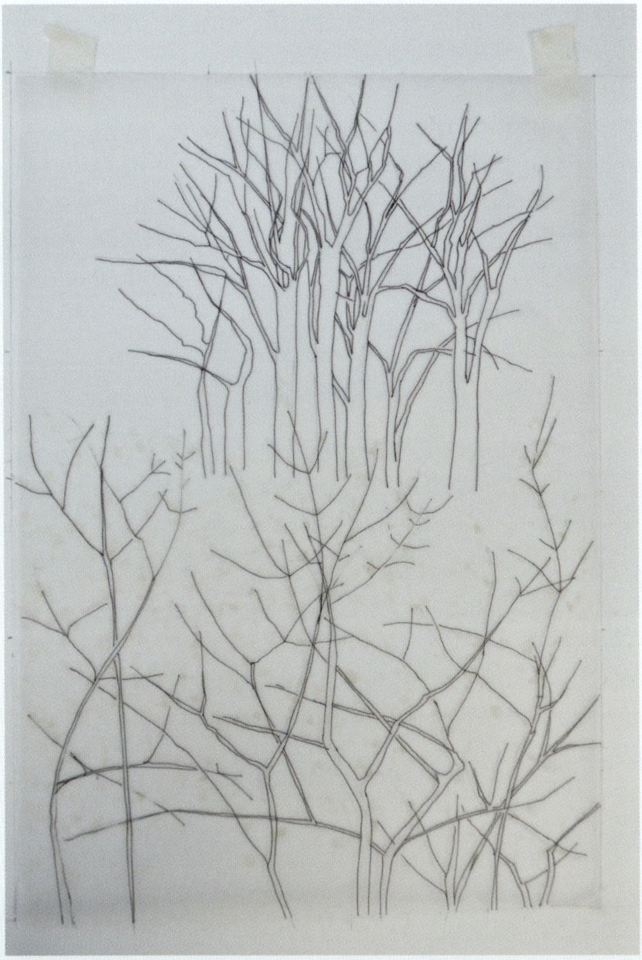

Step 1: Draw the outlines of the trunks and main branches on to the watercolour paper, then produce a tracing of this drawing.

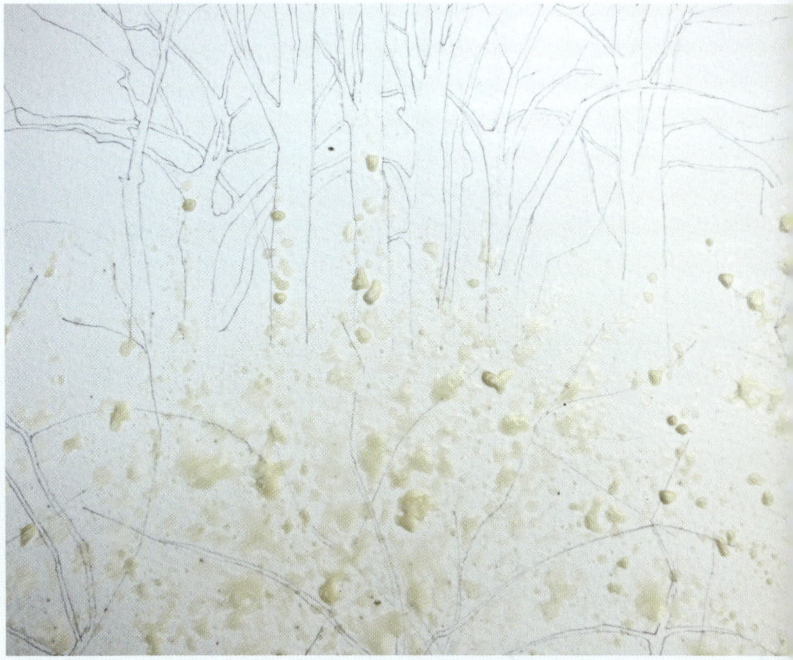

Step 2: Use masking fluid to reserve the white of the flowers.

Step 1: On the stretched watercolour paper, draw in the outlines of the main trunks and branches with pencil. Keep the drawing to a minimum; you need to establish only the placement of the trees. The finer details will be added directly with paint; working this way will enable you to paint more loosely and hence keep the painting fresher.

When you have completed the drawing, make a tracing of the outlines as an insurance policy against disasters. Working loosely involves an exciting element of risk, and creating a tracing removes some of the tension, as you have the opportunity to easily start the painting again.

Step 2: The blackthorn flowers are tiny but arranged in clumps along the branches. Since it will not be possible to paint around them, the white of the paper needs to be reserved by using masking fluid.

Imagine the masking fluid to be white paint, and 'paint' the flowers in by applying the masking fluid with a colour shaper or small masking-fluid brush.

Place the dots of masking fluid carefully in the area of the focal point, where the flowers are more spread out and distinct at the tips of the branches and will show clearly against the dark tree trunks behind. In the area where the flowers are more dense, the masking fluid can be applied more loosely. Begin by placing some masking fluid along the branches to establish the shapes of the clumps of flowers and their growth habit. When you feel that there are almost enough flowers, flick more masking fluid into this area; this will help to prevent the image becoming too tight.

Allow the masking fluid to dry completely before continuing with your painting.

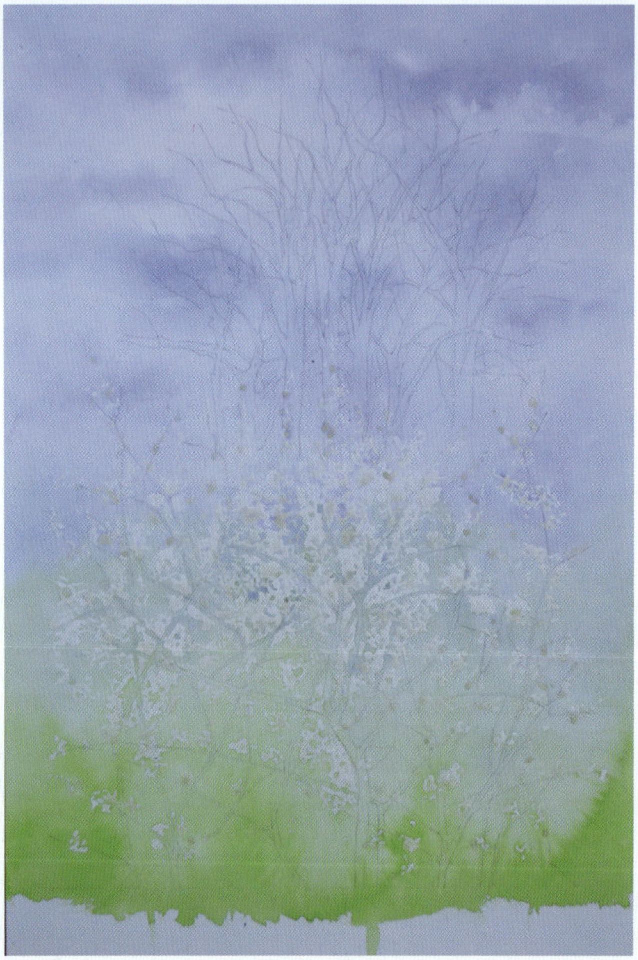

Step 3: Working wet in wet, paint in the sky, lifting out soft clouds as you work, and then paint in the green of the background.

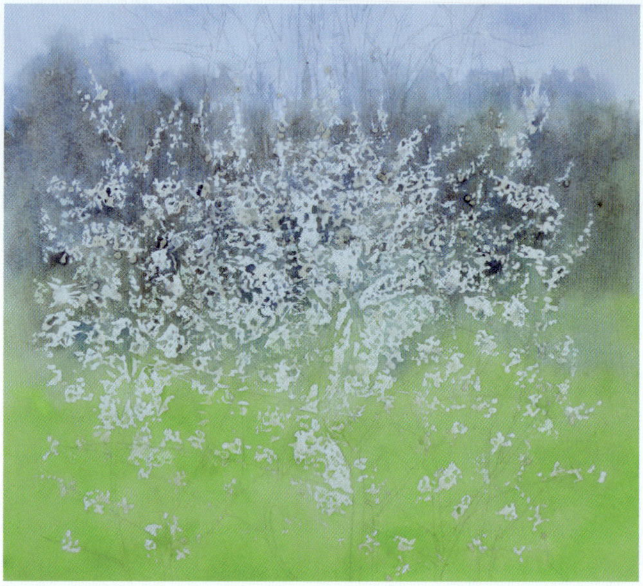

Step 4a: Paint in the underwash for the background hedge, keeping the top edge soft.

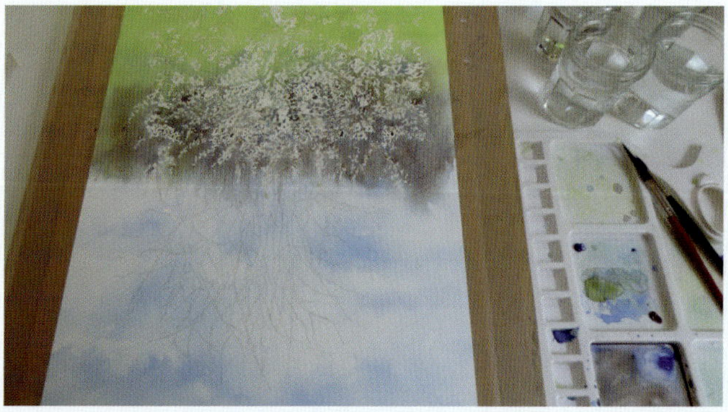

Step 4b: Turn the painting upside down to work wet in wet, to ensure that the paint flows in the right direction to achieve the desired effect.

Step 3: Using a midtone mix of cobalt blue and cerulean blue, paint in the sky. Work wet in wet and at a slight angle, allowing the paint to run down the paper. While the paint is still wet, use a barely damp brush to lift off some of the colour, to form some subtle clouds. (Be careful, if the brush is too wet, it will cause cauliflowers to form.) Alternatively, you could lift off some of the damp paint with kitchen roll; if the kitchen roll is very slightly damp, it will give nice, soft edges to the depicted clouds.

Continue applying paint under the area of the hedge in the background, increasing the amount of cobalt blue in the mix. From the bottom of the hedge, begin to add May green to the cobalt blue. This turquoise mix will form the base for the greyer areas within the mass of flowers. Grade the colour towards green in the lower third of the painting, where the grass is visible behind the blackthorn.

When the paint is complete dry, add a little more masking fluid over this first layer of paint, to reserve some flower shapes within these applied colours. This will help to give an impression of depth within the mass of flowers. Allow the masking fluid to dry completely before continuing.

Step 4: Make up a range of mixes of soft greys by using cobalt blue and burnt sienna. Also prepare a puddle of May green. The mixes should be made up to a midtone slightly darker than that required as, when applied to wet paper, the tones will become lighter.

Turn the painting upside down, so that the water will flow in the correct direction to create a soft edge along the top of the hedge. Wet the paper thoroughly to beyond where the top of the hedge will be.

Beginning at the bottom of the image (that is, where the grass is located, which is now at the top of the paper), apply a wash of May green, allowing it to flow down the paper towards the depicted hedge. As the paint approaches the

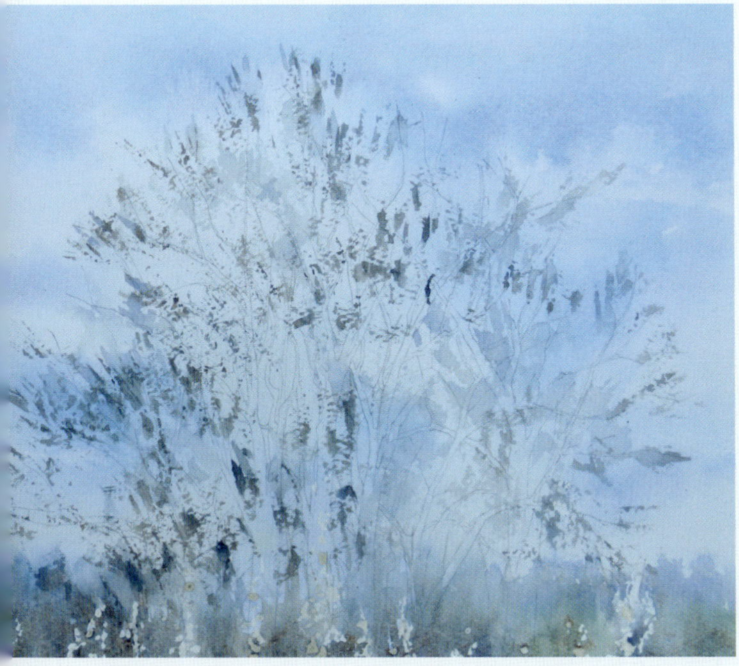

Step 5: Make marks to depict areas of fine twigs at the ends of the branches.

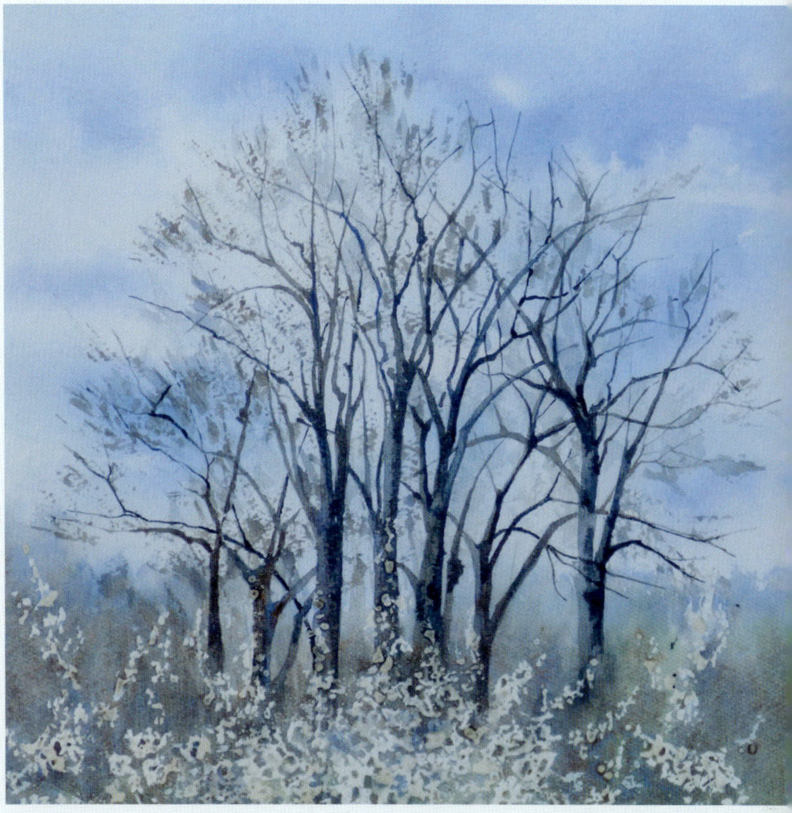

Step 6: Paint in the trunks and branches of the tall trees.

bottom of the hedge, start adding some greys to the mix, choosing different colours from the prepared mixes. Allow the green and greys to blend wet in wet. As you progress into the area of the hedge, use just the grey colours, varying them across the page and allowing them to blend. Stop applying paint just short of where you want the top of the hedge to be, and allow the water to carry the paint further over the page, giving a soft edge to the top of the hedge. (For further information on creating a soft edge, *see* the section 'Watercolour: Tips and techniques' in Chapter 2, Materials and Techniques.)

Step 5: Turn the painting back to its original orientation (with the depicted grass again located at the bottom of the paper).

At the ends of the branches, there are areas of fine twigs that, because of their number, can appear almost as patches of colour, rather than being visible as individual twigs.

Using the same mix of soft greys as used for step 4, load a round brush with paint. Laying the tip of the brush very gently on to the paper, roll it to create a small patch of colour. While the paint is still wet, repeat this manoeuvre with a brush loaded with clean water. The marks produced should have a mixture of soft and hard edges, giving texture to the patches of depicted twigs.

Step 6: Darken the tones of the grey mix slightly by adding more cobalt blue and burnt sienna. Paint in the main trunks and branches of the tall trees, varying both tone and colour as you work. Blend the bottom of the trunks into the hedge, so that the trunks merge into it.

Although these tall trees appear almost black and silhouetted in the photograph, I have kept them lighter. While they need to be quite dark, the branches of the blackthorn in the foreground need to be darker; making the tall trees too dark will make achieving the necessary tone for the blackthorn branches impossible. Keeping the tall trees a little lighter will also give more depth to the image, putting the tall trees at a slight distance behind the blackthorn.

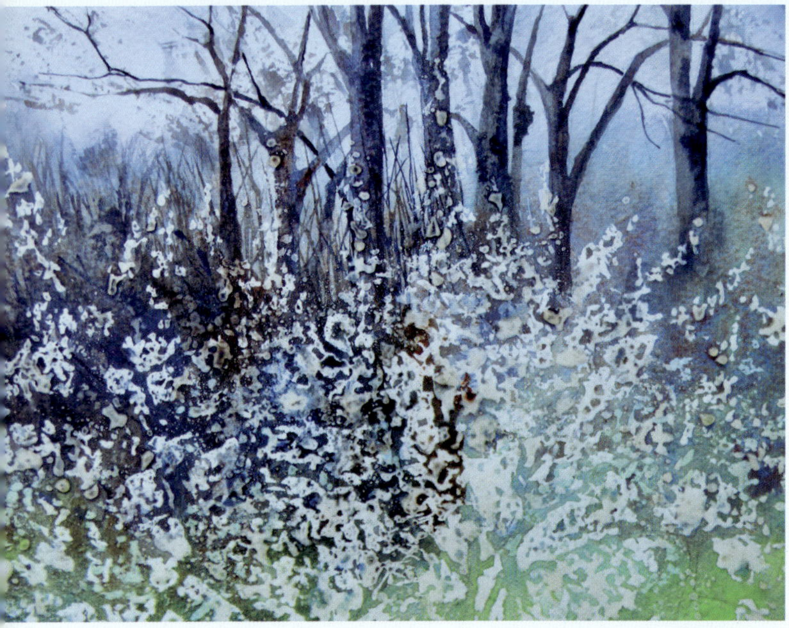

Step 7: Paint in the hedge behind the blackthorn, by working slowly across the page.

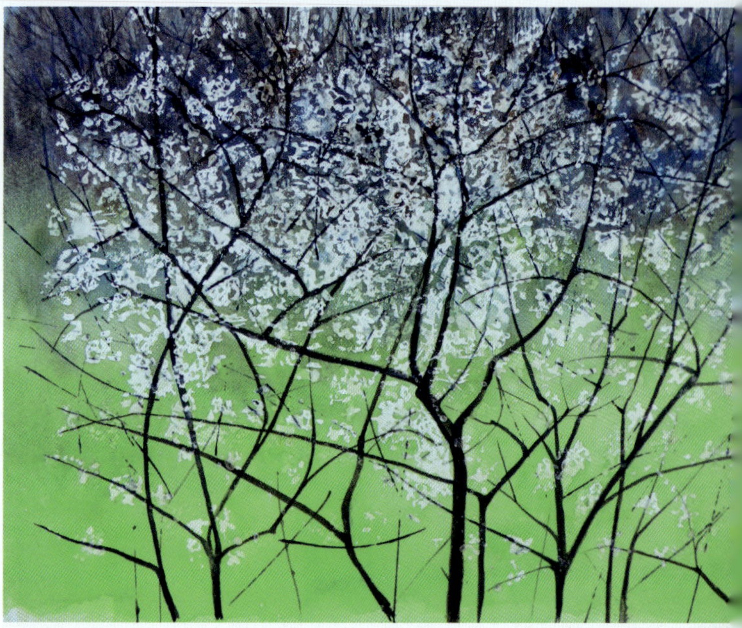

Step 8: Carefully paint in the trunks and branches of the blackthorn in rich, dark tones.

Step 7: Make a mix of cobalt blue, ultramarine blue and burnt sienna in the palette, ensuring that you keep some neat colour at the edges of the mix (*see* the section 'Watercolour: Tips and techniques' in Chapter 2, Materials and Techniques, for instructions on how to mix colours). Also have more May green prepared.

Paint in the hedge behind the blackthorn, working carefully across the page a little at a time. Work on dry paper, but make sure that you keep all of the edges of the paint wet as you work.

Apply paint to the middle band of the depicted hedge, using a round brush.

At the lower edge of this band of paint, blend it into the green. (It may be easier to continue the green to the bottom of the image to avoid an unwanted hard line.)

At the upper edge, while the paint is still wet, use a fine brush, such as a swordliner or rigger, to pull the paint upwards, to create fine lines for the representation of branches and introduction of texture at the top of and within the hedge.

As you work, pick up different colours from the mix, as areas of neat colour will enhance the interest of the painting.

Step 8: Make up a rich, dark mix of ultramarine blue and burnt sienna; the paint should be quite thick.

Using a round brush, paint in the trunks and branches of the blackthorn. Paint these in carefully, as they give the structure and shape of the blackthorn.

Make sure that the paint is dark enough to still be visible once you paint over the region of the hedge; it should be darker and blacker than that of the background.

Once you have painted in the drawn branches, cut a strip of watercolour paper, and dip the long edge into the paint in your palette. Use this to randomly print more branches – do not worry if they do not all join up! This printing technique will stop the image becoming too rigid and will add depth and busyness to the mass of flowers.

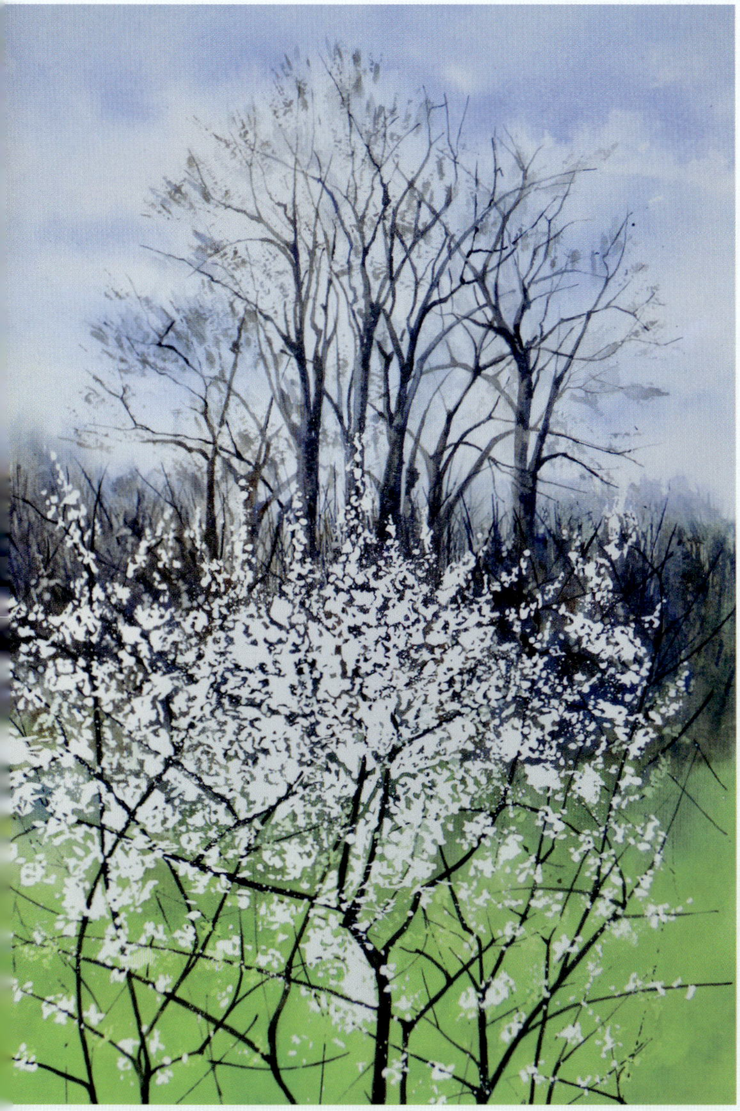

Step 9: Remove the masking fluid.

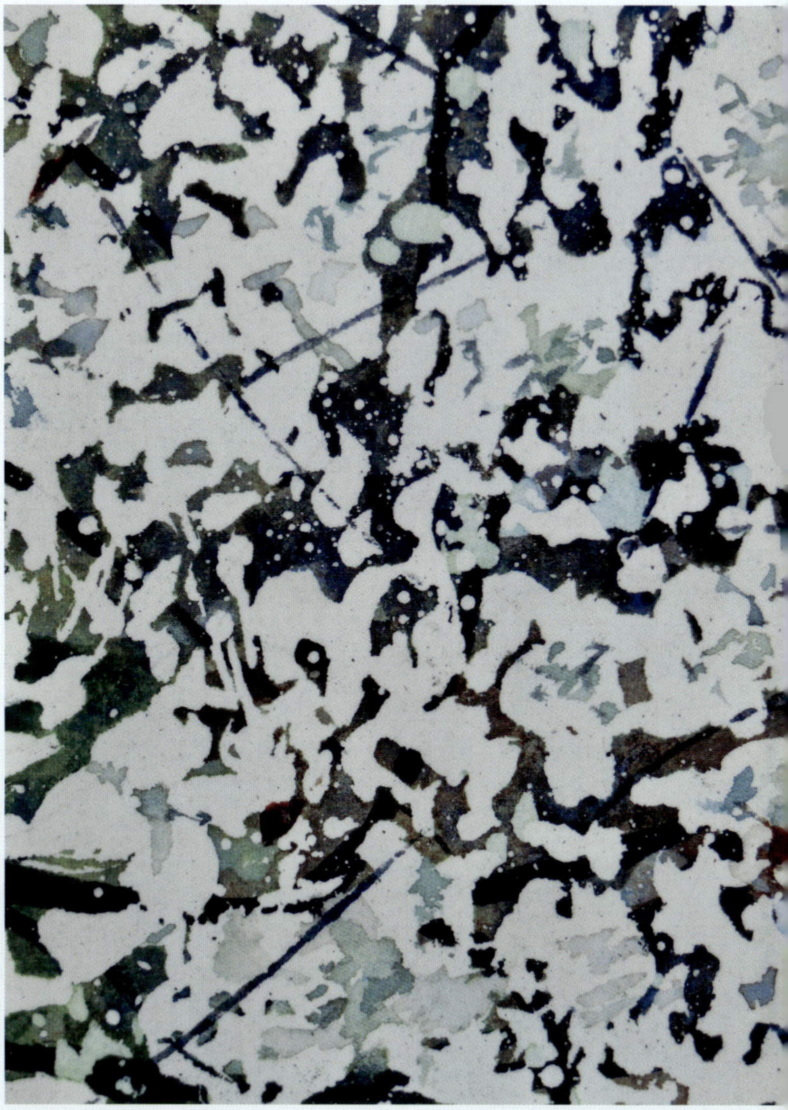

Step 10: Add depth to the blossoms.

Step 9: When the paint is completely dry, remove the masking fluid to reveal the white of the flowers.

Tip: At this stage, the white of the mass of flowers should be quite stark and bright against the background. Take a moment to assess your painting.

If the white does not stand out enough, it is because the background is not dark enough. It is the relative difference between the tonal values that causes the white to appear to be bright. Since you cannot make the paper whiter (white paint or ink is not a bright as the paper), you have to make the background darker. To achieve this at this stage means reapplying the masking fluid! Frustrating though this may be, it is worth the effort!

Step 10: Having previously masked the patches of blossom, some of these patches may now have a slightly odd appearance. Using a pointed brush and a mix of pale colours (cobalt blue and May green or some pale greys), randomly add some marks to break up the larger patches of white. Do not be overly concerned with painting neat flower shapes; this is a mass of blossom where individual flowers are not really visible.

Also print a few more twigs across the areas of blossom by using a short piece of watercolour paper dipped into the mixed paint.

Step 11: Finally, stand back to assess the painting. If necessary, add a few more marks or adjust the tone before declaring the painting finished.

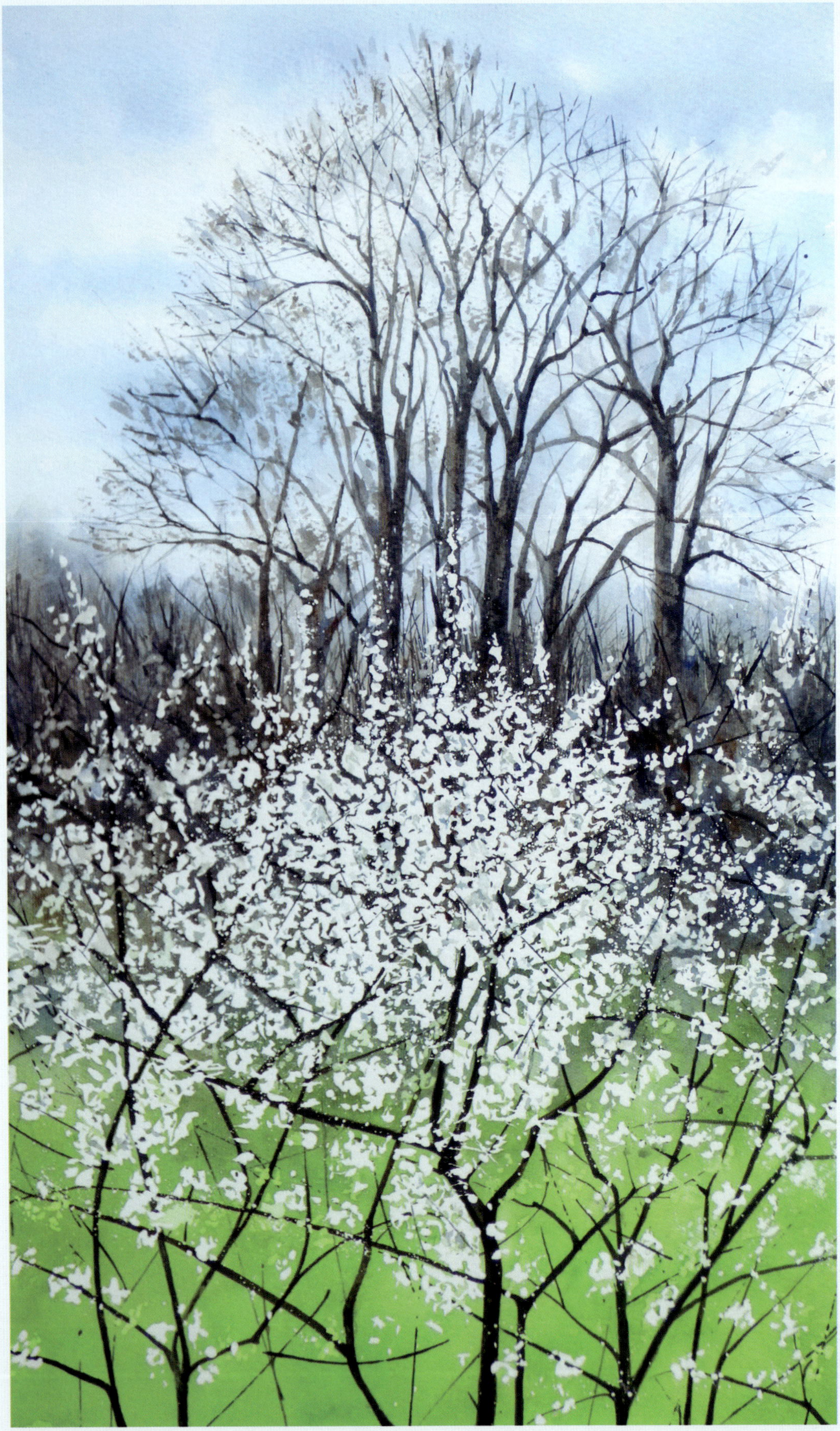

The finished painting:
Spring Blackthorn,
watercolour, 29cm × 46cm
(11½in × 18in),
Siân Dudley.

PROJECT

Spring in the Lane

Rob Dudley

The Inspiration

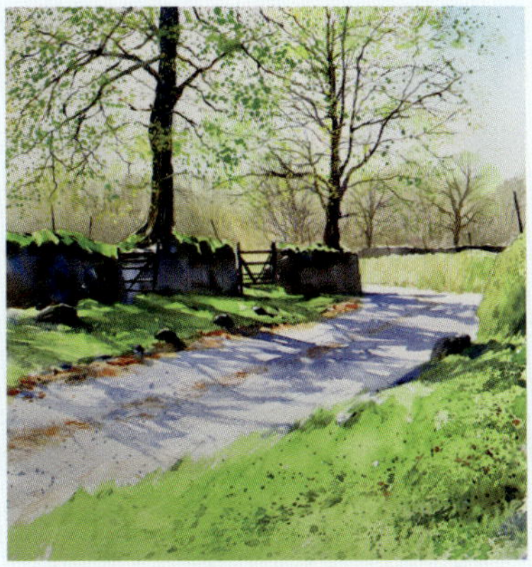

Spring is a wonderful time for the artist. With the days gradually lengthening and temperatures rising, it is a welcome relief from the days spent in the studio to get outside with paints and sketch pads and lay some colours down.

Gradually, winter trees begin to burst into fresh, green life. The greens at this time can be very tricky to capture, especially some of those relating to the growth of new leaves; the greens can look too bright or zingy, particularly if the strengthening spring sunlight is shining through the leaves. Spring leaves need careful observation, and their depiction needs careful execution, to create a believable interpretation.

I particularly like springtime. The light seems to freshen, the trees begin to come into life and everything seems to be full of possibilities. It is a very exciting time to venture out from the studio with paints, sketch pads and a camera, to see what catches the eye. On this occasion, I was walking near to my studio in a lane that I know well, and I came upon this light, airy scene. The tall beech trees were beginning to put on leaves and were casting wonderful shadows across the road. Their dark trunks acted as a contrast to the bright leaves and the sunlit wall tops. The colours were almost too bright, as if spring were announcing itself by shaking off the muted colours of winter.

Developing the Idea

I wanted to paint the scene almost as I had seen it, with very few adjustments. The light and airy quality of the day was something that I was keen to try to capture; for me, it was the very essence of spring. The tonal contrast would give a real kick to the painting; the shadowed wall and dark trunks of the beeches would be useful in this respect, by juxtaposing these elements against the lighter passages within the painting.

Information Gathering

I was able to make some quick pencil sketches and a few colour notes and to take some useful photographs to bring with me to the studio. When taking the photographs, I not only took several of the overall scene but also zoomed in on specific details; the light hitting the gates, the sunlit wall tops, and the shadows cast from the trees. These would be useful in providing detailed references for application when creating the painting.

Designing the Painting

Layout

On returning to the studio, I reviewed the drawings, notes and photographs made in the lane and proceeded to rough out some loose thumbnail sketches, exploring at first which format would best suit the painting that I was planning.

After a couple of quick, exploratory format sketches, I decided on an almost square format. A more square format offers a compact, focused and more contained composition especially when compared to that of a portrait or landscape format.

The strong diagonal of the lane makes a useful contribution towards the strength of the overall design of the painting, in that it leads the viewer down the lane and into the painting. It also leads the viewer to a strongly contrasting tonal passage within the painting: the shadowed wall and brightly lit lane. This contrast adds a real kick within the watercolour painting and, although not a key focal point, it still provides a point of interest.

I made the decision quite early when planning the design of my watercolour not to paint both of the main trees in their entirety. To include their full height would have made the design too tall and would have necessitated a different format. The extra height needed to include the full trees would take away some of the emphasis from the lane itself, which is not what I wanted and would have resulted in a different painting altogether.

The painting would have two key focal points: the left-hand foreground tree and the dark gate almost in the centre of the painting.

Note how the slightly broader trunk of the tree on the left, compared to that of the tree on the right, brings it just slightly forward within the design, adding to the sense of recession along the lane.

Tone

After making a few tonal sketches to assess possibilities, I decided to use a full range of tones, focusing in particular on creating dramatic impact by the careful positioning of bright lights and strong darks. The strongest tones would be reserved for the trunks and walls. Paler tones would be employed in the background, to create a sense of recession and distance within the design.

Colour

If it were possible to describe the colours used for this painting with only a single word, it would be 'bright'! I wanted the colours to have real impact. Even the darks seem to have a brightness about them.

The occasion when I encountered this scene was on one of the first warm days of early spring, and the rising temperatures had encouraged leaves, grasses and hedgerows to put on a really bright display. They seemed to be crisp, happy colours. So too would be the colours in my palette.

Texture

The texture within the painting, particularly for the leaves and foreground verge, would be achieved through both laying of washes and spattering. The texture of the trees' fresh leaves, being of particular interest, would benefit from a spattered, lively approach in execution. The rest of the painting would be made up from simple, unfussy washes, either wet in wet or wet on dry.

The texture of the chosen paper was selected in order to offer a relatively smooth finish for the washes. Too rough of a paper would have resulted in too many visually disruptive textural elements being created within the painting.

Painting the Image

Materials and equipment

- Watercolour paper:
  - Bockingford NOT 300gsm/140lb, stretched and taped to a board
- Watercolour brushes:
  - No. 10 pointed sable
  - No. 6 pointed sable
  - No. 2 pointed sable
  - Fine rigger
  - Medium stencil brush
- Artist-quality watercolours:
  - Burnt sienna
  - Cobalt violet
  - Lemon yellow
  - May green
  - Neutral tint
  - Quinacridone gold
  - Raw sienna
  - Ultramarine blue
  - Winsor blue (green shade)
  - White acrylic gouache
- 2B pencil
- Dip pen
- Kitchen roll
- Palette
- Scrap watercolour paper

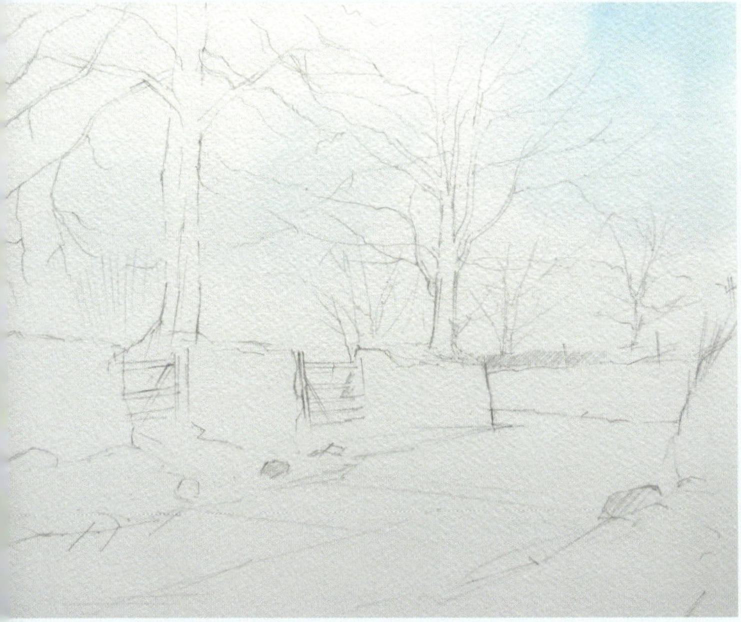

Step 1: Draw in the image outlines with pencil, and paint in the sky.

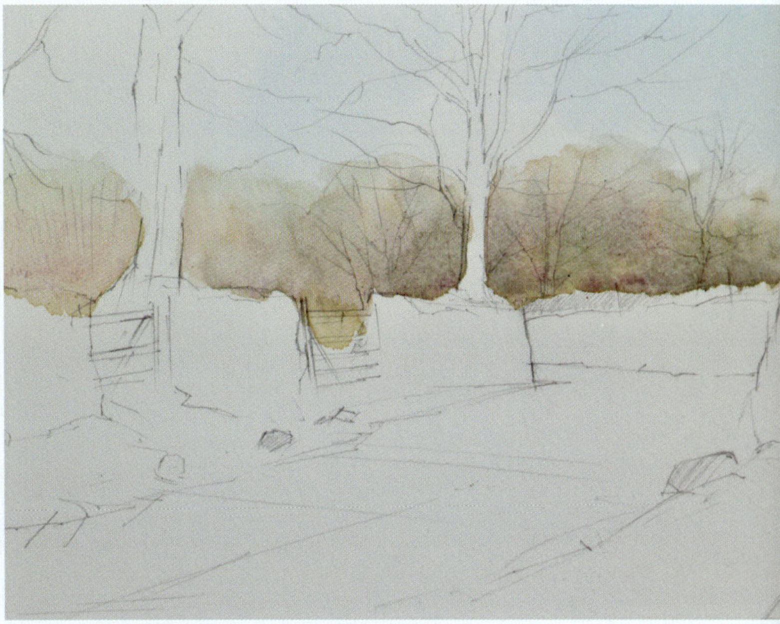

Step 2: Add the first washes for the distant trees.

Step 1: After carefully drawing in the image on the stretched piece of paper by using a 2B pencil, mix a puddle of Winsor blue, being careful not to make the mix too strong. Test its strength on a piece of paper, and allow it to dry before committing it to the painting. Make certain that you test it on the same type of paper that you are going to paint the picture on. Dampen the sky area with clean water and, with the board at a slight angle, drop in this blue paint with the No. 10 sable, keeping the wash stronger to the right. With the board at the same angle, allow the paint to dry.

Step 2: Mix puddles of quinacridone gold with ultramarine blue and cobalt violet. Using a No. 6 sable, lay down washes for the distant trees. Allow the washes to dry slightly but, while the paint is still damp, touch in some cobalt violet.

Keep the tops of the depicted trees uneven; avoid creating a straight line. When the paint is dry, using a fine rigger, indicate some of the main trunks and branches with a stronger mix of the quinacridone gold and ultramarine blue. Allow the paint to dry.

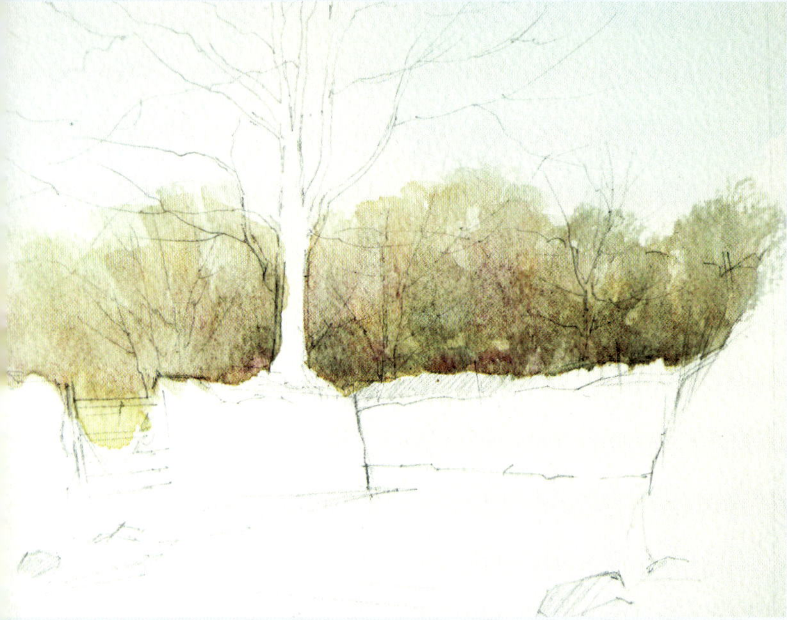

Step 3: Strengthen the distant trees.

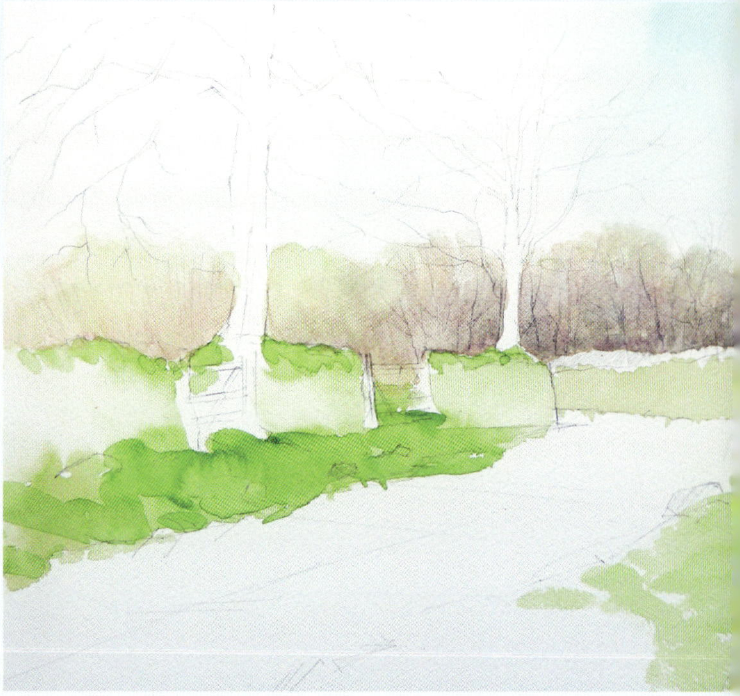

Step 4: Add the initial verge, wall top and hedge washes.

Step 3: Prepare a mix of raw sienna and ultramarine blue and, with the No. 10 sable, begin to develop the distant trees by pulling this paint mix across the previous washes with some dry brushstrokes. Check the effect of your strokes on some scrap watercolour paper before using them on the painting. Kitchen roll often proves useful for taking off any excessive paint, or water, from the brush before proceeding with making a dry brushstroke.

Step 4: Having made certain that the last step is completely dry, add a wash of May green with a little raw sienna to the wall top and neighbouring verge and a paler version to the wall itself and opposite verge by using the No. 10 sable. Allow the paint to dry.

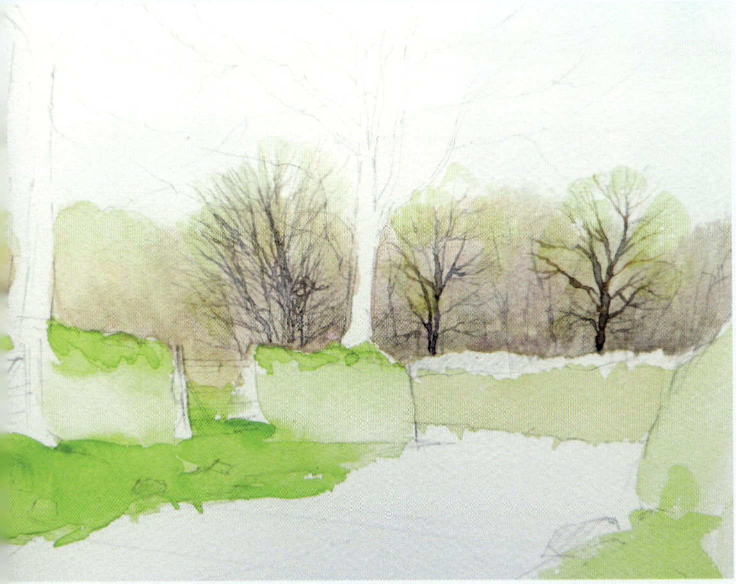

Step 5: Develop the middle-ground trees.

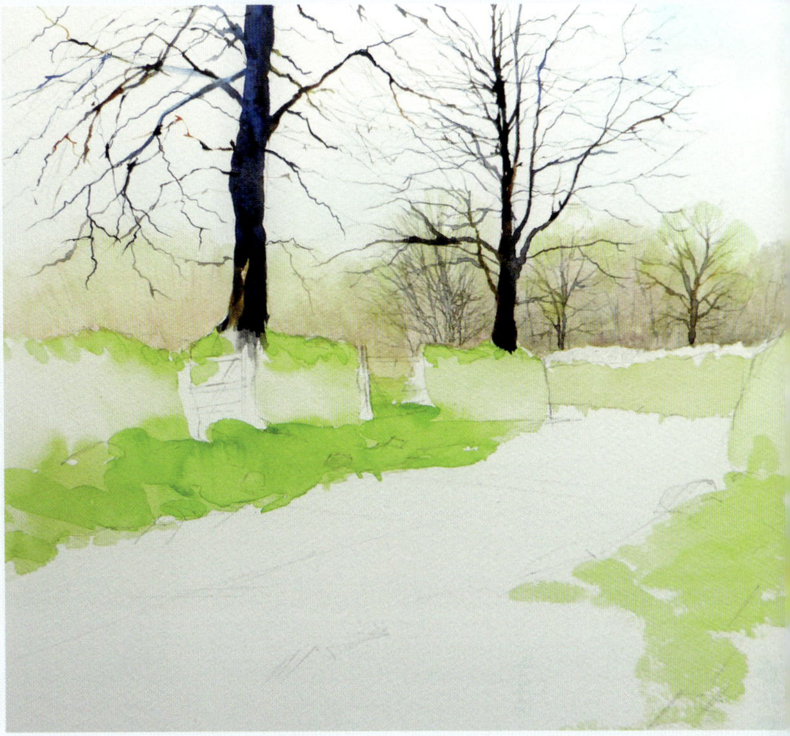

Step 6: Paint in the main beech trees.

Step 5: With a mix of ultramarine blue and burnt sienna, use both the fine rigger and dip pen to draw the trunks and branches of the middle-ground trees. Don't make the mix too dark, as this will seem to bring the trees too far forward within the design and reduce the sense of space and distance. Work from the bottom and pull both pen or brush upwards to make strokes: trees grow from the ground; the strokes should do the same!

Step 6: After checking that the previous step is completely dry, use a stronger version of the mix used in step 5 and, with a No. 6 sable, fine rigger and the dip pen, paint in both of the main trees. Vary the strength and predominant colour of the mix as you go. When the paint is dry, add a dilute wash of May green to the trees' shapes. Allow the paint to dry.

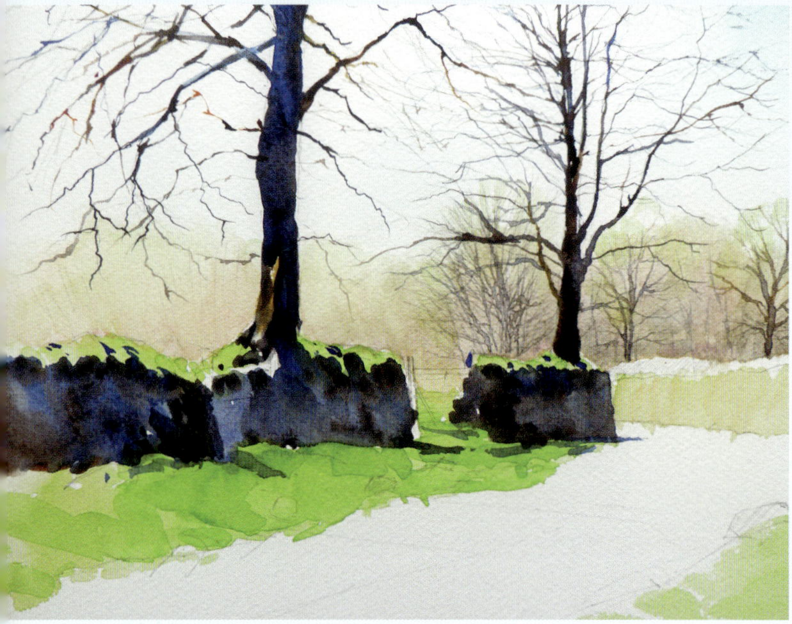

Step 7: Add the strong wall shadows.

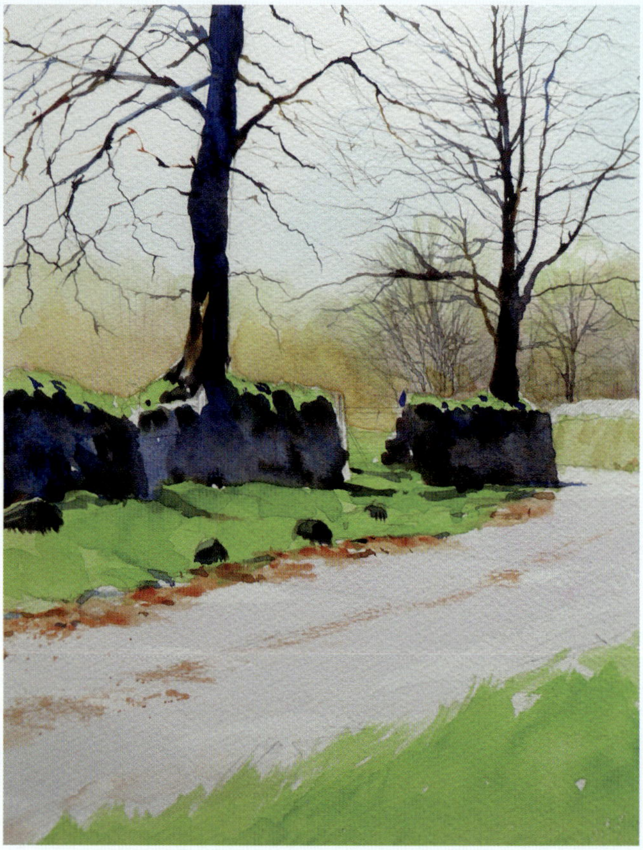

Step 8: Add verge, lane-surface and roadside initial washes, and paint in the verge-side stones.

Step 7: Taking a strong, dark mix of ultramarine blue and burnt sienna, paint in the shadow side of the wall. Don't try to depict each and every stone; the result of trying to do so can often look unconvincing, somewhat akin to rural Lego! Vary the mix as you paint, so long as it stays dark. While the wash is still damp, touch in pure ultramarine blue along the top of the wall, to indicate darker shadows cast from some of the grasses on top of the wall. Working with the larger brush minimizes the risk of overdetailing the wall. Wash in a mix of May green and burnt sienna for the hedge, allowing the colour to get paler as the depicted hedge disappears around the distant bend.

Step 8: With the same shadow mix as used for the previous step, paint in some of the verge-side stones.

Add further washes of May green, to build up the foreground verge.

Take a pale mix of ultramarine blue and burnt sienna, and loosely indicate the surface of the lane, being careful to keep the bend in the lane paint-free.

Keeping the bend free from any paint, and therefore of the palest of tones, will result in a greater tonal contrast between the unpainted paper of the lane and the dark tones of the wall. This contrast will bring a brightness and a kick to the painting.

When the paint is dry, make a dryish mix of burnt sienna and quinacridone gold, and touch it into the depicted roadside. Dry brush the centre of the lane to indicate the leaf litter and road debris that often seem to gather at these points.

Step 9: Add some burnt sienna, ultramarine blue and raw sienna to white acrylic gouache. This will create an opaque paint that will allow the painting of a lighter colour over a dark one, in this case, for the depiction of lighter branches over the darker trunks.

With a fine brush, indicate some of the branches growing out from and in front of the trunks. The inclusion of these branches will help to create the trees' three-dimensionality. Without these branches, the trees might look very flat and one-dimensional. Allow the paint to dry.

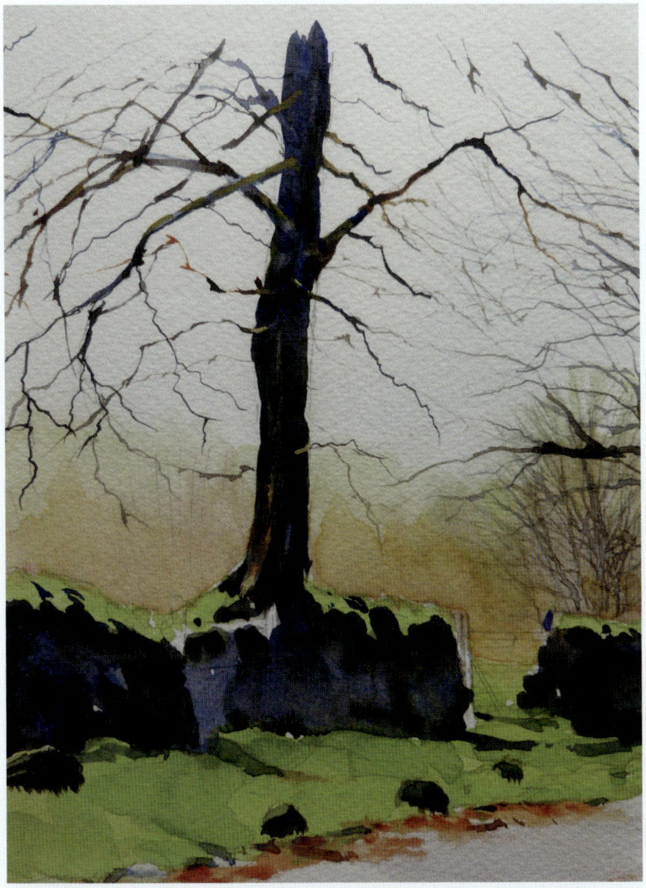

Step 9: Add detail to branches of the main trees with a gouache mix.

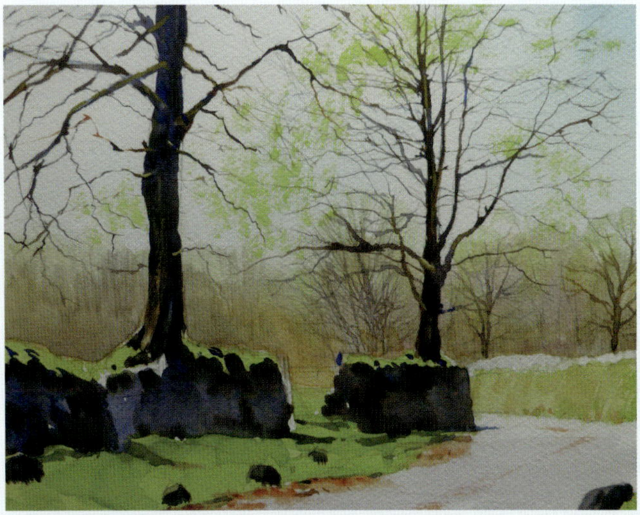

Step 10: Add background foliage to the main trees.

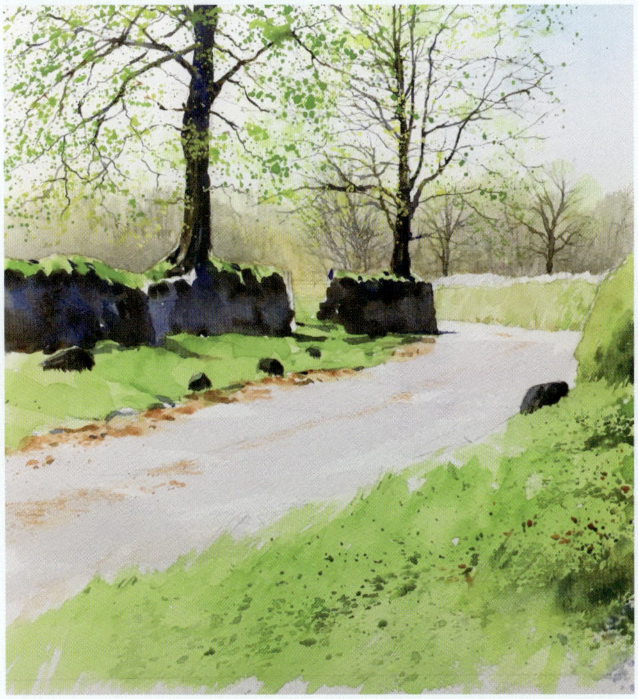

Step 11: Add spattering to depict the leaves of the main trees.

Step 10: After checking that the previous step is completely dry, use the stencil brush to stipple a mix of lemon yellow and May green to parts of the right-hand tree.

Step 11: This step requires the application of three different stages, or layers, of spattered paint. Allow each of the layers to dry before moving on to creating the next.

- The mixes for the subsequent layers are:
- White acrylic gouache with lemon yellow
- White acrylic gouache with May green
- White acrylic gouache with both May green and lemon yellow

The mixes should be thin enough to flick them easily from a brush. Make up the mixes when you need them – not before – as they will dry quite quickly.

With some scrap watercolour paper, torn to size, to protect the rest of the painting from unwanted paint, mask around the main shape of the trees. To prevent the masking paper from moving, weigh it down with a few coins.

With the No. 6 brush, flick the white-and-lemon-yellow mix over the tree area. Be careful not to overdo the flicking; this painting represents early spring, and not too many leaves are out yet. Allow the paint to dry.

Repeat the above application technique with the remaining two mixes.

Note: Sometimes, the masking paper can act like a wick, drawing paint to it and transferring it to the paper below. Therefore, at the end of each stage, carefully remove the protective paper to avoid any unwanted paint creeping on to parts of the painting where it is not wanted.

Make up a separate puddle of May green and burnt sienna paint, and flick this mix on to the foreground verge.

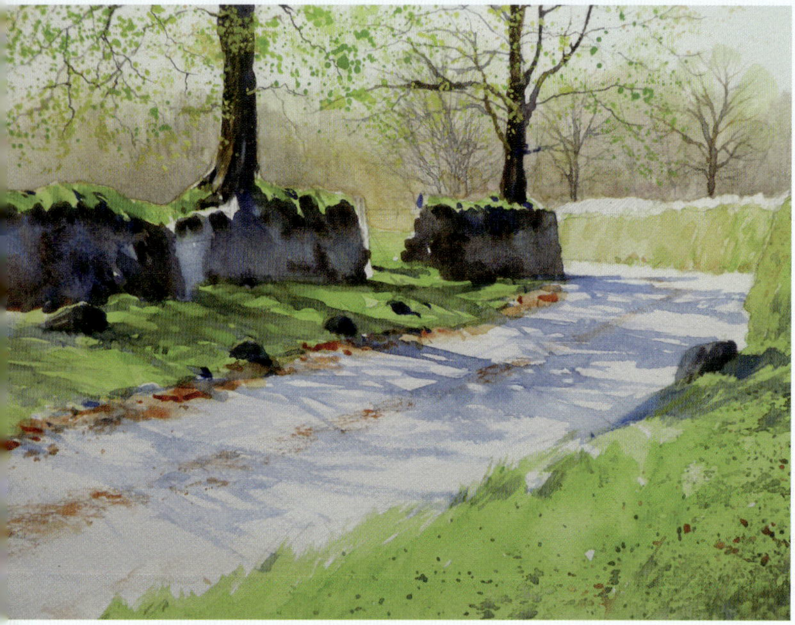

Step 12: Add tree shadows in the lane.

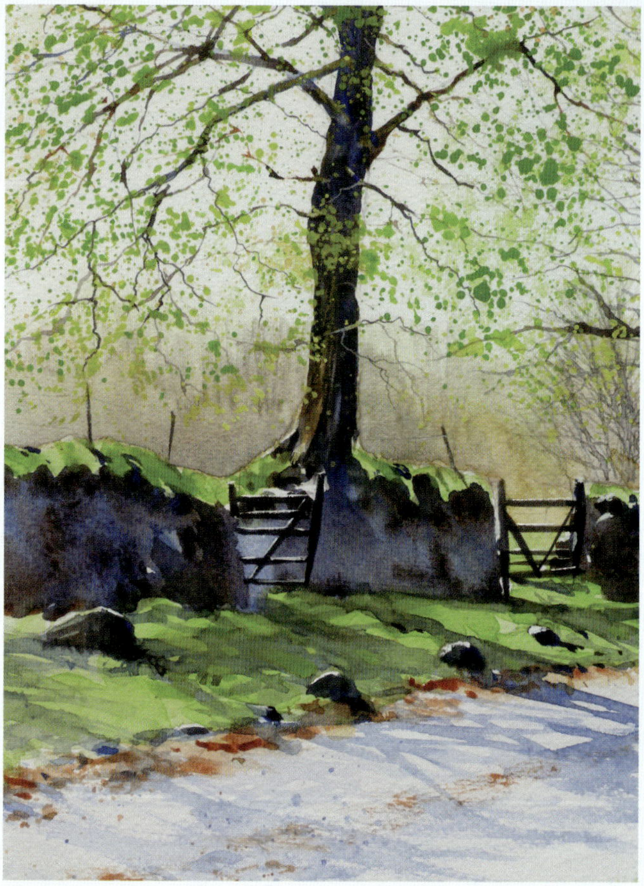

Step 13: Add finishing touches, to include additional structure and details.

Step 12: The shadows falling across the lane are very important to the overall success of the painting. They not only fill an otherwise empty area within the design but also link both sides of the painting together. Take a mix of ultramarine blue and a little neutral tint and, with the No. 6 brush, paint the shadows in. Paint quickly and vigorously. Vary the strength of the mix as you go: weaker and paler for the weaker shadows, and stronger for the more distinct ones. Allow the paint to dry.

Step 13: With a strong, dark mix of burnt sienna and ultramarine blue, paint in the gate and the fence posts, and touch the mix into some of the depicted roadside stones.

With a paler version of the previous mix, drop in the middle-ground hedgerow, being careful to keep the top of the hedge free from paint; this is to give an indication of the spring sunlight hitting the hedge top.

Spatter the lane with the same mix to create a little more texture, and, with some pure burnt sienna, add some touches along the lane edges.

Allow the paint to dry.

With the finest sable and some white acrylic gouache, paint in the strong highlights of some of the stones and, after checking that the paint for the depicted gates is completely dry, do the same for the top-lit rails and bracing bars.

At this stage, be careful not to overwork these finishing details.

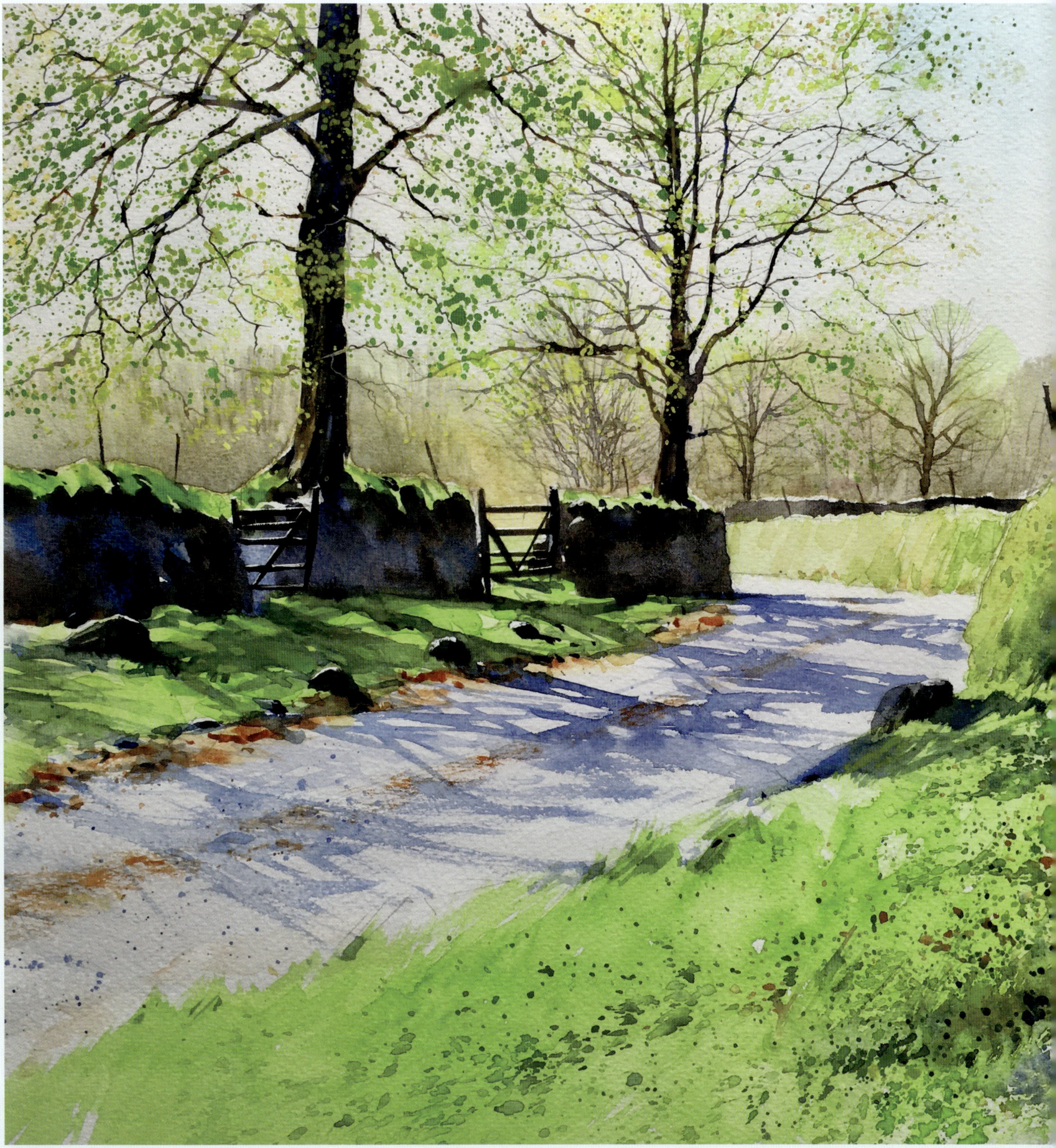

The finished painting: *Spring in the Lane*, watercolour, 32cm × 33cm (12½in × 13in), Rob Dudley.

PROJECT

Bluebell Woods

Siân Dudley

The Inspiration

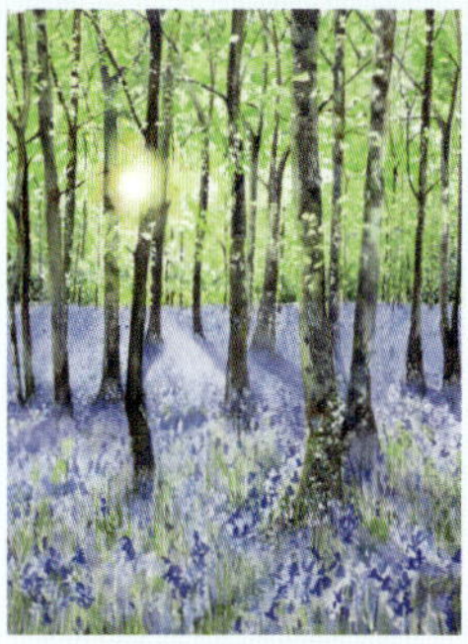

What can be said to explain the inspiration that one feels on entering a bluebell wood? The mass of colour, the joyous dancing of the bluebells, the scent, the fresh green leaves on the trees, the sun peeping through the branches… it is a rare landscape artist who has not been inspired by bluebell woods at some point in their career!

The plaintive cry that we often hear is 'I'd love to paint that, but I have no idea where to start!' This project is an answer to that cry. It is by no means the definitive way to approach the subject, but it should prove to be a sound starting point for many artists who want to capture this archetypal English scene in paint. The inspiration for this piece is, of course, the delight that I feel when walking in a bluebell wood, but it is also about wanting to help others to get started with this subject matter.

Developing the Idea

I wanted to include a method of capturing the mass of blue in the distance. I decided that this could be slightly exaggerated. When we think of the carpet of bluebells, we often forget the scrubby undergrowth of the woodland floor. These tatty-looking bushes and clumps of grasses do not make the most beautiful subject matter and I, at least, choose to blot them from my memory when I reimagine the scene. They will be left out. Unless you are lucky enough to live near one of the rare woods that do not have this undergrowth amongst the bluebells, I suggest that you do the same. Why complicate the painting?

When we stand in a bluebell wood, the individual bluebells near us attract our attention because of their beauty. Tempting though it might be to include a clump of them, it will complicate the design; adjusting the layout to accommodate a group of bluebells and the trees and to keep everything in proportion is a difficult task. All that is needed here is enough information in the foreground to indicate that the large patch of blue paint should be read as bluebells, that is, to provide context.

The trees are a supporting act in this image. They are there to describe a wood, the freshness of the season and a feeling of airiness and, of course, to give context for the bluebells! Having said that, it is a fairly major supporting role and due consideration needs to be given as to how the trees are to be painted.

Information Gathering

Photographs are an extremely useful tool for capturing scenes such as these. Breezy, spring days have pretty clouds scudding across the sky that add to the delight of the scene but also restrict the opportunity for capturing the light effects of sun through trees, sometimes to just a few seconds. There is not time to capture the shadows and bright patches of sun highlighting clumps of bluebells in a sketch; instead, use your camera.

On the other hand, cameras flatten landscapes. What you see in front of you as a vast patch of blue can often be reduced to a narrow strip by the camera lens. This is what you need your sketchbook for. Make sketches to capture the proportions of the scene. Make thumbnail sketches to plan out the layout for your composition before making some sketches; compare these sketches with what you see through your camera lens. Remember, it is your response to the scene that is correct.

Since the bluebells in the foreground will provide the context for how the blue patch in the painting is to be read by the viewer, it is important to make a note of their shapes while you are in the wood. I take close-up photographs and then use these to discover the outline shapes, the silhouettes, of the bluebells. (Since they dance in the slightest breeze, it is very difficult to do this *en plein air*!) Painting in these shapes will be enough information to render the bluebells in a loose, painterly manner in the painting.

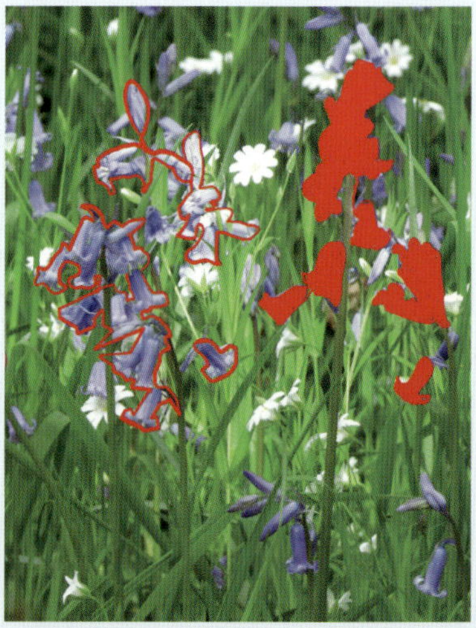

Close-up photograph of bluebells, with added outlines and filled shapes of the silhouetted bluebells.

Designing the Painting

Layout

This painting was composed by using a number of photographs. The scene includes a bright spot of sunshine coming through the trees that acts as a focal point. The trunks and shadows will lead the viewer's eye from the focal point to the region of bluebells, where it will be free to roam around, while the viewer imagines standing amongst the bluebells, before the viewer's eye will be led up via the trunks, to begin the journey around the painting again.

Tone

Bluebell woods rarely allow for us to see very far, so the tonal range over distance is not a large one. However, care must be taken to ensure that this range is there in the painting. As the bluebells recede, they will become paler, as will the leaves on the trees.

For the depicted sun to shine through the leaves, there must be a strong tonal difference between the patch of sunlight and the darks of the tree trunks. The darks are essential for the lights to glow. This also applies to the shadows of the tree trunks; they must be dark enough for the patches of sunlight falling on the bluebells to be discernible.

Colour

This painting can be made by using a limited palette. In this case, choose the blues first, and note that bluebells are usually actually a bluish purple. Ensure that the yellows and greens that you choose make fresh colours when mixed with the blues; many greens that are mixed from typical palettes (for example, with ultramarine blue and cadmium yellow) make duller greens that are more typical of summer trees. Finally, add a brown with which to mix the greys for the tree trunks.

Texture

This painting includes a lot of spattering. The texture in the distance will involve very fine spattering of both masking fluid and paint, achieved by using a toothbrush. For the leaves and bluebells in the middle distance, spattering should be achieved by using an assortment of paintbrushes, to give different shapes and sizes of paint marks. In the foreground, more-definite marks can be made by painting them in with paintbrushes.

Techniques to practise

1 Spattering paint by using a toothbrush.
2 Spattering by flicking paint from a variety of brushes, to discover the sizes and shapes of spattered marks that you are able to make.

Painting the Image

Materials and equipment

- Watercolour paper:
  - Bockingford NOT 300gsm/140lb, stretched and taped to a board
- Watercolour brushes:
  - Da Vinci Series 35, size 4 (pointed round)
  - Swordliners, large and medium
  - Dagger
  - ¼-in flat
- Artist-quality watercolours:
  - Burnt sienna
  - Cobalt blue
  - Dioxazine purple, PV23 (Daler Rowney permanent mauve or Winsor & Newton Winsor violet)
  - Lemon yellow (not the nickel-titanate version)
  - May green (Schmincke)
  - Permanent rose
  - Sap green (Daler Rowney)
  - Ultramarine blue
- 2B pencil
- Eraser
- Tracing paper
- Black pen
- Masking fluid
- Small masking-fluid brush
- Colour shaper
- Toothbrush
- Palette
- Kitchen roll

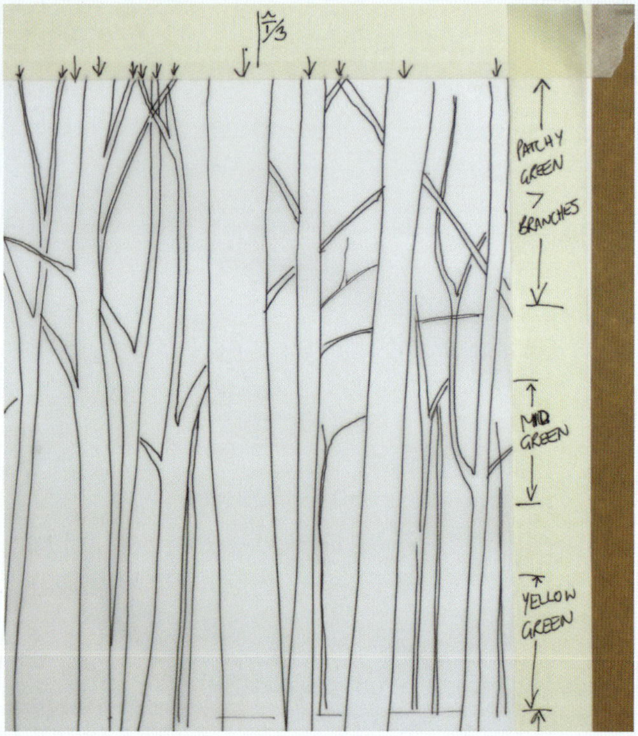

Step 1: Draw in minimal outlines, and then trace them. Make notes around the edge of the painting for guidance.

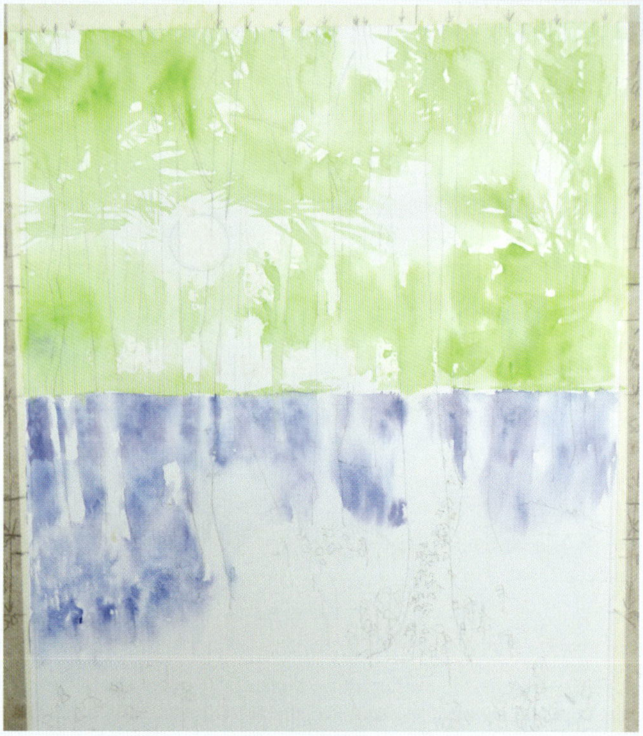

Step 2: Apply the first washes of pale tones to the leafy area and to the area of bluebells, varying the colours as you work.

Step 1: Begin by drawing in the positions of the trees with a 2B pencil. Add in a few of the main branches – enough to give some structure to the composition. Mark the position of the sunlight coming through the trees; in addition to this main area of sun, also mark the area lower down, where there is light coming through between the tree trunks. Draw a line across the page where the bluebells meet the foliage and also draw in a few bluebell silhouettes in the foreground.

This type of outline drawing can be very confusing in a woodland painting – what is tree trunk and what is the gap between the trees? To overcome this, I mark the tree trunks with arrows on the adjacent gum strip attaching the paper to the board, as shown. (I prefer not to mark within the painting area, as the marks can easily be lost under paint.)

Similarly, I have also written notes down the side of the image, as a guide for the application of colour and tone, according to the plan that I made when designing the painting. This scene will be painted quite loosely, and making such notes is a useful device for staying on track. In a design such as this, where the changes of colour and tone are quite subtle, it is easy to lose the features that will make the painting sing.

Finally, make a tracing of the image; it is easier to apply paint loosely if concerns about having to start again are reduced by having a tracing to return to.

Step 2: In the palette, prepare some puddles of lemon yellow and May green. Wet the top half of the paper, using a large brush such as a swordliner. Be sure to leave some of this region of the paper dry and avoid wetting both the area where the sun will be depicted and the area immediately around it. Using the same brush, apply paint with loose, gestural hand movements across this top region of the page, in the directions that branches grow. Vary the tone of the paint, and avoid completely covering the paper's surface; for the brightest highlights, white paper needs to be reserved.

Make up a mix of cobalt blue, dioxazine purple and ultramarine blue in the palette (*see* the section 'Watercolour: Tips and techniques' in Chapter 2, Materials and Techniques, for instructions on how to mix colours), so that you can choose different hues from within this mix. Dampen the paper of the bottom half of the painting: do not have this too wet. Working quite slowly, drop in selected colours from the mix in the palette, allowing variation in tones and colours and allowing some texture to develop. Be careful to keep the tones paler nearer the horizon line in the distance. Paint about halfway down the area of bluebells.

Do not be concerned with avoiding the tree trunks. This layer need to be loose; you do not need to be restricted by painting around the tree trunks. The depth of tone being applied here will easily be managed later on.

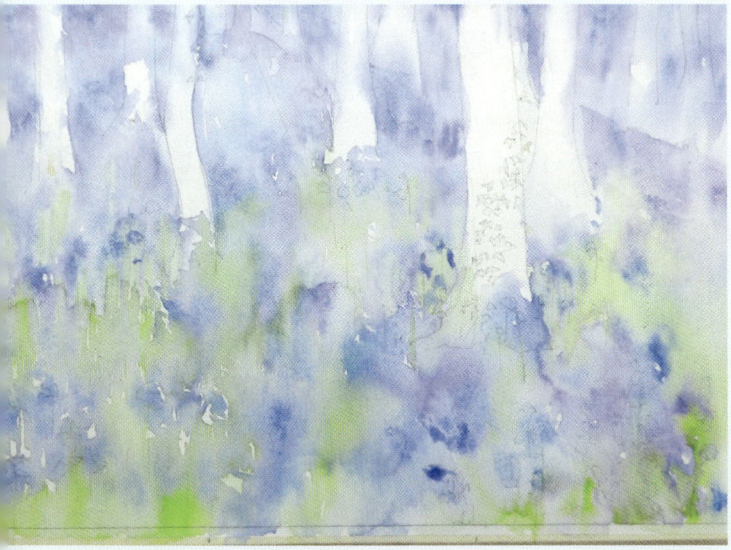

Step 3: Continue working down the page, adding some green areas amongst the depicted bluebells.

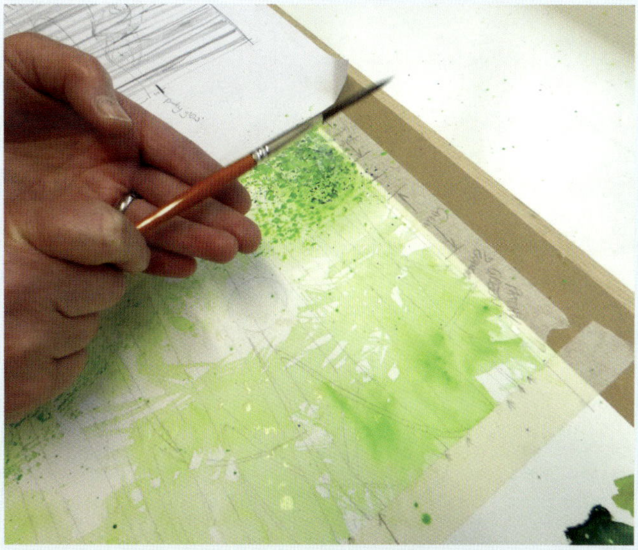

Step 4a: Begin building up layers of foliage by spattering paint.

Step 4b: While the paint drops are still wet, gently roll a brush over them, to create leafy shapes.

Step 3: When you get to the foreground, keep working as in step 2, but now add some May green to the mix. Make sure that you are not working with the paper being too wet, otherwise the colours will blend together too much. Strengthen the tones in the foreground as you near the bottom of the page, but remember that these are the palest tones in this area, so take care not to make them too dark. You are aiming for blotchy paint, varied in both colour and tone.

When all of the paint is completely dry, apply some masking fluid. Where the trees meet the bluebells (in the distance), apply a fine spatter of masking fluid, especially over the bluebell base layer, by using a toothbrush.

Higher up the image, spatter some masking fluid from a colour shaper or masking-fluid brush, to reserve very light leaf shapes.

Use the colour shaper to draw, with masking fluid, some bluebell silhouettes in the foreground and some of the ivy leaves that are located up the nearest tree trunk.

Step 4: Begin to apply paint to depict the foliage of the trees. The foliage needs to be built up in layers, to give the feeling of depth to the wood, so do not get carried away! Keep an eye on what is happening and, if everything begins to blend together too much, stop, allow it all to dry, then continue.

Begin by spattering a mix of greens across the painting. Pick up different colours from your palette; choose greens that you have mixed, yellow and some blue. Using a swordliner brush, spatter lines that imply leaves along the length of a branch.

While these drops of paint are still wet, take a round brush and, laying the length of the brush tip's filaments on to the page, roll the brush tip through the wet paint. This will break up some of the lines and produce randomly shaped leaves. It will also allow the different colours to mix and blend, producing a wide variety of greens! (Again, do not attempt to avoid the tree trunks.)

Allow the paint to dry.

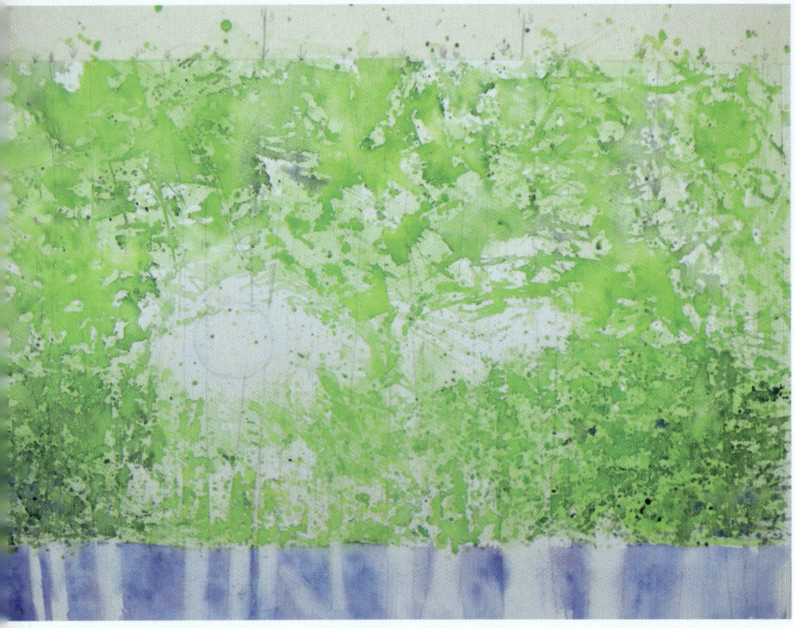

Step 5: Repeat step 4, until you are happy with the result.

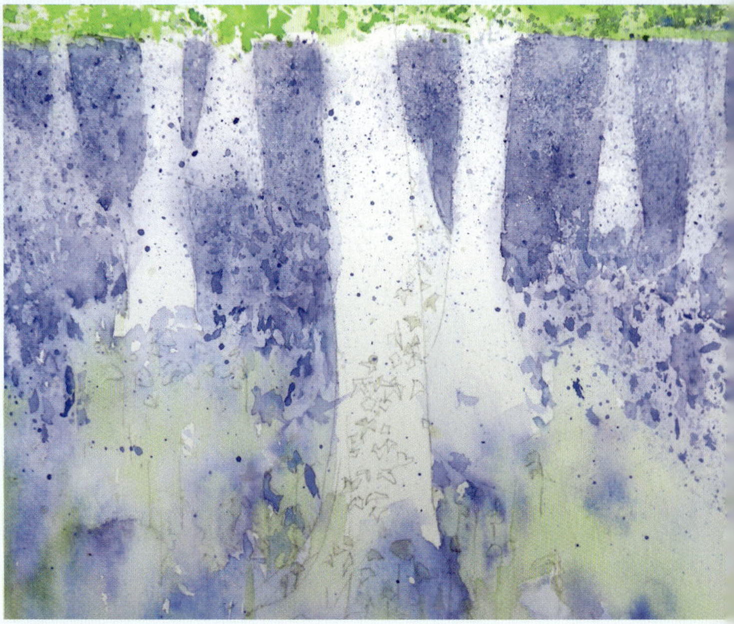

Step 6: Spatter a mix of blues across the region of the bluebells, keeping the marks smaller in the distance and increasing their size towards the foreground.

Step 5: Repeat step 4! As well as building up layers of depicted leaves and foliage, painting in layers in this manner gives you the opportunity to adjust tone and colour. Refer to the original design and make adjustments as necessary.

You may find that you need to repeat the application of this layer.

Step 6: Using a toothbrush, spatter a range of blues in mid-tones across the region of bluebells in the distance. Moving down the page, change to using a brush, and spatter some larger marks, remembering to vary the colours as you work. Allow the tones to become deeper as you near the bottom of the image.

As you getter closer to the bottom of the image, use more of a dabbing action to produce shapes that are comparable to those of bluebell silhouettes.

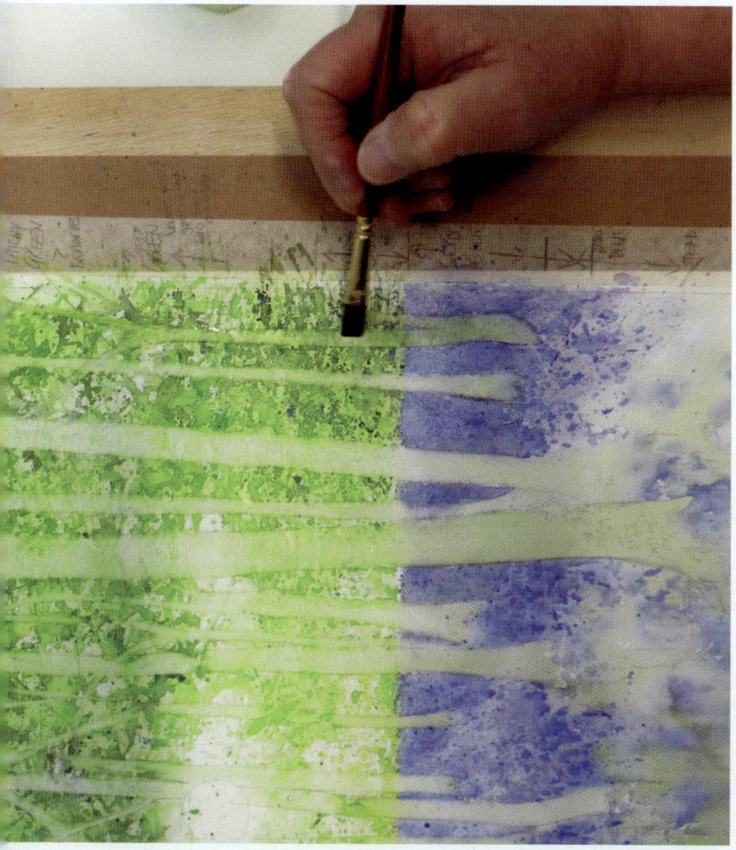

Step 7: Prepare the tree trunks for being painted, by carefully removing the paint from the first washes. Leave a little green paint in place.

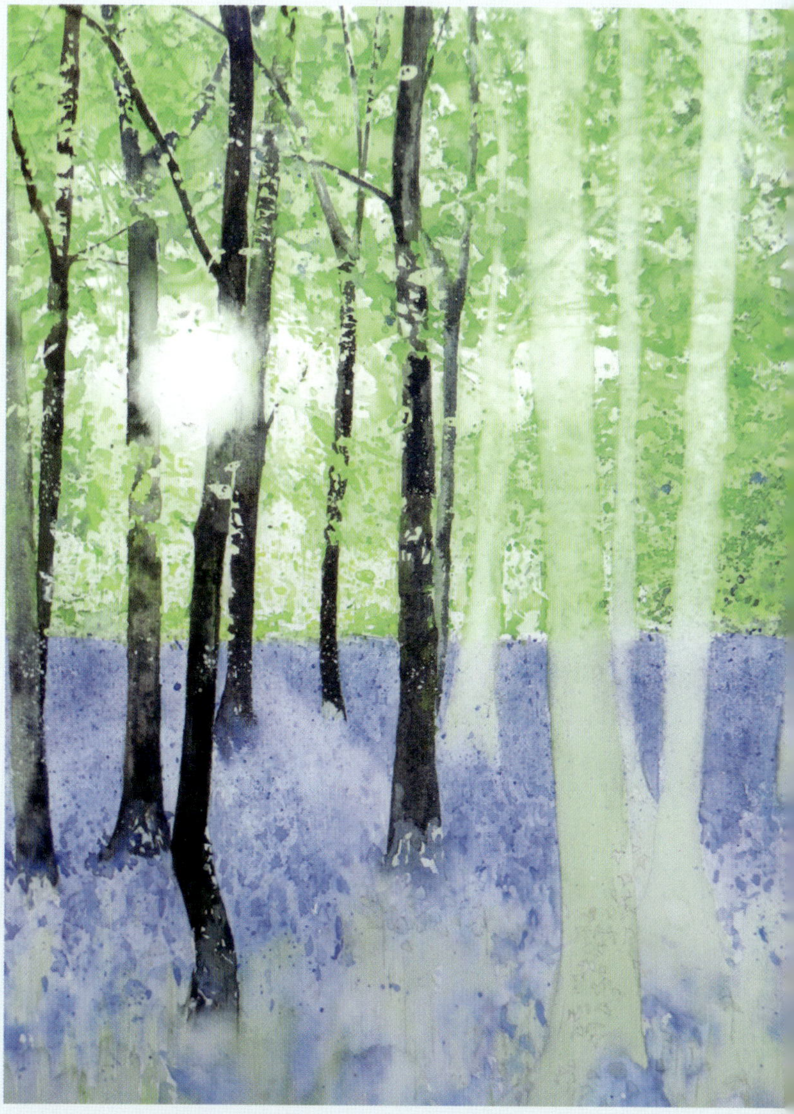

Step 8: Using a brush, paint in the tree trunks, leaving some green patches for the depiction of leaves.

Step 7: Using a flat brush and clean water, wet the paint that has landed on the tree trunks. Give the paint a moment to soften, then lift it off with the brush or, if necessary, kitchen roll. The thin, pale layer of paint that is left over the regions of the tree trunks will add to the colour of the trunks.

Work slowly along the edges of the trunks, leaving some of the paint in place. This will form the shapes of leaves in front of the trunks.

Step 8: Paint in the tree trunks. Mix up a range of grey-browns, green-browns and greens in the palette. Be sure to make thick mixes – the tones of the trunks need to be very dark for the foliage to glow.

Wet the tree trunks with water, being careful to wet around the green paint that is still in place (this is to represent the leaves in front of the trunks).

Drop in a selection of colours from the mix in your palette into the wet areas on the trunks. Drop in the paint at an angle for one edge of each trunk; the paint will bleed across the trunk and give it the appearance of having a rounded shape. Wait a few moments, then drop in either more colour or water, as seems appropriate having looked at what has already appeared on the paper; this will produce textural marks for the representation of the bark.

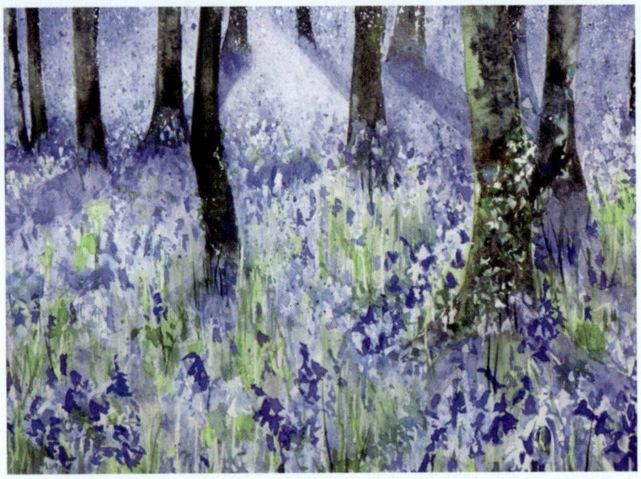

Step 9: Build up texture in the foreground, using fine lines for painting in grasses and a round brush to begin adding some bluebell shapes.

Step 9: Begin to build up some more-defined texture in the foreground. Using a green mix and the swordliner brush, lightly paint in some blades of the grasses. Keep the lines very lightweight, airy and randomly spread across the image. These brushstrokes will only hint at grasses; the design does not call for clumps of grasses or bluebell leaves. Rather, these marks are to break up an expanse of blue in the foreground, which might otherwise look unnatural.

Also, using a round brush, paint in some loose bluebell shapes. Paint just enough of these shapes to give context to the rest of the painting. Base the shapes on the silhouettes of bluebells, and choose to use paint mixes of a range of different colours and tones. Do not be overly concerned with detail: all that is needed is enough form and character to give context to the blue marks in the rest of the painting.

Finally, add the shadows. Make reference to the information you gathered when you took your photographs: shadows do not always follow a predictable course!

Painting the shadows takes courage, as it means painting a well-defined wash over previous layers. As painting each shadow is best done in one wash, you may choose to subtly mark where the shadows are to be. Using a very pale wash, and a very light touch, paint each shadow in with one stroke.

Step 10: The painting is nearing completion now. Remove the masking fluid, then take time to stand back to assess whether there are areas that need further adjustment. Putting the painting upright and standing back to look at it across a room can be very informative.

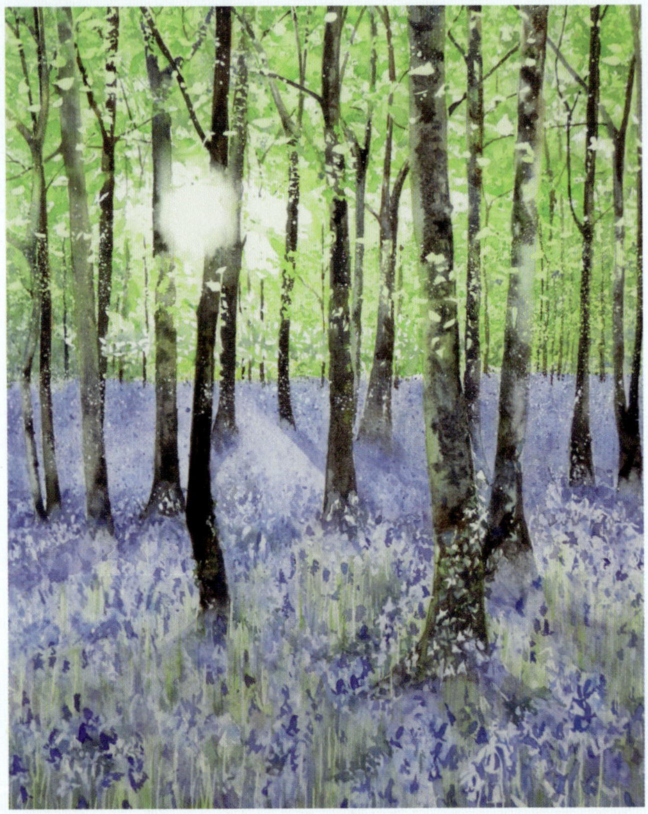

Step 10: Stand back to assess the painting, to decide whether adjustments are needed.

At this stage, this painting needs some adjustments:

The tones along the lower edge of the tree foliage (near the horizon) need to be deeper, to allow the areas where the sun shines through to appear to be brighter. This was achieved by adding more foliage, using darker, bluer mixes of greens.

The very bright area around the sun needs a suggestion of warmth. A delicate, gradated glaze of permanent rose was added in a halo shape around the sun.

The greens (of grasses) in the foreground need a little more definition and possibly the foreground needs a few more-defined bluebell shapes. Using darker tones of blues and greens as appropriate, more grasses and bluebells were painted in.

Assess your own painting and make any adjustments that you feel are necessary. To avoid overworking the painting, take time to assess and make all adjustments carefully, assessing again each time before you make an additional change.

The finished painting: *Bluebell Woods*, watercolour, 33cm × 42cm (13in × 16½in), Siân Dudley.

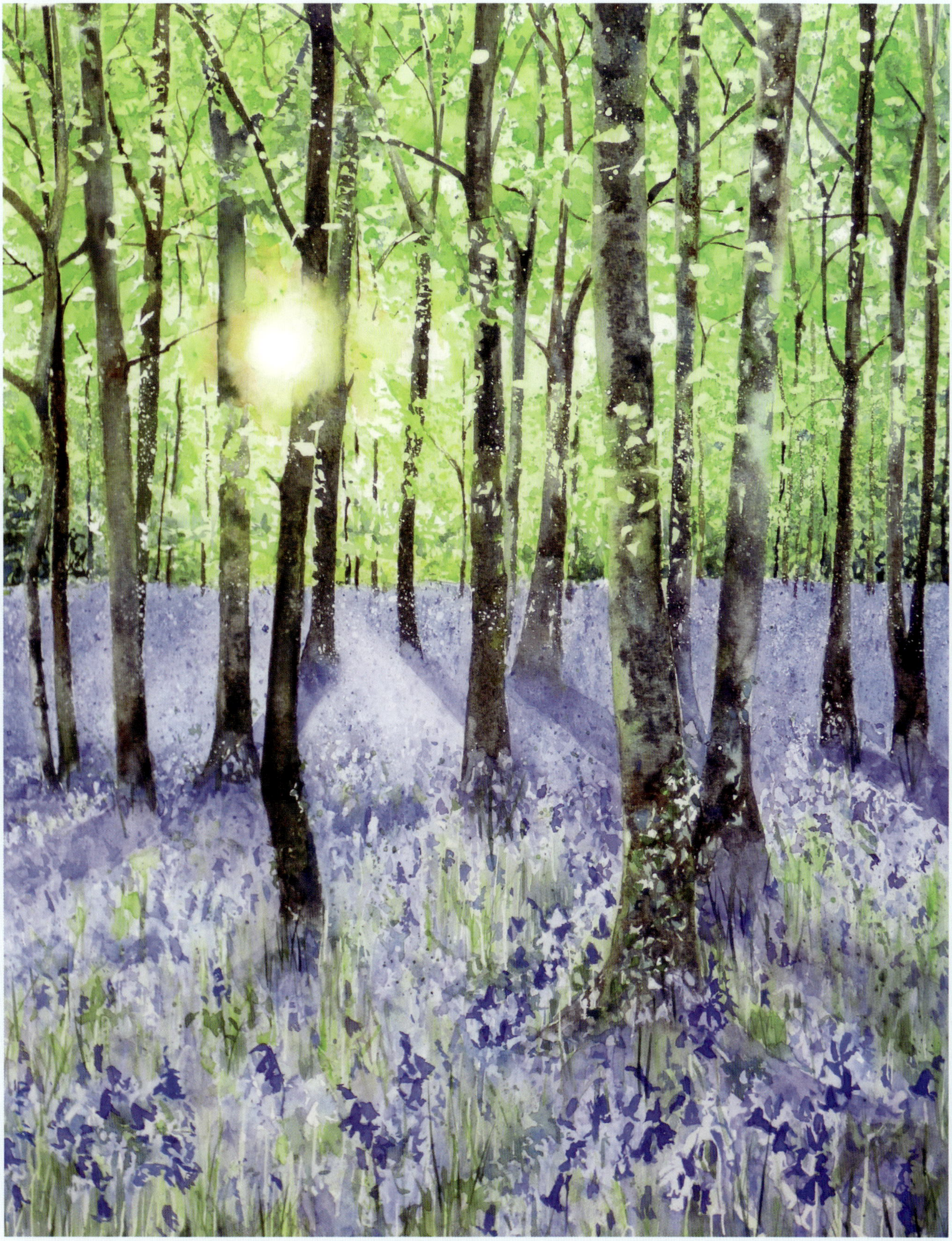

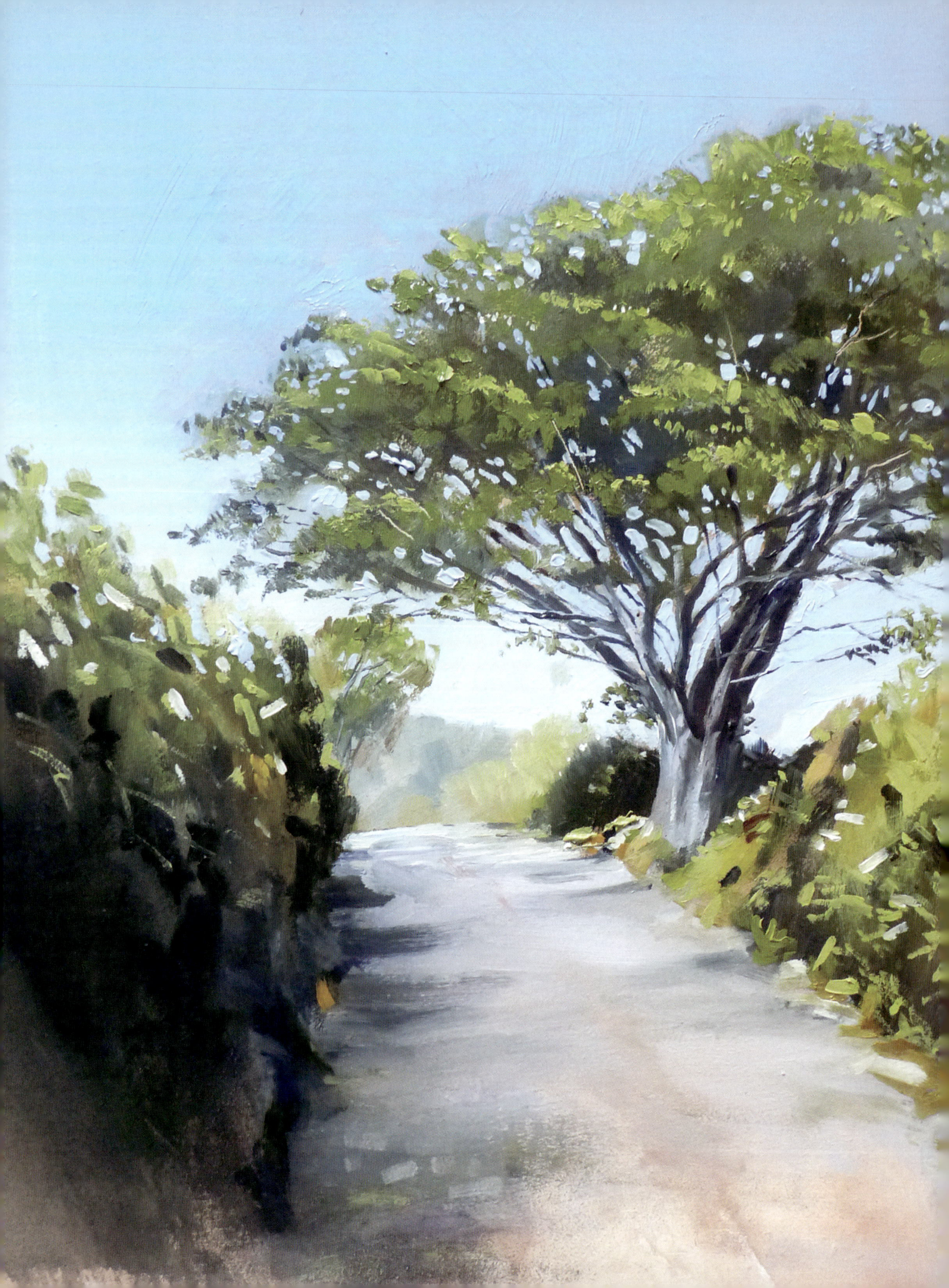

Chapter 6

Summer

For many people, summer is their favourite season of the year. Amongst the trees, the bright, acid greens of spring are replaced with the richer, more mature colours of summer. As the branches fill with leaves, so too do they sag under the weight of the extra foliage. The trees seem to be full of birds and buzzing insects; they seem to hum in the summer sunlight and they cast deep, dark shadows on the ground below.

The days are long and the weather is warmer and (a little) more stable, which for artists means easier days of sketching and painting *en plein air*. With less chance of rain and longer hours of daylight, the whole experience can be so much more relaxed. The romantic ideal of sitting beneath a tree, sketching the meadow in front of you, is one that never loses its appeal!

The mature, summer greens are richer than those seen in spring, requiring a change of palette. Choose colours that are softer, for example, substituting raw sienna for lemon yellow and olive green for sap green. Consider the weight of the extra foliage; this heaviness can be subliminally implied by choosing to use opaque paints.

The supporting skeleton of the tree – its trunk, branches and twigs – will often be hidden from view in summer; the leaves obscure much that would have been visible only weeks before. It has been estimated that a mature oak tree can have over 200,000 leaves. In the summertime, it is wonder that we can see any branches at all! When sketching, observe how branches disappear amongst the leaves, reappearing in unexpected places. Note how the richness of the dark tones in the shadows add to the apparent density of the tree canopy.

Sitting in the shade has benefits beyond the avoidance of sunburn, which is all too easily acquired when time is lost in concentrating on painting; it also takes the glare off of the paper or canvas, is much easier on the eyes and means it is often possible to assess colour and tone without the need for sunglasses.

The Big Beech Tree: Summer, water-mixable oils on board, 26cm × 30cm (10¼in × 11¾in), Rob Dudley.

THE BIG BEECH TREE: SUMMER

Rob Dudley

Trees in summer can often appear to be heavy with leaves. The Big Beech Tree seemed to almost groan under the weight of its foliage. This was my starting point for *The Big Beech Tree: Summer*. Gone were the lighter characteristics of spring: the heaviness of summer had taken over. To paint this heaviness, I decided to work in oils; the oil paint complements this approach, as marks made with oils appear heavier compared to the lighter touches of watercolours.

Although the beech tree would have hundreds of thousands of leaves, my approach in painting them was not to consider them as individuals but as blocks of leaves. These blocks would appear to add to the weight of the tree, thereby helping to emphasize the point that I was trying to illustrate.

PROJECT

Summer Tree

Rob Dudley

The Inspiration

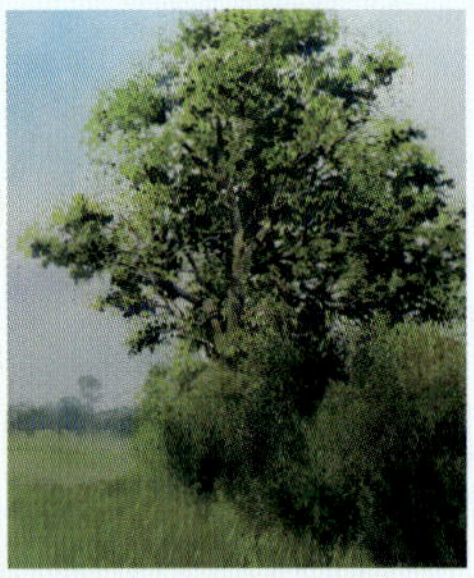

While tutoring a watercolour course late one summer, during the lunch break, I took the opportunity to walk some of the local footpaths, to discover whether any spots would make good painting grounds for my students. I came across this wonderful oak tree at the side of a large field. It seemed to dwarf the hedgerow bushes and smaller trees that it was growing amongst. There was something quite captivating about it, full of dark shadows and dusky, summer greens. It was almost calling out 'paint me!'

Developing the Idea

The idea behind this painting was very simple: a study of an oak tree set in a late-summer landscape. The painting was also to show the depth and volume of the tree, the shadows on both its foliage and its boughs, and the variations of greens within this single tree. The painting would not be a pixel-perfect copy of the tree, but it would be based on my response to and interpretation of this tree. My sketch and photographs would be the starting point for the painting, not the destination.

Information Gathering

I didn't have long to gather information; I was tutoring at the time at nearby Flatford Mill and had to get back to run the afternoon session. So, I had to rely on a very quick sketch and some hastily taken photographs. This was a painting that would have to wait until I returned to my studio in Devon.

Designing the Painting

Layout

Back in the studio, some months later and working from the simple sketch and photographs that I had taken, I experimented with some tonal and format thumbnails in order to arrive at my preferred design.

Very quickly, I settled on a slightly elongated portrait format to make the painting being, as it was, a portrait of a rather splendid oak tree. A more traditional landscape format, I felt, would leave too much space on each side of the tree, which in turn would take attention away from the oak itself. The portrait format would reduce the chances of this happening.

Tone

Much of my memory of the scene, and it is important not to ignore one's memories and feelings of a scene, was about the shadows on the branches and within the cavernous depths of the tree, and the lights, the darks and the chinks of sky seen through the foliage. To capture these elements, I would have to work with a broad tonal range: from the lightest lights to the darkest darks and those tones in-between. When selecting my palette of colours, I would have to ensure that I could mix the wide range of tones required.

Colour

When I encountered this scene, the sun was shining brightly, and summer was hanging heavy in the air. The oak tree's colours were not as vibrant as they would have been earlier in the season, with some of the leaves having just a hint of brown about them.

I tend to think of the leaves in late summer as being of a weary, dusty, end-of-summer green, so different to the bright, fresh greens of spring.

I chose a palette of colours from which I could mix both a full range of these weary greens and some deep, dark shadow colours.

Although I had already decided that I would use masking fluid for certain effects, I also chose to include some white acrylic gouache amongst my chosen paints. With the addition of a little watercolour to this gouache, I could use its strong opacity to touch in leaves, branches and even patches of sky over some of the previously painted passages – light over dark.

Texture

One of the most important aspects of this painting is the texture that the leaves create both in the oak and along the hedgerow. I wanted to create the illusion of this leafy texture but without having to paint every individual leaf. It not only would have taken far too long but also would have likely ended up looking far too contrived and lacking in visual credibility. I therefore chose to flick and spatter the paint on to the paper's surface, in order to create a leaflike effect rather than blocks of colour, building up the texture of the leafy layers as I went.

I chose to work on a paper that had a nice tooth to the surface and would complement the spattering effect. This paper would also allow for the application and successful removal of masking fluid, something that I would be using quite a lot of for this watercolour painting.

Technique to practise

This project involves spattering. This can be achieved by using a variety of brushes and techniques. Some people are able to flick paint off of the brush simply by tapping the brush with a finger of the hand that they are holding the brush with. Others find that they need to make more of a flicking action, maybe even tapping the brush on to a finger of the other had. Whichever technique you find easiest, you will find that different brushes will give different-sized and different-shaped spatters.

Some guidance will be found in the text but, before beginning this project, it is advisable to spend some time practising spattering techniques until you achieve marks that you feel would be suitable for this painting.

Painting the Image

Materials and equipment

- Watercolour paper:
  - Bockingford NOT 300gsm/140lb, stretched and taped to a board
- Watercolour brushes:
  - No. 14 pointed sable
  - No. 8 pointed sable
  - No. 6 pointed sable
  - No. 2 pointed sable
  - Fine rigger
  - Medium stencil brush
- Artist-quality watercolours:
  - Burnt sienna
  - Cobalt blue
  - Green gold
  - Lemon yellow
  - May green
  - Neutral tint
  - Permanent rose
  - Raw sienna
  - Sap green
  - Ultramarine blue
  - Winsor blue (green shade)
  - White acrylic gouache
- 2B pencil
- Masking fluid
- Scrap paper
- Masking tape
- Maskaway eraser
- Dip pen
- Kitchen roll
- Palette

Step 1: Draw in the image outlines with pencil, and mask out relevant parts of the image.

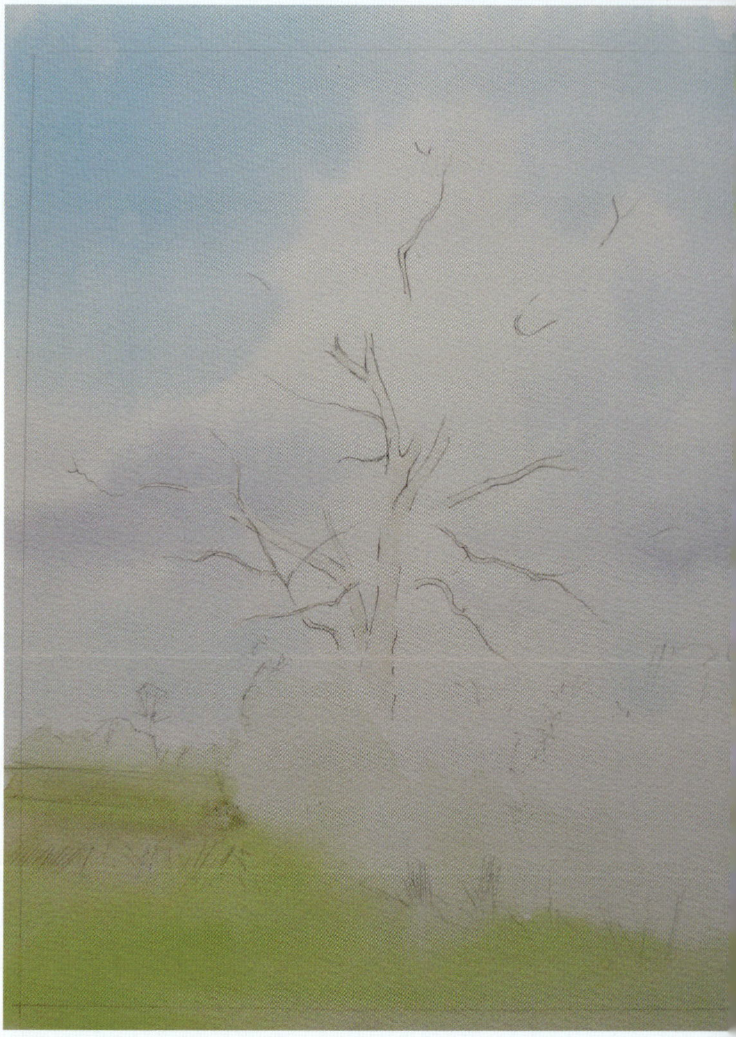

Step 2: Add washes for the sky and distant and foreground fields.

Step 1: On the dry, stretched piece of watercolour paper, use a 2B pencil to draw in the design. For the main tree, it is not necessary to draw in every leaf or branch; include just the main trunk and key branches.

With masking fluid, mask out the trunk and branches of the main tree. Spatter some masking fluid over the region of the hedgerow bushes. Allow the masking fluid to dry completely before moving on to the next step, as any wet masking fluid can have a ruinous effect on good watercolour brushes!

Step 2: With the board at a slight angle, dampen the entire painting. Allow the water to soak into the paper a little; you want the paper to be damp but not to have water floating on its surface.

Mix puddles of Winsor blue with ultramarine blue, permanent rose and neutral tint, and wash in the sky by using a No. 14 sable. Make a mix of cobalt blue and May green with a touch of raw sienna, and use this mix to paint in the distant fields and trees, strengthening the tone of the mix as you move forward within the painting. Leave the board at the same angle as that for when you were painting, and allow the paint to dry completely.

Step 3: Strengthen the distant trees.

Step 3: With a mix of cobalt blue and May green, strengthen the distant tree line by applying the mix with a No. 8 sable. While the paint is still wet, soften the bottom of some of the depicted trees by dampening the paint in these regions with clean water. Be careful not to make the tree tones too strong; the trees are in the distance, and the chosen tone should reflect this. Note that paler tones tend to recede, whereas stronger tones come forward. Allow the wash to dry fully.

Step 4: Tear scraps of paper to use as a mask, and place them around the tree shape, to protect the rest of the painting from unwanted spatter. Sometimes, it is useful to stick these paper pieces together with tape, and weigh them down with coins, to prevent any movement of the mask.

Make a good puddle of paint of lemon yellow, May green and a touch of sap green (you will be surprised at how much paint you will need for this step). Make sure that the mix is not too strong; this is the lighter first layer of spatter, and subsequent layers will add the darks. Tap the loaded brush to spatter the mix on to the paper, to create the main tree's shape. Use the same mix to spatter in the hedgerow bushes. I find that a No. 6 or a No. 8 brush works well for this.

When you have finished the spattering, carefully lift the mask away from the wet paint. This will prevent any paint from creeping under the mask to areas where it is not intended to reach.

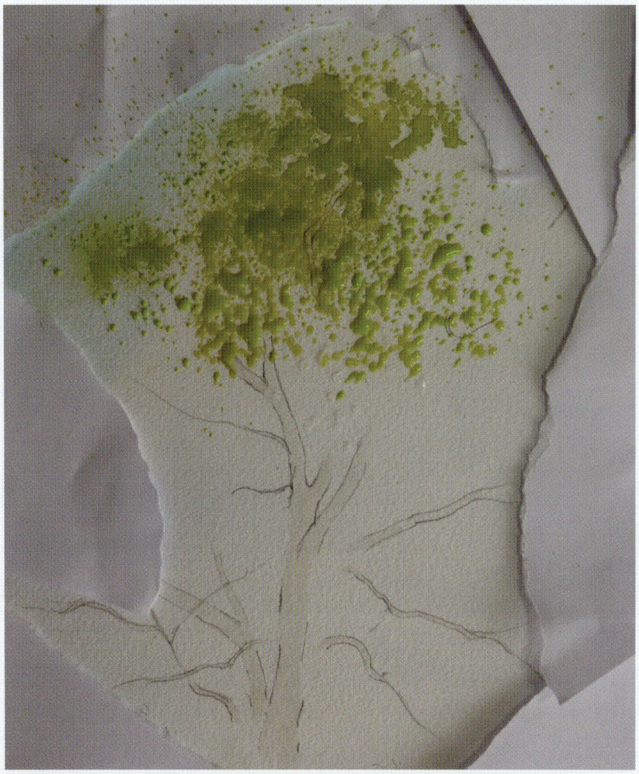

Step 4a: Spatter on the first layer of paint through a paper mask for the depiction of the main tree's foliage.

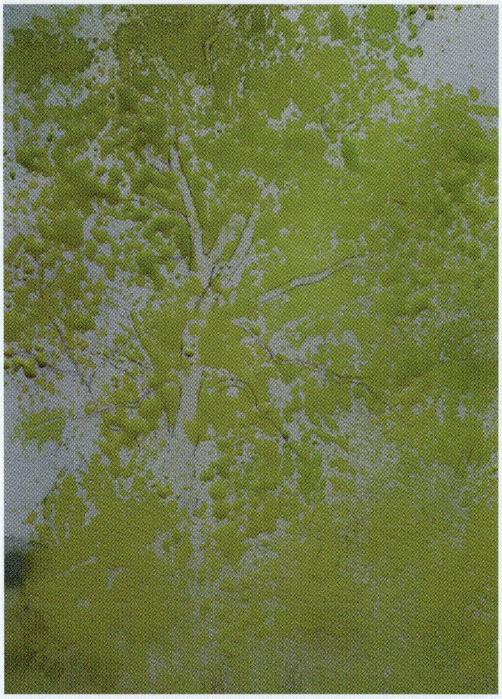

Step 4b: Continue spattering paint, until the tree's shape is formed.

This step must be left to dry completely before the next layer of spattering is applied, otherwise the textural effect of the depicted leaves will be lost, as the wet droplets of paint will coalesce into a wash.

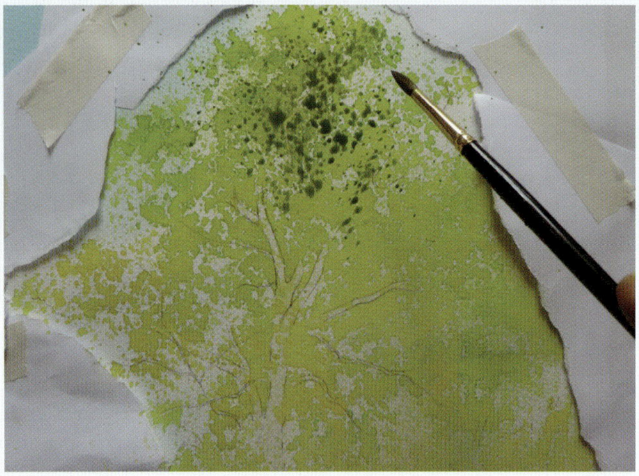

Step 5a: Build up the foliage with layers of spatter, using a brush for the depiction of larger leaves.

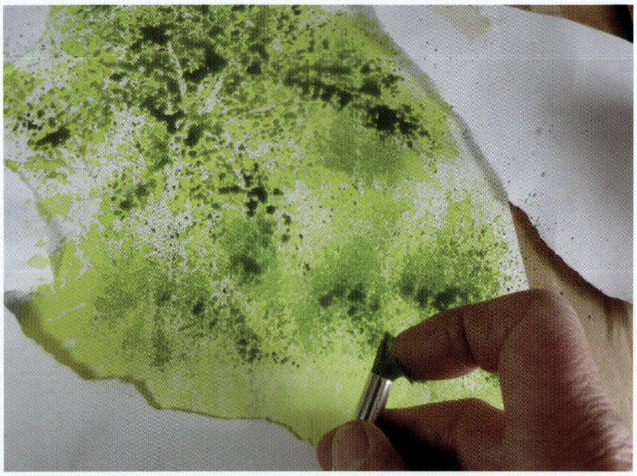

Step 5b: Add spattering by using a stencil brush, to create the effect of smaller leaves in the tree and hedgerow.

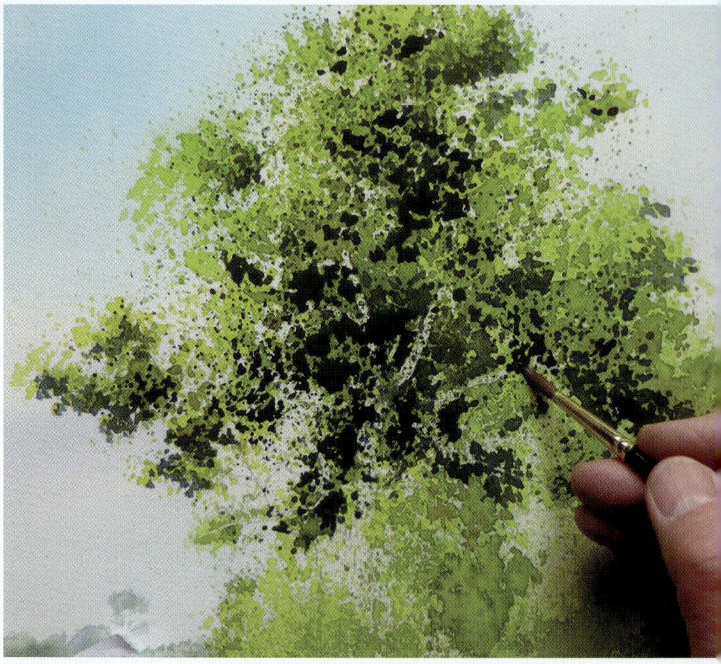

Step 6: Add the dark shadows to the main tree's foliage.

Step 5: As for the previous step, mask around the oak tree with scraps of torn paper. If the paint on the previously used mask is completely dry, this mask can be reused.

Strengthen the mix used in step 4 by the addition of ultramarine blue and spatter the next layer. As before, when finished, carefully lift the mask away from the wet paint to prevent creeping.

Using a stencil brush, paint in the hedgerow, not by stencilling but by using the brush to spatter and flick paint from. Using the stencil brush in this way will result in a different series of marks compared to those marks forming the oak, creating a different leaflike texture for the hedge.

Allow the paint to dry.

Step 6: Remask the painting and carefully spatter a dark mix of ultramarine blue, sap green and a little burnt sienna over the oak tree, making certain that the mix is dark enough. Concentrate the areas of spatter to define the shadowed parts of the tree, particularly on the underside of boughs and the interior of the body of the oak.

Remove the mask and, with a No. 6 brush, pull some of the spatters together; this action is to define some of the shadows more precisely. Repeat this spattering application of the darker mix for the hedgerow but by using the stencil brush and then drawing together of some of these spatters with the No. 6 brush. Allow the paint to dry.

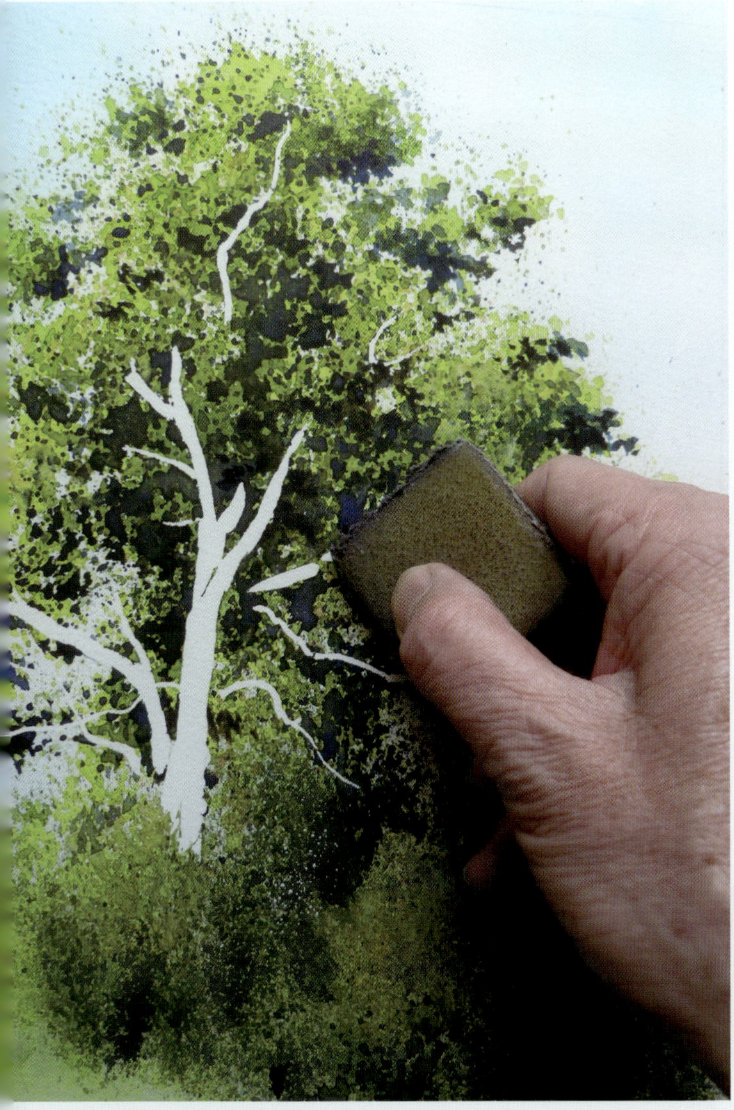

Step 7: Carefully remove the masking fluid.

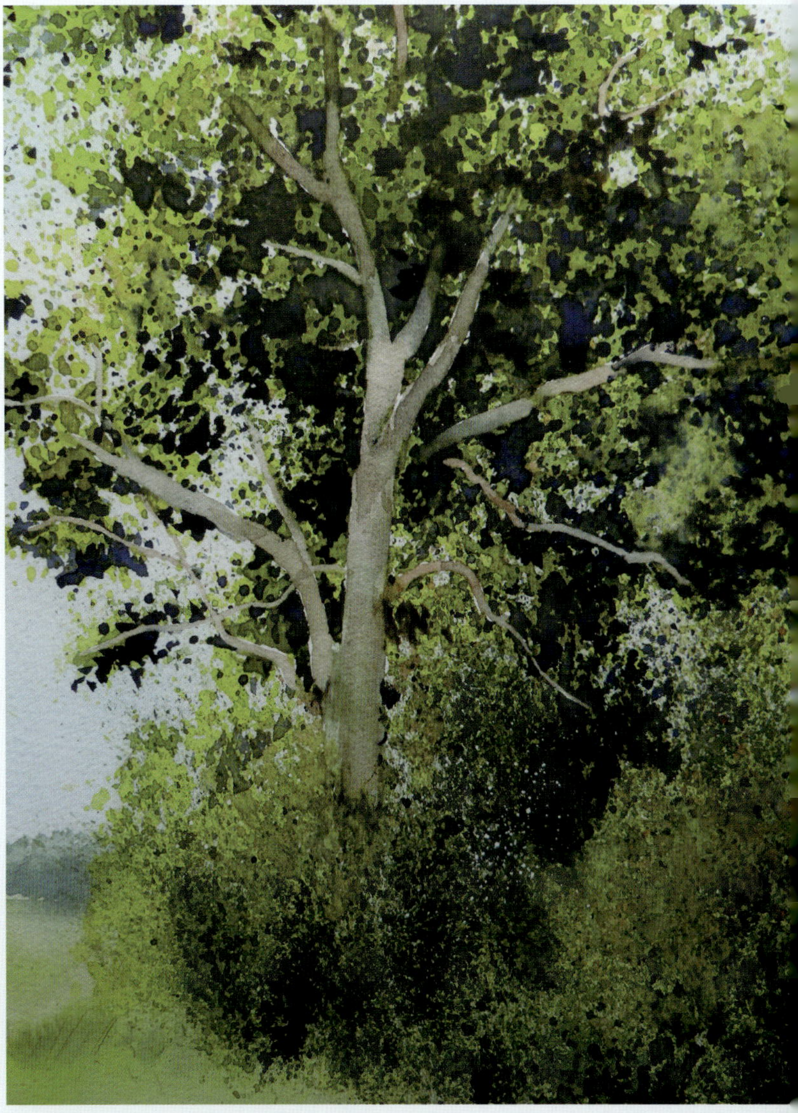

Step 8: Paint in the main tree's trunk and branches.

Step 7: It is imperative to make certain that the previous step is absolutely dry before attempting to remove the masking fluid. If the paint is not dry in all parts of the painting, it is extremely likely that, while removing the masking fluid, unwelcome paint smears will appear where they are not wanted!

Use a Maskaway eraser or clean fingers to remove the masking fluid. Don't rub too frantically or pull at the dried masking fluid, as this might tear the watercolour paper.

Step 8: With a well-pointed No. 6 brush, paint in the oak's trunk and branches, with varying mixes of burnt sienna and ultramarine blue.

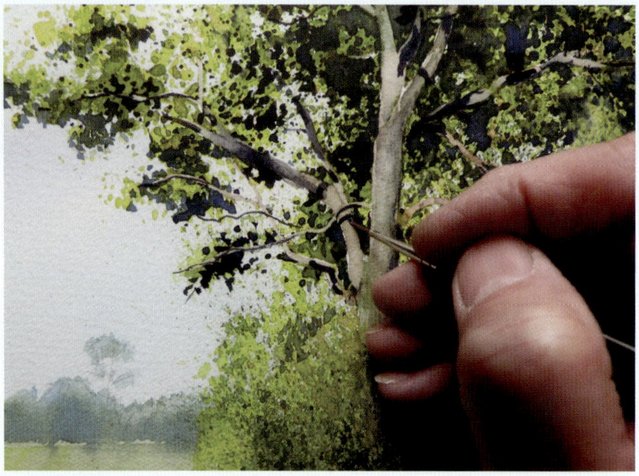

Step 9: Add shape and form to the trunk and branches, by introducing shadows.

Step 9: Darken the trunk mix of burnt sienna and ultramarine blue by the addition of neutral tint. Use this mix to darken some of the branches and add shadows to the trunk and branches. Note how the rounded shapes of the shadows define the form of the branches.

Step 10: Sky holes are simply holes in the tree's foliage through which the sky is visible, or through which birds can fly! Summer trees will obviously appear to have fewer sky holes than, say, the same trees in spring or winter, but they are still there and should not be ignored. Without the sky holes, the tree will look solid, even top-heavy, and false.
With some ultramarine blue added to the opaque white acrylic gouache, paint in some sky holes. Keep the shapes irregular and in proportion to the shapes within the rest of the tree. Paint in a few sky holes, then step back to assess the progress that has been made. Avoid painting in too many sky holes, as too many can end up looking as false as can too few.

Step 11: Having made certain that the previous step is dry, mix together some raw sienna with the white acrylic gouache, and paint in some of the smaller branches. Use a dip pen or fine rigger for creating these thinner branches.
With a mix of green gold and May green, paint in the foreground grasses. Flick the rigger or No. 6 brush upwards when painting these grasses, with the movement of the brush indicating the grasses' direction of growth. These directional marks will make for a more interesting and varied foreground. Add a touch of burnt sienna to this mix and flick a little of it into the region of the hedgerow.

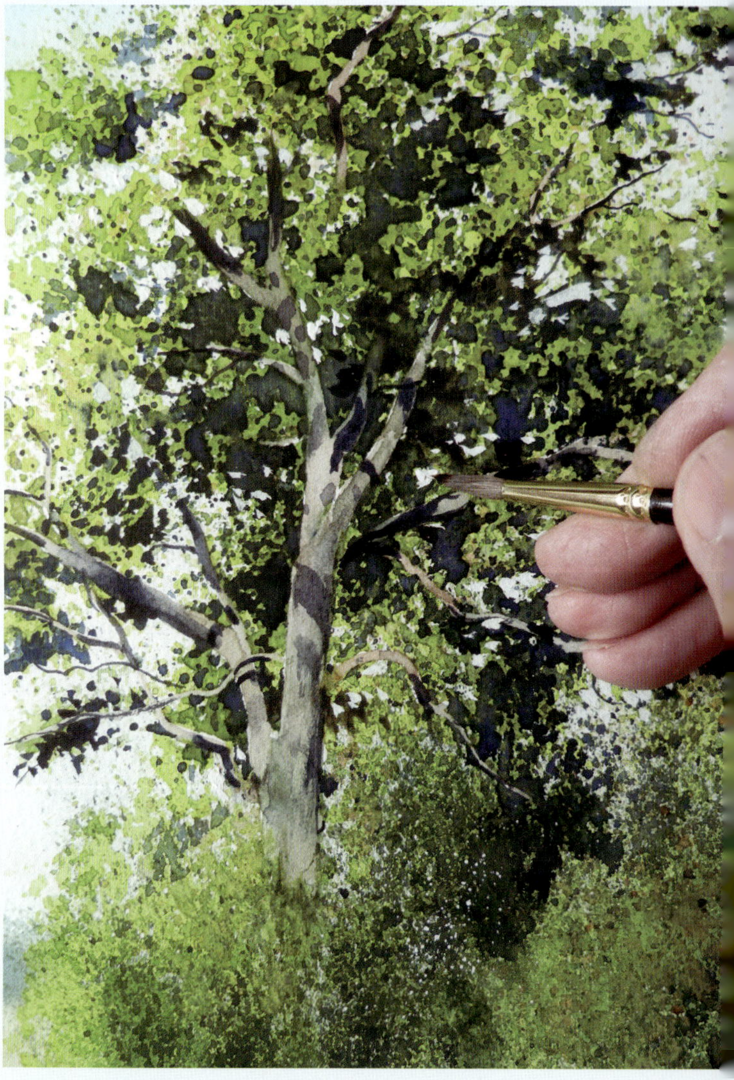

Step 10: Add the sky holes by using acrylic gouache.

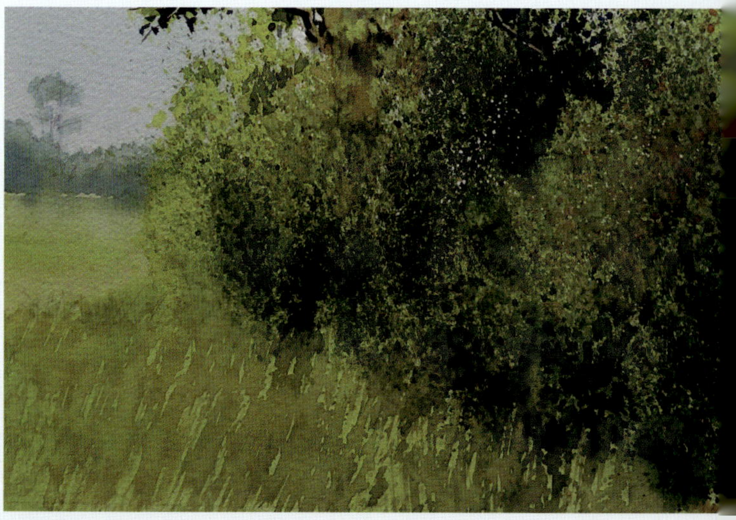

Step 11: Paint in the foreground grasses and add finishing touches.

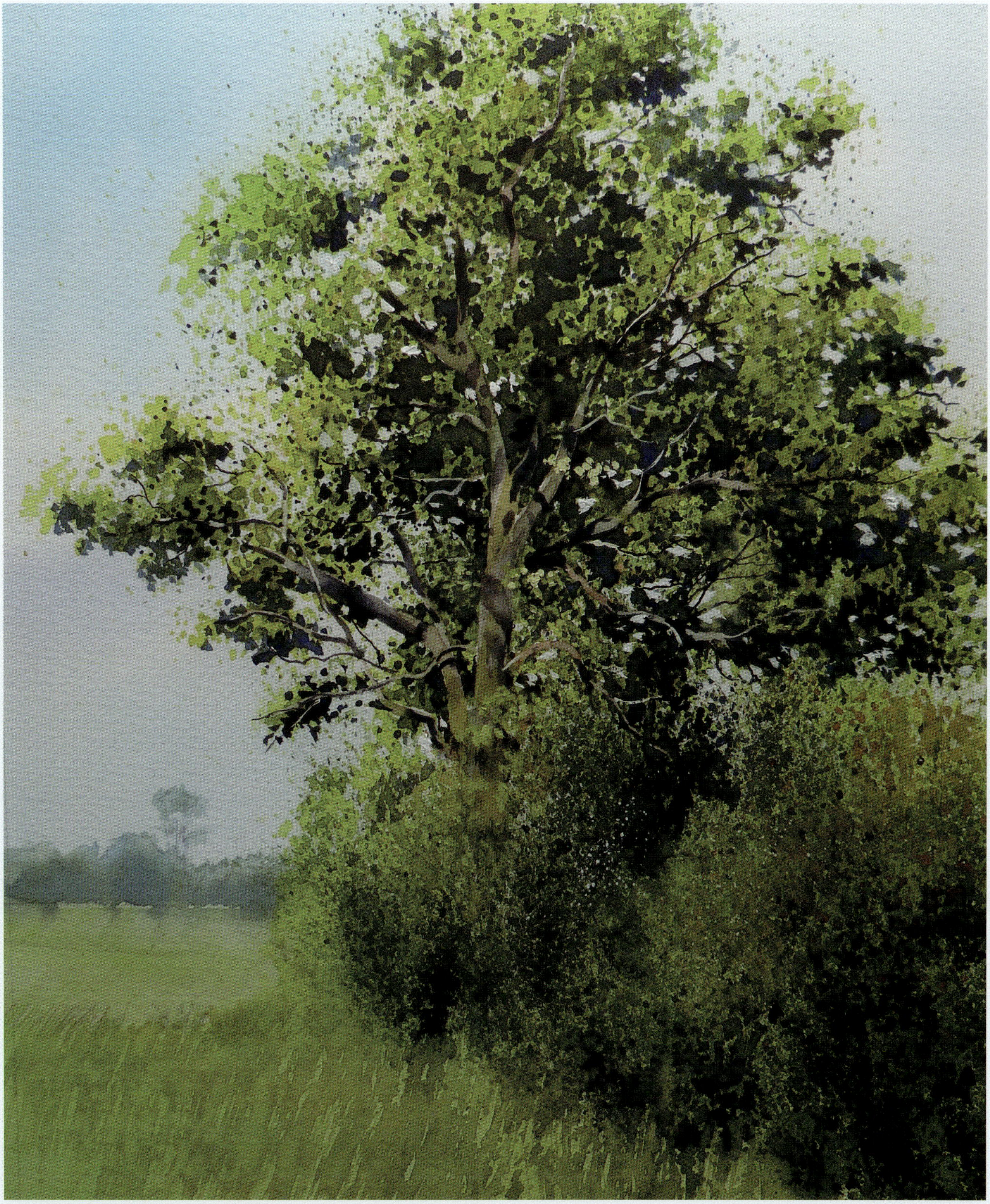

The finished painting: *Summer Tree*, watercolour, 28cm × 34cm (11in × 13½in), Rob Dudley.

PROJECT

Summer Shade

Siân Dudley

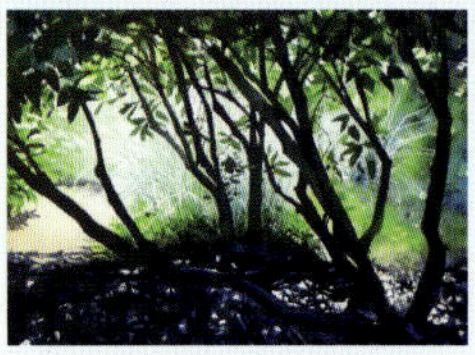

The Inspiration

The inspiration for this painting came in an instant, during a visit to a formal garden. It was a very hot afternoon, the sun was beating down and my eyes needed a rest from the strength of the light. I often choose not to wear sunglasses, in order to enjoy the colours of my surroundings in natural light and to avoid the softening of tonal contrast. As we walked around a bend, I was greeted with a magical scene: a cool tunnel formed by trees growing across the path, with a wonderful, beckoning glow of light beyond, enticing a visitor to walk through it to discover what was beyond. I was particularly inspired by the shapes of the trunks and branches that twisted and turned into fascinating shapes. The glow on the grasses beyond highlighted the negative shapes between the trunks and it was this effect that made me want to capture the scene in a painting.

Developing the Idea

Since it was the glowing negative shapes that really interested me, the image was planned to emphasize these elements rather than the trees or the grasses occupying the negative shapes. This painting had to be about colour and tonal contrasts.

This scene would have been nothing without the delightful shapes of the trunks and branches; although I wanted the viewer to look through the trunks and branches to the brightness beyond, I also wanted these elements to be interesting in themselves, to lead the viewer's eye around the painting, on a visual journey that would be pleasurable in its own right.

When summarizing the role of the trees in this painting, it is worth noting that it is an odd one. The focal point of the painting is the sunlit grass, followed by the play of light on foliage throughout the painting. For this to be the case, the trees have to fall to the background in the viewer's mind, yet they are positioned in the foreground of the painting.

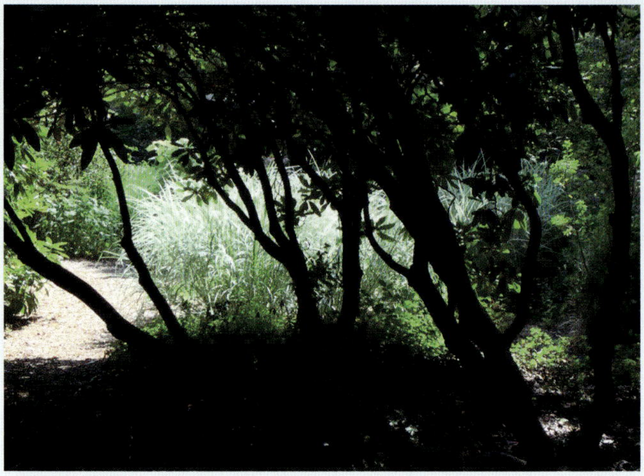

The main photograph of a set that was used for reference for this painting.

Information Gathering

There was little opportunity to sketch on this occasion, so I began by looking long and hard at what was in front of me, taking time to identify what was important to me and to begin forming a composition in my mind. Imaging yourself drawing a particular scene can also help to commit the scene to memory. I then took time to use a camera to gather the information that I needed.

Firstly, I moved around, using the viewfinder to compose a photograph that captured the shapes and view that I was looking for. Just a slightly different angle altered the shapes of the trunks and the negative shapes between them, so it is important to carefully observe what you are seeing in the viewfinder or screen, as well as to directly observe the scene that you are photographing. If your camera allows it, review the photographs before leaving the scene.

Once I was happy with the composition, I then altered the settings on the camera (exposure and colour bias) to capture the other information that I needed; I worked from the whole set of photographs, not just a single photograph.

Designing the Painting

Layout

I was pleased with the composition of one of the photographs and based the composition on it with very little alteration.

Tone

Similarly, the tonal contrasts captured in the photograph were well balanced to lead the viewer's eye through the tree tunnel. It will be important to ensure that the darks are very dark, as it is the contrast between the lights and darks that will enable the light areas to glow.

It is worth noting that this image contains a mixture of lost and found edges, which will be used to lead the viewer's eye around the painting. Where the trunks cross the path, there is a huge tonal difference between the tree trunks and the sunlit path; the shapes are clear and well defined. However, in the shadows, there are lost edges, where it is difficult to identify, for example, what is trunk and what is branch. These lost edges are important, as the lost detail will cause the viewer's eye to keep moving, looking for something to focus on. They also help to simplify what could otherwise be an extremely busy painting!

Colour

As ever in nature, the range of greens was almost infinite, and this would need to be simplified for the painting. As a result of the planting of the garden, within the scene was a lovely arrangement of glaucous-blue grasses, appearing almost white in the sun, and some gorgeous, bright yellow-greens. These were the colours needed to draw the viewer's eye through the image to the path beyond the shade under the trees. Bright bismuth yellow and Winsor blue (green shade) are the basis for the necessary paint mixes, with the addition of a little sap green and cobalt blue.

The rich, dark greens will be made from mixes of dioxazine purple, sap green, indigo and cobalt blue. There were warmer greens in the summer foliage, which could act as a bridge between the palest greens and the rich, dark greens of the trees themselves. However, this huge range of greens would not serve the purpose of the painting, so it could be simplified by mixing the warmer greens from the paints used for the bright, pale greens and the rich, dark greens of the leaves on the trees.

In such strong sunlight, the trunks appeared to be almost black; although I wanted strong contrasts, black deadens an otherwise vibrant image, so it is to be avoided. To keep the extremely dark areas lively and interesting requires some very dark mixes: mixes that appear almost black but still have a range of colours within them. These can be achieved with indigo, dioxazine purple and sap green. The addition of cobalt blue to this mix both softens and cools it, helping to give the impression of a cool tunnel under the trees.

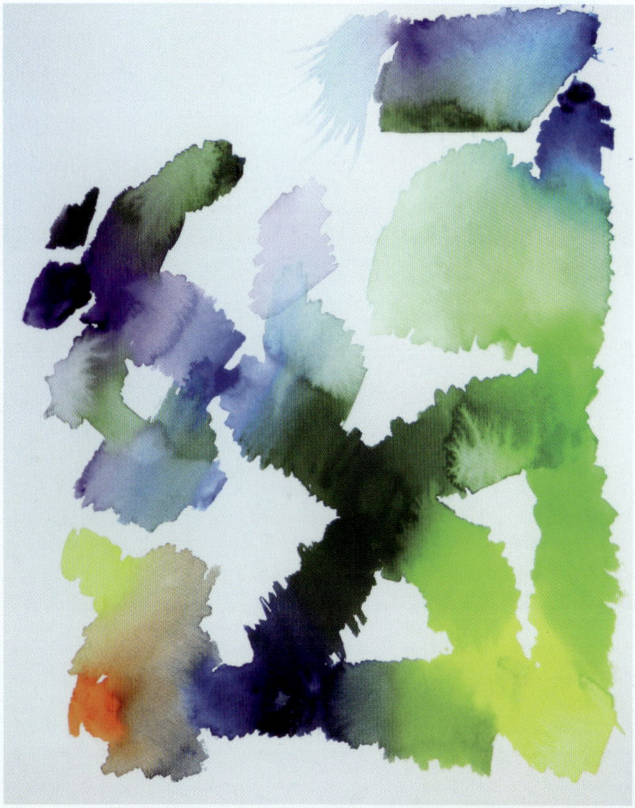

When choosing the colours to use, make sure that you can produce the full range of colours that you will need. For this painting, it is important to check whether a colourful range of very dark tones can be produced by using the chosen palette.

Also important in avoiding flat, uninteresting darks is the use of glazing. It is used throughout this demonstration to build up layers of tone and colour. As more layers of paint are applied, it is possible to build up colour and tone, thus giving a richer, more interesting finish than can be achieved with just a single layer of paint. The use of glazing also makes it easy to leave patches of the lower glazes peeping through, which in this image will be read by the viewer as dappled light.

Texture

It would be easy to be drawn into producing a very busy, highly textured image, particularly when working from a photograph. Keeping the inspiration in mind, the texture of the foliage is not that important in this image, so it makes sense to keep it as simple as possible. Using round brushes and daggers to print enough leaf shapes to encourage the viewer to read the rest of the marks as foliage is all that is needed – the danger here is overworking the painting! Stop regularly to assess how the painting is developing.

Painting the Image

Materials and equipment

- Watercolour paper:
  - Bockingford NOT 300gsm/140lb, stretched and taped to a board
- Watercolour brushes:
  - Da Vinci Series 35 size 4
  - Swordliners, medium and small
  - Dagger, medium and small
- Artist-quality watercolours:
  - Bismuth yellow (Daler Rowney)
  - Cobalt blue
  - Indigo (Daler Rowney)
  - May green
  - Permanent mauve (dioxazine purple, PV23, Daler Rowney)
  - Sap green (Daler Rowney)
  - Winsor blue (green shade) (Winsor & Newton)
- 2B pencil
- Eraser
- Tracing paper
- Black pen
- Masking fluid
- Mapping pen
- Colour shaper
- Palette
- Kitchen roll

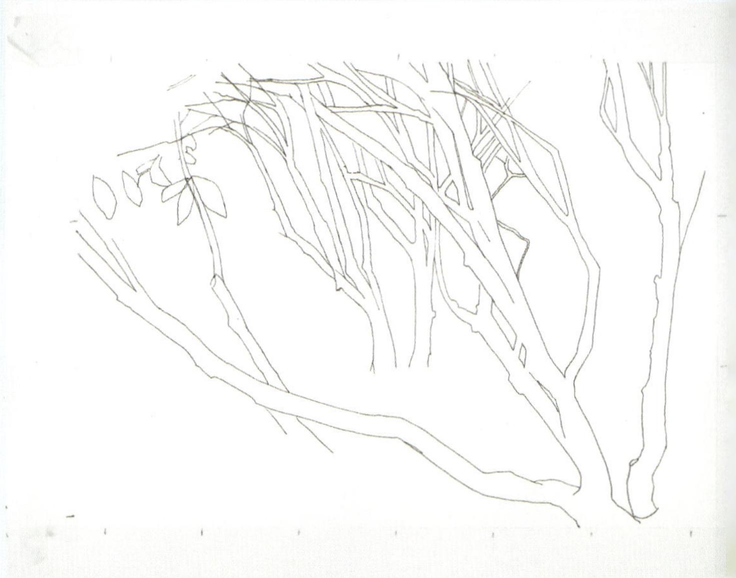

Step 1: Draw in the outlines of the tree trunks by using a 2B pencil. (The outlines are shown here drawn in ink, for clarity.)

Step 1: Lightly draw in the outlines of the trees on to the watercolour paper by using a 2B pencil. Take care to ensure that the negative shapes are interesting. As a result of the dark shadows, some of these silhouetted shapes may look a little unnatural at this stage. Take care to ensure that the shapes form an interesting pattern on the paper.

NON-DRAWING DAYS

Sometimes I have what I call a 'non-drawing day', when, no matter how hard I try, I cannot make my pencil go where it should. The first time that I attempted this project was one such day. I persisted but, by the time I was satisfied with the drawing, I had ruined the surface of the watercolour paper by erasing my many mistakes, so I could not paint on it. I sensibly stopped trying to be creative and did some research instead.

The next day, feeling more creative, I began by drawing over my pencil lines with black, permanent ink. This confirmed that I was happy with the design. I was then able to trace this ink drawing and transfer the composition to a new piece of watercolour paper. This tracing also serves as insurance, should the painting go wrong, as the composition can be redrawn quickly by using the tracing.

You will find a copy of this ink drawing in the appendix; you can use this drawing to create your own tracing. If you prefer to work with a different image size, try photocopying the drawing and printing it off at your required size before tracing it.

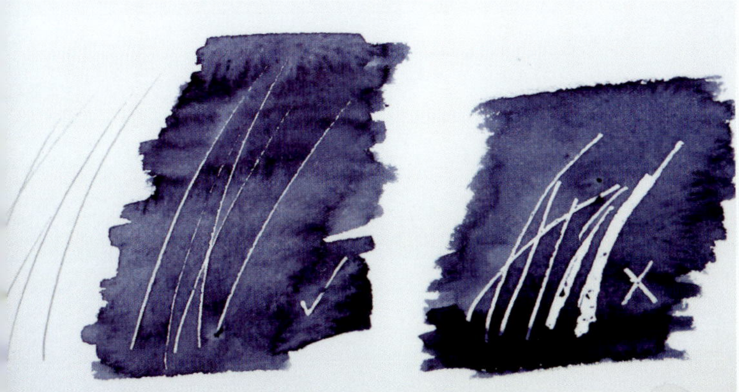

Step 2: Apply the masking fluid, using similar strokes with the pen as those that you would use when drawing with a pencil. (These strokes are shown here against a wash of indigo paint, for clarity.)

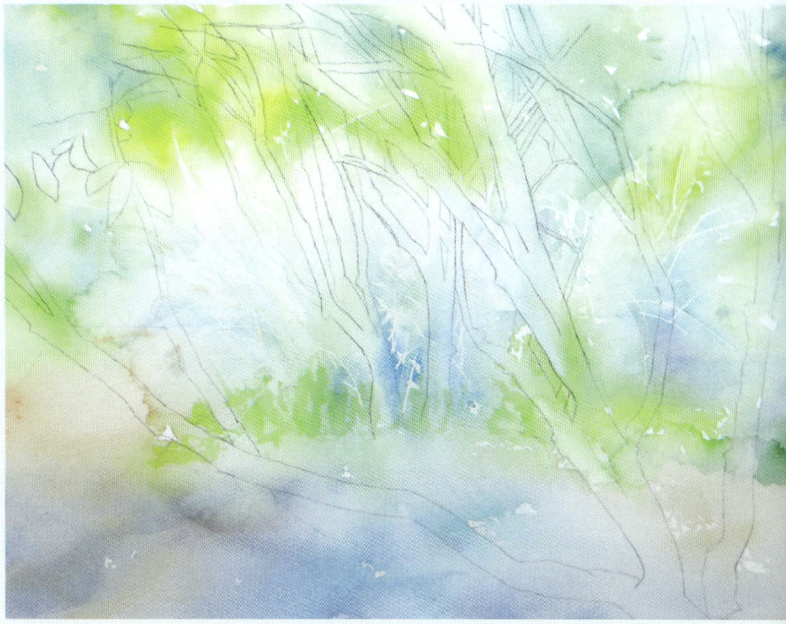

Step 3: Apply washes across the surface of the painting, working wet in wet and varying the colours as you work.

Step 2: By using a mapping pen, apply masking fluid for the depiction of a few grasses and to reserve highlights.

Take care to apply the masking fluid as if you were drawing, using similar hand movements as you would use with a pencil, to achieve the tapering effect needed to depict a blade of grass, that is, lift the pen towards the end of each stroke.

Tip: Practise first, using the same type of watercolour paper that you will be working on for the painting. When the masking fluid is dry, apply a dark paint (for example, indigo) so that the masking-fluid lines show up easily. This practice will give you more confidence when making this painting, as the pale tones and colours used for the texture of the grasses are indistinct and difficult to see.

Step 3: First, apply varied washes wet in wet. Use the photograph to guide the placement of the various mixes of paint. Keep the tones very light, as this layer will provide highlights. Paint straight across the tree trunks, as painting around them will inhibit the making of loose hand movements and the flow of paint. This layer of paint being under later layers of much darker paint on the trunks will add interest and depth.
Keep this wash loose. Work only while the paint is very wet. Once it starts to dry, unwanted cauliflowers may occur, so stop before there is a danger of this happening. Do not worry if the application of paint doesn't work out exactly as you had hoped. This approach involves layering paint, and corrections can be made in subsequent layers; this layering approach is preferable, rather than losing freshness by trying to be too precise and controlled while applying a single wash.

Allow the paint to dry thoroughly.

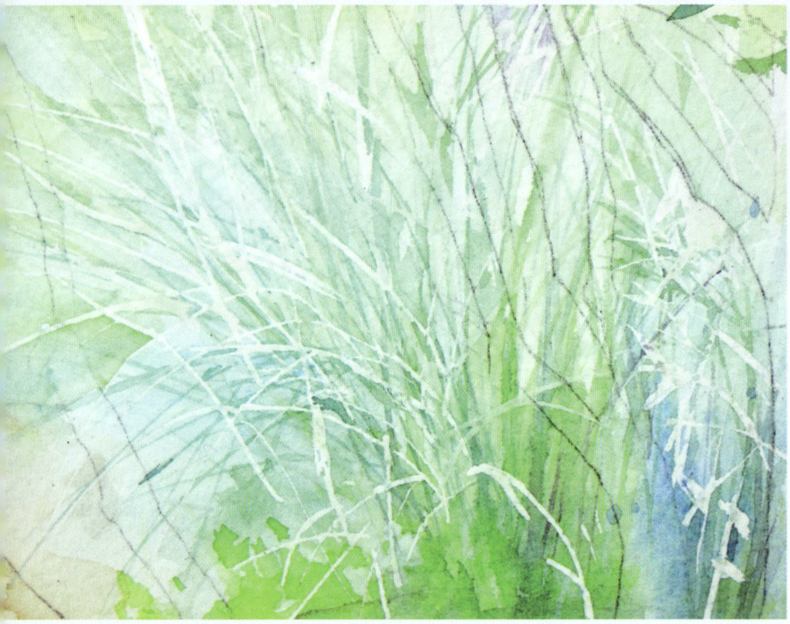

Step 4: Paint in the bright, sunlit grasses under the trees. Using a swordliner brush, apply very pale colour in fine lines.

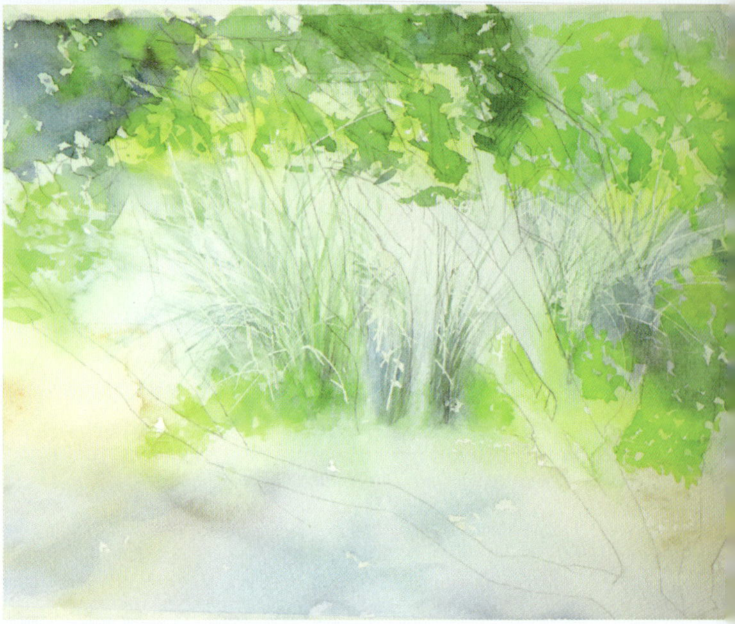

Step 5: Begin to build up the foliage, using brush techniques to hint at leaf shapes, and leaving some of the lighter, lower layer of paint showing through.

Step 4: Over the dry paint, draw in some grasses by using masking fluid applied with a mapping pen or colour shaper. Also reserve a few areas of highlights across the painting by applying masking fluid to those regions, using the photograph as reference for the placement of these highlights.

Paint in the grasses under the trees, using a very pointed brush such as a swordliner or small rigger. Use a mix of May green, Winsor blue and cobalt blue. The paint for the shadows on the right of the image may have a touch of the dioxazine purple added to the mix. Keep the tones light.

It may help to paint some of the grasses, then, while the paint is still wet, paint some more blades of grass by using just water. The water and paint will run together, giving very pale grass-blade shapes.

To avoid overworking this aspect of the painting, do this step by creating a layer, allowing it to dry, then repeating this action, until you are satisfied with the texture of the depicted grasses. Work across the tree trunks so that you do not restrict your hand movements.

Step 5: Apply a second layer of paint to begin building up the foliage, making adjustments as necessary to both tone and colour. Tone will deepen with a second layer of paint, so be careful not to lose highlights. Use a mix of yellow-greens to depict where the light peeps through, as indicated by the photograph. Use a mix of blue-greens in the more shaded areas; including cobalt blue will give a soft haziness.

Work in smaller patches than were covered in step 3, still working wet in wet and dropping colours in according to the colour placement of the reference photograph. Use brush techniques that will begin to hint at the shapes and textures of foliage and leaves, especially at the edges of each patch as you work it.

Do not work too quickly, and take care to leave gaps so that the lighter tones underneath show through. The gaps between leaves are usually quite angular and random, so random shapes left by your brush will be a good way to achieve a natural-looking effect.

Do not rush working this layer. Work quickly enough to avoid tightening up and including too much detail but slowly enough to make deliberate choices of marks and colours.

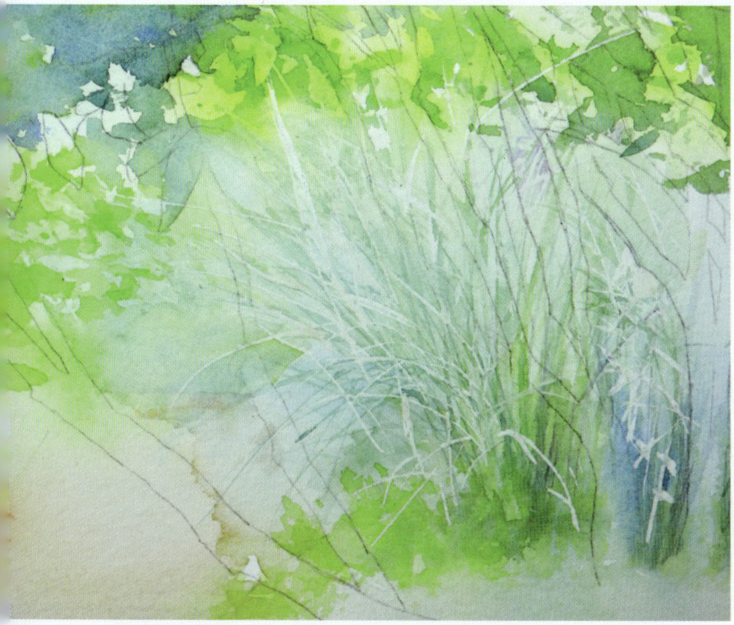

Step 6: Paint in the bush behind the grasses in pale tones, keeping texture and detail to a minimum, to lose detail to increase the impression of bright sunlight shining on to the grasses.

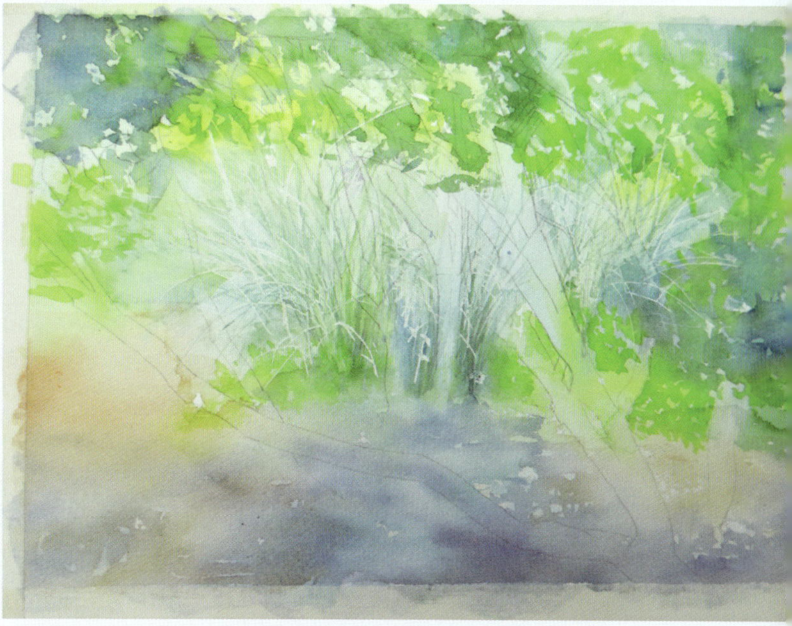

Step 7: Begin to build up the tones in the shaded area under the trees, leaving patches of the first washes showing through.

Step 6: In the photograph, the lightest grasses under the trees are set against a bush that is midtone, which defines the edge of the grasses.

In bright sunlight, detail is often bleached out. By keeping this bush of a paler tone within the painting, softening the detail (compared to that visible in the photograph) and blurring the boundary between the grasses and the bush, the viewer's eye continues to move along the path, and the impression of the scene occurring on a hot, sunny day is increased. Keep the texture of the bush very subtle by applying a little more colour (pale blue-greens and yellow-greens) to this area, adding just enough paint so that the masked grasses will show up.

Step 7: Begin to build up the midtones and textures across the lower part of the painting, by applying a layer (a glaze) of slightly thicker paint.

Add a layer of colour to the region of shade under the trees. Use a mix of dioxazine purple and blue-browns, allowing the colours to blend on the paper. Use browner hues where the path is sunlit and bluer colours where the shadow is deep and rich, under the trees. Again, take care to allow patches of the first layer of lighter tones to show through, to negatively paint the dappled light coming through the trees.

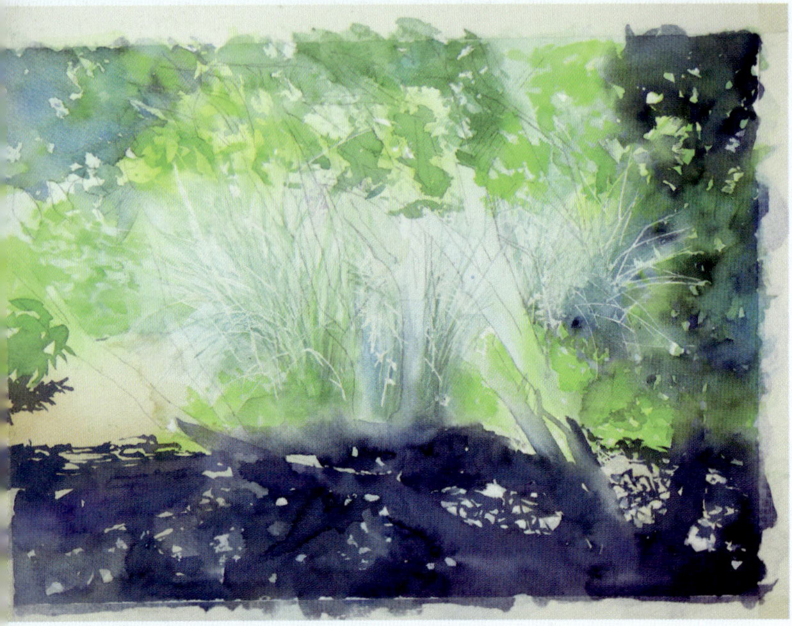

Step 8: Begin to add some rich, dark tones to the shadowy areas, varying the colours as you work.

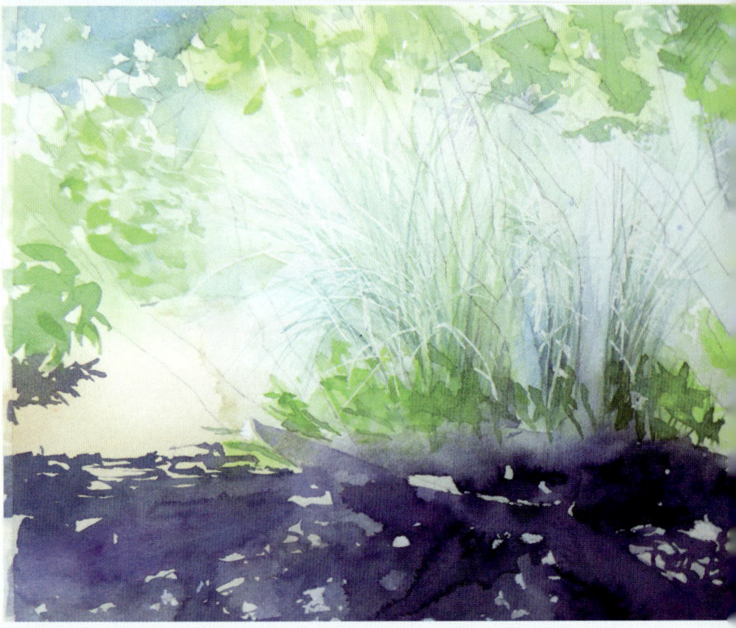

Step 9: Using midtone greens, add shadows at the bases of the grasses.

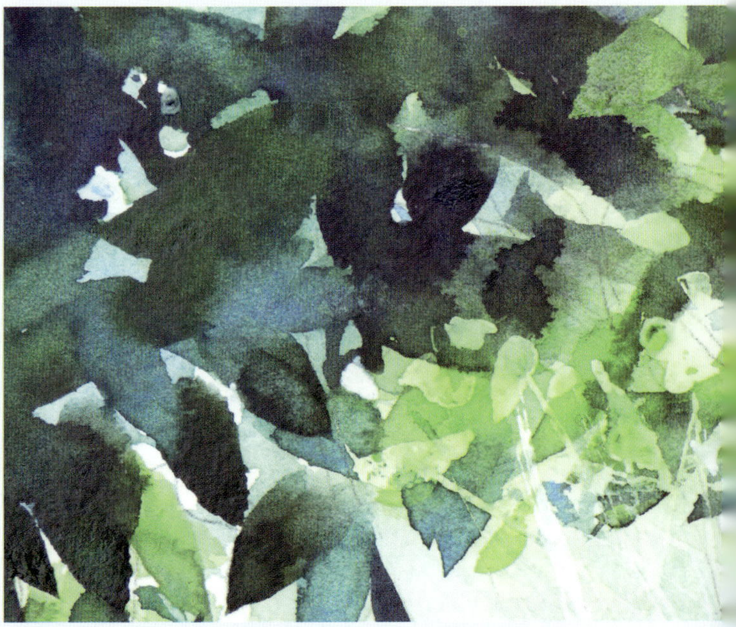

Step 10: Using a variety of dark greens, paint in the foliage on the trees.

Step 8: This step requires you to have a degree of boldness, to apply a rich glaze of strong colour. Using midtones to dark tones of a purple–blue–grey mix, paint in strong shadows under the trees. Work slowly, negatively painting patches of sunlight by allowing some of the paler layers underneath to show through. Do not rush this layer, otherwise you risk losing the depiction of the dappled patches of sunlight! Continue working up the right-hand side of the image, adding some green to the mix. This will be the final layer in this area, but keep the mark-making quite loose, as detail here will draw the viewer's eye away from the main focal point of the painting.

Step 9: The grasses will need to look as if they are growing, not floating; there needs to be a transition between the dark glaze of the shadows and the depicted very pale, sunlit grasses. Using rich midtones in a range of greens, paint in the shadowy area at the base of the grasses.

Step 10: Using a range of greens, and strong dark tones across all of the colours, paint in the leaves across the top of the painting. Use brush techniques that easily make leaf shapes (*see* the section 'Watercolour: Tips and techniques' in Chapter 2, Materials and Techniques). Change colours frequently, washing the brush between the use of different colours, to keep the colours fresh. Allow the shapes to overlap while the paint is wet, so that soft edges are created. Also paint on to dry paper so that hard edges appear, making definite leaf shapes, giving context to the other marks.

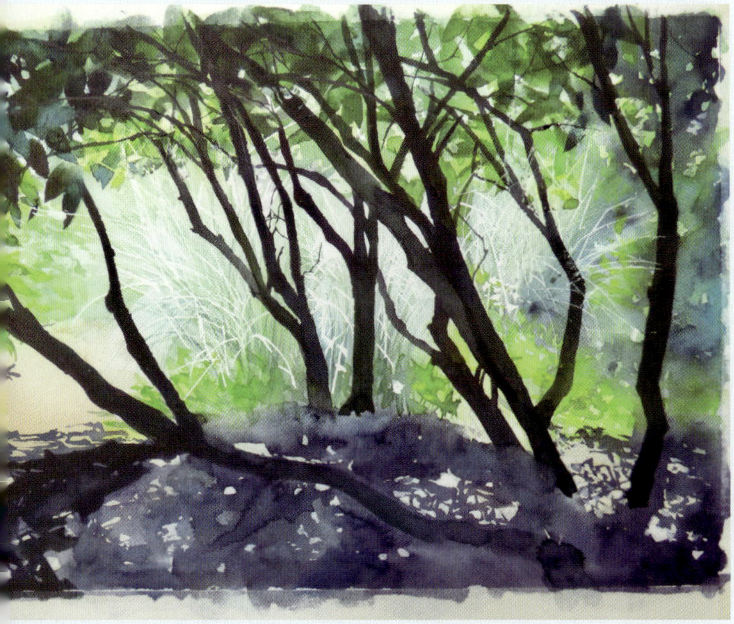

Step 11: Remove the masking fluid, paint in the tree trunks, and add a final glaze for the depiction of shadows on the ground.

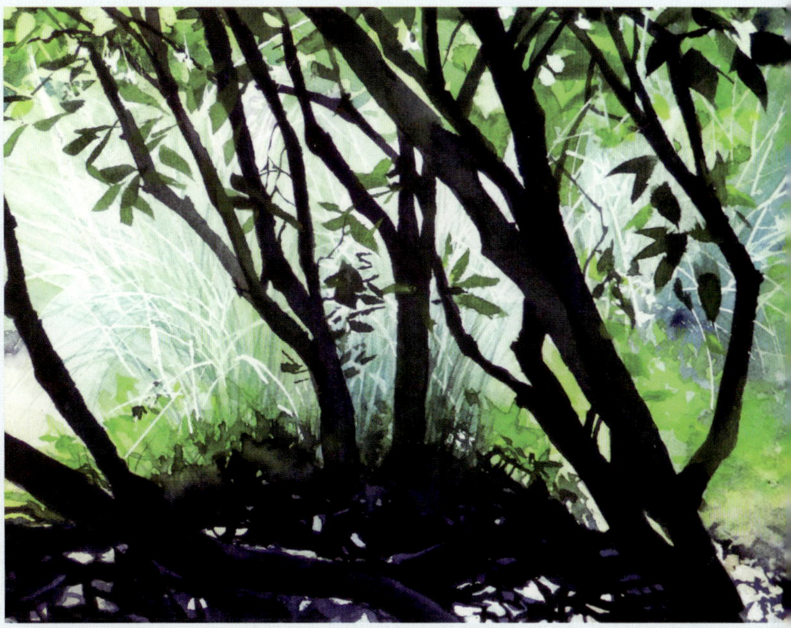

Step 12: Complete the painting by adding well-defined leaf shapes in rich, dark tones across the grasses.

Step 11: Remove the masking fluid that was applied for the depiction of grasses and the reservation of highlights, by gently rubbing the dried masking fluid with your fingers. Using dioxazine purple, indigo, cobalt blue and sap green, mix a range of colours in the darkest tones possible. Choosing different colours from within the mix as you work, paint in the tree trunks and branches. Be bold: these trunks need to be extremely dark!

Continue to paint in the final glaze for the depiction of the shadows across the ground. Again, leave small patches of the lower glazes showing through, to increase the effect of tiny patches of sunlight on the ground.

Take care that you keep everything dark enough. In places, in the reference photograph, the edges of the tree trunks are lost in the shadows, so be careful that you match the tones well on the painting.

Step 12: Finally, stand back to assess the painting. Make any final adjustment to colour and tone, before adding the final touches.

Using very dark tones, paint in some shapes along the top edge of the shadows on the ground and at the base of the grasses.

To complete the painting, paint in some well-defined leaf shapes around the branches and tree trunks, using the very darkest green mixes. Place some of these leaves across the very bright grasses; the very wide tonal range in this region of the painting will enhance both the brilliance of the grasses and the depth of the shadows.

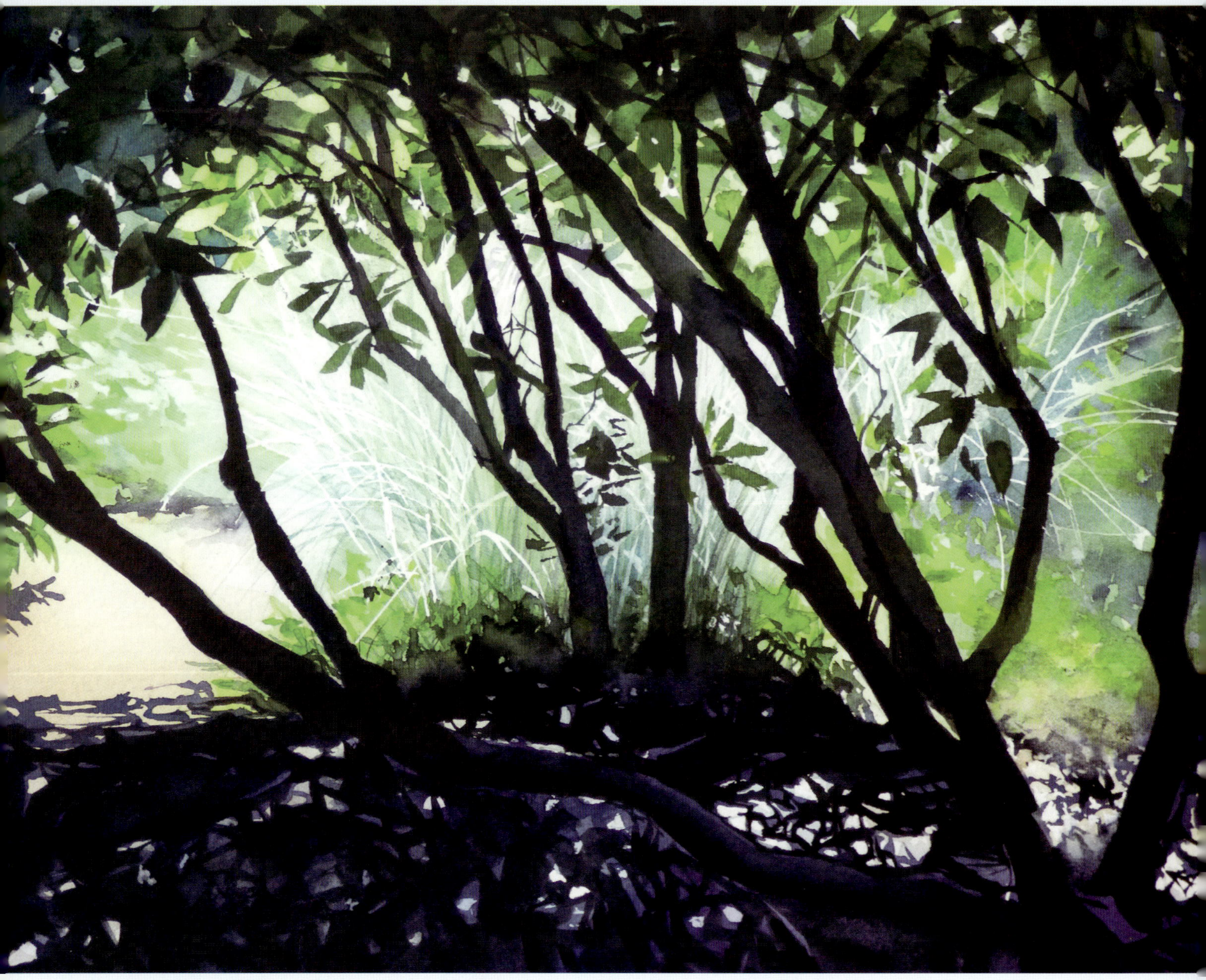

The finished painting: *Summer Shade*, watercolour, 29cm × 21cm (11½in × 8¼in), Siân Dudley.

PROJECT

Summer Fields

Rob Dudley

The Inspiration

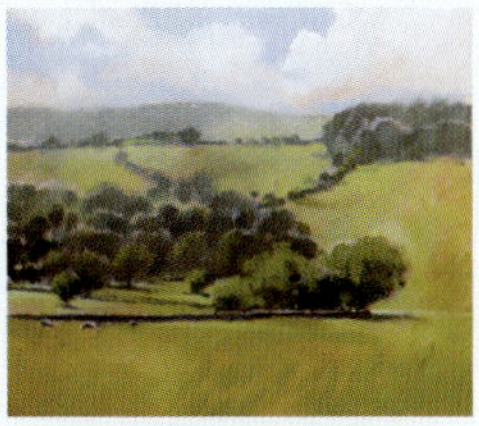

I am fortunate to live on the southern side of Dartmoor, an area rich in artistic pickings, and I can always find an excuse to pop up on to the moor with paints and brushes at the ready.

Devon is known for many things: its famous cream teas (remember, cream then jam, as is the Devon way), cider and Devon lanes. In parts of the county, Devon lanes are deep and precariously narrow, with high banks on each side, and can often feel quite enclosed. So, when a gap or the opening to a field appears, I will always take a moment to look at the view. Stopping on this occasion, I was met with a view across fields towards some trees, more fields and, in the distance, the open moor. Apart from the obvious beauty that lay before me, I was also attracted to the variation visible within the greens of the scene.

There were bright yellow-greens seen in the foreground field; strong, warm summer greens and blue shadows seen within the nearest trees; and softer, pale grey-green trees seen in the distance. It was this variation that I decided to make my painting about; one might even consider it to be an exercise in green rather than a painting.

Developing the Idea

When working *en plein air*, it is as important for you to spend time planning and developing the idea as it is when working in the studio: in many ways, more so! One might think that, with time against you, it would be imperative to get some paint down quickly. I would advise caution against this approach. I have seen too many paintings started without proper consideration and preparation, resulting in disappointing messes.

In *Summer Fields*, I wanted to observe and record simply and directly the change of colour and tone within the trees and the landscape before me: nothing more, nothing less. While making all of my decisions when planning the painting and when applying the water-mixable oil paints that I chose, I would have this simple aim in mind. Adding to this that, when working on location, time and therefore speed is of the essence, I couldn't get too caught up in detail, as the light might change or the weather might close in, and what made me reach for my brushes in the first place might have been gone forever.

Designing the Painting

Layout

Even when working *en plein air*, it is still essential to consider layout. I always carry a small sketch pad and will produce some rapid thumbnail sketches before working on a prepared panel for the actual painting. It is far better to work out the design, the format of the painting and the placement of tone in advance, rather than discovering halfway through the painting that the design is flawed.

When painting outside, I carry a number of differently sized boards to work on. These range from small 15cm × 20cm (6in × 8in) boards, to 20cm × 30cm (8in ×11¾in) boards and up to 40cm × 30cm (15¾in × 11¾in) boards. Sometimes, even if time is short, a larger board can be easier to work on, as it allows for larger, less fiddly, broader brush movements to be made.

Tone

Summer Fields is essentially a tonal painting, made from very few colours and some closely related tones. The tonal range from foreground to background is quite narrow, and within the middle-ground trees even narrower still. For the sense of distance to be created within the painting, the tones would have to be carefully assessed and be equally carefully rendered.

Colour

I try to keep my painting kit to the bare minimum when painting outside, carrying as few brushes, pens, pencils, paints and panels as I can get away with. Therefore, my colours would be mixed from the few that I carry. The colours haven't been chosen at random or scooped up from my studio table as I pack my sketching bag. Quite the opposite; they have been selected to allow me to mix the broadest range of colours from the least number of paint tubes.

Texture

This wasn't to be a painting about the textures within the landscape. Any texture would be picked up from the prepared board itself and texture was not something that I would concern myself with when making this painting.

Painting the Image

Materials and equipment

- Gessoed MDF board:
  - Prepared with a ground of a mix of French ultramarine blue and burnt sienna, 30cm × 25cm (11¾ × 9¾in)
- Oil-painting brushes:
  - No. 1 round
  - No. 4 flat
  - No. 8 filbert
- Water-mixable oil colours:
  - Cadmium yellow light
  - French ultramarine blue
  - Sap green
  - Titanium white
- Sketch pad
- 2B pencil
- Palette
- Palette knife
- Dipper for water
- Field easel

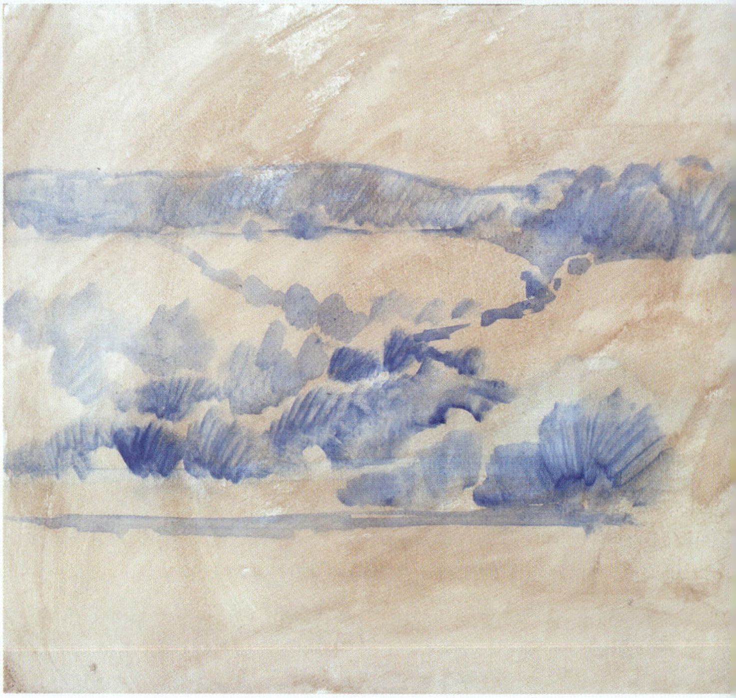

Step 1: Loosely sketch in the key elements of the landscape.

Step 1: Based on your separate thumbnail pencil sketch and with a dilute mix of French ultramarine blue, loosely sketch in the key elements of the design, by using a No. 1 round. Don't try to include any detail; establish the big shapes, not the small details. Consider this step as a way of discovering how the shapes interlock and relate to each other.

Give some indication of the tonal arrangement within the painting: the lights and darks. Any mistakes can be wiped off with an old rag and correct applications be made in their place.

Such a dilute mix as used for this step won't take long to dry, allowing you to soon move on to the next step.

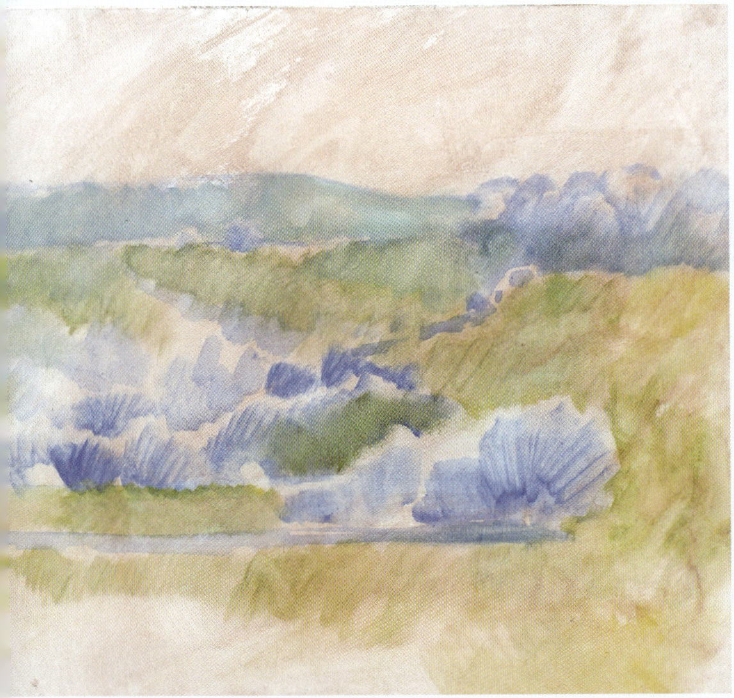

Step 2: Add the initial shapes and colours.

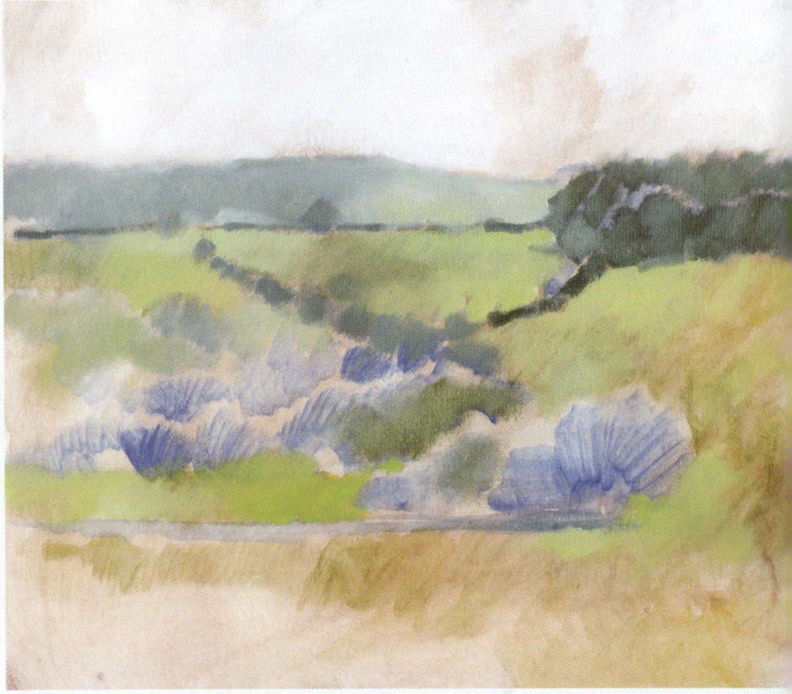

Step 3: Paint in the distant hills, fields and copse.

Step 2: Using cadmium yellow light, sap green, French ultramarine blue and titanium white, begin to block in the basic shapes within the design. Move around the painting as you go; don't concentrate on one area alone, as this can make it difficult to assess the overall relationships of both tone and colour across the whole of the painting.

Be careful not to add too much paint; it is preferable to scuff the paint on by using the side of the brush. Too much paint easily and often results in control being lost, as the painting's surface becomes slippery.

Step 3: In order to assess the tones within the landscape more easily, add some titanium white with a touch of French ultramarine blue, and loosely brush in the sky by using the No. 4 flat. This will give a base against which to compare and relate other tones as the painting progresses.

Begin to introduce more colour, and more paint, for depiction of the distant hills, fields, copse and individual trees. Use various mixes of cadmium yellow light, sap green, French ultramarine blue and titanium white. Use more white in the mix to reduce the strength of the tone when painting in the distant hills. If the mix for the distant hills is too tonally strong, the hills will appear to come too far forward, and the sense of recession and distance within the painting will be lost.

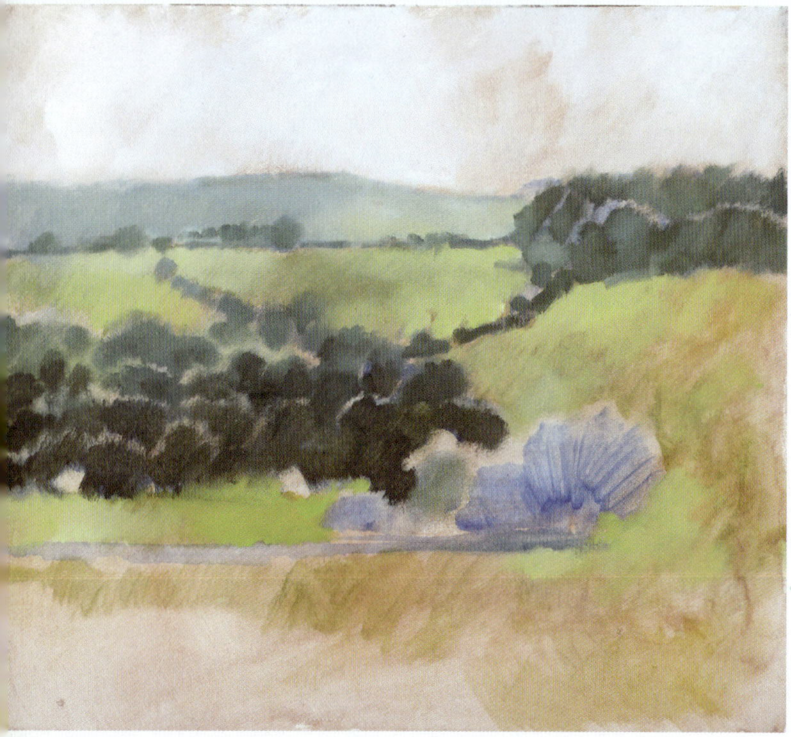

Step 4: Build up structure.

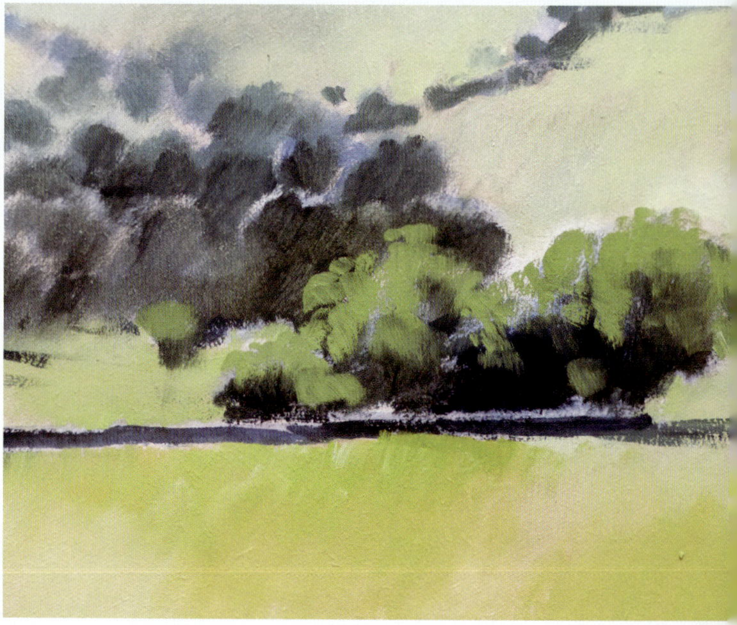

Step 5: Paint in the main trees and finishing touches.

Step 4: Move around the painting, strengthening colours and tones by using more paint and tonally stronger mixes than those used in step 4. Note how the tones are paler in the distance, becoming stronger as they move towards the foreground. The trees are painted by using a brush known as a filbert. Its rounded tip makes it perfect for use when you are trying to paint the shapes of summer trees. Indicate some of the field boundaries, the walls and the bushes with the same mixes of paint.

Step 5: Using a dark mix of sap green and French ultramarine blue, paint in the main trees. Allow this applied paint to become slightly tacky – this normally takes only a few minutes – before painting the sunlit parts of the trees with a mix of sap green and cadmium yellow light. Use a well-loaded brush, and pull or drag the brush over the underpainting.

In order to bring a little life to the painting, use a dark mix and a small brush to paint in a few sheeplike shapes. When these applications are slightly dry, paint in some white, to indicate the sunlight hitting the backs of the depicted sheep.

Indicate some highlights on the foreground wall with a mix of white that includes a touch of sap green and French ultramarine blue, to grey it slightly. The brightest white should be reserved for the depictions of the sunlit sheep, not the wall.

Strengthen the blue of the sky, leaving some cloudlike shapes unpainted. These shapes can then be picked out with white, particularly towards the top of the clouds.

Note how the original coloured ground shows through in some parts of the painting and helps to tie the work together as a whole.

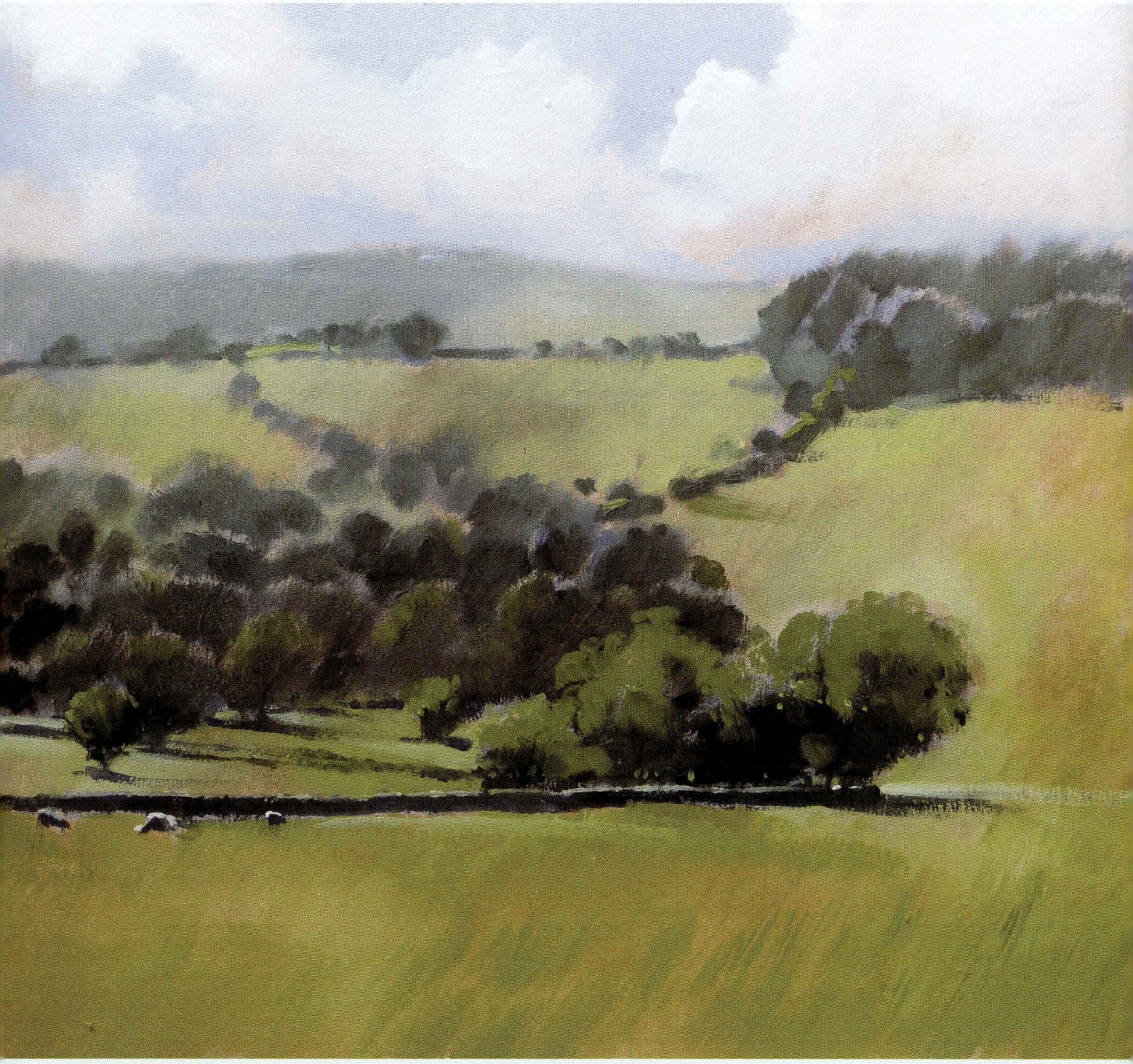

The finished painting: *Summer Fields*, water-mixable oils on board, 30cm × 25cm (11¾in × 9¾in), Rob Dudley.

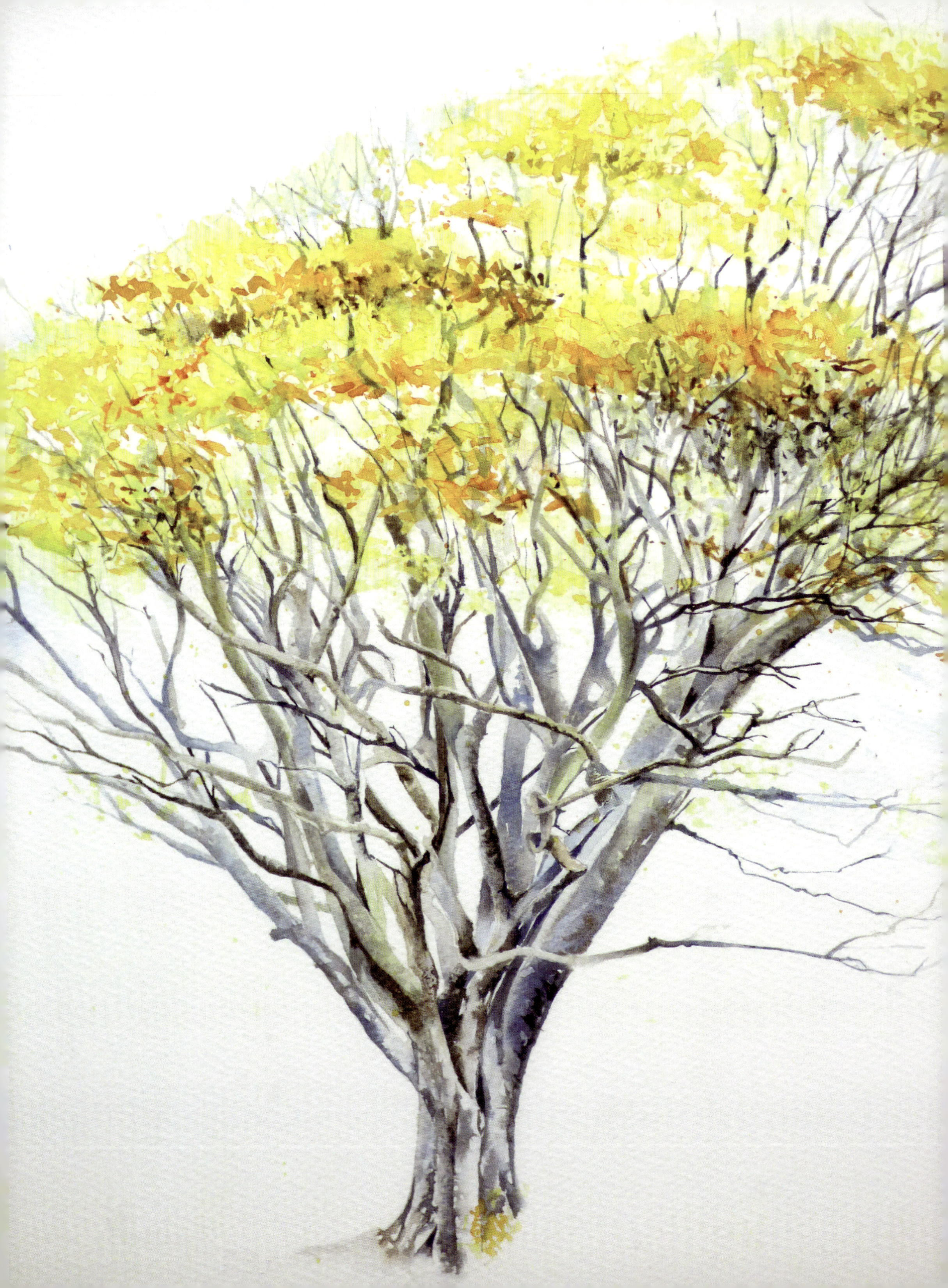

Chapter 7

Autumn

If just one word could be used to describe autumn, it would have to be 'colour'! Who could not fail to be captivated by the reds, golds, yellows and russets of a bright autumnal day?

As the trees slip from late summer towards autumn, many will change in colour from dusty greens to reddy golds. In parks and gardens, from field to moor, this transformation seems to be the trees letting out all of the captured summer sunshine in one final performance, before winter cloaks the land.

For the artist, the autumnal colour is an undeniable inspiration. Once again, it requires a change of palette to properly portray the season. On bright days, the softer colours of summer seem to need spicing up to achieve the fieriness of autumn, to be both warm and vibrant. Try adding colours such as quinacridone gold, green gold, transparent yellow and translucent orange to your palette. On cooler, misty days, perhaps later in the season, the trees can appear to be of soft, warm browns and russets; paints such as burnt sienna and cobalt blue will soften the other colours as you mix them in.

When out gathering information, take paints with you, so that you can make colour notes. Practise mixing the more obvious hues, but look too for less-expected hues. In spite of orange and blue being complementary colours, and hence easily assimilated into the design of a painting, one of the great joys of autumn is to see brightly lit yellow-gold trees set against dark indigo-grey skies. Look again too at the colours of the tree trunks; on sunny days, the trunks reflect the colour of the remaining leaves, themselves taking on golden hues.

Keen observation will reveal that it is not just colours that alter the appearance of the trees. As the season progresses, the leaf distribution through the canopy changes too; twigs, branches and trunks hidden by the dense summer foliage are revealed once more as the leaves fall. This changing leaf distribution varies hugely from species to species, and also as a result of location. Some trees lose their top leaves first, while others can be bare near the trunk, with a few stalwart leaves clinging to the twigs at the very ends of the branches. A tree can lose all of its leaves on the side facing the prevailing wind and yet remain almost fully clothed in leaf on the sheltered side.

The trick is not to make assumptions but to get out into the landscape to make your own observations.

The Big Beech Tree: Autumn, watercolour, 29cm × 38cm (11½in × 15in), Siân Dudley.

THE BIG BEECH TREE: AUTUMN

Siân Dudley

I have loved the grandeur and stature of this tree since I first set eyes on it, many years ago. I am particularly fond of the trunk, the huge size of the branches, and the very obvious wind pruning, which has clearly taken place over decades!

Standing in the lane looking up at this tree, I am impressed by its height. On the particular autumn day that inspired this painting, I was very aware of the leaf distribution, as yet untouched by a seasonal storm. The leaves lay in golden, horizontal bands across the branches. Many had fallen already, allowing the outer branches to reappear above each band, as the branches reached upwards. I was attracted by the contrasts between the horizontal and vertical elements.

The sun shone brightly through the remaining leaves, generating a golden glow on parts of the trunk. In the centre of the tree, the combination of thick branches and remaining leaves produced deep, indigo shadows. The tones emphasized the depth and girth of this grand, old tree, while the complementary colours emphasized the autumnal glow.

I decided to work in watercolour, as I felt that the qualities of this medium best expressed the fragility of the attachment of the remaining leaves and would suit the expression of the subtle blends of colour that I had observed for the trunk and branches. The colours that I had observed excited me, so I decide to enhance them slightly in the painting.

PROJECT

Tennis Club Trees

Siân Dudley

The Inspiration

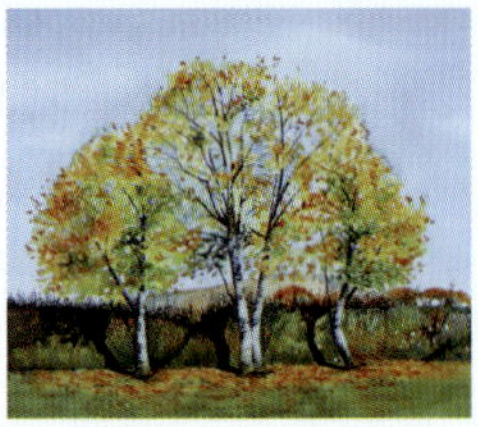

Autumn colour is always inspiring, but sometimes the complexity of a woodland or a stand of trees can be overwhelming. When I came across this little group of trees at our local tennis club, I was impressed by the simplicity of the arrangement, which would allow a simple composition to be made and enable me to concentrate on other aspects of the painting. This project is included here so that you can focus on finding paints to portray the autumn colours that delight us so much, while also practising a range of brushstrokes.

What follows is a step-by-step project with instructions for how the final image was produced. These instructions are a good starting point. However, being for a simple composition, this is an ideal project to repeat, while changing colours, tones or the way that you apply the paint, and so take steps towards developing your own style.

Tip: Make a tracing of your drawing so that you can easily make another painting, concentrating on the colours and textures, rather than spending time drawing out the composition again.

Developing the Idea

There were various aspects of the scene that were interesting. Being able to see under the tree canopy to the top of a distant hill was a pleasant change from the trees being set against a hillside. The way that the canopies of the trees in the field beyond echoed the shape of the hill in the distance was amusing (keeping it simple, they reminded me of umbrellas). The Devon hedge immediately behind the trunks provided an area of deeper tones to exaggerate the light colour of the trunks, and the play of shadows across the trunks, branches and hedge added interest. A Devon 'hedge' is usually an overgrown stone wall (drivers, beware!), so painting this in slightly darker tones seemed fitting.

This image also lends itself to practising a technique for painting of the sky holes in a tree without using masking fluid, while maintaining a relaxed, loose approach.

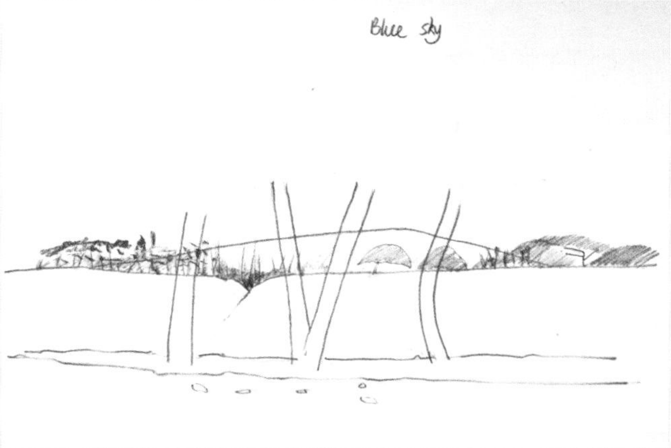

A quick sketch to note the shapes of the tree trunks.

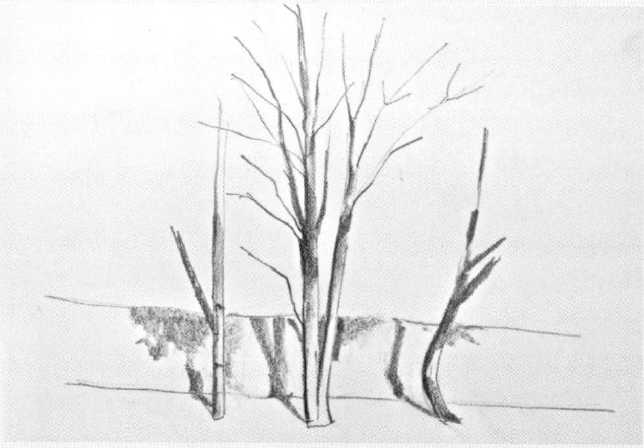

A thumbnail sketch to help me to design the layout of the painted image.

A quick sketch to note the shape of the shadow along the ground and up the bank.

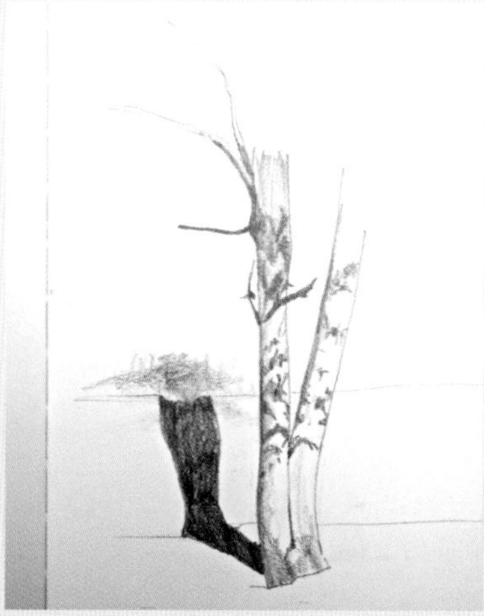

Information Gathering

This stage consisted of drawing a few very quick sketches, allowing me to to make notes of the shapes of the tree trunks, the shadows that they cast and the texture of the bark. These were used alongside photographs as references for the painting.

Designing the Painting

Layout

The trees themselves make a delightful group, so there is no need to rearrange them on the page. In spite of the obvious simplicity of this arrangement, a quick thumbnail sketch was made to ensure that the concept of being able to see the top of the hillside between the tree trunks would work well on the page and that there was still room to place the trees in the field behind, along the top of the hedge, in a manner that was balanced and visually pleasing.

Tone

Autumnal colours are bright, and need to be as such in this painting and, as a tree loses its leaves, the canopy become less dense; keeping the tones light at the tops of the trees would bring out these two features. To emphasize the brightness of the autumnal colours and to give weight to the tree trunks, darker tones are required under the trees, in particular where the shadows fall.

Colour

The autumnal colours were the main inspiration for this painting, so the starting point for the paints to be used has to be the colours for the leaves: a mix of yellows, golds and light browns. These colours will be emphasize by setting them against a bright, blue sky, such as we often see on crisp, autumn days. The following selection of colours over the page, made a lovely range of autumnal greens, without the need to add any other colours to the palette.

Treat the paint list below as a starting point. Remember that one of the reasons for the simplicity of this project is to allow easy experimentation with different colours and textural marks. Try making choices based on your personal preferences or simply on what paint colours you already own!

Texture

This project includes very simple mark-making, using brushes to make loose, dabby marks, to represent leaves, and broad wet-in-wet washes. Experiment with your brushes to find shapes and marks that you feel would be appropriate for this image. Trying to make this painting several times using different brushes and marks will increase your repertoire for those more complicated images!

Technique to practise

On a sheet of watercolour paper of the same type that you intend to use for the painting, practise making leaf shapes with different brushes and hand movements. *See* Chapter 2, Materials and Techniques, for inspiration and advice.

Painting the Image

Materials and equipment

- Watercolour paper:
  - Bockingford NOT 300gsm/140lb, stretched and taped to a board
- Watercolour brushes:
  - Da Vinci Series 35, size 4
  - Swordliners, medium and small
  - Daggers, medium and small
- Artist-quality watercolours:
  - Burnt sienna
  - Cobalt blue
  - Lemon yellow
  - New gamboge
  - Paris blue (Schmincke)
  - Quinacridone gold
  - Ultramarine blue
- 4B pencil
- Eraser
- Tracing paper
- Black pen
- Palette
- Kitchen roll

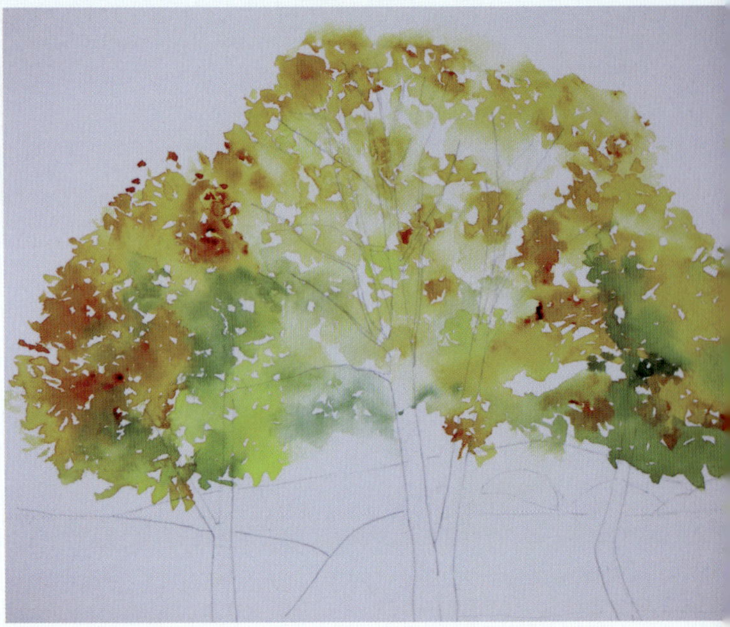

Step 1: Apply the first layer of paint, varying colour and tone as you work.

Step 1: Draw in the image with pencil, using outlines to place the trees, hillside and vegetated bank on the paper. Keep this drawing as minimalistic as possible, as detail will be added by using paint.

In the palette, prepare mixes of lemon yellow, new gamboge and quinacridone gold. In a separate well, prepare a mix of quinacridone gold and cobalt blue.

Using a dagger, apply the paint with a dabbing action, changing the angle of the brush to give differently shaped marks. Choose to use different colours and tones from your mixes as you work.

Do not work too quickly, and remember to make sure that some paper is left clear of paint, to avoid the trees becoming one amorphous mass.

For some areas, work on to dry paper. In other areas, before applying paint to them, dampen the paper with clean water first, using the same brush and hand movements as will be used for the paint application. It is important to do this so that, as the paint flows into the wet areas, the shapes remain appropriate and do not become a flat wash.

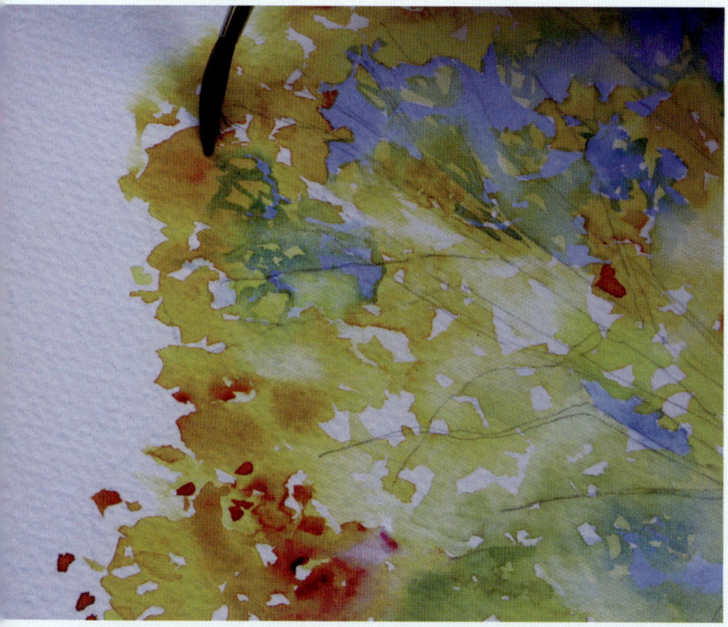

Step 2: Using blues, paint in the sky holes within the trees' foliage. Use the blue paint to negatively paint in some yellow leaf shapes, using glazing to create some green shapes in the canopy.

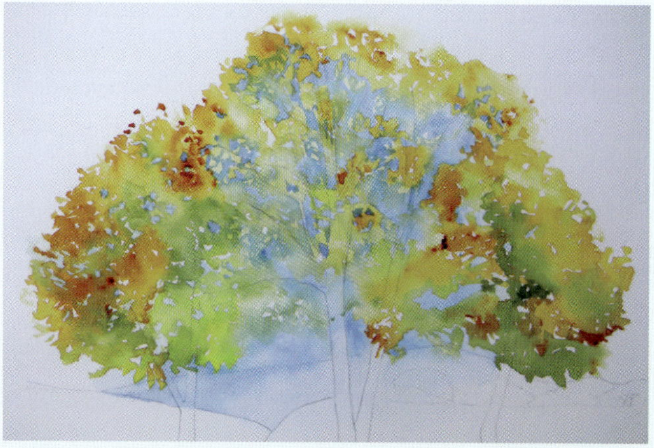

Step 3: Underwash the distant hill with blue paint.

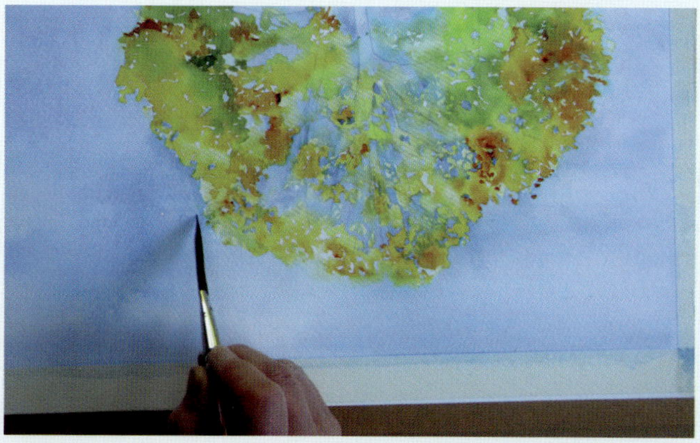

Step 4: Turn the board upside down to paint the sky by using wet-in-wet washes.

Step 2: Using Paris blue and cobalt blue, prepare some blue paint of the correct tone for the depiction of the sky behind the tree. Begin by filling the sky holes, that is, the gaps between the leaves.

Continue applying this colour over the yellows that were applied in step 1. As you do this, negatively paint some leaf shapes, allowing the blue to glaze over the paint below, to alter both colour and tone within the depicted canopy. Use clean water to soften the edges of some of the shapes, creating a variety of hard and soft edges.

Step 3: Paint a wash of blue across the region of the hill in the distance. Carry this wash across the tree trunk, as it will enhance the shadows that will be painted later on. This will add an element of aerial perspective, by replicating the blueing of colour that we experience when looking over distance in a landscape.

Step 4: The sky needs to be depicted by using a gradated wash. If painted from the top down, this may result in a hard line across the top of the depicted leaf canopy. The solution for this is to turn your board upside down and position it at a slight angle before applying this wash.

Wet the paper from along the top of the bank and across the top of the leaves. Using the prepared mix of blue paint, apply a wet-in-wet wash of paint. Where the sky meets the bank, start applying the wash at the line of the bank. Although there is water across part of the tree canopy, drop in the paint outside of the line of leaves. The paint will flow very slightly up the slope to give a soft edge where the leaves meet the sky, without developing a hard edge.

Continue applying the wash across the area of the sky. Use any uneven patches to make clouds. By lifting out some of the paint with a slightly damp brush, you will achieve lovely, soft clouds; for more-definite clouds, try lifting out the damp paint with kitchen roll.

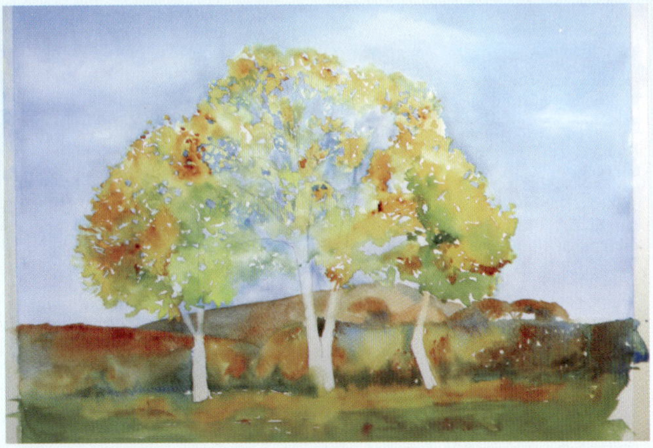

Step 5: Using a variety of colours, paint in the distant hill. Use the same colours in slightly deeper tones as underwashes for the foreground.

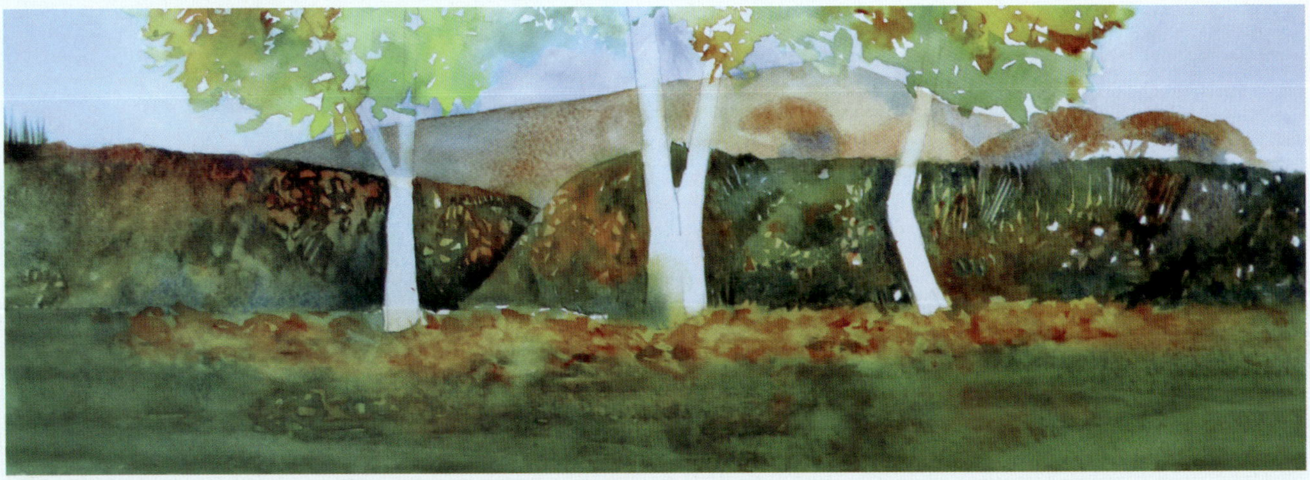

Step 6: Using a variety of colours and brushmarks, paint in the vegetation of the bank.

Step 5: In the palette, mix up a range of colours in fairly pale tones.

Turn the painting back to being the right way up. Wet the paper from the top line of the hill down to the bottom of the paper, but keep the tree trunks dry.

Using pale blues and browns, apply a variegated wash to the distant hillside.

Using the same colour mixes but in deeper tones, bring these colours into the region of the vegetated bank. Allowing the colours to mix on the paper, apply the blues where the shadows need to be depicted. As you come down the page, introduce yellows and greens, aiming for a patch of yellows to be the base layer of paint where the lying, fallen leaves are to be painted.

While painting in the bank, using the same tones, add some tree shapes to the middle ground, pulling a little paint down to join the bank.

By not working too quickly, you can allow textures to appear in the paint, for example, created by cauliflowers, which will add to the perceived textures of the grass and vegetated bank.

Step 6: Working slowly across the page, and choosing different colours from your mixes as you go, continue to paint in the vegetated bank. Vary your brushmarks, allowing some of the underwashes to show through.

Note that masking fluid has not been used here; the underwashes show through as a result of negatively painting around shapes with the darker tones and different colours. (Applying masking fluid on the first, dry wash is an alternative way of reserving the underwashes.)

Using a range of deeper golds and yellows mixed in the palette, paint in the fallen leaves by applying leaf-shaped marks under the depicted trees.

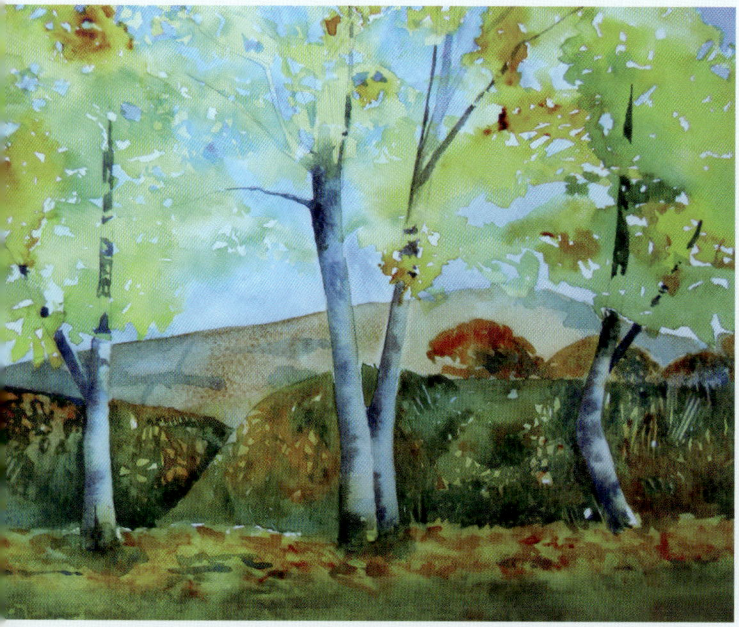

Step 7: Paint in the tree trunks and the main branches.

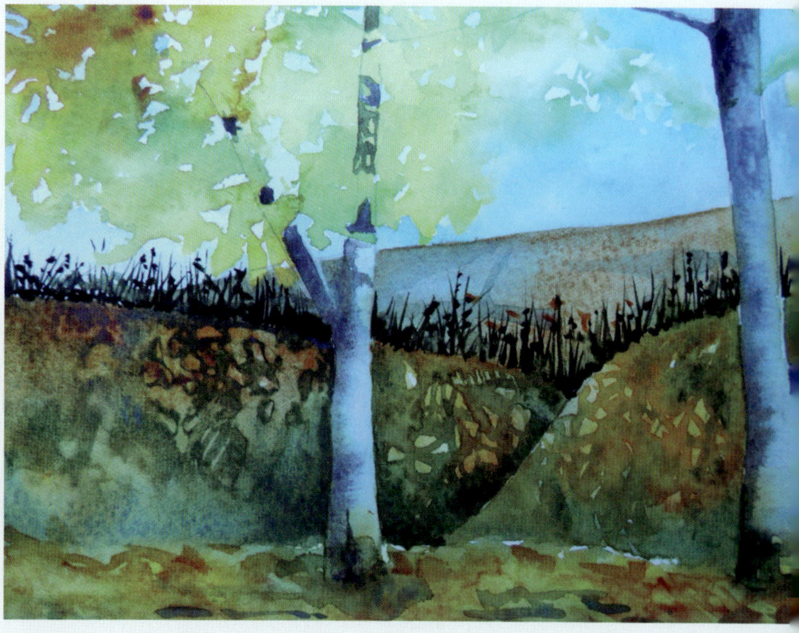

Step 8: Paint in the silhouettes of the grasses along the top of the bank.

Step 7: Paint in the tree trunks by using a silvery grey mix that is made with cobalt blue and burnt sienna. Have a darker tone of the same colour ready to drop in down one side of each of the trunks while the first wash is still damp. This will bleed across the trunk, giving it a rounded appearance. As the first wash begins to dry, the darker mix can also be dropped in to produce cauliflowers, to give the bark some texture.

Using the same mix, paint in some of the main branches. Lift the brush off as you move along each branch, to leave the impression of leaf shapes extending across the branch.

Step 8: Using a thick mix of dark colours, paint in the silhouettes of the grasses along the top of the bank. Take care to avoid painting across leaves that hang below this line. I have used a very dark green here, mixed from quinacridone gold, burnt sienna and ultramarine blue. Although it is very dark, it is not black, and there is variety within the mix.

Step 9: Paint in more branches. Take care to leave gaps along their length, as a representation of branches disappearing behind leaves. It is almost impossible to follow a single branch from the trunk to the branch's tip! Use a dark mix of greys, and take the opportunity to add some of this mix to the trunks, for the creation of more texture in the bark.

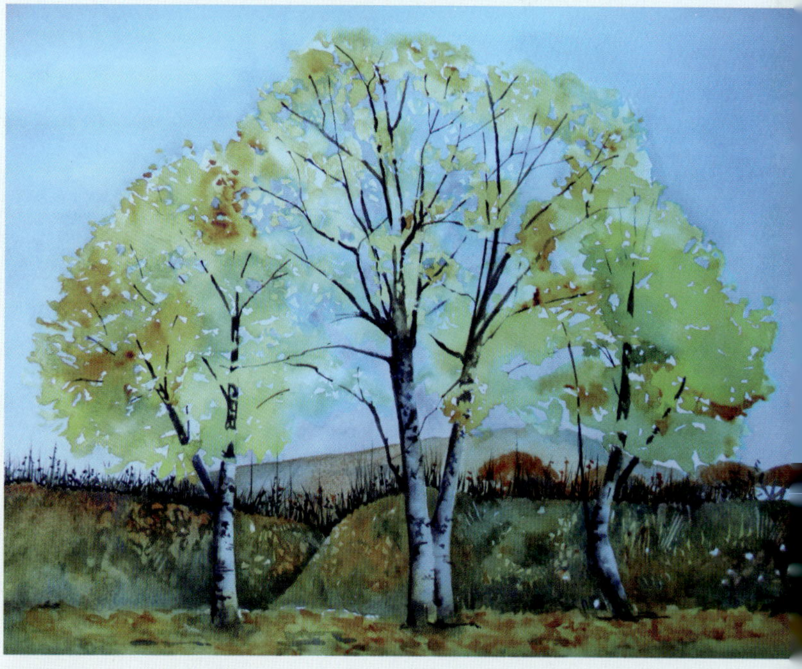

Step 9: Paint in more branches.

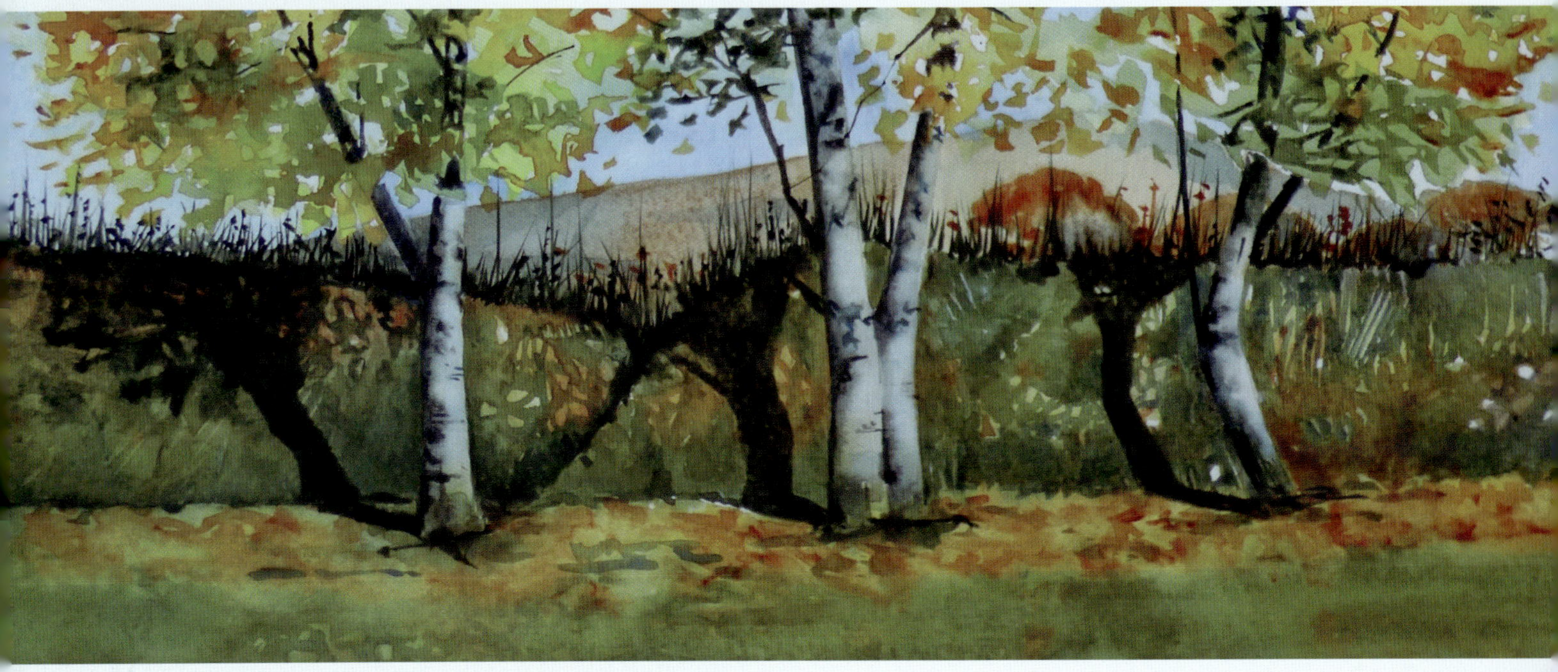

Step 10: Paint in the shadows cast against the bank by the trunks.

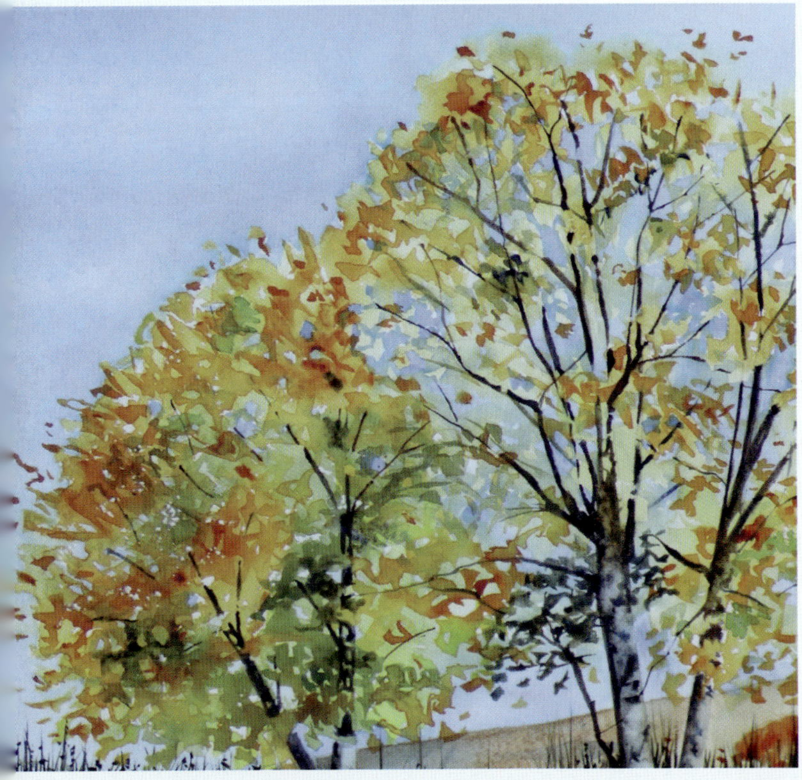

Step 11: Paint in more leaves, to complete the painting.

Step 10: Take courage, and paint in the trees' shadows that fall across the bank. This needs to be done boldly and with thick, dark tones. These shadows will describe the shape of the bank.

Paint the shadows confidently, as being too tentative will result in disturbance of the washes underneath. At this stage, you do not want to make a mess! Do not be overly concerned if the shadows are not exactly the shapes that you intended them to be. Your viewer will simply read the bank as being of a slightly different shape.

Step 11: Using a wide range of yellows, golds and light yellow-browns prepared in your palette, add more leaves. Vary the tone as you go – some of these leaves can be quite dark – and vary the brushmarks too. Finally, add some marks to depict dark-green leaves in the shadowy areas.

As you work, take care not to cover up the sky holes, and be very careful not to add too many leaves. Remember, these are autumnal trees that have already lost a lot of foliage, so you do not want the canopy to look too dense.

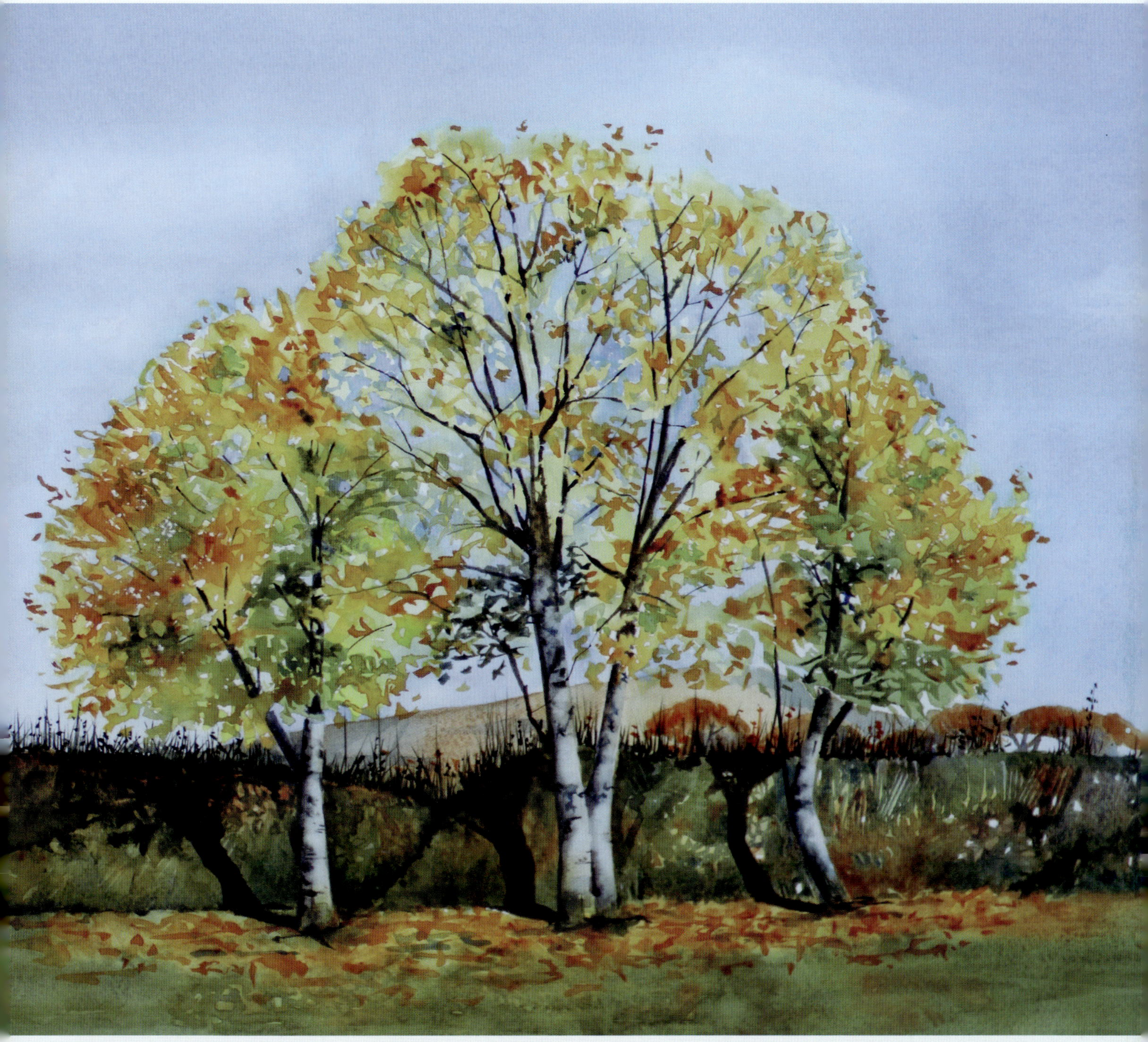

The finished painting: *Tennis Club Trees*, watercolour, 40cm × 30cm (15¾in × 11¾in), Siân Dudley.

PROJECT

Autumn in Longtimber

Rob Dudley

The Inspiration

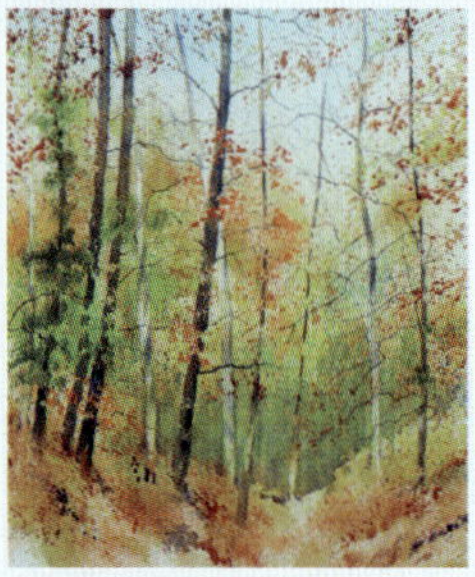

I came across this scene when out walking by our local river, the Erme, on a sunny afternoon in late October. Walking is such an ideal way to search out new painting spots! I was struck by the bright, autumn colours of the leaves, which festooned the nearby trees. With the sun hitting them, they seemed to be glowing. I overheard a couple describing it as 'a good display'; it certainly was.

The inspiration for this particular painting was very simple: it was the colour of the leaves. Or, more accurately, the colours, there were so many; indeed, how could the inspiration be anything else!

Developing the Idea

Although it was walking by the river that led me to discover the scene, it was not about the river. The painting would be about the wonderful autumn colours, the towering quality of the trees, and the colours and play of light on the trunks.

I decided to work in watercolour, the reason being that I felt it would be the most appropriate medium with which to portray the texture and colours of the leaves within the painting, by building up layers of paint by using the spattering technique.

Information Gathering

I was able to make some sketches, colour notes and photographs, paying particular attention to the colours within the background trees and undergrowth. I would work from these back in the studio, and also, of course, from my memory and feelings of the experience of walking through a wood in autumn.

Designing the Painting

Layout

Having returned to the studio, I decided upon the layout very quickly, after working through some basic thumbnail sketches.

The format that worked best was portrait, from the format lending itself to emphasizing the height of the foreground trees. Indeed, the wood is known locally as 'Longtimber'. The strong upright elements within the design were balanced by the inclusion of the roughly horizontal undergrowth.

The suggestion of the path was a useful device, in that it leads the viewer's eye into the painting and helps to create a sense of distance and recession within the wood.

Tone

For the painting to be successful, it would need to have a full range of tones. The dark tones of the foreground trees would be particularly important, as they would not only provide a tonal kick when contrasted with the lighter tones present but also help to establish a sense of depth within the painting.

Colour

When choosing colours for the painting, I had to consider the emotional qualities that they would evoke in addition to the physical qualities of each paint; how they would mix, would they granulate, were they liftable and would they stain?

I felt that it was important to include some passages of green within the design, and these greens would offer a nice, complementary kick when juxtaposed with the red of the autumn leaves.

Texture

One of the reasons for working in watercolour would be that it would allow me to create some interesting textures for the background. By spattering layers of colour, I would not only build up some pleasing colour effects but also create some useful leaflike textures.

Painting the Image

Materials and equipment

- Watercolour paper:
  - Bockingford NOT 300gsm/140lb, stretched and taped to a board
- Watercolour brushes:
  - No. 10 pointed sable
  - No. 6 pointed sable
  - No. 2 pointed sable
  - Fine rigger
  - Medium stencil brush
- Artist-quality watercolours:
  - Burnt sienna
  - Green gold
  - Lemon yellow
  - Quinacridone gold
  - Raw sienna
  - Sap green
  - Translucent orange
  - Ultramarine blue
  - Ultramarine violet
  - Winsor blue (green shade)
  - Winsor green
- Dark-green or dark-grey pencil crayon
- 2B pencil
- Masking fluid
- Medium masking-fluid brush
- Maskaway eraser
- Palette
- Kitchen roll

Step 1: Draw in the image outlines with pencil, and mask out relevant parts of the image.

Step 1: On the stretched watercolour paper, using a 2B pencil, draw in the design. It is not necessary to draw in every branch and twig; at this stage, focus on the main structures of the trees.

Mask selected trunks with masking fluid by using a medium masking-fluid brush. Allow the masking fluid to dry fully before moving on to the next step.

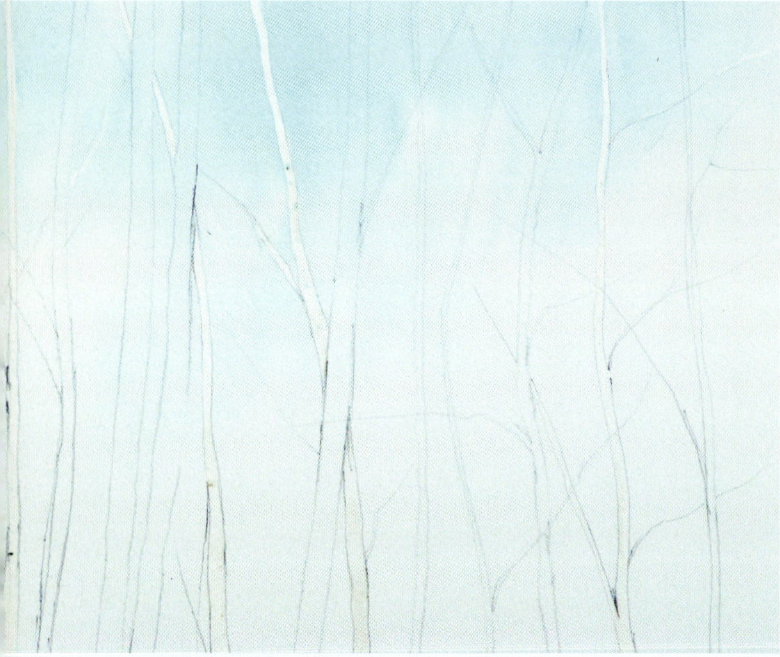

Step 2: Add the sky wash.

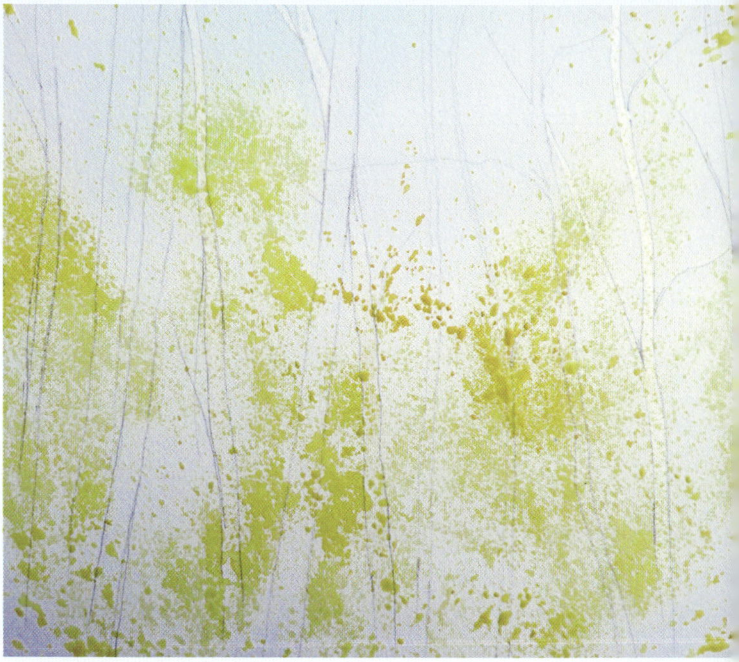

Step 3: Add first-stage spattering.

Step 2: With a large brush, dampen the sky area with clean water, allowing it to soak into the paper; adding paint too soon will make the application of colour less controllable, by causing paint to float on the surface of the paper into areas that the paint is likely to be unwanted. Drop in some Winsor blue, and allow this paint to dry, keeping the stretched paper at the same angle as that it was painted at. To alter the angle of the board at this stage would risk the formation of cauliflowers.

Step 3: To build up the background texture of the foliage requires spattering layers of colour on to the paper, while allowing each layer to dry before adding the next. The tonal strength of the colours increases from layer to layer, until the desired effect is arrived at.

After making certain that the previous step is thoroughly dry, spatter lemon yellow on to the painting. Concentrate the spatter towards the base of the depicted background trees.

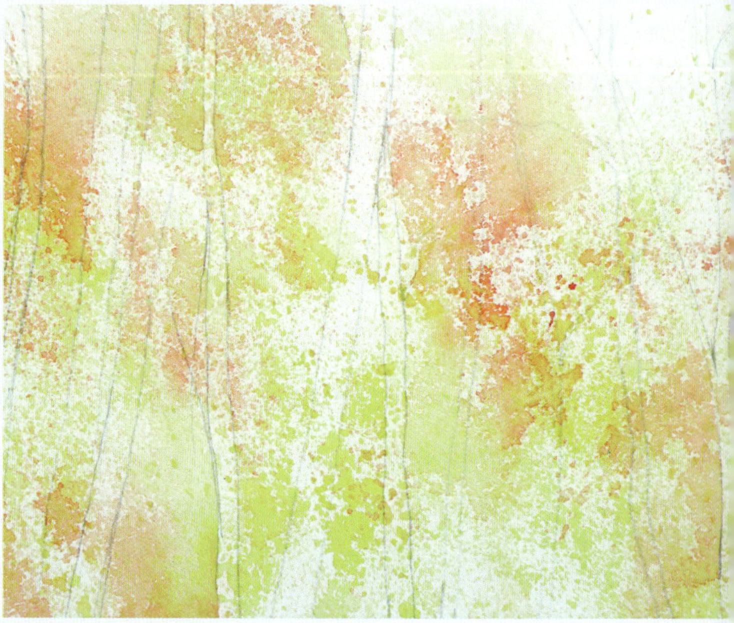

Step 4: Add second-stage spattering.

Step 4: Having made sure that the previous step is dry, spatter washes of translucent orange and quinacridone gold over the regions where the autumnal foliage is to be depicted.

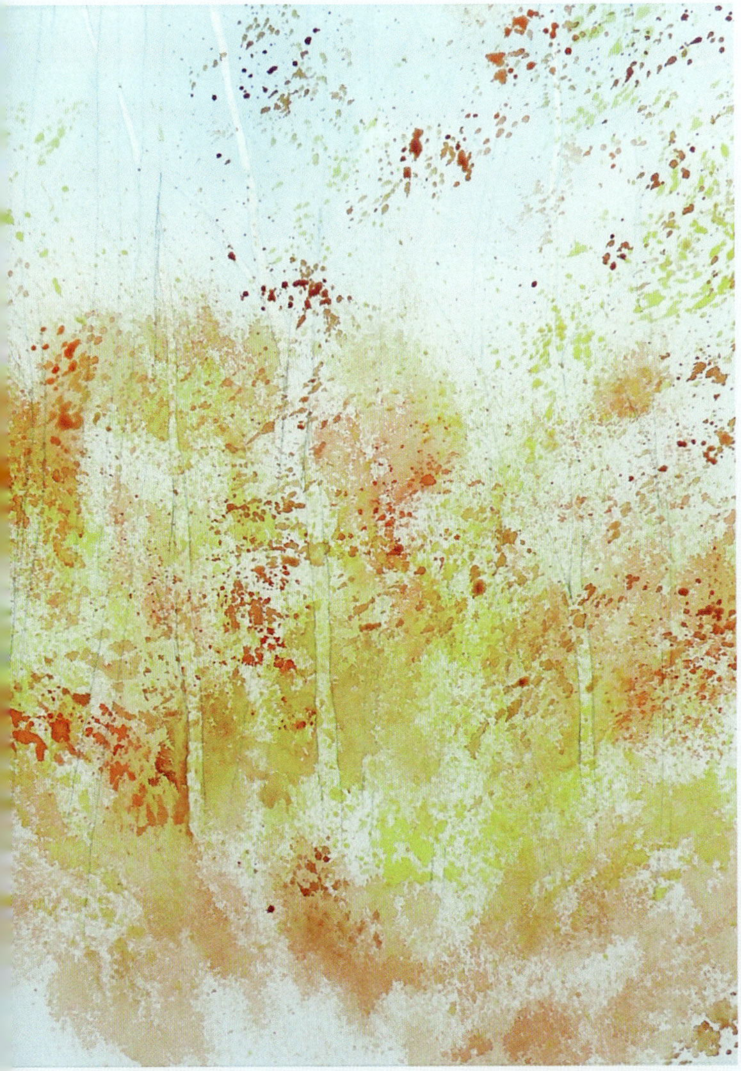

Step 5: Add third-stage spattering.

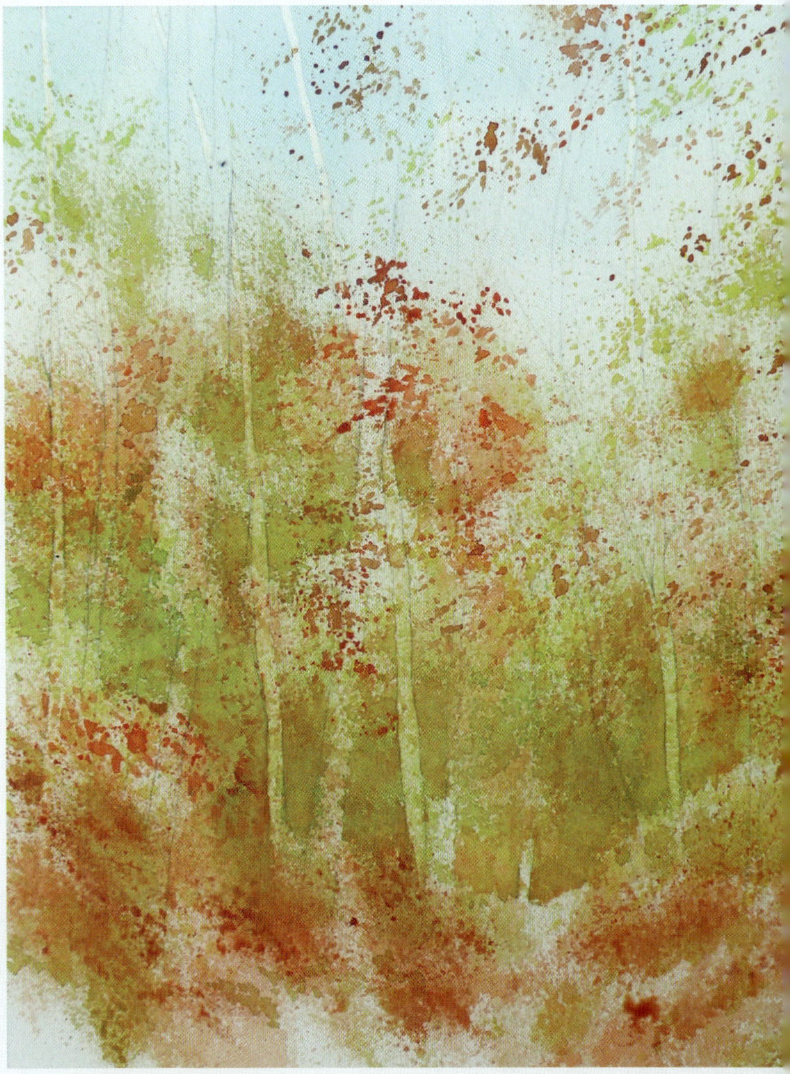

Step 6: Develop the foreground.

Step 5: Continue building up the foliage layer by spattering on mixes of green gold and quinacridone gold. Allow the paint to dry.

Step 6: With the application of spatters of burnt sienna, begin to develop the foreground. With a No. 6 brush, draw some of the spatters together, with their direction describing the shape and fall of the land. With the same mix, add some spatters to the depicted foliage. While the paint is still damp, drop in some green gold, and define the distant foliage with it. Allow the paint to dry.

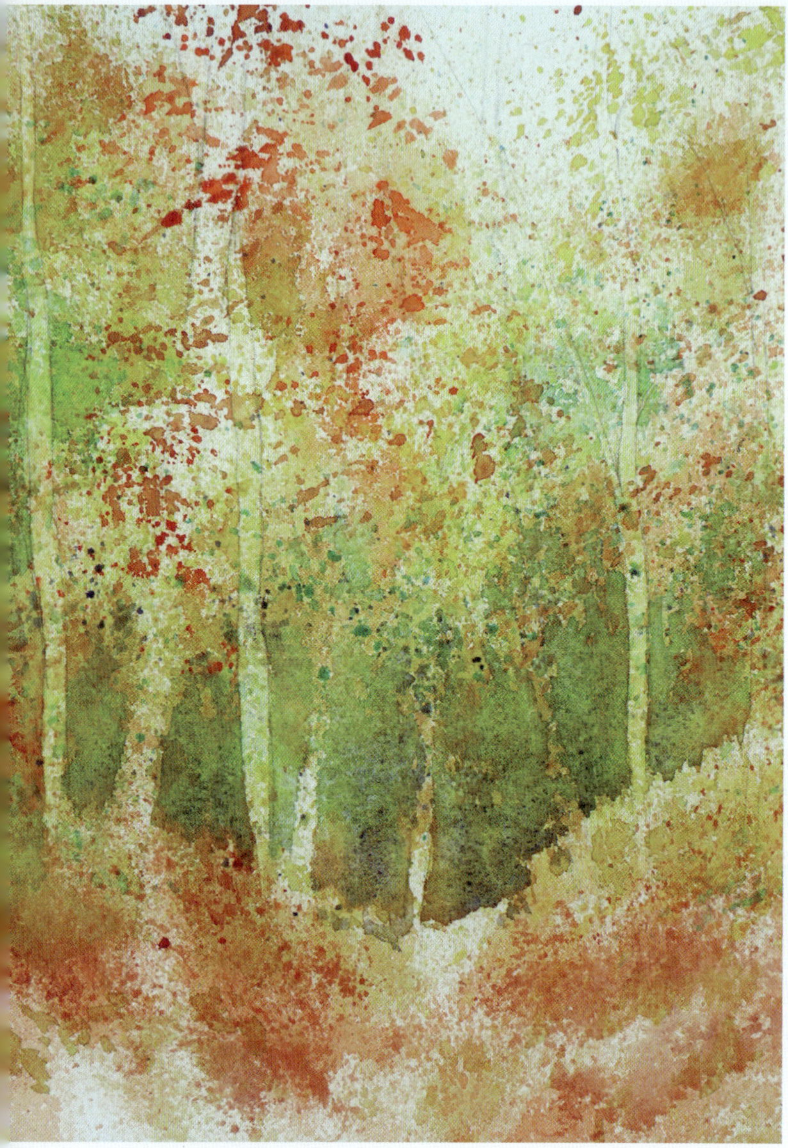

Step 7: Build up the distant trees.

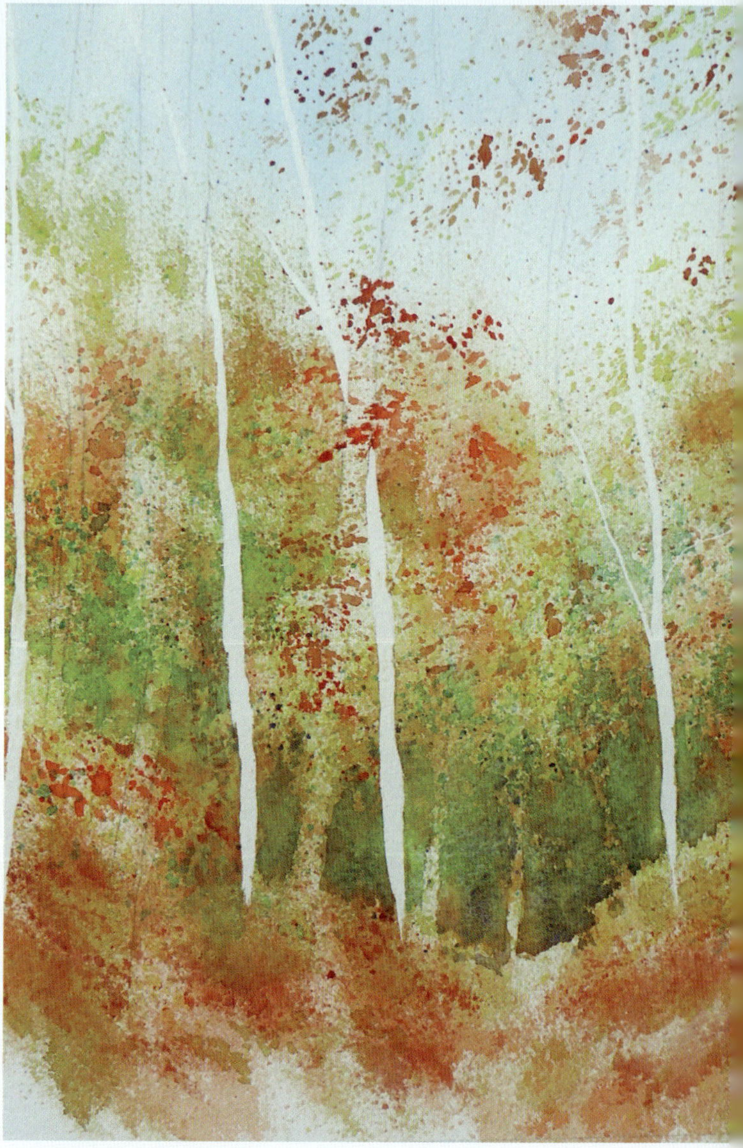

Step 8: Remove the masking fluid, to allow painting in of some of the main tree trunks and branches.

Step 7: Dampen the areas where the distant trees are being depicted. Drop in some ultramarine violet, paying particular attention to the bottom of the region of foliage. With a mix of green gold and Winsor green, spatter this paint into the distant trees, allowing some spatters to land on the still-damp ultramarine violet.

Step 8: To make absolutely certain that the previous step is completely dry, test the painting's surface with a piece of kitchen roll. If the kitchen roll picks up some still-wet paint, allow the painting's surface to dry for a little longer, before attempting to remove the masking fluid. Use a Maskaway eraser to remove the masking fluid.

Using mixes of raw sienna, green gold and ultramarine violet, paint in some of the trunks. Be careful not to paint in the trunks with too dark of a tone; remember, the trees within the scene were being hit by sunlight, and to paint their representations in too strongly will reduce this effect.

When the paint is dry, with a dark pencil crayon, draw in some of the thinner branches of the trees.

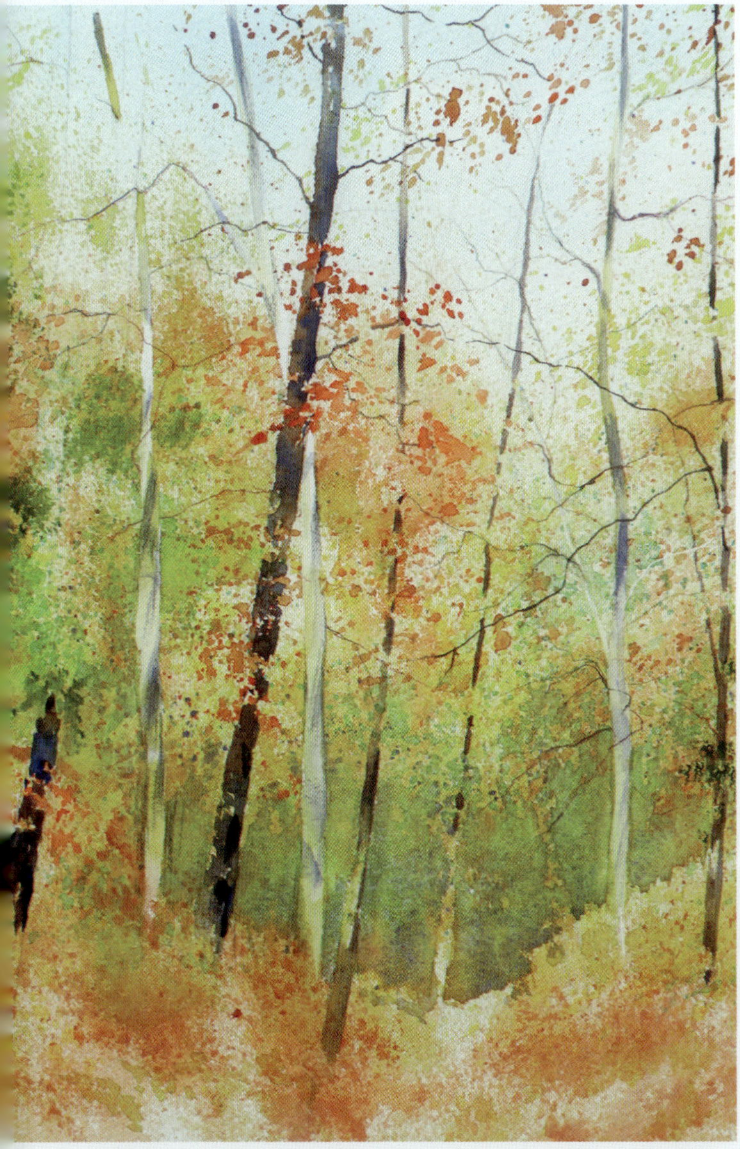

Step 9: Paint in the rest of the main tree trunks and branches, and apply additional finishing touches.

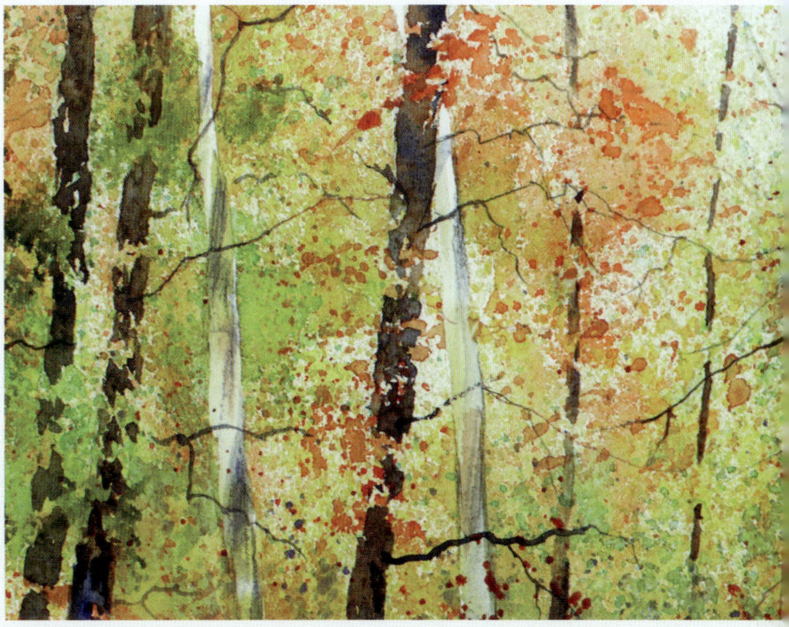

Step 10: Use a pencil crayon to draw in some of the finer branches.

Step 9: To suggest the ivy growing up some of the trunks, take some sap green mixed with some green gold and, with a fairly stiff mix, stipple this on by using a medium stencil brush.

As this stippled paint is drying, with strong mixes of ultramarine blue and burnt sienna, paint in the rest of the main trunks and branches, by using the No. 6, No. 2 and fine rigger brushes; the size of brush used is dictated by the relative size of the trunk or branch being painted in.

Note how, by not painting parts of the trunks or branches, the effect of leaves covering parts of the tree is suggested.

As the paint for depicting the trunks is drying, add some detail to the foreground with ultramarine violet.

Step 10: Once the paint is completely dry, with a dark pencil crayon, pick out and draw in some of the thinner branches.

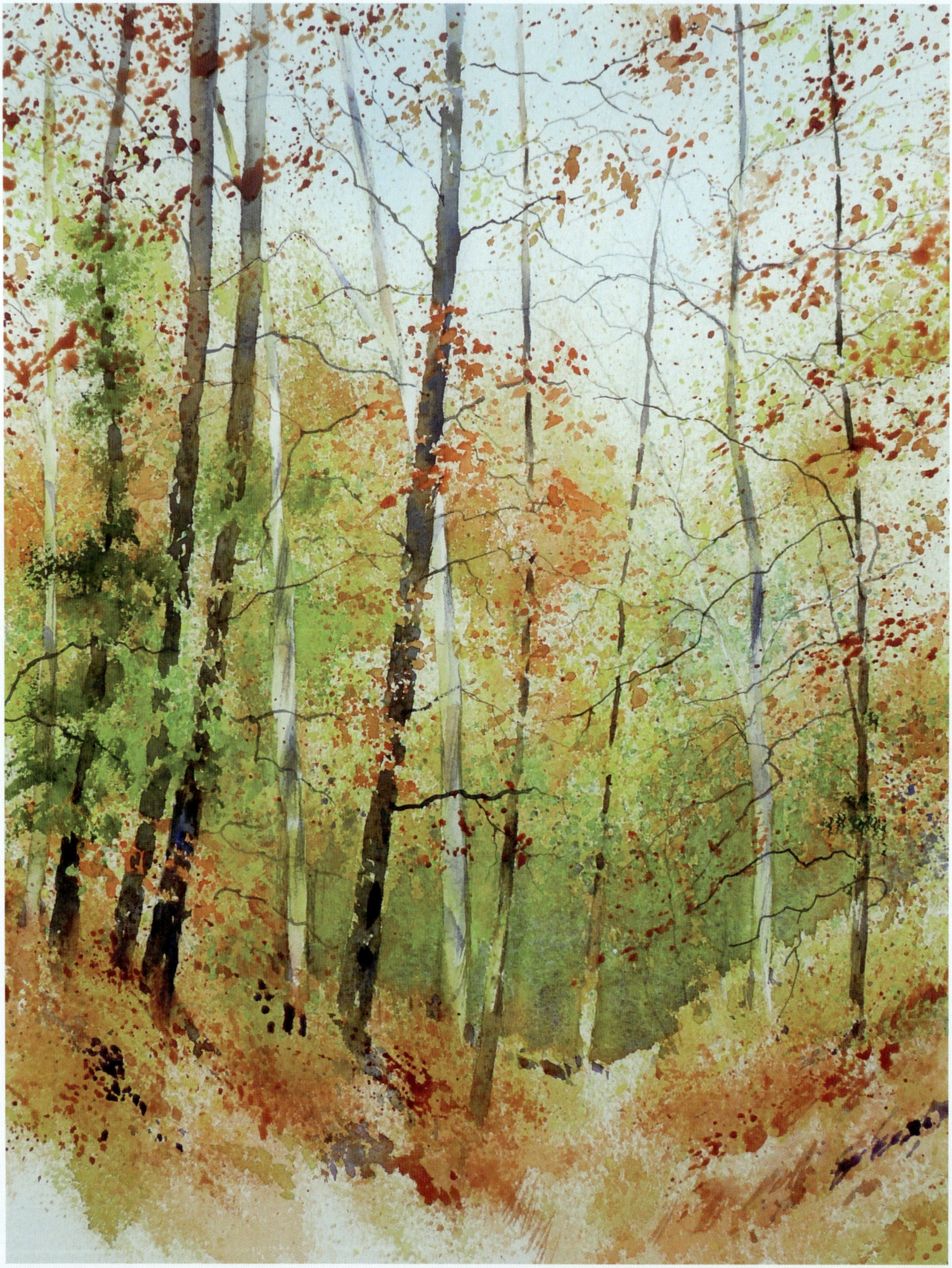

The finished painting: *Autumn in Longtimber*, watercolour, 32cm × 40cm (12½in × 15¾in), Rob Dudley.

PROJECT

Autumn Road

Rob Dudley

The Inspiration

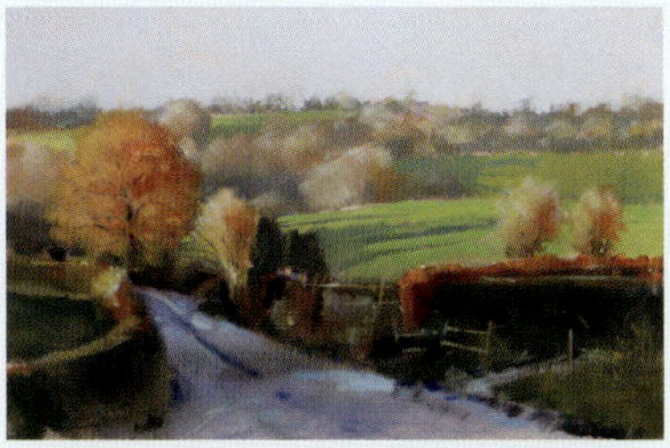

If you ask a group of people to describe the autumn, it won't be too long before they mention the wonderful autumn colours. For many, the season is *all* about the colours: the rich reds, bright russets and glorious golds of the turning leaves; these colours are the headline acts. But, if you search beyond the vibrant colours, you will also be rewarded with displays of subtle browns and soft grey-greens, and by blue shadows. They are not so showy, perhaps, as the headline colours, but they are not a bad supporting cast and are definitely something worth exploring in paint.

The soft light of an October afternoon was the starting point for this painting. I had been travelling back after a weekend away and took a little detour to an area a few miles from home that I did not know well and felt was worthy of investigation. Driving down a narrow lane, I came across this scene before me. I was hooked.

It had the bright, showy trees of autumn, combined with the soft grey-browns in the distance. The shadows were fingering across the sunlit fields with the merest suggestion of mist forming in the valley.

It was simple in its subject matter – a lane and some trees, fields and shadows – yet utterly captivating. It just had to be painted!

Developing the Idea

In developing the idea, I knew that one of the key things that I wanted to try to convey was the distinct quality that the autumnal light had on that particular afternoon. It seemed to possess a stillness about it, a soft delicacy. The light had a way of softening colours and tones, merging edges in part of the landscape, while bringing others into sharp focus. It was a lot to ask for in a little painting and a challenge, definitely, but it was worth the attempt and was something to aim for.

In order to allow me as much working time as possible to blend and soften the colours, I decided to use water-mixable oils, as they would stay workable for longer than watercolour or gouache was likely to.

Information Gathering

I had some paints and a couple of sketchbooks with me and started to make some quick drawings and colour notes. There wouldn't be time to make the painting on site: the light was already beginning to change, so, within a few minutes, I had to gather as much useful information as I could, to work from back in the studio.

Designing the Painting

Layout

I felt that this image would work best as a small, intimate painting – nothing too large and expansive. The marks used would be direct and simple and, for that reason, they probably wouldn't work on a larger scale, as they would end up getting lost in the expanse of the painting. I tried various formats, in the end choosing a landscape format. This I felt complemented the width of the scene, emphasizing, as it did, the fields, distant trees and shadows, for example.

Tone

As always, tone was going to be the key to the success or otherwise of this little oil painting. The tones were so close in value that they would require careful consideration and handling. If too many strong contrasts were introduced, they would unbalance the design and take away the softness of the afternoon light of the scene being represented. These close tonal values contribute to the softening of the edges, particularly for the middle-ground and background trees. The juxtaposition of strong tonal contrasts tends to produce sharp edges and, other than its use in a few key areas of strong sunlight, I was mindful that this was something that I wanted to avoid.

It was because of these close tones and soft edges that I very quickly decided to work in oils, as their longer drying time allowed me plenty of time to soften and blend edges.

Colour

I worked with a carefully selected palette of just six colours, from which I knew that I could mix a range of subtle greys and soft browns and, of course, the brighter autumnal golds.

I chose to work on a coloured ground; very dilute burnt sienna was painted loosely on to the board and allowed to dry. This would not only make it easier for me to pitch my tones and colours in the early stages of painting but also offer a unifying effect to the whole painting, by linking together any areas that remained unpainted.

Texture

This painting was not really about texture; in fact, I wanted to play down any texture within it and concentrate instead on producing soft, texture-free blends. Inclusion of too much texture, by the use of thick paint, might take away attention from the blended colours, and I was mindful to avoid this from happening.

Painting the Image

Materials and equipment

- Gessoed MDF board:
  - Prepared with a ground of very dilute burnt sienna, 30cm × 20cm (11¾in × 8in)
- Oil-painting brushes:
  - No. 1 round
  - No. 4 flat
  - No. 8 filbert
- Water-mixable oil colours:
  - Alizarin crimson
  - Burnt sienna
  - Cadmium yellow light
  - French ultramarine blue
  - Sap green
  - Titanium white
- Palette
- Palette knife
- Dipper for water

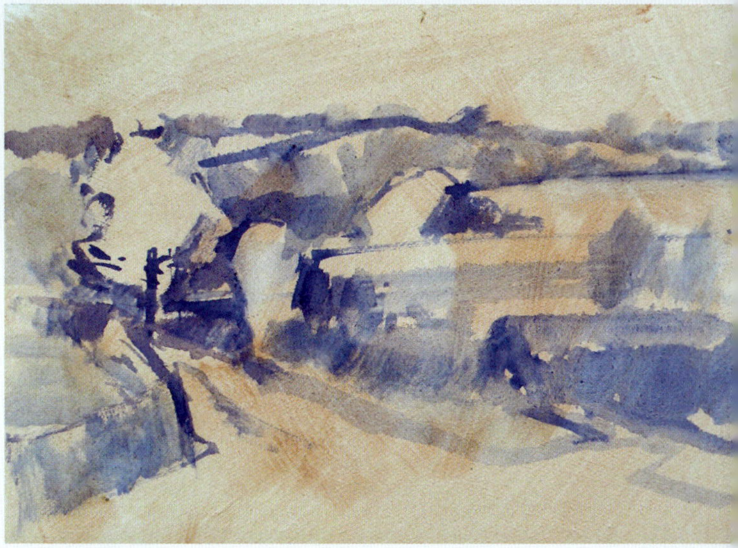

Step 1: Add first impressions of the features of the scene.

Step 1: Using French ultramarine blue and alizarin crimson, mix a dilute pool of paint. With this mix, working on the prepared board, having ensured that the coloured ground is completely dry, very loosely paint in the key features of the scene, indicating some of the tones as you go.

Avoid the temptation of working with a small brush for this step, as it will likely encourage the inclusion of too much detail, which is something to be avoided so early on in the painting's life. At this stage, it is all about finding your way around the painting; finding out where the lights and darks are, how the balance of the painting is working and how the shapes interact with each other.

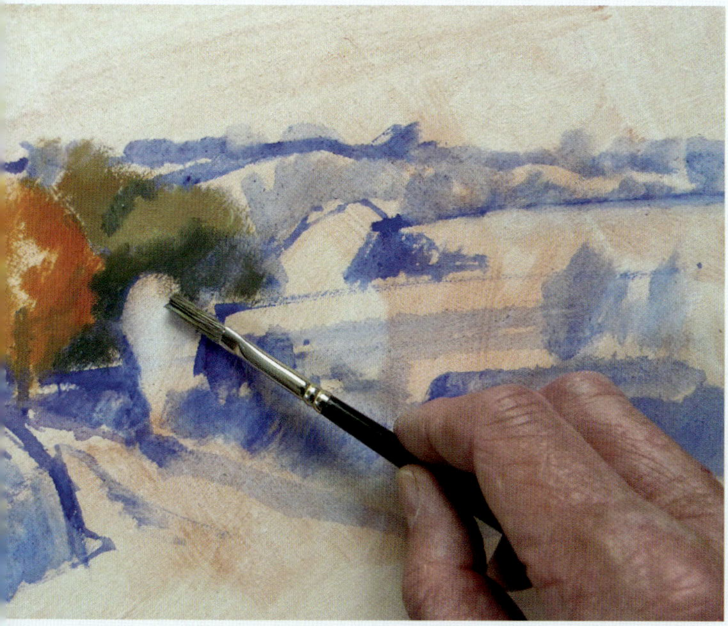

Step 2: Apply the first indications of colour.

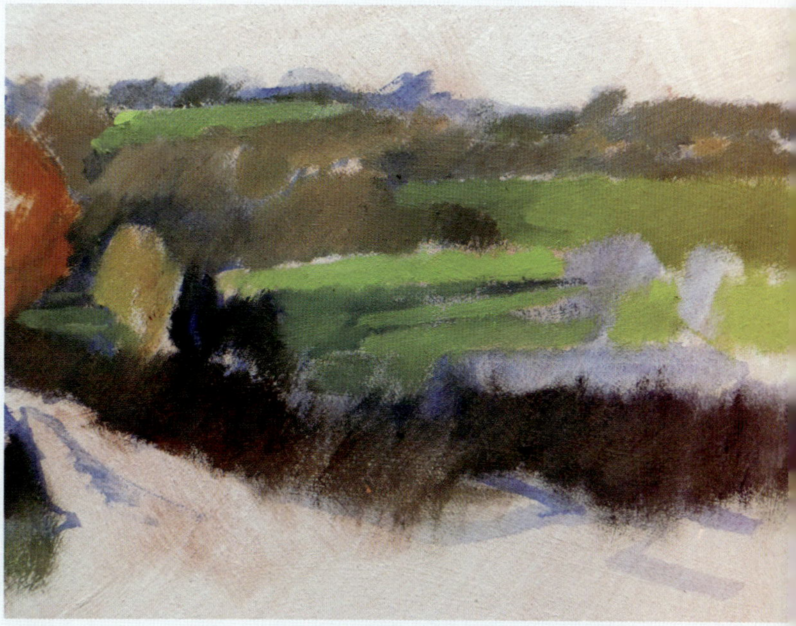

Step 3: Paint in the distant trees and middle-ground fields.

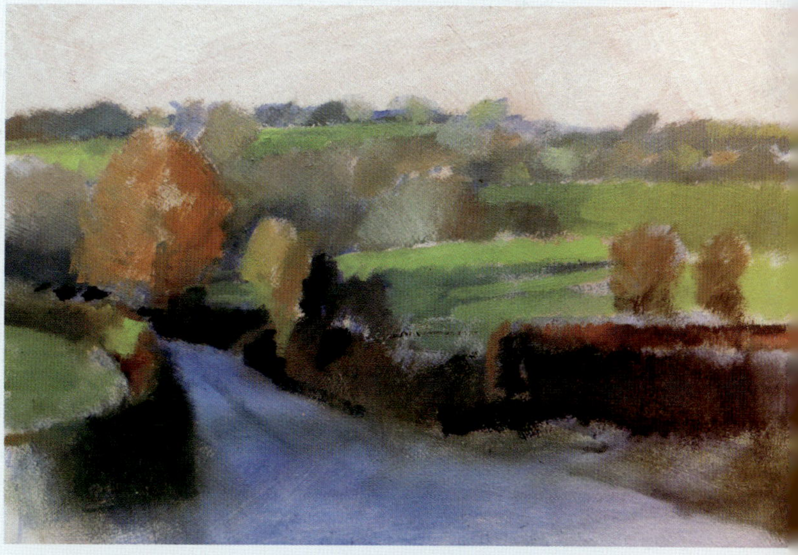

Step 4: Strengthen the trees and build up the shadows.

Step 2: Create a variety of colour mixes using the paint colours suggested. Vary your choice of colour selected from these mixes as you work.

Loosely block in the depictions of the trees and hedgerows, giving some indication as to the placements of lights and darks. Use the side of the brush to scuff paint on to the board. Be careful not to add too much paint and too much detail.

Step 3: With a mix of sap green, cadmium yellow light and titanium white, paint in the areas of the fields. Vary the mix as you go; paint some areas with a little more yellow, others with a little more green. Add a touch of French ultramarine blue to the mix for the depiction of shadows.

For the suggestion of distant fields, use the same field mix of paint as above but with the inclusion of a little more white. By reducing its tonal strength, the mixed paint will appear to recede within the painting, adding to the sense of distance.

Step 4: Add a touch of titanium white to a mix of French ultramarine blue and burnt sienna, and begin to pick out the sunlit side of the middle-ground and distant trees, by scumbling over the previously applied colours. For the scumbling technique to work successfully, I find it best to let the underpainting dry slightly before proceeding.

Add some suggestions of foreground shadows with a mix of French ultramarine blue and burnt sienna.

Paint in the road with a mix of French ultramarine blue and alizarin crimson; scuff the colour on, allowing some of the board's coloured ground to show through.

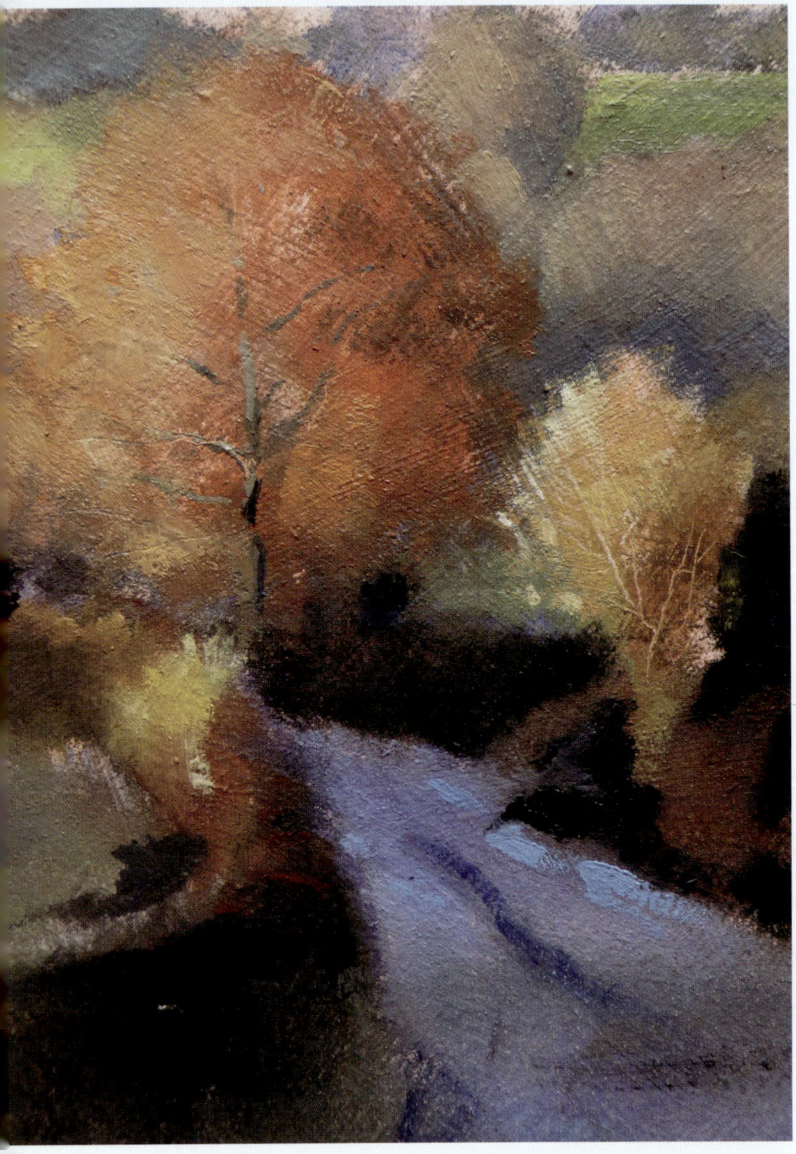

Step 5: Add structure to the main tree and hedgerow.

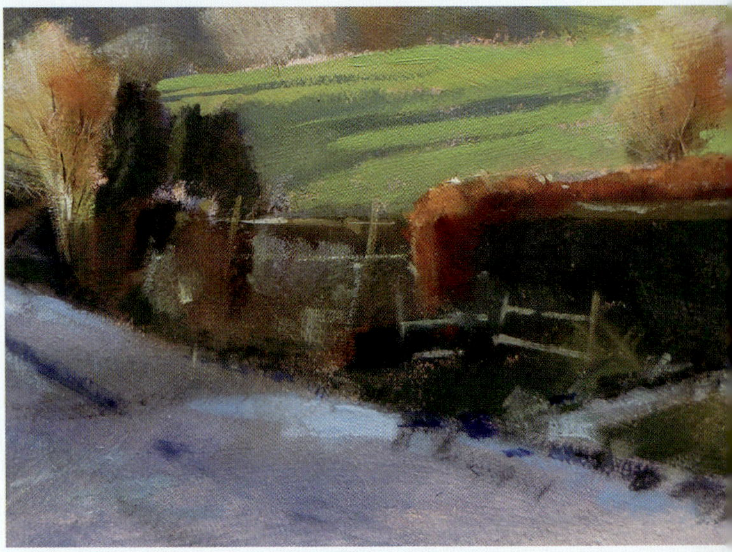

Step 6: Pull it all together with the addition of final details.

Step 5: Begin to add structure and detail to the depicted main tree and right hedgerow, with mixes of cadmium yellow light, burnt sienna and titanium white. Paint in some indications of the trunk and branches. Use similar mixes but with a touch more titanium white for the depiction of the bright hedgerow tree. With the palette knife, scratch in some suggestions of branches.

Step 6: This is the time that I am probably the most cautious about when painting: so close to finishing but also so close to losing the painting by overworking it.

Add structure and detail to the painting to bring it all together. Be careful; if too much detail is added, it can fragment the work, rather than unify it, by offering the viewer almost too many things to look at.

Therefore, at this stage, it is important to add touches very sparingly; add a few and then review the painting as a whole.

Paint in the sky with a mix of French ultramarine blue, titanium white and a hint of alizarin crimson, allowing some of the coloured ground to show through. Note how the distant tree line is shaped by this painting in of the sky.

To finish this painting, a few touches of pale blue were added to the roadsides, some fence posts were touched in, along with simple indications of vegetation for the right foreground, and highlights added where applicable.

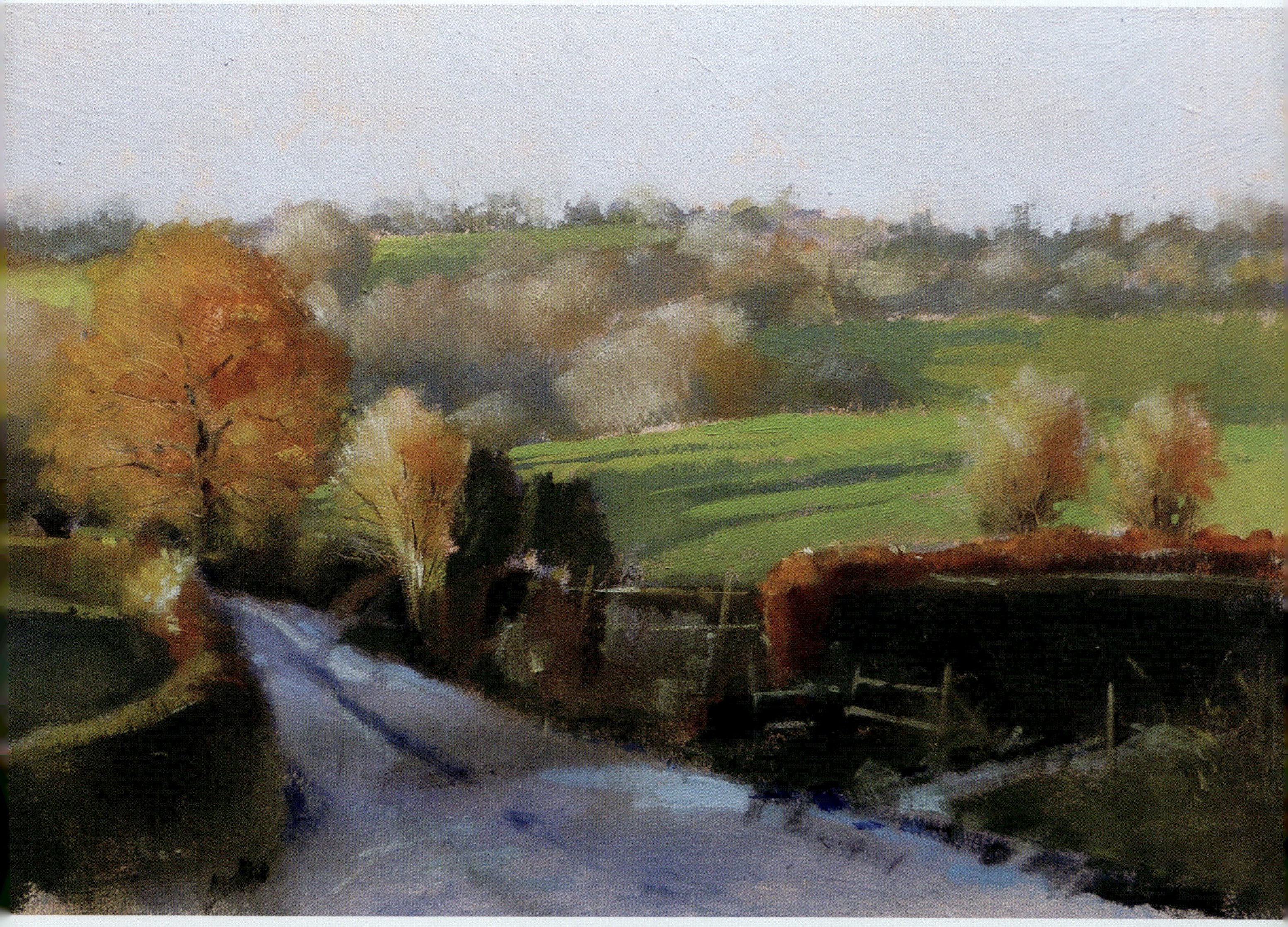

The finished painting: *Autumn Road*, water-mixable oils on board, Rob Dudley, 30cm × 20cm (11¾in × 8in), Rob Dudley.

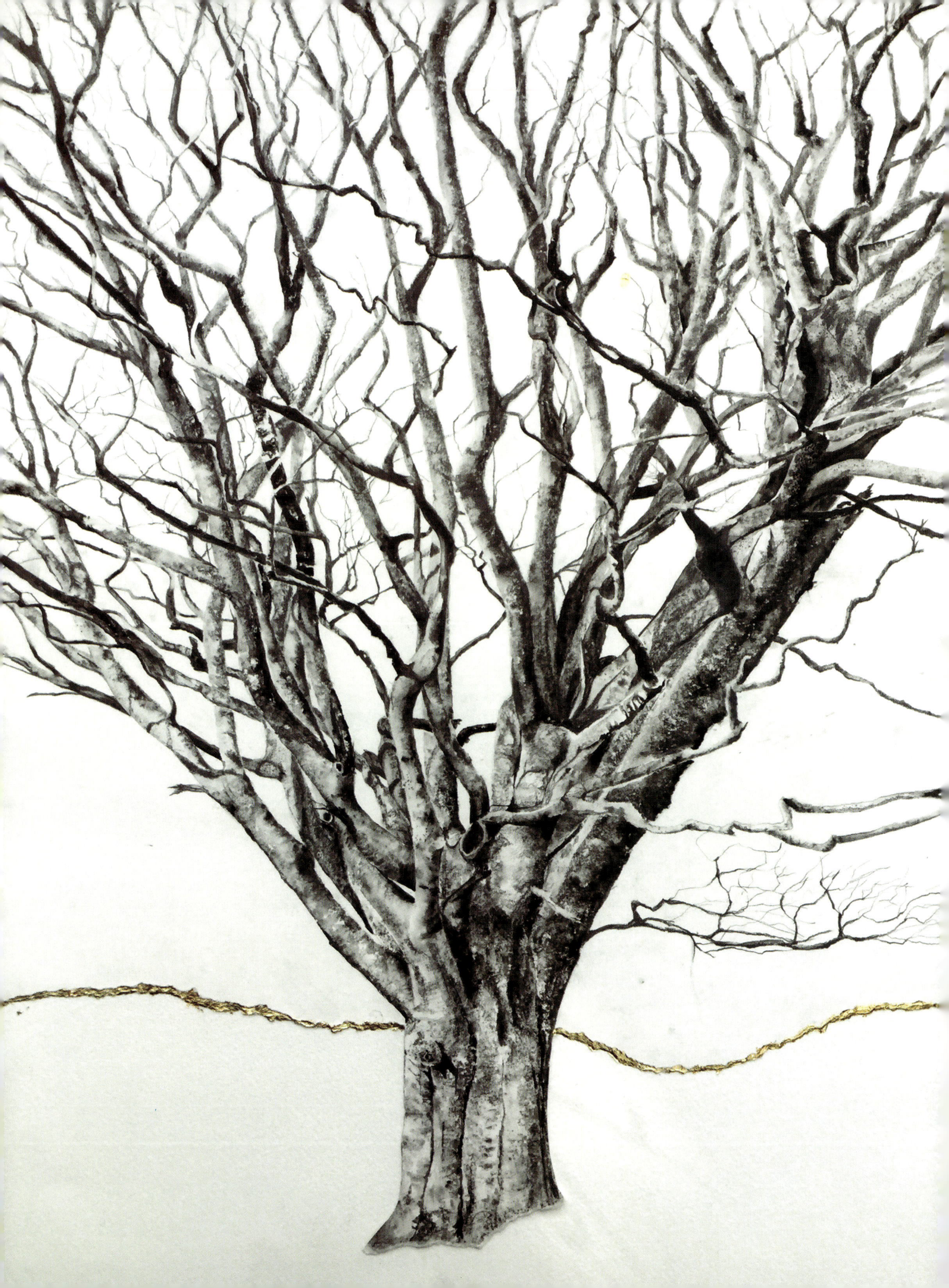

Chapter 8

Winter

For some people, winter is the time of the year to shut the door, to snuggle up with a good book in front of a roaring fire and to venture out as little as possible, while looking forward to the spring. But behaving as described would mean missing out on so much that the season has to offer. Embrace the elements! This is the time to wrap up warmly and discover the beauty of winter.

Wearing fingerless mittens keeps your hands warm enough to hold a pencil with which to sketch or draw. Choose your materials for creating artwork carefully; watercolour is not the best choice on damp days or in sub-zero temperatures! Before setting out, deciding that, in the available daylight hours and current weather conditions, a realistic goal is to produce a small pencil sketch frees the mind to spend the time being creative with that pencil.

Some might see winter trees as stark, skeletal forms, lacking leaves, and lacking in interest. These skeletal versions of trees can be immensely inspiring in their own right! The lacy effect of the branches, the shadows that they cast, and the shapes and patterns that they create each have their own beauty. The play of light on the bark brings out colours and textures that are unseen in summer. Unencumbered with heavy foliage, a wooded hillside can appear soft, light and airy.

The observant artist will see bare trees as ideal opportunities to study the trees' underlying structure, getting to know the shapes of oak, ash and beech and how these shapes differ. This knowledge is useful when painting trees, particularly summer trees, when this underlying structure is lost from view.

A camera is useful too, for capturing fleeting light effects. With the sun low in the sky, the shadows of trees are longer than those cast in summer and can be quite dramatic. In describing the fall of the land, they can appear to increase the steepness of a slope or exaggerate distance. Clouds move quickly in winter and, on a windy day, shadows are often too transient to catch with a drawing. The large puddles found in winter can be the source of beautiful reflections, which can be a useful addition to the design for a painting, if not being the painting's inspiration themselves.

Winter colour is subtle, inspiring restful paintings. A woodland of deciduous trees offers a fabulous display of soft minky-browns and grey-greens. Colours should be chosen to reflect the cold of winter, so consider using paint colours such as cobalt blue and burnt umber instead of ultramarine blue and burnt sienna.

More water in the atmosphere can affect aerial perspective. This means that even on a clear day, the visibility is often less in winter than that in summer. Consider using opaque paints or adding a white (for example, titanium white) to your palette, to aid you in achieving this misty effect.

The Big Beech Tree: Winter, 56cm × 74cm (22in × 29¼in), graphite and metal leaf, Siân Dudley.

THE BIG BEECH TREE: WINTER

Siân Dudley

The bareness of The Big Beech Tree in winter accentuated its grandeur and its solidity. I was fascinated by the intertwining of the branches and the negative shapes between these branches. I loved the way that shadows appeared in unexpected places, hinting at hidden branches. As the sun reflected off the trunk, the trunk appeared to be almost silver. Most of all, I loved the way that the sun highlighted the texture of the bark.

I wanted to make an image that would capture a sense of the enormity of the tree, in a way that would draw attention to the fine details of the texture of the bark. The laciness of the intertwining branches and the variety of tones would lead the viewer's eye continually around the image, hopefully for it to find the last leaf left en route.

I decided to use graphite, which instantly gave me the silvery colour that I desired, and it could be burnished in places to a slight sheen. I used both powdered and pencil forms, applying it both wet and dry, to achieve the marks and effects that I wanted. The gold-coloured metal leaf that I used to finish the painting represents the autumnal colour of the single remaining leaf and the majesty of this great tree.

PROJECT

Winter Landscape

Rob Dudley

The Inspiration

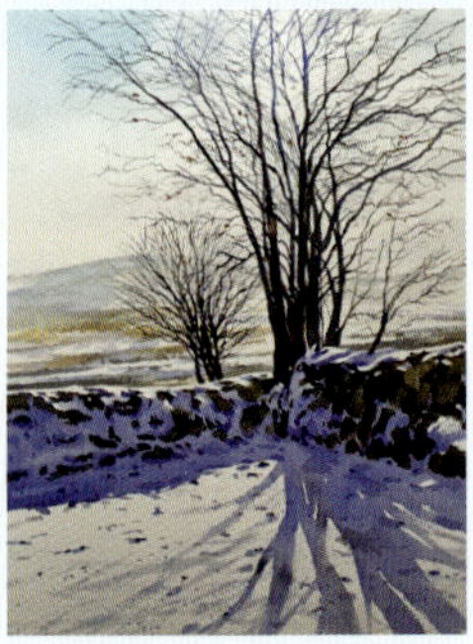

I do enjoy painting scenes like this one. The combination of bright lights, crisp darks and the architectural beauty of winter trees has me coming back time and again.

I first spotted this scene while sketching on Dartmoor. The sky was heavy with cloud and the light was flat, with no sign of shadows: lovely, but lacking a real kick, with no real contrast in tones – it all seemed rather flat. But, within a few minutes, the clouds had parted, the sun shone and the entire moor was transformed; sunlight and shadows were everywhere. There seemed to be a painting in every direction. However, I focused on the wonderful darks in both walls and trees set against the bright lights of the sunlit snow. This was my inspiration.

Developing the Idea

Developing the idea was relatively simple; it was about the tracery of the winter trees. I wanted to emphasize the contrasts between the dark of the trunks, the bright white of the snow and the wonderful purple-blue shadows. By balancing these elements correctly, the painting would have real impact.

Information Gathering

I was able to both make sketches and take photographs when gathering information. I chose not to make colour notes, although paints and brushes were available in my bag, as I was concerned that, as quickly as the weather had changed, it might do so again, and the wonderful light would be gone before I had had a chance to record the scene.

Designing the Painting

Layout

Back in the studio, working from both sketches and photographs, I produced some tonal and format thumbnails, to assess the potential success or otherwise of the painting's design, eventually settling on a slightly elongated portrait format. This would allow for the generous proportions of the main trees, and their shadows, to occupy much of the design. A traditional landscape or even a square format would have been too constraining to the composition, either by cutting off too much of the trees or the shadows within the design. I wanted to use the walls and the thrusting diagonals to lead the viewer into the painting, with their eye continuing upwards towards the treetops.

Tone

It was pretty obvious when planning this painting that a full range of tones would be employed, with particular emphasis given to the strong contrasts between the lights and darks: the key, in many respects, to the overall success or otherwise of the painting. The dark of the tree trunks and the granite stones of the wall juxtaposed with the bright white of the snow gives a real kick to the painting. With paintings such as this, the painter has to commit to dark darks and bright lights; there can be no half-hearted measures. In particular, if the dark is not strong enough then the contrast will undoubtedly be lost, and the painting will be weaker as a consequence.

Colour

I decided that I would work with a simple, restricted range of watercolours, ensuring of course that the colours were obviously harmonious and able, when mixed, to produce some bright darks. Two of the key colour choices were the selections of ultramarine blue and burnt sienna. When mixed, they would not only produce some useful greys and strong darks, essential for the wide tonal range that the subject demanded, but also settle out and granulate as these paints dry, creating some pleasing textural effects, especially within the depicted stones of the snow-covered walls.

Some areas of the painting would be protected with masking fluid that, when removed, would reveal the white of the paper, to indicate lying snow.

White acrylic gouache would also be used to strengthen the depictions of snow or to add further touches of snow to the painting, where needed.

Texture

The choice of paper on which to paint is always an important one when working with watercolour. In this case, I chose a stretched piece of Bockingford NOT 300gsm paper. It has a rather nice texture to its surface and thereby would encourage some pleasing granulation effects from the paints chosen, which is particularly useful for painting in the snowy shadows and the granite stones within the moorland wall. It would also allow for the successful application and removal of the masking fluid that would form an essential element of the painting's execution.

Painting the Image

Materials and equipment

- Watercolour paper:
  - Bockingford NOT 300gsm/140lb, stretched and taped to a board
- Watercolour brushes:
  - No. 10 pointed sable
  - No. 6 pointed sable
  - Fine rigger
- Artist-quality watercolours:
  - Burnt sienna
  - Cobalt blue
  - Green gold
  - Neutral tint
  - Permanent rose
  - Raw sienna
  - Transparent oxide brown
  - Ultramarine blue
  - Winsor blue (green shade)
  - White acrylic gouache
- 2B pencil
- Masking fluid
- Medium masking-fluid brush
- Maskaway eraser
- Dip pen
- Palette
- Kitchen roll
- Scrap paper

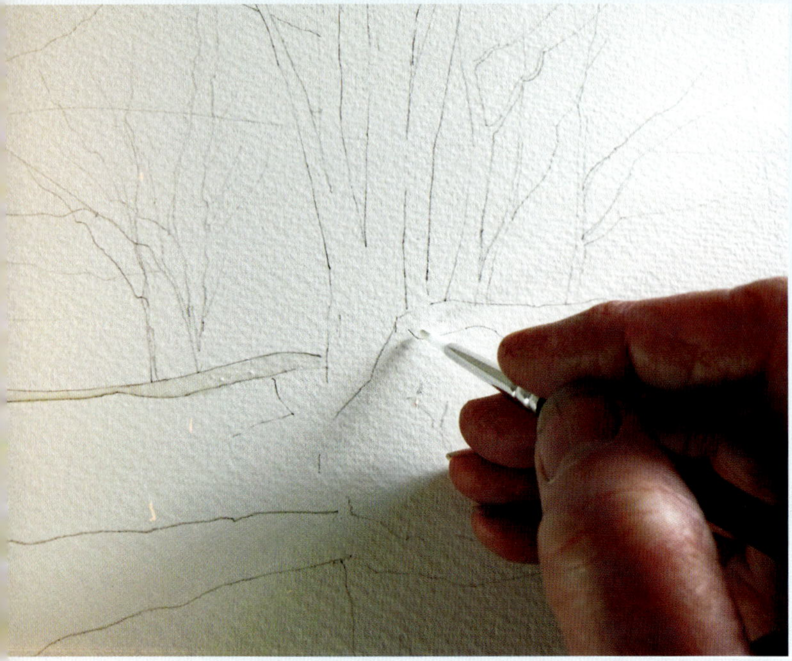

Step 1: Draw in the image outlines and mask out the wall tops.

Step 2: Add the sky washes.

Step 1: Use a 2B pencil to draw in the design for the painting. It is not necessary to draw in all of the small branches, just the main ones. Mask out the regions of the tops of the walls where the snow is to be shown lying by using a medium masking-fluid brush. By masking these wall tops, the white of the paper would be preserved which, when at a later stage, the dried masking fluid is removed, would depict the snow. This masking also allows for the sharp-edged juxtaposition between the white of the snow and the dark of the wall or trees, creating dramatic impact, which is vital in this painting. Allow the masking fluid to dry thoroughly before continuing on to the next step.

Step 2: Having made sure that the masking fluid is completely dry, dampen the sky area of the painting with clean water.

Prepare a puddle of Winsor blue – but make certain that it is not too strong – and a mix of ultramarine blue with permanent rose. With the No. 10 sable, wash in the Winsor blue on each side of the main tree and use the mix of ultramarine blue and permanent rose to indicate some clouds near to the sky line. Allow the paint to dry.

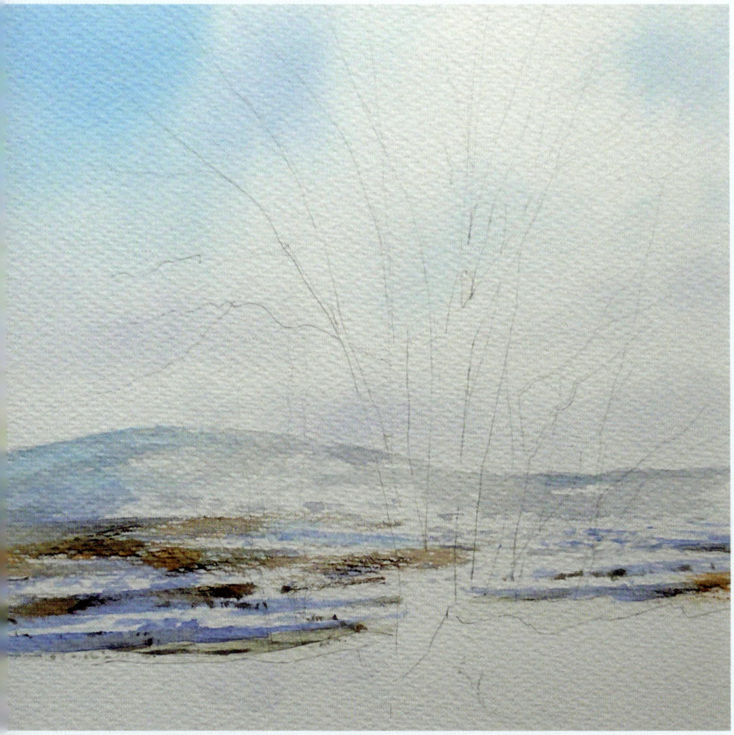

Step 3: Add distant- and middle-ground moor washes.

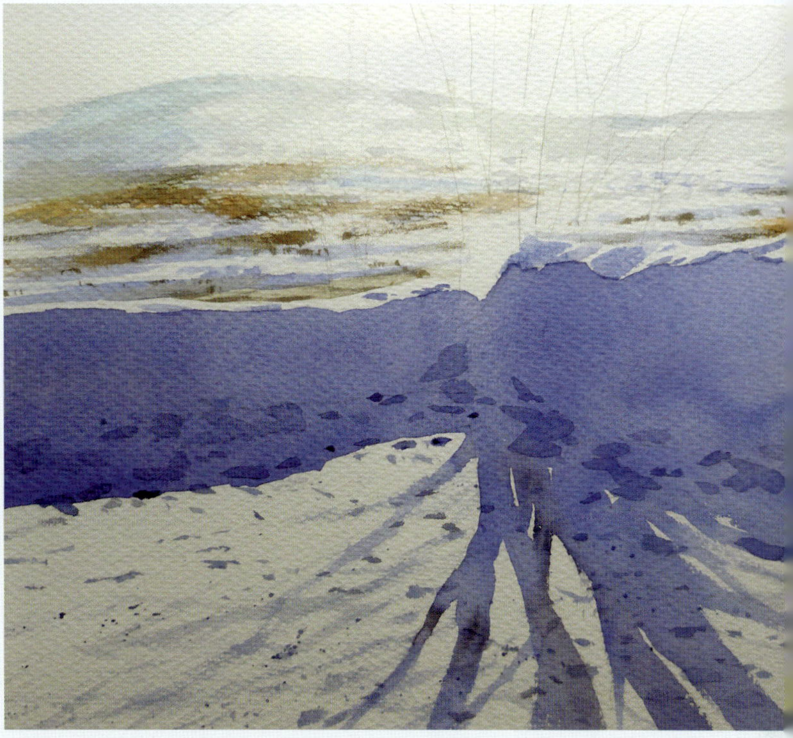

Step 4: Paint in the first stage of the walls and shadows.

Step 3: Having made certain that the previous step is completely dry, mix puddles of burnt sienna and raw sienna, ultramarine blue with cobalt blue, and raw sienna with neutral tint; use these preparations to paint in the distant moor. Keep the colours paler in the distance of the painting, with them becoming stronger as they get closer to the foreground. These changes of tone will help to convey a sense of distance and recession within the watercolour painting.

Use a variety of techniques to create the moorland landscape, including the application of washes, dry brushstrokes and layers. Allow the paint to dry.

Step 4: Make up a puddle of ultramarine blue with a little touch of permanent rose added to it. The resultant mix should be predominately blue but with a slightly purple cast. Using the largest brush, paint in the walls and tree shadows quickly, with as few passes of the brush as possible; don't keep going back into the wash, particularly if it is beginning to dry, as this is likely to create unwanted cauliflowers, or back runs.

When this applied paint is completely dry, using the same mix, indicate a little texture for the snowy foreground and bottom of the wall, with the addition of some smaller brushmarks.

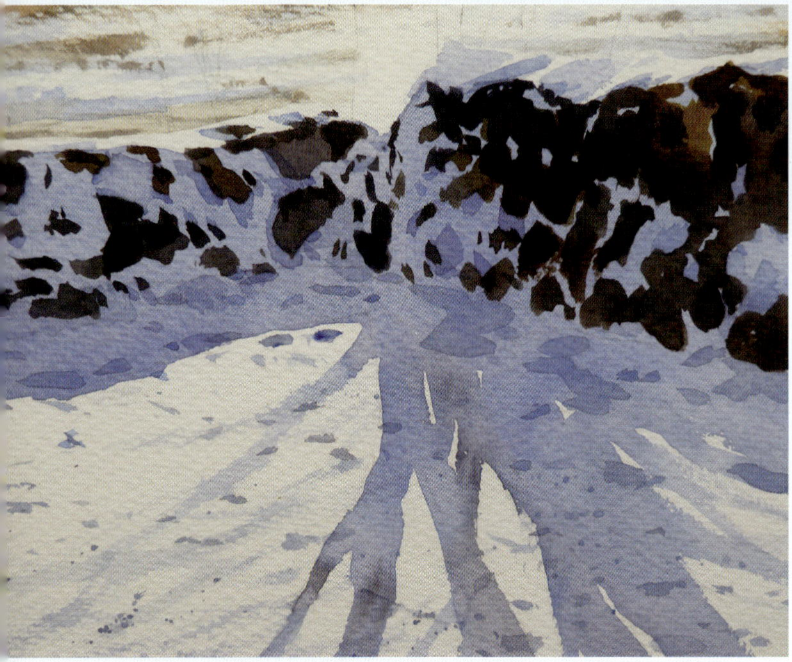

Step 5: Build up the walls and shadows.

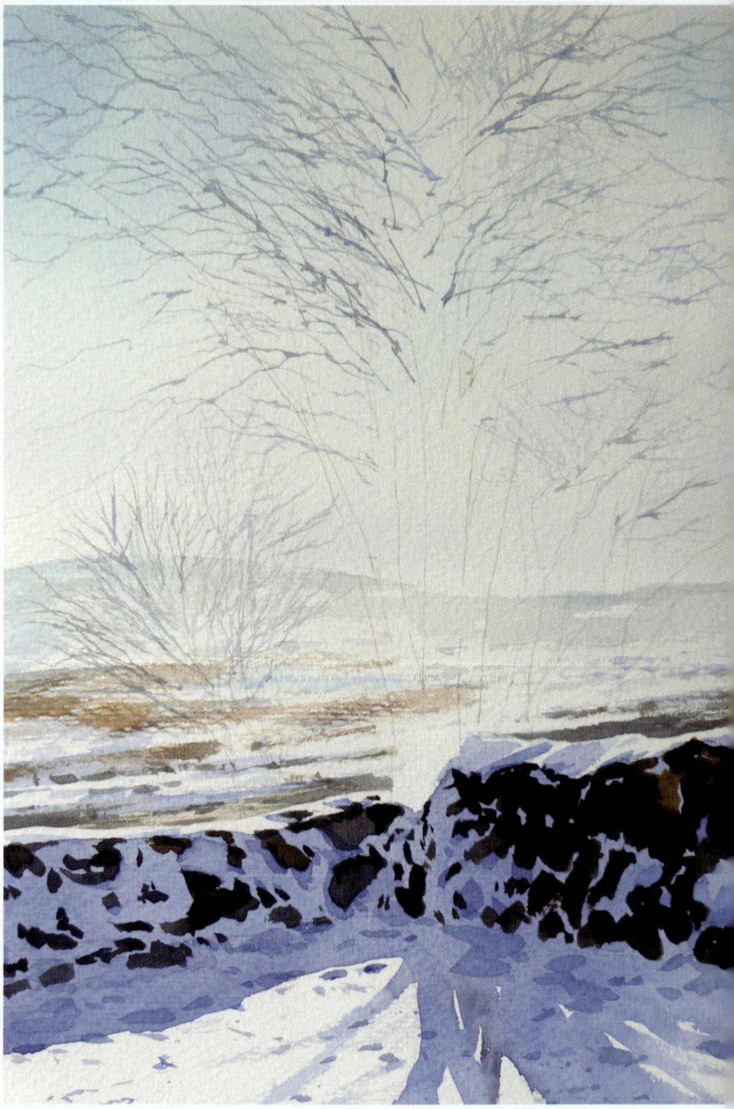

Step 6: Paint in the first stage of the trees' branches.

Step 5: Having verified that the previous step is thoroughly dry, mix ultramarine blue, transparent oxide brown and neutral tint, and make a puddle of pure green gold.

Using the mix, paint in some of the wall stones that are visible through the snow. Vary the mix as you go, dropping in some green gold to one or two of the stones when the applied mix paint is still damp. After allowing all of the paint on the paper to dry fully, with the shadow mix used for step 4, paint in some suggestions of shadows in and around the wall stones.

Step 6: Using a rigger and a pale mix of ultramarine blue and neutral tint, paint in some of the branches for both the smaller and the larger trees. It is by painting in these paler branches and overlaying them at a later stage with darker ones that a sense of depth within the trees will be created. Without these paler branches, the trees would look rather flat. Allow the paint to dry.

Note: At this stage, upon reviewing the painting, I decided that I needed to strengthen some of the tones behind the wall, in order to increase the contrast between the wall and the moorland. To achieve this, I mixed a little neutral tint with some raw sienna and painted it in accordingly.

Tip: Remember to review a painting throughout its progression, making adjustments along the way as necessary.

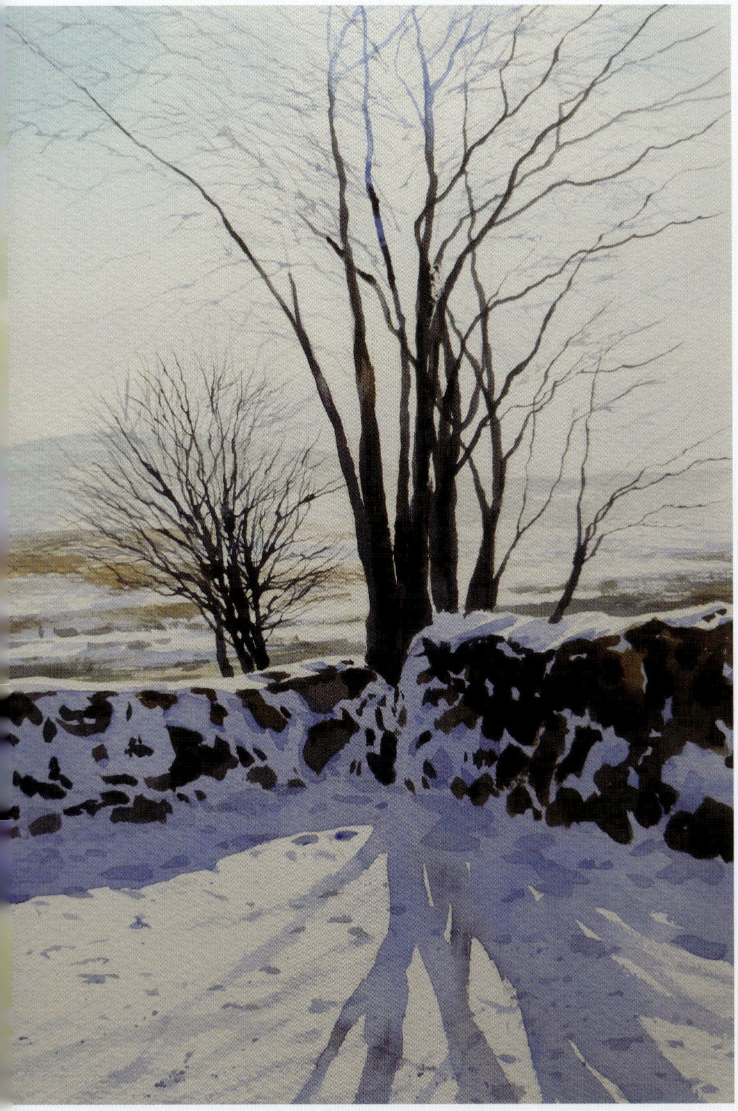

Step 7: Paint in the main trunks and branches.

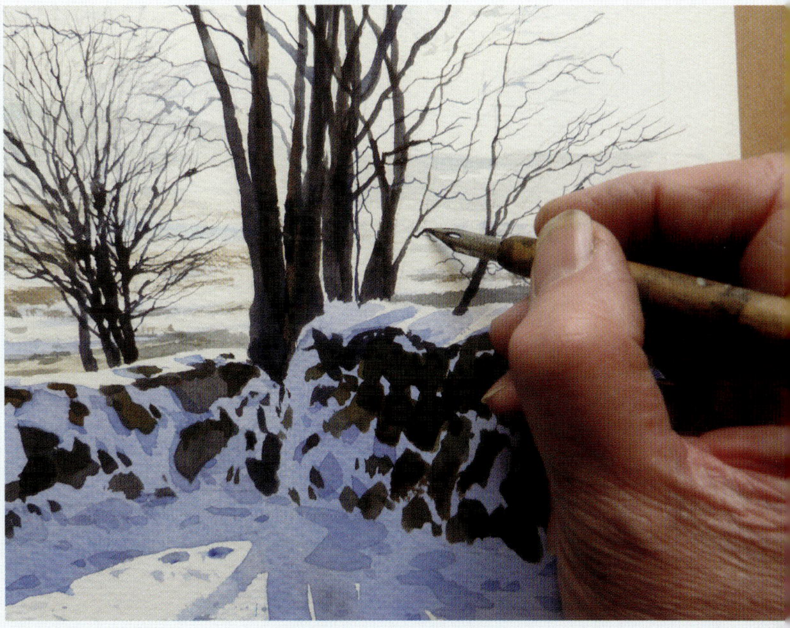

Step 8: Use the dip pen to draw in the finer branches.

Step 7: With mixes of ultramarine blue, neutral tint and burnt sienna, use the well-pointed No. 6 sable to paint in the main trunks and branches of the trees.

For the branches towards the top of the main tree, mix a palish wash of ultramarine blue and neutral tint. This lighter-toned wash is to indicate the bleaching effect of the strong sunlight coming through the trees' uppermost branches. Think of this stage as not so much painting but something more like drawing with paint.

Step 8: This step flows on almost seamlessly from the previous one, in that it works best if the previous step is still wet, as the paint applied with the dip pen will run into the still-wet paint of the branches, thereby avoiding an unnatural join. Using the same mix of ultramarine blue and neutral tint with burnt sienna, use the dip pen to draw out some of the finer, thinner branches. Don't worry if not all of the twigs and branches join up, any missing parts of the twigs or branches will be lost in the overall effect. As before, I like to think of this as drawing with paint.

Sometimes, the paint applied with a dip pen does not flow as freely as one would like when working with this drawing tool. It often helps to test the flow of paint first on a scrap piece of paper, before using the dip pen and paint mix on the painting.

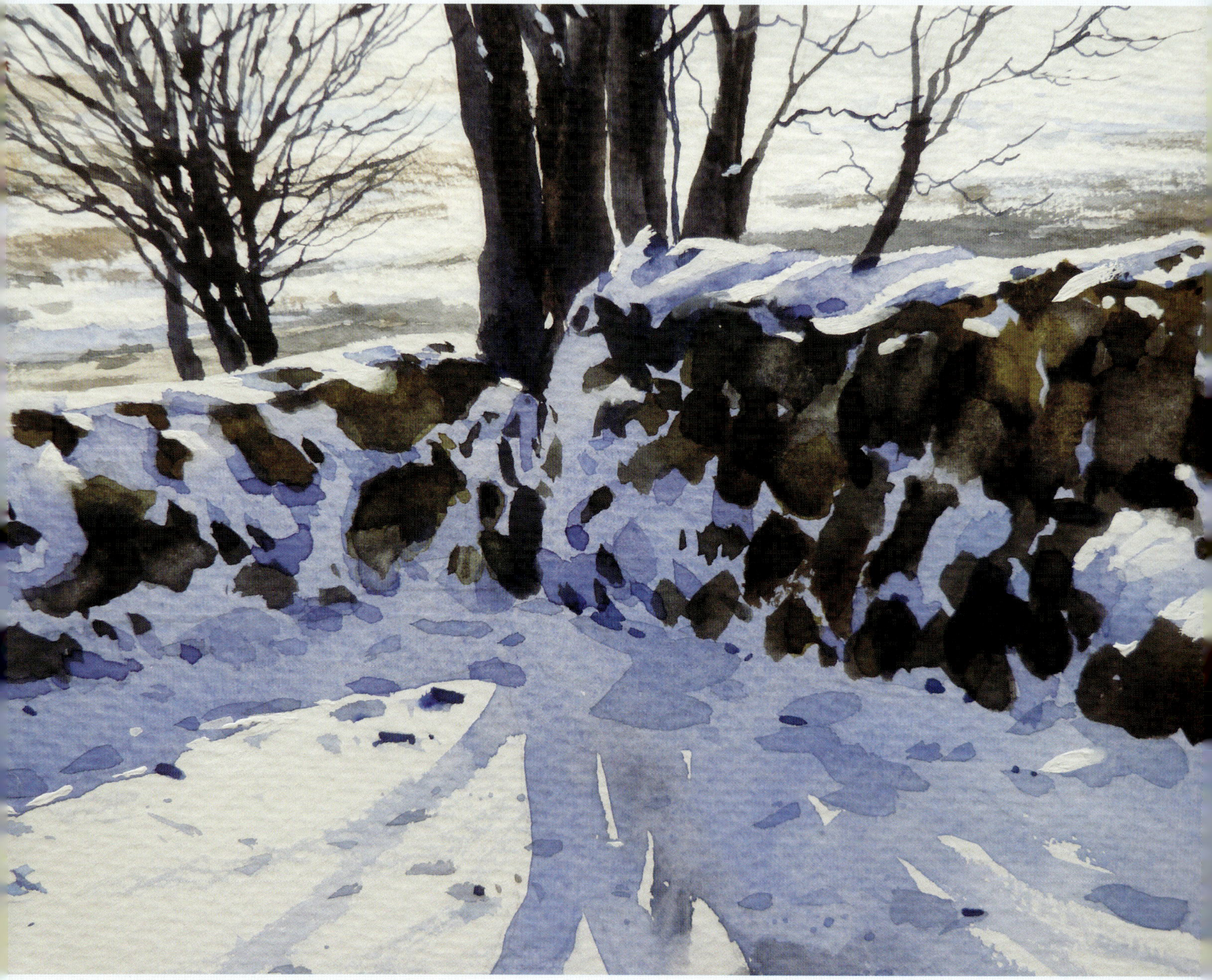

Step 9: Add the finishing touches.

Step 9: Having made certain that the previous step has completely dried, remove the masking fluid from the painting by using a Maskaway eraser. With clean water, lift some paint from some of the depicted wall stones to soften their edges. Add any final shadows, if needed. Use white acrylic gouache to touch in and define some of the snow on the wall tops, where appropriate. Add touches of white acrylic gouache with a little ultramarine blue to depict snow caught in and on some of the branches.

Finally, touch in a few leaves that have been caught in the tree since the autumn, with a mix of burnt sienna and ultramarine blue.

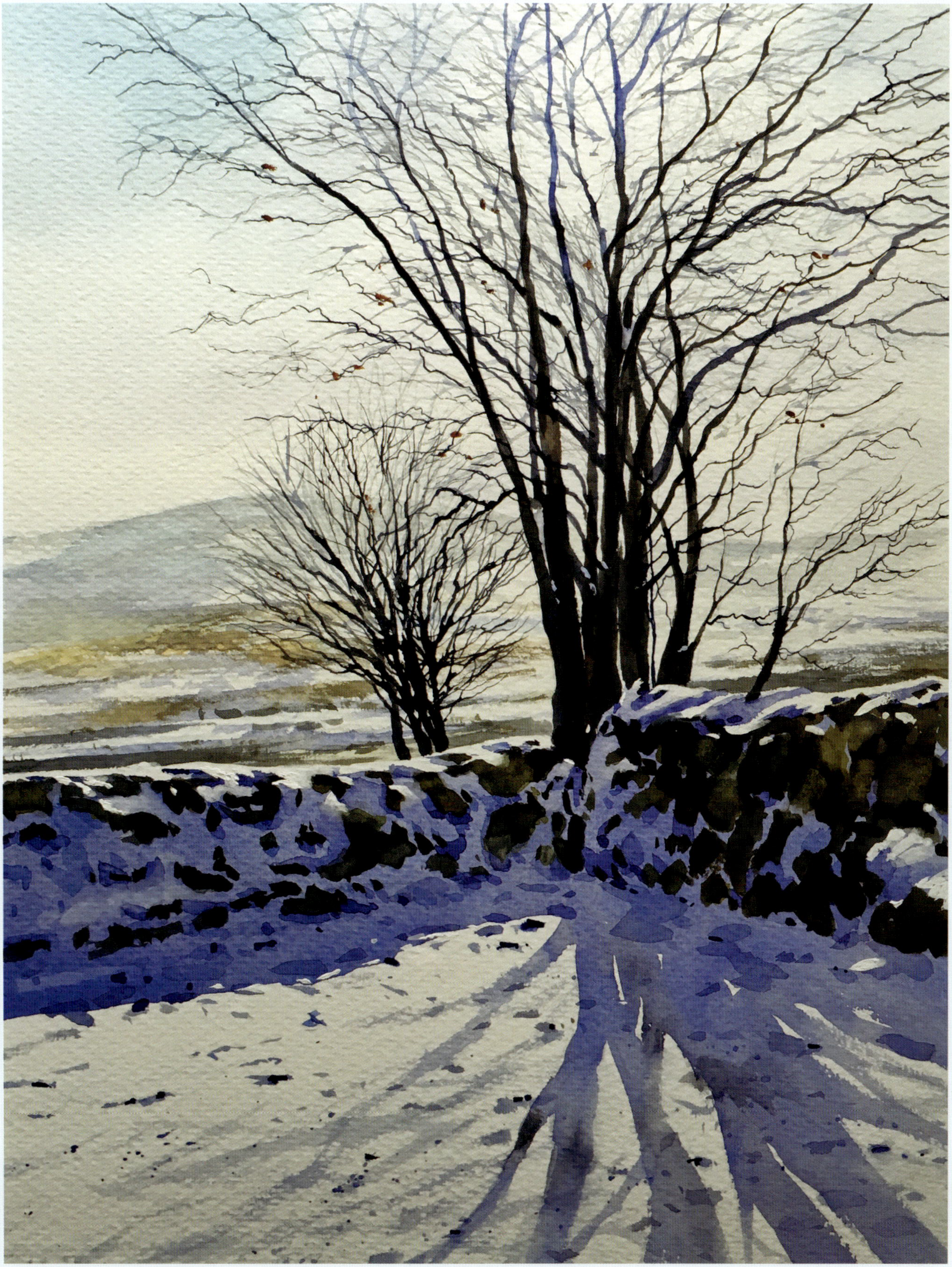

The finished painting: *Winter Landscape*, watercolour, 29cm × 38 cm (11½in × 15in), Rob Dudley.

PROJECT

Nearly All Gone Now

Rob Dudley

The Inspiration

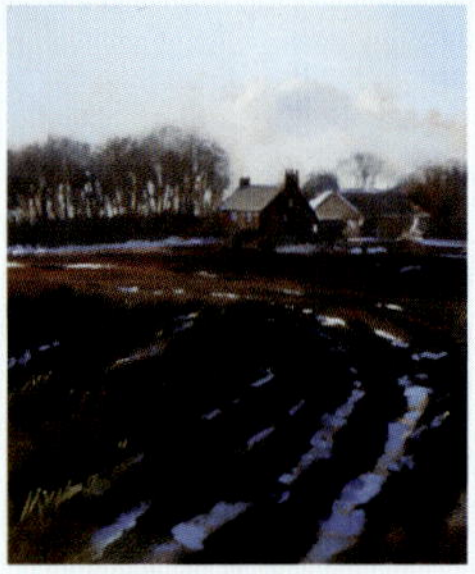

Living as I do in south Devon, it doesn't snow very often, so, when it does, I try to get out into the landscape to sketch and photograph the snow's all-too-fleeting visit, with the aim to make some paintings featuring snow. Such was the case one day in late winter. It had snowed overnight, and snow covered the fields near to my studio with a light, white, dusting of the elusive stuff! I wasn't able to get out until late in the afternoon; after a bright sunny morning with relatively warm temperatures, much of the snow was beginning to melt. I needed to get a move on. With the light just beginning to fade towards early winter twilight, I came across this scene: a cosy-looking farm cottage, framed by a stand of winter trees, with the last patches of shadowed snow sitting in the furrowed field. A very traditional English scene, the like of which has inspired countless generations of landscape painters, and I was no exception to this inspiration. I was hooked; it was a painting waiting to happen.

Developing the Idea

The melting had caused many of the footpaths and fields to become wet and squelchy underfoot. Water was beginning to run freely. The feel of the land was beginning to become heavy; the crispness and lightness of snow was being replaced by something far heavier and cloying. Because of this, I decided, before even getting back to the studio, to use oil paints for this piece, as I felt that they complemented the conditions within the landscape. The use of watercolour, by its very nature being light and airy, would have resulted in a different feel to the painting than that I was trying to convey.

The painting would be just as much about the wonderful blue-shadowed snow and its bright highlights as it was about the cosy cottage. The wonderful, curving furrows play a key role in leading the viewer's eye towards the cottage; without the cottage, the furrows would have pointed towards nothing, which would be likely to prove somewhat of a visual anticlimax. Both the furrows and the cottage strengthened the design, because of the presence and the influence that each brought to the other.

In the few minutes that I spent looking at the scene before me, I became aware that, as the late-afternoon light levels began to drop, the tracery of the trees seemed to close in, becoming denser, ever more solid. Where minutes before the branches had seemed etched on the sky, as I watched, they began to be lost within it.

The edges to the buildings, furrows, walls, hedges and shadows seemed to soften and merge. The only sharp areas were the bright patches of snow, a sunlit roof and some brightly lit stalks of foreground grasses.

But is it about trees…?

This painting might not at first glance appear to be about trees at all. The snow in the field and the farm buildings may appear to play a more leading role.

However, without the trees, the painting would have lacked scale and interest and would have been a lesser thing without the trees' inclusion. This is a case of the supporting act being is as important as the leading role. Don't forget that the Oscars are given to leading actors *and* to actors in supporting roles; each needs the other to shine!

Information Gathering

Producing a sketch or quick colour study was not possible because of the rapidly changing light conditions. Therefore, I decided to take some quick photographs by using my phone; these really were snapshots, and normally I would choose not to work from such reference material, but on this occasion it was my only option. I managed to take about ten shots before the light changed and the view had become significantly different to the one that had caused me to stop.

With so few photographs and no drawings to work from, I spent as much time as I could committing key aspects of the scene to memory.

These remembered details combined with the photographs would be my starting point for the making of the painting.

Designing the Painting

Layout

After producing some small thumbnail sketches, I decided to use a portrait format for the painting, incorporating a low viewpoint into the design. This low viewpoint would in turn raise the horizon, allowing me space below it to include some of the foreground features and patterns, crucial for the painting's overall design to succeed. Using the rule of thirds as the underlying grid structure to the layout, I placed the farm buildings and cottage along the top third line, using the field furrows to lead the viewer's eye from bottom left up towards the buildings. The trees to both sides of the farm act to frame the buildings and, by so doing, prevent the viewer's eye from falling out of the painting.

Tone

The tonal range – lights and darks – within much of the painting would be quite narrow, with just a few punchy contrasts: the sunlit snow lying on the dark field, for example. The considered distribution and balance of tones throughout the painting would be important to the painting's overall success or failure. For instance, the strong tonal contrasts between the darks of the field and the lights of the sunlit snow can be used to create interest within the painting, whereas the closer, more subdued tones of the farm buildings will cause these buildings to recede into the background, creating the impression of distance.

Colour

The colours chosen were very similar to those within the actual landscape. Working with just six well-chosen colours, I ensured a harmony for and balance to the palette, with nothing standing garishly out of place, much like the feeling of the scene at that particular time of day.

Just as my choice of colours was very important, so too was my choice of ground to paint on. I chose to work on a grey, midtoned board. This colour and tone would make it easier for me to assess the lights and darks of the paining and, in addition, to pull the whole painting together in the later stages, when areas of the coloured ground would peep through.

Texture

When working with oils, I tend to think of texture in three ways: the texture of the board or canvas that I am working on and the influence that this has on the painting, the texture of the subject matter, of the tree trunks, twigs, dried grasses and so on, and the texture of the applied paint itself. For this painting, I worked on a comparatively smooth, gessoed board and chose to work with relatively thin paint, in order to prevent the surface of the paint from becoming too thick.

When painting on a small scale such as for this painting, I am wary about applying the paint too thickly; it can easily become a feature in its own right, taking away some of the attention from the subject. I wanted to avoid this from happening.

Painting the Image

Materials and equipment

- Gessoed MDF board:
  - Prepared with a ground of a dilute mix of French ultramarine and burnt sienna, 25cm × 29cm (10in × 11½in)
- Oil-painting brushes:
  - No. 1 round
  - No. 4 flat
  - No. 8 filbert
- Water-mixable oil colours:
  - Alizarin crimson
  - Burnt sienna
  - Cadmium yellow light
  - French ultramarine blue
  - Sap green
  - Titanium white
- Palette
- Palette knife
- Dipper for water

Note: Other than for step 1, where the paint mix needs to be thinned to a watery consistency, in order to draw in the main shapes, all other mixes are either arrived at by using paints straight from their tubes or, when the neat paints are too stiff to work, by the addition of just a few drops of water to the paints.

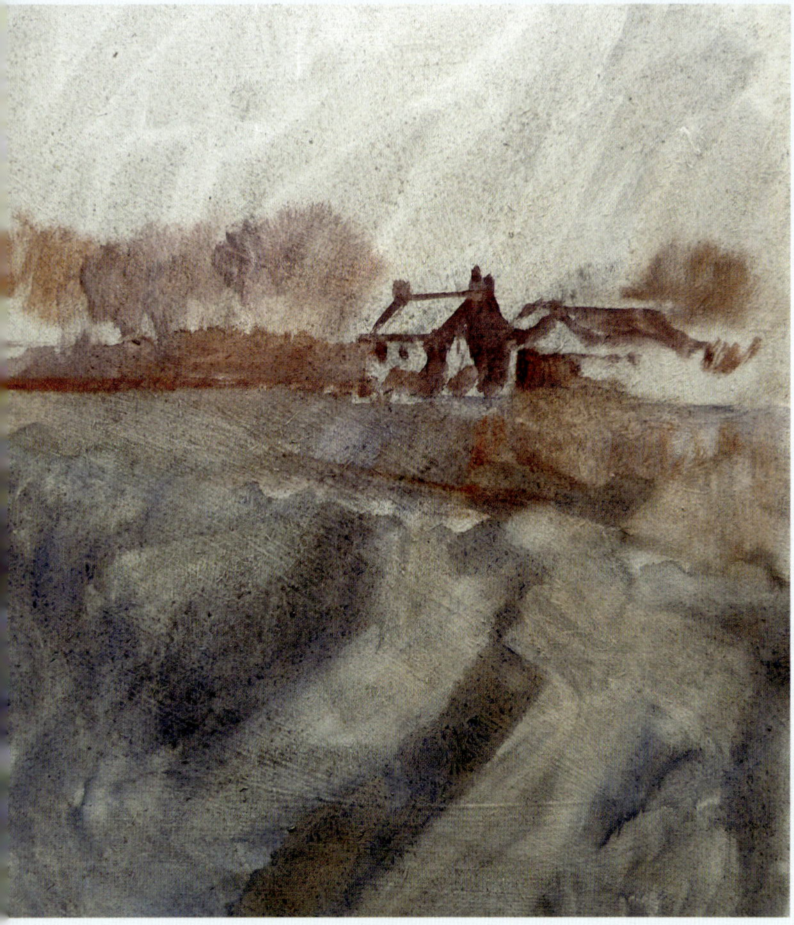

Step 1: Sketch in the initial shapes.

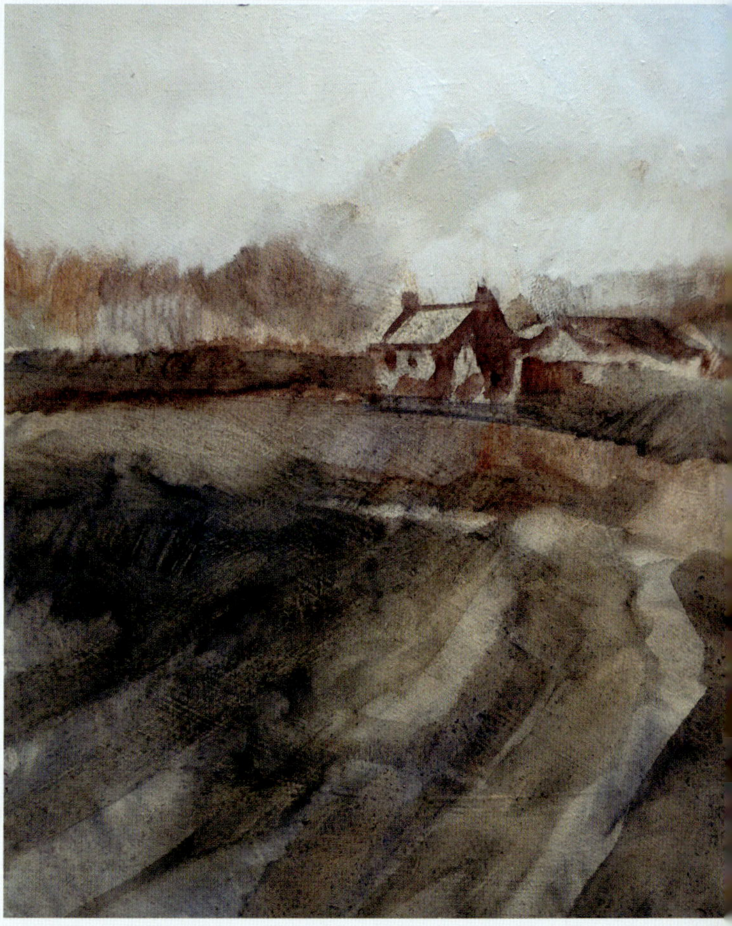

Step 2: Introduce the sky.

Step 1: With a watery mix of alizarin crimson, French ultramarine blue and some burnt sienna, rough out the main shapes of the design by using the flat brush. Resist the temptation to draw in any detail. This stage is about getting down some basic shapes and an indication as to where some of the darks are likely to be. A painting takes time to emerge; it has to be coaxed and encouraged, so don't try to rush it into existence.

Allow the paint to dry for a few minutes.

Step 2: I wanted to give an indication of the depicted sky's tone early on, as this would help me to assess the other tones within the landscape below it. The sky is by no means finished at this stage, and I will return to it later, to strengthen it accordingly. With a mix of titanium white, French ultramarine blue and a touch of burnt sienna, using the flat brush and vigorous strokes, roughly paint in the sky, being careful not to use too much paint. Control can often be lost in the early stages of an oil painting, if too much paint is applied too soon.

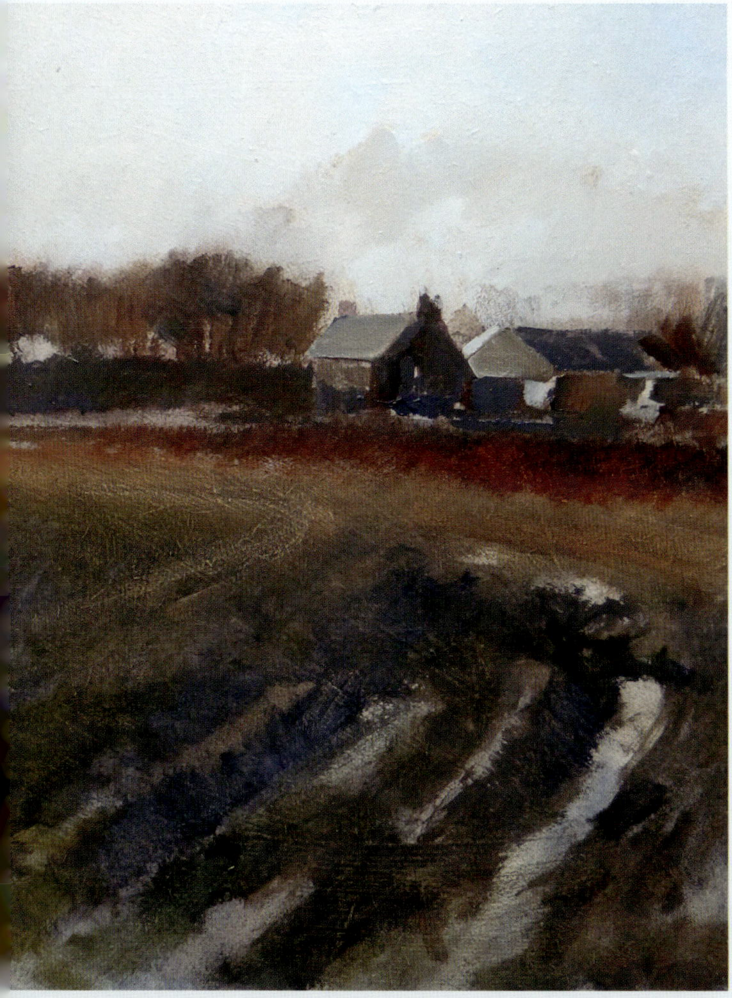

Step 3: Begin to establish the shapes of the buildings and furrowed field.

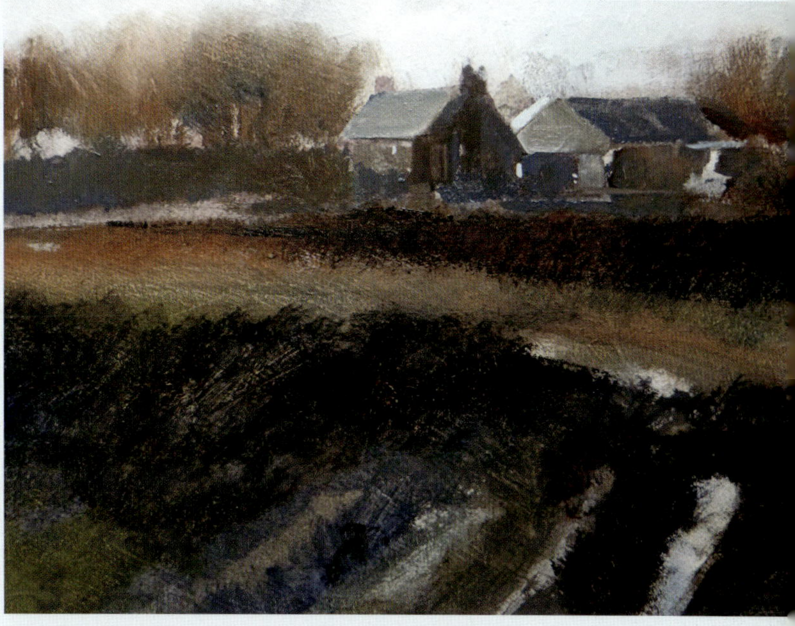

Step 4: Strengthen the farm buildings and foreground.

Step 3: Working with mixes of French ultramarine blue, burnt sienna and titanium white, loosely block in areas of colour and tone for depictions of the farm buildings and distant trees. Again be careful not to add too much detail and structure at this stage.

Moving to the depiction of the field, use a mix of burnt sienna with French ultramarine blue to loosely scumble in the field and its furrows.

Use a mix of sap green with cadmium yellow light to suggest some of the grasses in the left foreground.

Step 4: Working with stronger mixes of burnt sienna, French ultramarine blue and a touch of titanium white, tighten up the structure of the depicted farm buildings. Even at this stage, be careful not to overdo the detail. Using a larger brush will prevent too much detail from being added. With stronger, darker mixes of the above colours, reinforce the foreground furrows, with the movement of the brushmarks indicating the furrows' direction within the field.

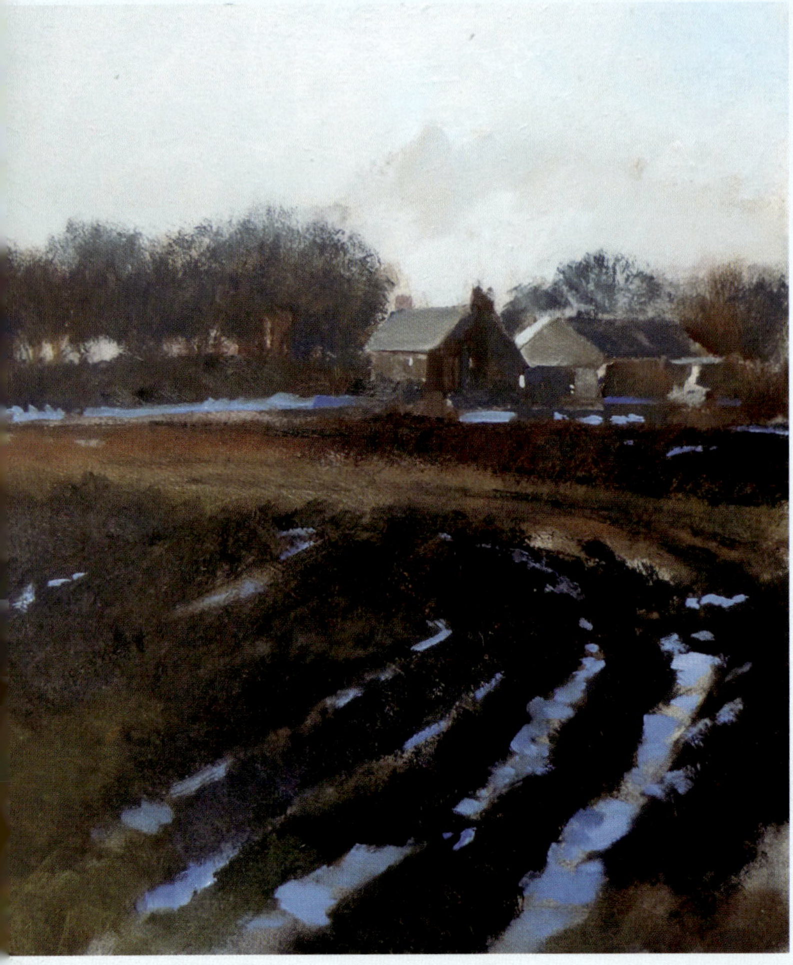

Step 5: Add snow and develop the trees.

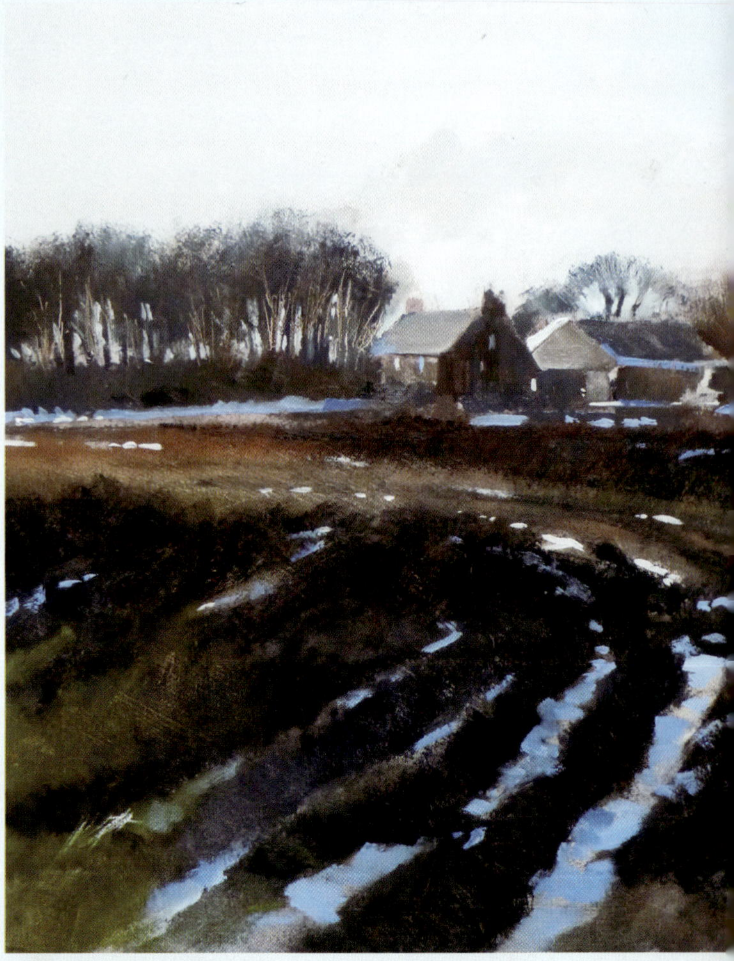

Step 6: Add some highlights.

Step 5: For the next stage, use the filbert brush and a mix of French ultramarine blue with burnt sienna. Hold the brush loosely, so that the paint hardly touches the board and lightly touch in the tree shapes on each side of the group of farm buildings. Using this technique to indicate the trees allows for some of the previously applied colour to show through in patches, which in turn creates a richer, more interesting effect, rather than a flat, solid layer of colour.

Then, with a mixture of titanium white and French ultramarine blue, touch in the patches of snow lying in the furrows and along the bottom of the hedgerow.

Note how the snow sits in the bottom of the furrows, with the lines of snow appearing to get narrower as they run further away from the viewer. This strong diagonal movement into the painting helps to move the viewer's eye from foreground to background in an unfussy, almost effortless transition. Think of these furrows as signposts pointing the way.

Step 6: With the No. 1 round and pure titanium white, add some touches of paint to indicate the brightly lit snow. Be careful not to add too many touches, however; it is easily done, and too many will create too much attention. With the minimum of fuss, hint at the farmhouse windows. This is not the time to put in six panes of glass and the curtains! Subtlety is key. With the end of the brush, scratch in a few suggestions of trunks and branches for the surrounding trees.

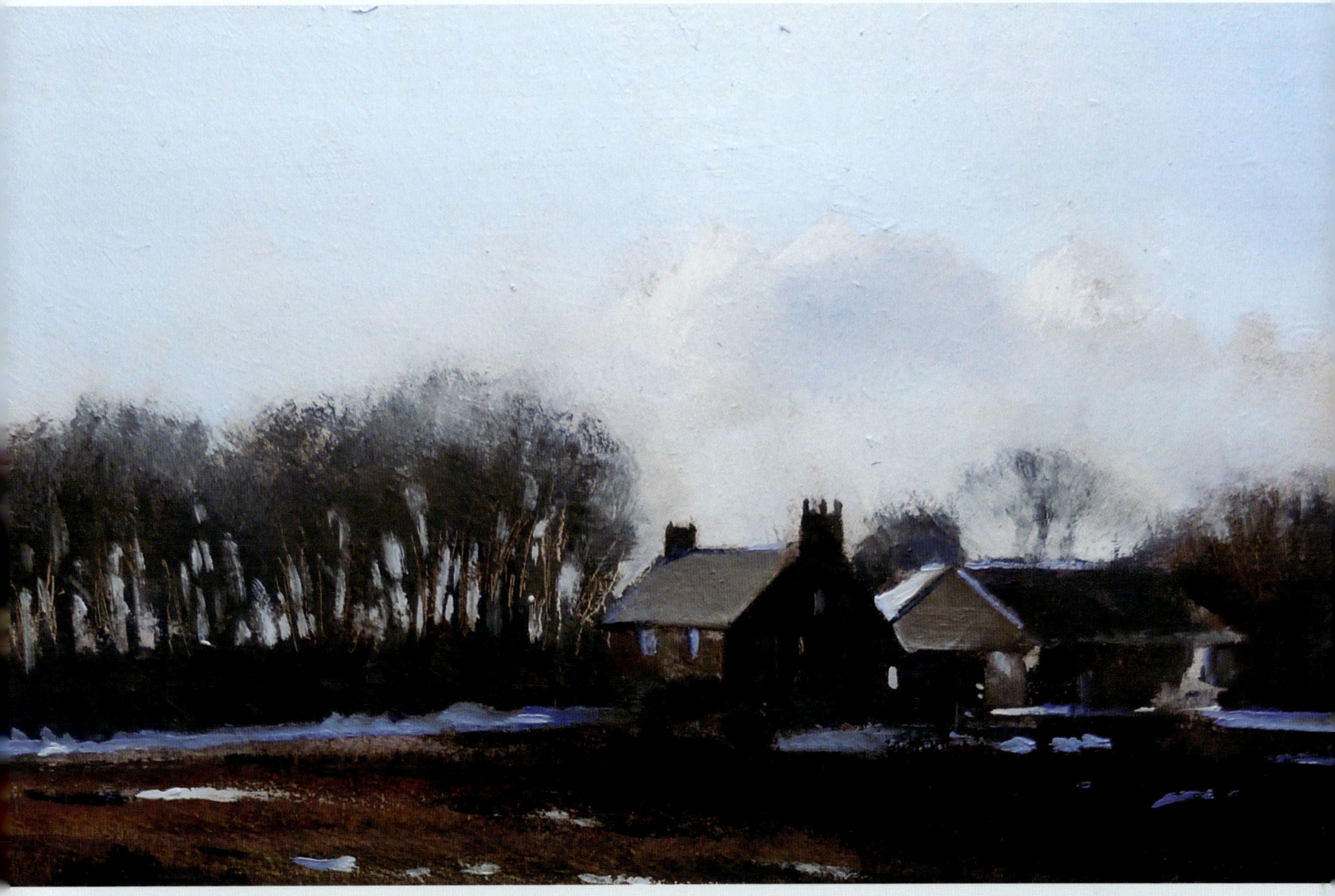

Step 7: Add the finishing touches.

Step 7: With the No. 4 flat and a mix of titanium white and French ultramarine blue, paint in the sky, varying the mix, leaving a few cloud shapes towards the skyline. Touch these clouds in with titanium white and a little burnt sienna, with their shadows being created by the addition of French ultramarine blue.

Use the sky mix to indicate some of the sky showing between the trunks of the trees along the hedgerow.

Mix a bright yellow-green from the sap green and cadmium yellow light, and flick in this mix to depict some of the foreground grasses.

At this stage, I felt that the trees seen above the roof of the barn were rather lumpy and heavy and somewhat distracting to the overall design of the painting. So, with the sky mix still on the palette, I lightly painted over the trunks and scuffed some colour over the rest of these trees. The effect was to lessen both the tone and the detail of the trees, overall reducing their impact on the painting.

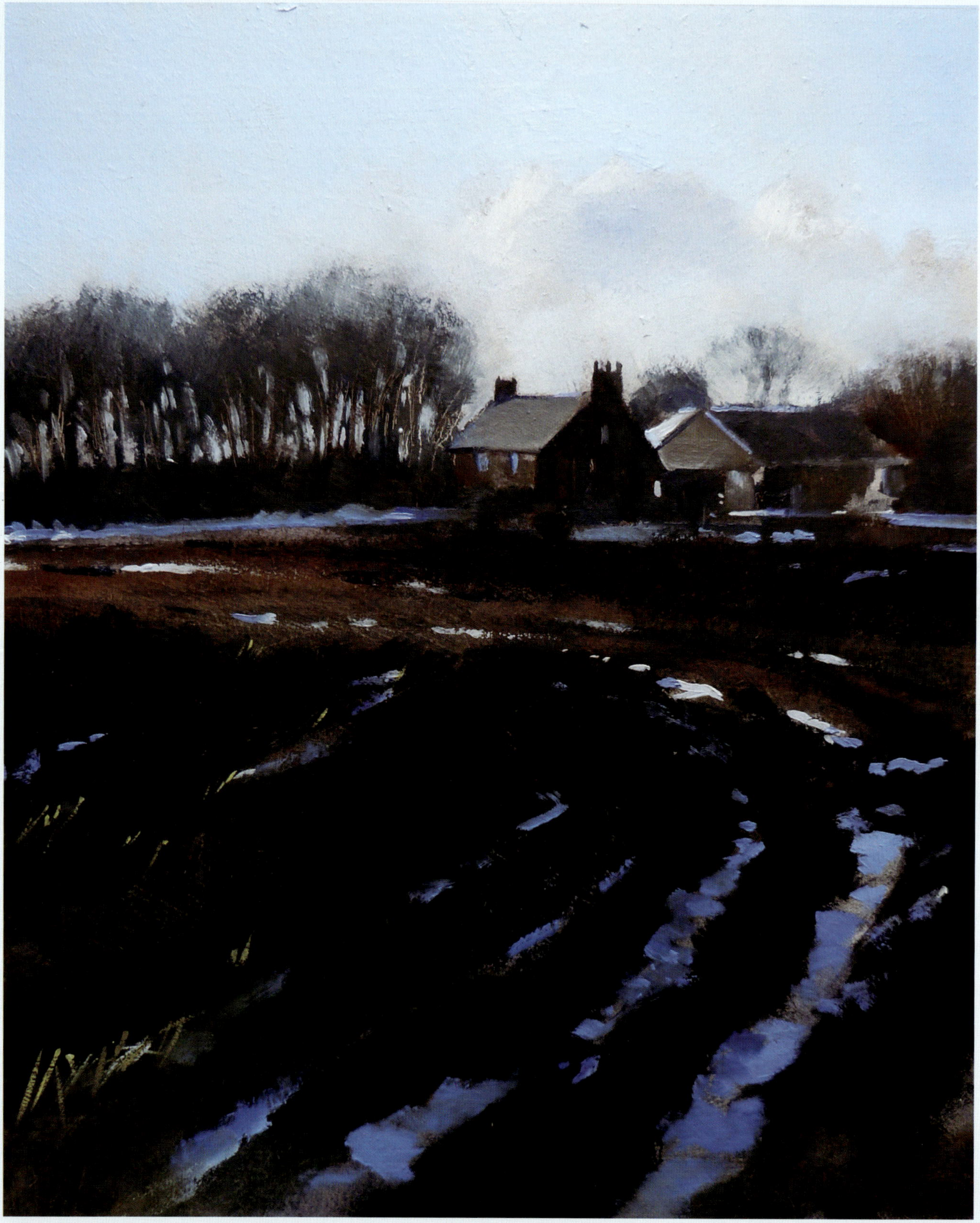

The finished painting: *Nearly All Gone Now*, water-mixable oils on board, 25cm × 29cm (9¾in × 11½in), Rob Dudley.

PROJECT

Winter Sunset

Siân Dudley

The Inspiration

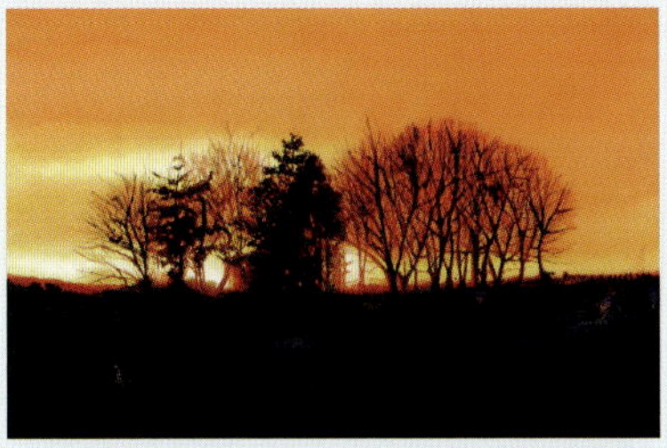

There is something wonderful about sunsets that never fails to draw our attention. During a walk on Dartmoor one winter's day, we were struck by the intensity of colour that we witnessed as the sun went down. It was more like a summer sunset than a winter one, so, when I spotted the stand of trees with their wintry laciness on the horizon, I couldn't resist taking a few photographs. The tracery of the trunks and branches against the orange glow was breathtaking.

Developing the Idea

As usual for quick snapshots, the photographs were a little disappointing. The camera software had reduced the intensity of the orange glow and diminished the variation in tone and colour in the landscape to a flat black.

This painting was about the silhouettes of the trees against the sky, which the flat blackness of the landscape exaggerated. Taking inspiration from this, I decided to lose all detail in the landscape to focus attention on the trees.

Making a painting glow so much that the viewer feels the need to squint at its brightness is a challenge. This is an ideal subject with which to accept that challenge! This painting should be very bright, with strong tonal contrasts, to emphasize the brilliance of the sun shining through the trees.

Information Gathering

Sunsets rarely allow you enough time to take colour notes with paint. This photograph was the main physical information available for this painting but, of course, everyone has memories of sunsets. This is a prime example of relying heavily on memory for the information needed to make the painting. While witnessing the sunset, I took particular mental note of the colours that I was seeing. The value of a good, hard stare should not be underestimated in enhancing the memory for later reference!

This sunset project is also a good example of having to take particular care to focus your attention on your intentions for the finished painting. This will enable you to make decisions as you work. How bright of an image would you like to hang on your wall? In doing this painting, how important is it to produce an image to frame, compared with the importance of what you might learn during the painting of the image? If learning takes precedence over creating something for display, you may well decide to make the painting much more orange than you would if you were planning to hang it in your living room. This type of information is not directly practical in the way that a sketch would be, but it is just as valid to use this knowledge when planning a painting.

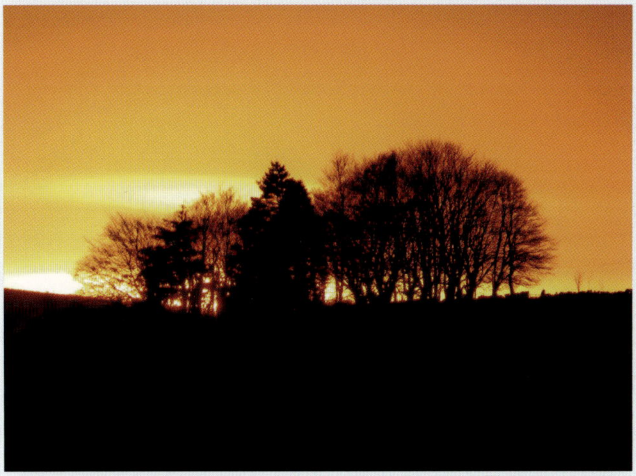

Reference photograph for *Winter Sunset*.

Designing the Painting

Layout

The original photograph was cropped to give a more balanced composition. Using the rule of thirds, the most intense area of light was placed near the intersection of the lower left thirds. The silhouettes of the stand of trees lie across the middle third of the painting.

Tone

This painting requires a huge range of tonal values, with the juxtaposition of the lights and darks and the visual bridge between the two extremes being vitally important to the success of the image.

Colour

This painting needs to glow, so the paints chosen need to be fresh and bright and to retain their intensity upon drying. Glazing techniques will be invaluable here, as they result in richer colours than are achievable by the application of a single layer of a homogenous mix. The application of glazing techniques means that the colours used for the lower layers must be transparent (opaque colours move too easily) and, if possible, of a staining character. Schmincke's translucent orange naturally retains a good depth of colour and vibrancy when dry that is intensified when it is glazed over lemon yellow. This orange also mixes with blues to give a range of browns, which will be useful for the paler tones of the depicted trees.

Around the edges of the orange glow was a sliver of red. I chose to mix permanent rose with the translucent orange to achieve this colour, as this mix does not dry flat in the way that some reds do.

In a painting, a flat, black lower section would be boring; what is needed in order to paint this region of the painting is a very dark tone mixed from a selection of colours, allowing the different colours to show within the mix, while keeping the tone extremely dark. Glazing this over an orange base layer would also help to add interest.

This same mix could be used for the darks of the trees. A suitable mix can be achieved by using indigo, ultramarine blue and burnt sienna.

Texture

This painting is about the colour and the shapes of the silhouetted trees. As such, textural marks do not play a huge part in this image. Having said that, the lower, very dark section of the painting would be boring if it were completely devoid of texture, so a selection of broad, sweeping brushmarks could be used here to *very* loosely imply the form of the landscape.

Painting the Image

Materials and equipment

- Watercolour paper:
  - Bockingford NOT 300gsm/140lb, stretched and taped to a board
- Watercolour brushes:
  - Da Vinci Series 35, size 4
  - St Petersburg round, size 10
  - Swordliners, medium and small
- Artist-quality watercolours:
  - Burnt sienna (Daler Rowney)
  - Indigo (Daler Rowney)
  - Lemon yellow (Daler Rowney)
  - Permanent rose
  - Translucent orange (Schmincke)
  - Ultramarine blue
- 4B pencil
- Eraser
- Tracing paper
- Black pen
- Palette
- Kitchen roll

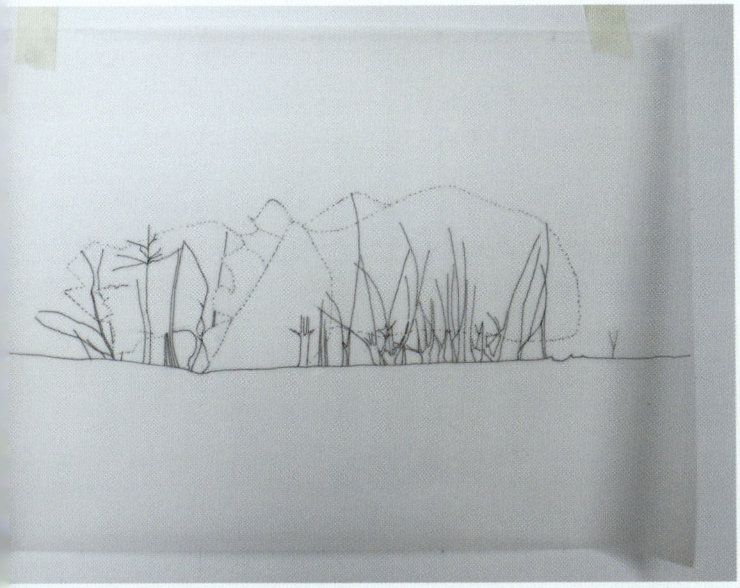

Step 1: Draw in the horizon line and the outlines of the trees, then produce a tracing of this drawing.

Step 2: Apply a variegated wash of lemon yellow, leaving the highlights unpainted and white.

Step 1: Begin by drawing in the horizon line, then continue by drawing in the outlines of the tree trunks, to place them on the page. There is no need to draw in more than the outlines of the main trunks and branches, as the trees can be 'drawn' in with paint and a paintbrush as you work, allowing you to work more freely. Lightly mark in the edges of the trees as a guide. I have drawn very little; if you feel the need to draw more than this, you should, but try not to overdo it.

It is a good idea to make a tracing of this drawing; in the unfortunate event of a big wash going wrong, it will be quick and easy to start again by using the tracing to replicate the composition.

Step 2: Using lemon yellow and water, apply a very wet wash. As you work around the area of the sun, decrease the tone, fading it to white. Do not wet the area of the brightest light, so that paint cannot flow into this area of the paper. While the paint is still very wet, use an almost dry brush to lift off some of the paint, to create a soft edge. (As a warning, this brush should be almost dry to avoid the risk of creating cauliflowers. Touch it on to kitchen roll to remove excess water before using it on the painting.)

In other areas of the painting, increase the tone as you move down the paper.

Allow the paint to dry thoroughly.

Tip: I have not used masking fluid here, as the patch of intense white light is large enough work around. If you would feel more confident in creating your painting by masking the very centre of the white area, do so. This type of wash needs to be carried out confidently, as being tentative causes delays that are often long enough to result in unwanted cauliflowers.

Step 3: Apply a variegated wash of translucent orange, leaving a little of the yellow wash visible near the highlights.

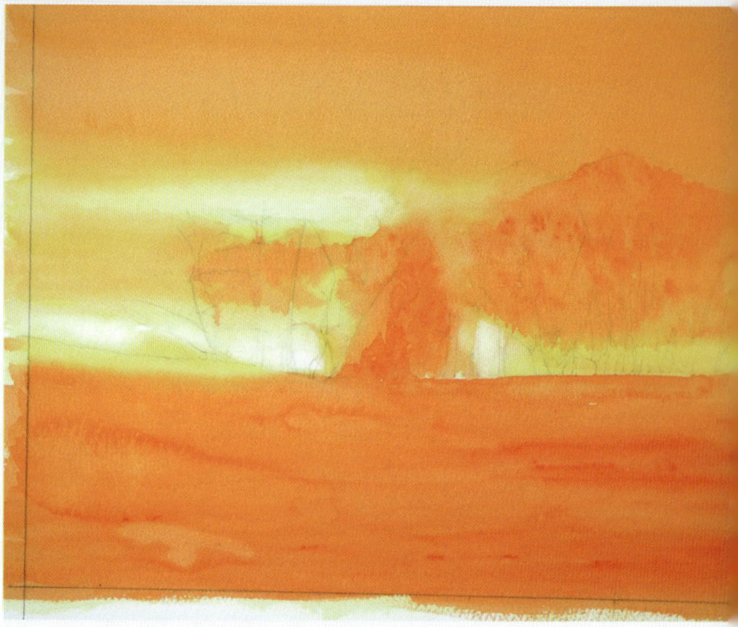

Step 4: Strengthen the tones on the landscape and behind the trees.

Step 3: When the first layer of paint is completely dry, apply translucent orange by using the same techniques as those described in step 2. Keep the colour even across the sky, gradating the tone towards the highlights and allowing some of the yellow base layer to show through.

In the area below the trees, the paint can be applied more unevenly; a few cauliflowers here will help to imply the texture of the landscape.

Allow the paint to dry thoroughly.

Step 4: By using a medium tone of the translucent orange, increase the overall tone of the landscape. Working with a slightly drier mix of the paint and water, move the brush horizontally across the page. Allow a few cauliflowers to develop.

Using this same medium tone, add some paint to the darker areas within the area of trees.

The sky itself is not darker here; the darker appearance is actually due to fine branches. Rather than paint in every branch, they can be suggested by using a deeper tone of the orange.

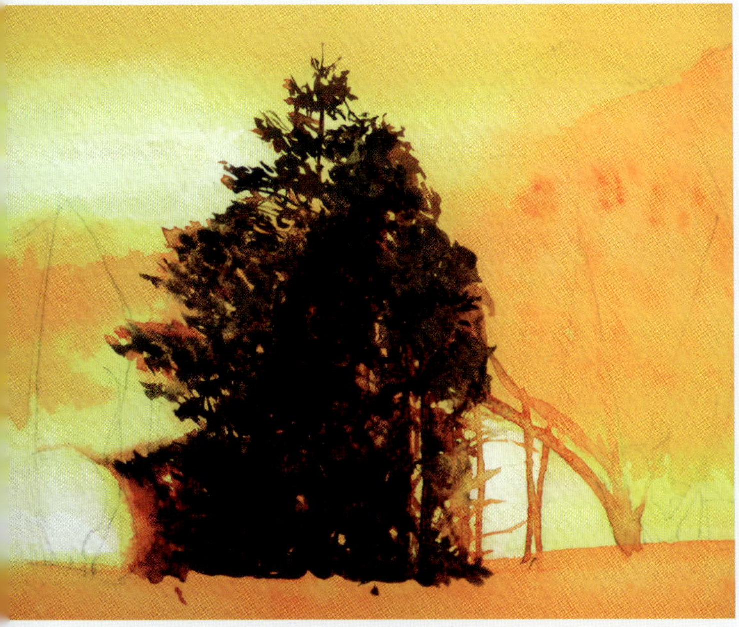

Step 5: Paint in the large conifer silhouetted by the sun, gradating the colour at the edges where the sunlight appears to melt the tree.

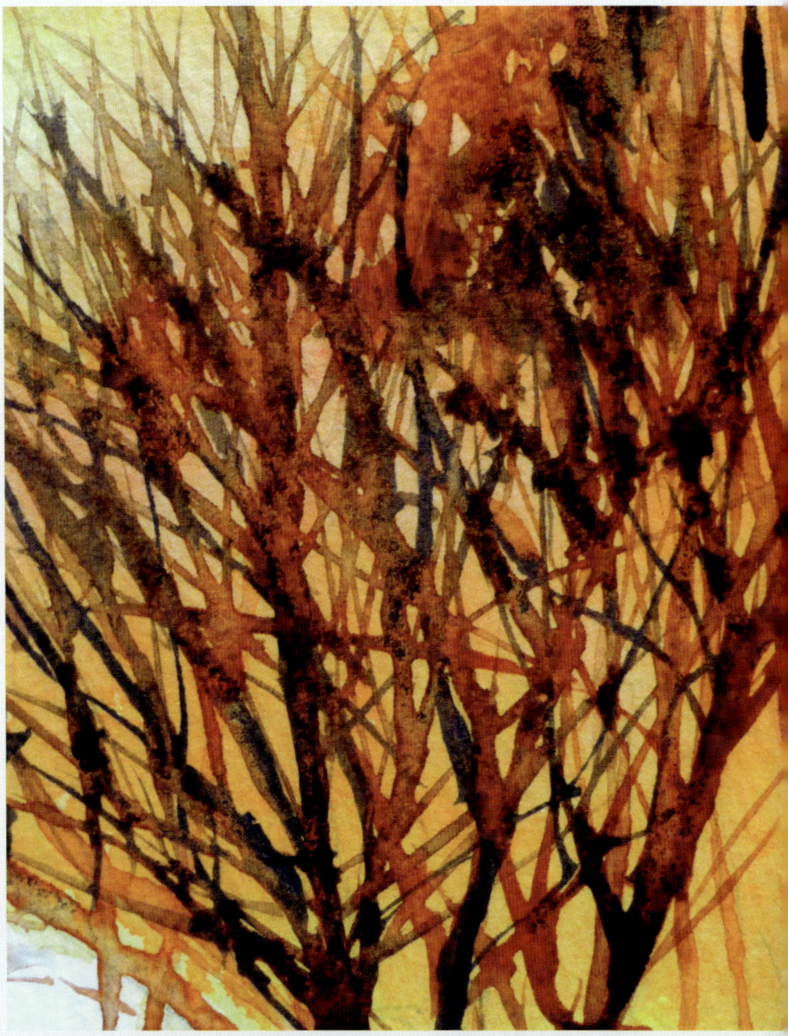

Step 6: Paint in the tree trunks and branches, varying the colours to reflect the direction of the sunlight.

Step 5: Make up a red-orange mix by using permanent rose and translucent orange and a rich orange-brown mix by using translucent orange, ultramarine blue and burnt sienna. Keep the paint mixes quite thick, to produce dark tones.

Using a brush with a good point, paint in the dark conifer in the centre of the stand. Leave patches of the underwashes showing through. Use the redder colour at the edges, allowing it to run into the browns towards the centre of the tree. Soften any hard edges near the area of intense light.

Tip: Do not wet the area of the highlight. Work from the light area towards the darks, to reduce the risk of paint running towards the highlight.

Step 6: Using the red-orange mix, begin to paint in the tree trunks. While the paint applied for the trunks is still wet, drop in a little of the browner mix, allow the colours to mix on the paper.

Take care that the sides of the trunks nearest the highlights are red and darken the trunk edges that are away from the sun.

Have a variety of colour mixes ready. Using a swordliner brush, paint in the branches of the trees. Draw the branches up, and out, from the trunks. Vary the pressure on the tip of the brush to achieve different thicknesses of branches. Having rinsed the brush, draw more branches by pulling the brush though the still-wet paint, allowing the water to dilute the tones. Again, while the paint is still wet, drop in other colours, allowing them to run together.

Use the pencil guidelines to establish where the tops of the trees are. Keep stepping back to assess the painting. If in doubt about whether you have enough branches, stop! Reassess, and add more branches only if you need to.

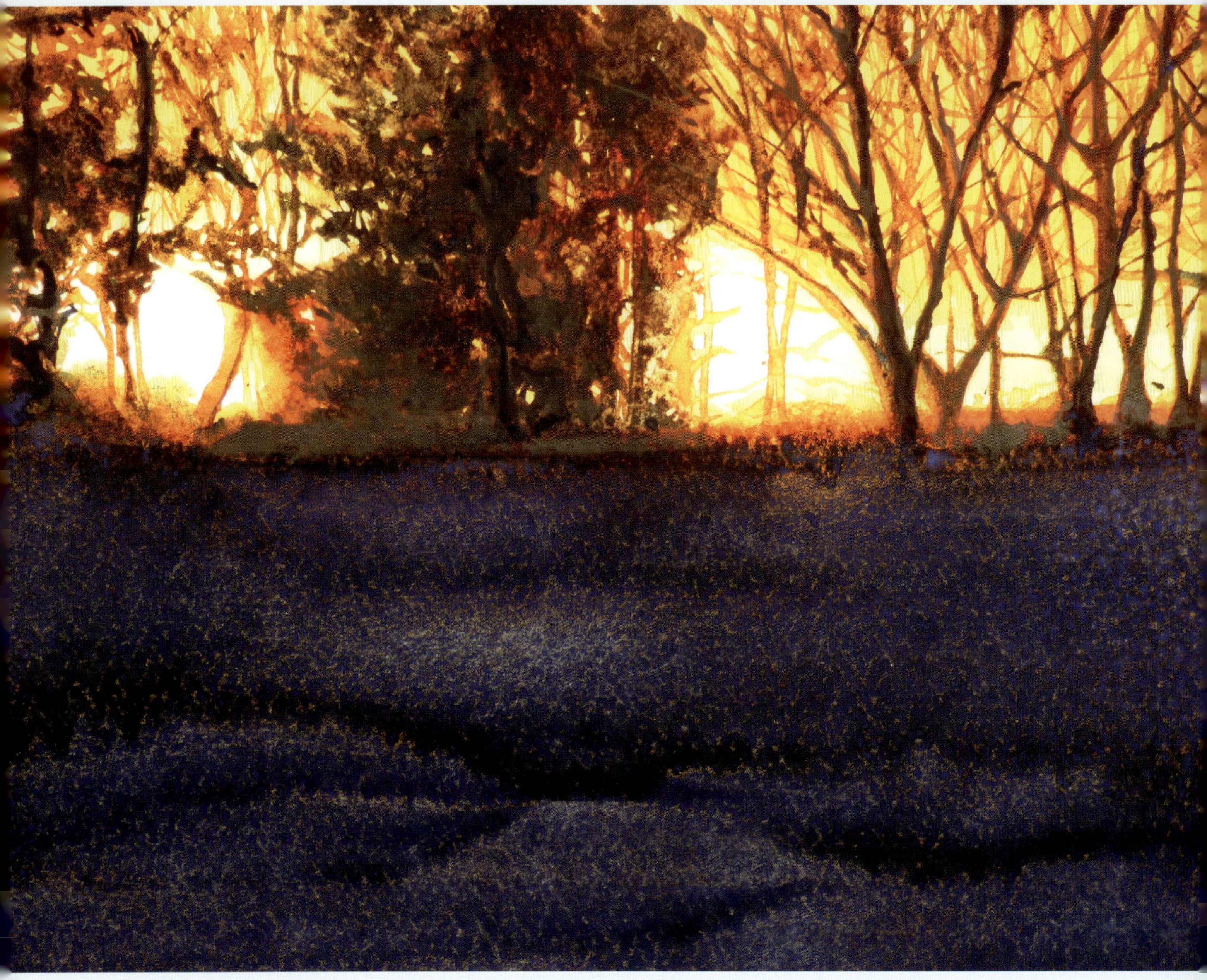

Step 7: Using a very strong, dark mix, apply a wash to the landscape, allowing some of the underwash to show through in places.

Step 7: Mix up a very strong, dark mix of indigo, ultramarine blue and burnt sienna. Make sure that you have enough of this mix to cover the lower section of the painting. Try to paint this layer in one wash, repainting this section to obtain the dark tone needed for it only if absolutely necessary.

Using a large brush and horizontal hand movements, paint in the shadowy landscape. Work at a slight angle on to dry paper, catching the bead of paint as you move down the page. Begin this application by adding a thin line of water across the top edge of the depicted land, to give the impression that the glow of the sunset is melting the edge of the land. Allow some lines to develop. This area of the painting is inspired by – not of – the landscape and it should be so dark that very little detail shows.

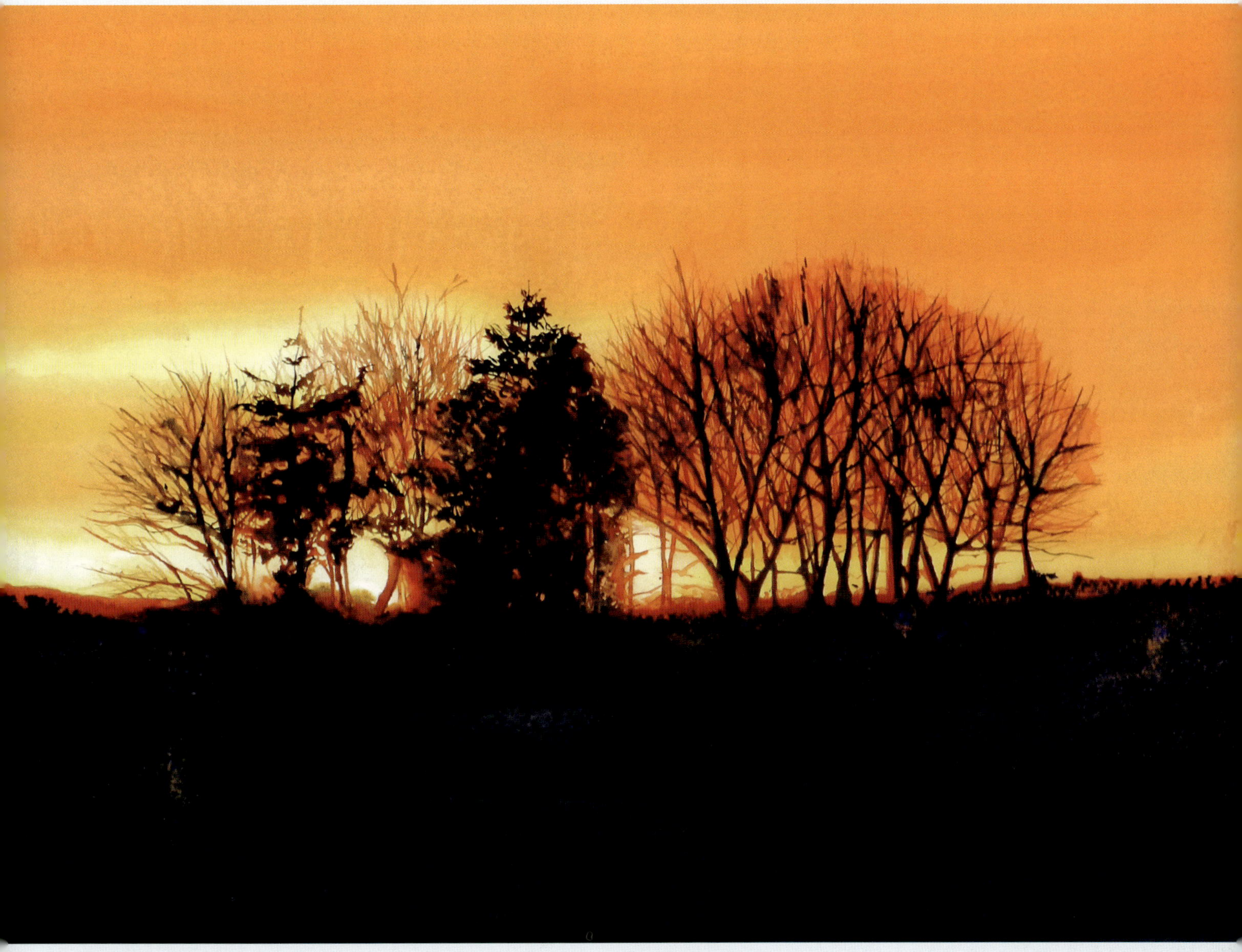

The finished painting: *Winter Sunset*, watercolour, 42cm × 29cm (16½in × 11½in), Siân Dudley.

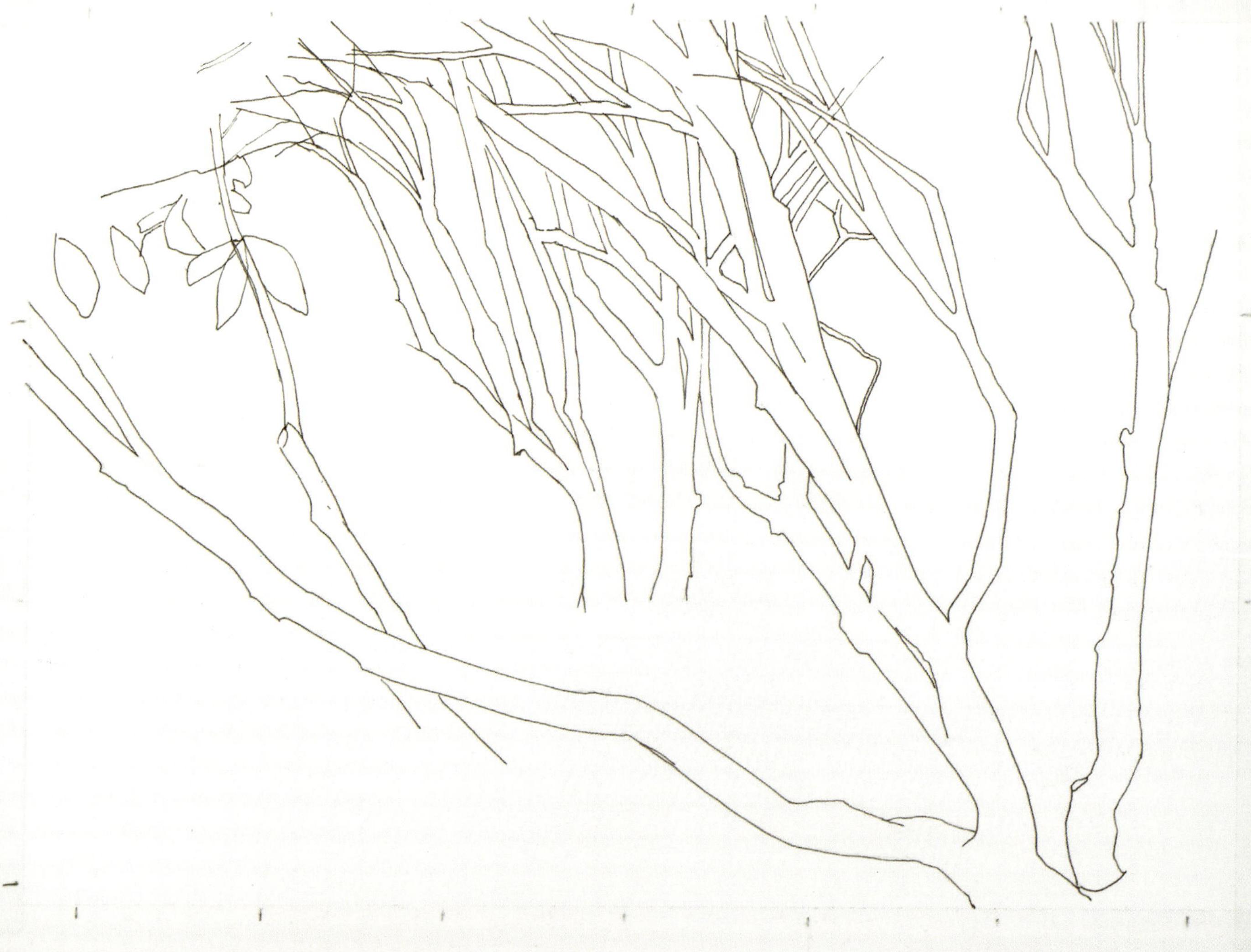

Further information

Resources: websites and videos

Siân and Rob Dudley live in Devon, England. Together, they run Moor to Sea Arts, sharing their expertise and enthusiasm for painting.
www.moortoseaarts.co.uk

Siân and Rob have made numerous tuitional videos with ArtTutor. Their videos include a course on basic watercolour techniques and cover a wide variety of subject matters.

ArtTutor is a website dedicated to a very high standard of art tuition across all media.
www.arttutor.co.uk

Suppliers

Jackson's Art Supplies
1 Farleigh Place
London
N16 7SX

020 7254 0077
www.jacksonsart.com

Ken Bromley Art Supplies
Unit 13 Lodge Bank Estate
Crown Lane
Horwich
Bolton
BL6 5HY

01204 690114
www.artsupplies.co.uk

Two Rivers Paper
Pitt Mill
Mineral Line
Roadwater
TA23 0QS Watchet

01984 641028
www.tworiverspaper.com

Index

RELATED TITLES FROM CROWOOD

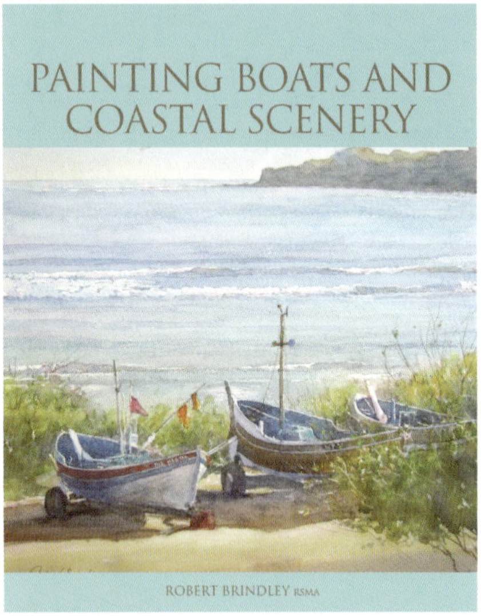

978 1 84797 119 7

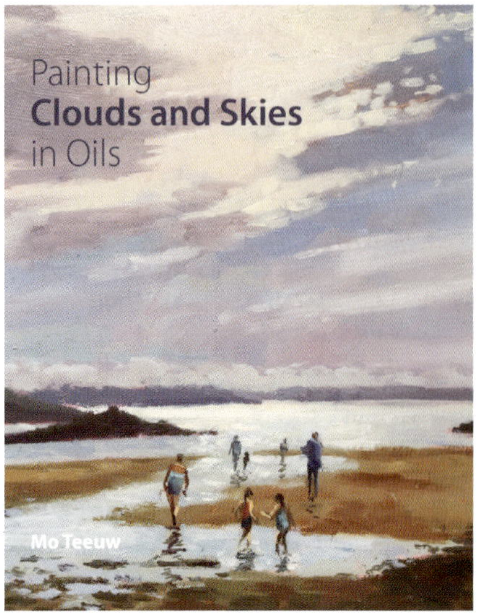

978 1 78500 345 5

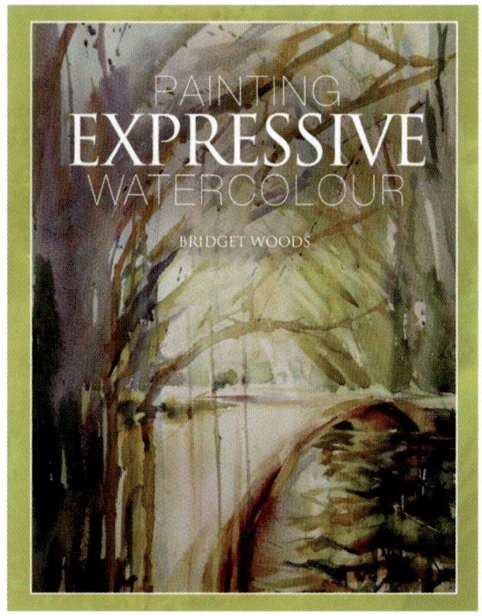

978 1 84797 750 2

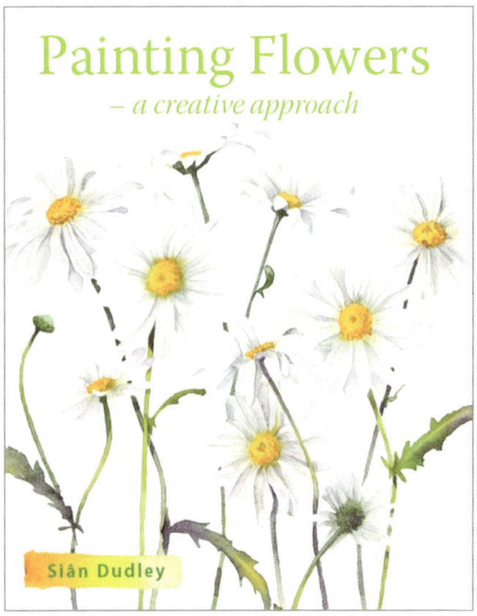

978 1 78500 371 4

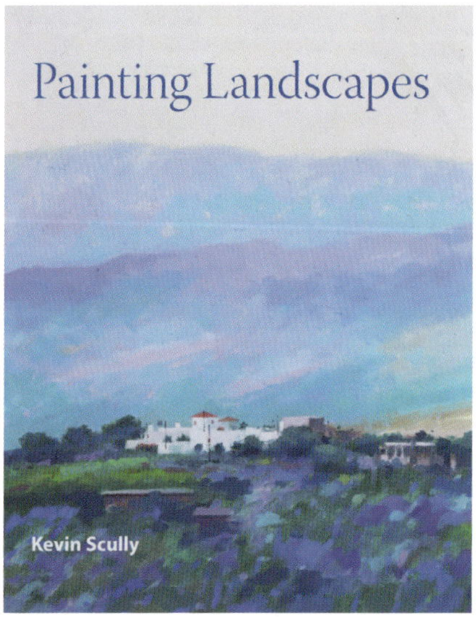

978 1 78500 383 7

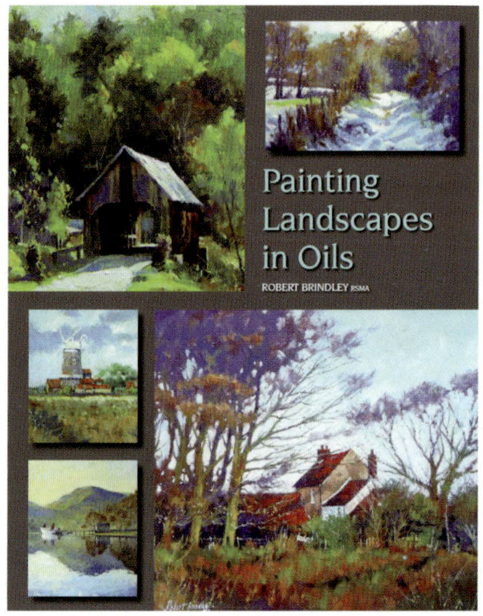

978 1 84797 314 6

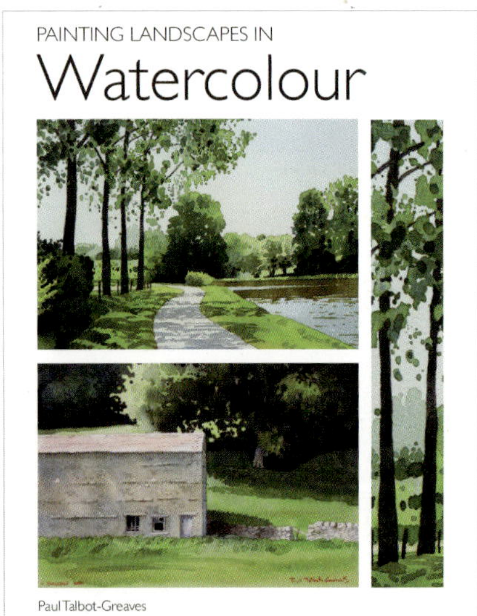

978 1 84797 085 5

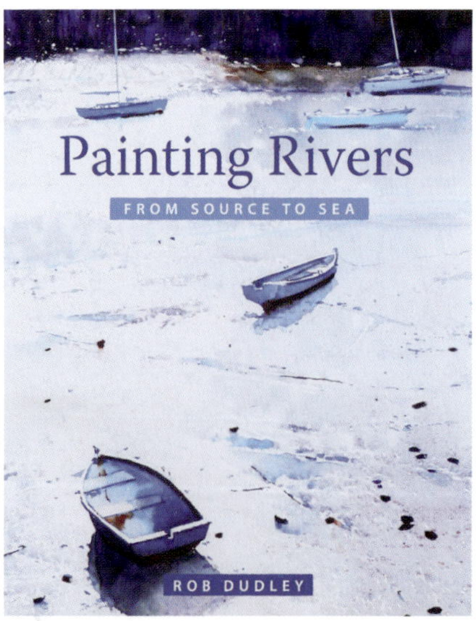

978 1 78500 359 2

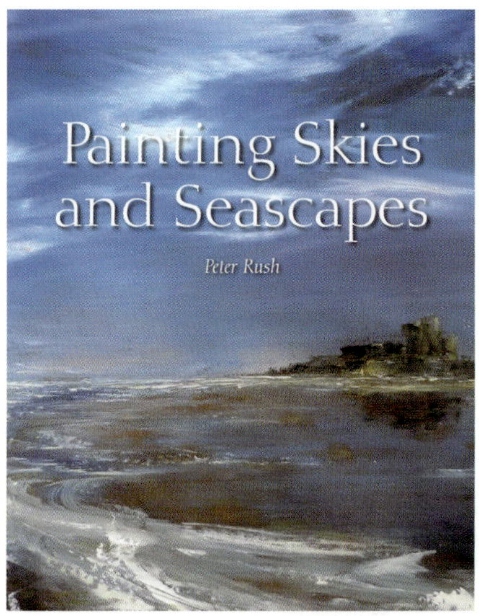

978 1 84797 621 5

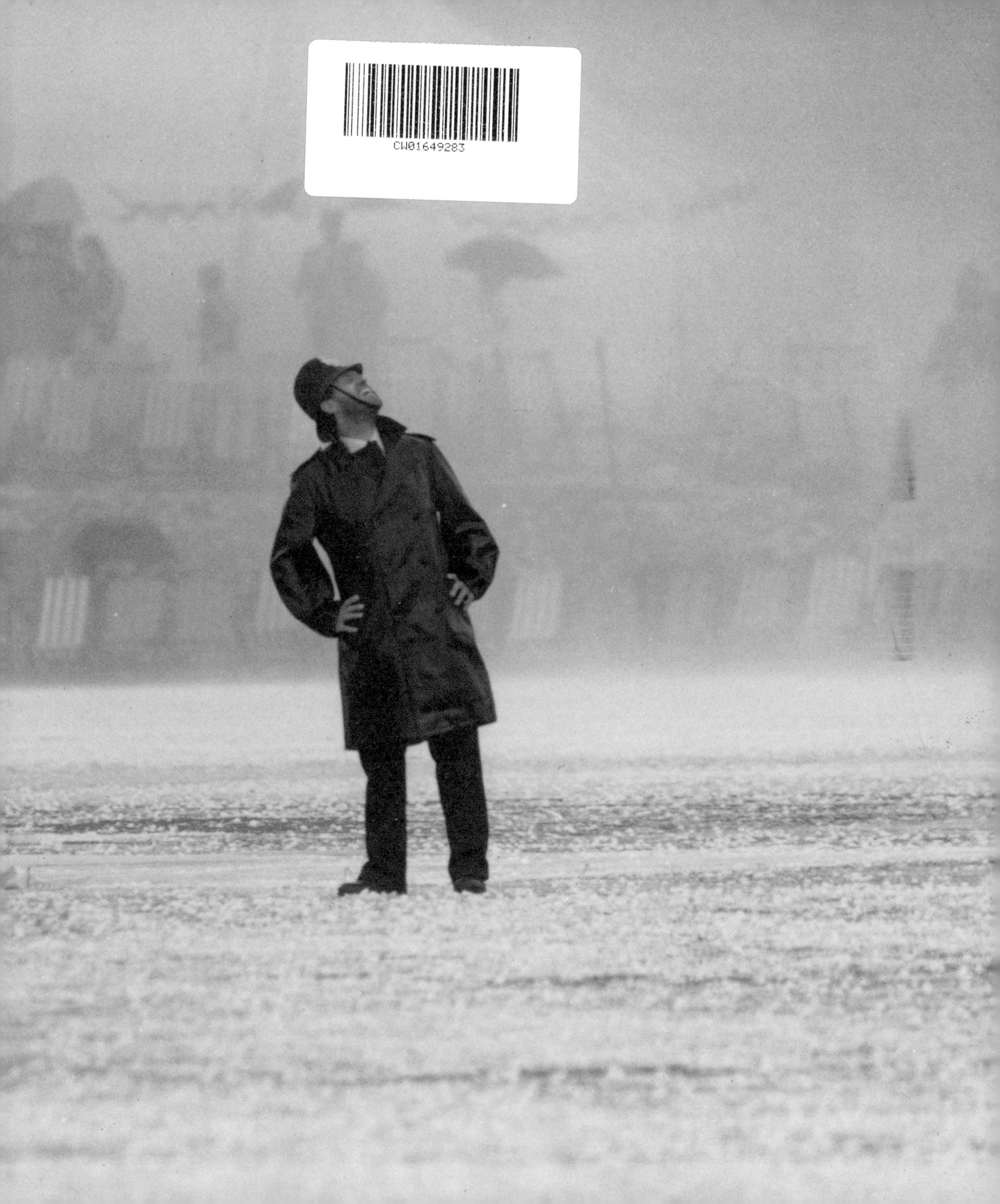

CRICKET IMPRESSIONS

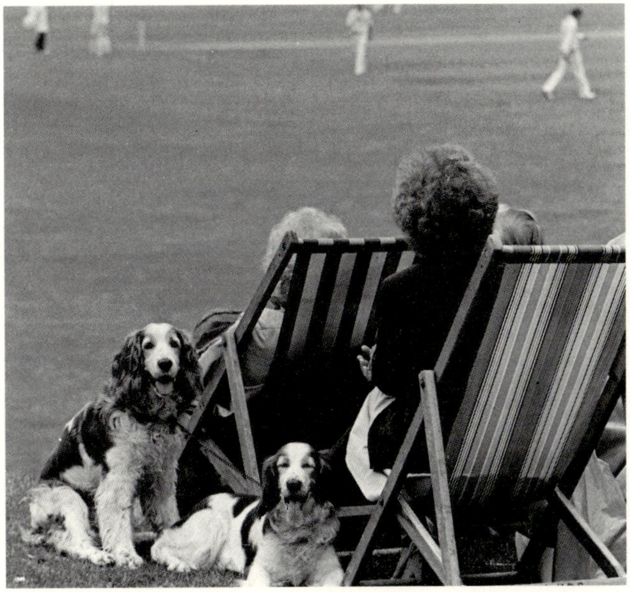

Adrian Murrell

THE KINGSWOOD PRESS

The Kingswood Press
an imprint of William Heinemann Ltd
10 Upper Grosvenor Street, London W1X 9PA
LONDON MELBOURNE TORONTO
JOHANNESBURG AUCKLAND

First published 1987

0 434 98095 1

Designed by Mary Hamlyn

Photoset by Rowland Phototypesetting Ltd,
Bury St Edmunds, Suffolk

Printed and bound in Hong Kong by
Mandarin Offset

To my parents Renee and Bill

Introduced by

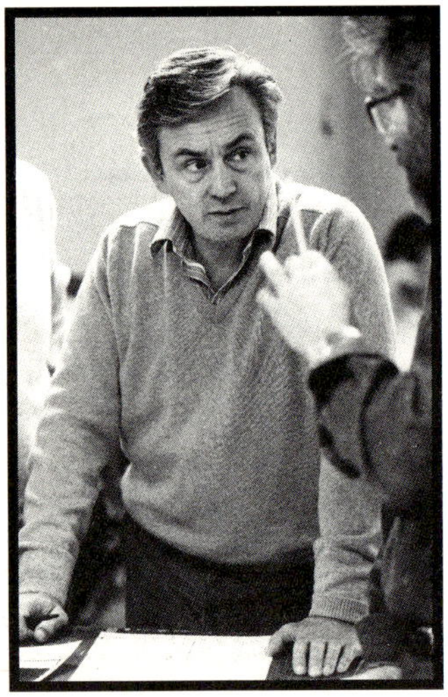

Donald Trelford, Editor of the *Observer*. He loves cricket and cricket photographs because they capture one moment in the style of a player.

'I think cricket photography is a marvellous and relatively new art.

'The problem is that the photographer has to sit so far away and because much of the formal movement of the game is slow, the lens has to be constantly focused on the player, to wait for that one moment when the emotions of the player are revealed. Adrian's got great news sense, a profound understanding of the game and a desire for the picture to be seen now – not as an exhibition print years later. They are some of his many qualities, combined with a sense of where the story is coming from and where it's going next. He's always at least one step ahead.'

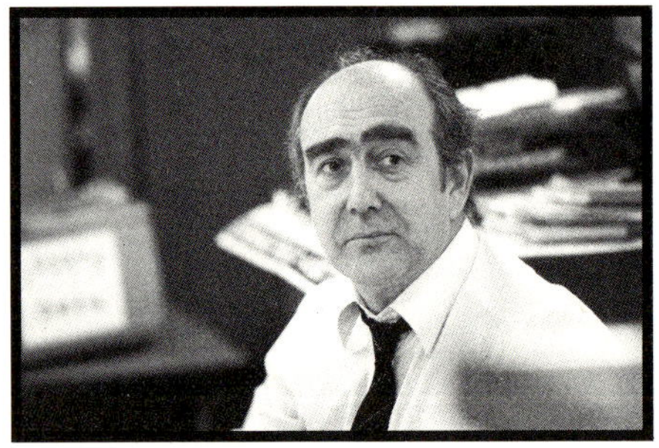

Peter Corrigan, Sports Editor of the *Observer*.

'Adrian understands the game and knows what he's looking for. He's a brilliant photographer. He came on the scene about six years ago and works very hard. When you send him off on a job you know he'll come up with the goods.

'We use pictures big: they help to enhance the written word. The readers notice photographers on our paper more than others, because the pictures are good. They tend to look for the by-line – they want to know who took it.

'For the first edition I ask Adrian for the shape we are locked into. When we are remaking the back page for the second and third editions at about 6 o'clock, we build it around the picture, unlike all the other papers, and whether the picture is landscape or upright, we hope to accommodate it. (Even so, that may not last long because the printers are trying to make us fit a modular shape, with the same shape for the picture through all the editions. This means we would have to be much less flexible with the pictures.) Sometimes it's soul destroying, but on a Saturday night I'm not interested in their portfolios – it's not the Tate Gallery.'

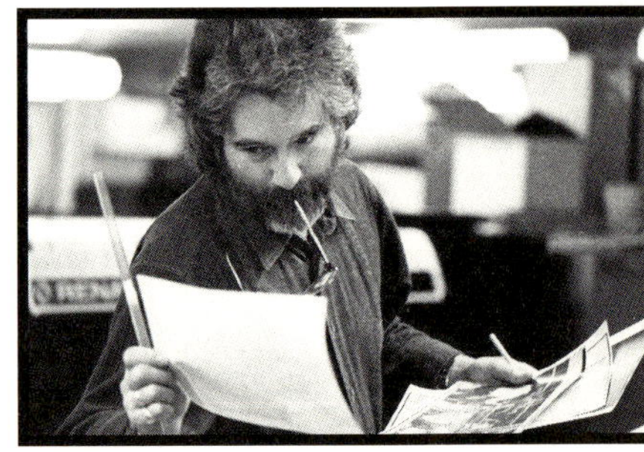

Tony McGrath, Picture Editor of the *Observer*.

'I know very little about cricket, so I'm looking for a shape. My whole operation is to stop people turning the page. If I put a picture of Botham scoring the winning run, it may be historically important, but visually it doesn't mean a thing.

'Adrian is incredibly committed. There are times when he comes in through the door panic-stricken, soaked in sweat – because he cares. For instance, he'll cover a five-day test match from day one and start sending us stuff from the Friday's play: everything he has shot that day, and all through the Saturday, will be sent to the office by a messenger or on a train. He will identify anything which he thinks is good by shooting a blank frame after it. This way, he can tell us if there is anything special to look out for, and we can discuss it on the telephone. Of course, he won't actually see it until he brings in the last lot of film on a Saturday for the last edition, so on his two- or three-hour car journey back he will live in his own nightmare – did he get a shot, or will there be a hole in the page? Or, two minutes after he left the ground did Botham knock someone out when bowling?

'He captions all his pictures, unglamorous and routine: but very important. Without a caption it might as well go straight in the bin.

'He is superb at his special subject, cricket. But he proved his versatility when he was sent to cover the assassination of Indira Gandhi. He already had a visa for the cricket tour, so he went straight out for the *Observer*, and we got a nine-column front-page picture, the only one in Fleet Street. A sports photographer wiping the floor with a hard news story!'

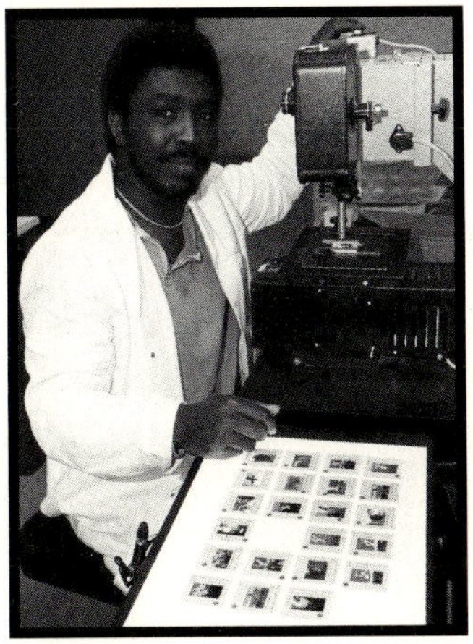

John Gichigi, processes and prints all Adrian's pictures at All-Sport Photographic. 'Adrian will come in with colour film from matches, which I process here and then dupe (make identical copy transparencies) straight away, to send out to several clients at once. Then the black and white is processed, printed, filed and sent to newspapers and magazines all over the world.

'Adrian uses XP1 film as his main black and white. In processing the silver in it is bleached away, leaving a fine-grained, even-toned image which is very good for showing the detail in predominantly white and green images. However this film has a comparatively long processing time, so it is not suitable for quick day-to-day newspaper use, but the quality is much better for reproduction. I think it is worth the extra time, and you don't have to "burn in" (expose certain areas for longer) or "dodge" (hold back certain parts of the image) like you have to with HP5 or Tri-X.

'Adrian shoots up to 200 rolls of film, both colour and B & W, during a busy week in the domestic season. These might include a three-day county match, the start of a Test and perhaps a portrait of a player. He rarely panics because he plans his week out quite carefully, so generally we know what to expect. At least that way if there's a crisis, we all know about it.'

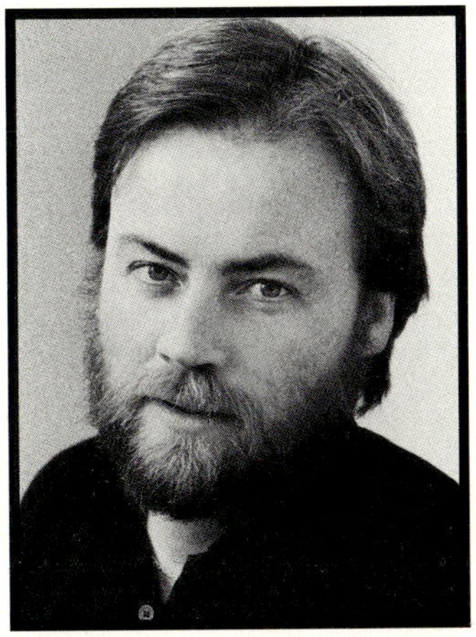

Eamonn McCabe, four times Sports Photographer of the Year and picture editor of *Sportsweek*. (He was formerly the *Observer* sports photographer.)

'You can tell an Adrian Murrell picture, it reflects soul and emotion, his images are unique. His type of picture complements what I do, and the sports pages look good because of that. I also find his quality staggeringly good – the clarity in his pictures is excellent for reproduction in the paper. The trouble with sport photographers is that we get banded together within our areas – football, cricket, rugby – whereas we're really photographers who take sports pictures. I don't know how he takes pictures at county level, week in, week out – he has a very professional attitude which means he gets consistently good results.

'I've certainly never seen him as a threat. We work well together – dovetailing in our sports. I've always found him easy to work with; we're close friends and we criticise and encourage each other – we both know when we've got a good picture.'

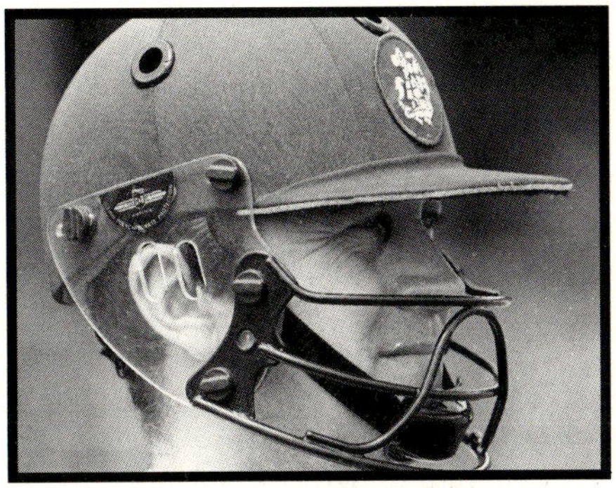

Phil Edmonds, Middlesex and England cricketer.

'It would seem odd that as a professional sportsman I have become progressively less interested in the sports pages in general. I do remain, however, a real sucker for special talent and therefore pictures of the Platinis and Maradonas of this world still catch my eye.

'From a personal point of view I am obviously flattered when my own picture is included in the paper – not so much as an ego trip per se, but more because it generally indicates an achievement on the field the previous day. A good action photograph also enables one to analyse technique albeit to a limited degree. Although I know that an immense amount of work goes into the lay-out of the sport pages, I'm sure that the majority of us take things partly for granted. I am concerned that I have never fully appreciated the difficulties there must be for the photographer in obtaining and transmitting the pictures to home base.'

Acknowledgements

For the help and advice I have received I should like to thank friends and colleagues at All-Sport, particularly Matt Homes who spends hours filing my pictures; also the long-suffering John Gichigi, Ian Down and Simon Bruty in the darkroom; Bob Martin for technical assistance; and Mavis Streeton, Tony Duffy and Steve Powell. Also I'd like to extend my warm appreciation to my colleagues at the *Observer* for their encouragement, in particular Tony McGrath, picture editor, Eamonn McCabe, now of *Sportsweek*, and Tony Martin and David Watkinson in the darkroom. Thanks are due also to Scyld Berry and Peter Smith who on tour have kindly let me sleep on their hotel room floors! And I'd like to thank Christopher Martin-Jenkins, Andrew Longmore and Amanda Ripley at the *Cricketer* for their support and Derek Wyatt, my publisher at William Heinemann, who started it all off. Also my special gratitude to Mary Hamlyn and Mary Lou Grimberg for their creativity, time and tremendous patience, which made this book possible. Finally, I must thank my brother-in-law Clive Limpkin who lit the fuse!

Foreword

Cricket is a sport. Photography is a hobby. It occurred to me at the end of 1976 that putting them together might provide an agreeable way of wintering in India.

As a child I had not been academically distinguished, but when I was sixteen my sister had married Clive Limpkin, a photographer with the *Daily Mail* and on his advice I had attended a photography course at the Guildford College of Art and Design. By September 1976, however, my career had progressed no further than making the tea and running errands for an advertising photographer. I was going nowhere.

Is there a tide in the affairs of men? I don't know, but just as India had traditionally offered opportunities to adventurous young men back in Imperial days, so it did to me now. An England cricket tour was going there and, although my experience of the game was limited to my school second XI, I persuaded the *Daily Mirror* to let me cover it for them as a freelance.

Fortunately for me – as well as for Tony Greig and his team – England won the series 3–1 and back in Fleet Street the tour was good news. I managed to have forty pictures published with my by-line. While in Bombay I was also lucky enough to meet the publisher of the *Cricketer International*, who about a year later signed me up as a special photographer.

It all sounds so easy, but at first it was a real struggle to survive. For a start it can take up to £15,000 simply to equip oneself properly. A Nikon 600 mm lens, for example, costs £3,000. (I admit that on that first tour I was an innocent abroad with just one camera and forty rolls of film. Now I travel with so much gear that the excess baggage charges and insurance premiums alone are frightening.) Foreign travel is expensive too, but I found the odd assignment here and there and after securing a foothold at the *Observer* with an agreement to cover the domestic cricket season things gradually improved. Then in 1979 I joined All-Sport, Europe's largest sports photographic agency, headed by Tony Duffy.

Cricket Impressions is the result of the past ten years on the road. The pictures have been chosen for the behind-the-scenes insight they offer and for their photographic merit; they are not a chronological set of action shots. Also, I should like to point out that although this is a book of cricket pictures, which I sincerely hope will be a source of pleasure to cricket lovers young and old, with or without cameras, I *am* a photographer, and I naturally should like to think that some of my knowledge and experience might be of help, or interest, to other photographers. Therefore, in addition to the comments I make throughout the book on photographic problems and how to overcome them, I have also included a small section of technical data relating to three of the more unusual or interesting techniques which have been used.

All the pictures, however, have one thing in common – I enjoyed taking them and, whether your interest is in the cricket or in the photography, I hope to pass some of that enjoyment on to you.

Adrian Murrell, September, 1986

Technical terms

burning in is a method used during printing to give more exposure to parts of a black and white print

camera motordrive is an attachment for the camera that automatically winds on the film, frame by frame at up to 6 frames a second

the converter is basically a lens which extends the focal distance. It's a very small object – a couple of inches wide – and it fits between the long lens (which is your normal working lens of 600mm) and the camera body. The normal converter is a 2 × which means that if you stick it on a 600mm lens it brings the focal distance up to 1200. A 1.4 is, literally, a 1.4 × converter which means that on a 600mm it brings the focal distance approximately up to 840mm length with a loss of 1.5 stops. A converter is an essential piece of equipment for a cricket photographer

dodged is a method used during printing to reduce the exposure in certain areas of a black and white print, to darken or lighten the subject matter

a fish-eye lens is an extremely wide-angle lens, similar in its range to the eye of a fish. The view thus obtained is, of necessity, distorted when flattened and printed

focal length is computed for the camera lens by measuring the distance between the centre of the lens and the plane of sharp focus on the film while the camera is focused on infinity

frames per second means the speed at which a camera with a motordrive can take pictures, i.e. six frames per second means that the camera can expose six frames per second

600mm F4 lens is an immensely powerful telephoto lens with a very good maximum aperture. Slow film can therefore be used in dull conditions

a nebula filter is similar in effect to a starburst filter, but further it refracts the light from the highlights, splitting it into primary colours – cyan, magenta, yellow – round that starburst effect

a panned shot means moving the camera lens in synchronisation with the subject whilst using a slow shutter speed. This keeps the main subject sharp but blurs the background giving a sensation of movement in the picture

pushed two stops gives the film extra time in the developer thus increasing the effectiveness and sensitivity of the film. Pictures can be shot in extremely low light, for example – night cricket in floodlight conditions

a starburst filter splits the light into a star by means of a grid pattern on the filter

shutter speed the period of time light is allowed to pass through the lens and reach the film in the camera to expose it correctly

1/250 sec; 1/500 sec; 1/1000 sec; these are all shutter speeds fast enough to enable the action to be 'frozen'

Technical information

The information on this page is for the more serious photographer, who perhaps has his or her own darkroom, rather than for the casual hobbyist. It deals with three pictures which are technically unique within the context of this book. I would also say that I found these three among the most stimulating and satisfying to produce.

Cover picture

This effect was not achieved whilst taking the shot but shows useful application of darkroom printing techniques.

The initial photograph (single image) was taken with a 600 mm Nikon F4 lens with a 1.4 converter, shot at 1/1000 sec at F5.6. You lose a stop using this particular teleconverter. However, it facilitated the lens being extended to 840 mm. It was necessary to shoot the picture at 1/000 sec to 'freeze' the bowling action – 1/500 is not fast enough to prevent lateral movement, particularly of hands and feet. Filmstock was Ilford XP1 rated at 400 ASA. Once processed the single image film of Lawrence was taken to the darkroom.

Darkroom procedure was as follows:

1. Mark the baseboard with five or six parallel lines approximately 10 mm apart. (Use masking tape for this to avoid defacing the baseboard.)
2. Establish correct exposure for the multiple images so that the cumulative exposure time results in a correctly exposed print.
3. Movement effect is created by moving the paper held in the printing easel after each exposure, using the lines as an accurate guide.
4. The final exposure must be double the previous exposure to give it prominence and a strong image.
5. For the cover, this shot was printed on a surface compatible with retouching techniques. Colour was then added by commercial retouchers.

Botham stands out in a crowd – page 43

I used a Nikon 300 mm 2.8 telephoto lens. To throw the foreground and the background out of focus, I used the widest aperture possible, ie 2.8 mm, which also gave me a fast shutter speed (1/500 sec) to avoid movement and camera shake. Filmstock was Fuji 100 ASA transparency. The result achieved was that one's eye is immediately drawn to Botham and a stronger emphasis is given to his profile – a good portrait technique.

Tony Greig – page 102

This shot has a studio feel about it although it was shot on location, using the floodlight from the tower at Sydney Cricket Ground. It was taken using 100 ASA film, with a 35 mm lens, at a very low shutter speed, as it was dark except for the light from the floodlight. To a large extent it was hit or miss whether the shot would come out sharp, and in fact I took six shots and this was the only sharp one. Apart from handholding the camera and not using a motor drive (to avoid camera shake) the really difficult problem was lining up Greig's head correctly to achieve a rim-lighting effect. If his head moved literally an inch either way it would have caused flare into the lens and ruined the photograph. Due to lack of daylight the aperture was only F2 at 1/30 sec, consequently this gave a shallow depth of field. (Look at the picture, the face is sharp, but the arms are not.)

All the photographs in this book were taken using Nikon equipment.

All black and white photographs were taken on Ilford HP5 and XP1 film and printed on Ilford paper.

The vast majority of the colour photographs were taken on Fuji film, which is ideally suited to cricket photography.

I should like to acknowledge my indebtedness to all three companies.

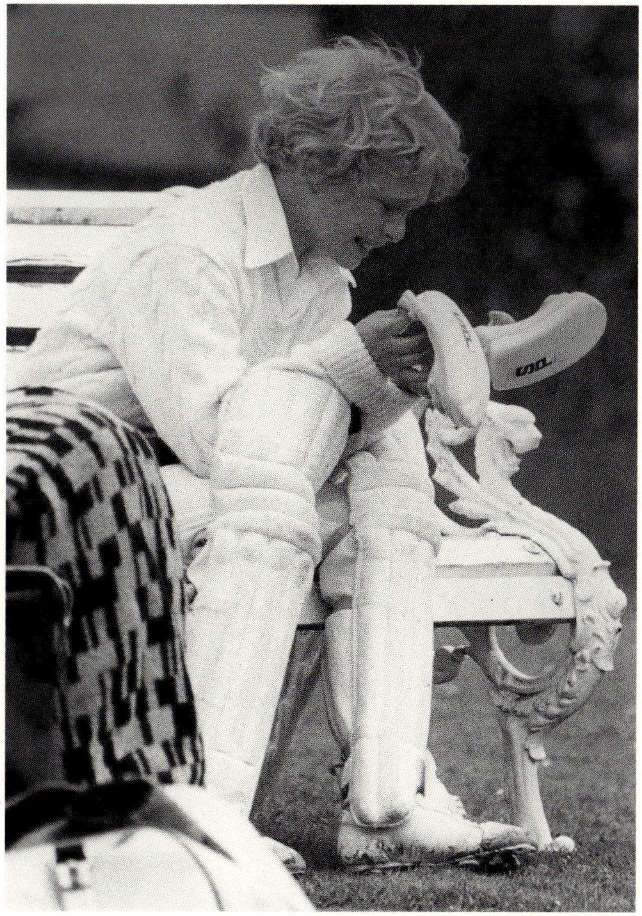

It's only a game

This was my first commission for the *Cricketer*. I went along to an under 11's colts match to see this boy, who was the star batsman. He was out first ball. *George Cox's Farm, Sussex, May 1979*

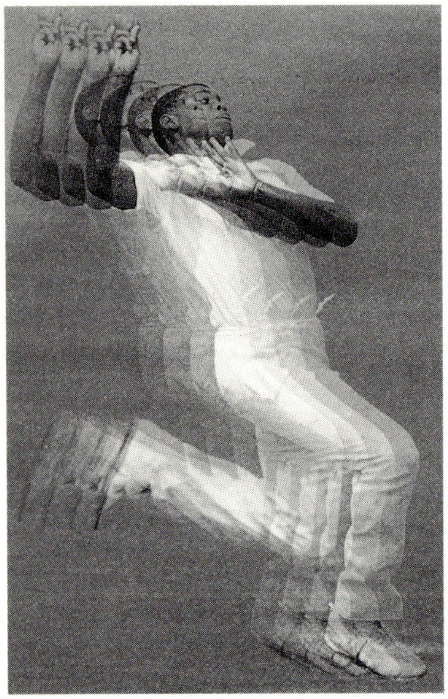

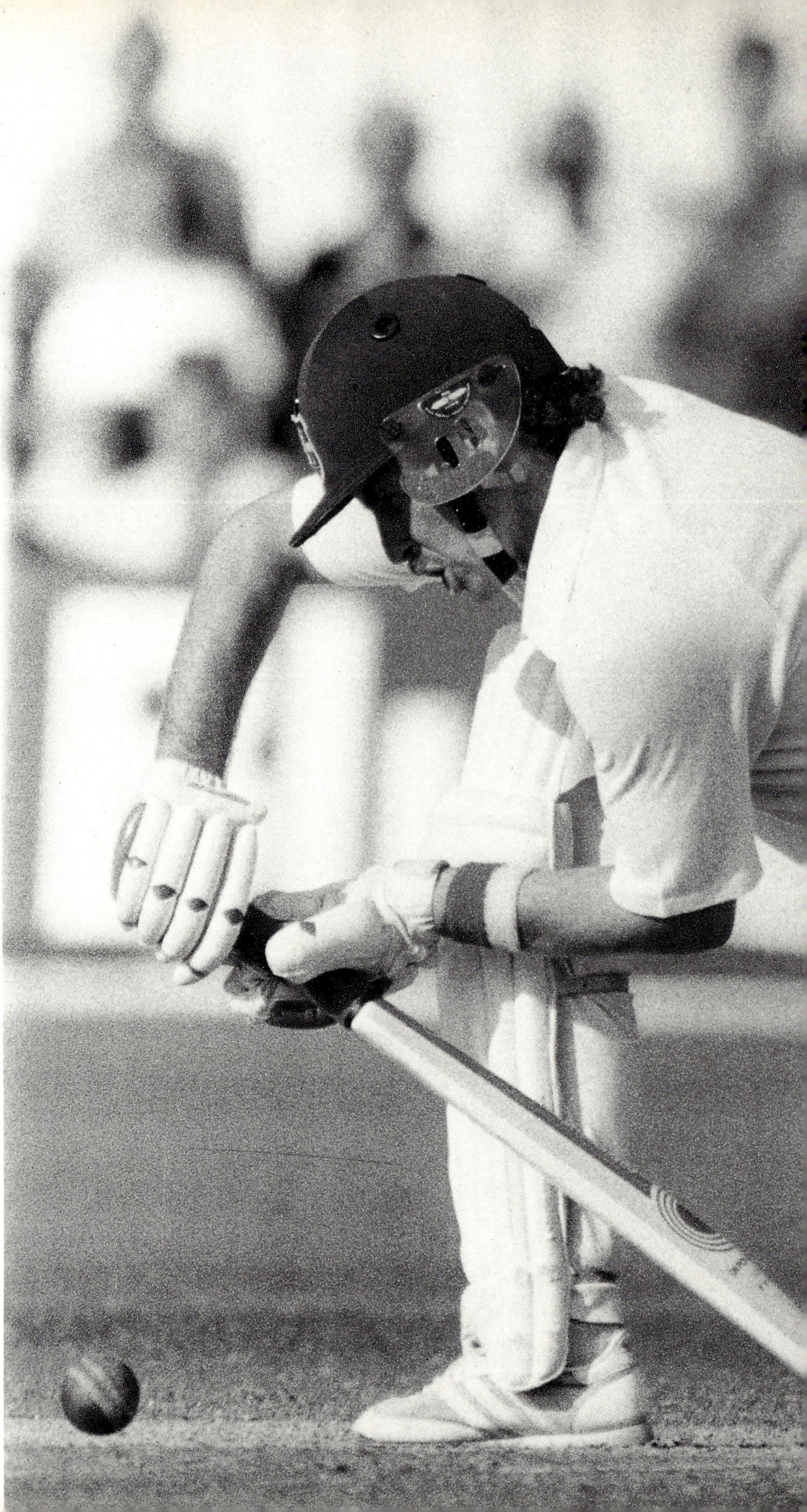

During the Australians' 1985 tour in England, Graeme Wood (pictured here) was under some pressure to prove himself as a world-class batsman. It had been rumoured that he had considered joining Kim Hughes, Rodney Hogg, Graham Yallop, *et al* in the rebel Australian side which went to South Africa. In the event he opted for respectability and the official tour, but he was

Graham Wood on his way to making a century, third Test, England v Australia, Trent Bridge, July 1985

above: *David Lawrence, the Gloucestershire pace bowler, Middlesex v Gloucestershire, Lord's, July/August 1985*

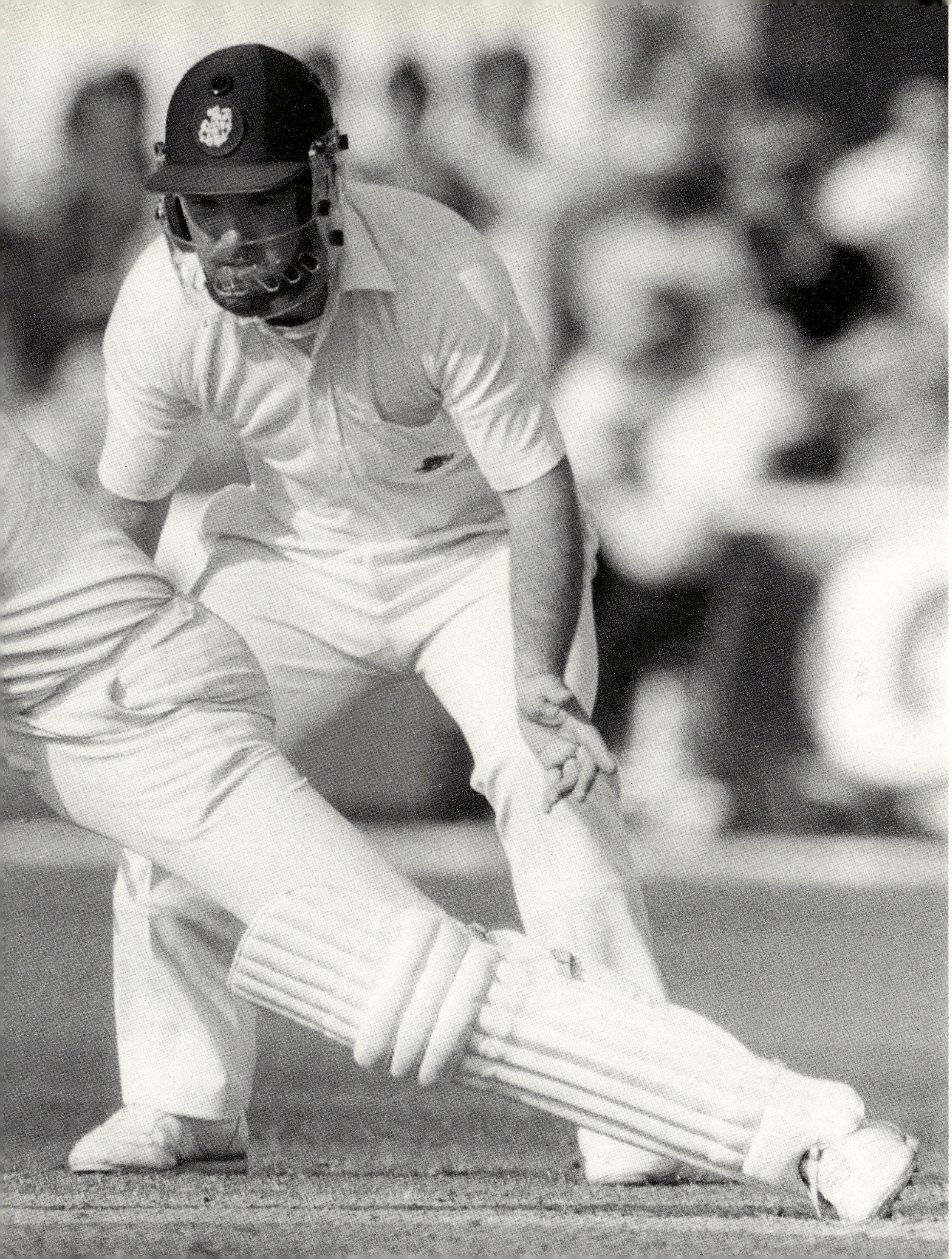

perhaps tainted by the threatened disloyalty. Hence the need to re-establish himself. Also the Australian side was young and inexperienced, having lost so many seasoned players to the rebels, and Wood was one of the few remaining 'old guard', so for this reason also he was under pressure to score. All in all he was news. From this particular match I needed a picture for the early edition of the *Observer* and I decided to go for something a little different. The fashion in sports photography is very much to go for the dramatic, the bizarre, and relating this to batsmen, photographers will station themselves down the wicket for the dynamic head-on shot. On this occasion, however, I deliberately eschewed the dramatic and waited on the square leg boundary for this forward defensive stroke. I knew that the *Observer* is always looking for something beyond the obvious, but I was surprised – and very gratified – when they ran this picture through all that Sunday's editions.

Later that year I entered it for the Sports Photographer of the Year competition. I hoped that the picture's calm timelessness would evoke – originally for the readers of the *Observer* and subsequently for the judges – the sound of bat on ball. Then in 1986, I entered it for the Benson and Hedges award, where it won a Highly Commended, so perhaps I, at least in part, succeeded.

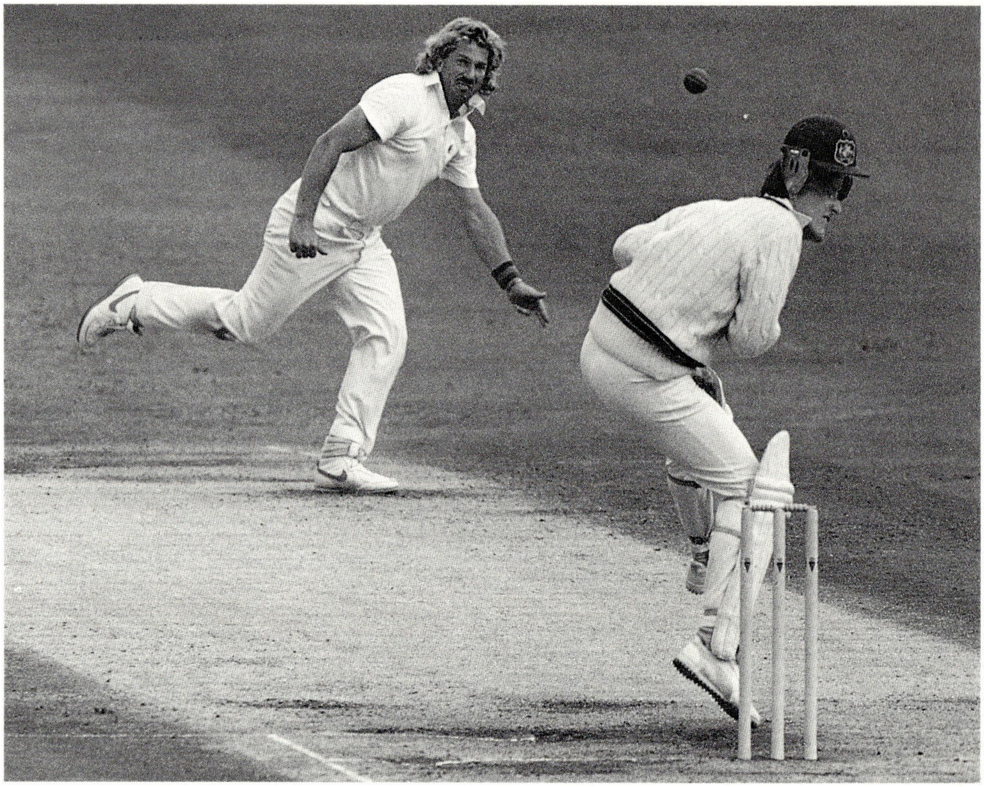

Ian Botham bowls Geoff Lawson a bouncer in the first Test, England v Australia, Headingley, June 1985

Tim Robinson of England runs out Ravi Shastri of India, fifth Test, India v England, Kanpur, February 1985

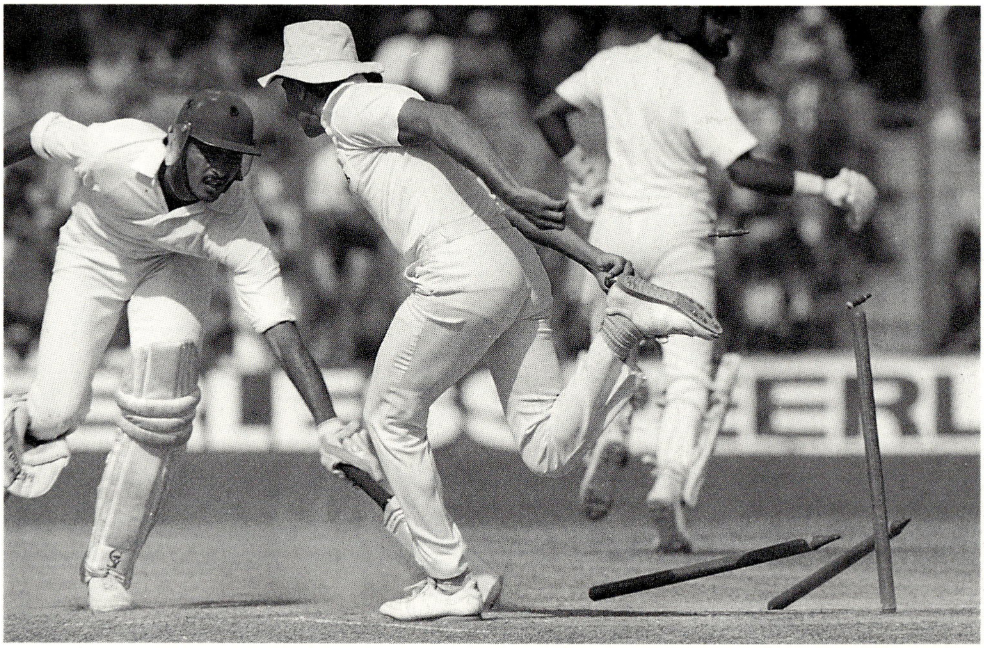

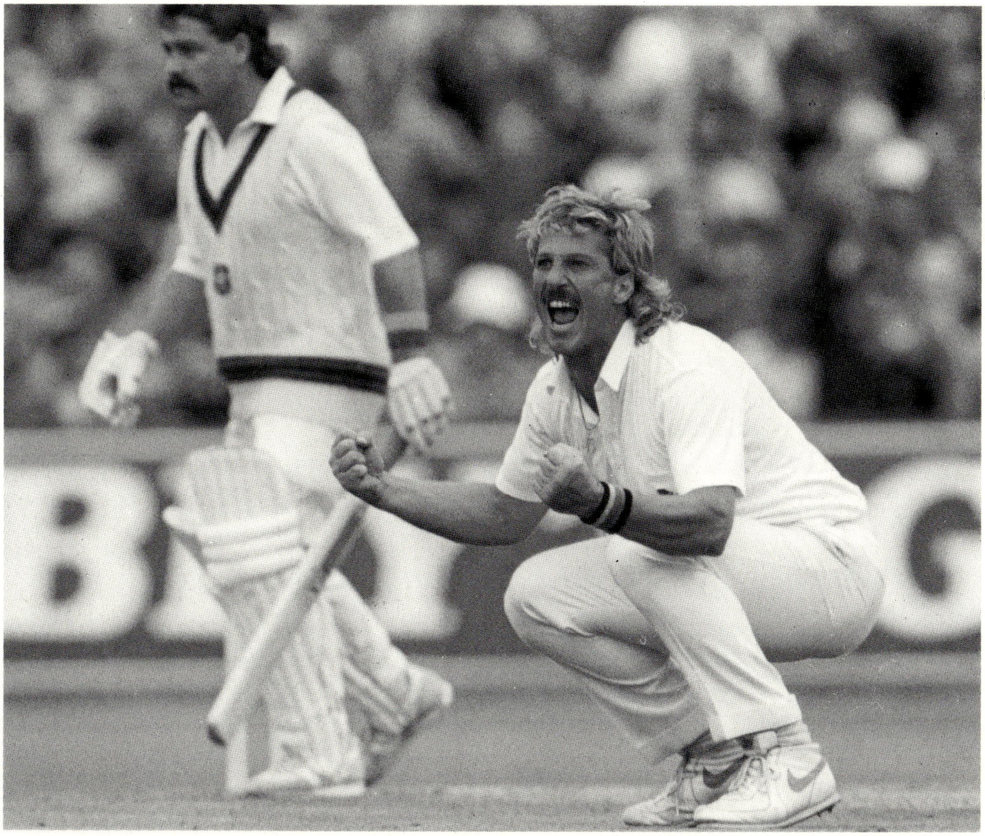

Ian Botham captures the wicket of David Boon in the fourth Test, England v Australia, Old Trafford, August 1985

The first match played under lights at Melbourne Cricket Ground, England v Australia in the World Championship, February 1985

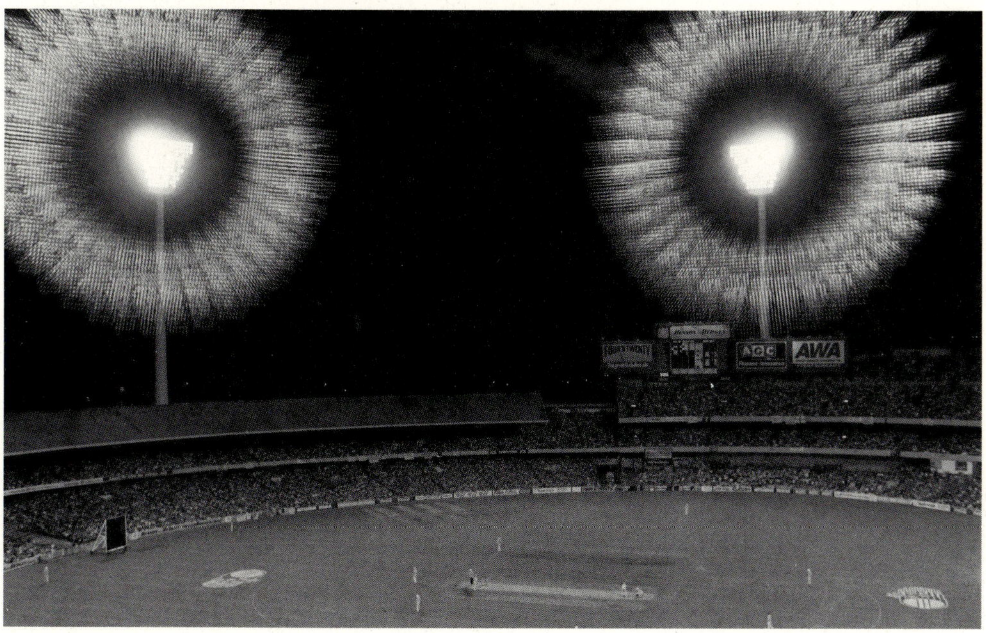

(Graeme Wood, incidentally, scored 172 in the single Australian innings in that test, which was drawn.)

The other pictures on this and the next four pages were also part of my entry for the 1985 Photographer of the Year competition. The two photographs which complete the portfolio can be found on page 47 (Botham at Edgbaston) and on page 129 (the flying Dujon).

When making a selection of your own work (which need not necessarily have been published) for such a competition, the key is not just to pick ten good action shots, but rather to consider the overall effect of the portfolio. This particular competition, unlike the Benson and Hedges, for which one enters individual cricket photographs, is not confined to cricket. You are competing against photographers whose portfolios might contain selections from all over the world – from ten different sports. These might range from national championships in perhaps tennis, golf or snooker to international events, such as World Cup soccer or Olympic show jumping, or indeed minor county cricket. (You don't have to go to the big events to get a good picture; the photograph of David Lawrence on page 12, and also used for the jacket of this book, was taken at a county match.) The competition is therefore very tough indeed. If you enter ten pictures all from one sport your selection *must* show variety – action, drama, emotion, mood.

I hope you can see from my portfolio that I tried to achieve not only variety: the dramatic wicket, the vicious bouncer, Gatting swearing at the umpire when a decision went against him, an elated Botham, but also careful balance, as supplied by the classic defence, and – even more removed from action and drama – the lights at Melbourne (page 15). That particular picture was taken in March 1985 at a one-day international between England and Australia. It was something of an historic event as it was the first time that floodlights had been used at the Melbourne Cricket Ground. It is not a great sports photograph but, by using a nebula filter, I was able to achieve the diffused halo effect which serves to emphasise the lights and convey something of the unusual background atmosphere.

Even if the portfolio is balanced, however, a mistake that is often made – by both amateurs and professionals – is in its presentation. Little finishing touches, such as borders around pictures, help to create the impression of care having been taken over the selection and add a certain unifying quality to the portfolio as a whole. The judges are not left with the feeling that the photographer just picked out the first ten pictures that came to hand and shoved them all together.

When I judged the Ilford Sports Photographer of the Year competition in 1985, I went through something like 500 pictures and what soon became obvious – and incidentally helped me make my final selection – was the importance of print quality. In fact I was surprised at the poor quality of some of the entries. Even if you have to make as many as ten prints of the same

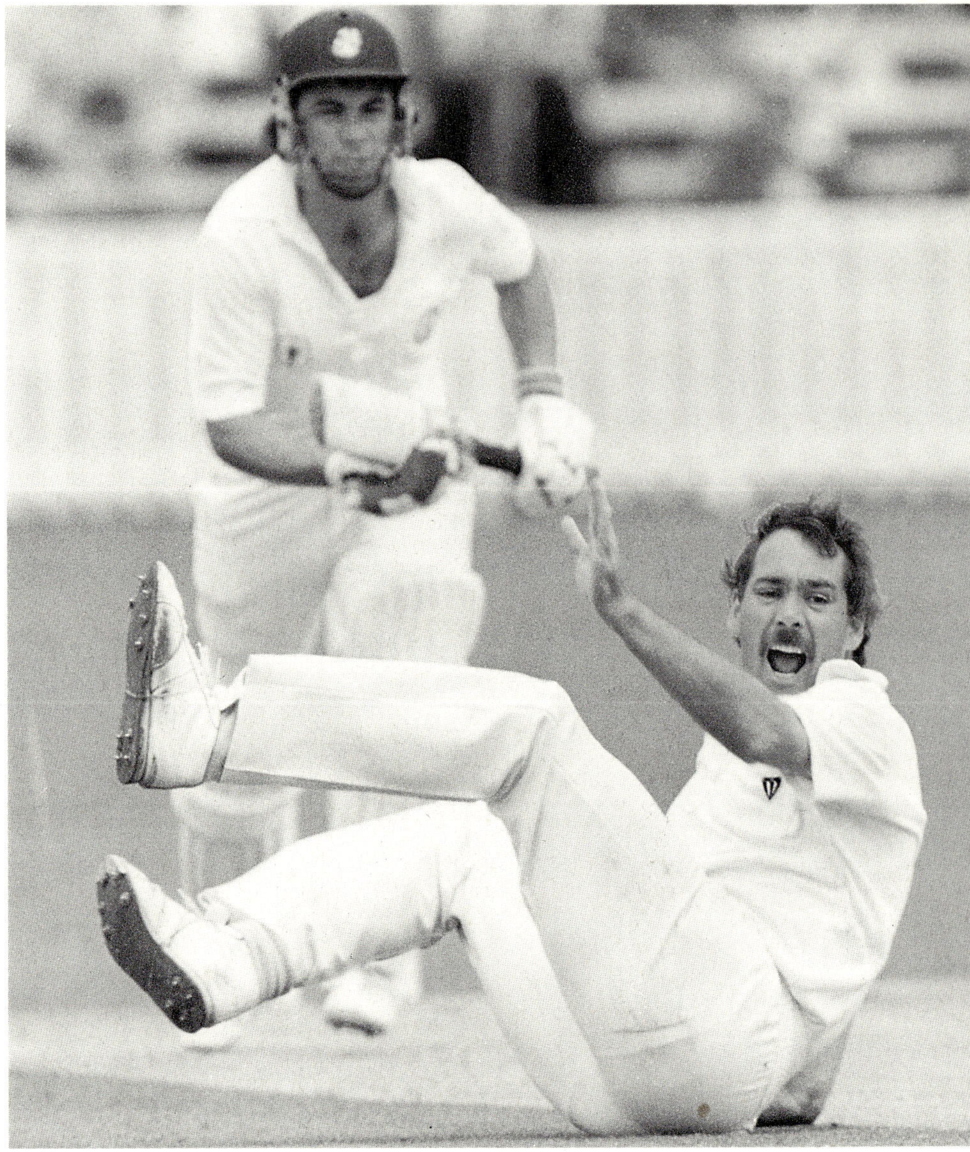

John Inchmore appeals for the wicket of Tim Robinson in the NatWest semi-final, Worcestershire v Nottinghamshire, Worcester, August 1985

opposite: *Mike Gatting's controversial swearing at the umpire in a one-day match, India v England, Chandrigarh, January 1985*

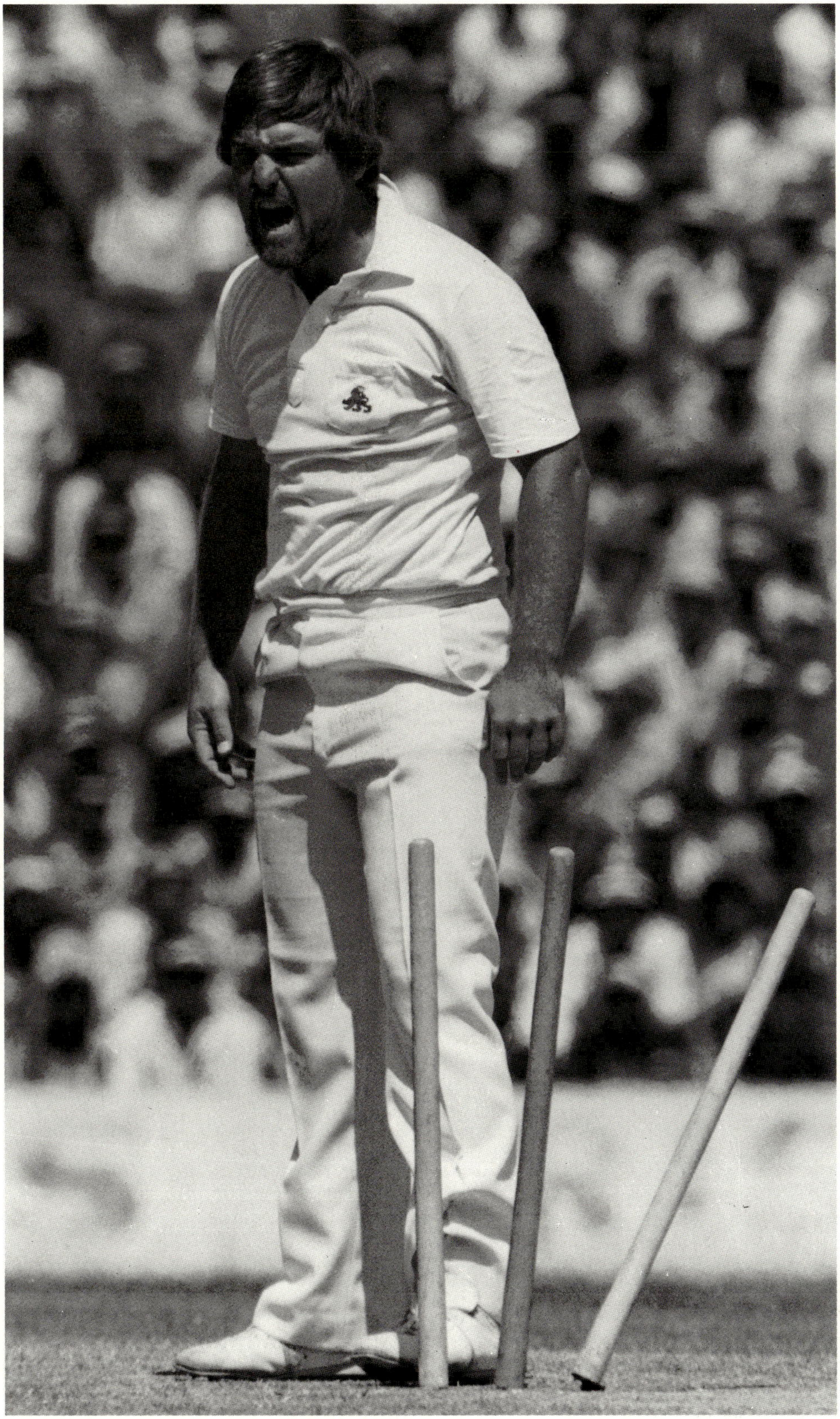

picture to get it right, it's worth it. It may be the deciding factor. Well, all that was the theory, the way I reasoned, but despite all my careful balancing, selecting and printing my portfolio didn't quite make it. I nearly got it right, but Chris Smith of the *Sunday Times* was the overall winner and I had to be content to be runner-up to him in the black and white section.

I would advise all beginners to start working with black and white film, which is in my view the best training for colour photography. There are fewer pitfalls and it is therefore easier to compose good shots, to learn from them, and then to improve on them. When shooting in black and white, you see something and you take it, but when taking colour photographs the various elements become more involved. Taking cricket pictures in India, for instance, you get magnificent colourful backgrounds – turbans banners, etc – but when taking a shot of a batsman or a bowler you have to think carefully about this background. In black and white the eye goes straight to the central image, a pylon behind the stand for example, is not so obtrusive as it would be in colour where it would stick out like a sore thumb. Also in black and white the background can be treated in the darkroom. It can be 'dodged' or 'burnt in' to give more impact to the main subject. This cannot be done so easily with colour, so it really is advisable to gain proficiency in black and white first.

Capturing the atmosphere surrounding cricket can be more difficult and more rewarding than achieving the great action shot. The picture here shows the 1983 World Cup Final crowds waiting for the victorious Indian team to appear on the balcony at Lord's; the mood of the supporters was vibrant. I endeavoured to catch it – I hope successfully.

When I took the photographs shown overleaf I was trying to convey some special uniqueness about each place: Lord's under snow, Melbourne under lights. The picture of Christchurch is different again, a study in contrast – the hills of Canterbury receding towards the horizon and half obscured by the shantytown 'hicksville' crowding the fence, and the symmetry of the circle of exercising players.

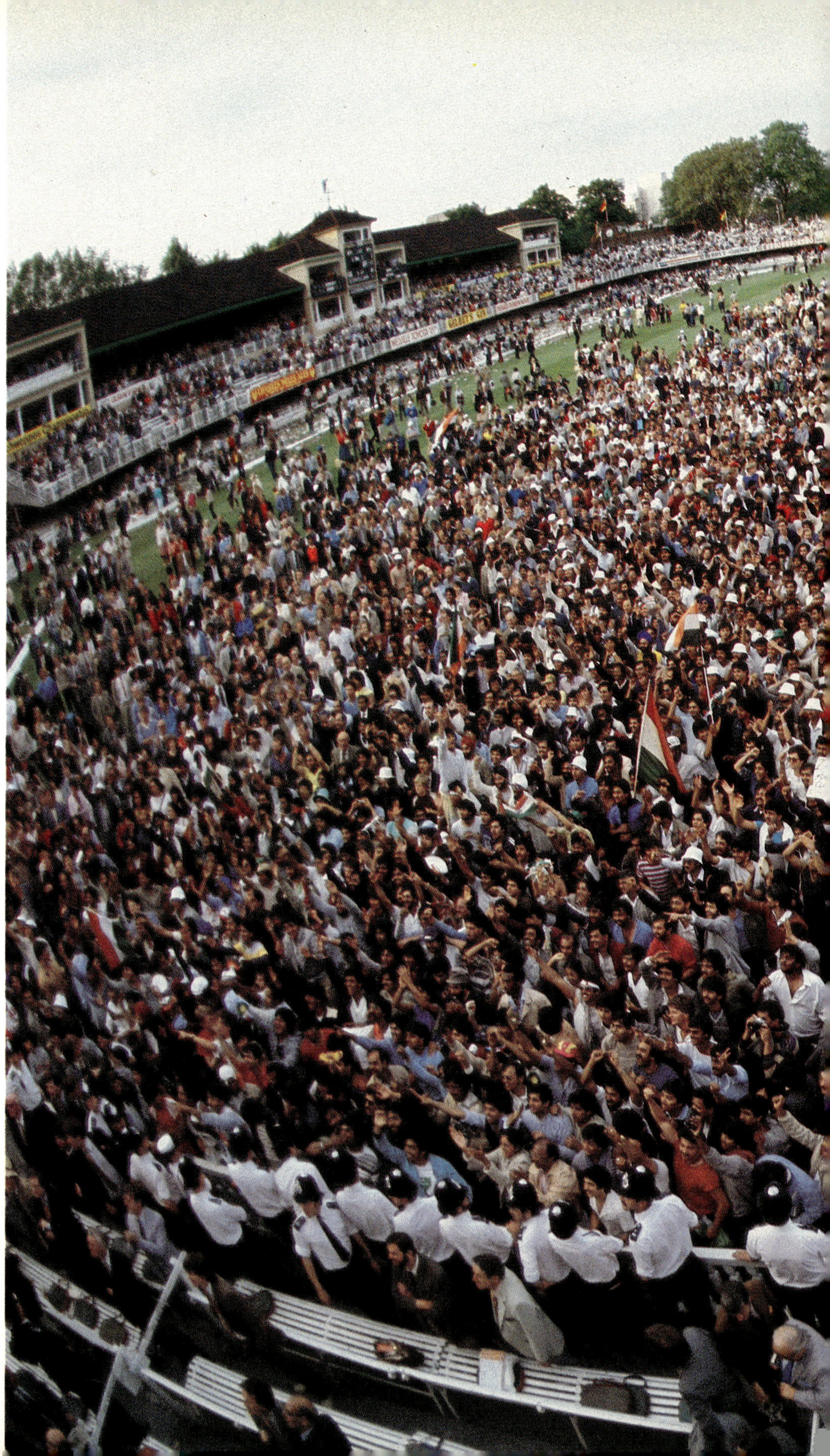

World Cup Final, West Indies v India, Lord's, June 1983

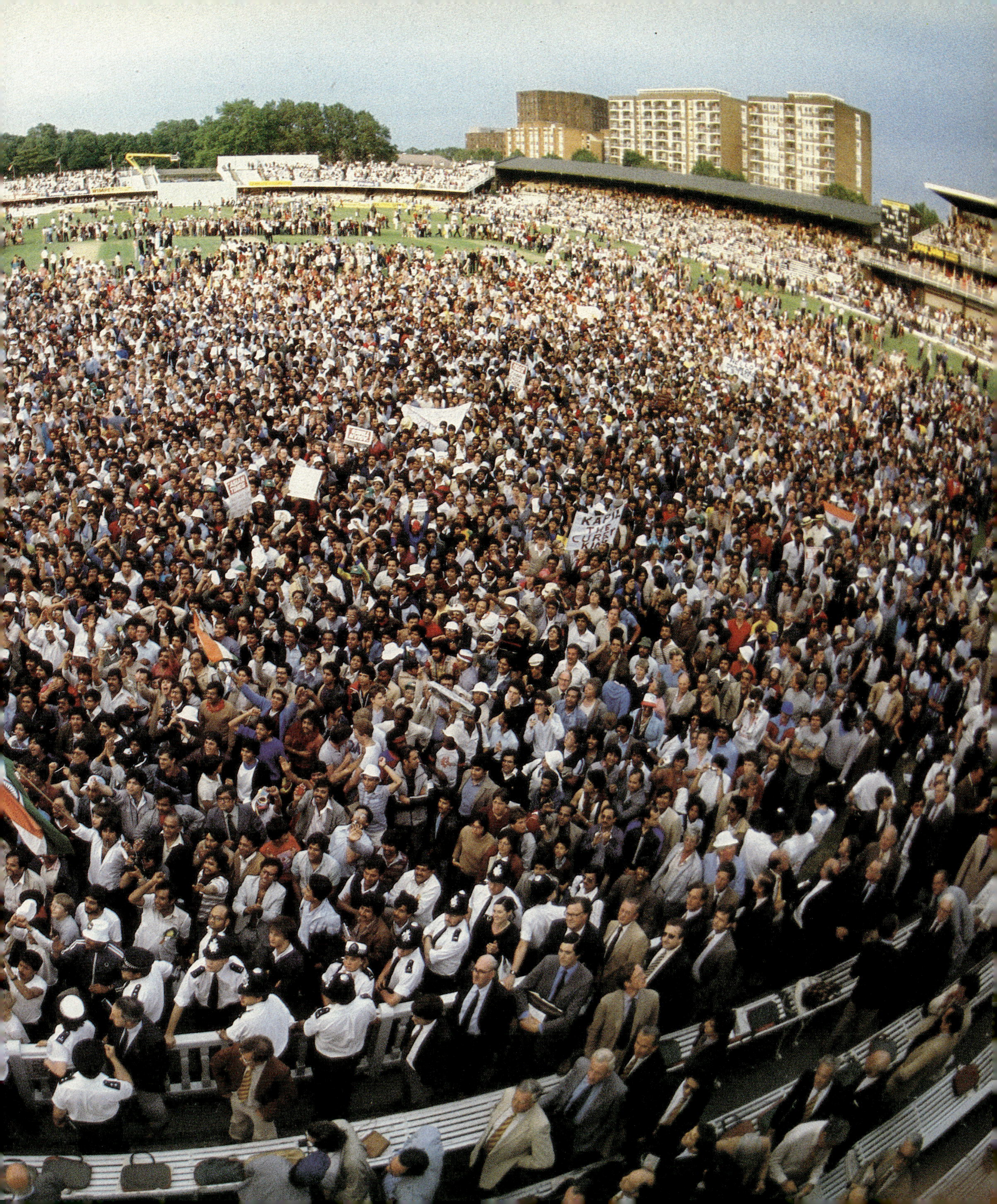
KAPIL
THE

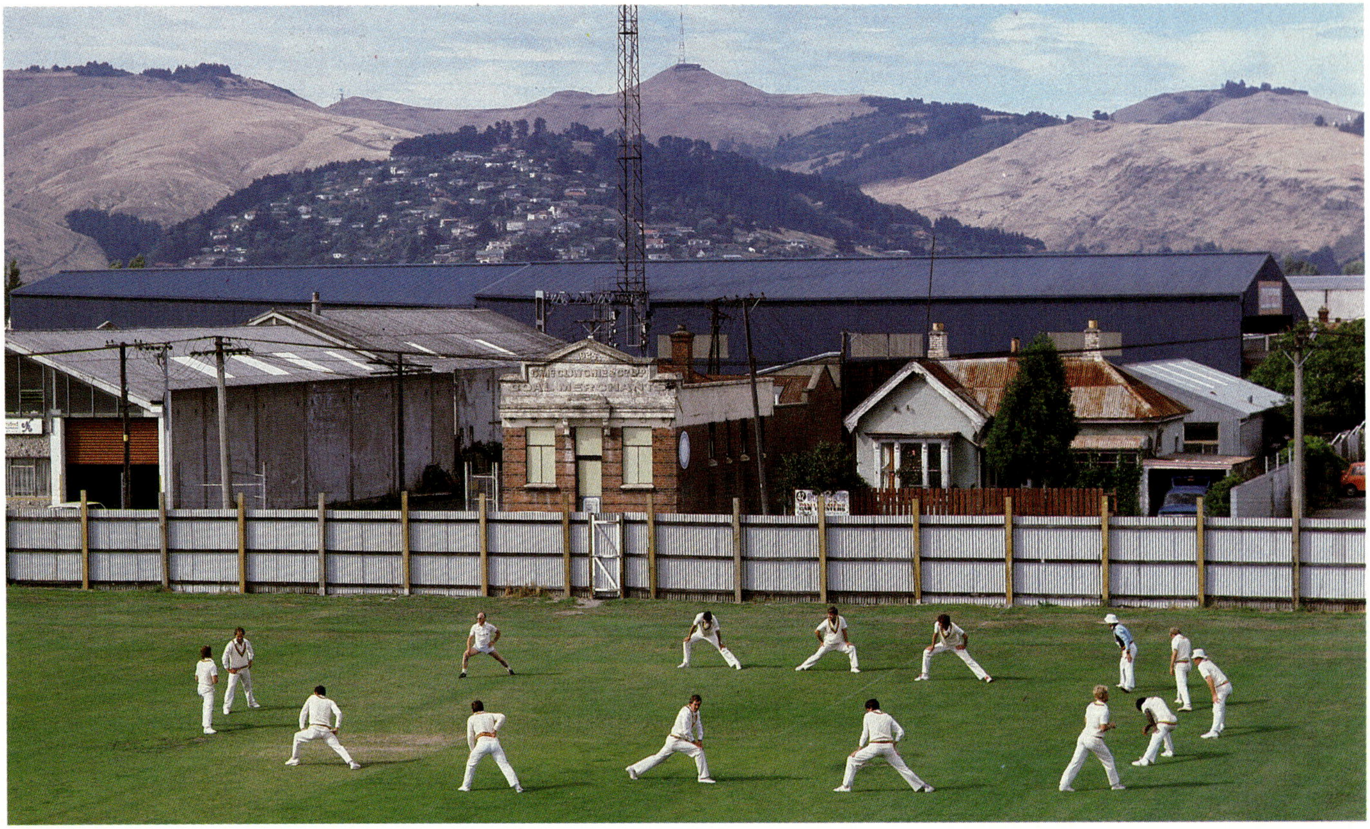

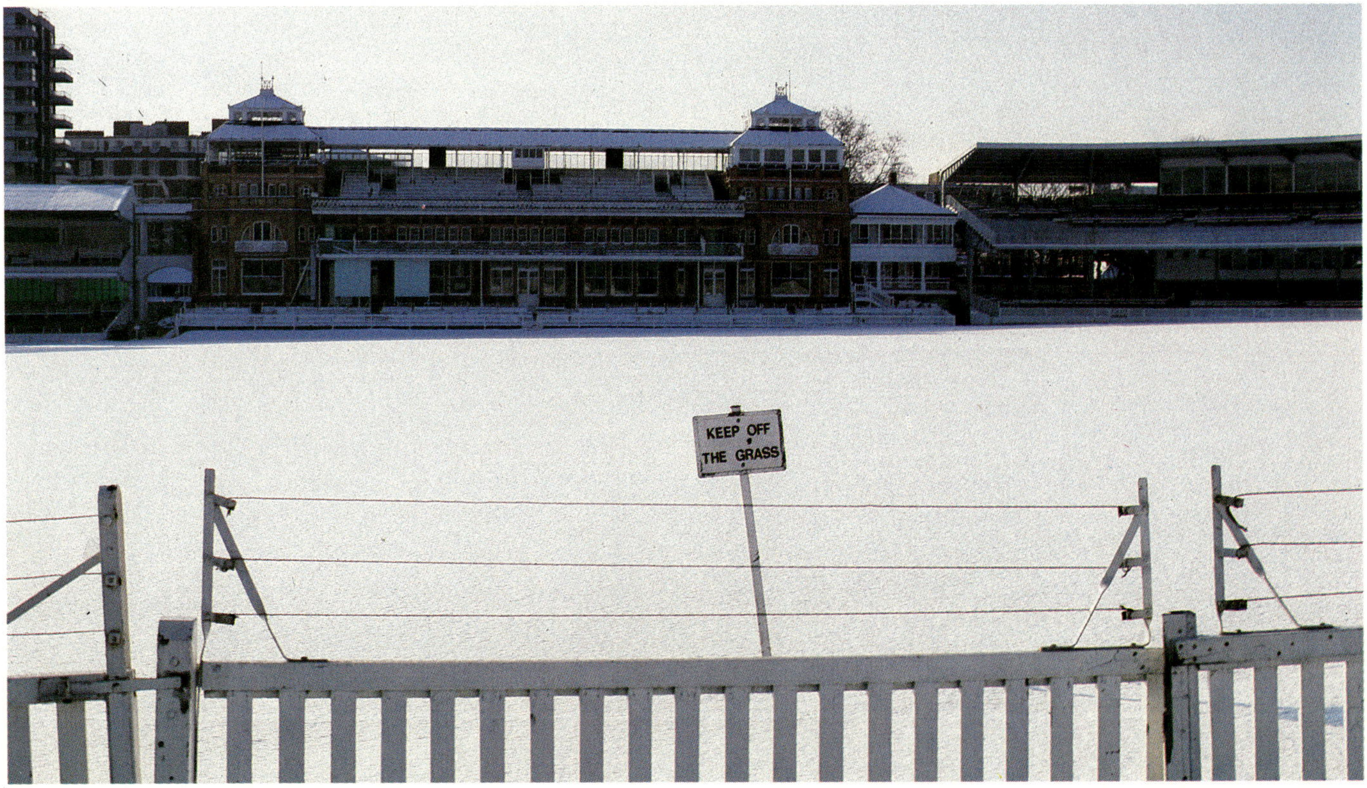
KEEP OFF
THE GRASS

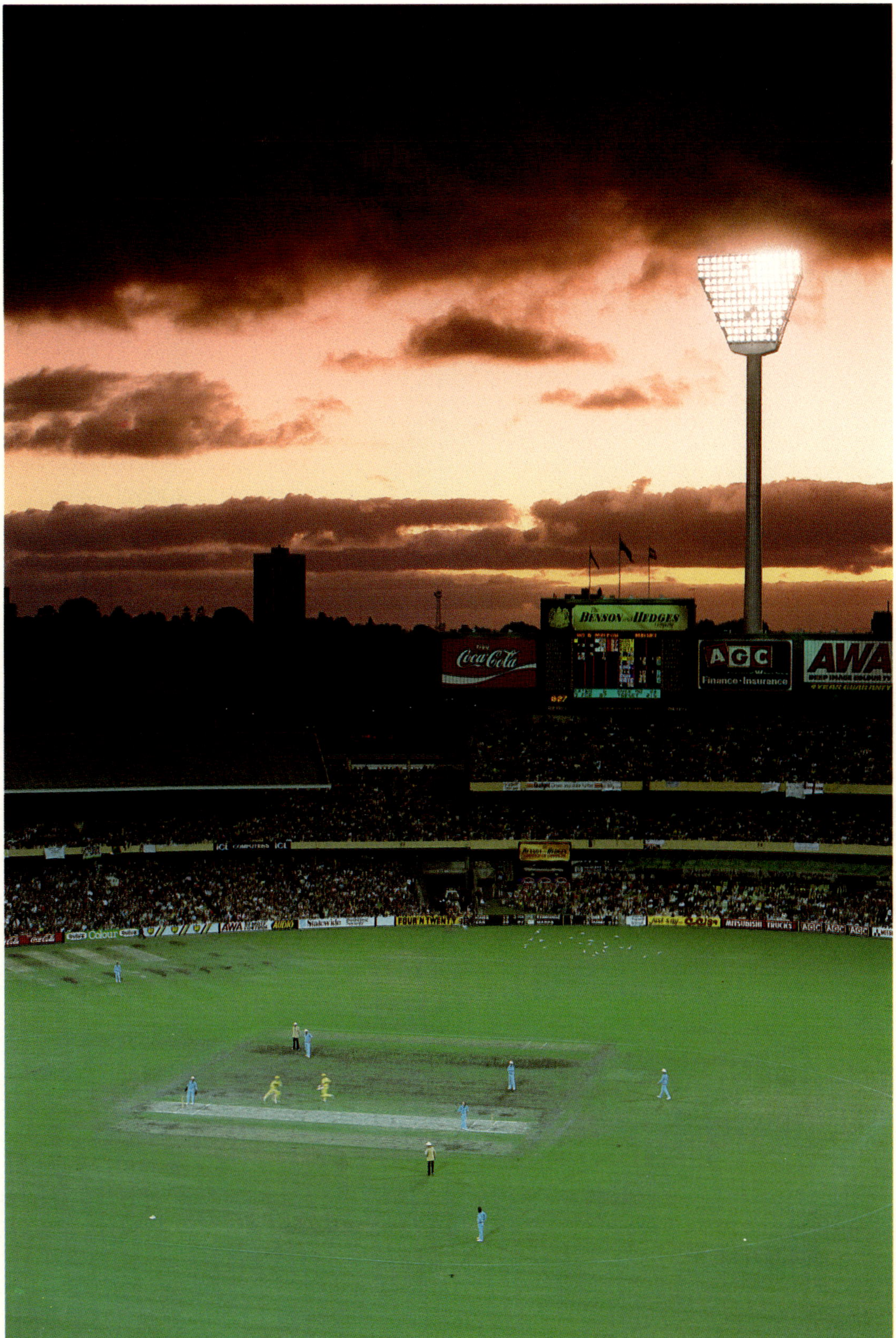

Even as recently as ten years ago you would not have seen an England team undertaking such formalised training. These days much more importance is attached to physical fitness, probably because of the larger and larger sums of money involved. The West Indians were the pioneers in this area and now they are superfit. So here we see the England players following suit. Mind you, it didn't do them much good – they were thrashed out of sight!

Australia v England, Melbourne, February 1985

opposite, above: *Christchurch, New Zealand, January 1984*

opposite, below: *Lord's, December 1983*

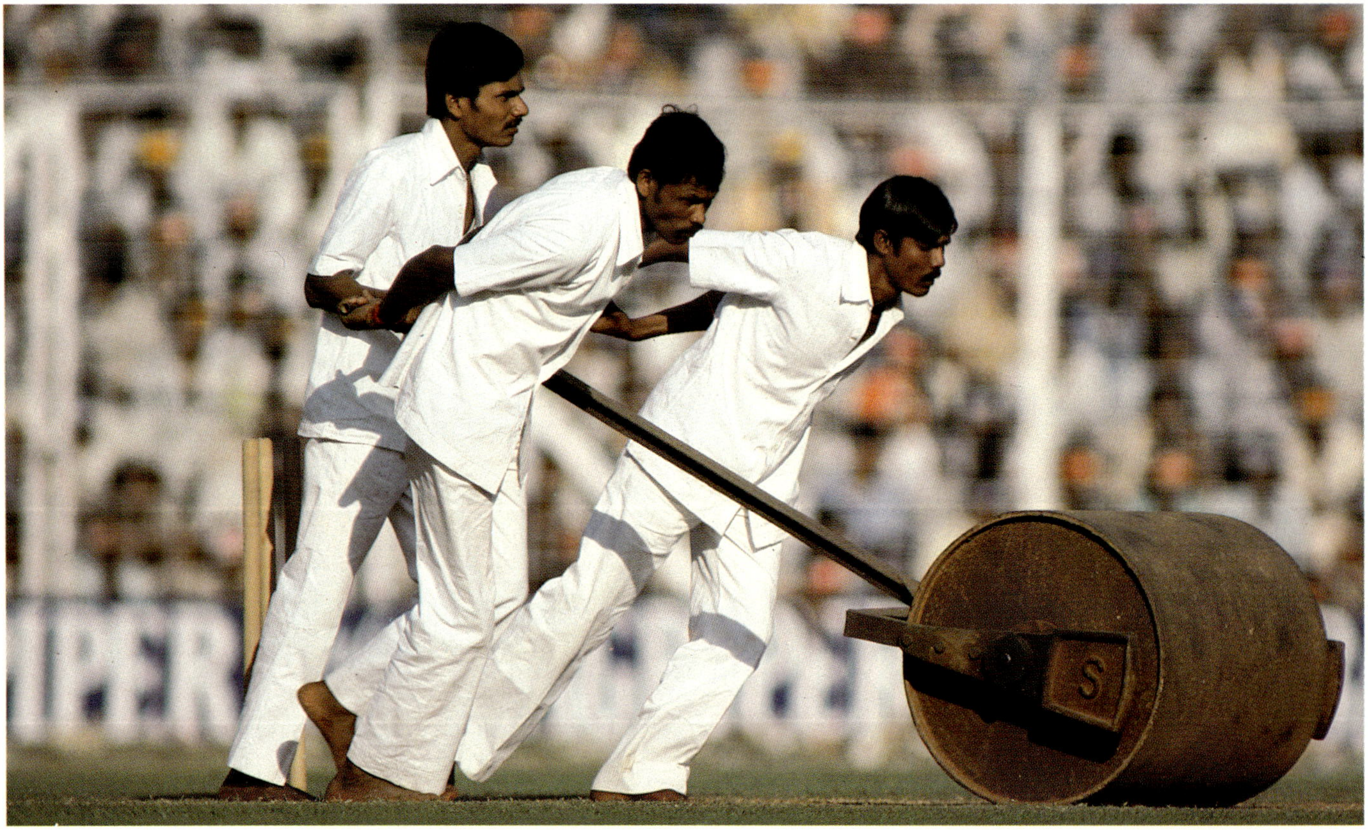

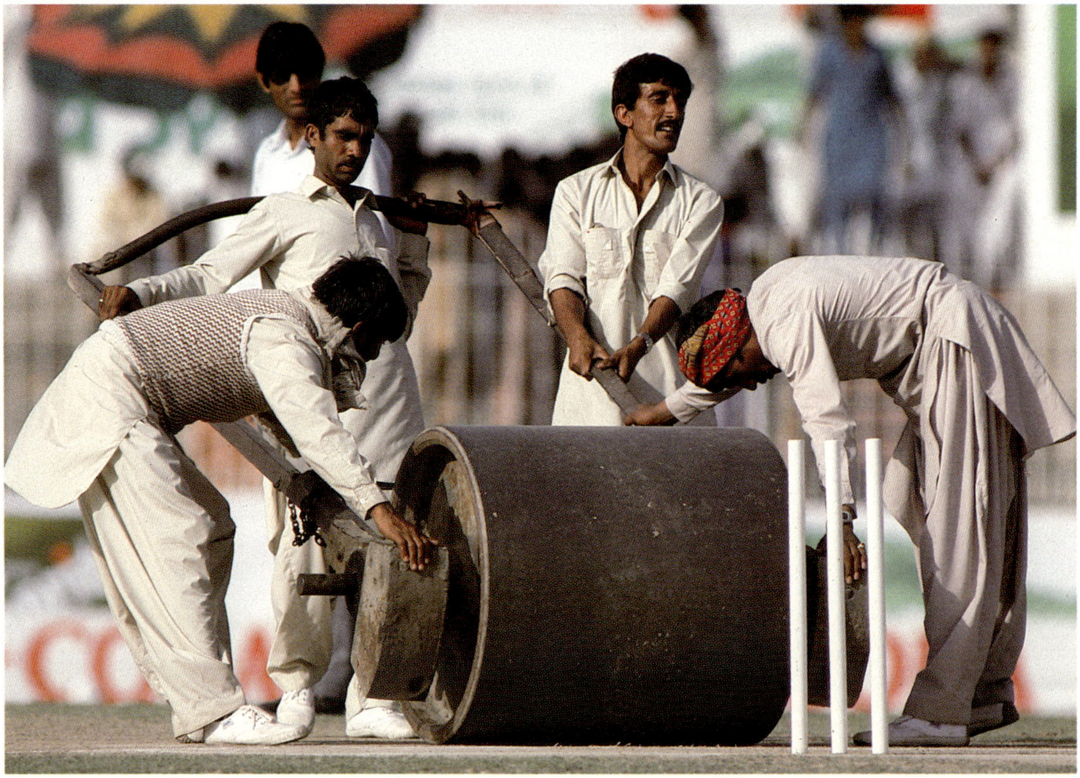

The groundstaff are as important a part of the atmosphere as are the surroundings.

Around the world –

above: *At Bombay, November 1981*

below: *At Faislabad, March 1984*

opposite, above: *At St Vincent, January 1981*

opposite, below: *At Lord's, September 1984*

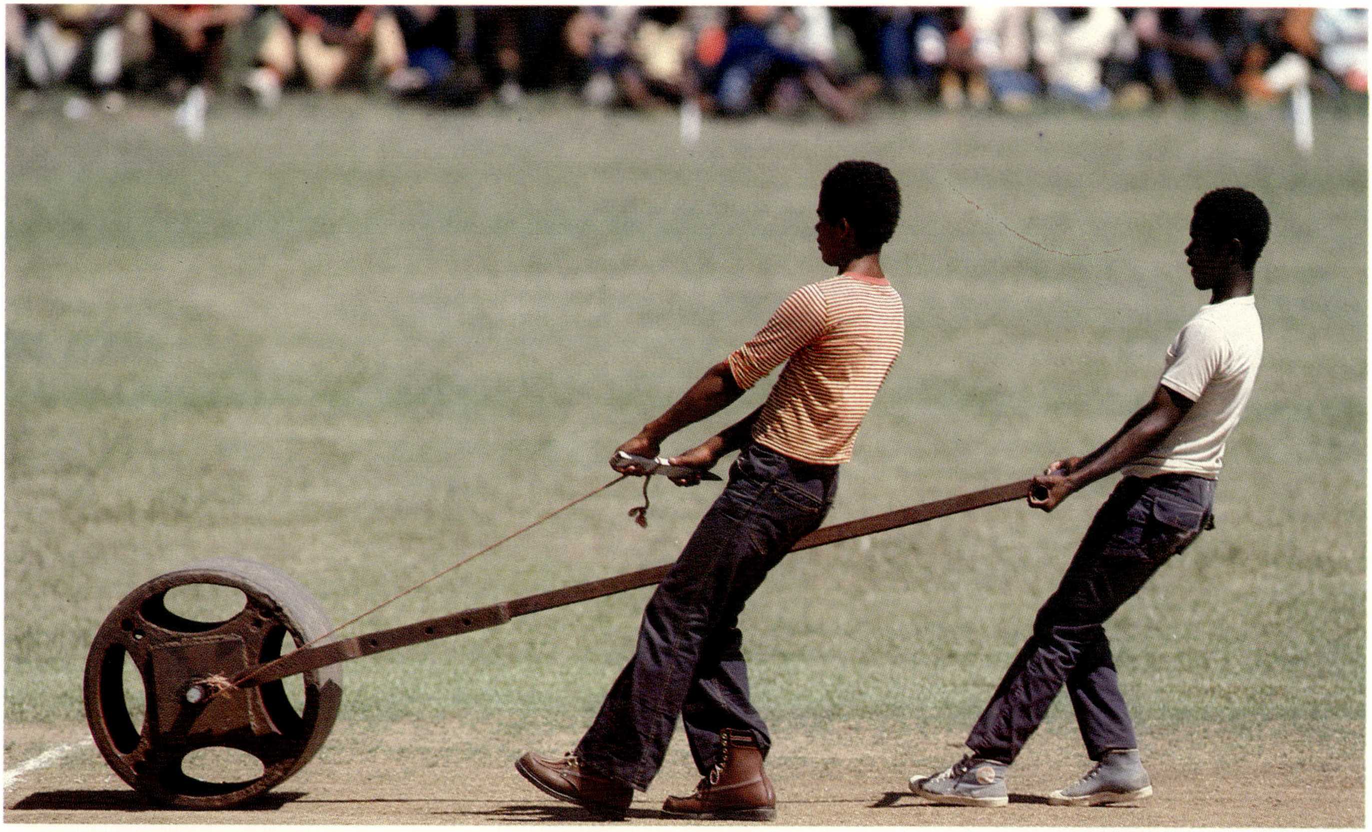

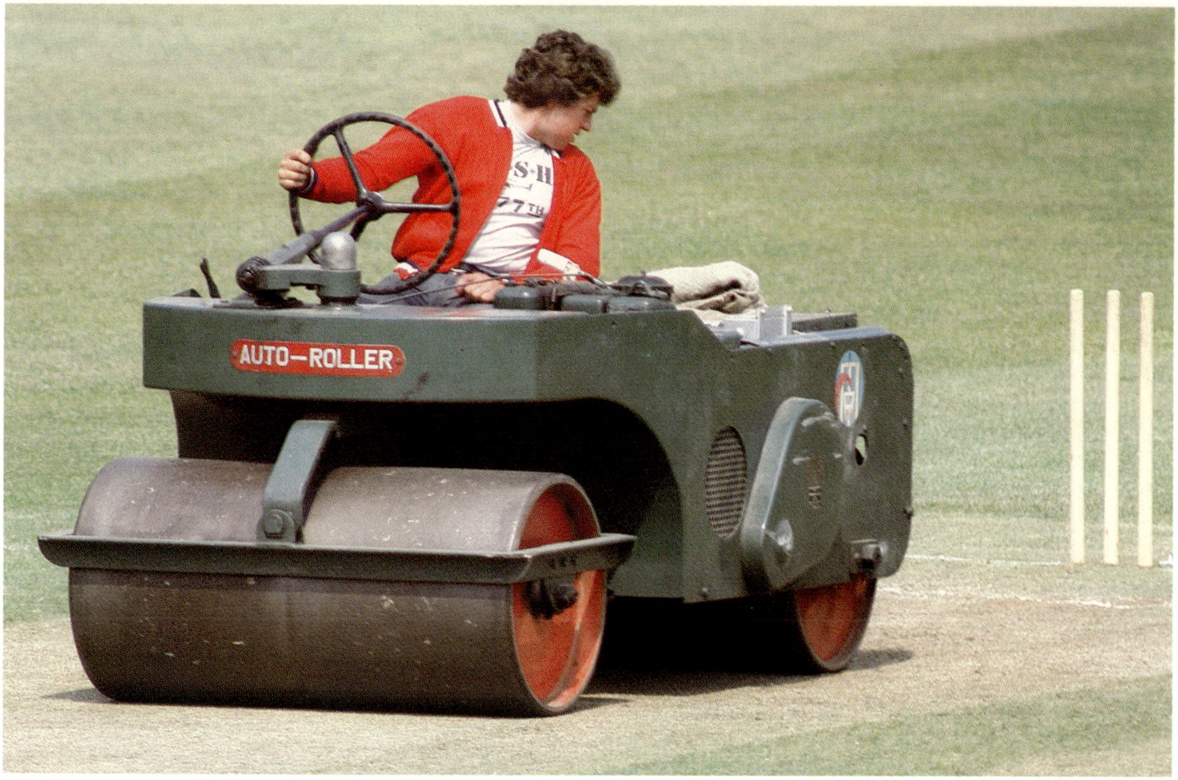
AUTO—ROLLER

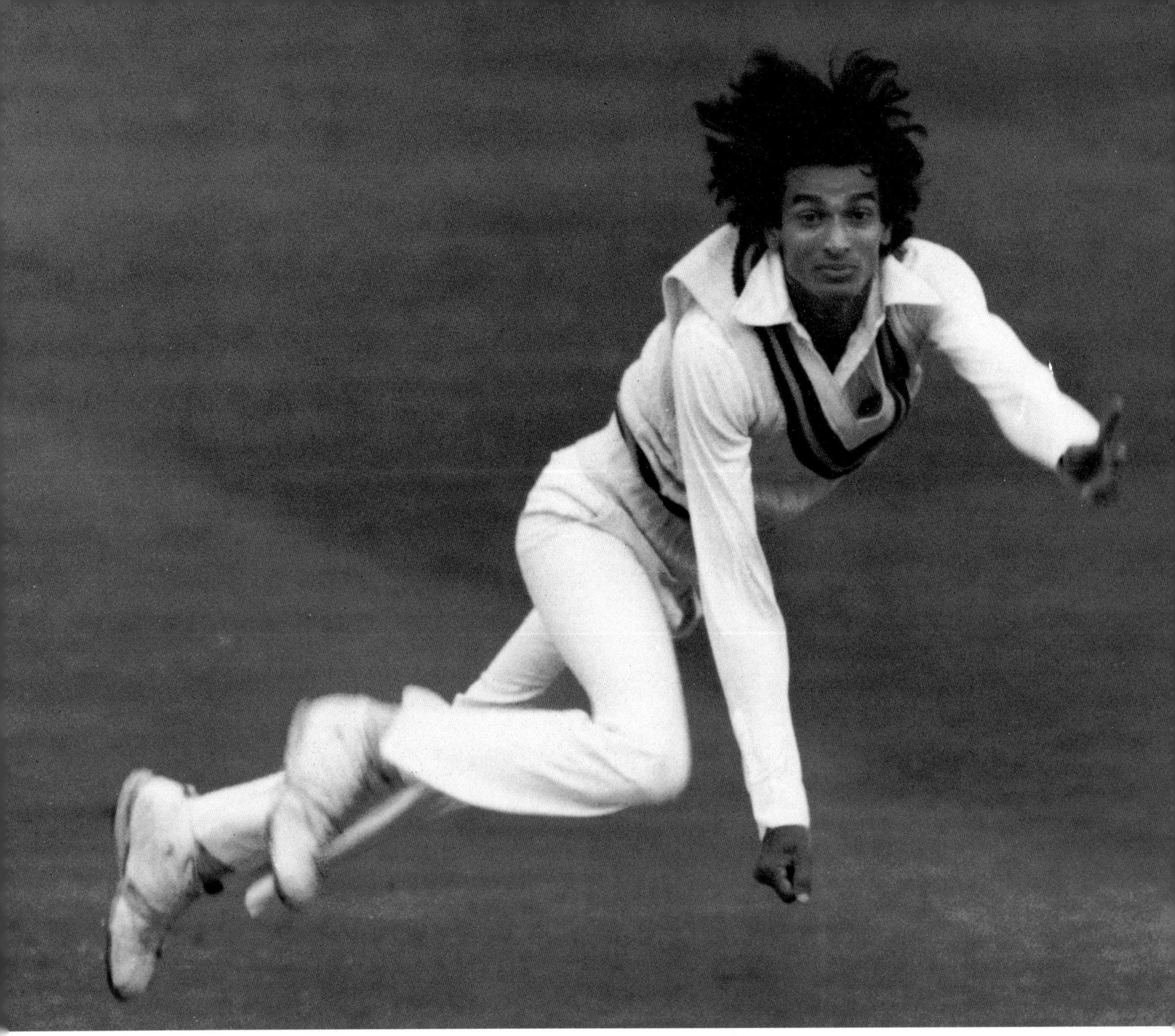

It is not easy to take good bowling pictures, because you really need to get in close. This applies especially in colour where other distractions in your print must be reduced to a minimum. If you're concentrating on the bowler's action you must ignore everything else, even though this may mean missing a catch or a wicket. However, there are always quiet periods in a day and, if you watch carefully, you will develop a sixth sense as to when is a good time to start shooting.

The photographs on this page were taken on a very long lens, 600 mm F4 with a 1.4 converter, bringing it to a focal length of 840 mm. This is a slightly hit or miss approach; it's impossible to know how successful you've been until after you've seen the negative.
Ten years ago a converter would give the effect of shooting the picture through a milk bottle – it would be very fuzzy and horrible. The advantage of the modern converter over the old one is that the sharpness is improved 100 per cent. In fact the advance in the last

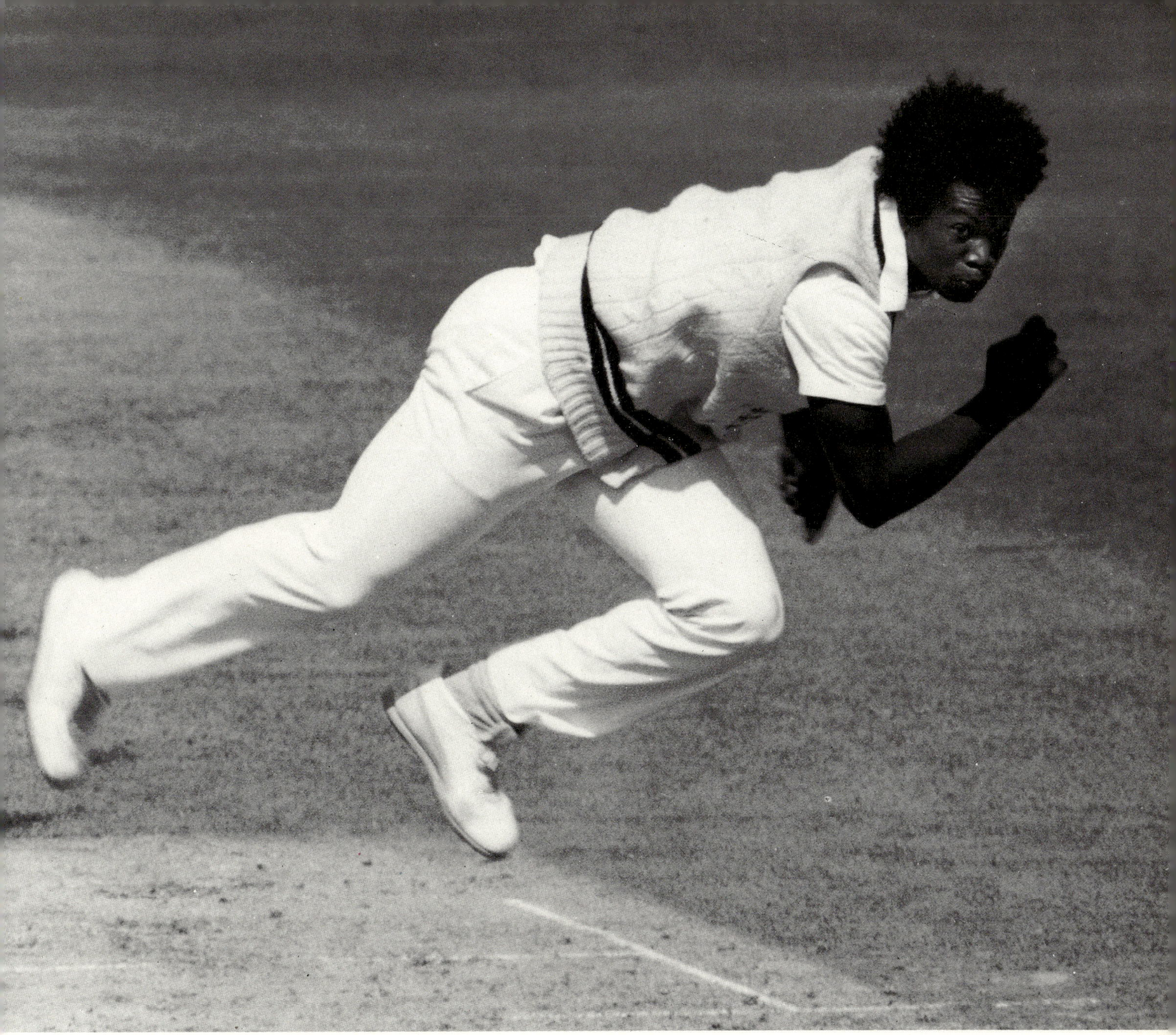

ten years by all the major camera manufacturers – Nikon, Canon, Pentax, Minolta – has been a great step forward in photography. With the 1.4 converter, which most cricket photographers use, you only lose one stop in light through the lens. This again is another breakthrough. Normally, on the 2× converter, one loses two stops and obviously, with the light in England, that could mean that you would be unable to get the speed from your camera necessary to 'freeze' your subject, ie the bowler, in mid-action. You have to shoot at 1/500

Norman Cowans, bowling for Middlesex, Middlesex v Surrey, the Oval, August 1982
opposite: *Sikander Bakht, third Test, England v Pakistan, Headingley, August 1982*

sec to guarantee that you will keep the movement in focus. Out of a complete roll of film you will probably only have a fifty per cent success rate with regard to sharpness. Also, you really need a motor drive to take these shots.

Having, by these somewhat uncertain methods, achieved some satisfactory shots, I have put the pictures of Bakht and Cowans together on pages 24 and 25 not only because the prints have similarities – both shots were taken from an elevated position thus giving totally uncluttered backgrounds – but also because so do the careers of the subjects. They both played for their respective countries, Pakistan and England, when they were relatively young and both looked like they might be high fliers. Neither, however, has really fulfilled that early promise.

By contrast, the shots of Kapil Dev and Joel Garner were taken from on a level down the wicket. This certainly adds to the drama, but you will see why you need to be really close in for bowling shots and aware of what background will show up in your print. The careers of the subjects may be compared also. Both Kapil Dev and Joel Garner are bowlers who, as they have grown older, have replaced whatever they may have lost in pace with more intelligent use of the ball.

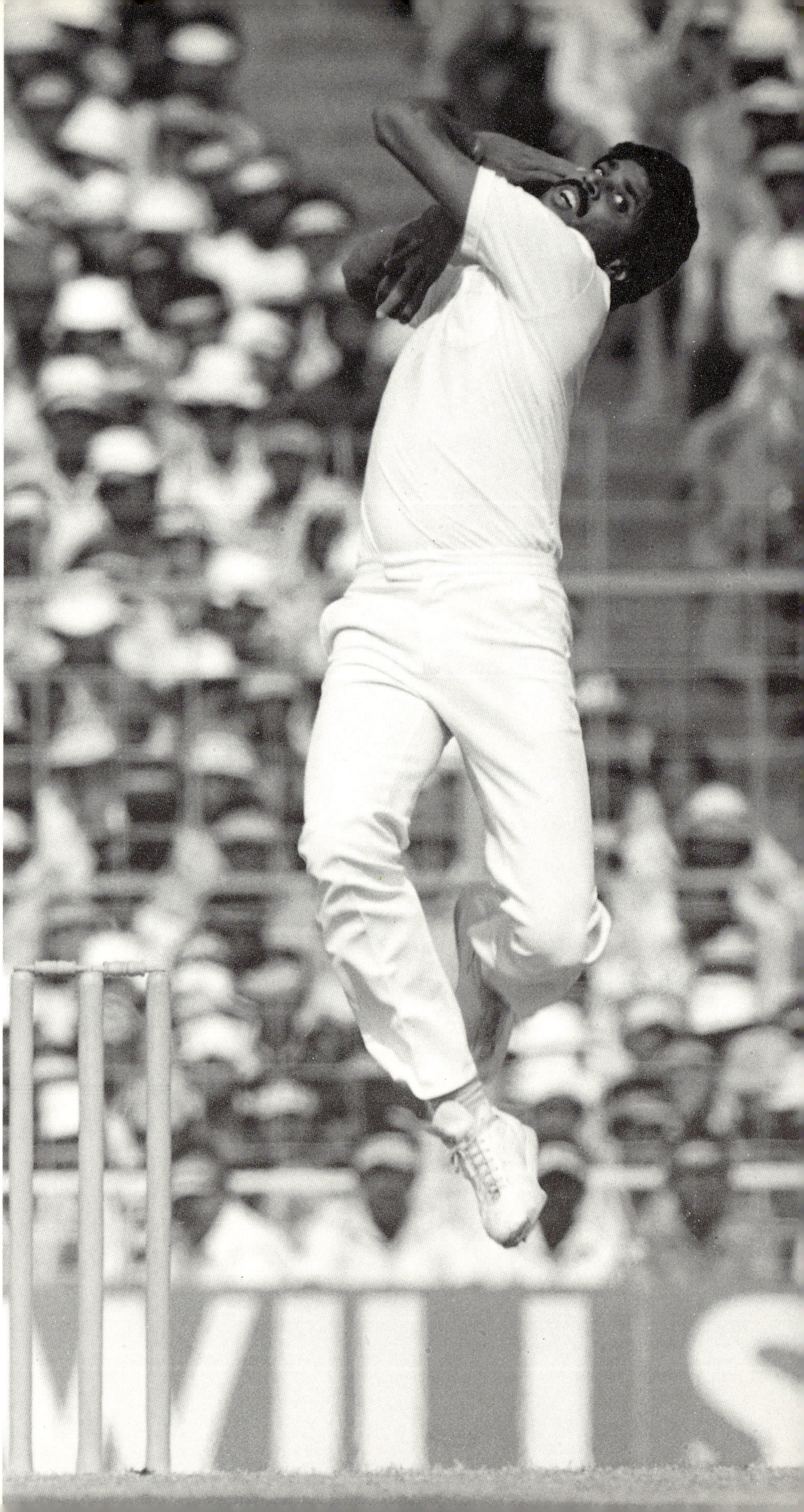

Kapil Dev of Worcestershire and India, fifth Test, India v West Indies, Calcutta, December 1983

opposite: *Joel Garner, Somerset and West Indies, Essex v Somerset, Chelmsford, May 1983*

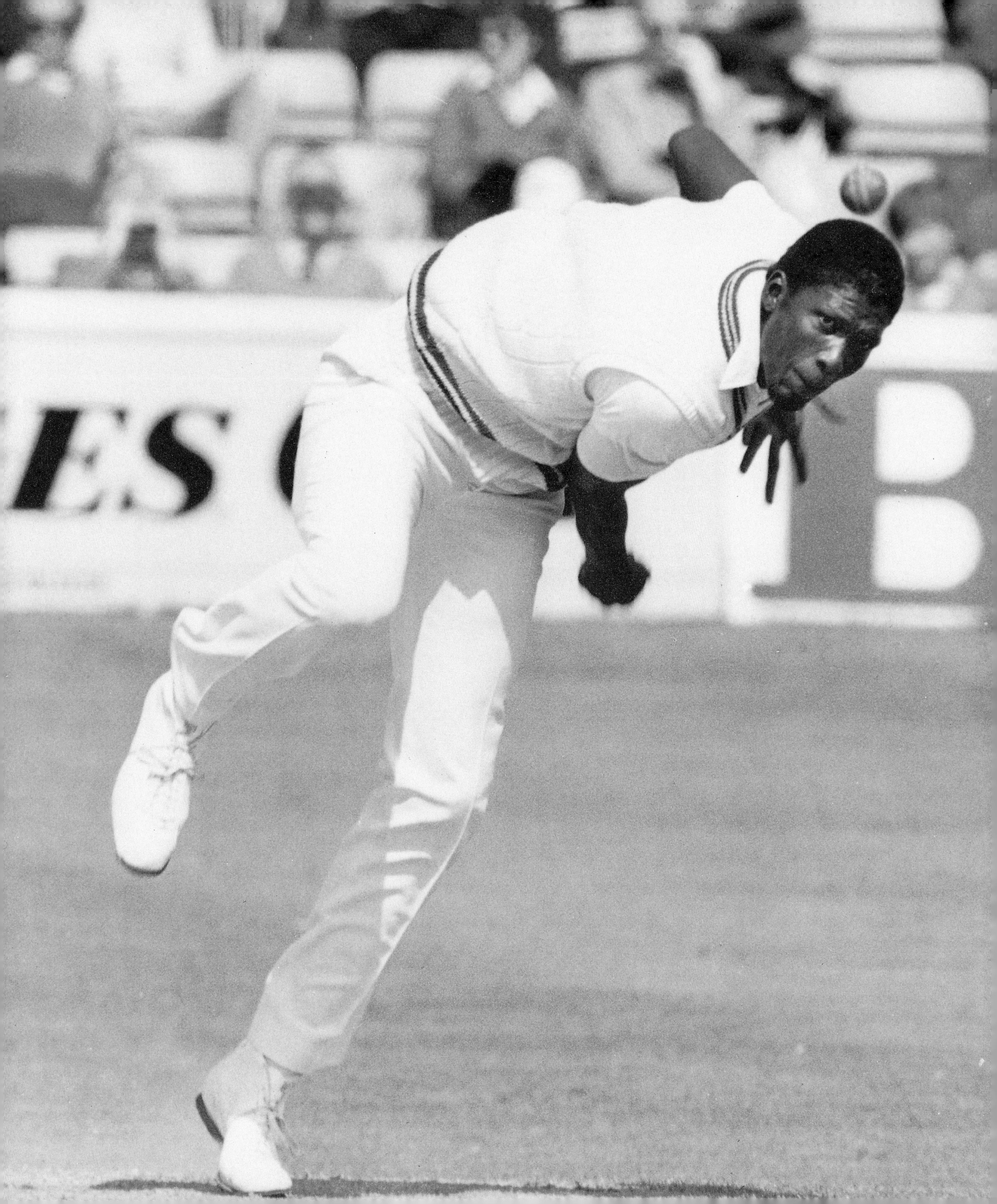

Fast bowling has won the West Indies an enviable record in the 1980s. Although England and Australia have produced such greats as Larwood, Truman, Lindwall and Lillee, it is the West Indians who have been consistently menacing since the 1960s and who now dominate the world fast bowling scene. For the photographer, as well as for the batsman, fast bowling presents a considerable challenge, because the batsman's reaction to a threatening ball is frequently bizarre and, if captured by the camera, rewardingly evocative of the tension of aggressive cricket.

Allan Lamb receives an Imran Khan bouncer, second Test, England v Pakistan, Lord's, August 1982

opposite: *Roland Butcher avoids a fast one from Malcolm Marshall, third Test, West Indies v England, Barbados, March 1981*

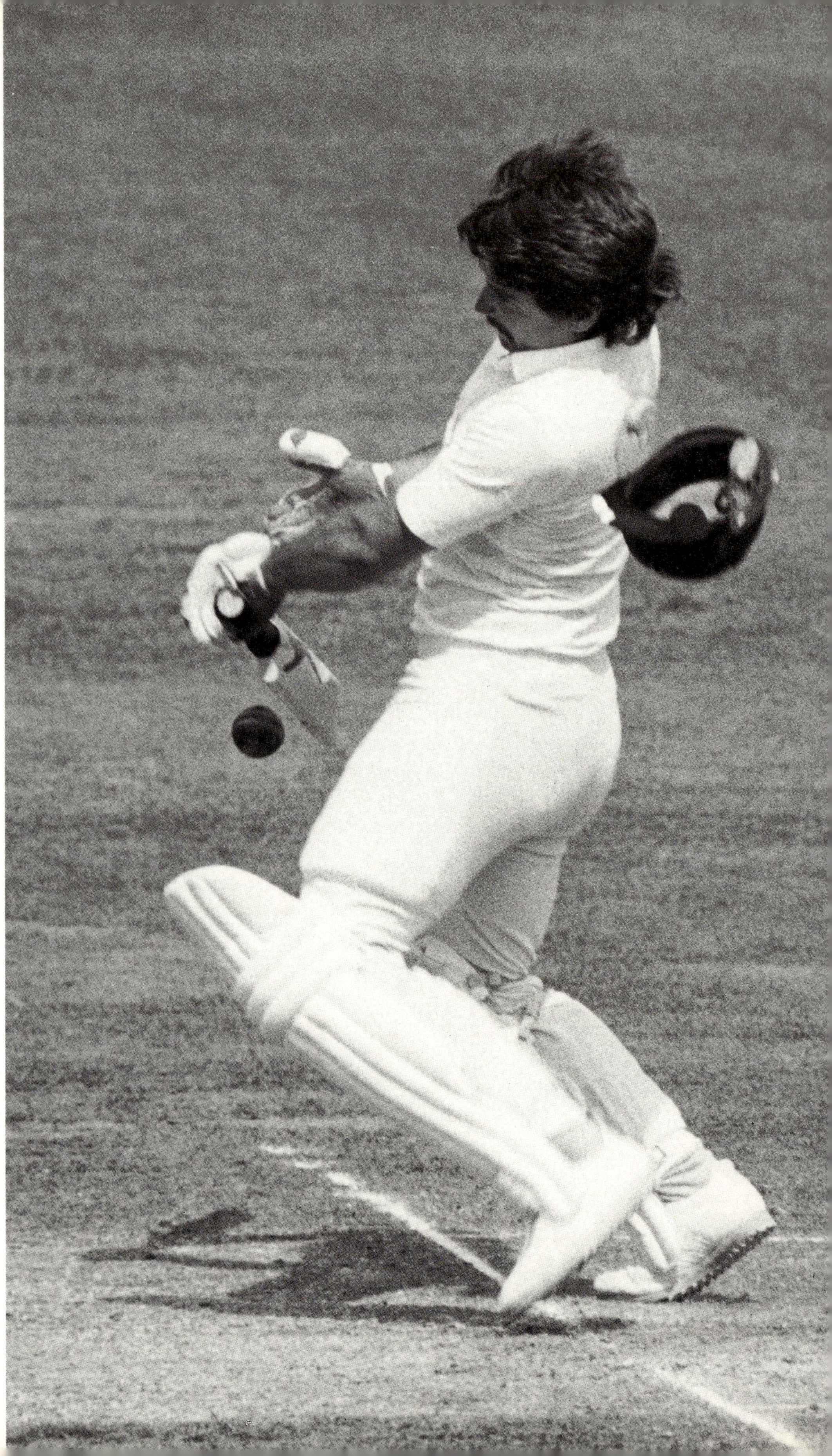

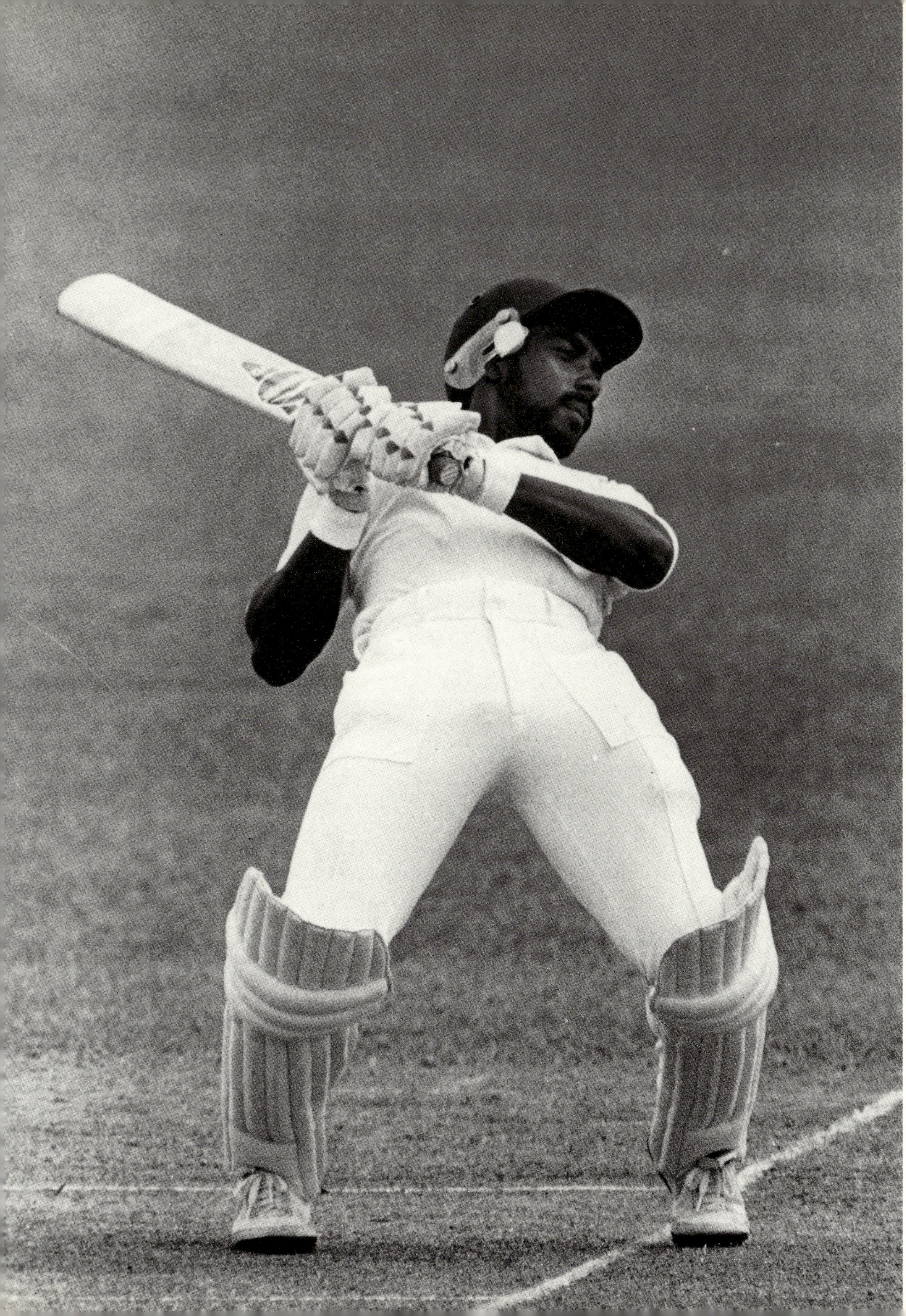

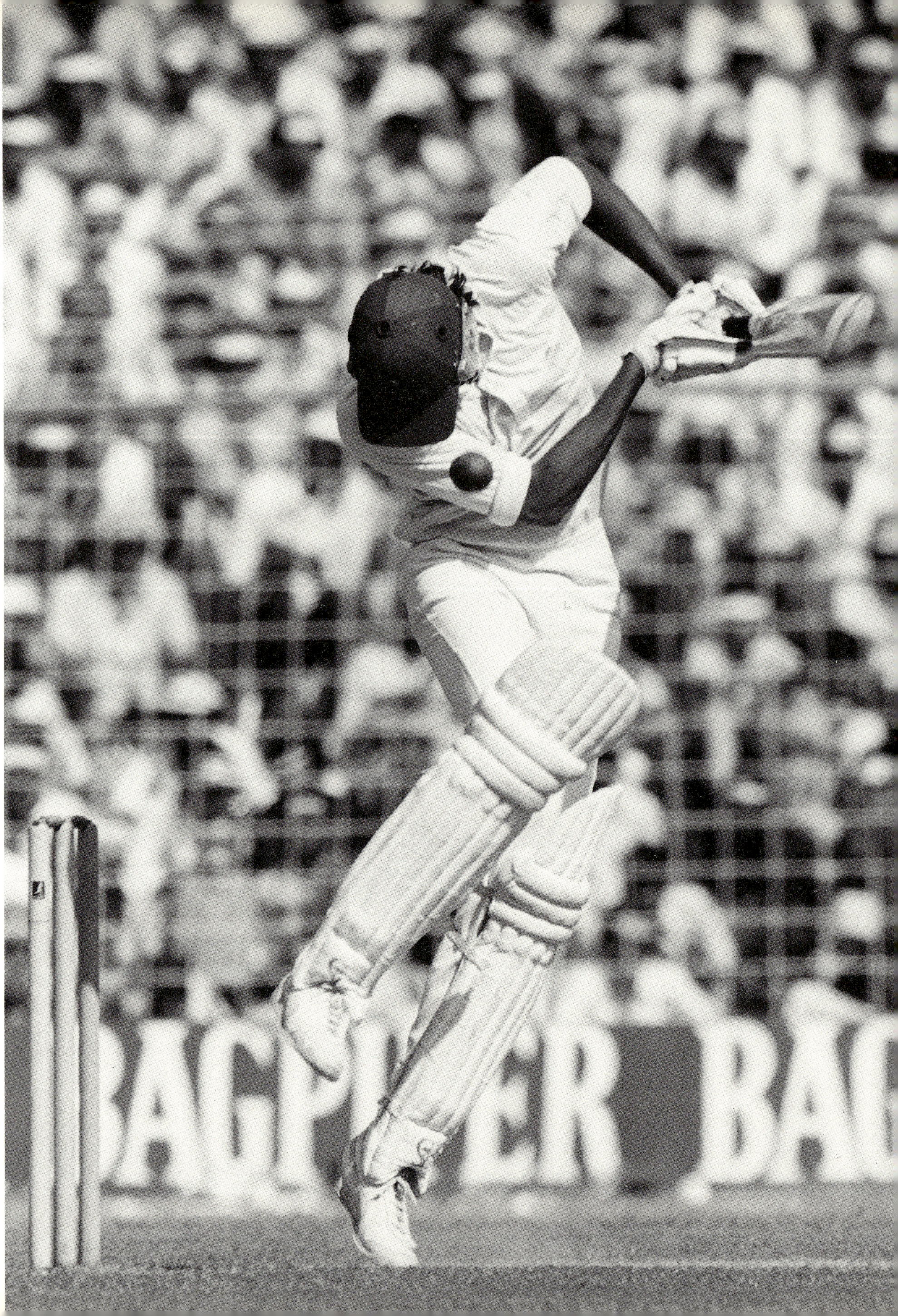

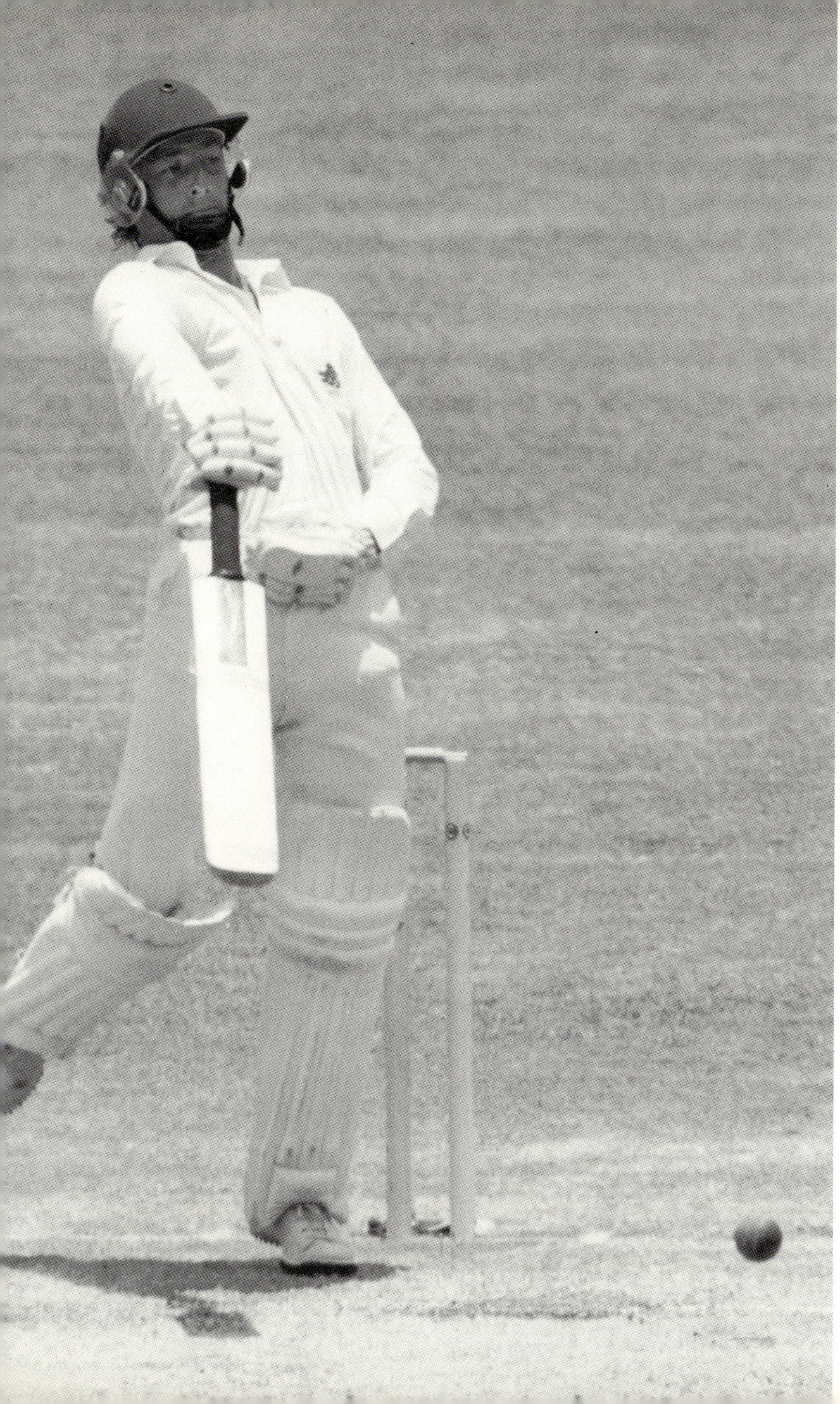

'Oh, what a lovely job you have!' says Joe Public to the cricket photographer, 'following cricket, sitting around and drinking beer'. Well, it's not like that. I do have a lovely job, but there's not much sitting around. You can have two or three overs when nothing much happens, but you have to be ready all the time for when something does happen. And *when* it does, your reaction must be as sharp as the batsman's.

Graeme Fowler performs his unique action after facing a fast ball from Joel Garner, second Test, England v West Indies, Lord's, June 1984

opposite: *Ravi Shastri moves away from a Marshall bouncer in the fourth Test, India v West Indies, Bombay, November 1983*

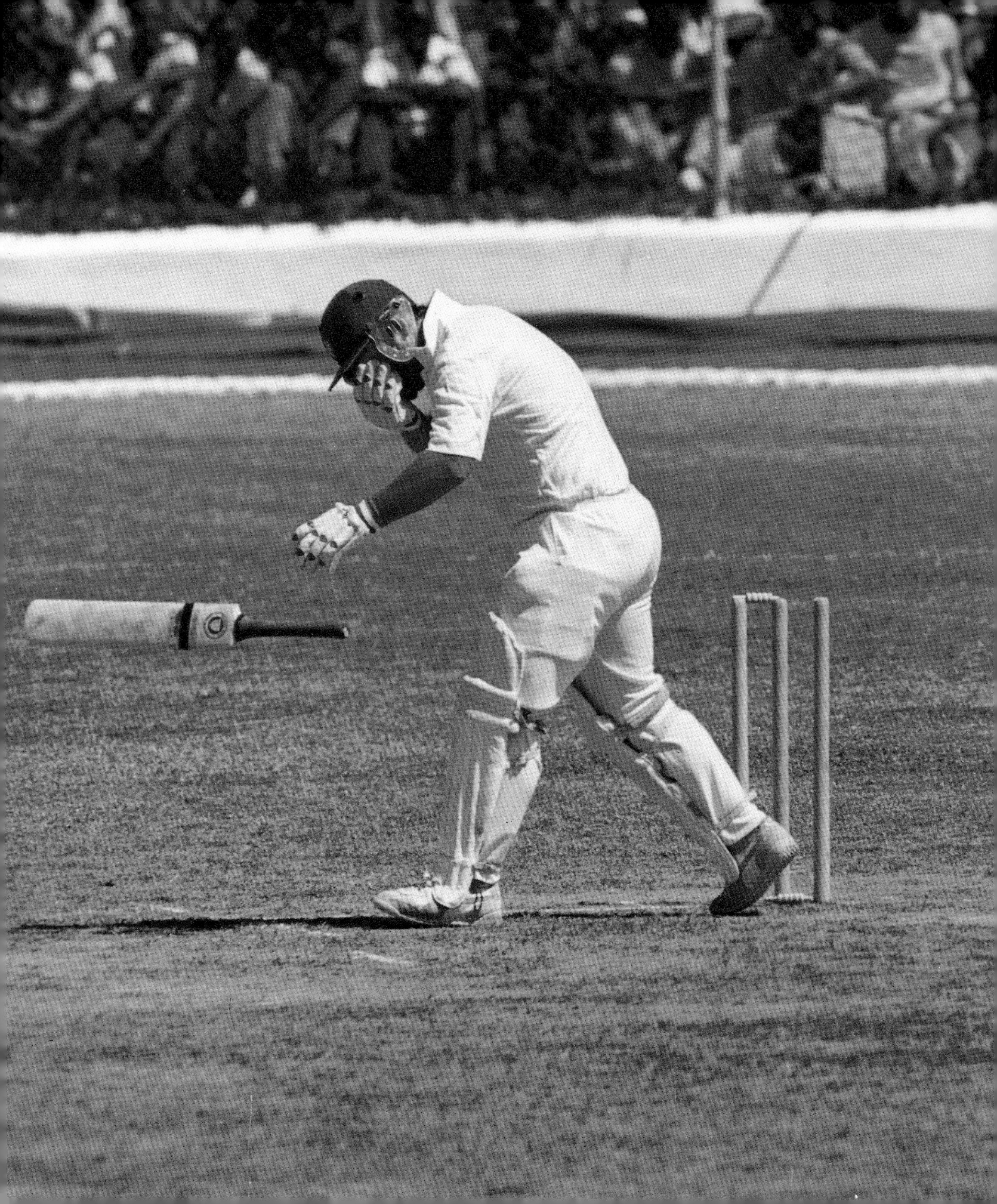

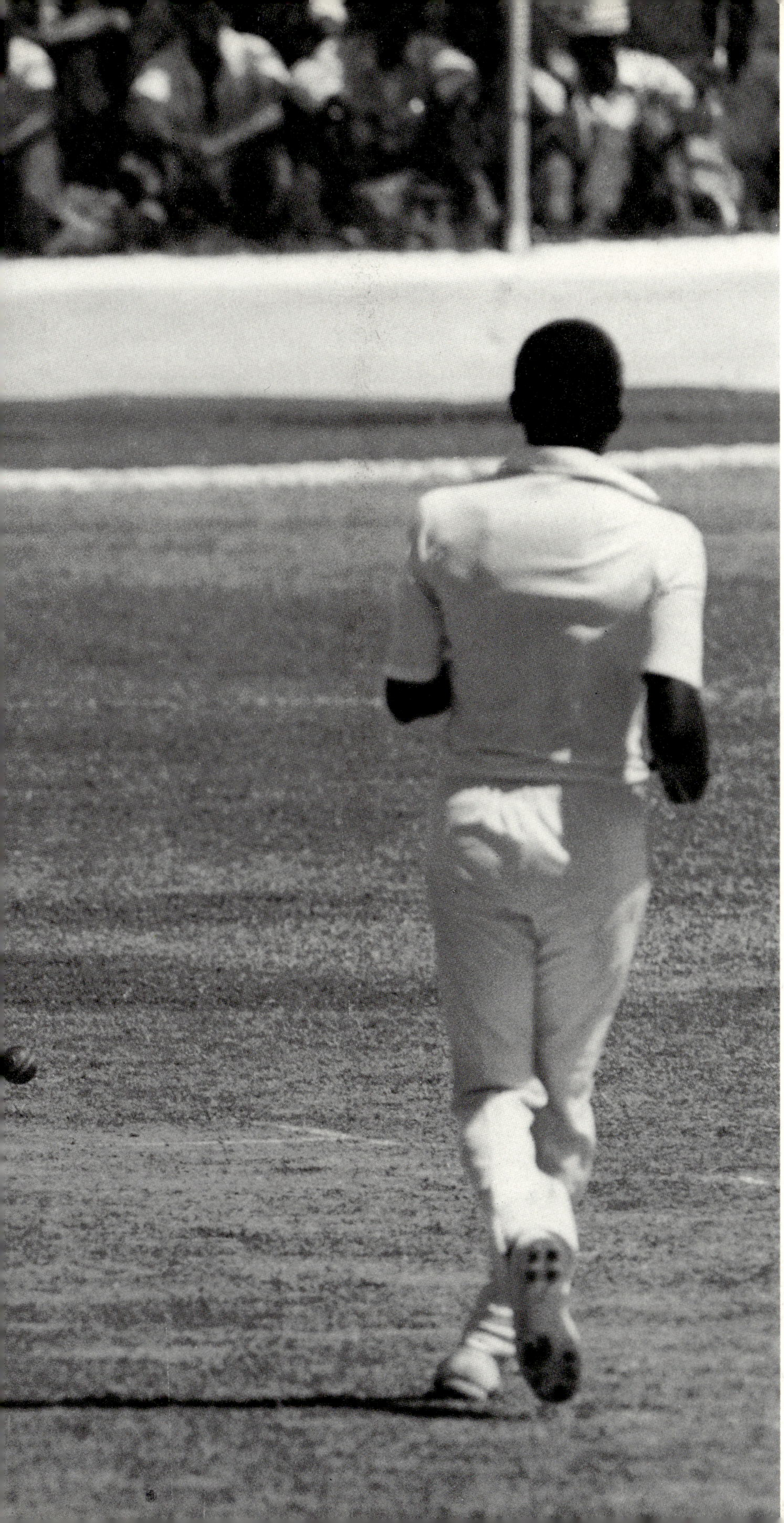

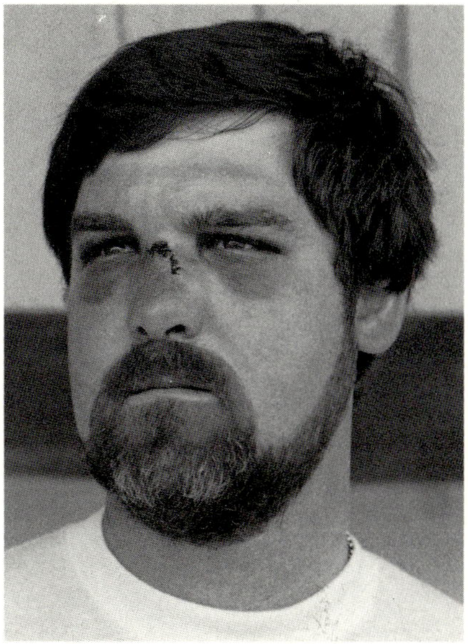

England went to the West Indies in 1986 full of optimism. They had won the Ashes the previous summer and the media were forecasting that they would certainly hold their own in the Caribbean. Then one split second of disaster shattered not only Gatting's nose but also England's hopes. The other England batsmen were shocked, almost traumatised. If Gatting, the most in form bat of all, could not survive – then who could? Morale plummeted. And fairly soon the press started predicting another 5–0 whitewash. Gatting returned to England for emergency surgery and, rather sadly, the scorebook records, not – as one might have expected – 'retired hurt', but out 'hit wicket'. Later he returned to the tour and with Olympian bad luck – broke his thumb.

Mike Gatting is smashed in the face by a fast, rising ball from West Indies pace bowler, Malcolm Marshall, one-day international, Jamaica, February 1986

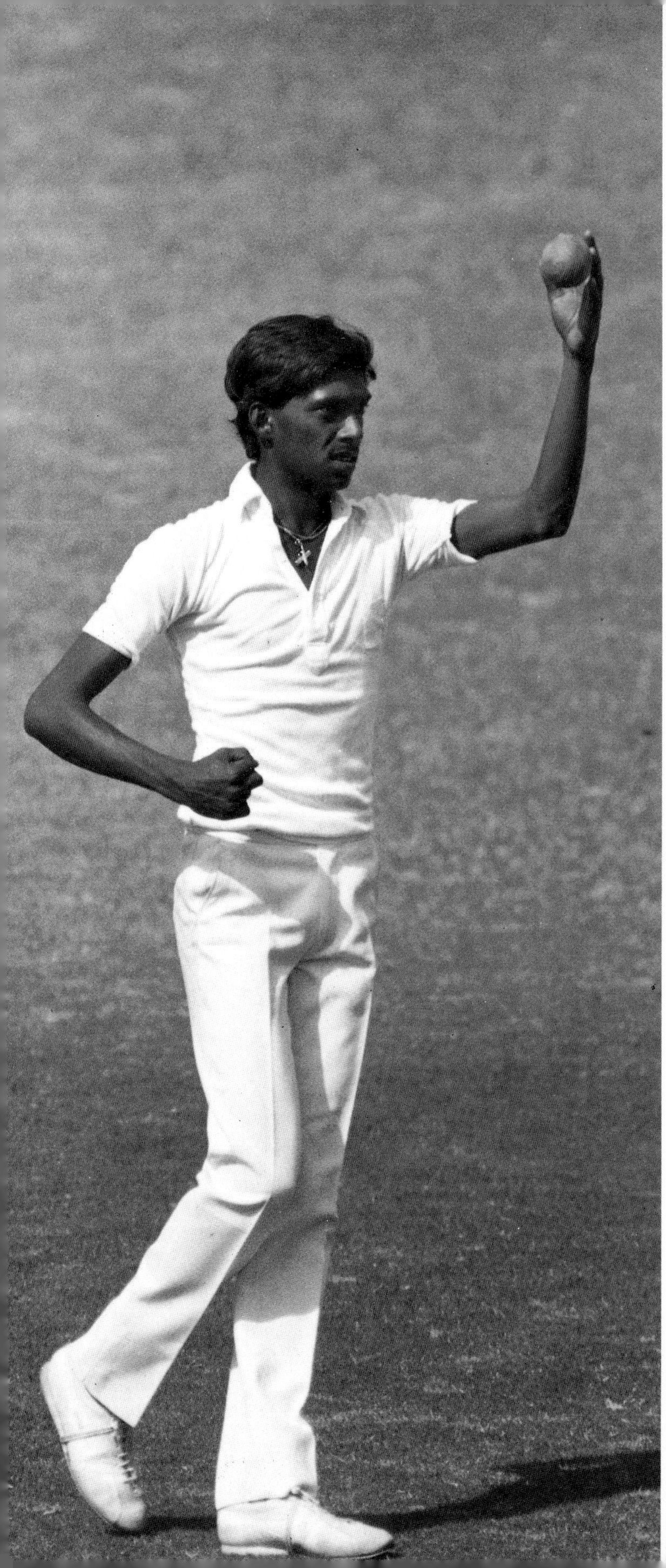

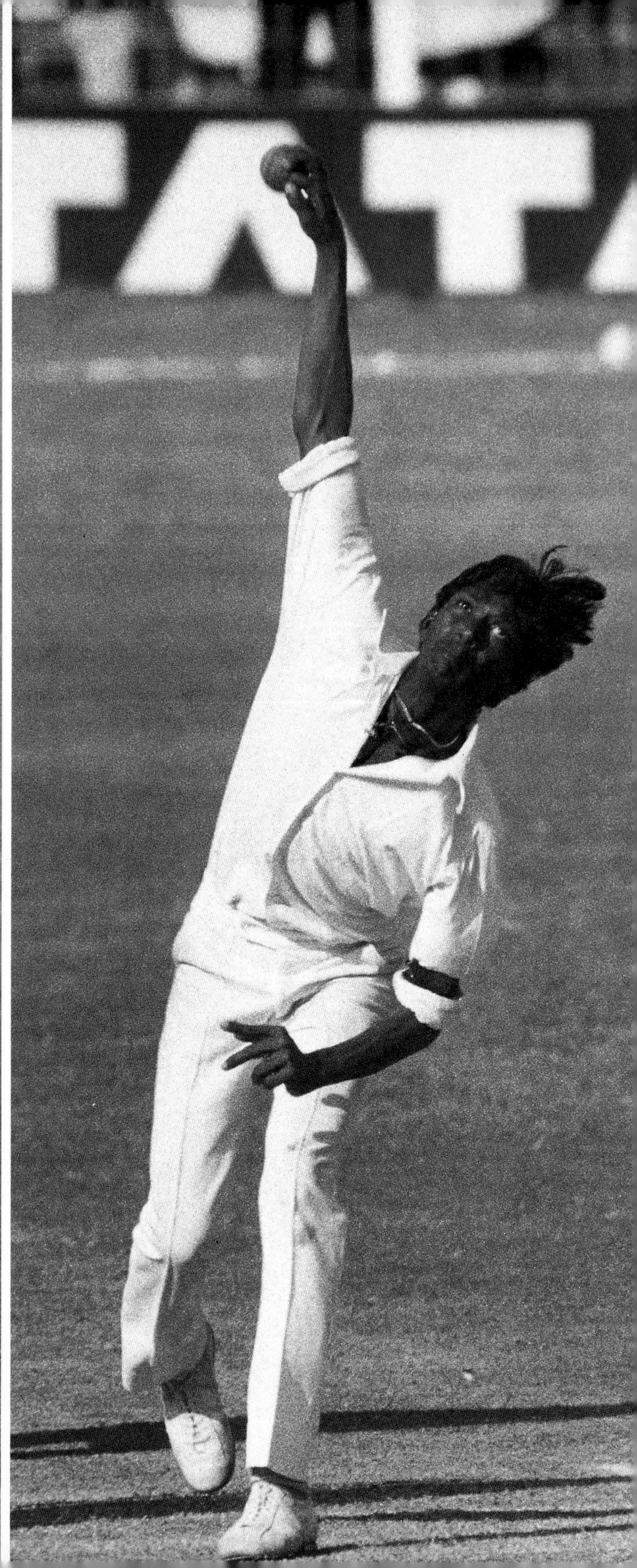

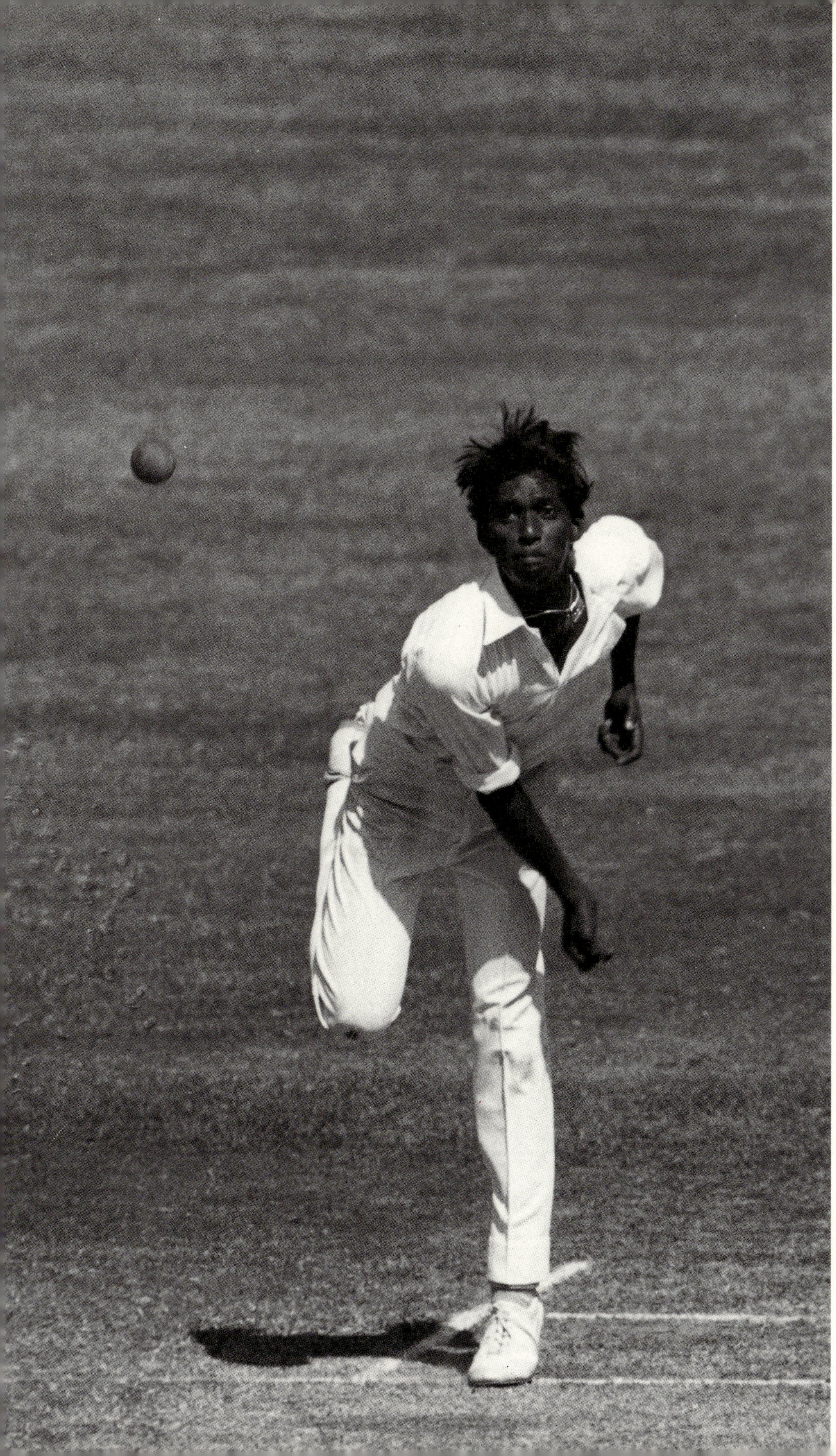

The incredible 90 mph bowling of the West Indians may have captured the attention and the imagination of cricket lovers around the world, but the leg-spin bowler has an art and poetry all of his own. The second two pictures of this spread, I think, demonstrate this and capture the distinctive action. The tension in Laxman Sivarama-krishnan's left hand the instant before releasing the ball is also eloquent.
Named after two Hindu gods and an epic warrior hero, Siva was nonetheless an unknown eighteen-year-old when he appeared on the test scene during England's tour of India in 1984/85. He took 20 wickets for an average of 31.43. However, leg-spin bowling is a dying art, perhaps because it is the fast bowler who gets the wickets, and after a disappointing tour in Australia in 1985 Sivaramakrishnan was dropped from the test side.

First Test, India v England, Bombay, December 1984

Although, because of my newspaper work, I am most at home shooting in black and white, I do enjoy working in colour also. It is, however, limiting. If you are using black and white you can usually get some decent shots even in fairly grim weather, but anything taken in colour in poor light will just look dingy. This is a major consideration in England, especially for a sports photographer, who can't choose his weather. Also, with colour the exposure has to be spot on to within half a stop, or you might as well throw the picture away; it cannot be saved in the darkroom the way an under- or over-exposed black and white shot might be. But some pictures, like this one, really do need colour. In this case it is the black and white prints which I shot at the same time that are lifeless by comparison.

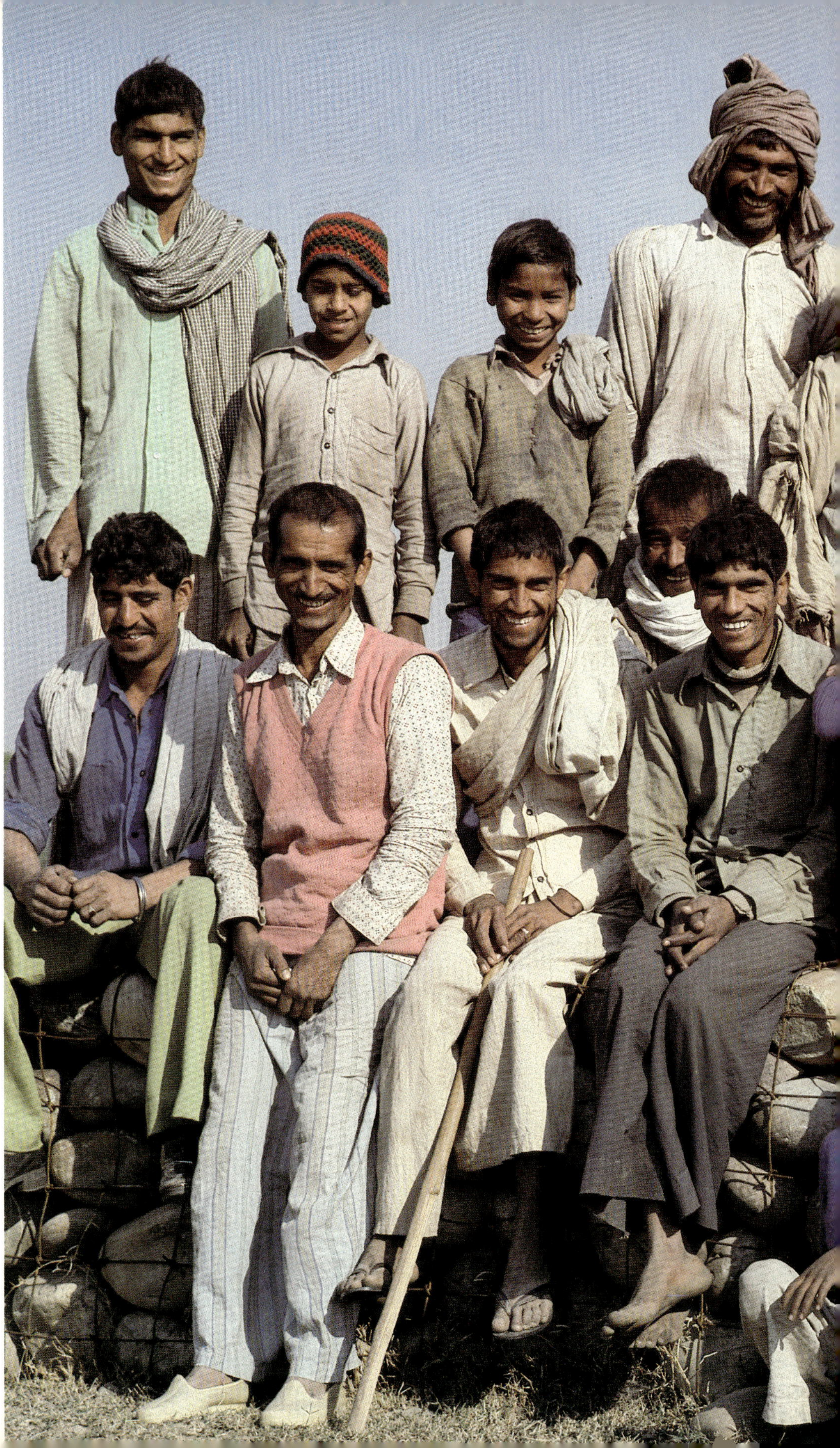

Local villagers come to beat for Ian Botham on a partridge shoot in Jammu in the foothills of Kashmir, December 1981

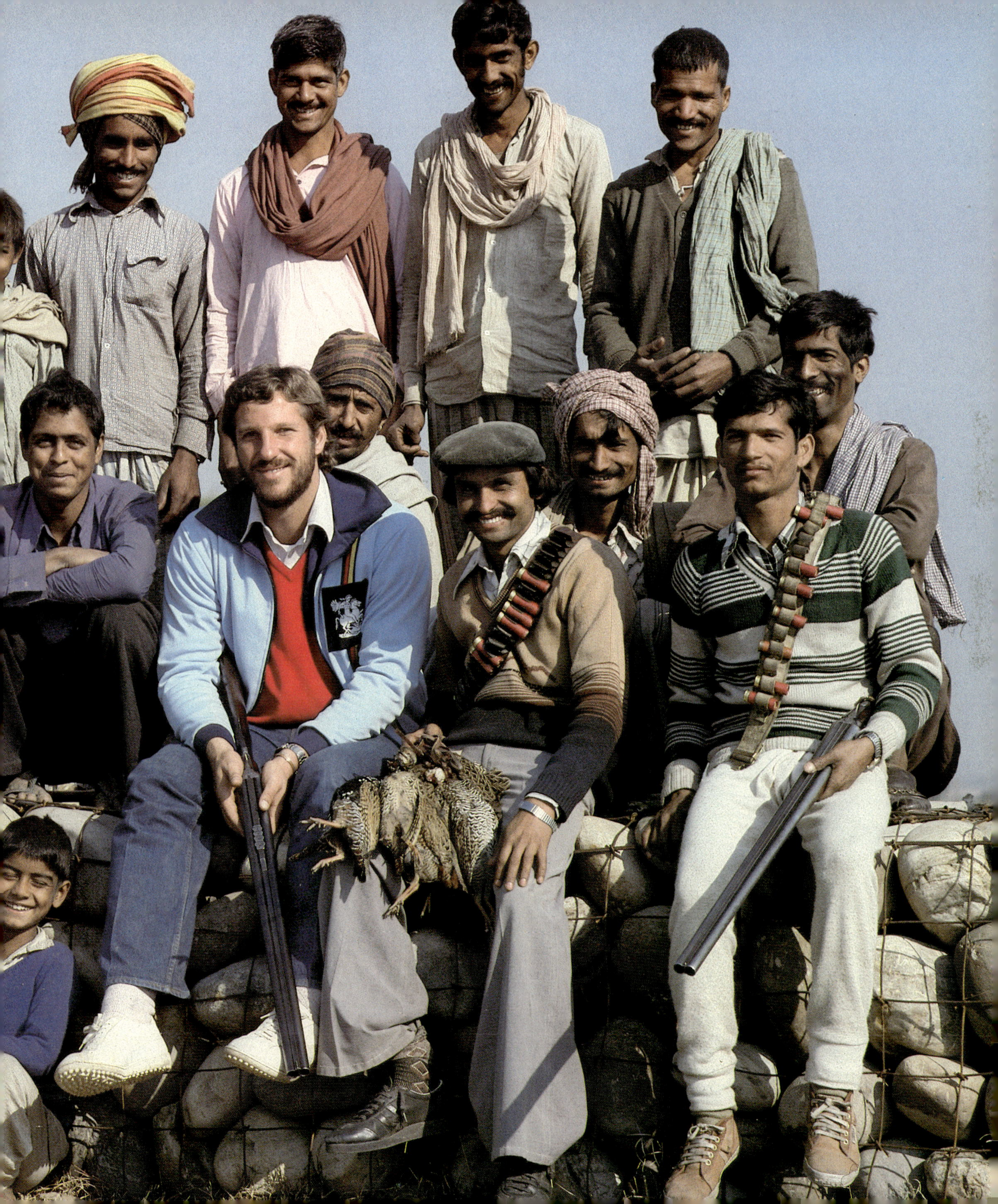

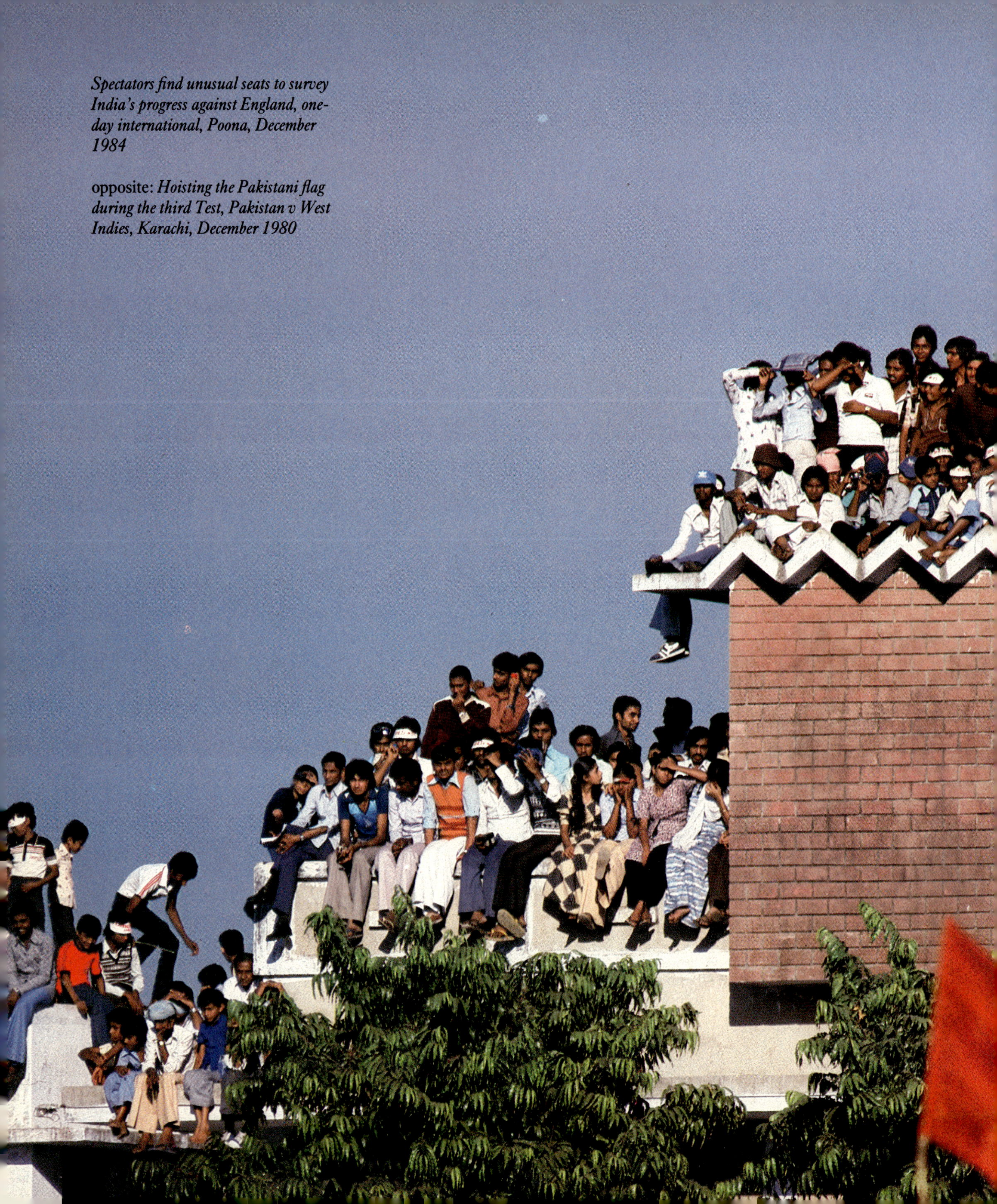

Spectators find unusual seats to survey India's progress against England, one-day international, Poona, December 1984

opposite: *Hoisting the Pakistani flag during the third Test, Pakistan v West Indies, Karachi, December 1980*

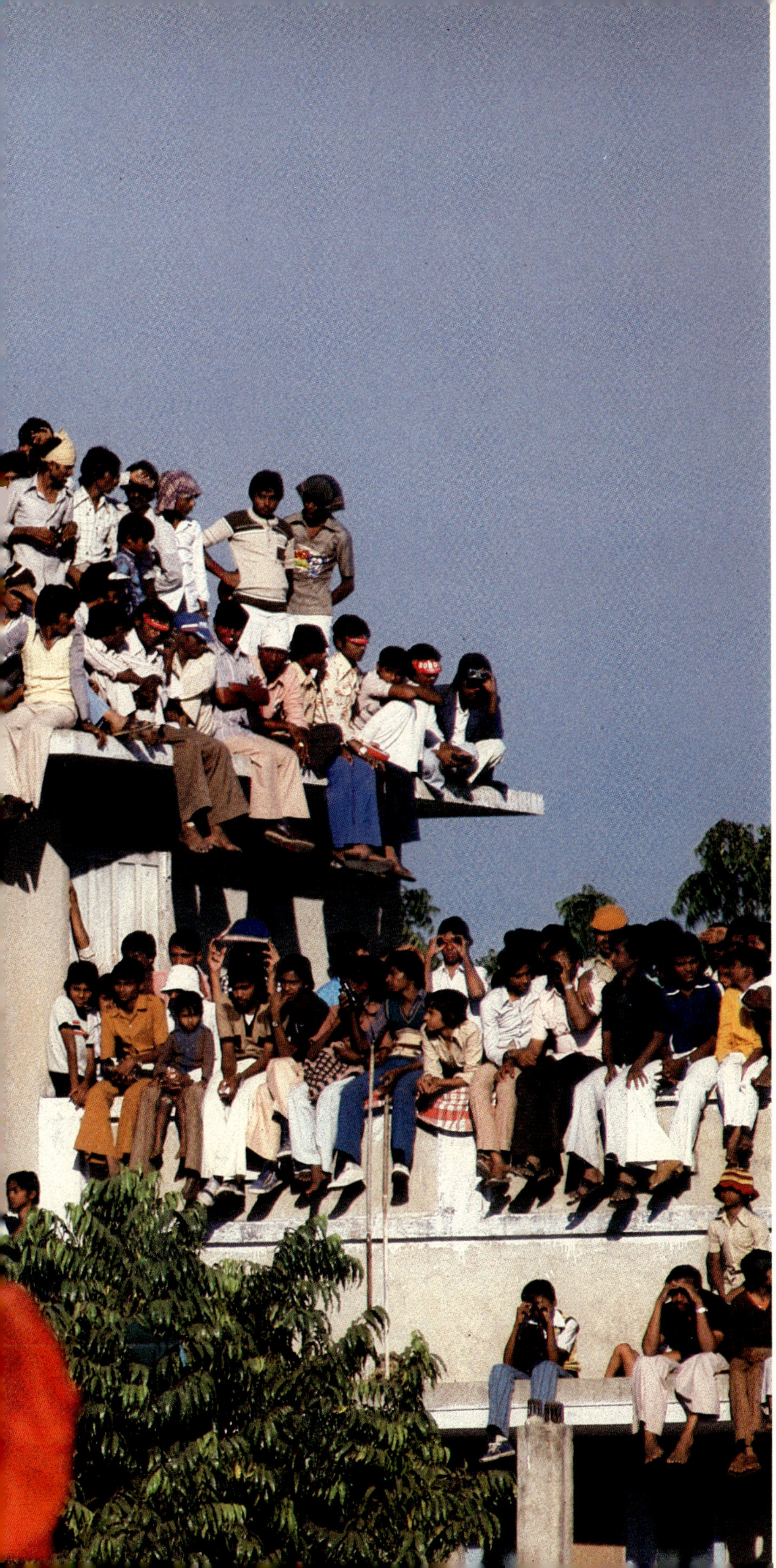

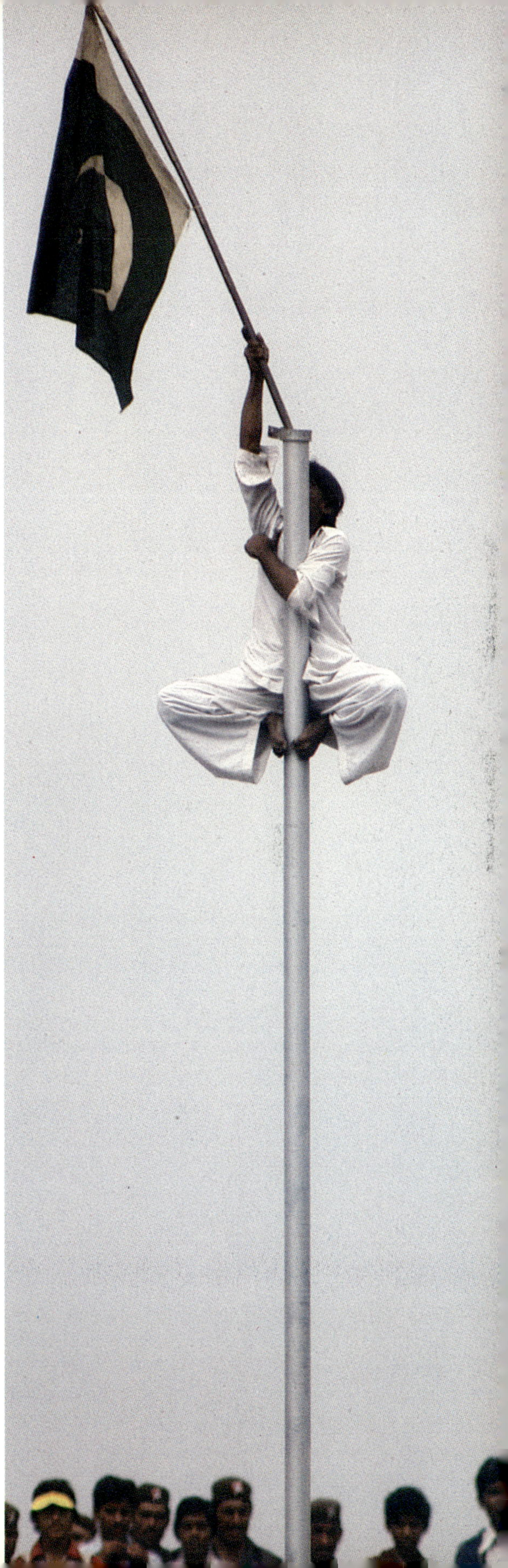

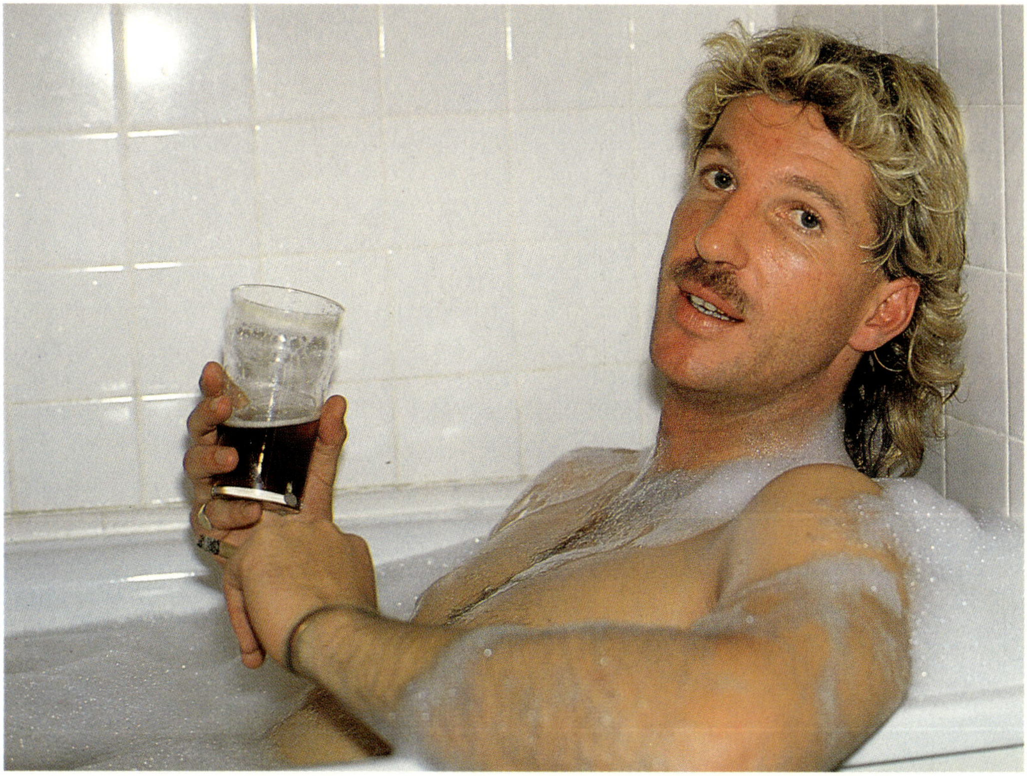

Every age produces a cricketing personality whose name becomes a household word – Grace, Constantine, Bradman, Compton – and the eighties have produced Botham. Love him or hate him you can't ignore him; his extraordinary vitality is almost tangible and this makes him an ideal photographic subject. I would go even further and say that sometimes test matches can be photographically boring when Botham isn't there. When he is playing, suddenly it becomes photographically exciting. Somehow he makes pictures.

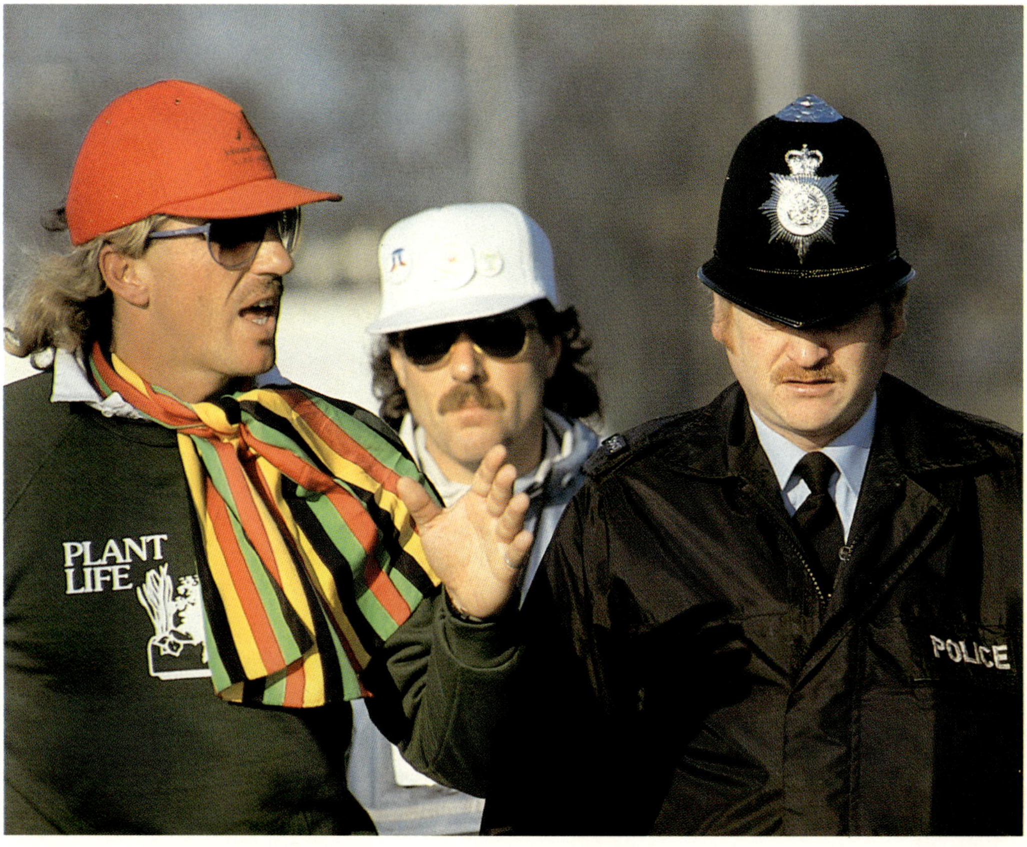

Plant life is the motto; 'Both' and Phil Rance and a troubled policeman on the Leukaemia Charity Walk, from John O'Groats to Land's End, November 1985

above: *In the hotel bath one evening towards the end of the same walk, which raised £800,000 for Leukaemia Research, November 1985*

opposite: *Gower and Botham, one-day international, England v Australia, Old Trafford, May 1985*

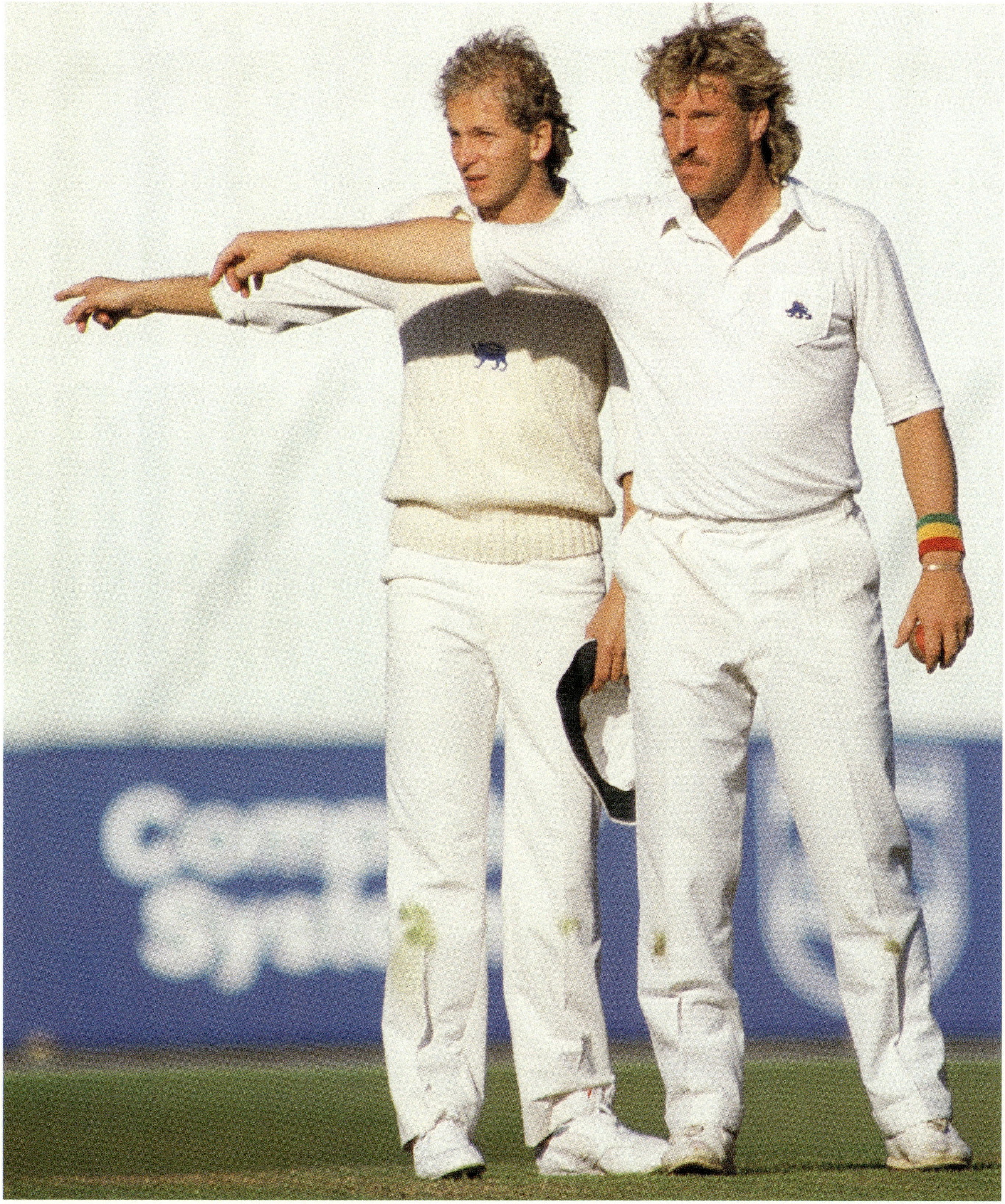

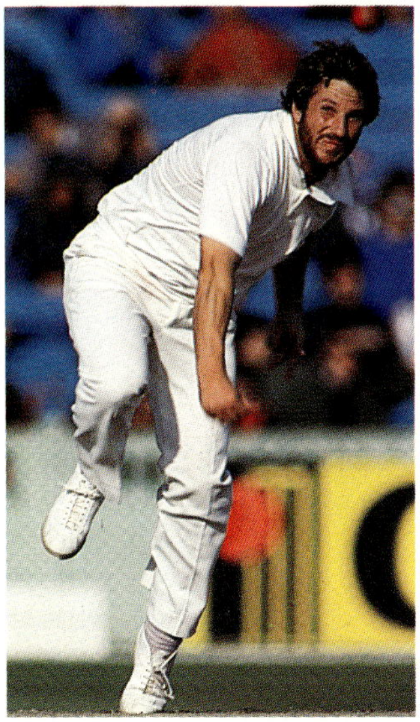
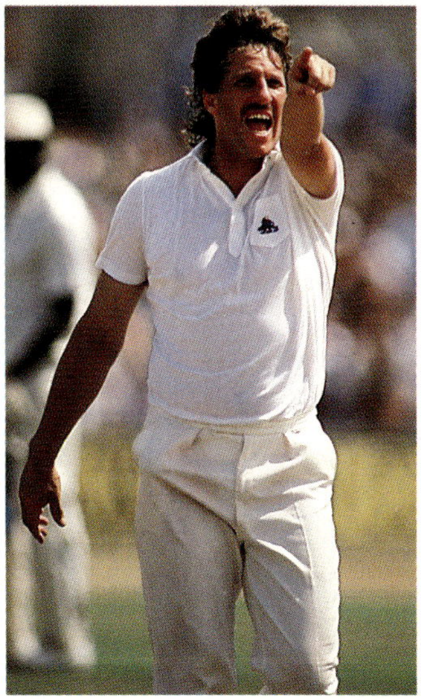
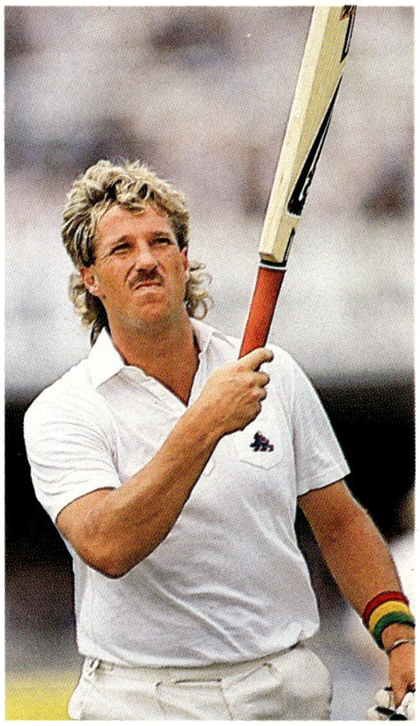
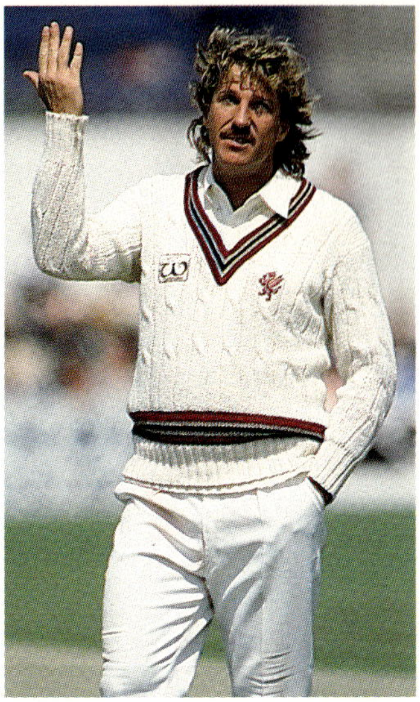
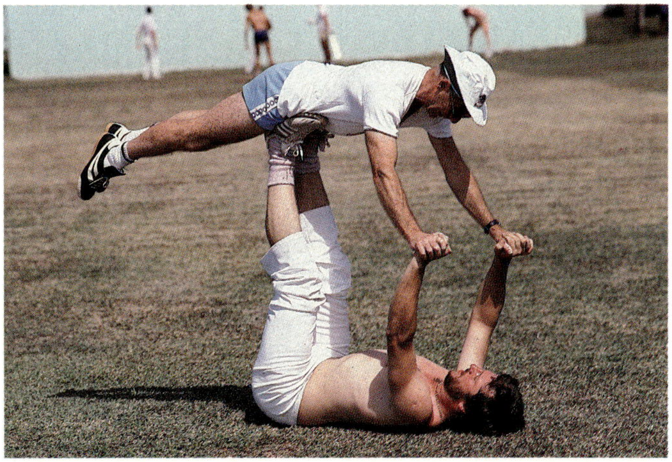
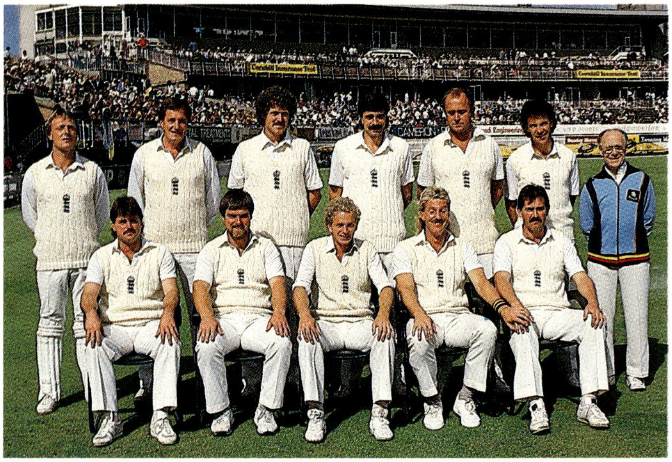
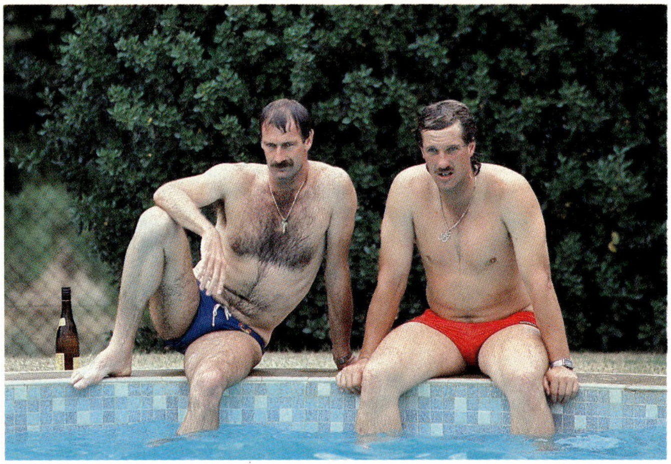
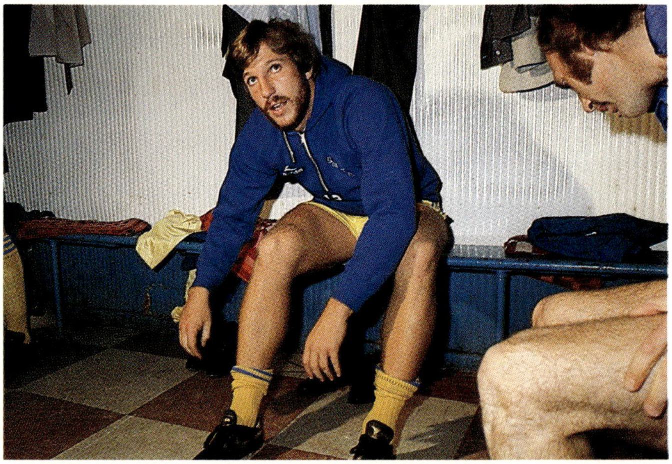

top line: *Aggressive bowler; Angry captain; Disappointed batsman; Well, what the heck? With close friend Viv Richards; With Allan Lamb as seen on cover of* Lamb's Tales; *Receiving the Courage Award at Great Ormond Street Hospital after walking through London to raise money for Leukaemia Research*
middle line: *Captain Ian fools around with Bernard Thomas in*

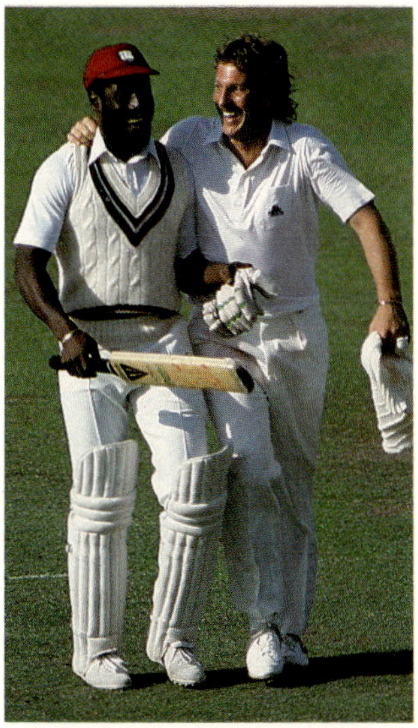
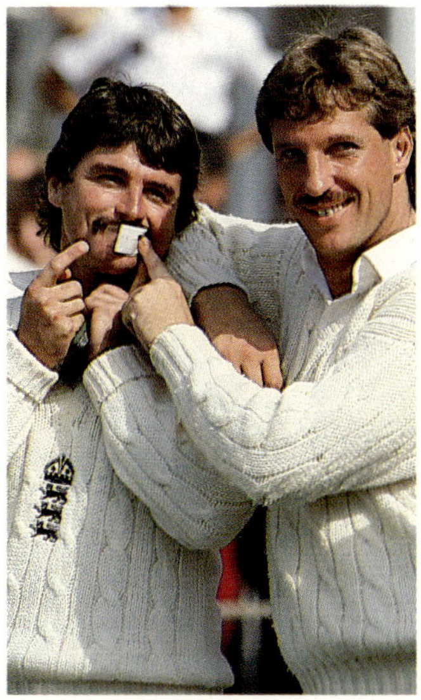
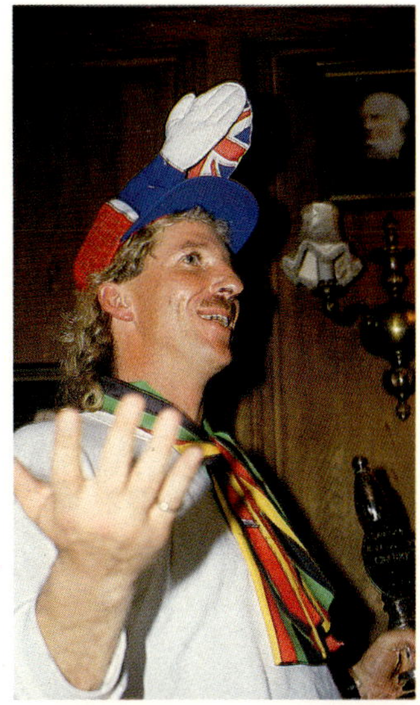
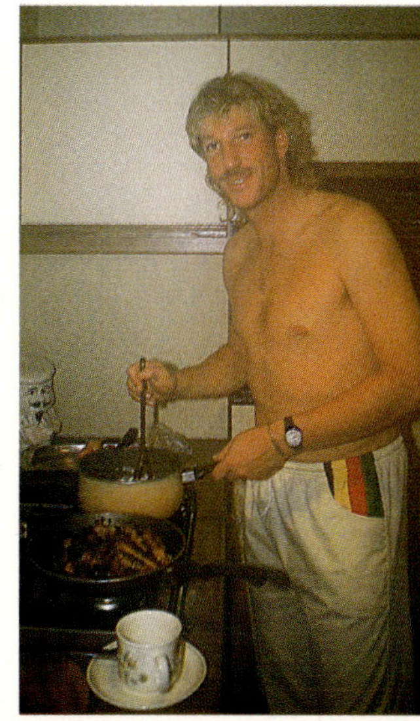
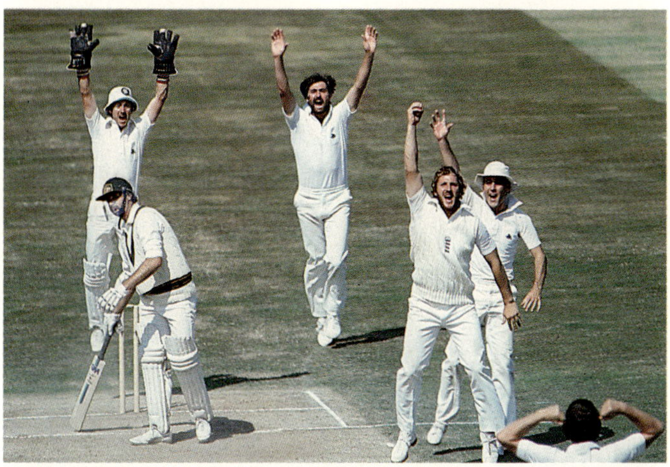
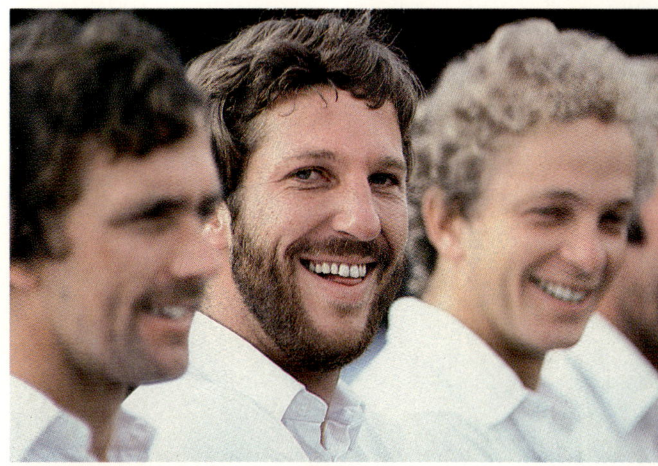
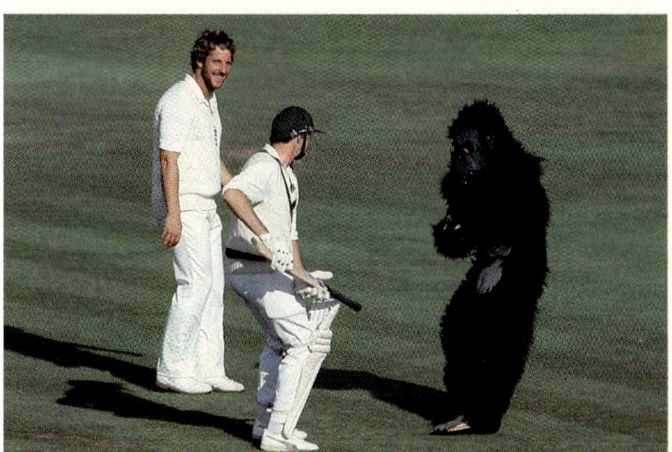
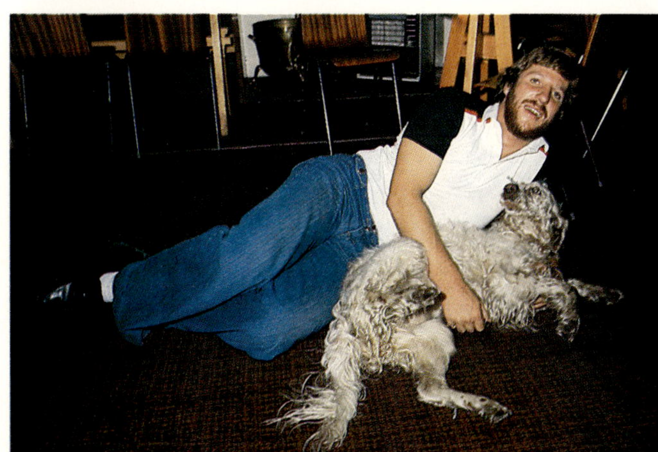

the West Indies; Always the dressing room joker, here he 'makes friends' with Graham Gooch; Enthusiasm means competitiveness; Standing out in the crowd

bottom line: *With Dennis Lillee; Turning out for Scunthorpe United; Making friends with Yallop and 'Guy' the gorilla (no relation); At home*

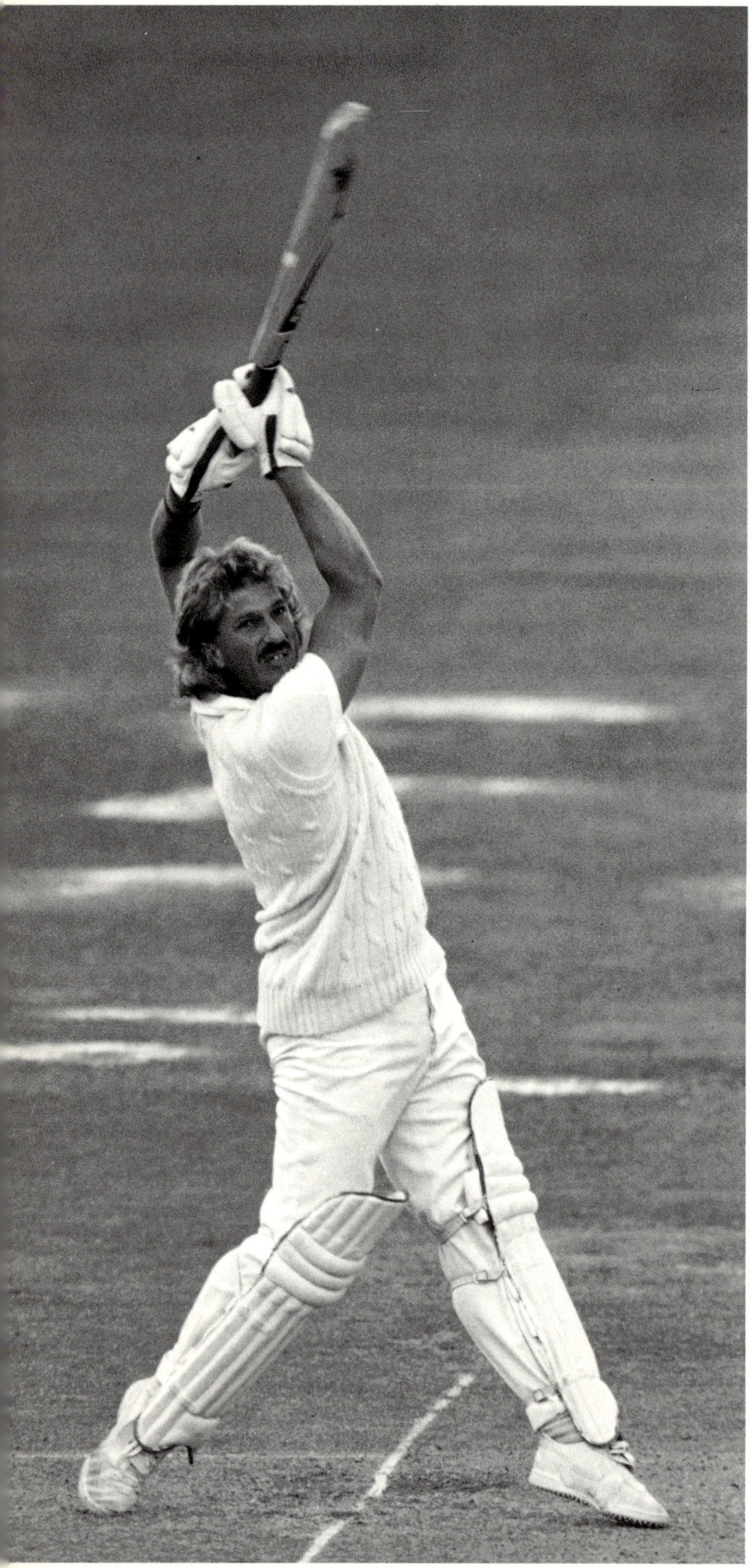
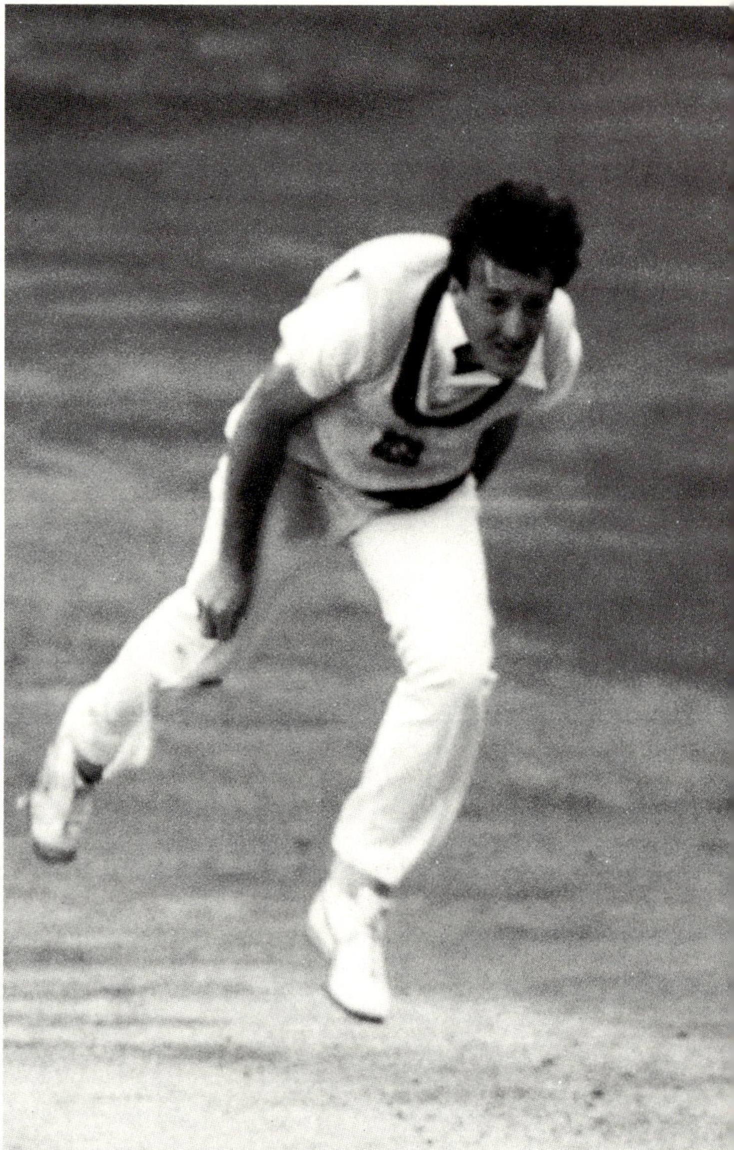
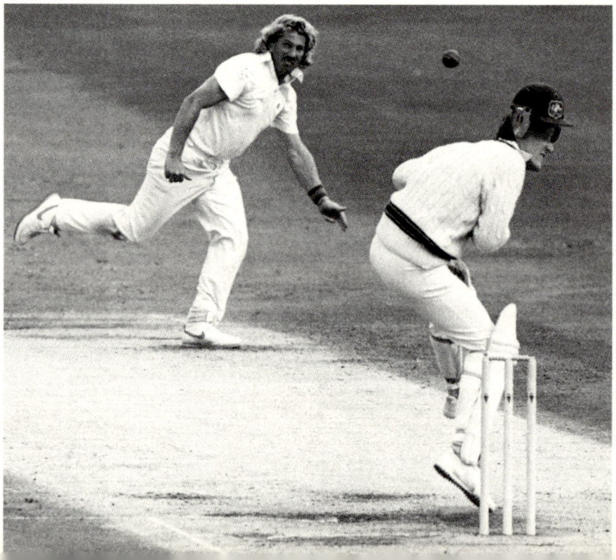

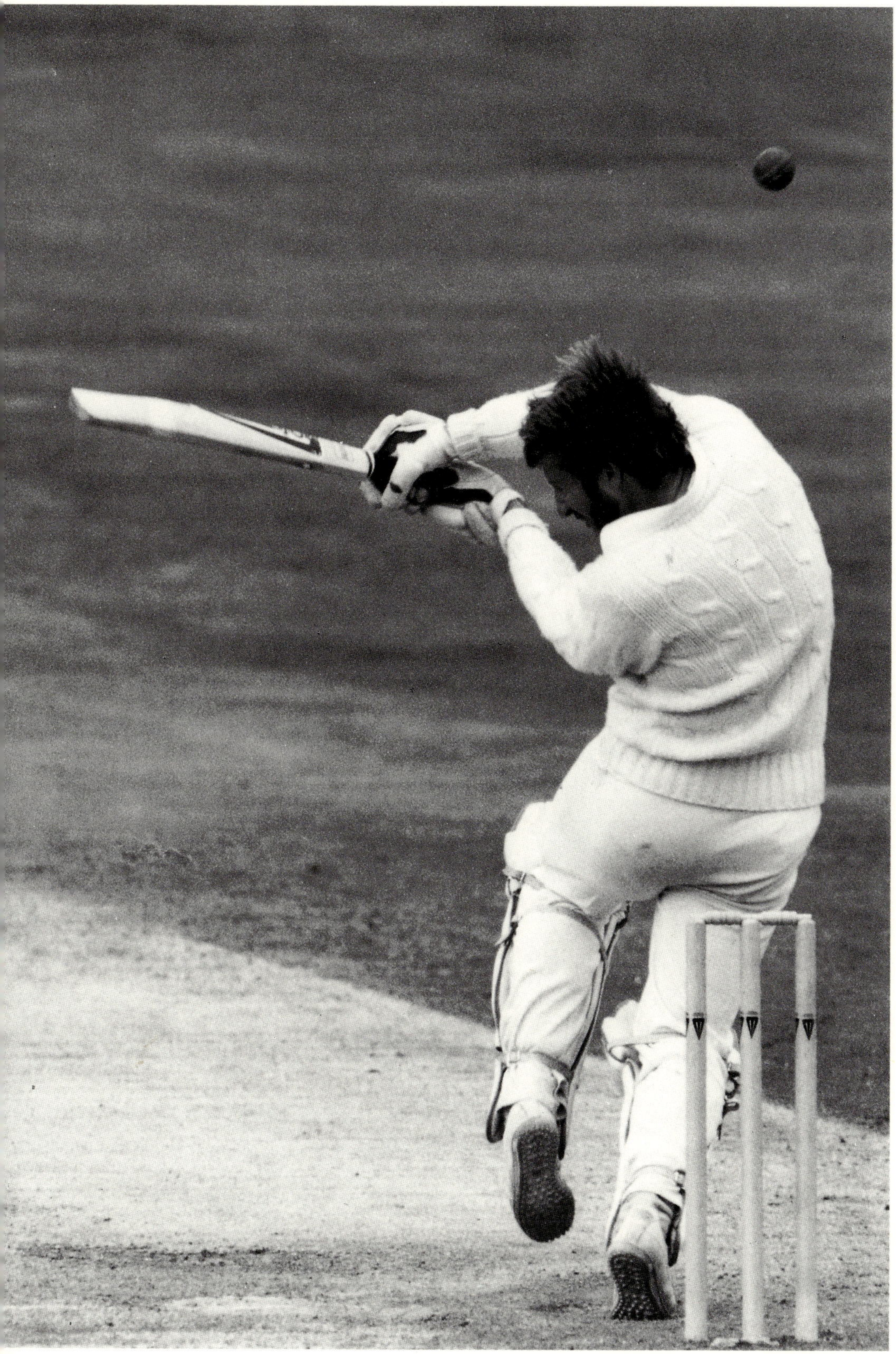

In 1981, in the third Test against the Australians at Headingley, Botham scored an epic century in really bad light. Soon after he had made his hundred, Lawson bowled him a really vicious beamer, doubly dangerous because the light was bad. The unhelmeted and inspired Botham, instead of ducking like any earthbound mortal, tried to hook it. He missed, but luckily the ball also missed him. He went on to make 149, not out. Unmollified (apparently) by this, four years later, on exactly the same ground in the Ashes series, with the roles reversed Botham returned the compliment with a truly fierce bouncer to Lawson.

Botham tries to hook a Lawson 'beamer', third Test, England v Australia, Headingley, July 1981

inset: *Botham returns the compliment, first Test, England v Australia, Headingley, May 1985*

opposite: *On this occasion this typical shot was Botham's downfall, second Test, England v Australia, Lord's, June 1985*

You have probably guessed that I have always had a soft spot for Botham, and he certainly brought me luck on this occasion. These two pictures were both Highly Commended in the Benson and Hedges Cricket Photographer of the Year competition. As I said – he is the ideal photographic subject.

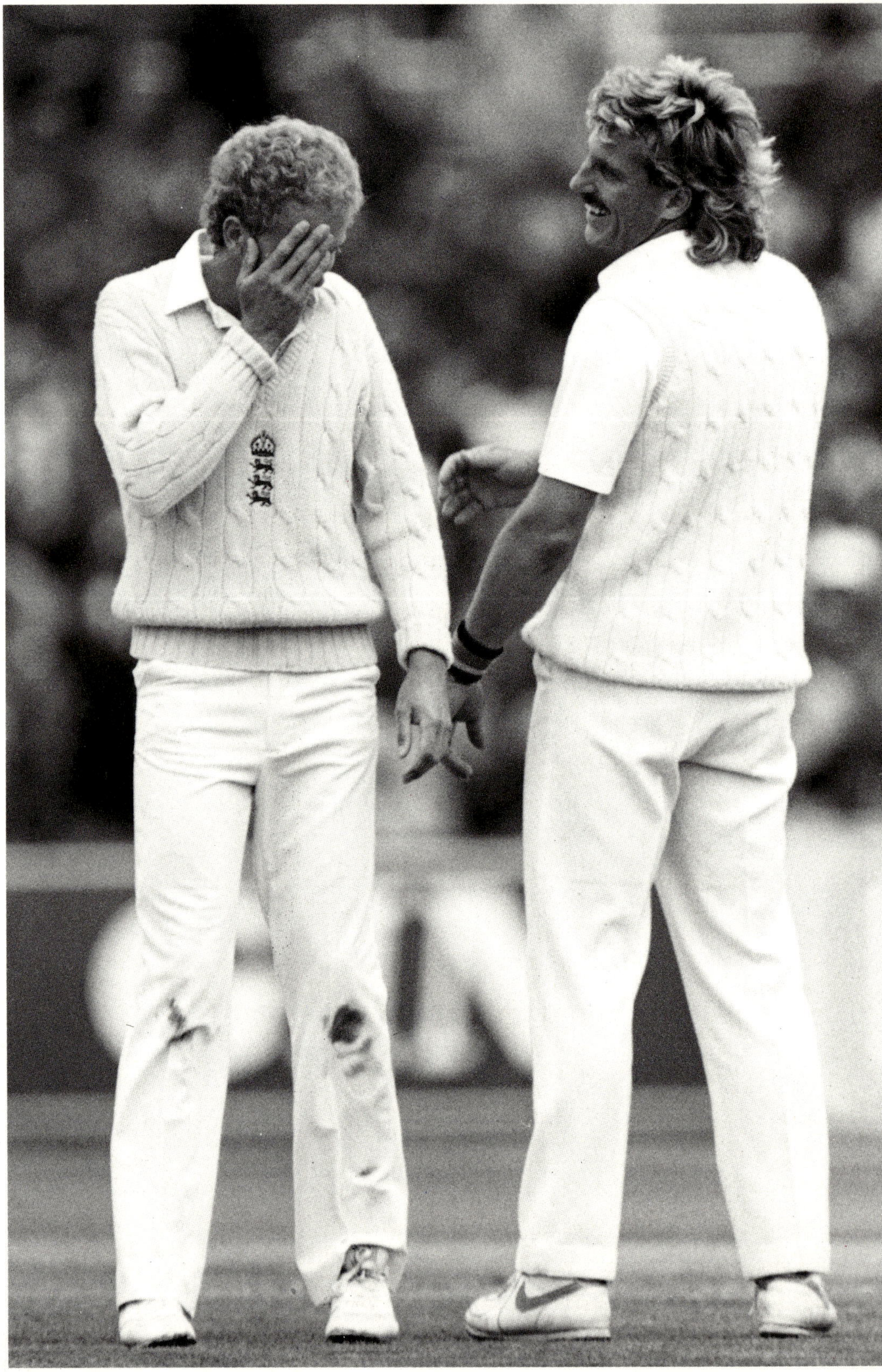

One in the eye for captain Gower, fifth Test, England v Australia, Edgbaston, August 1985

opposite: *Ian Botham thinks that something stinks in the fifth Test, England v Australia, Edgbaston, August 1985*

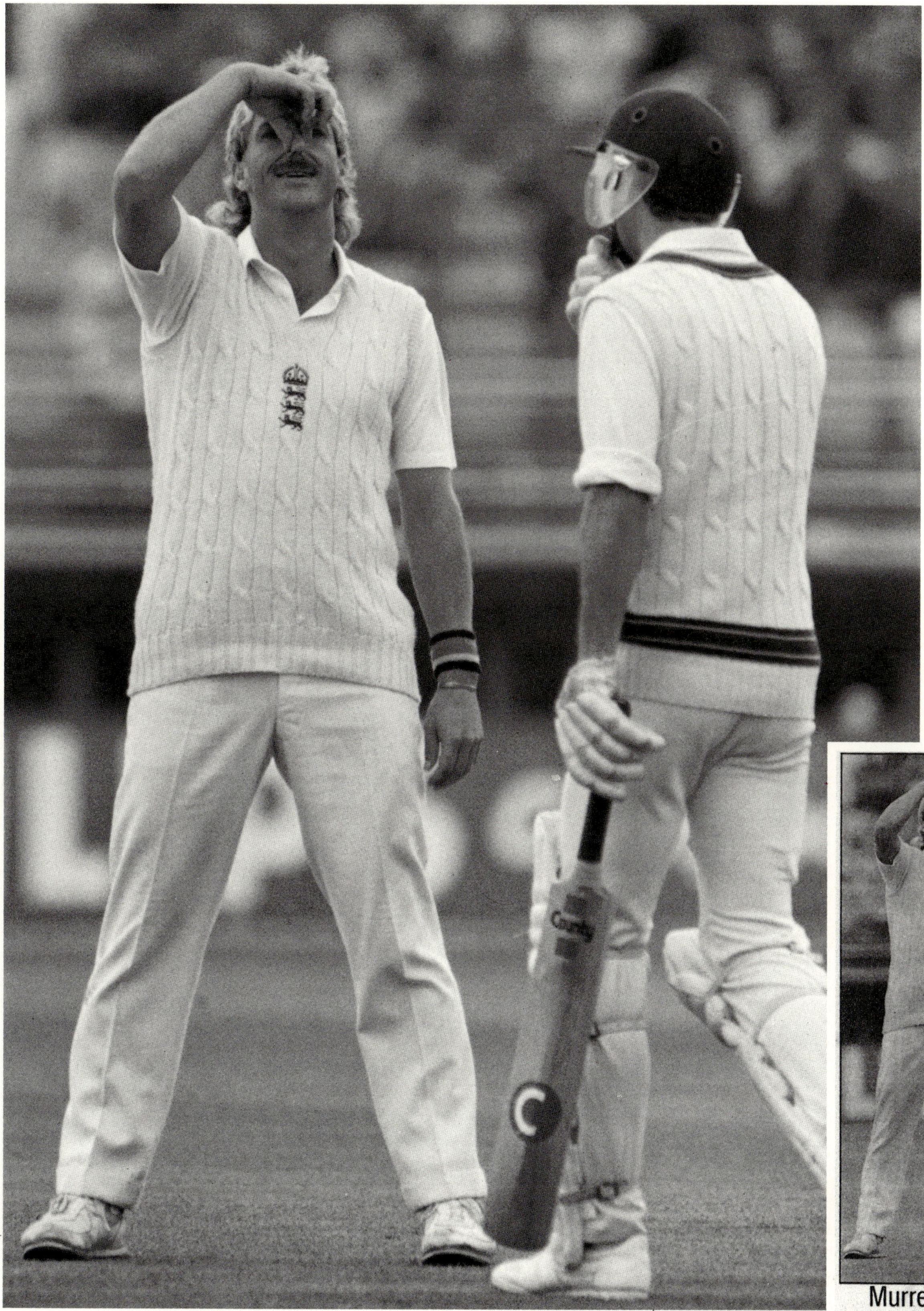

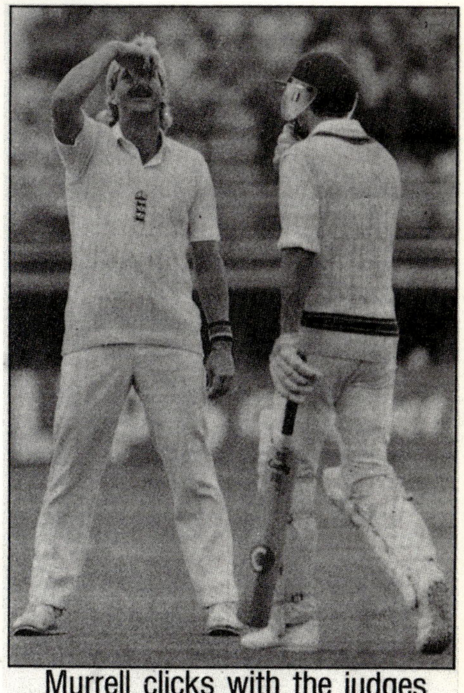

Murrell clicks with the judges

It may be only a pinch on the nose for Ian Botham, but for *Observer* photographer Adrian Murrell it was one of a collection of pictures that almost swept the board at the awards ceremony held by the Benson & Hedges Cricket Year book. Murrell took not only the first prize, but four of the 10 highly-commended awards as well. Murrell was a runner-up for the past two years in the competition to capture the outstanding cricket

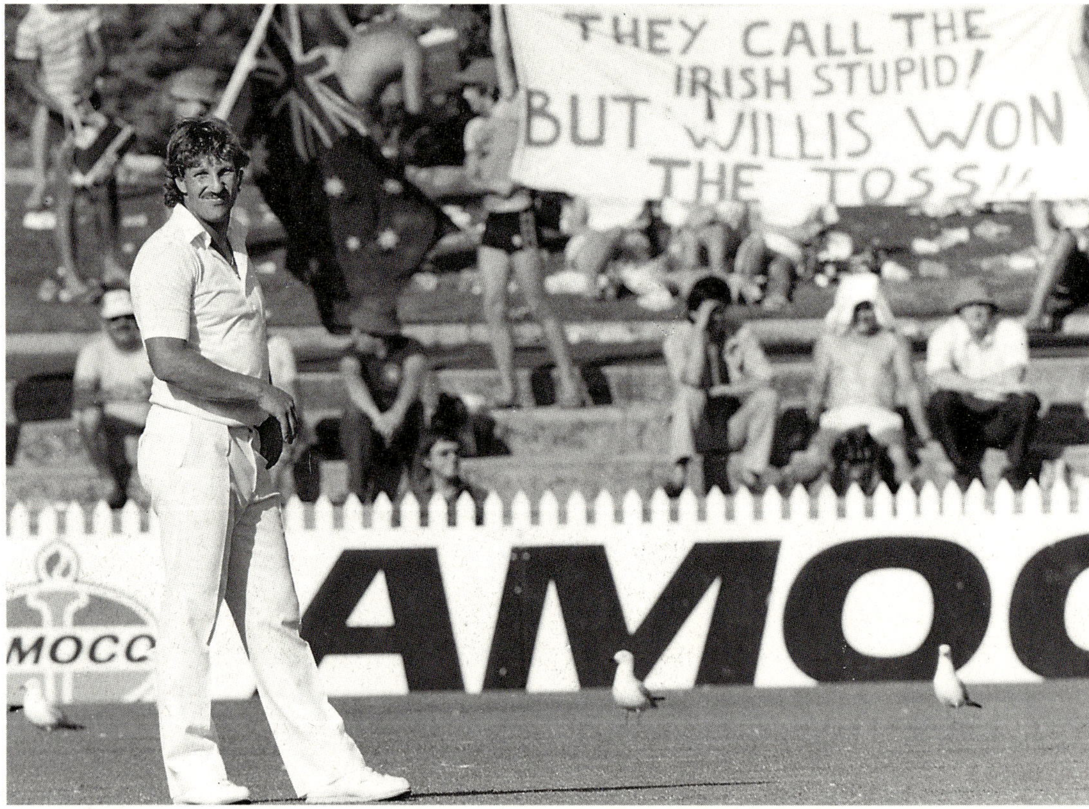

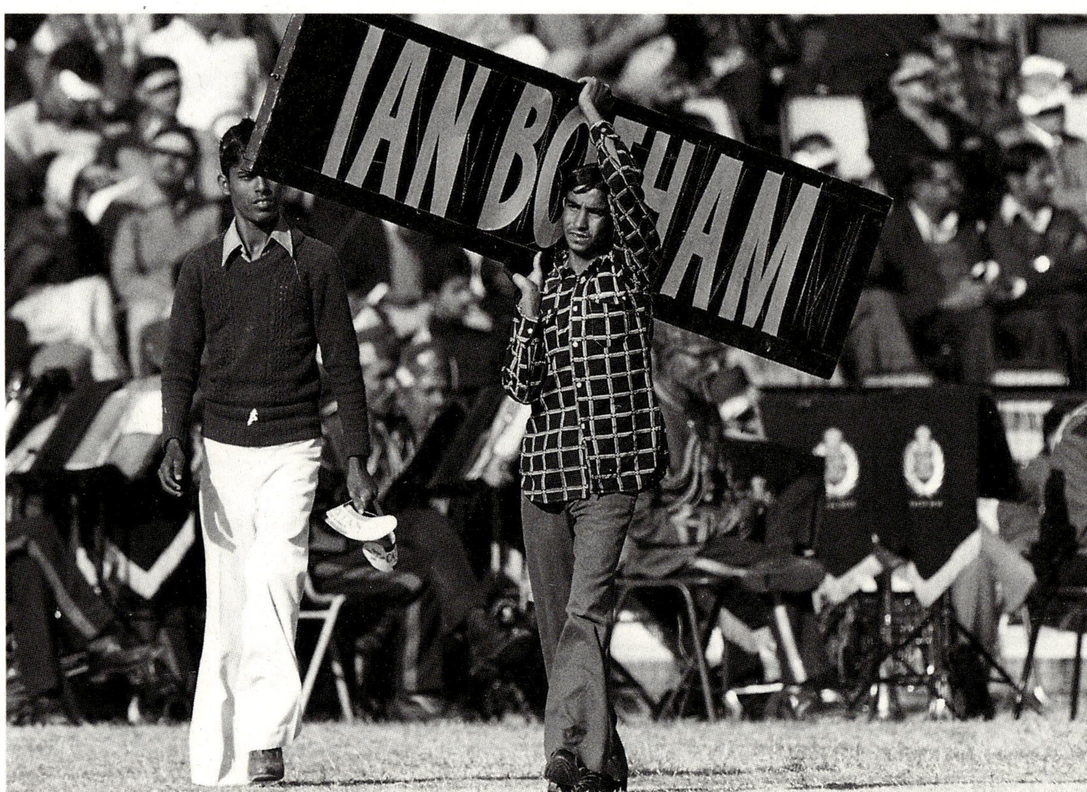

Unhappy spectators remove sign as Botham was not playing, North Zone v England, Kashmir, December 1981

above: *Ian Botham during the third Test in Adelaide, Australia v England, December 1982*

opposite, above: *Australia v England, fourth Test, Melbourne, December 1982*

opposite, below: *Yet another banner, second Test, England v India, Old Trafford, July 1982*

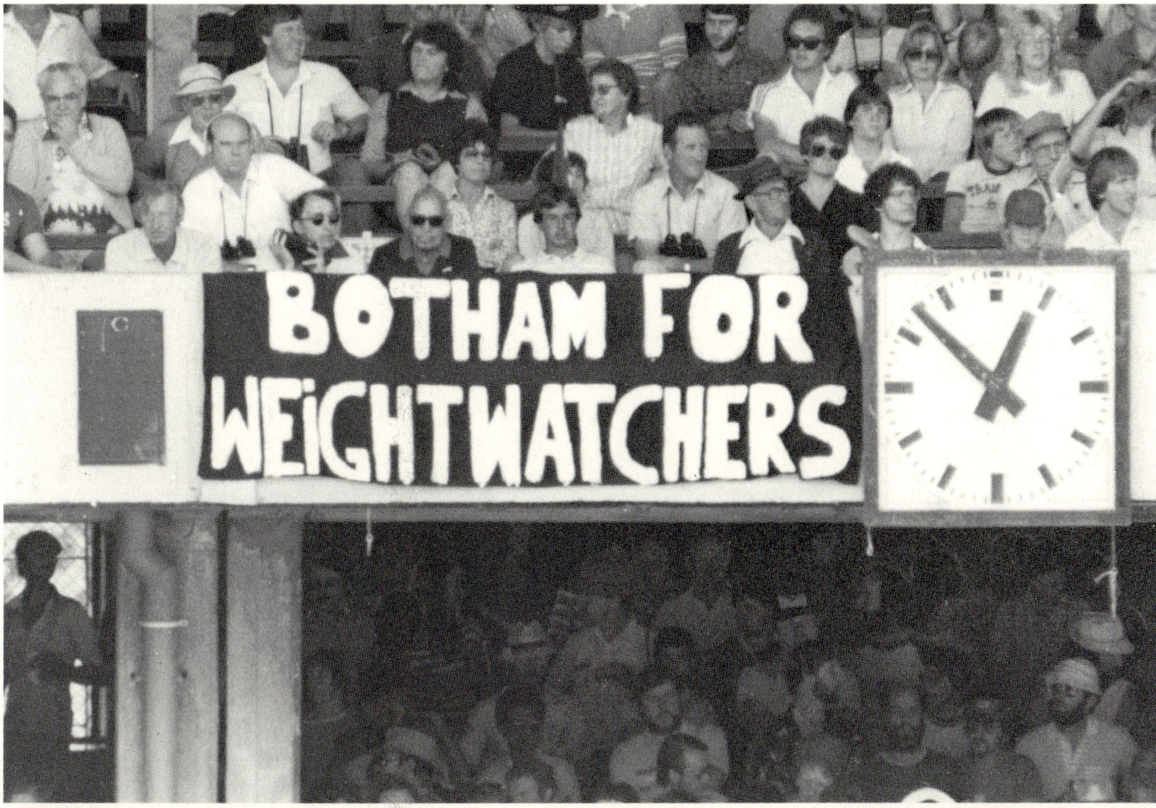
BOTHAM FOR
WEIGHTWATCHERS

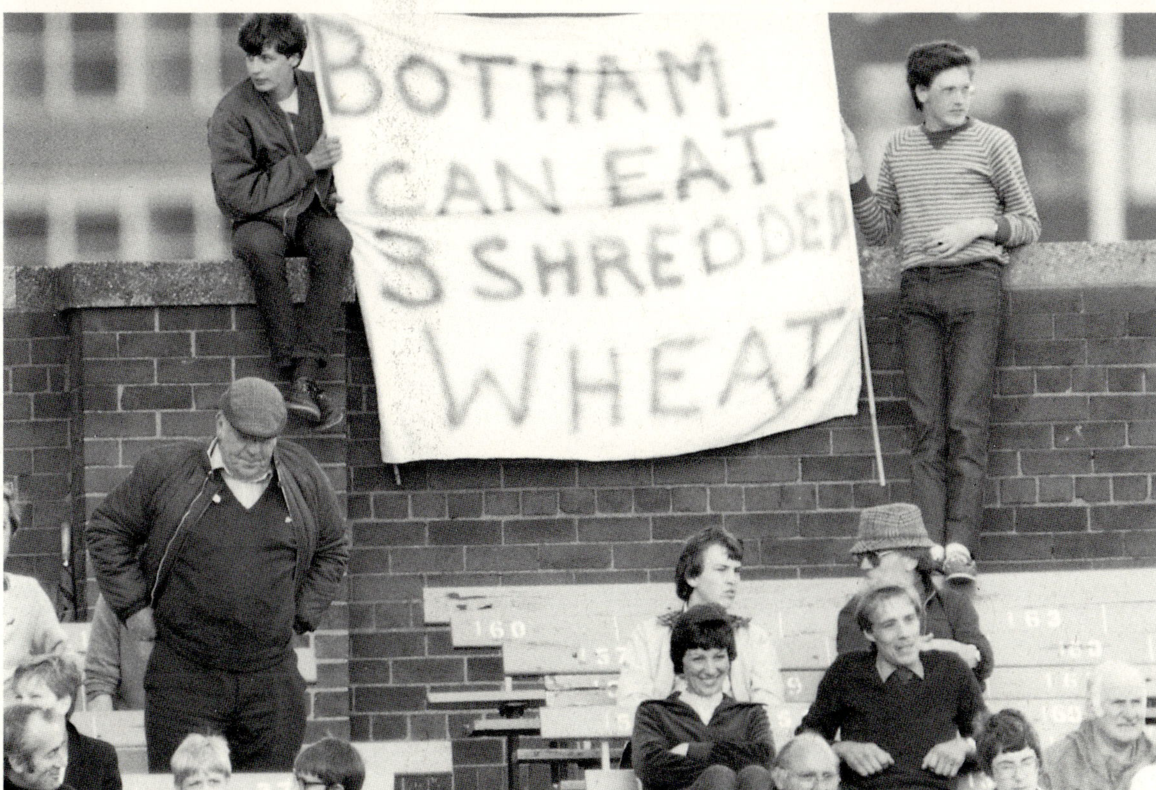
BOTHAM
CAN EAT
3 SHREDDED
WHEAT

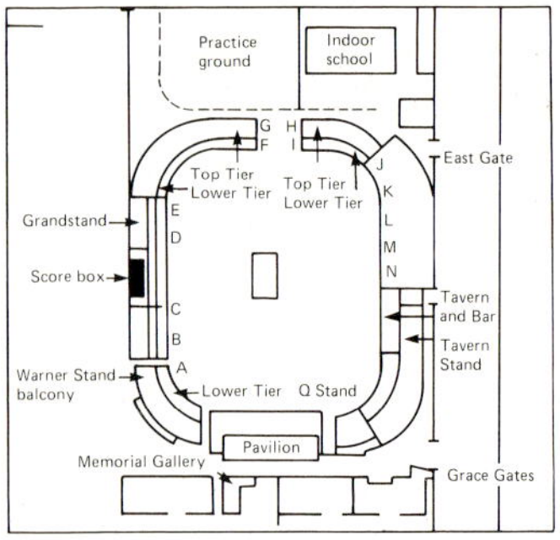

Lord's

Every day is a new challenge to a photographer. The light is never the same and the tension and the shape of a cricket match is utterly unpredictable. I usually turn up at the ground at least an hour and a half before the captains toss so that I can set up my tripod early, check angles and positions, and make certain there is adequate shelter if it is cold or wet. There are certain grounds that favour certain types of pictures. Lord's is outstanding for dramatic bowling or batting shots, because you can photograph from an elevated position under the scoreboard, this elevation gives an uncluttered background. You do, however, require a special pass. It obviously also makes an enormous difference to your photography if you have an understanding and knowledge of the game. It pays, for example, to watch the captain carefully. The pictures on the far right were taken at the Oval where the batsman, Alan Butcher, had persisted in scoring high in the air and freely down to long leg. A fielder was then positioned in front of long leg and I took up my own position on the boundary in line with his. The result, I think, was rewarding.

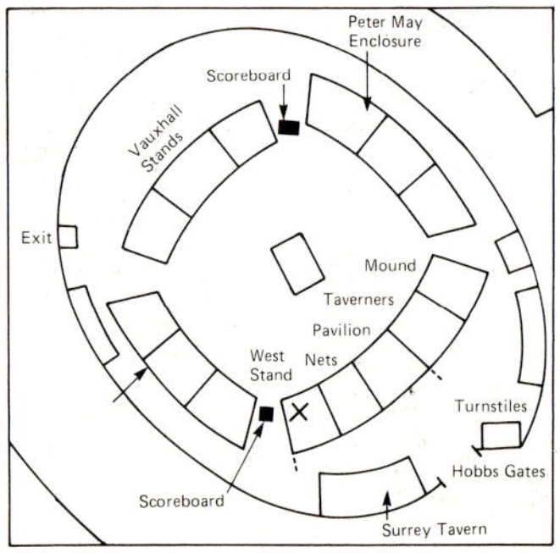

The Oval

I stood at × on the upper tier to achieve the shot on page 51.

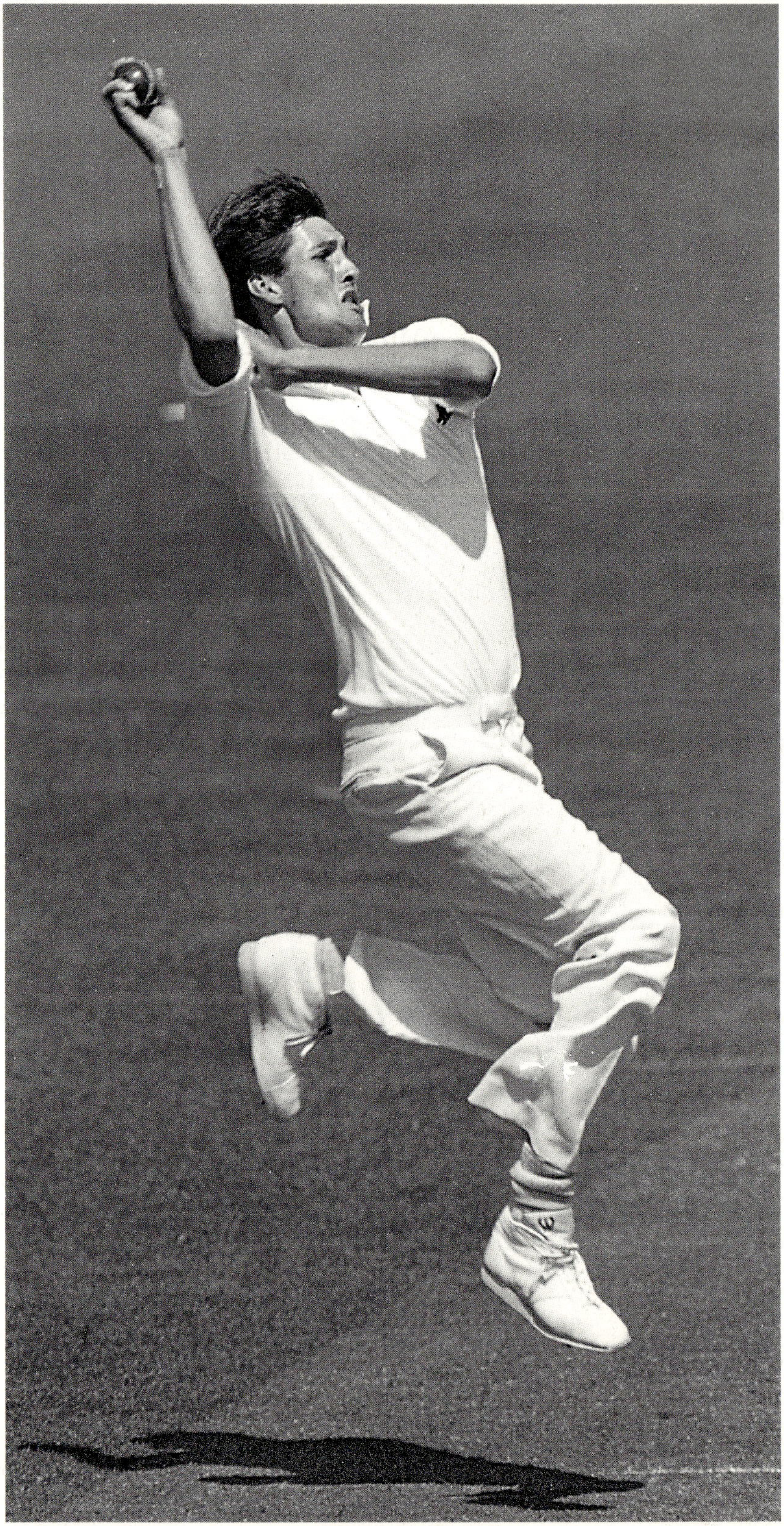

England and Essex fast bowler Neil Foster at Lord's, May 1985

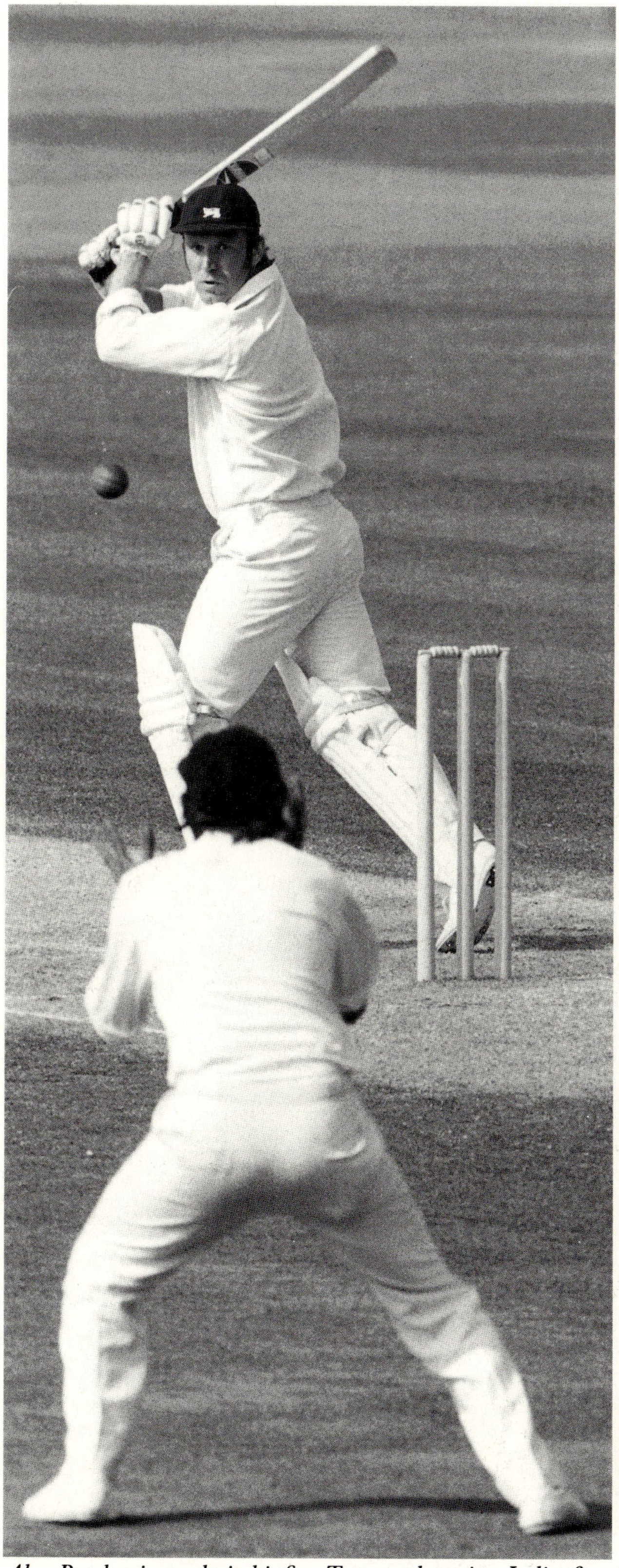

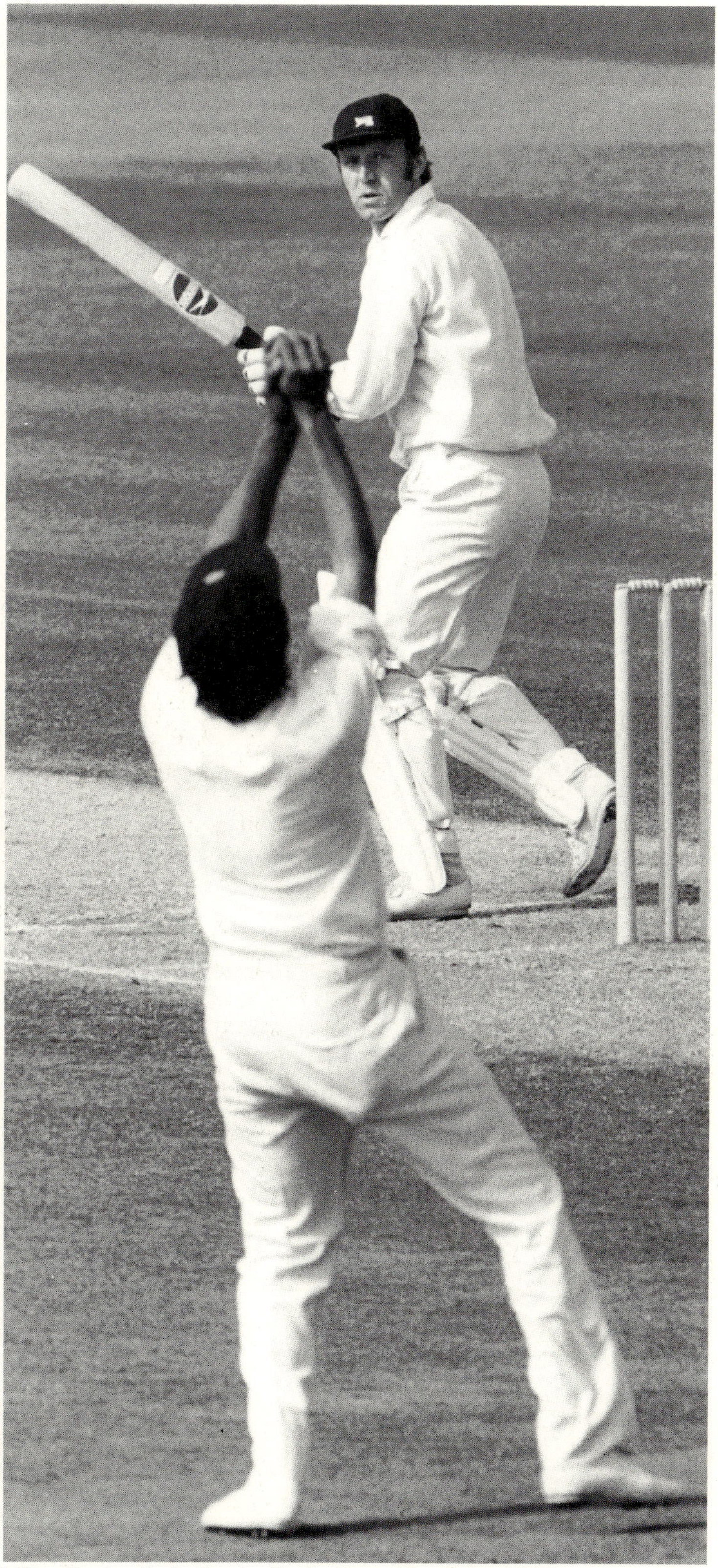

Alan Butcher is caught in his first Test match against India, fourth Test, England v India, the Oval, August/September 1979

Both these shots are slightly in and out of focus. The concentration on Mike Brearley's face gives the viewer an idea of what it is really like to face the blurred image of fast bowler Jeff Thomson. The second picture shows Kim Hughes running between the wickets at Lord's during a one-day World Cup game. It was a panned shot taken on a 600 mm F4 lens, and the *Observer* used it the following day, despite Hughes' partner, Graeme Wood, being out of focus.

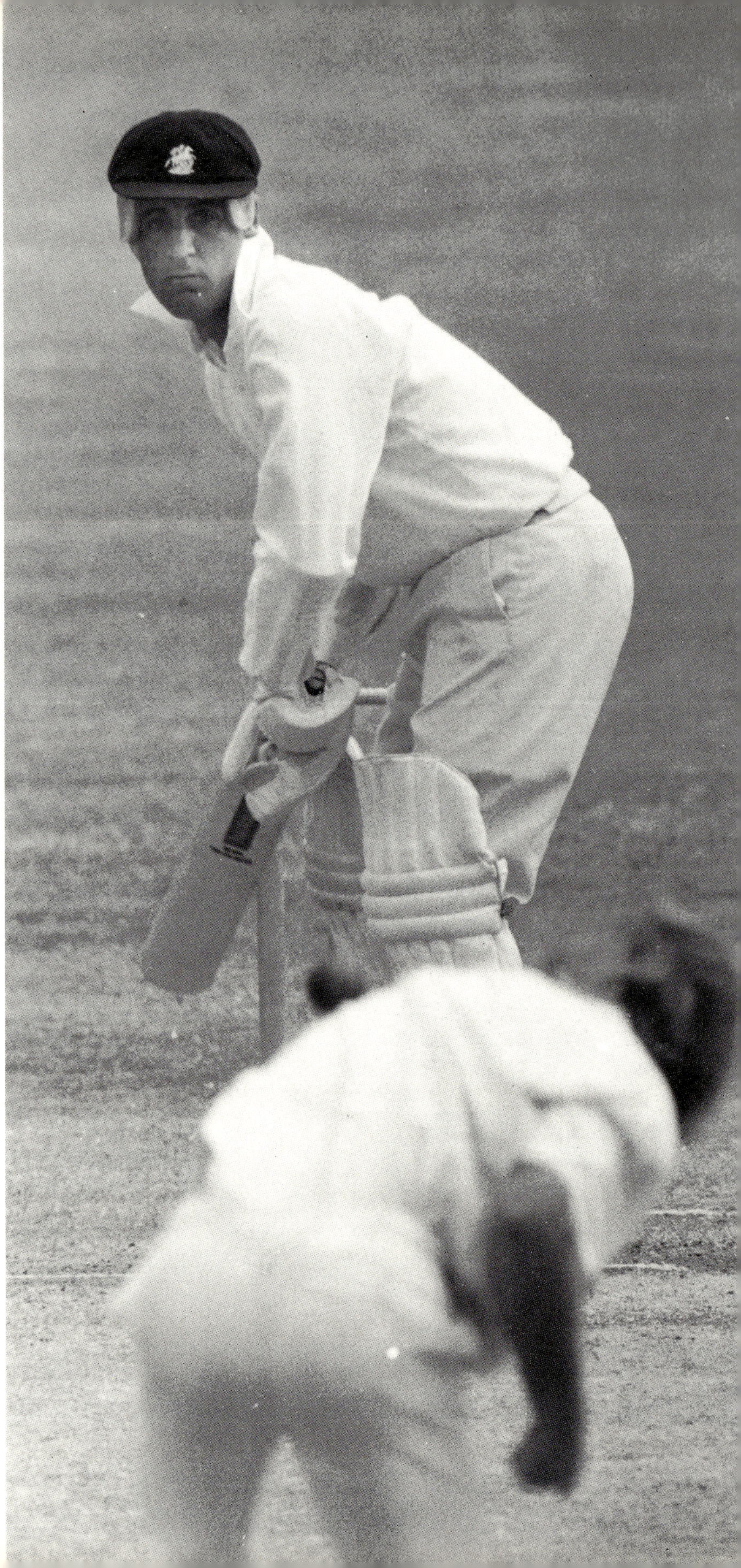

Mike Brearley faces the bowling, first Test, Australia v England, Brisbane, December 1978

opposite: *Kim Hughes and Graeme Wood, World Cup match, Australia v West Indies, Lord's, June 1983*

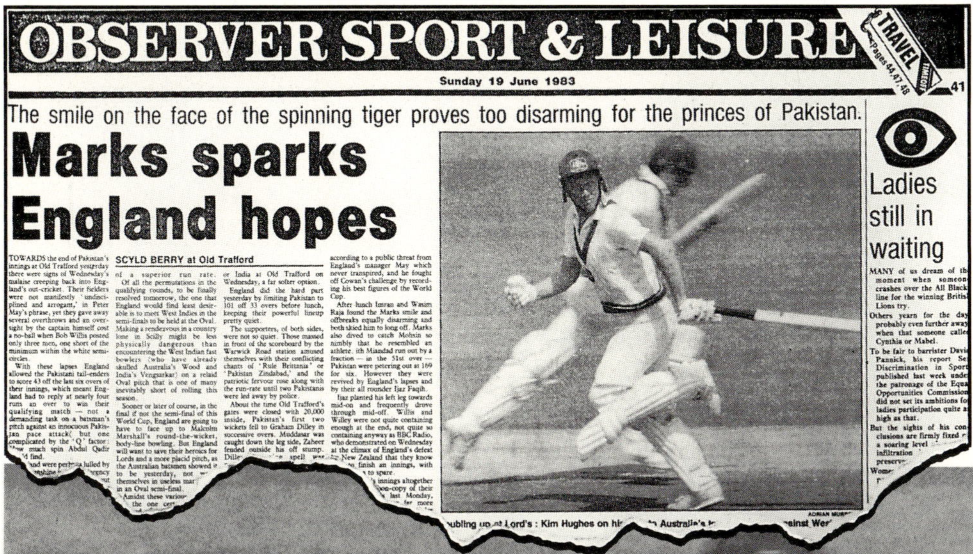

OBSERVER SPORT & LEISURE

TRAVEL Pages 44, 47, 48

Sunday 19 June 1983

41

The smile on the face of the spinning tiger proves too disarming for the princes of Pakistan.

Marks sparks England hopes

SCYLD BERRY at Old Trafford

TOWARDS the end of Pakistan's innings at Old Trafford yesterday there were signs of Wednesday's malaise creeping back into England's out-cricket. Their fielders were not manifestly 'undisciplined and arrogant,' in Peter May's phrase, yet they gave away several overthrows and an oversight by the captain himself cost a no-ball when Bob Willis posted only three men, one short of the minimum within the white semi-circles.

With these lapses England allowed the Pakistani tail-enders to score 43 off the last six overs of their innings, which meant England had to reply at nearly four runs an over to win their qualifying match — not a demanding task on a batsman's pitch against an innocuous Pakistan pace attack(but one complicated by the 'Q' factor: [illegible] much spin Abdul Qadir [illegible] find.

[illegible] and were per[illegible] lulled by [illegible] [illegible] of a superior run rate.

Of all the permutations in the qualifying rounds, to be finally resolved tomorrow, the one that England would find least desirable is to meet West Indies in the semi-finals to be held at the Oval. Making a rendezvous in a country lane in Scilly might be less physically dangerous than encountering the West Indian fast bowlers (who have already skulled Australia's Wood and India's Vengsarkar) on a relaid Oval pitch that is one of many inevitably short of rolling this season.

Sooner or later of course, in the final if not the semi-final of this World Cup, England are going to have to face up to Malcolm Marshall's round-the-wicket, body-line bowling. But England will want to save their heroics for Lords and a more placid pitch, as the Australian batsmen showed it to be yesterday, not [illegible] themselves in useless mar[illegible] in an Oval semi-final.

Amidst these vario[illegible] the one cer[illegible] [illegible] or India at Old Trafford on Wednesday, a far softer option.

England did the hard part yesterday by limiting Pakistan to 101 off 33 overs before lunch, keeping their powerful lineup pretty quiet.

The supporters, of both sides, were not so quiet. Those massed in front of the scoreboard by the Warwick Road station amused themselves with their conflicting chants of 'Rule Brittania' or 'Pakistan Zindabad,' and the patriotic fervour rose along with the run-rate until two Pakistanis were led away by police.

About the time Old Trafford's gates were closed with 20,000 inside, Pakistan's first two wickets fell to Graham Dilley in successive overs. Muddasar was caught down the leg side, Zaheer fended outside his off stump. Dille[illegible] spell was [illegible] according to a public threat from England's manager May which never transpired, and he fought off Cowan's challenge by recording his best figures of the World Cup.

After lunch Imran and Wasim Raja found the Marks smile and offbreaks equally disarming and both skied him to long off. Marks also dived to catch Mohsin so nimbly that he resembled an athlete. ith Miandad run out by a fraction — in the 51st over — Pakistan were petering out at 169 for six. However they were revived by England's lapses and by their all rounder Ijaz Faqih.

Ijaz planted his left leg towards mid-on and frequently drove through mid-off. Willis and Willey were not quite containing enough at the end, not quite so containing anyway as BBC Radio, who demonstrated on Wednesday at the climax of England's defeat [illegible] New Zealand that they know [illegible] finish an innings, with [illegible] to spare.

[illegible]'s innings altogether [illegible]on-copy of their [illegible] last Monday, [illegible] for more [illegible]

[illegible]ubling up at Lord's: Kim Hughes on hi[illegible] Australia's [illegible] against We[illegible]

ADRIAN MURR[illegible]

Ladies still in waiting

MANY of us dream of th[illegible] moment when someon[illegible] crashes over the All Black[illegible] line for the winning Britis[illegible] Lions try.

Others yearn for the day probably even further away when that someone calle[illegible] Cynthia or Mabel.

To be fair to barrister David Pannick, his report Se[illegible] Discrimination in Sport published last week unde[illegible] the patronage of the Equa[illegible] Opportunities Commission did not set its ambitions fo[illegible] ladies participation quite a[illegible] high as that.

But the sights of his con[illegible]clusions are firmly fixed [illegible] a soaring level [illegible] infiltration [illegible] preserv[illegible]

Wome[illegible]

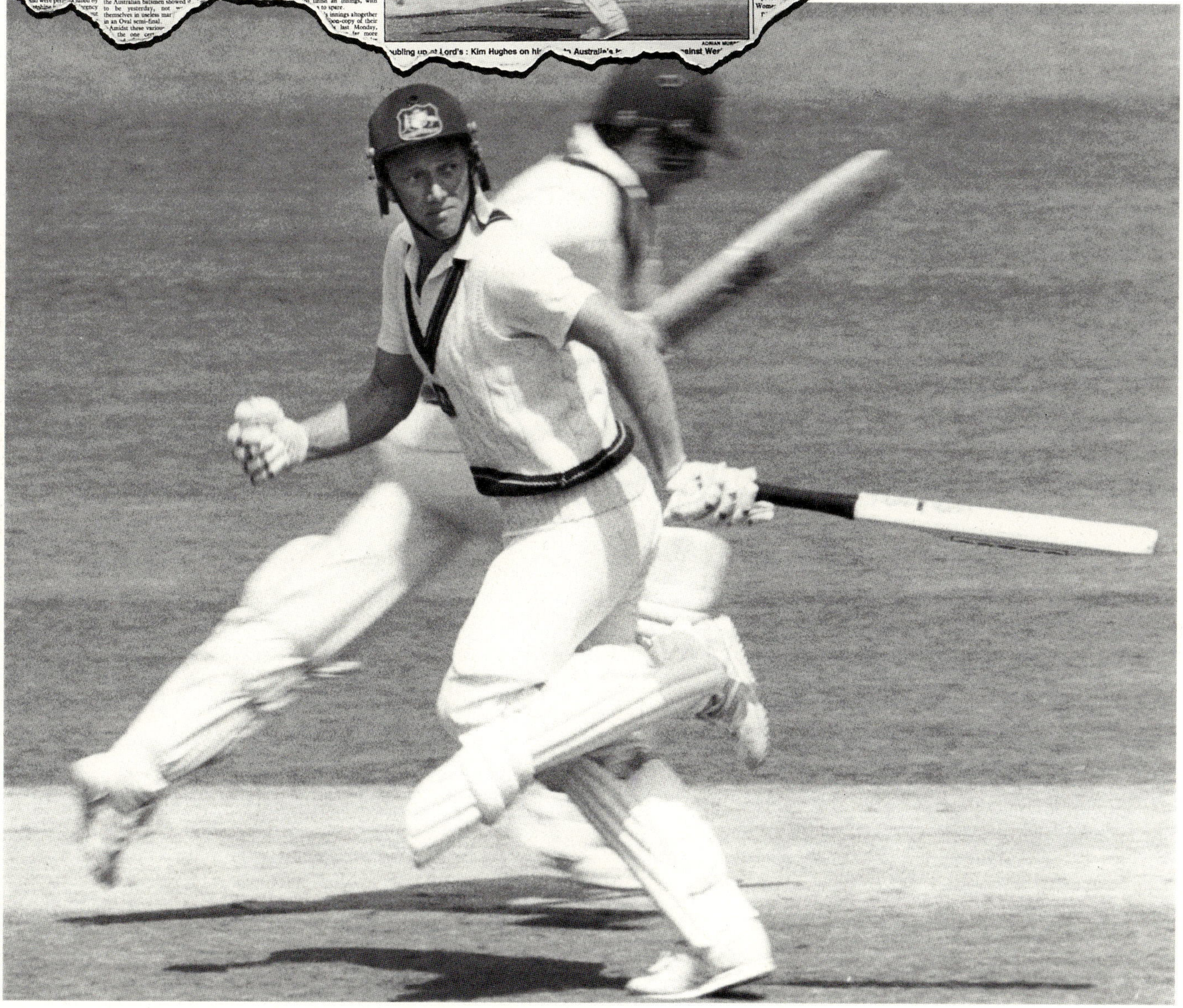

I worked really hard for the picture on page 55. It was taken at the first floodlit game England ever played in (when the photograph was taken it was still daylight). I wanted all the unusual features – the black sightscreen with the white ball right in front of it and the word CRICKET underneath, the distinctive clothing, the umpire in black – in one shot, and it took me a whole roll of thirty-six films to get it. By comparison the picture on this page is flukey. The composition is good (all-important in cricket photography) but I didn't – I couldn't have – plan it.

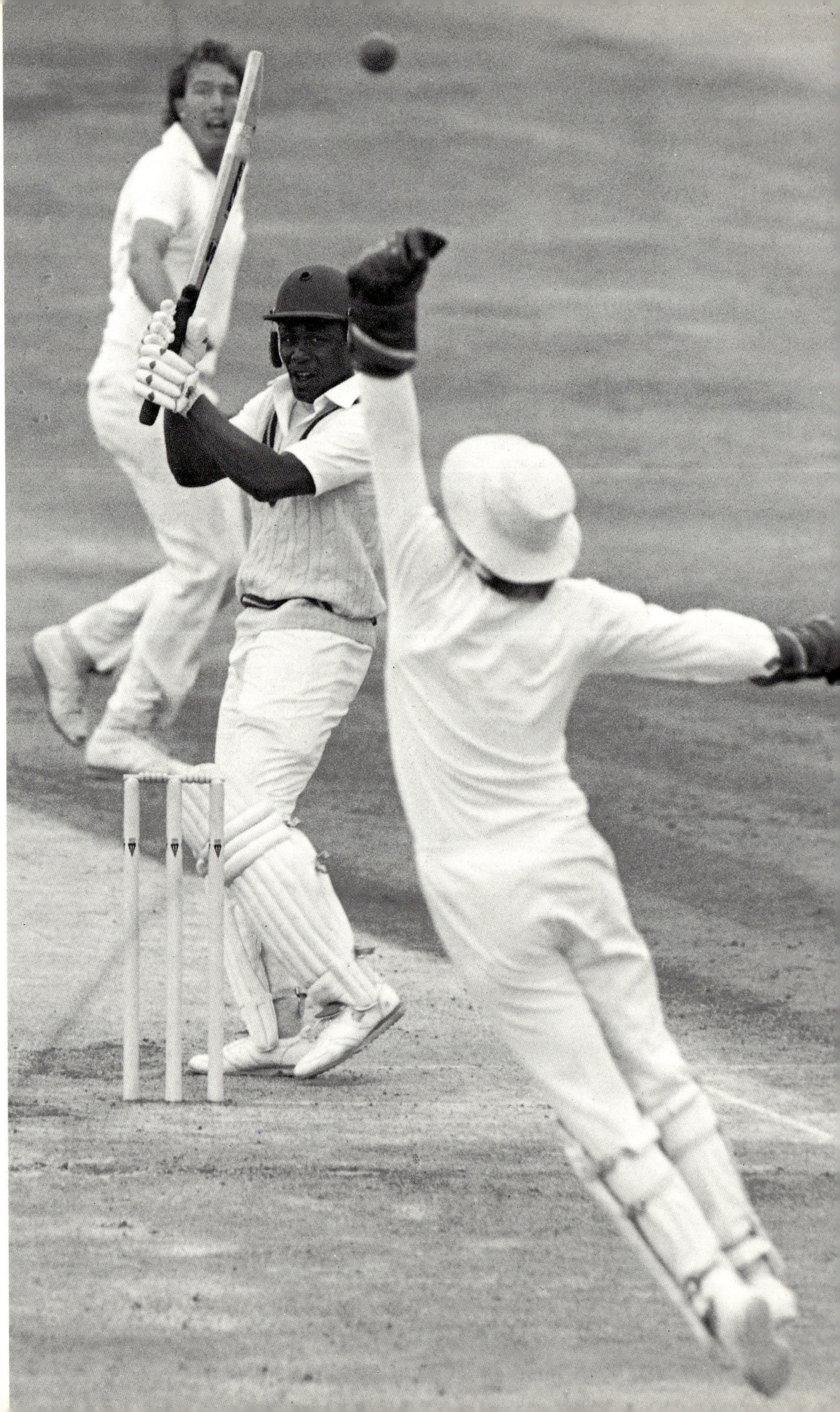

Desmond Haynes edges the ball for four over Downton off the bowling of Pringle, third Test, England v West Indies, Headingley, July 1984

opposite: *One-day international, England v West Indies, Sydney, November 1979*

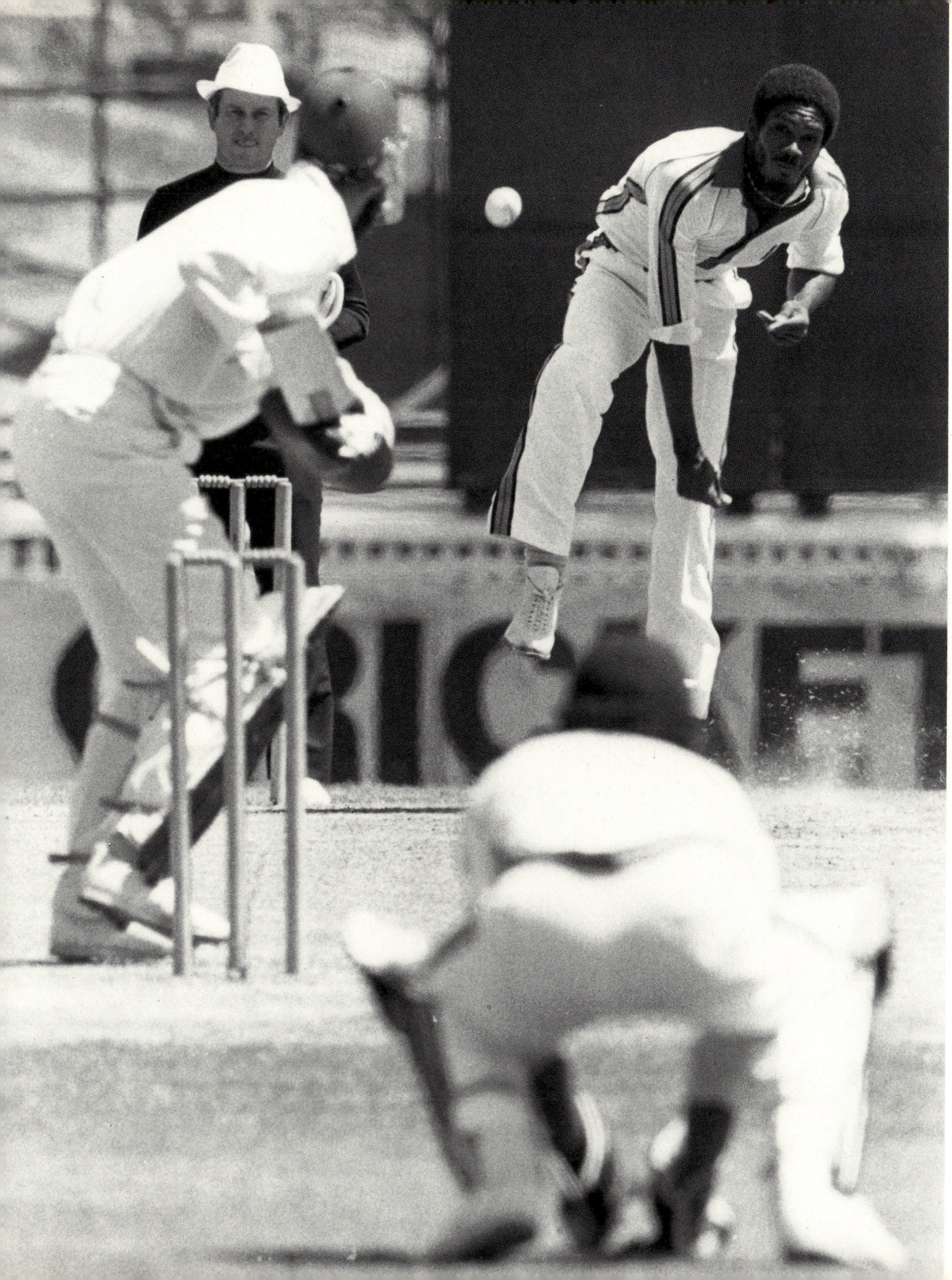

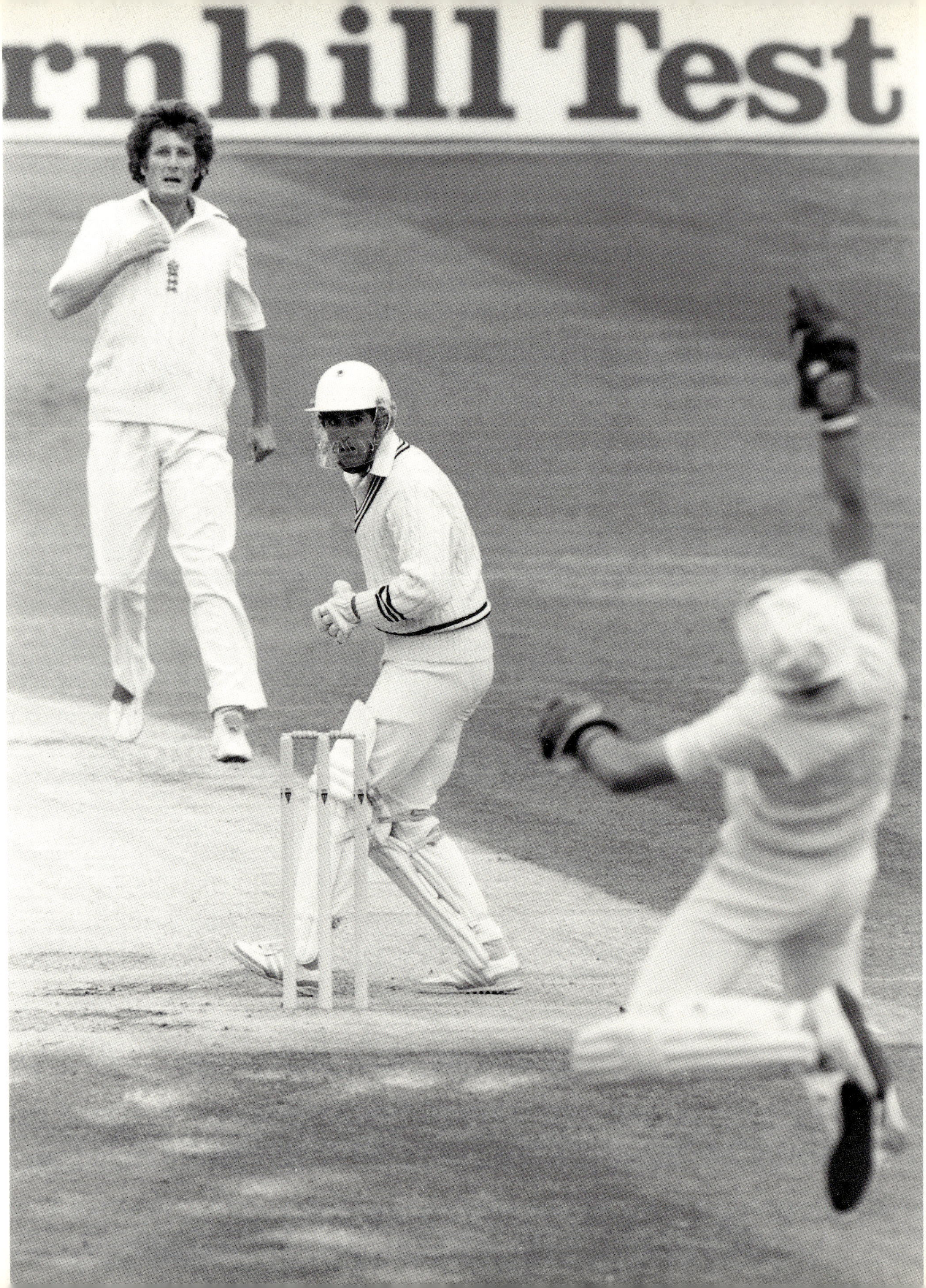
rnhill Test

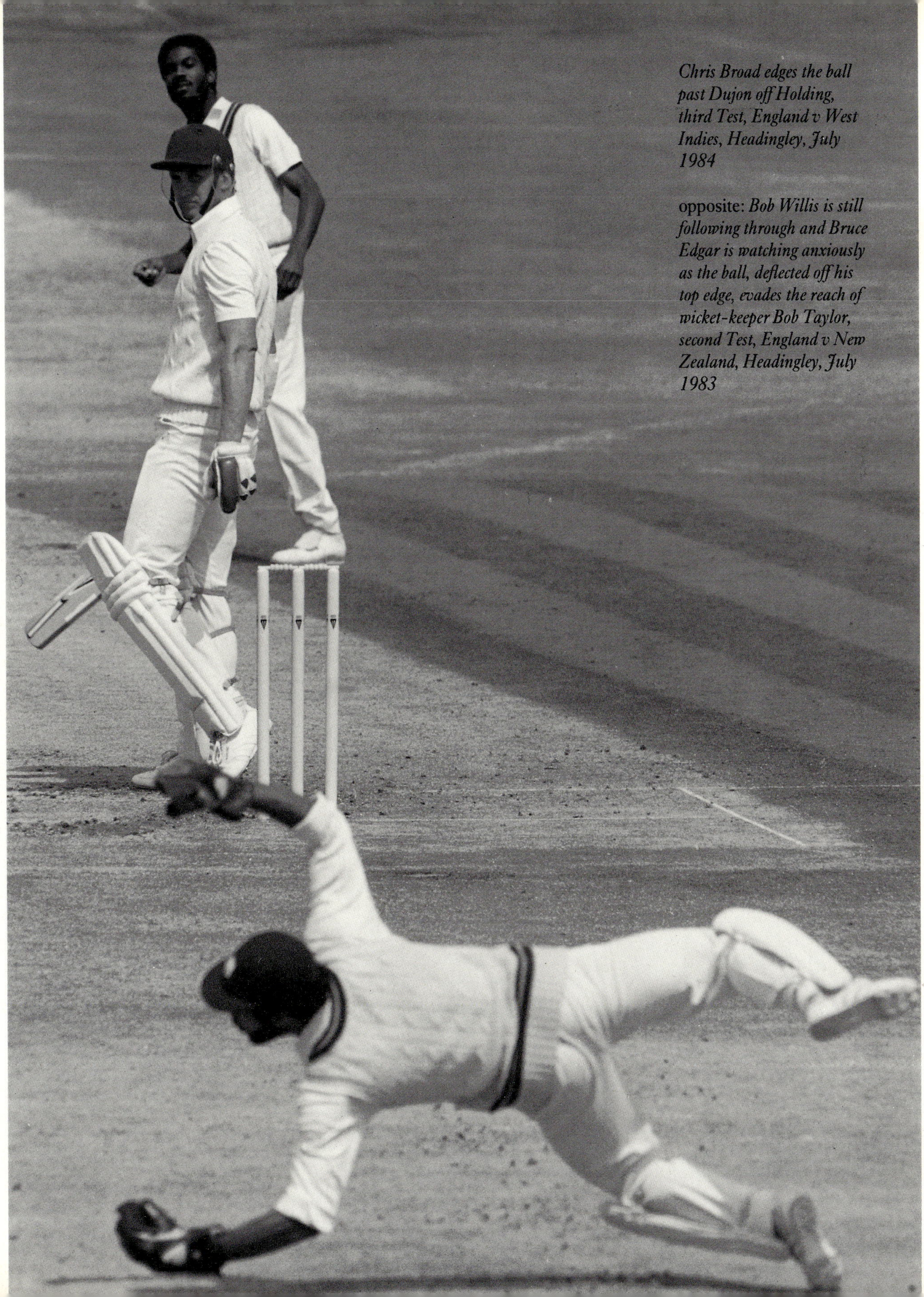

Chris Broad edges the ball past Dujon off Holding, third Test, England v West Indies, Headingley, July 1984

opposite: *Bob Willis is still following through and Bruce Edgar is watching anxiously as the ball, deflected off his top edge, evades the reach of wicket-keeper Bob Taylor, second Test, England v New Zealand, Headingley, July 1983*

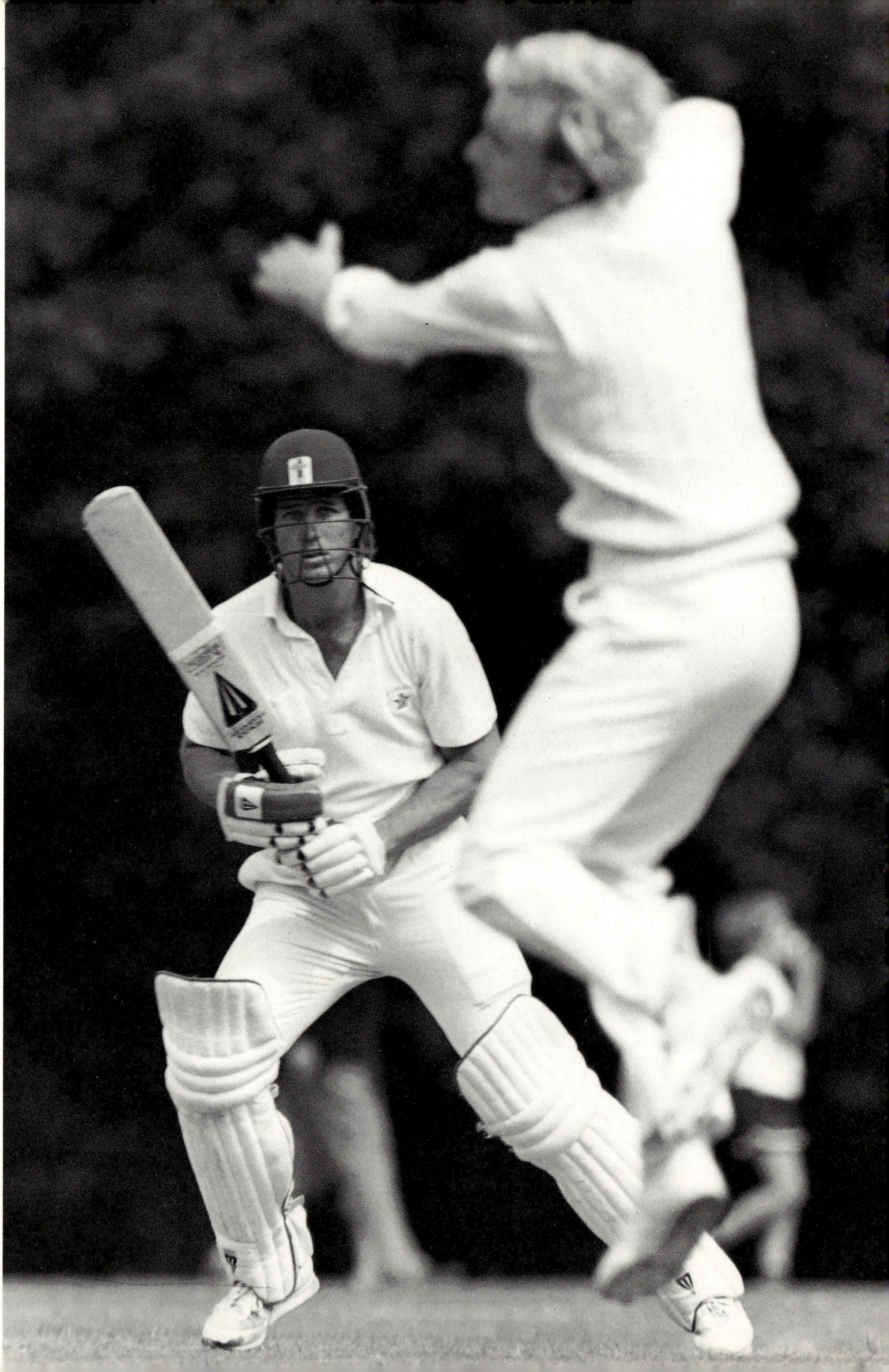

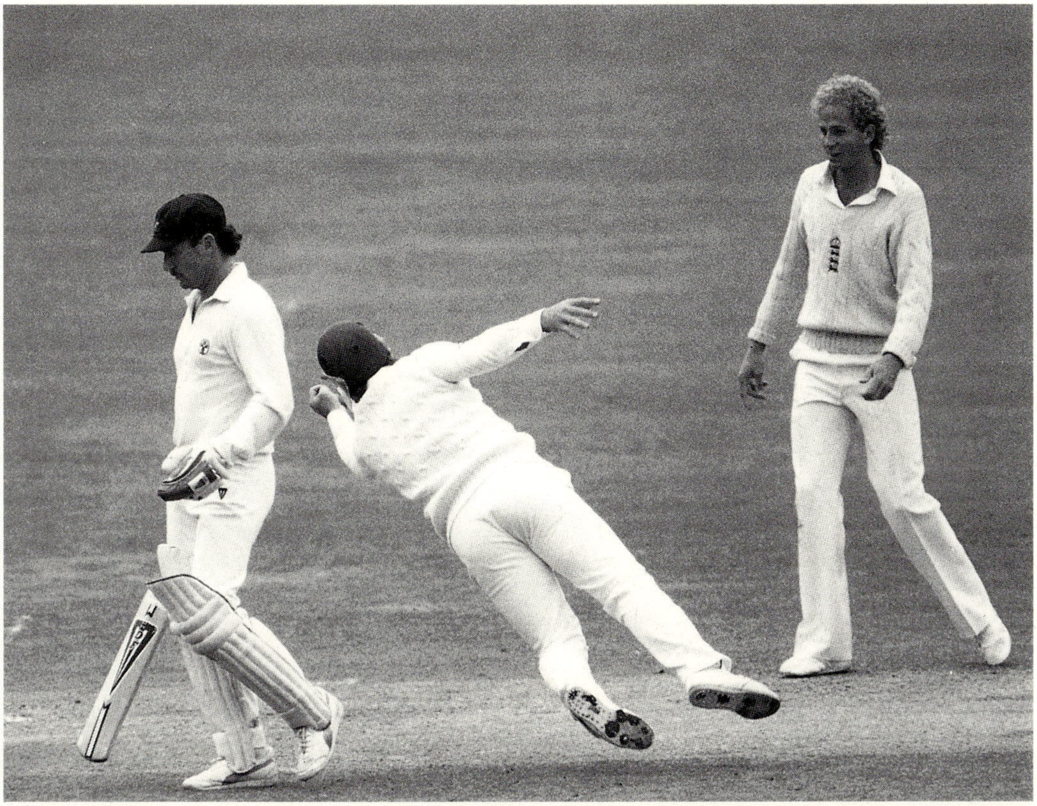

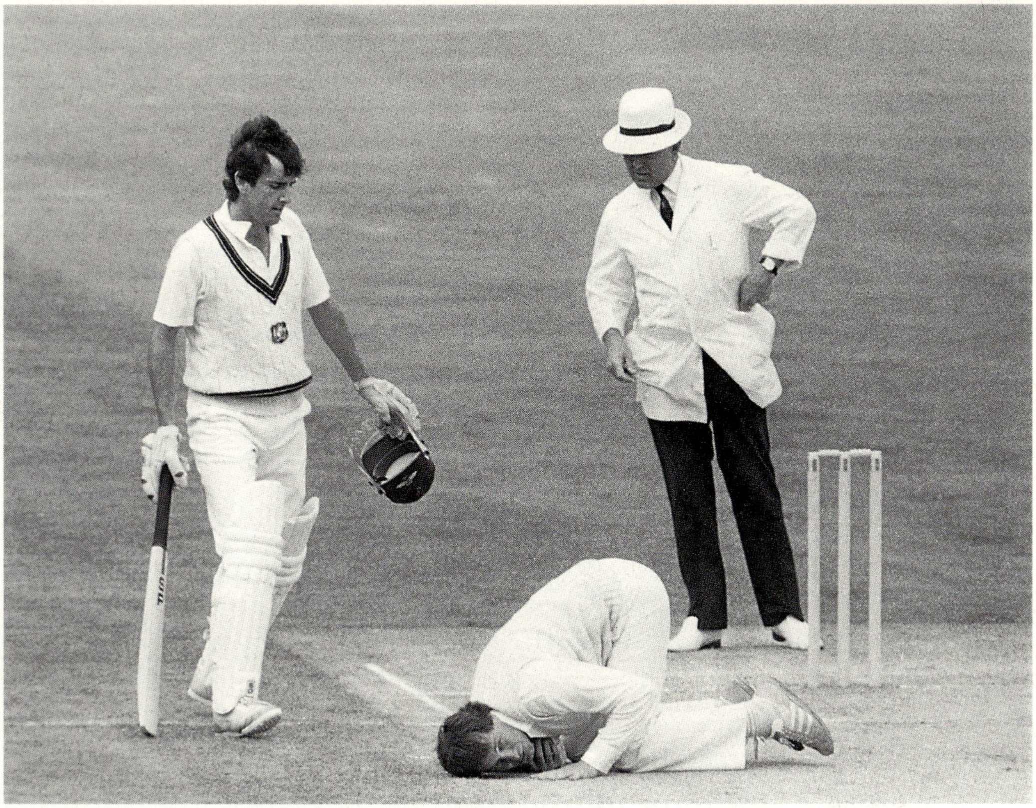

'Hush a moment, I think I hear a train coming!' John Emburey, sixth Test, England v Australia, the Oval, August/September 1985

above: *Despondent batsman Allan Border and delighted Gower as Gatting appears to bring off a tremendous catch, second Test, England v Australia, Lord's, July 1985*

opposite: *Grant Patterson of Zimbabwe hits four past diving fielder, Lavinia Duchess of Norfolk XI v Zimbabwe, Arundel, July 1985*

Even on tour a photographer needs a darkroom, and he needs access to it day and night. This can be a real problem, but bargains are struck. In 1977 I was able to do a deal with a Bengali newspaper in Calcutta. They liked a shot I took of Greig, which they used, and then I freelanced for them as well as for the *Daily Mirror*, and they let me use their darkroom.

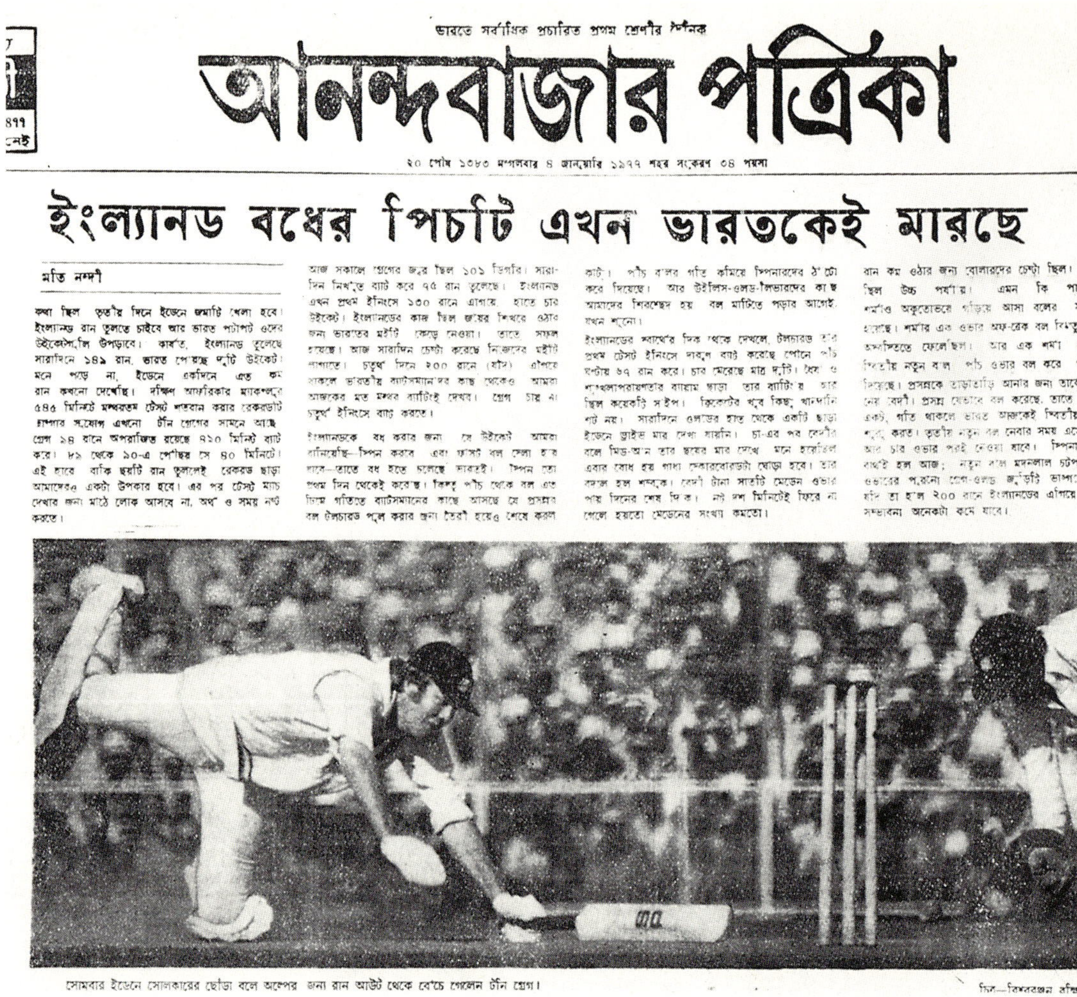

ভারতে সর্বাধিক প্রচারিত প্রথম শ্রেণীর দৈনিক

আনন্দবাজার পত্রিকা

২০ পৌষ ১৩৮৩ মঙ্গলবার ৪ জানুয়ারি ১৯৭৭ শহর সংস্করণ ৩৪ পয়সা

ইংল্যানড বধের পিচটি এখন ভারতকেই মারছে

মতি নন্দী

সোমবার ইডেনে সোলকারের ছোঁড়া বলে অল্পের জন্য রান আউট থেকে বেঁচে গেলেন টনি গ্রেগ।

চিত্র—বিশ্বরঞ্জন রক্ষিত

Tony Greig just escapes being run out by Kirmani, second Test, India v England, Calcutta, December 1976

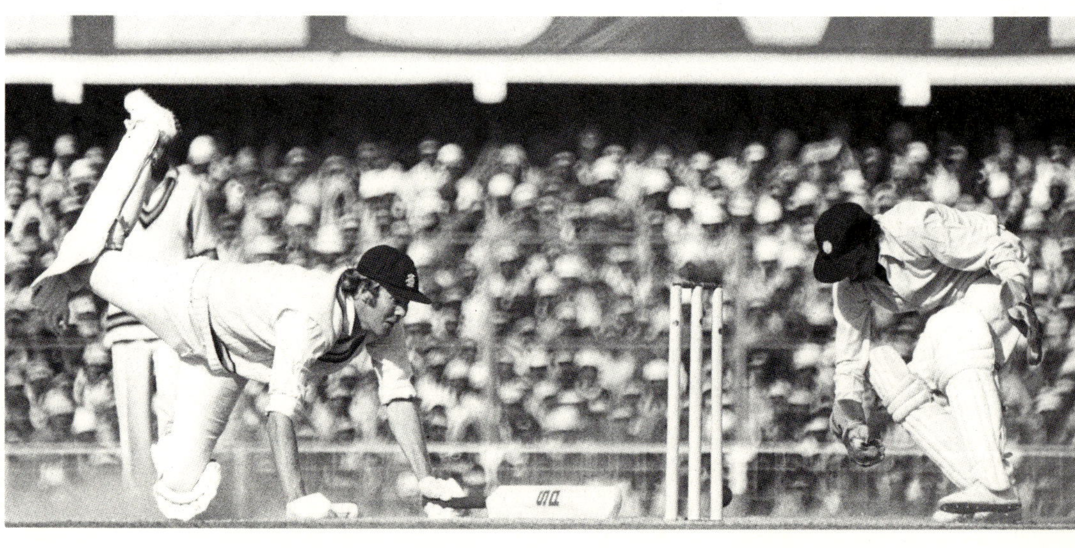

opposite, above: *Mike Gatting, watched by Phil Edmonds and Paul Downton, fails to catch a snick in the Benson and Hedges Cup, Middlesex v Somerset, Lord's, June 1982*

opposite, below: *Kepler Wessels just avoids being caught by Derek 'Arkle' Randall, second Test, Australia v England, Brisbane, December 1982*

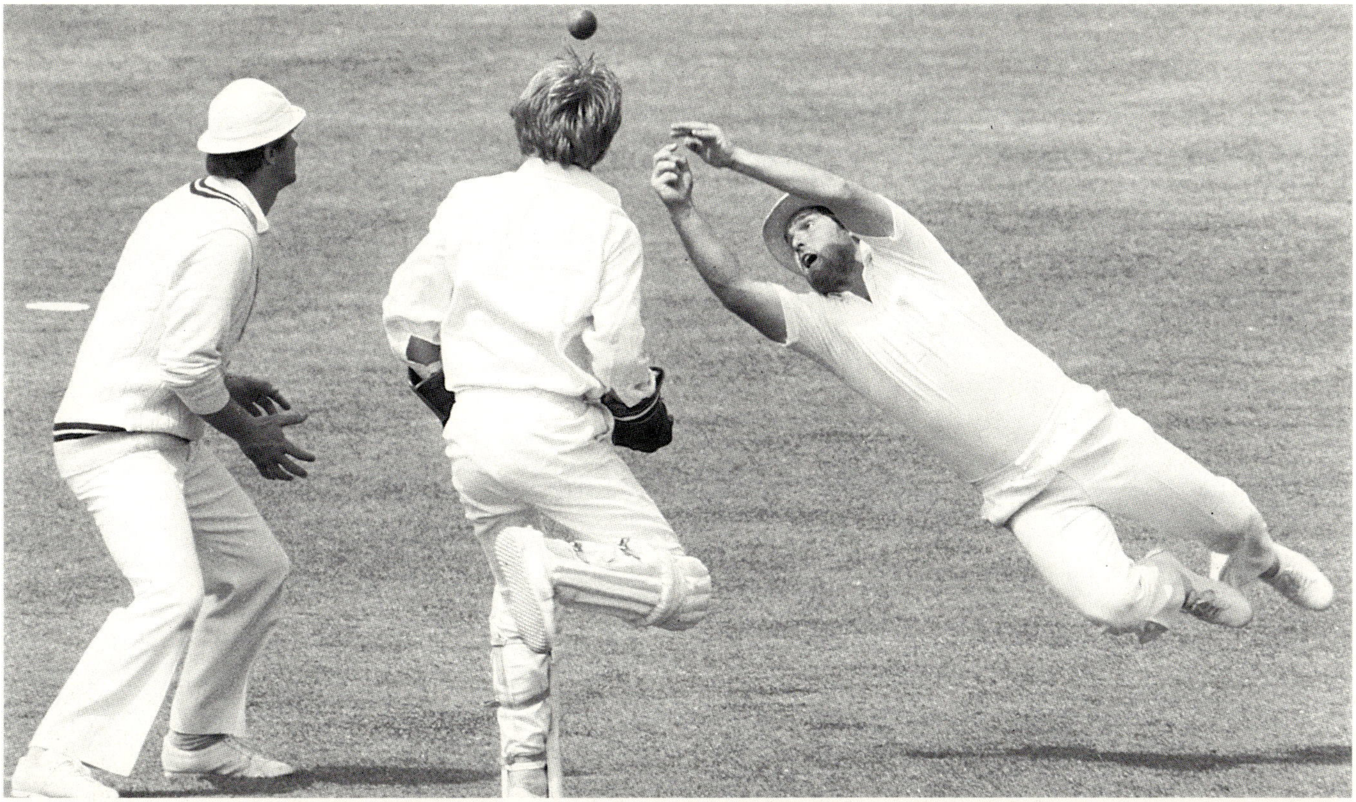

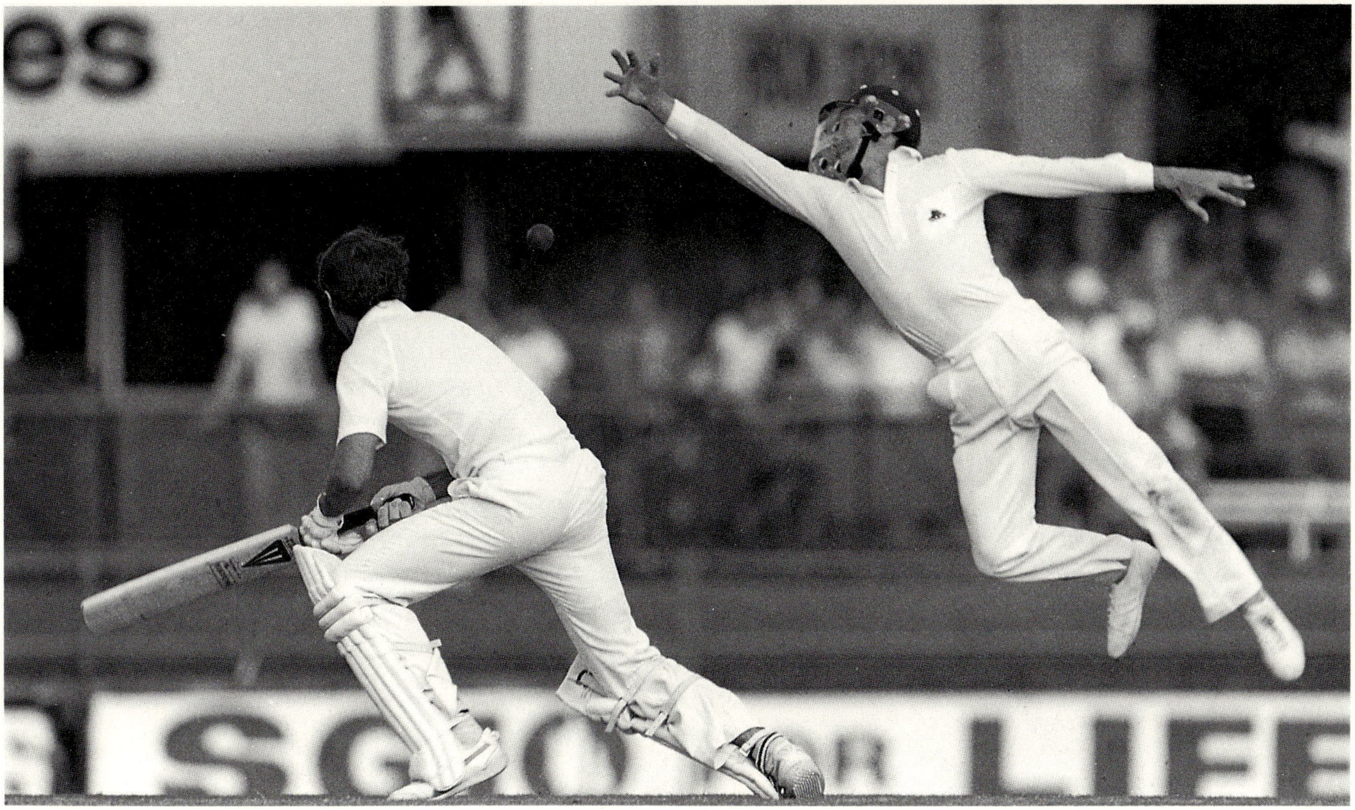

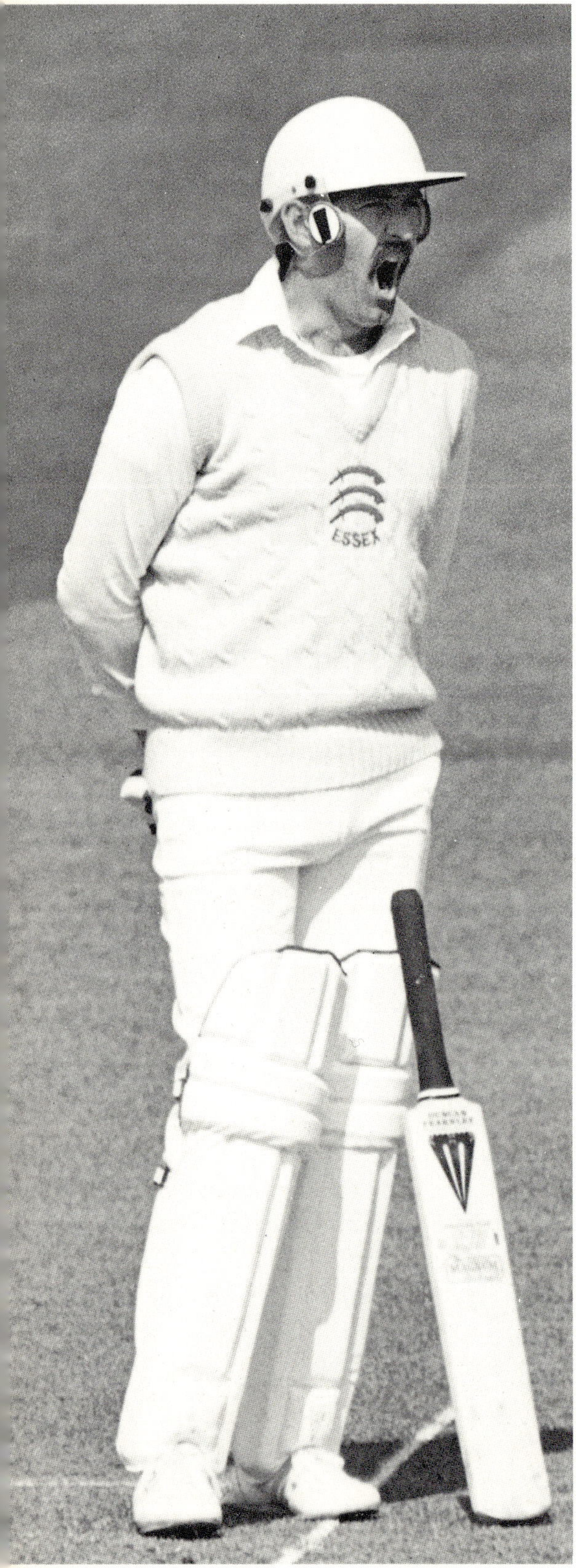
ESSEX

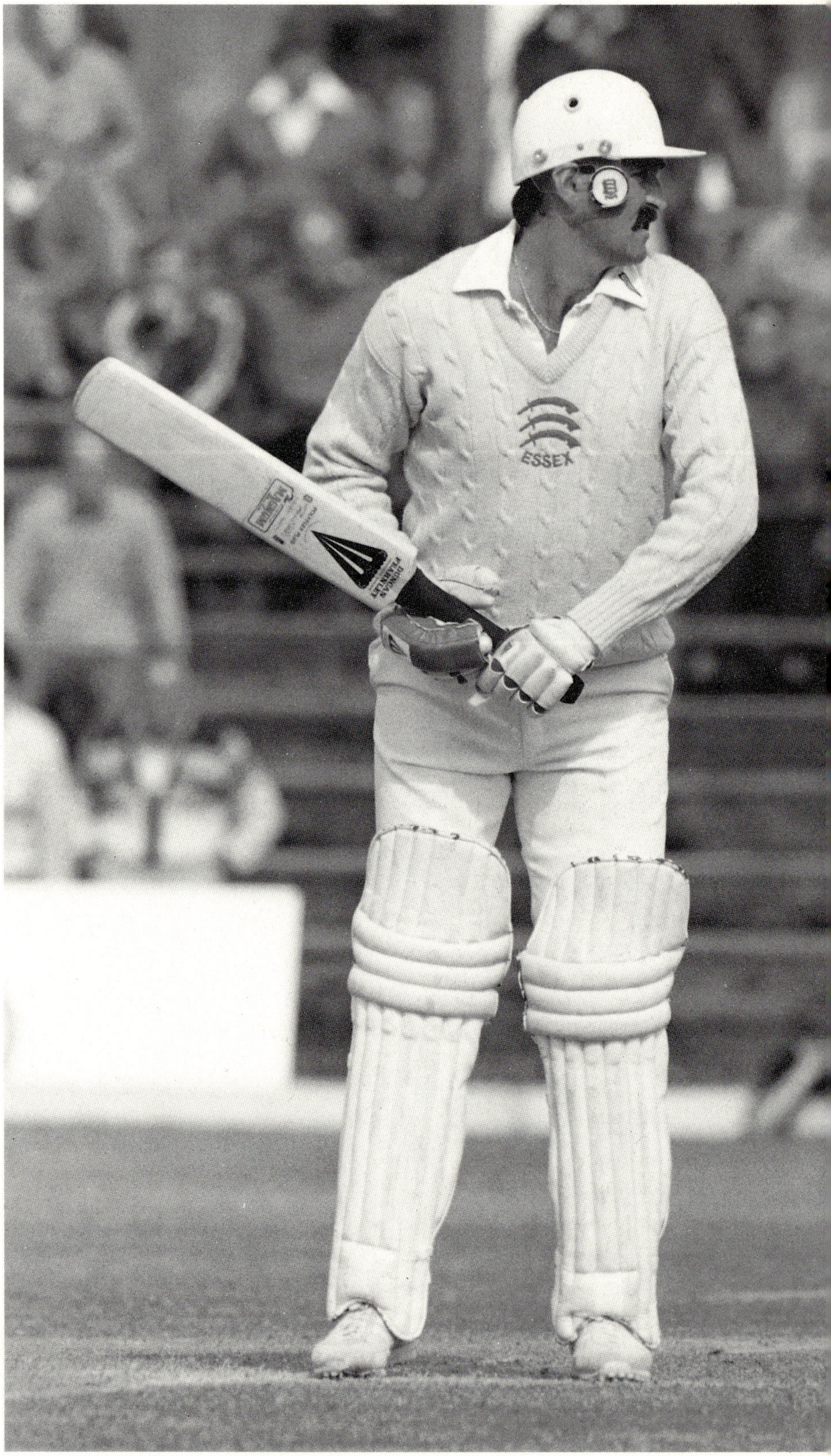
ESSEX

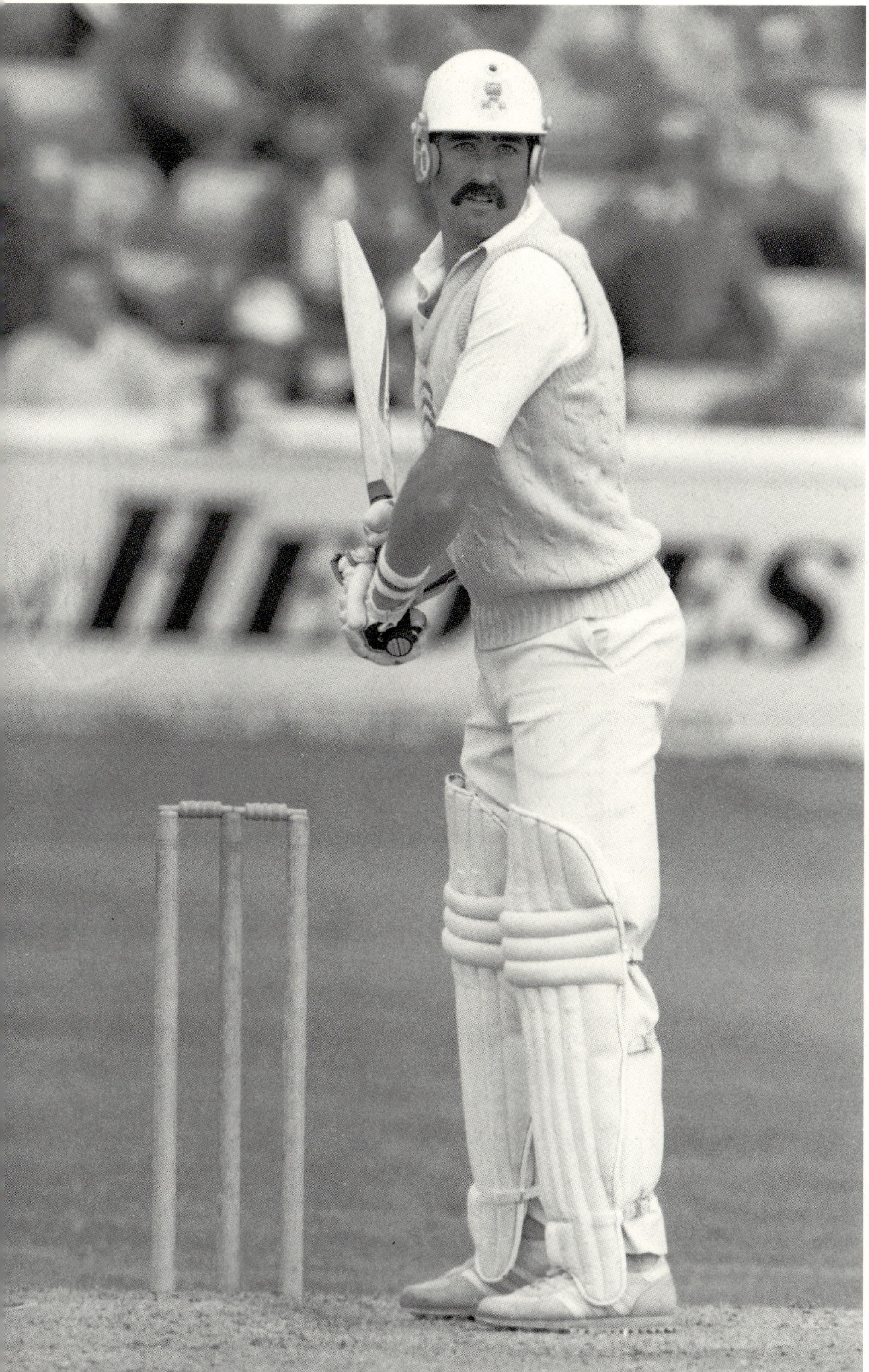

The personalities and moods of individual players can, perhaps, be interpreted from their body language. On this and the next two pages I have tried to capture these intangibles; always more difficult than taking a dramatic action shot, and if successful more rewarding than it is to 'freeze' the historic moment or immortalise the great player. Does Graham Gooch's distinctive upright stance say anything about the man himself? Certainly it shows an individual approach. He himself feels that his reactions are faster if he is upright. Others seem to agree, as he has many imitators, including Martin Moxon and David Smith.

Graham Gooch, Lord's, April 1985 and May 1983

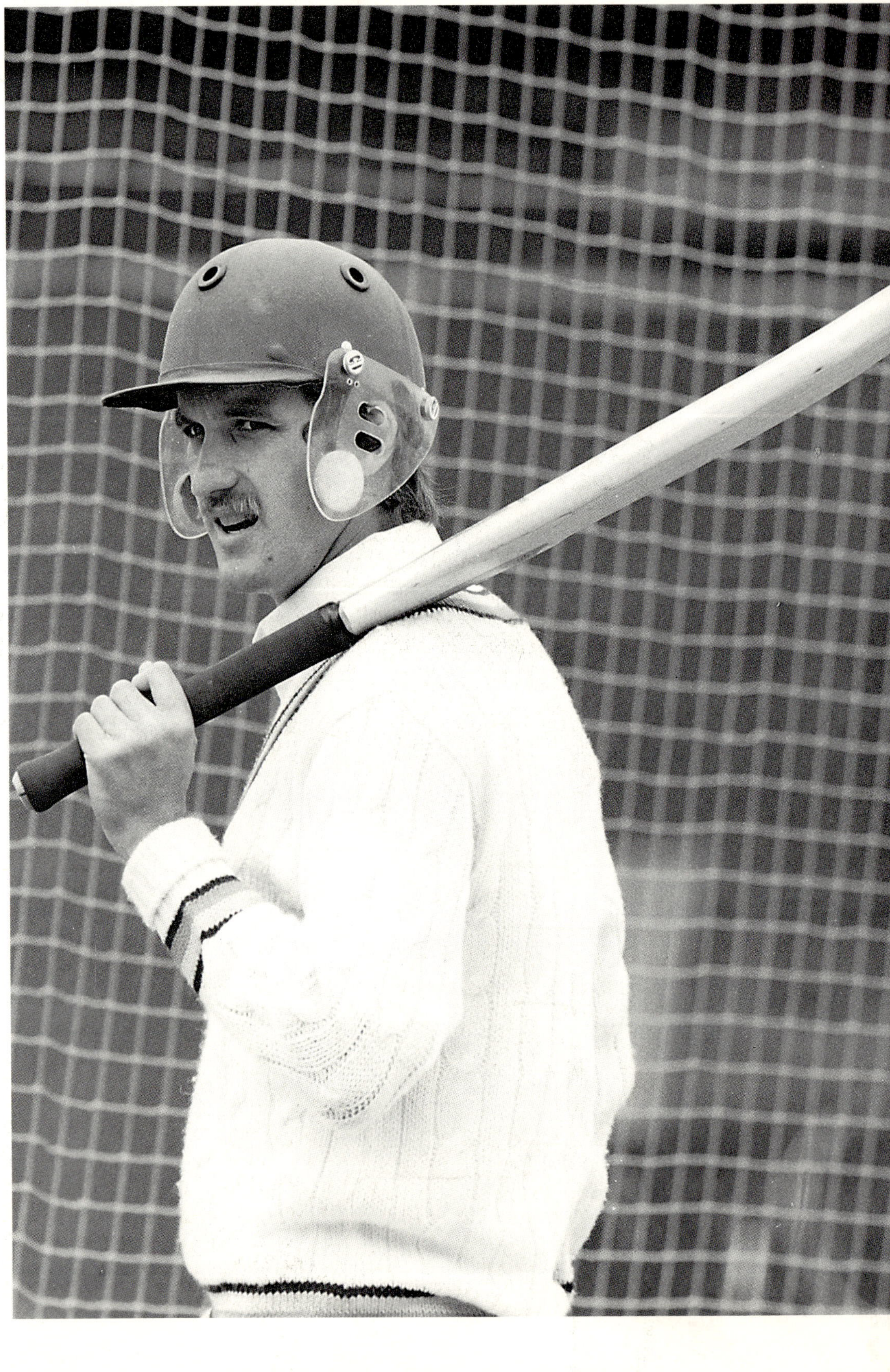

Chris Tavare, reflective cricketer, Christchurch, January 1982

opposite, left: *Greg Matthews, sleep-walking cricketer, Taunton, May 1985*

opposite, right: *Graeme Fowler, soldier cricketer, Headingley, September 1982*

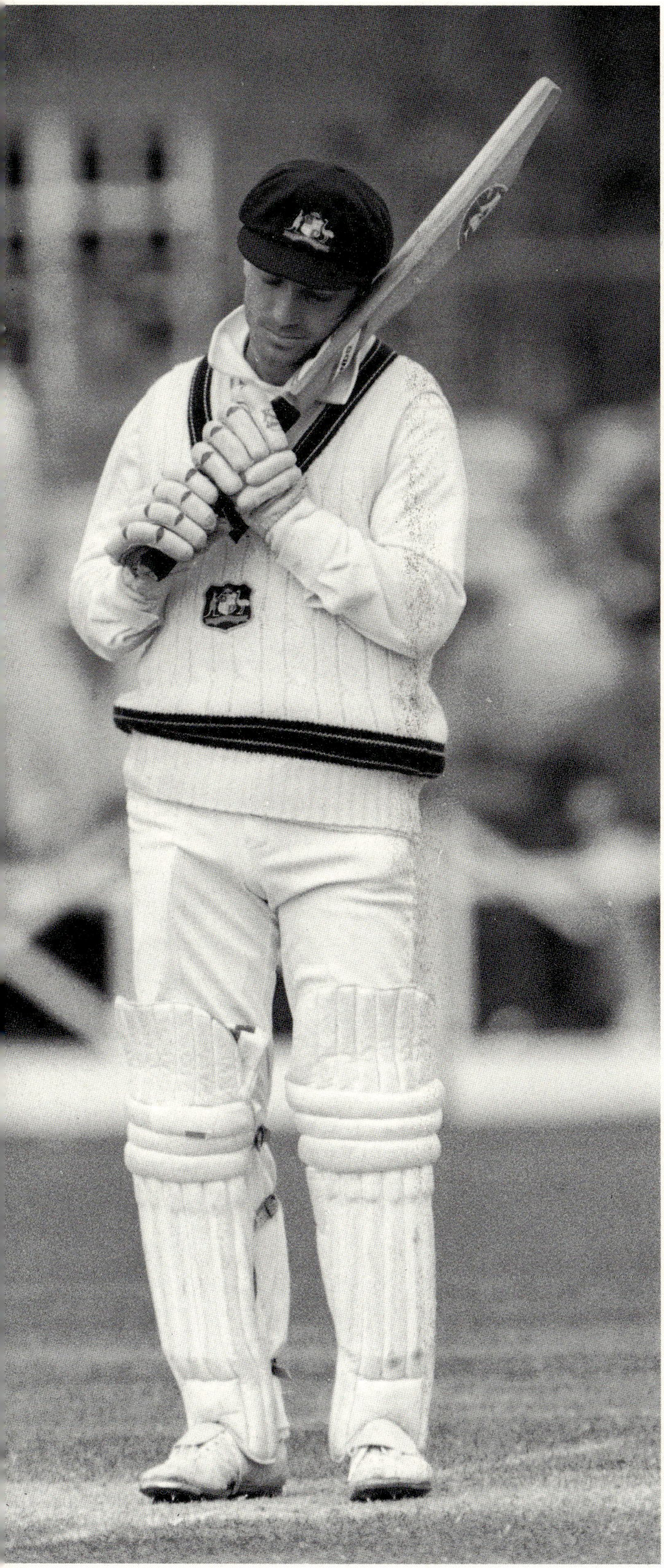

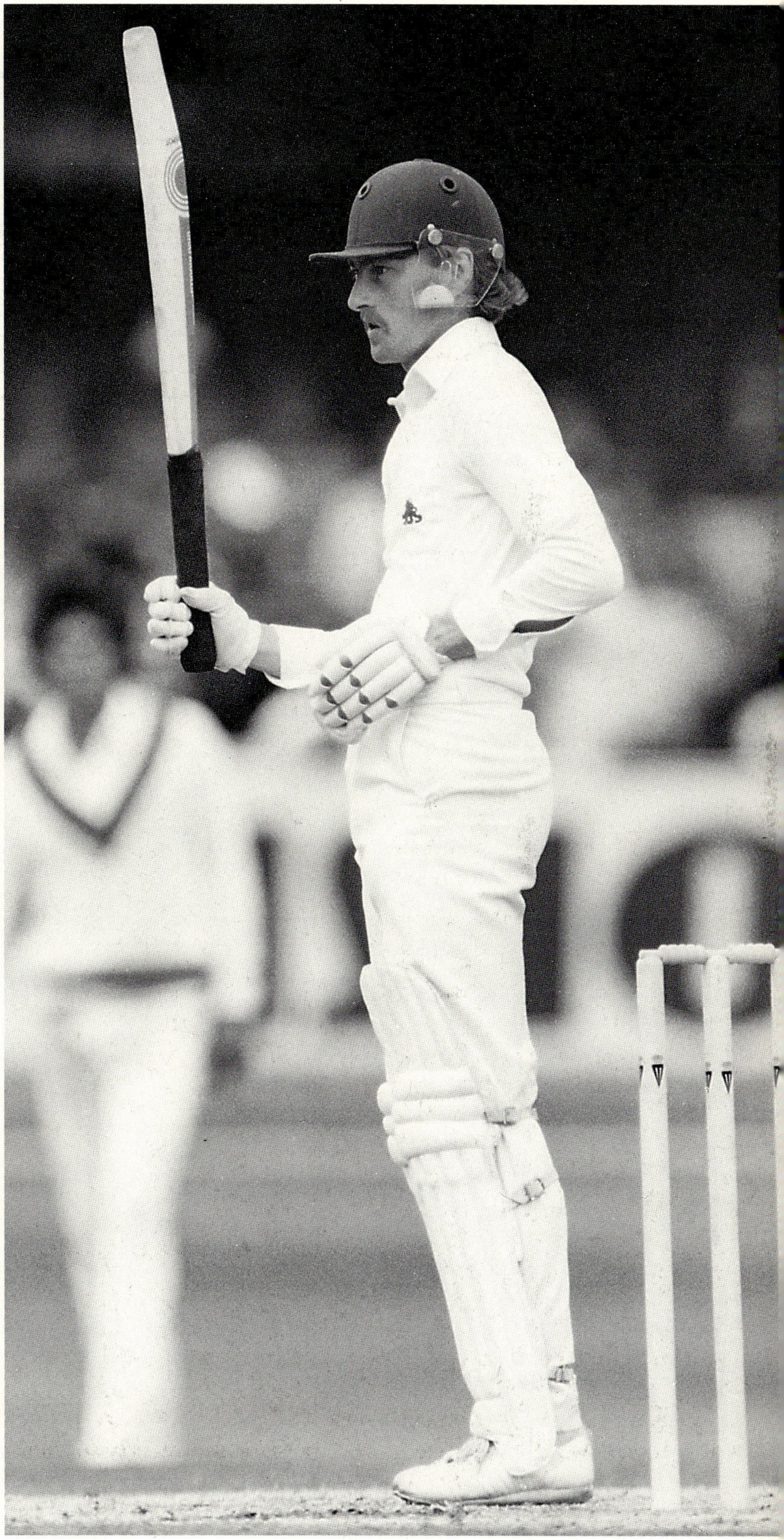

Controversy in almost any form is always good copy and makes for dynamic pictures – so too do violence and political upheaval – however much we may regret the circumstances behind the story or picture. This section only exists because of the dramatic impact and news value of discord.

The first incident concerns Robin Jackman and the sequence of events was as follows: Bob Willis had had to fly back from the West Indies for a knee operation and Robin Jackman was sent for as a replacement. He arrived in Georgetown, Guyana on 23 February 1981. He had, however, coached in South Africa and on 26 February his visitor's permit was withdrawn. As a result the England team decided to leave immediately. The picture on this page shows Jackman about to be served his deportation order.

I was in Guyana covering the tour on a freelance contract for the *Daily Express*, and all of us, cricketers and journalists alike, had been given strict orders not to

Pegasus Hotel, Georgetown, Guyana, February 1981

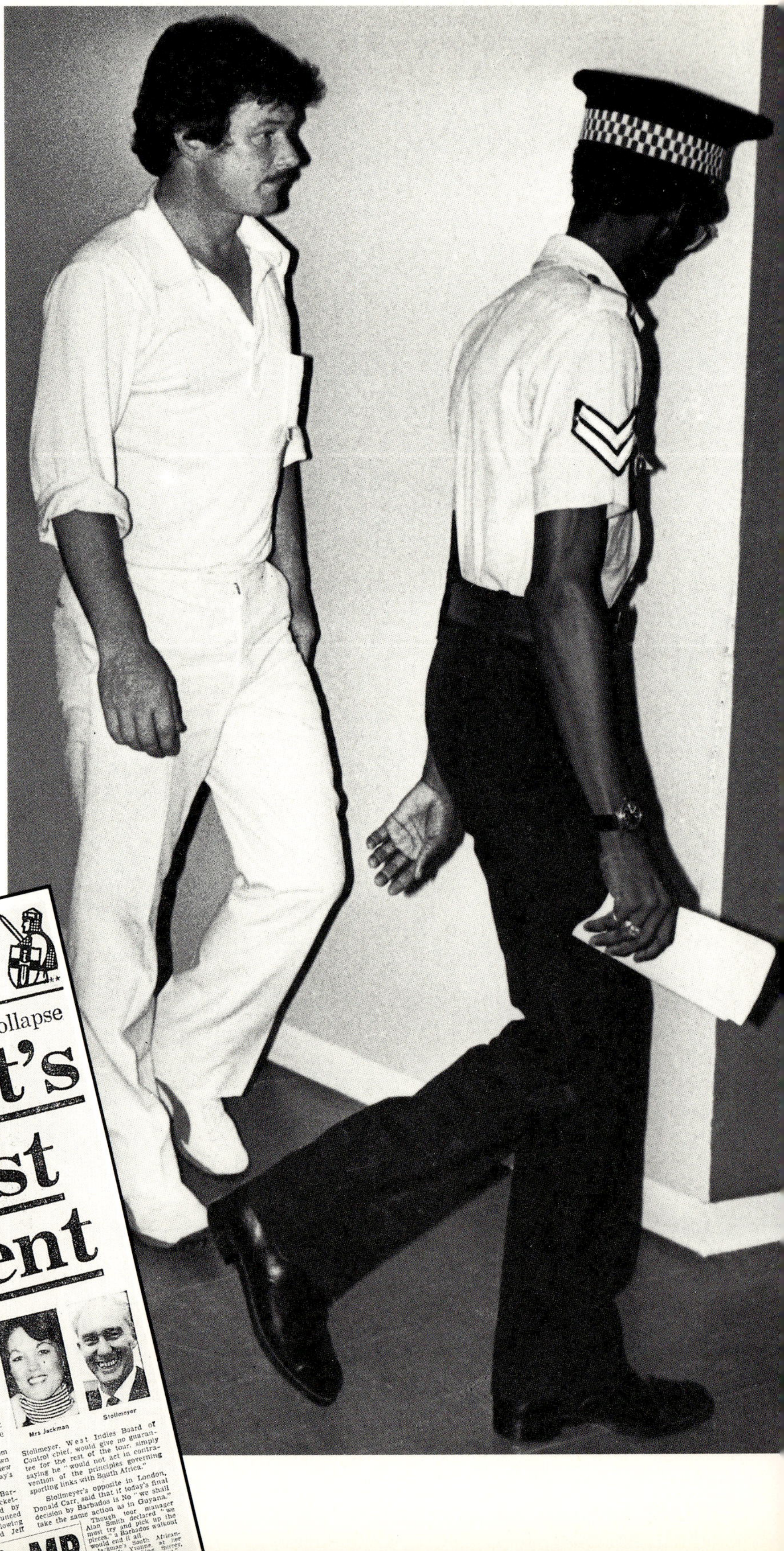

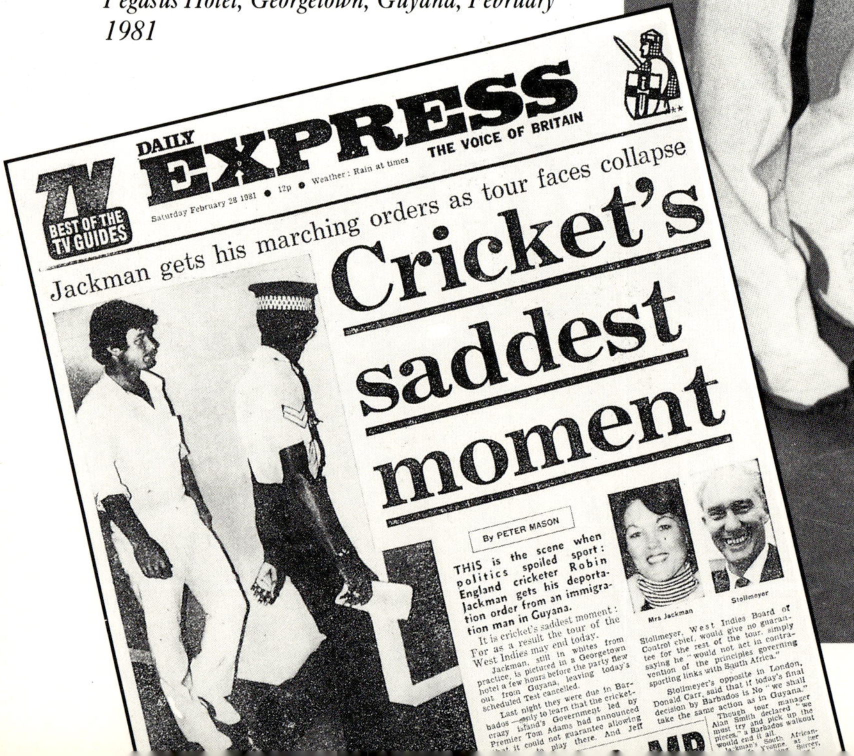

DAILY EXPRESS THE VOICE OF BRITAIN

Saturday February 28 1981 • 12p • Weather: Rain at times

BEST OF THE TV GUIDES

Jackman gets his marching orders as tour faces collapse

Cricket's saddest moment

By PETER MASON

Mrs Jackman

Stollmeyer

THIS is the scene when politics spoiled sport: England cricketer Robin Jackman gets his deportation order from an immigration man in Guyana.

It is cricket's saddest moment: For as a result the tour of the West Indies may end today.

Jackman, still in whites from practice, is pictured in a Georgetown hotel a few hours before the party flew out from Guyana, leaving today's scheduled Test cancelled.

Last night they were due in Barbados—only to learn that the cricket-crazy island's Government led by Premier Tom Adams had announced that it could not guarantee allowing ... to play there. And Jeff Stollmeyer, West Indies Board of Control chief, would give no guarantee for the rest of the tour, simply saying he "would not act in contravention of the principles governing sporting links with South Africa."

Stollmeyer's opposite in London, Donald Carr, said that if today's final decision by Barbados is No "we shall take the same action as in Guyana."

Though tour manager Alan Smith declared "we must try and pick up the pieces," a Barbados walkout would end it all.

... Jackman's South African ... Yvonne, at her ... Surrey, ...

leave the hotel. Nonetheless, having taken the picture, leave it I did – and headed straight for the local newspaper office. There, it was only with the greatest of difficulty that I persuaded the staff to let me use the developer. Worse, the local press office refused point blank to send the picture because of its political implications. Daunted but desperate, I rang Andrew Harvey, the *Daily Express* picture editor, at his home (2 am GMT) to ask his permission to fly to the nearest wire

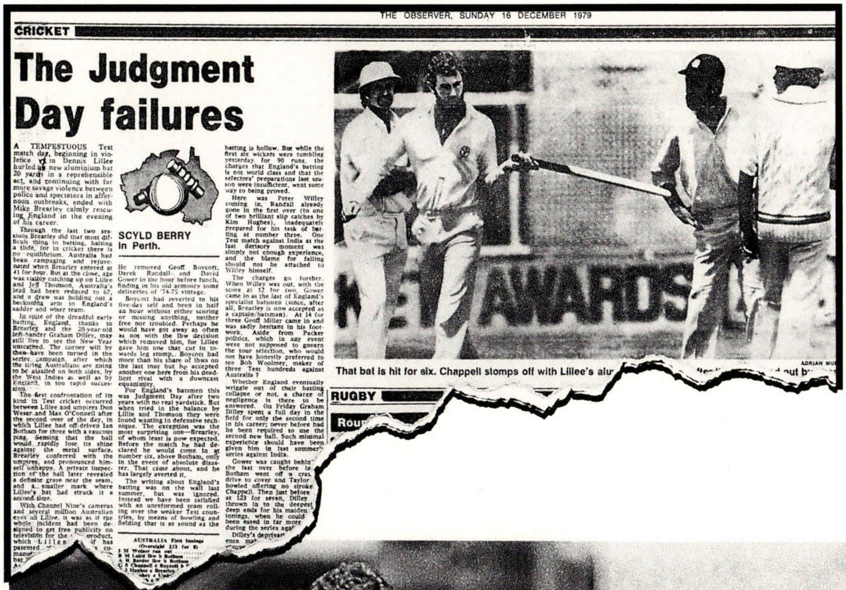

THE OBSERVER, SUNDAY 16 DECEMBER 1979

CRICKET

The Judgment Day failures

SCYLD BERRY in Perth.

A TEMPESTUOUS Test match day, beginning in violence when Dennis Lillee hurled his new aluminium bat 20 yards in a reprehensible act, and continuing with far more savage violence between police and spectators in afternoon outbreaks, ended with Mike Brearley calmly rescuing England in the evening of his career.

Through the last two sessions Brearley did that most difficult thing in batting, halting a slide, for in cricket there is no equilibrium. Australia had been rampaging and rejuvenated when Brearley entered at 41 for four. But at the close, age was visibly catching up on Lillee and Jeff Thomson, Australia's lead had been reduced to 67, and a draw was holding out a beckoning arm to England's sadder and wiser team.

In spite of the dreadful early batting, England, thanks to Brearley and the 20-year-old left-hander Graham Dilley, may still live to see the New Year unscathed. The corner will by then have been turned in the series campaign, after which the tiring Australians are going to be assailed on both sides, by the West Indies as well as by England, in too rapid succession.

The first confrontation of its kind in Test cricket occurred between Lillee and umpires Don Weser and Max O'Connell after the second over of the day, in which Lillee had off-driven Ian Botham for three with a raucous ping. Sensing that the ball would rapidly lose its shine against the metal surface, Brearley conferred with the umpires, and pronounced himself unhappy. A private inspection of the ball later revealed a definite graze near the seam, and a smaller mark where Lillee's bat had struck it a second time.

With Channel Nine's cameras and several million Australian eyes on Lillee, it was as if the whole incident had been designed to get free publicity on television for the product, which Lillee

He removed Geoff Boycott, Derek Randall and David Gower in the hour before lunch, finding in his old armoury some deliveries of '74-75 vintage.

Boycott had reverted to his five-day self and been in half an hour without either scoring or missing anything, neither free nor troubled. Perhaps he would have got away as often as not with the lbw decision which removed him, for Lillee gave him one that cut in towards leg stump. Boycott had more than his share of lbws on the last tour but he accepted another one here from his deadliest rival with a downcast equanimity.

For England's batsmen this was Judgment Day after two years with no real yardstick. But when tried in the balance by Lillie and Thomson they were found wanting in defensive technique. The exception was the most surprising one—Brearley, of whom least is now expected. Before the match he had declared he would come in at number six, above Botham, only in the event of absolute disaster. That came about, and he has largely averted it.

The writing about England's batting was on the wall last summer, but was ignored. Instead we have been satisfied with an unreformed team rolling over the weaker Test countries, by means of bowling and fielding that is as sound as the batting is hollow. But while the first six wickets were tumbling yesterday for 90 runs, the charges that England's batting is not world class and that the selectors' preparations last season were insufficient, went some way to being proved.

Here was Peter Willey coming in, Randall already gone in the first over (to one of two brilliant slip catches by Kim Hughes), inadequately prepared for his task of batting at number three. One Test match against India at the last derisory moment was simply not enough experience, and the blame for failing should not be attached to Willey himself.

The charges go further. When Willey was out, with the score at 12 for two, Gower came in as the last of England's specialist batsmen (since, after all, Brearley is now accepted as a captain/batsman). At 14 for three Geoff Miller came in and was sadly hesitant in his footwork. Aside from Packer politics, which in any event were not supposed to govern the tour selection, who would not have honestly preferred to see Bob Woolmer, maker of three Test hundreds against Australia?

Whether England eventually wriggle out of their batting collapse or not, a charge of negligence is there to be answered. On Friday Graham Dilley spent a full day in the field for only the second time in his career; never before had he been required to use the second new ball. Such minimal experience should have been given him in last summer's series against India.

Gower was caught behind the last over before lunch. Botham went off a crash drive to cover and Taylor bowled offering no stroke to Chappell. Then just before at 123 for seven, Dilley thrown in to the deepest deep ends for his maiden innings, when he could been eased in far more during the series

AUSTRALIA First Innings (Overnight 232 for 8)

J M Wiener run out
B M Laird lbw b Botham
A R Border lbw b Botham
G S Chappell c Boycott b
K J Hughes c Brearley

That bat is hit for six. Chappell stomps off with Lillee's alu

ADRIAN MU

RUGBY

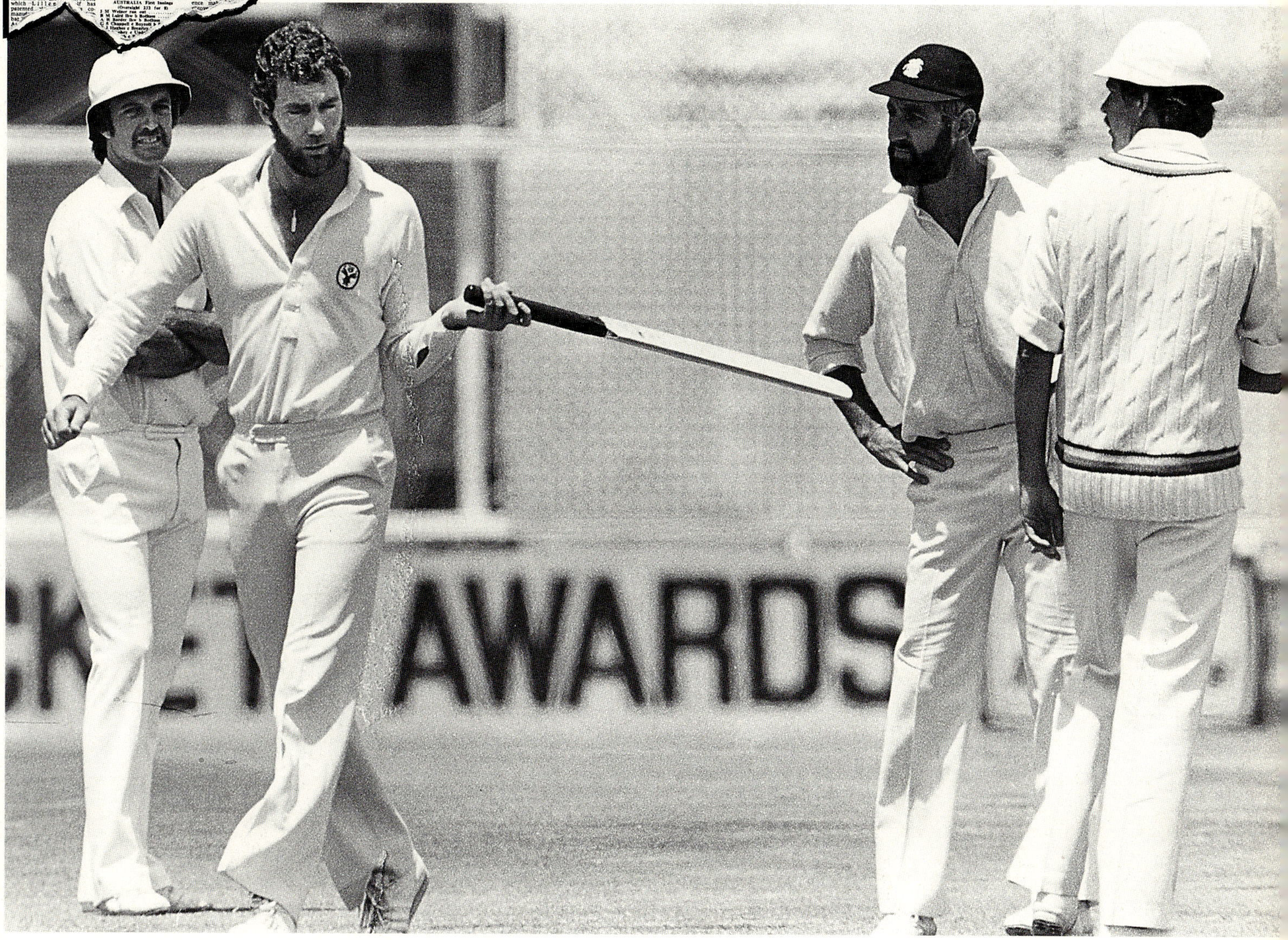

The aluminium bat, first Test, Australia v England, Perth, December 1979

office – at Miami, 2,500 miles away. He was enthusiastic and gave the go-ahead, and luckily I already had the necessary American visa.

The picture eventually cost the *Daily Express* £2,000 (the actual wiring costs were about £150 per photograph). I myself received £1,000 for achieving this world exclusive. Altogether it was a stimulating experience, despite (or perhaps because of) the 'secret' police who had followed me everywhere from the moment I left the hotel in Georgetown until I finally left the country.

The feedback from the *Daily Express* was wonderful. Ken Lawrence, the sports editor, was absolutely delighted and the story of how the photograph arrived at the newspaper became a feature in itself. Nonetheless, it was a sad day for cricket.

The next picture (page 67) shows a grumpy Greg Chappell, Australian captain during the England tour in 1979/80 removing – of all things – Lillee's aluminium bat. It was nothing special and why anyone should want one is a mystery. Anyhow, Lillee was experimenting with it and Mike Brearley (the England captain) objected, saying it took the shine off the ball, also that it dented it. The match was held up for ten minutes while they argued the point. The Cricket Council eventually banned the bat and it has never been heard of since, but it caused a lot of ill feeling at the time.

Even less entertaining, however, was the 1981 contretemps – also in Perth – involving Australian fast bowler, Terry Alderman. He had impetuously chased a fan who had tried to steal his sunhat when a boisterous element from the crowd invaded the pitch. This occurred during the first Test between England and

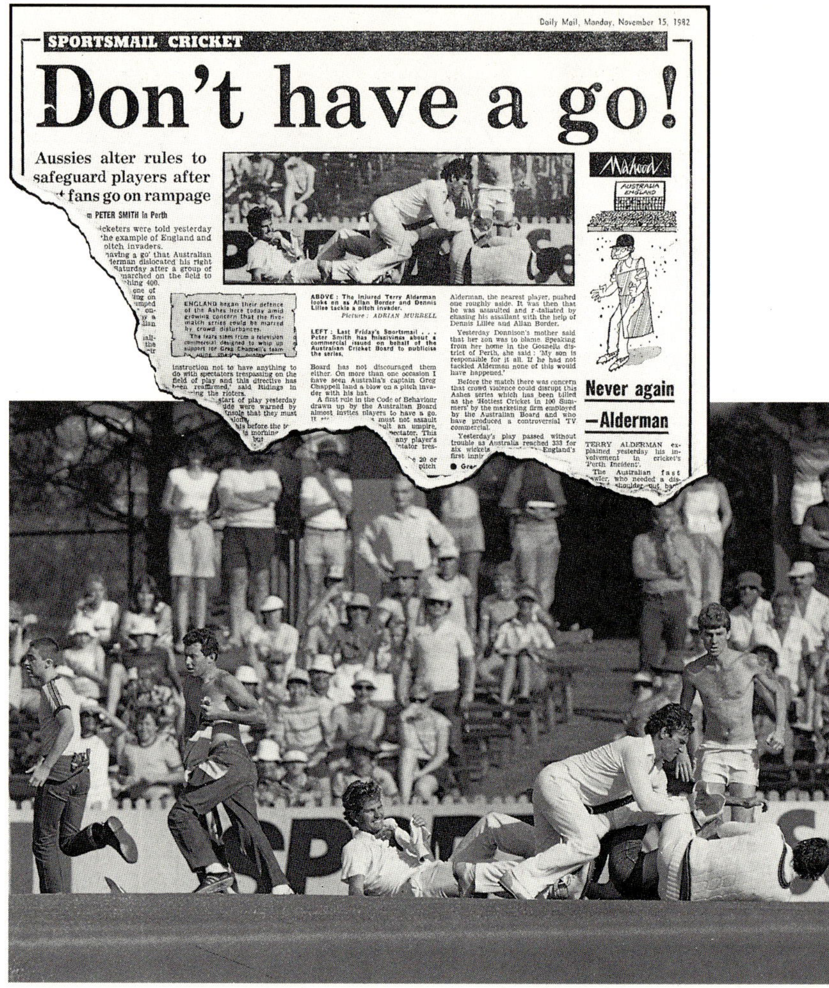

Daily Mail, Monday, November 15, 1982

SPORTSMAIL CRICKET

Don't have a go!

Aussies alter rules to safeguard players after fans go on rampage

PETER SMITH in Perth

icketers were told yesterday the example of England and pitch invaders.

having a go' that Australian derman dislocated his right Saturday after a group of marched on the field to hing 400.

ENGLAND began their defence of the Ashes here today amid growing concern that the five-match series could be marred by crowd disturbances.

The fears stem from a television commercial designed to whip up support for Greg Chappell's team

instruction not to have anything to do with spectators trespassing on the field of play and this directive has been reaffirmed,' said Ridings in ing the rioters.

start of play yesterday were warned by that they must

ABOVE: The injured Terry Alderman looks on as Allan Border and Dennis Lillee tackle a pitch invader.

Picture: ADRIAN MURRELL

LEFT: Last Friday's Sportsmail . . . Peter Smith has misgivings about a commercial issued on behalf of the Australian Cricket Board to publicise the series.

Board has not discouraged them either. On more than one occasion I have seen Australia's captain Greg Chappell land a blow on a pitch invader with his bat.

A first rule in the Code of Behaviour drawn up by the Australian Board almost invites players to have a go. must not assault an umpire, spectator. This any player's

Alderman, the nearest player, pushed one roughly aside. It was then that he was assaulted and retaliated by chasing his assailant with the help of Dennis Lillee and Allan Border.

Yesterday Donnison's mother said that her son was to blame. Speaking from her home in the Gosnells district of Perth, she said: 'My son is responsible for it all. If he had not tackled Alderman none of this would have happened.'

Before the match there was concern that crowd violence could disrupt this Ashes series which has been billed as the 'Hottest Cricket in 100 Summers' by the marketing firm employed by the Australian Board and who have produced a controversial TV commercial.

Yesterday's play passed without trouble as Australia reached 333 for six wickets England's first inn

Never again —Alderman

TERRY ALDERMAN explained yesterday his involvement in cricket's 'Perth Incident'.

The Australian fast bowler, who needed a dis- shoulder

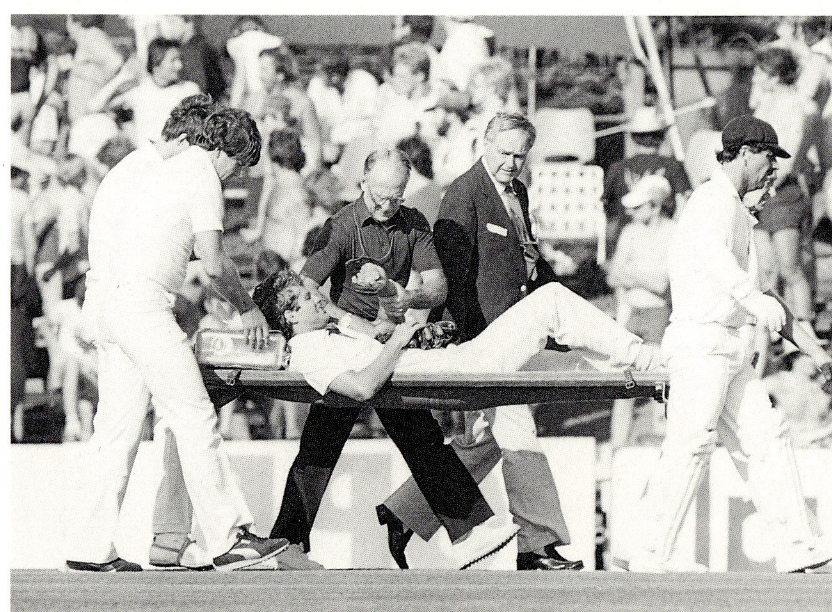

Terry Alderman, the first cricketer victim of crowd violence, first Test, Australia v England, Perth, November 1982

Australia. The mood became quite ugly and in the melee that followed Alderman dislocated his shoulder, put himself out of first-class cricket for the rest of the season and made world news.

The picture on this page shows a disconsolate Fletcher teaching his stumps a lesson – 'an unworthy reaction from someone who had been at pains to tell his team to accept the umpiring . . .' (*Wisden*, 1983). It was not only unworthy but also uncharacteristic and although he later wrote to apologise to the Indian Board the incident may well have cost him the captaincy for the 1983 season.

Fortunately for me, every tour that I have covered has had a major incident and my photographs have turned up on the front page as well as on the back. This is an absolute godsend to the freelance, who is frequently struggling anyway. However, it is one thing to be in the right place at the right time but, as I discovered in Guyana, it's quite another to be able to find a wire service to send the picture home.

A wire machine is rather like an old-fashioned typewriter. It has a drum on which a 10″ × 8″ print is fixed. A beam of light travels across relaying the image to a receiver in a newspaper office. It takes approximately ten minutes to transmit, and the system has enough sensitivity to sort out tones. The quality leaves something to be desired; it is good enough for newspaper reproduction but not for magazines. The system has been in use for forty years and the only improvement is that the machines have become smaller.

Sometimes, finding a wire machine is not the only problem and, due to political crises – as happened in both Guyana and India (see overleaf) – I even have difficulties processing the film.

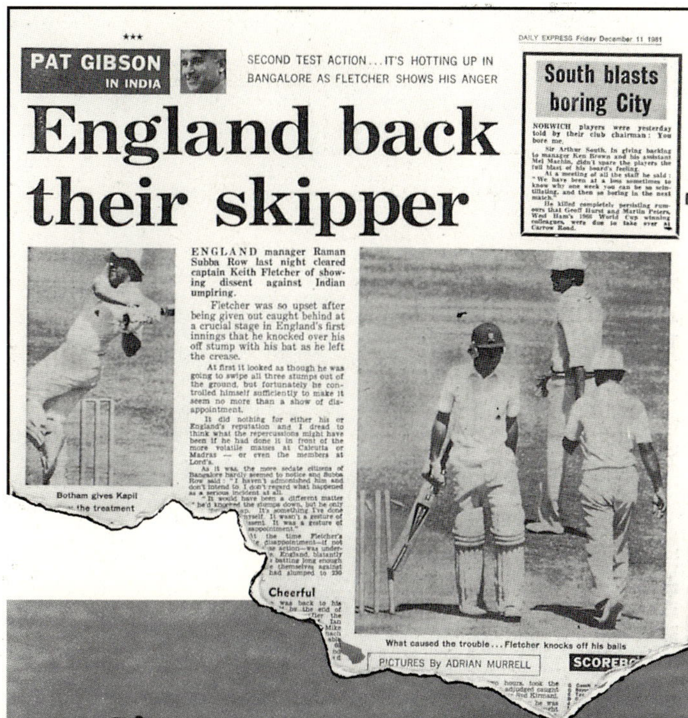

DAILY EXPRESS Friday December 11 1981

PAT GIBSON IN INDIA

SECOND TEST ACTION . . . IT'S HOTTING UP IN BANGALORE AS FLETCHER SHOWS HIS ANGER

England back their skipper

ENGLAND manager Raman Subba Row last night cleared captain Keith Fletcher of showing dissent against Indian umpiring.

Fletcher was so upset after being given out caught behind at a crucial stage in England's first innings that he knocked over his off stump with his bat as he left the crease.

At first it looked as though he was going to swipe all three stumps out of the ground, but fortunately he controlled himself sufficiently to make it seem no more than a show of disappointment.

It did nothing for either his or England's reputation and I dread to think what the repercussions might have been if he had done it in front of the more volatile masses at Calcutta or Madras — or even the members at Lord's.

As it was, the more sedate citizens of Bangalore hardly seemed to notice and Subba Row said: "I haven't admonished him and don't intend to. I don't regard what happened as a serious incident at all.

"It would have been a different matter if he'd knocked the stumps down, but he only ... It's something I've done myself. It wasn't a gesture of dissent. It was a gesture of disappointment."

... the time Fletcher's ... disappointment—if not ... action—was under... England, blatantly ... batting long enough ... themselves against ... had slumped to 230

Cheerful

... was back to his ... by the end of ... after the ... Ian ... Mike ...

Botham gives Kapil ... the treatment

What caused the trouble . . . Fletcher knocks off his balls

PICTURES By ADRIAN MURRELL

SCOREBO...

South blasts boring City

NORWICH players were yesterday told by their club chairman: You bore me.

Sir Arthur South, in giving backing to manager Ken Brown and his assistant Mel Machin, didn't spare the players the full blast of his board's feeling.

At a meeting of all the staff he said: "We have been at a loss sometimes to know why one week you can be so scintillating, and then so boring in the next match."

He killed completely persisting rumours that Geoff Hurst and Martin Peters, West Ham's 1966 World Cup winning colleagues, were due to take over at Carrow Road.

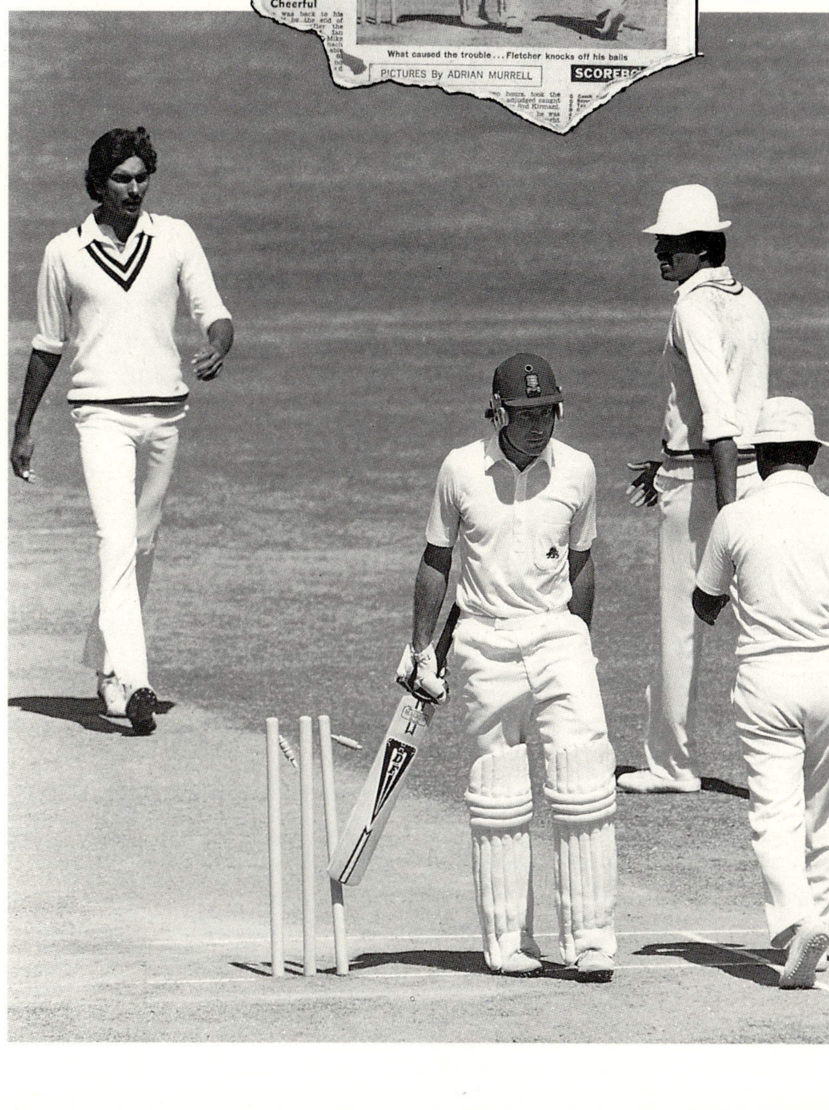

'Caught Kirmani, bowled Shastri', Fletcher disagreed, second Test, India v England, Bangalore, December 1981

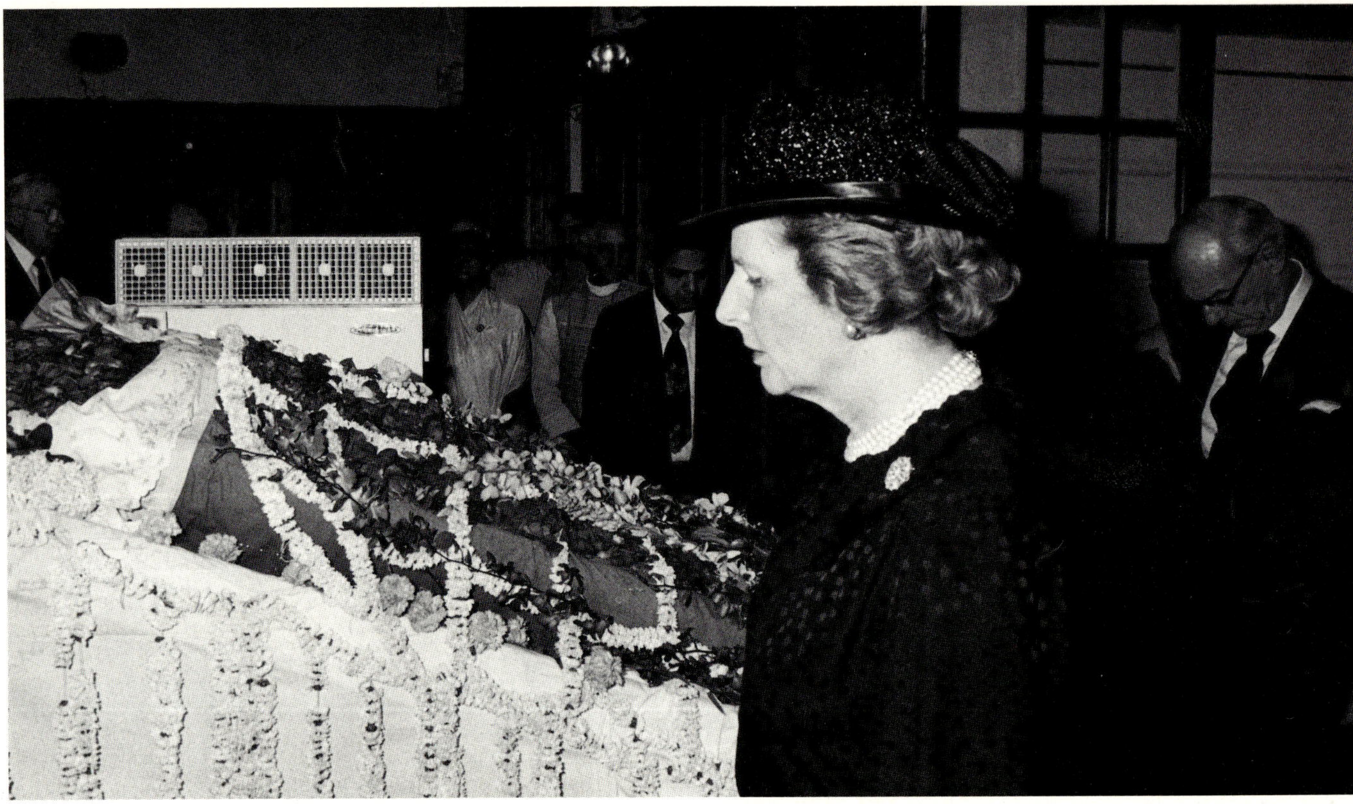

Prime Minister Indira Gandhi was assassinated on 31 October 1984 within hours of the England team arriving in India. At the time, I was working in England for All-Sport and had not flown out with the team as the *Observer* did not require pictures from the tour until the following weekend. None of the *Observer's* news photographers was able to obtain a visa from India House quickly enough to cover the immediate aftermath of the assassination, but I already had a visa. I was therefore sent on the earliest available flight to cover my first news story – in Delhi.

I arrived at Delhi airport at 1 am to find a strict curfew in force, but after bribing a maintenance-truck driver to get me through various check-points I was finally delivered to the hotel. It was full (fifteen TV crews had taken it over) and surrounded by security guards. More bribes, however, gained me access and I spent the night – in fact the next week – on the floor of Peter Smith's (cricket correspondent for the *Daily Mail*) hotel room.

The picture on this page shows Margaret Thatcher, who had herself survived a bomb attack in Brighton only nineteen days before the assassination, paying her last respects to Indira Gandhi. The photograph was wired from Associated Press (the film having been processed in a plastic bucket!) Back at the *Observer* the airconditioning unit was blacked out, throwing the two women's faces into sombre highlight.

The picture might have fetched up to £10,000 on the open market as a world exclusive had I been working as a freelance. As it was I was under contract – so I

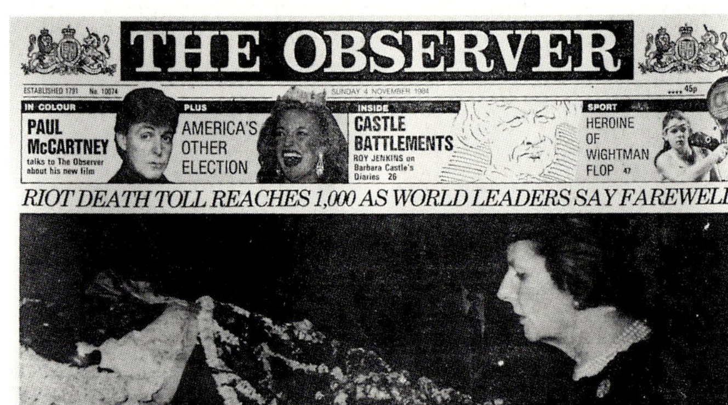

THE OBSERVER

ESTABLISHED 1791 No. 10074 SUNDAY 4 NOVEMBER 1984 45p

IN COLOUR PAUL McCARTNEY talks to The Observer about his new film

PLUS AMERICA'S OTHER ELECTION

INSIDE CASTLE BATTLEMENTS ROY JENKINS on Barbara Castle's Diaries 26

SPORT HEROINE OF WIGHTMAN FLOP 47

RIOT DEATH TOLL REACHES 1,000 AS WORLD LEADERS SAY FAREWELL

Delhi, 4th November 1984

received my normal fee, plus a small bonus.
It was in India six years earlier that my career had really got off the ground. At twenty-one years old, covering a cricket tour was a big deal in my life. I had arrived in Delhi with £250 lent to me by my parents, so I stayed in 50p-a-night hotels and Salvation Army hostels throughout India. On Christmas Eve, my first Christmas away from home and alone, I arrived in Calcutta from Delhi to find all the good (50p-a-night) hotels full, and the place I finally stayed at (25p-a-night) was disgusting. Still, there were many compensations. I saw England, under the captaincy of Tony Greig, take a series in India – the first time that this had happened since the 1933/34 tour under Jardine – and (thanks to John Lever) I got my first exclusive.
It was not much of a story really – more of a storm in an Indian teacup – but with temperatures in the low hundreds, as they were in Madras, silly things happen. It was because of this heat that John Lever had tied a gauze strip round his forehead to stop the sweat from running into his eyes. The Indians claimed that it was vaseline impregnated and that he rubbed grease onto the new ball to bring extra shine and thus increase the swing. As I said, it was not much, but it was all mine – or at least the picture was – and I was proud of it!
Another player who has been lucky for me – consistently so – is, of course, Ian Botham. However, despite the soft spot I have always had for him, friendship and professional integrity have to retain a precarious balance. On the 1984 tour to New Zealand and Pakistan, there was the inevitable Botham story. This time – as has so frequently been the case – about drugs. I could not simply ignore it. Knowing that the scandal was about to break (Botham knew it too), I took what I hoped was a sympathetic picture of him on the field of play, looking depressed. The other picture shown here was taken three years previously in Guyana as a stock picture, for much the same reasons. That is to say, it shows a thoughtful Botham, the picture to be used should the need – or the story – arise.

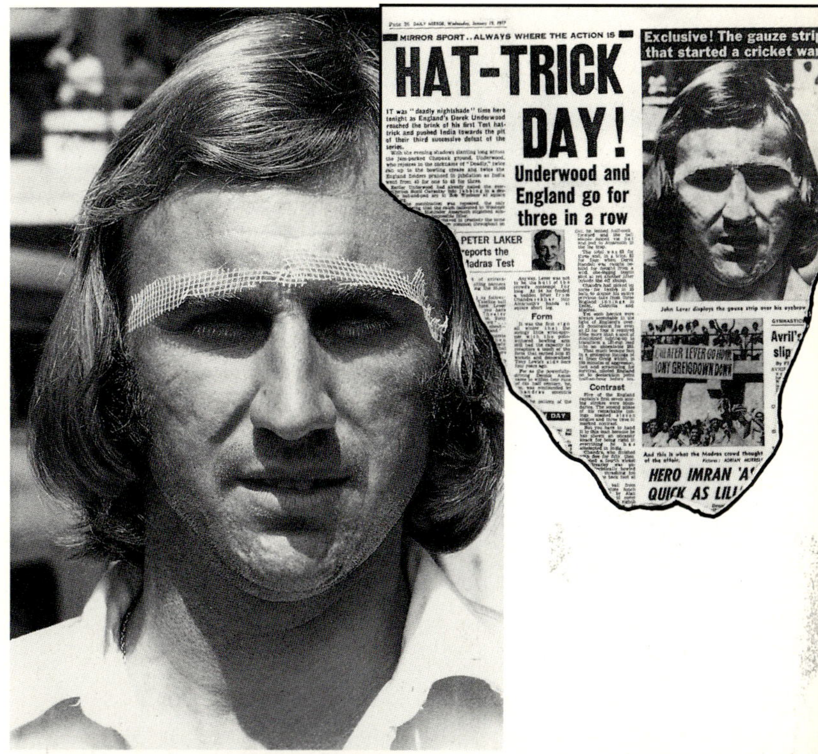

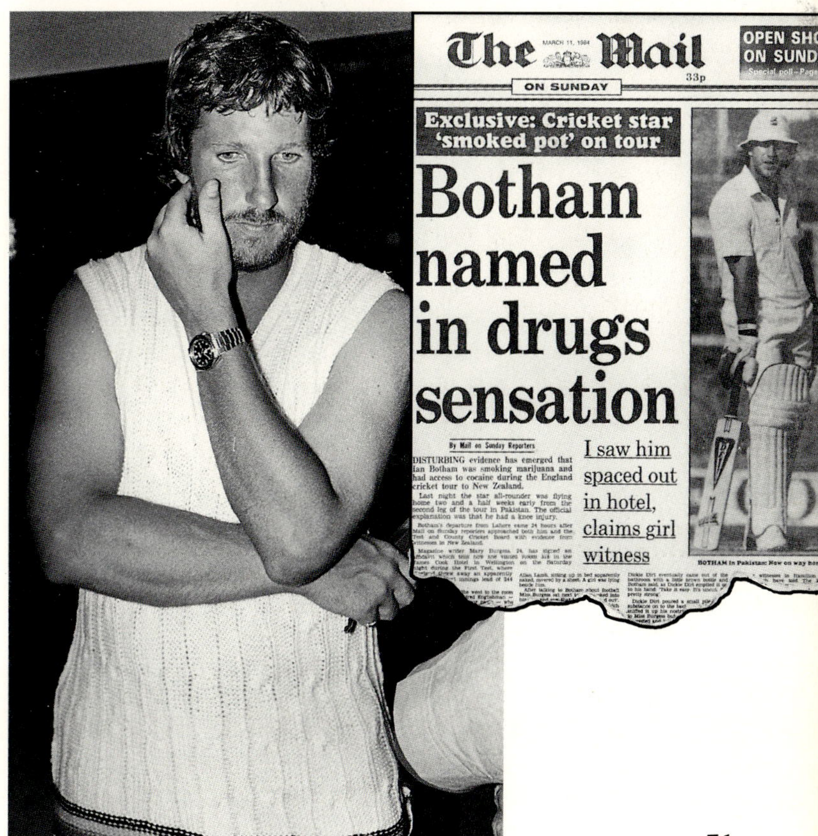

Botham thoughtful and Botham depressed –
left: *Georgetown, Guyana, January 1981*
right: *Pakistan, March 1984*

above: *John Lever, Madras, January 1977*

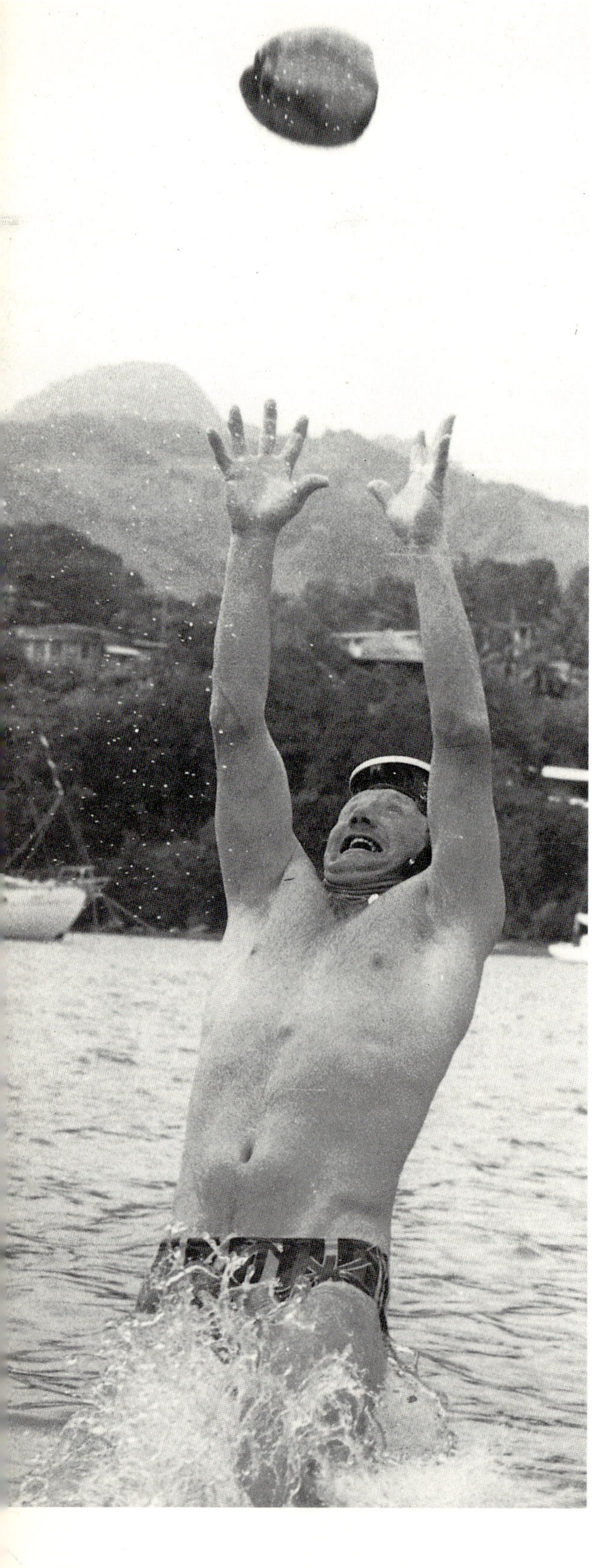
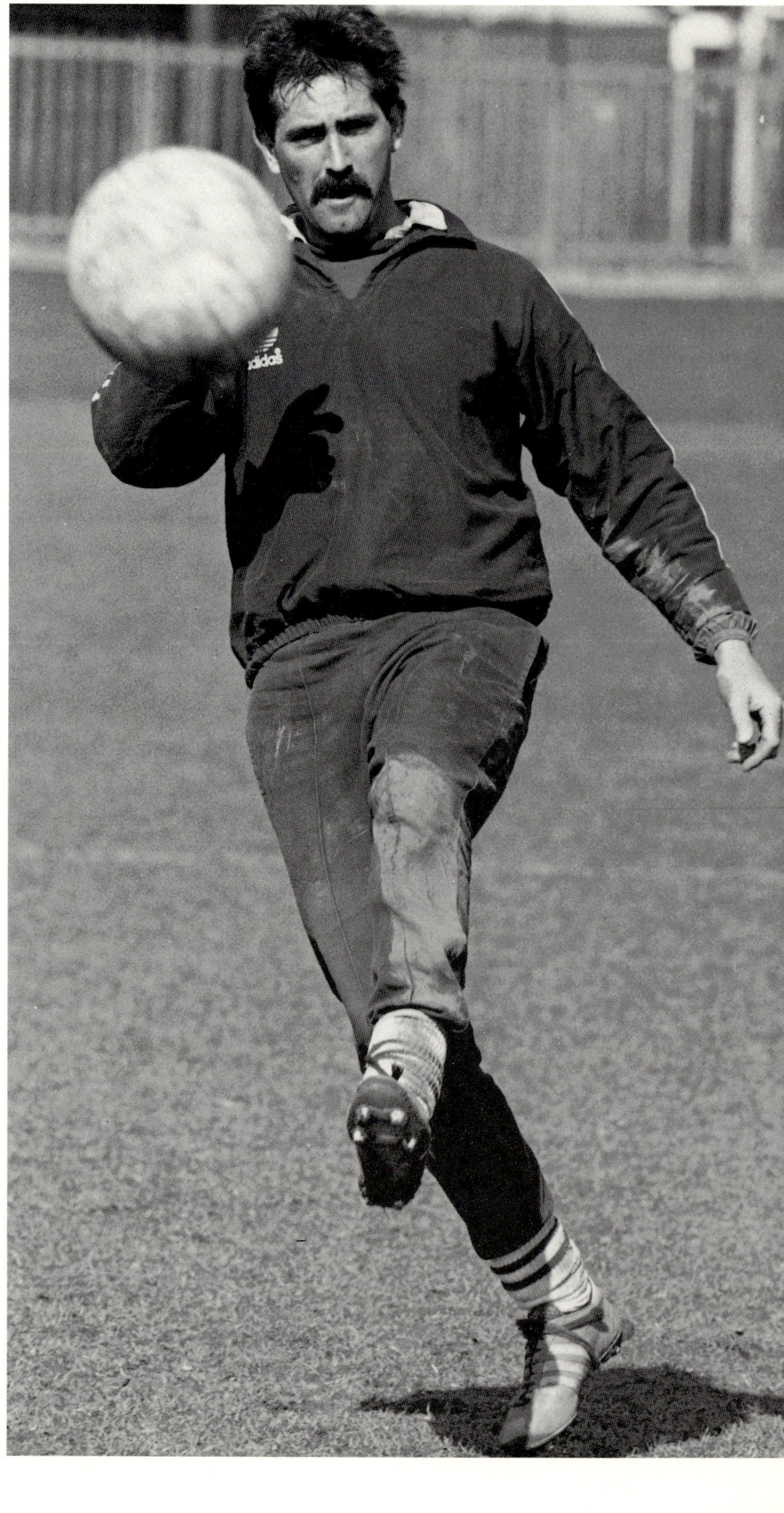

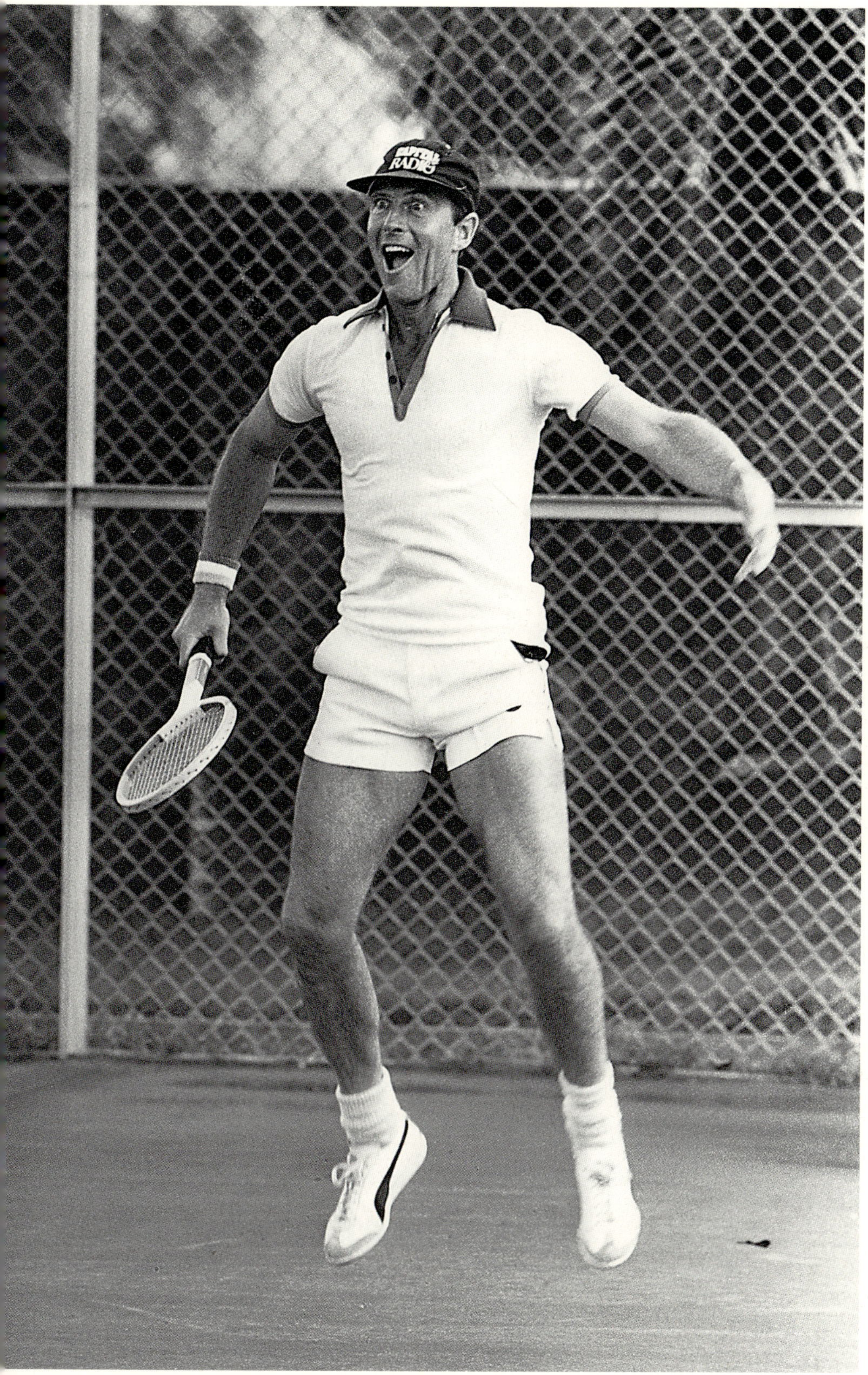

Tours take place in the depth of the English winter, so when the papers print a picture – say of Bairstow in the sea tossing a coconut – it catches the attention of the fogbound fan or the office-bound commuter. And that's what newspapers are about, catching the reader's attention.

Geoffrey Boycott (he cannot be serious), Georgetown, Guyana, February 1981

below: *John Emburey, Royal Golf Course, Calcutta, January 1981*

opposite, left: *David Bairstow, St Vincent, January 1981*

opposite, right: *Graham Gooch, not on tour but with West Ham, March 1985*

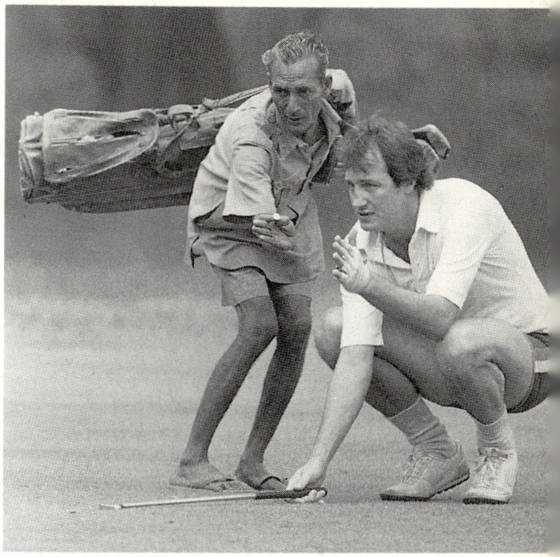

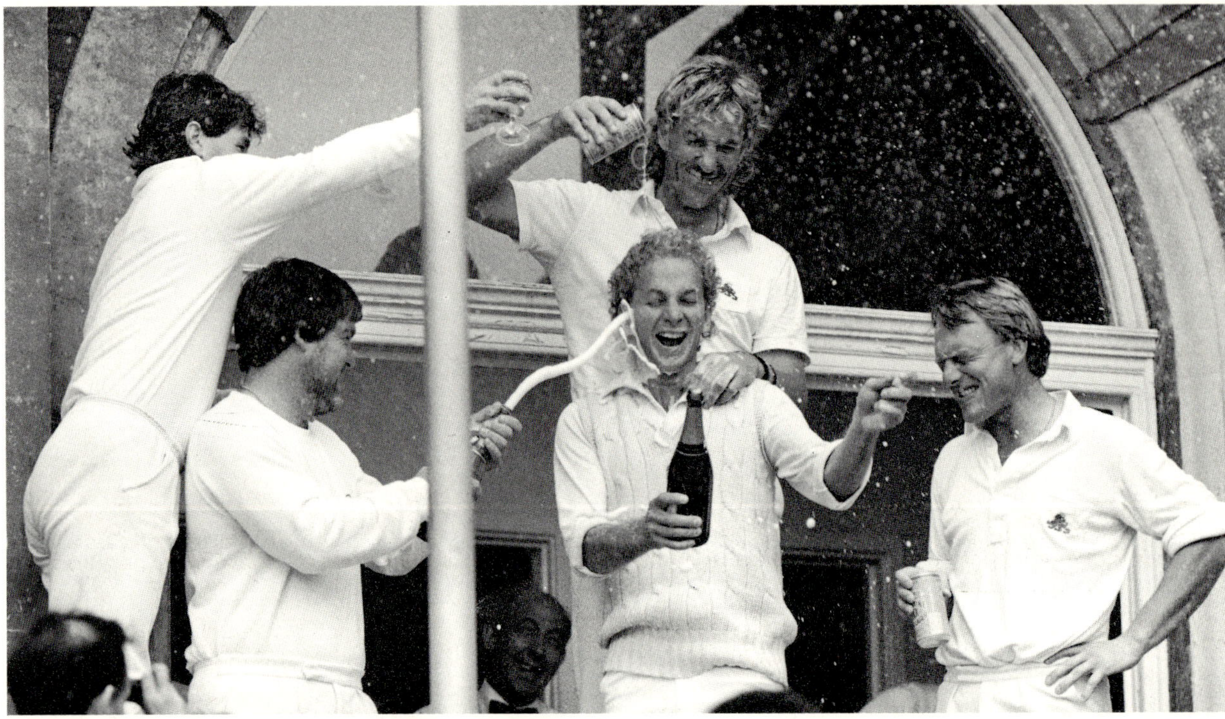

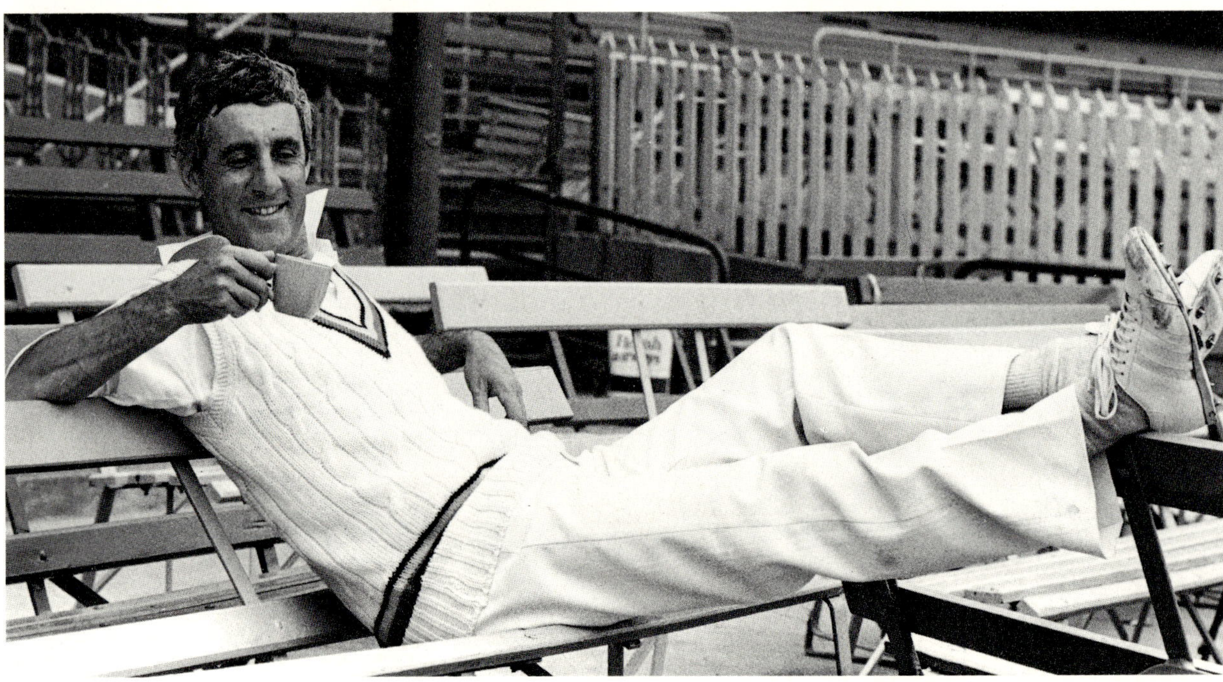

Captaining England has not always been a happy experience for David Gower (see page 121), but the summer of '85 at least ended in a blaze of glory, and the relaxed satisfaction of Mike Brearley (above) is also evocative of the best of cricket.

In fact, like fooling in the sea or unwinding playing tennis, celebrating in all its forms is yet another aspect of cricket and cricketers – that is, when there is anything to celebrate.

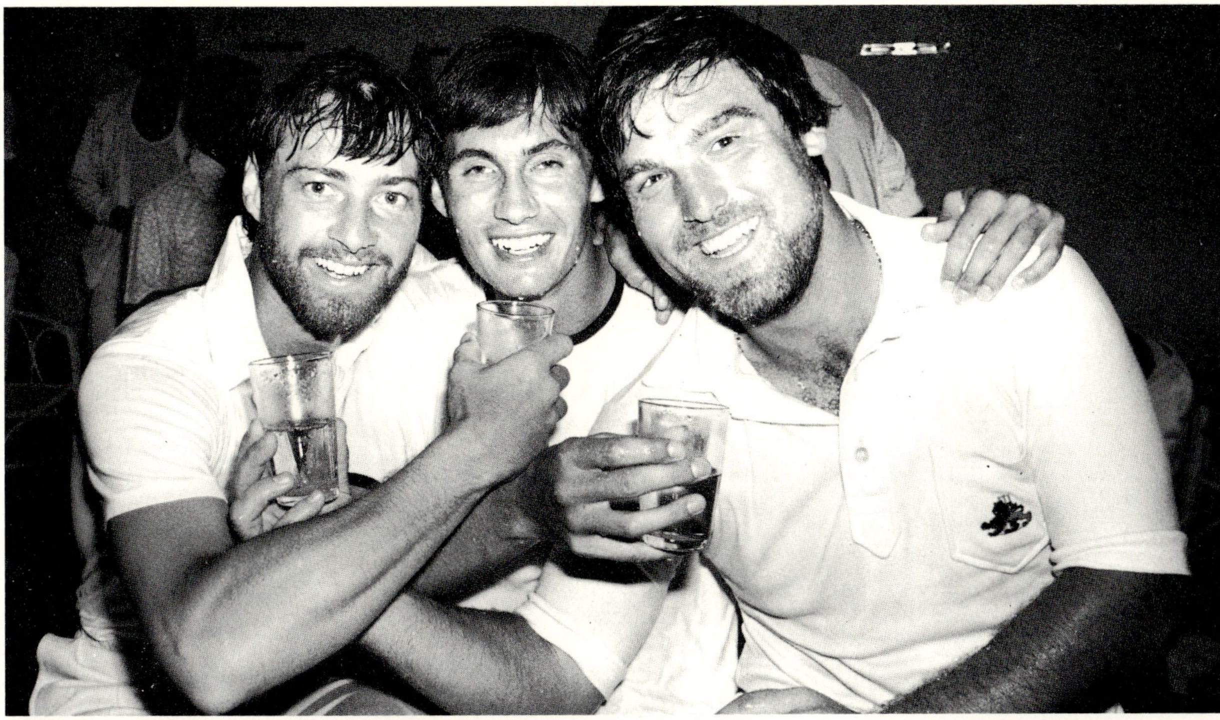

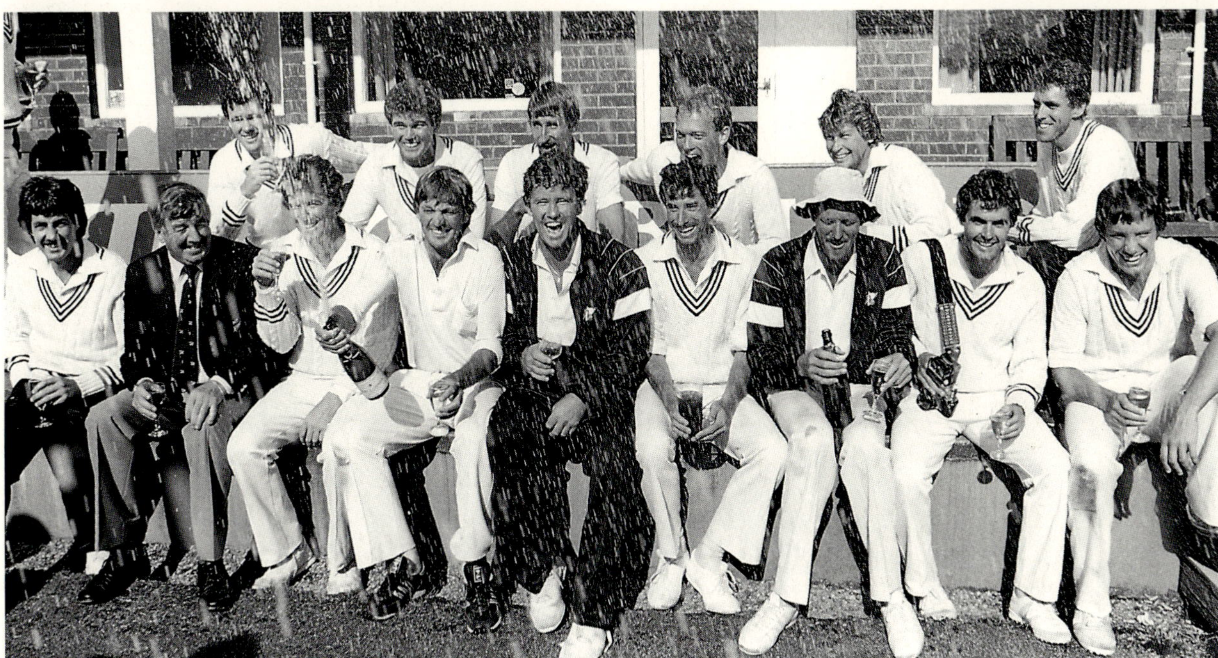

New Zealand celebrate their first win in England, second Test, Headingley, August 1983
above: *'Foxy' Fowler, 'Fast man' Foster and 'Fat-Gat' share a drink after coming back from one down to take the series 2–1 against India, Kanpur, February 1985*

opposite, above: *Gower celebrates the return of the Ashes at the Oval, September 1985*

opposite, below: *Mike Brearley looking pleased with himself after winning the Ashes series in Australia, February 1979*

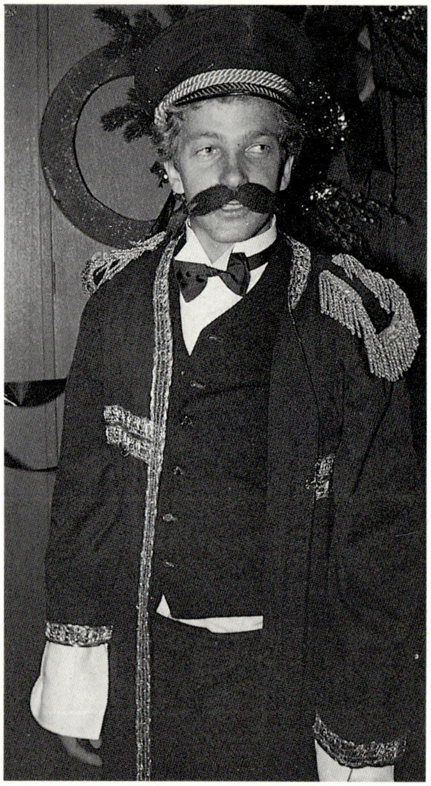

David Gower, Melbourne, 1978

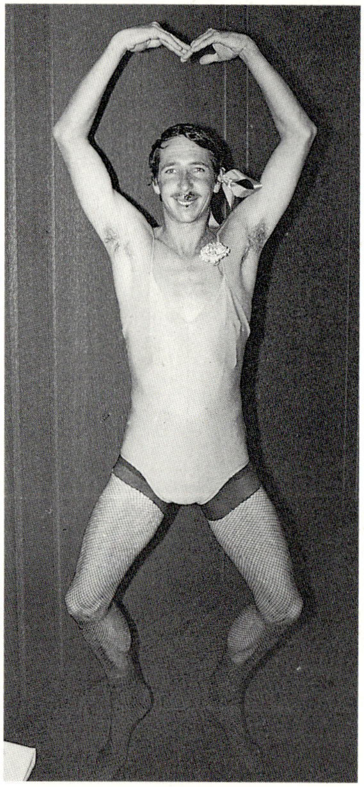

Derek Randall, Melbourne, 1982

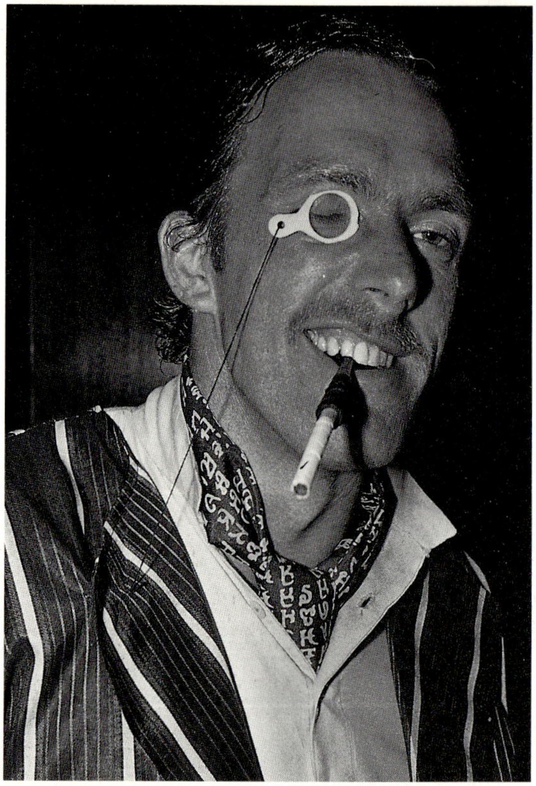

Geoff Cook, Delhi, 1981

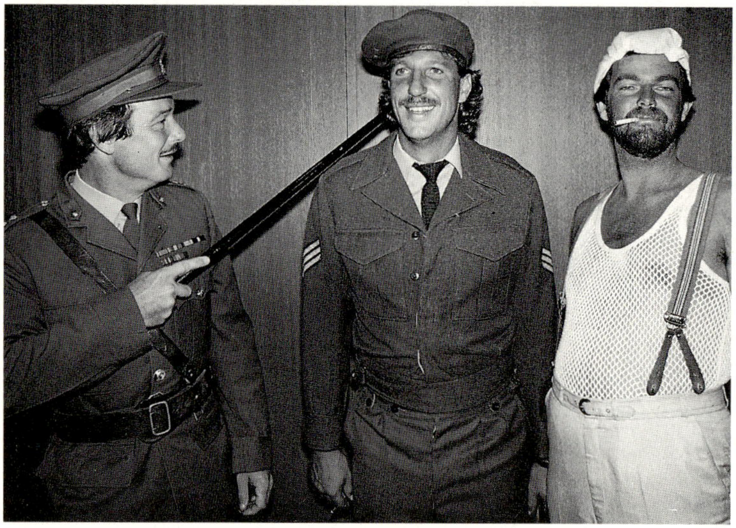

Jackman, Botham and Miller, Melbourne, 1982

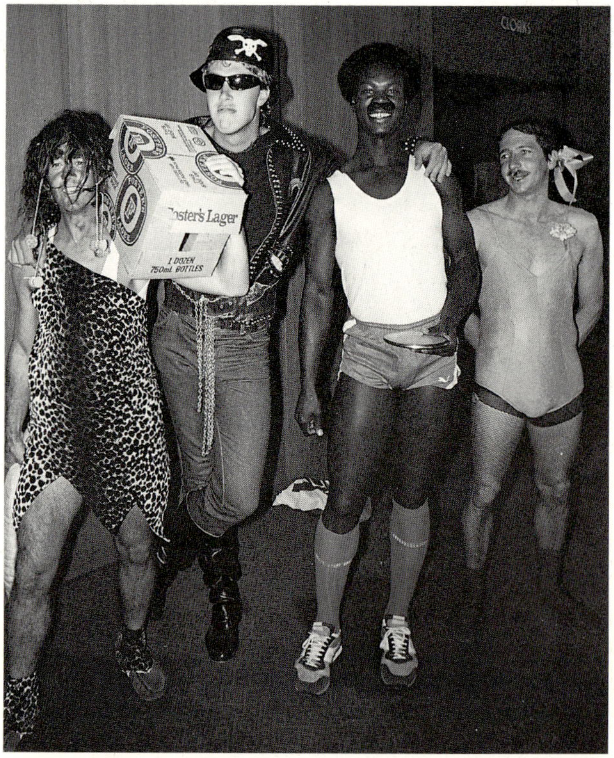

Taylor, Pringle, Cowans, Randall, Melbourne, 1982

The Christmas party on tour has become a special occasion for the England players. It gives them a chance to show off their alter egos.

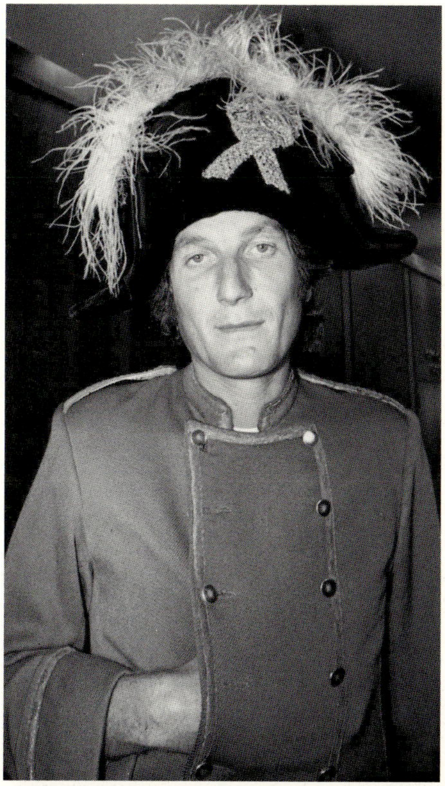

Captain Bob Willis, Melbourne, 1982

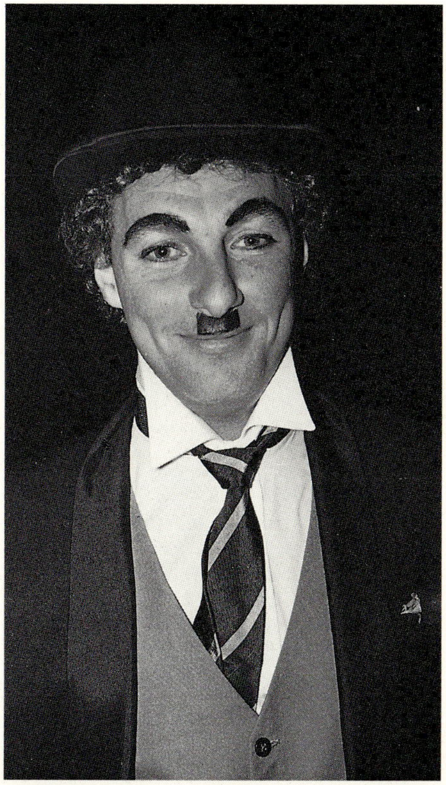

Jack Richards, Delhi, 1981

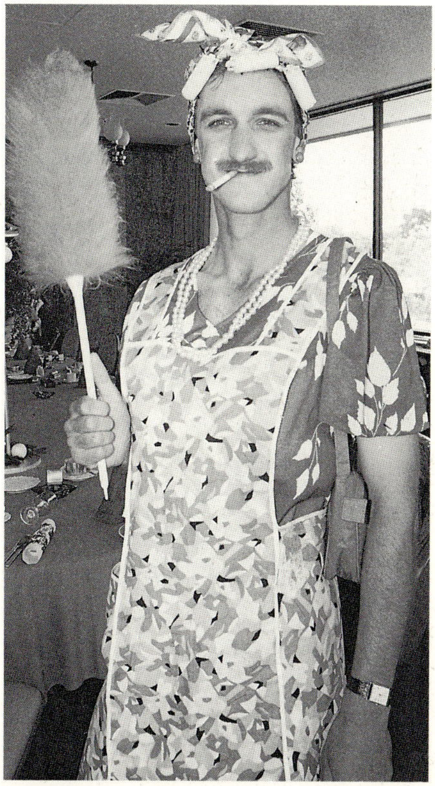

Chris Tavare, Delhi, 1981

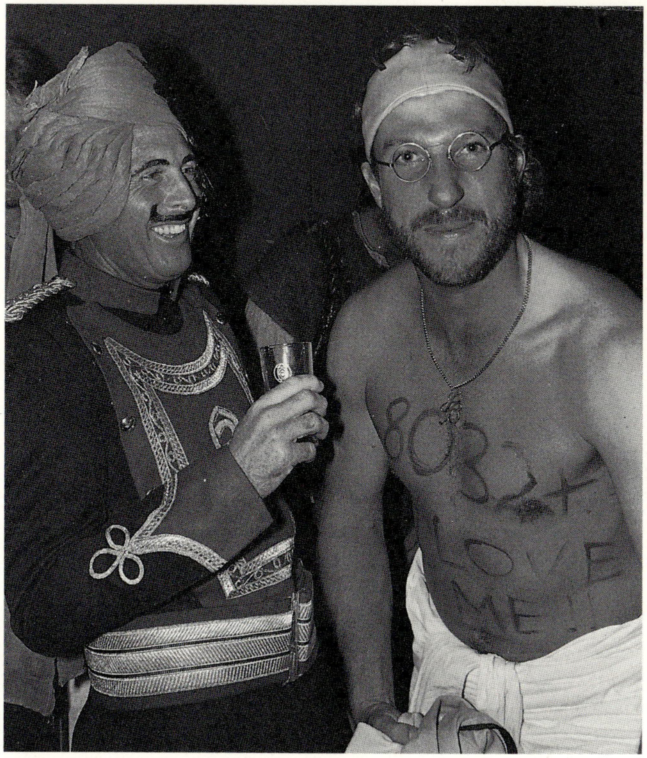

Boycott and Botham, Delhi, 1981

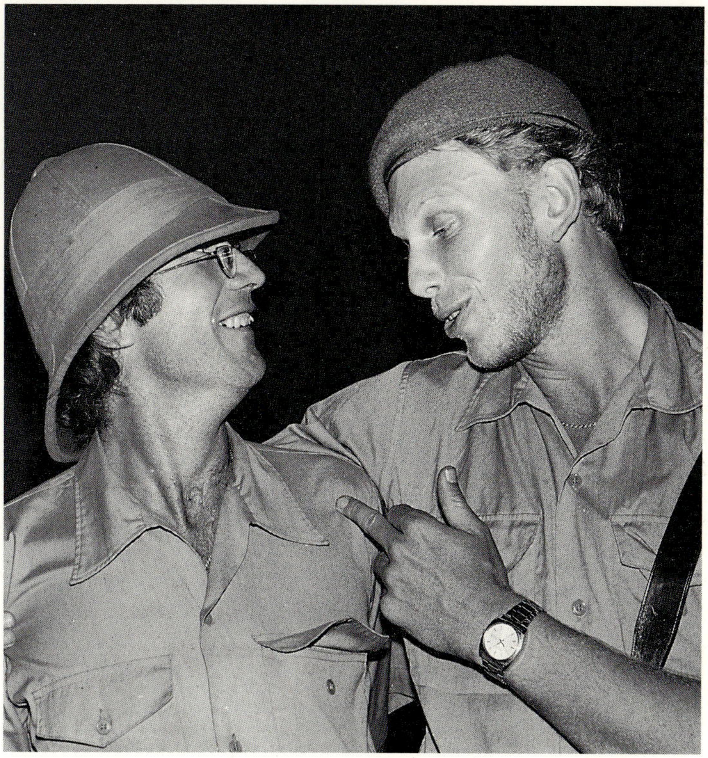

Keith Fletcher and Graham Dilley, Delhi, 1981

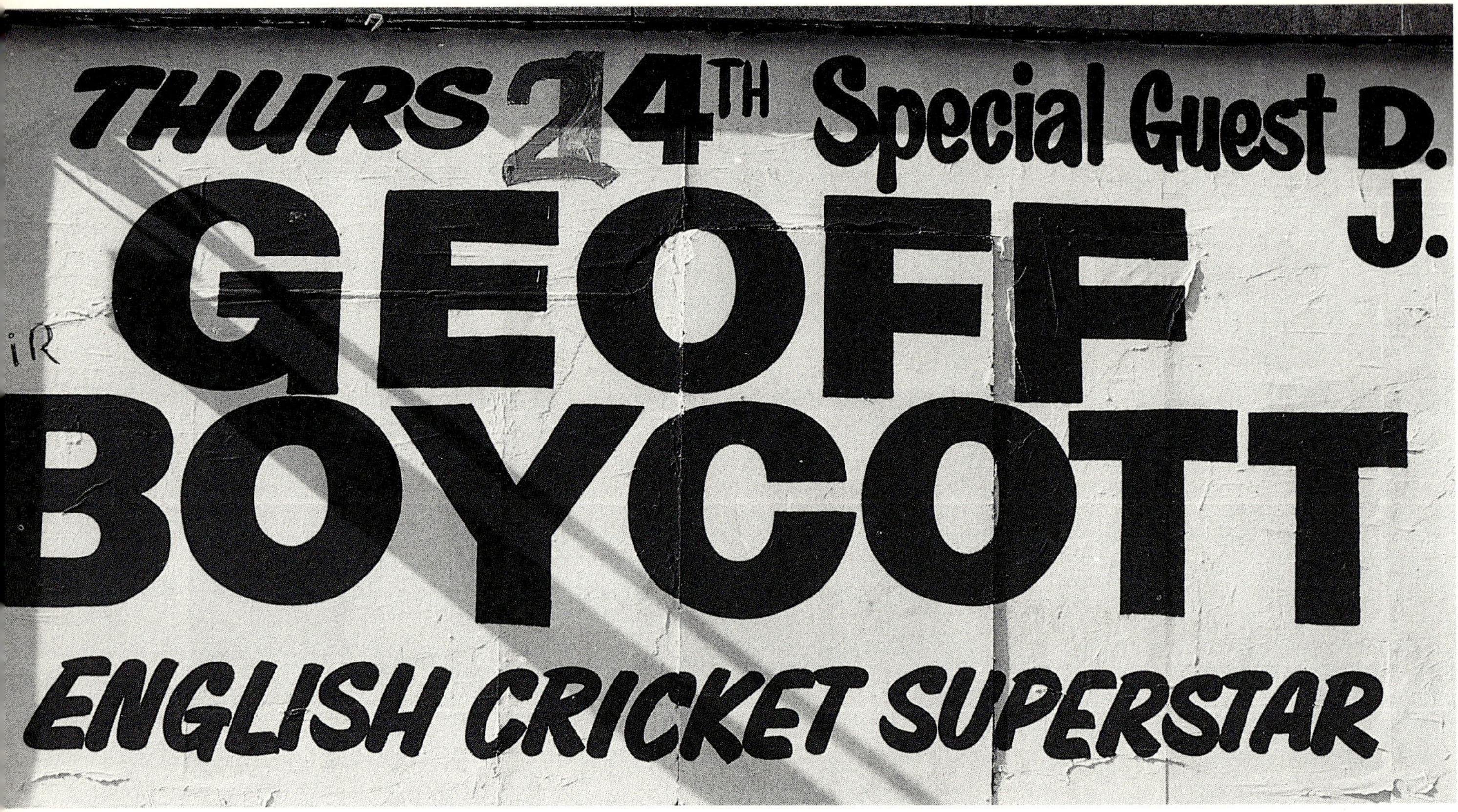

Boycott the DJ, Sydney, January 1980

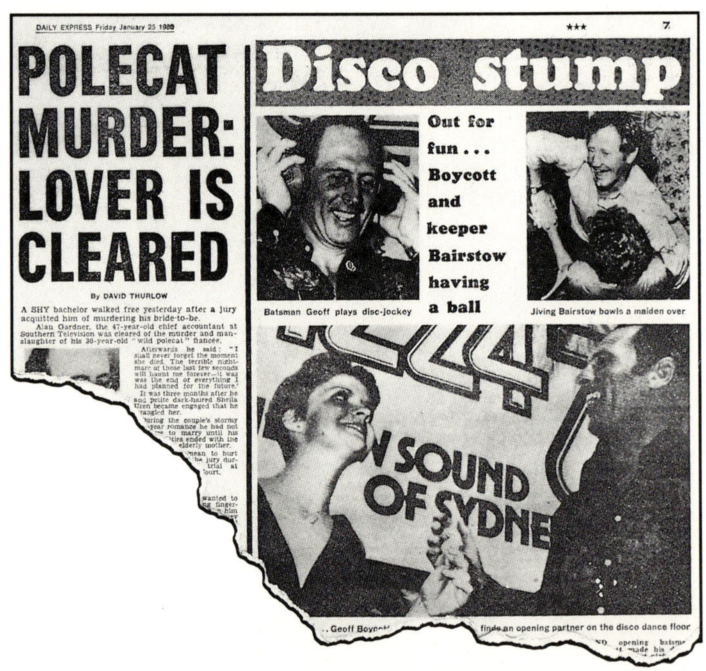

DAILY EXPRESS Friday January 25 1980 ★★★ 7

POLECAT MURDER: LOVER IS CLEARED

By DAVID THURLOW

A SHY bachelor walked free yesterday after a jury acquitted him of murdering his bride-to-be.

Alan Gardner, the 47-year-old chief accountant at Southern Television was cleared of the murder and manslaughter of his 30-year-old "wild polecat" fiancée.

Afterwards he said: "I shall never forget the moment she died. The terrible nightmare of those last few seconds will haunt me forever—it was was the end of everything I had planned for the future."

It was three months after he and petite dark-haired Sheila Uren became engaged that he ...rangled her.

...uring the couple's stormy ...year romance he had not ... to marry until his ...ties ended with the ... elderly mother.

...

Disco stump

Out for fun . . . Boycott and keeper Bairstow having a ball

Batsman Geoff plays disc-jockey

Jiving Bairstow bowls a maiden over

. . Geoff Boy... finds an opening partner on the disco dance floor

Geoffrey Boycott has always been something of an enigma – certainly not a gregarious extrovert – but without question a successful opening bat. Indeed, he is totally dedicated to the art of batting, but he is not the type of man to sit around drinking after a game or a training session. This has always meant that when things go wrong he's apt to be on his own, not drawing strength or support from the rest of the team. The last man, in fact, you would expect to find as a DJ in a night club.

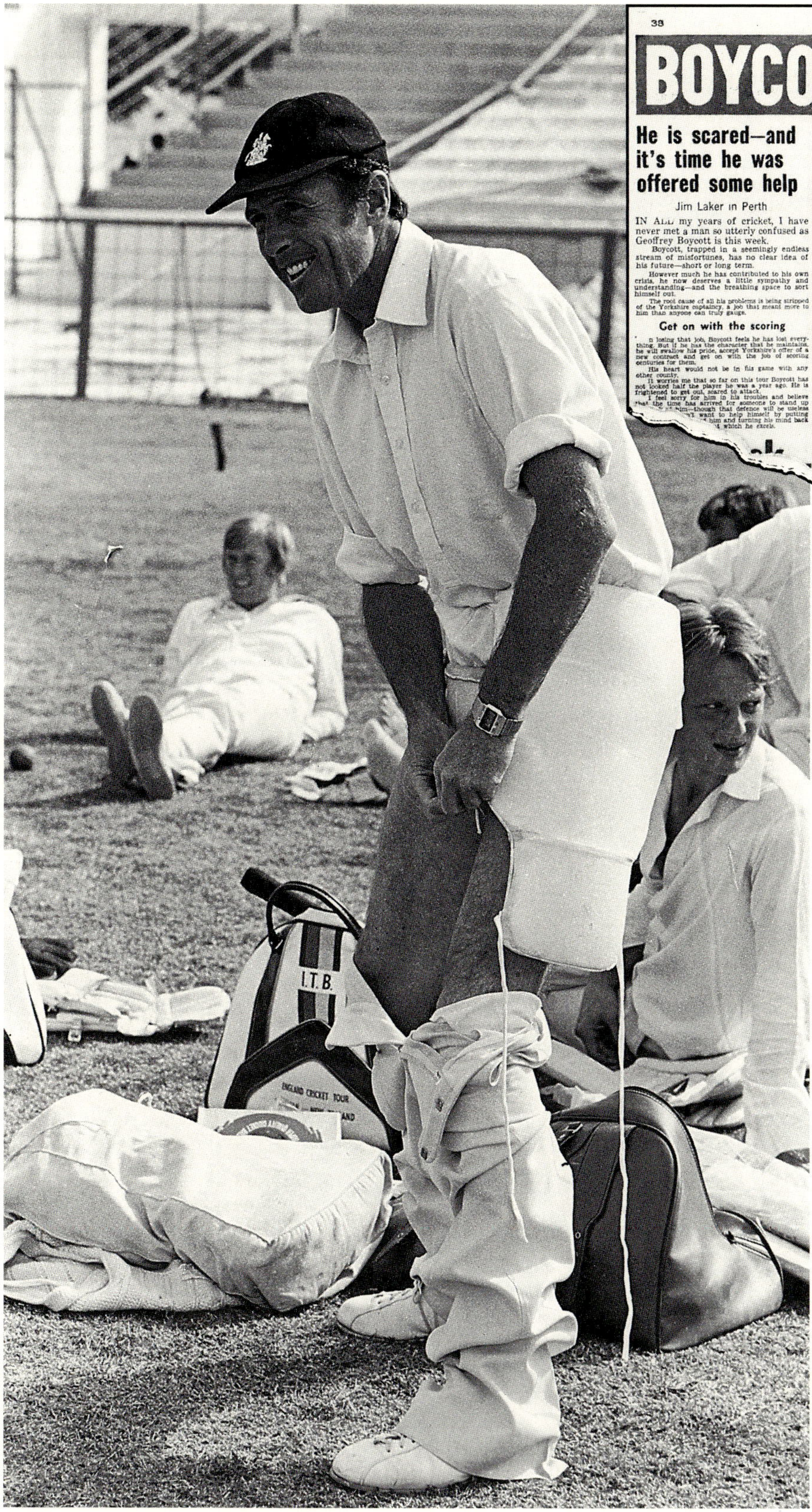

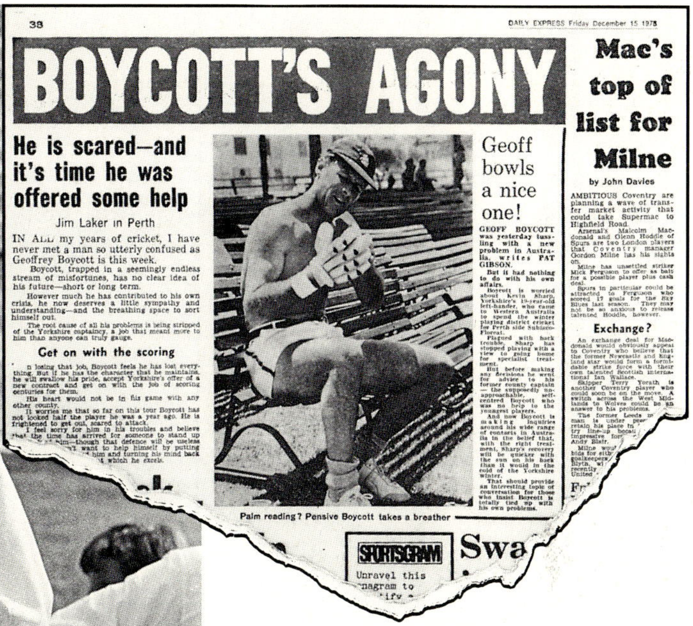

38 DAILY EXPRESS Friday December 15 1978

BOYCOTT'S AGONY

He is scared—and it's time he was offered some help

Jim Laker in Perth

IN ALL my years of cricket, I have never met a man so utterly confused as Geoffrey Boycott is this week.

Boycott, trapped in a seemingly endless stream of misfortunes, has no clear idea of his future—short or long term.

However much he has contributed to his own crisis, he now deserves a little sympathy and understanding—and the breathing space to sort himself out.

The root cause of all his problems is being stripped of the Yorkshire captaincy, a job that meant more to him than anyone can truly gauge.

Get on with the scoring

n losing that job, Boycott feels he has lost everything. But if he has the character that he maintains, he will swallow his pride, accept Yorkshire's offer of a new contract and get on with the job of scoring centuries for them.

His heart would not be in his game with any other county.

It worries me that so far on this tour Boycott has not looked half the player he was a year ago. He is frightened to get out, scared to attack.

I feel sorry for him in his troubles and believe that the time has arrived for someone to stand up ... him—though that defence will be useless ... want to help himself by putting ... him and turning his mind back ... which he excels.

Geoff bowls a nice one!

GEOFF BOYCOTT was yesterday tussling with a new problem in Australia, writes PAT GIBSON.

But it had nothing to do with his own affairs.

Boycott is worried about Kevin Sharp, Yorkshire's 19-year-old left-hander, who came to Western Australia to spend the winter playing district cricket for Perth side Subiaco-Floreat.

Plagued with back trouble, Sharp has stopped playing with a view to going home for specialist treatment.

But before making any decisions he went for advice to his former county captain — the supposedly unapproachable, self-centred Boycott who was no help to the youngest players.

And now Boycott is making inquiries around his wide range of contacts in Australia in the belief that, with the right treatment, Sharp's recovery will be quicker with the sun on his back than it would in the cold of the Yorkshire winter.

That should provide an interesting topic of conversation for those who insist Boycott is totally tied up with his own problems.

Palm reading? Pensive Boycott takes a breather

Mac's top of list for Milne

by John Davies

AMBITIOUS Coventry are planning a wave of transfer market activity that could take Supermac to Highfield Road.

Arsenal's Malcolm Macdonald and Glenn Hoddle of Spurs are two London players that Coventry manager Gordon Milne has his sights on.

Milne has unsettled striker Mick Ferguson to offer as bait for a possible player plus cash deal.

Spurs in particular could be attracted to Ferguson who scored 17 goals for the Sky Blues last season. They may not be so anxious to release talented Hoddle, however.

Exchange?

An exchange deal for Macdonald would obviously appeal to Coventry who believe that the former Newcastle and England star would form a formidable strike force with their own talented Scottish international Ian Wallace.

Skipper Terry Yorath is another Coventry player who could soon be on the move. A switch across the West Midlands to Wolves could be an answer to his problems.

The former Leeds ... man is under ... retain his place in ... try line-up becau... impressive for... Andy Blair.

Milne wou... bids for eith... goalkeepers ... Blyth, w... recently ... United ...

SPORTSGRAM Unravel this anagram to ...

Swa...

On 15 January 1978, in a minor match against a Sind XI in Karachi, Michael Brearley broke his arm. Geoffrey Boycott, as vice-captain, was the natural choice to replace him: England captain, more or less the peak of Boycott's ambition. Then, in September of that same year, Boycott's mother died, he lost the Yorkshire captaincy and he saw the position of vice-captain for the Australian tour go to Bob Willis. Finally, in Australia, his performance was disappointing. His batting had also suffered at the beginning of the year under the strain of the captaincy. In relation to this, Alex Bannister in *Wisden* (1979) makes the following rather pleasing comment: 'The obvious answer to any criticism of Boycott is to ask where England would have been without him.'

The beginning of a good year? – Karachi, January 1978

above: *The end of a bad year, Perth, December 1978*

Where do they come from? . . .

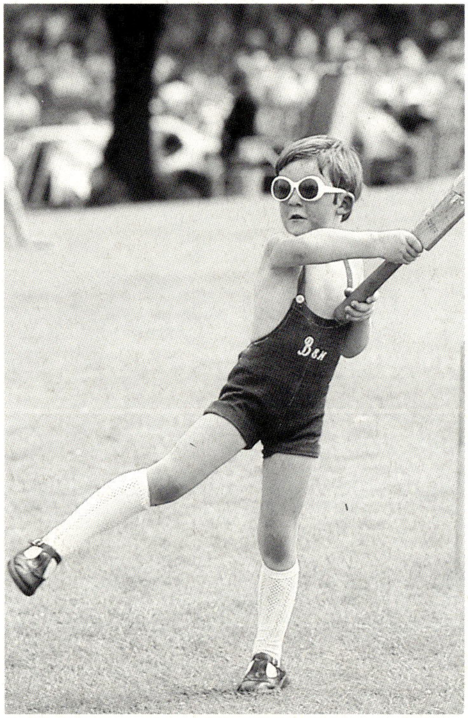

Hyde Park

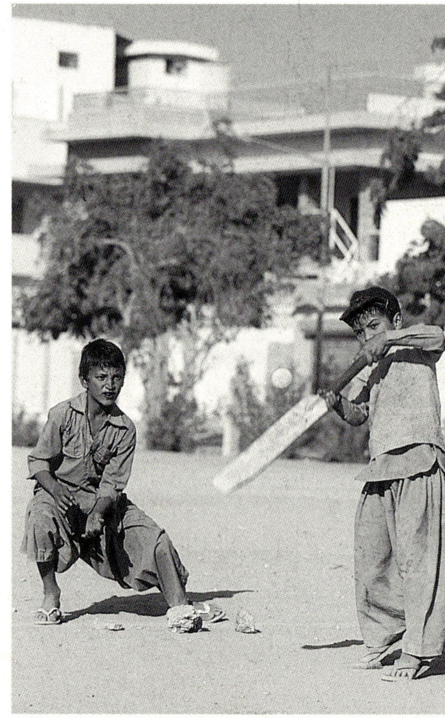

Karachi

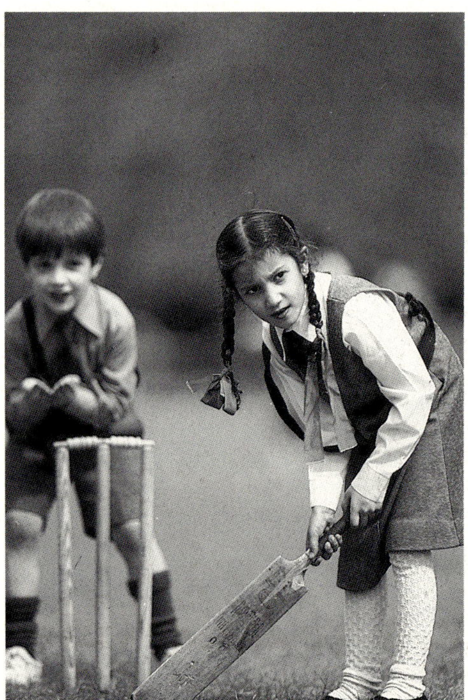

Chesterfield

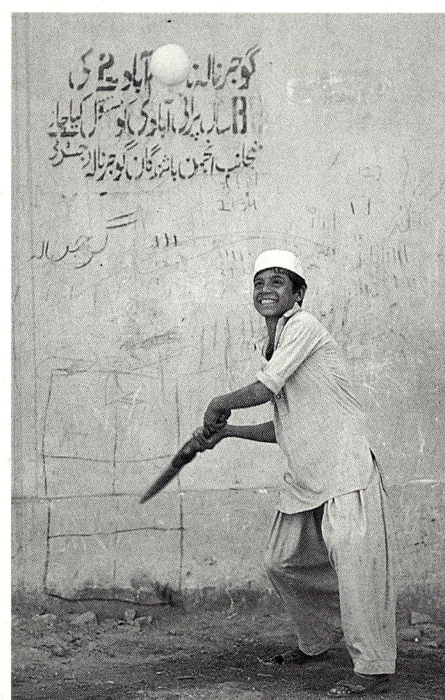

Lahore

. . . And where are they going? . . .

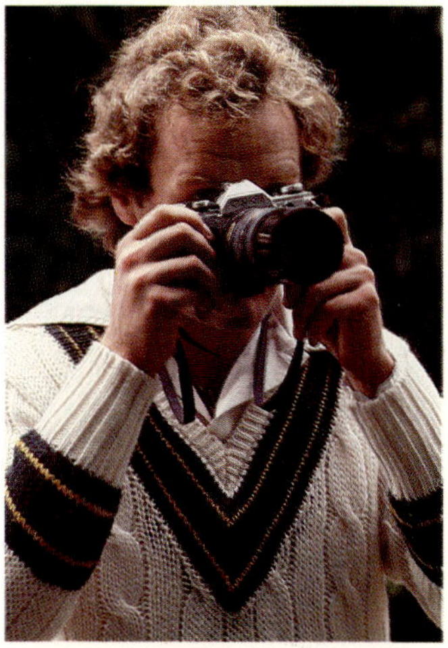

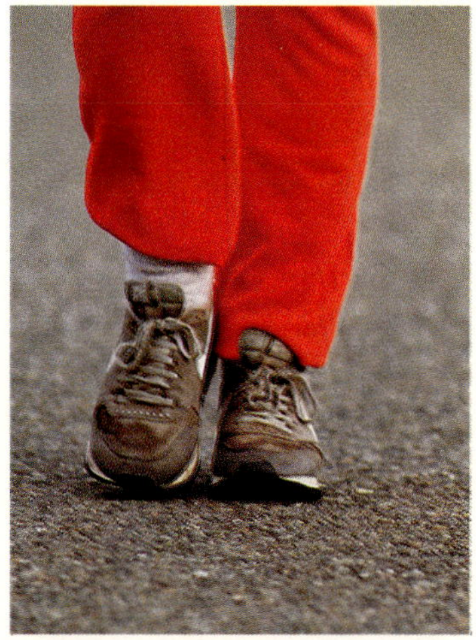

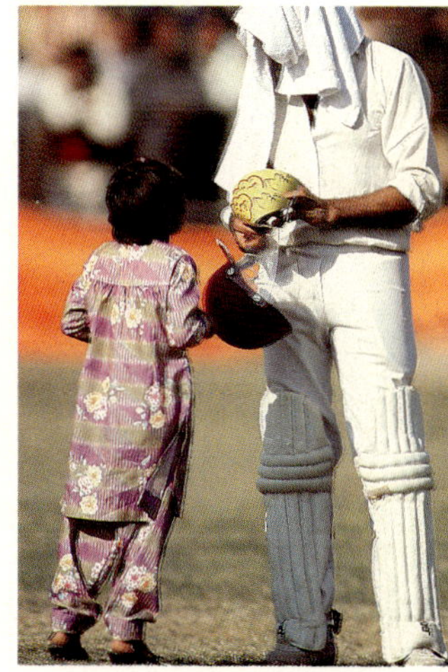

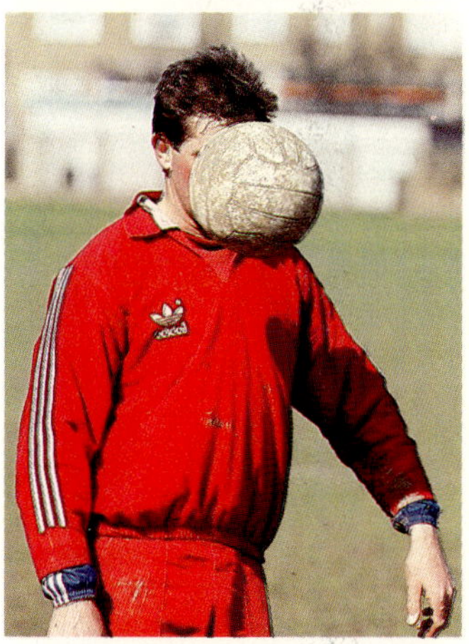

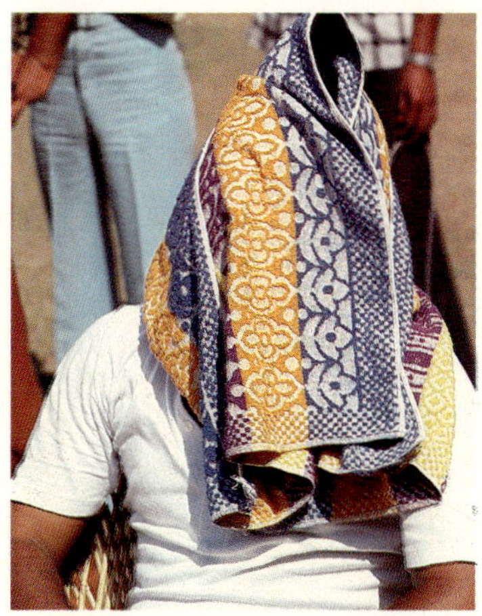

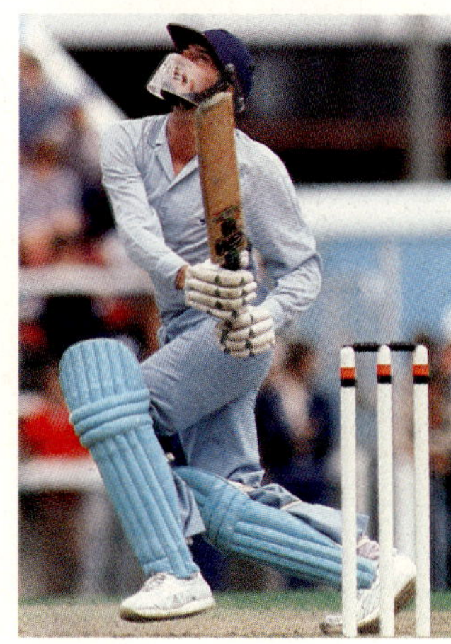

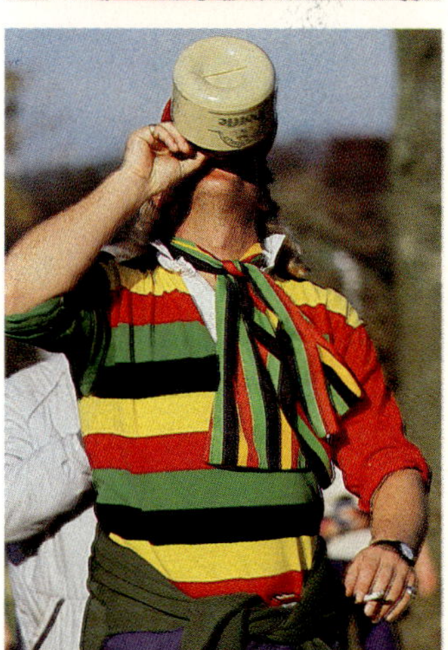

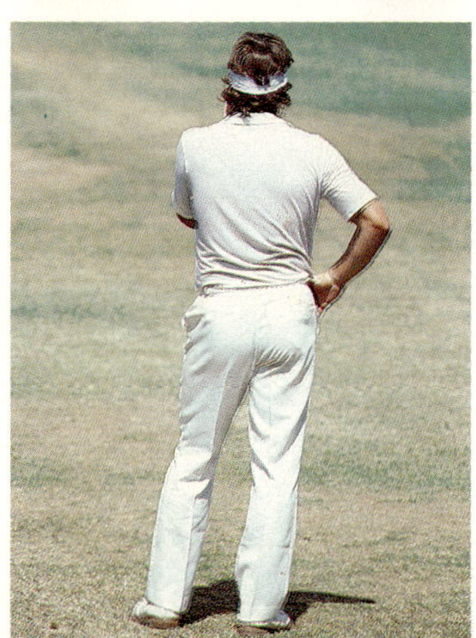

. . . I doubt if any of the children pictured opposite are headed for stardom (although I do admire the readiness of the earnest little wicketkeeper) so you'll never know their names. But if you haven't already identified the guy in the middle of this page with his head in a towel turn the book upside down.

top row, left to right: *Rodney Hogg, Ian Botham, Ashmat Rana* middle row, left to right: *Graham Gooch, Sunil Gavaskar, Derek Randall* bottom row, left to right: *Ian Botham, Ian Botham*

Graham Gooch, Courage International Batsman of the Year competition, the Oval, September 1979

below: *After scoring a century in the third Test against the West Indies, Barbados, March 1981*

opposite, left: *David Gower in the dressing room, Barbados, March 1981*

opposite, above: *Raising the Anthony Demelo Trophy after the Test series victory against India, fifth Test, Kanpur, January 1985*

opposite, middle: *Drinks break, the Oval, September 1985*

opposite, below: *Bangalore, January 1985*

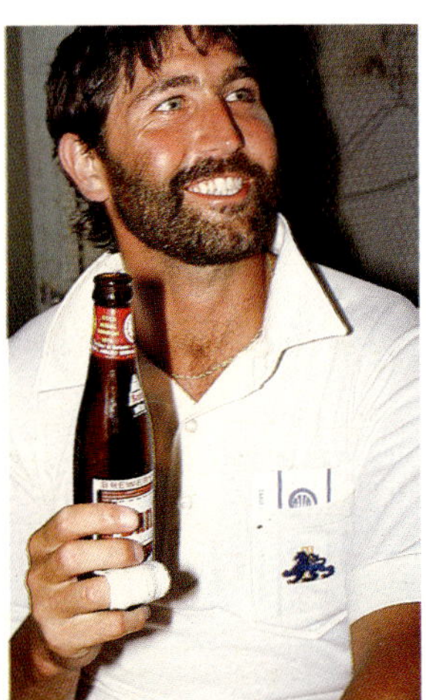

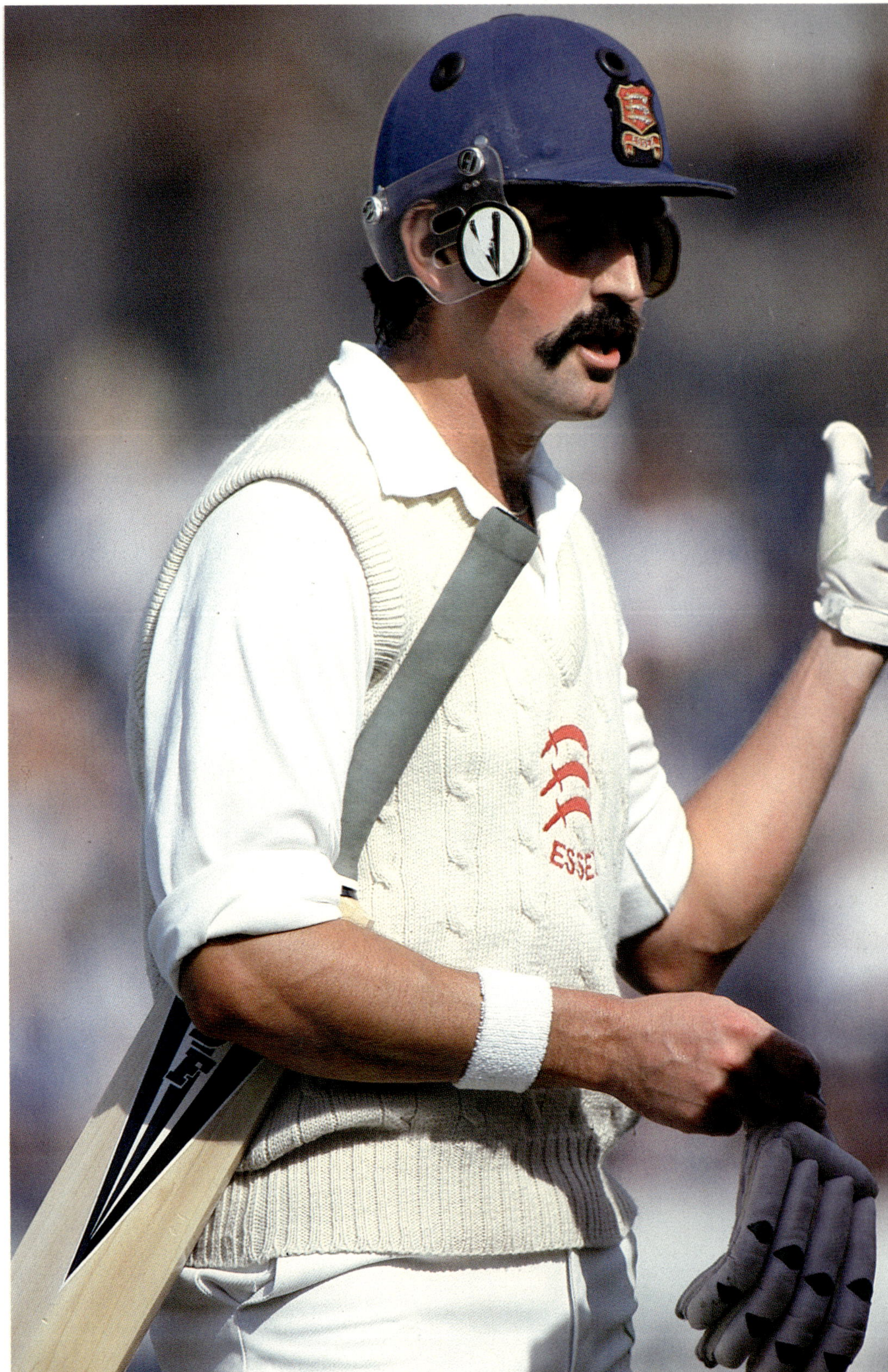

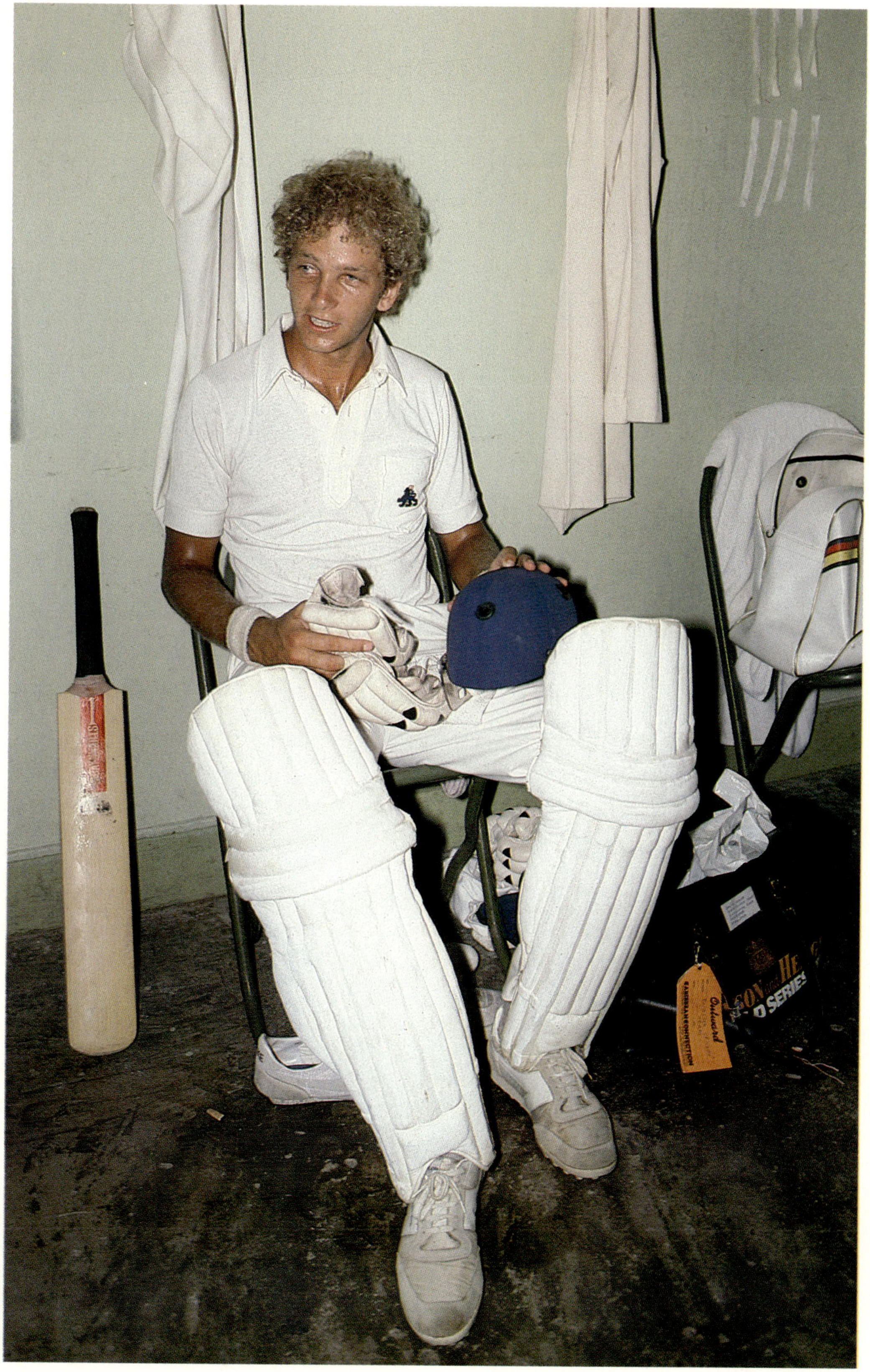

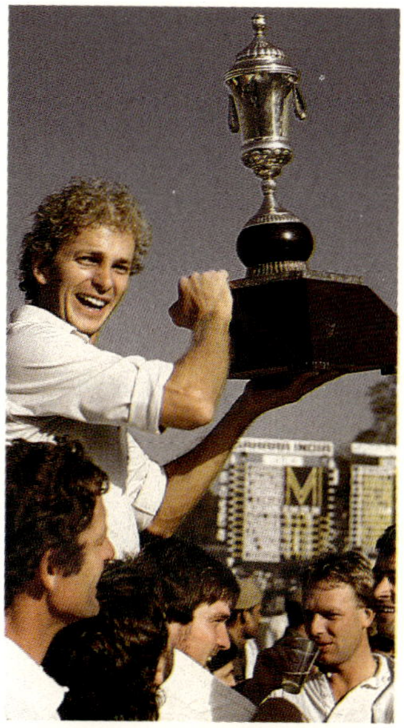

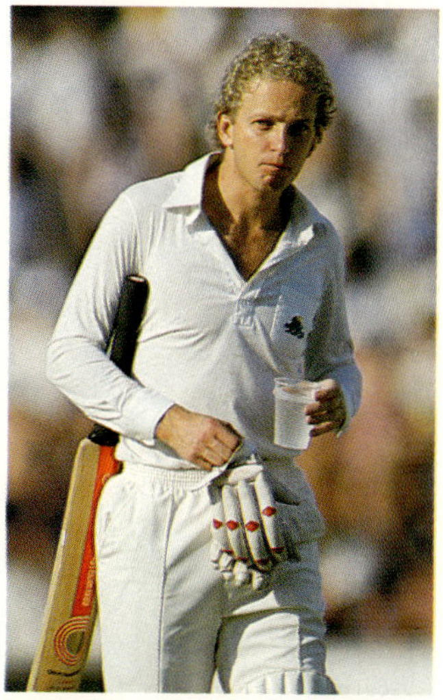

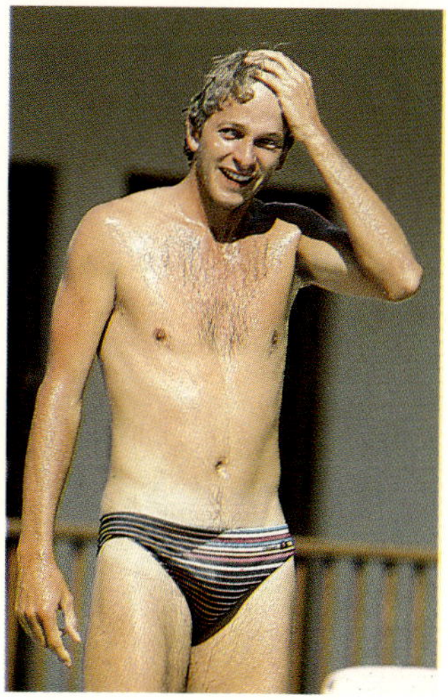

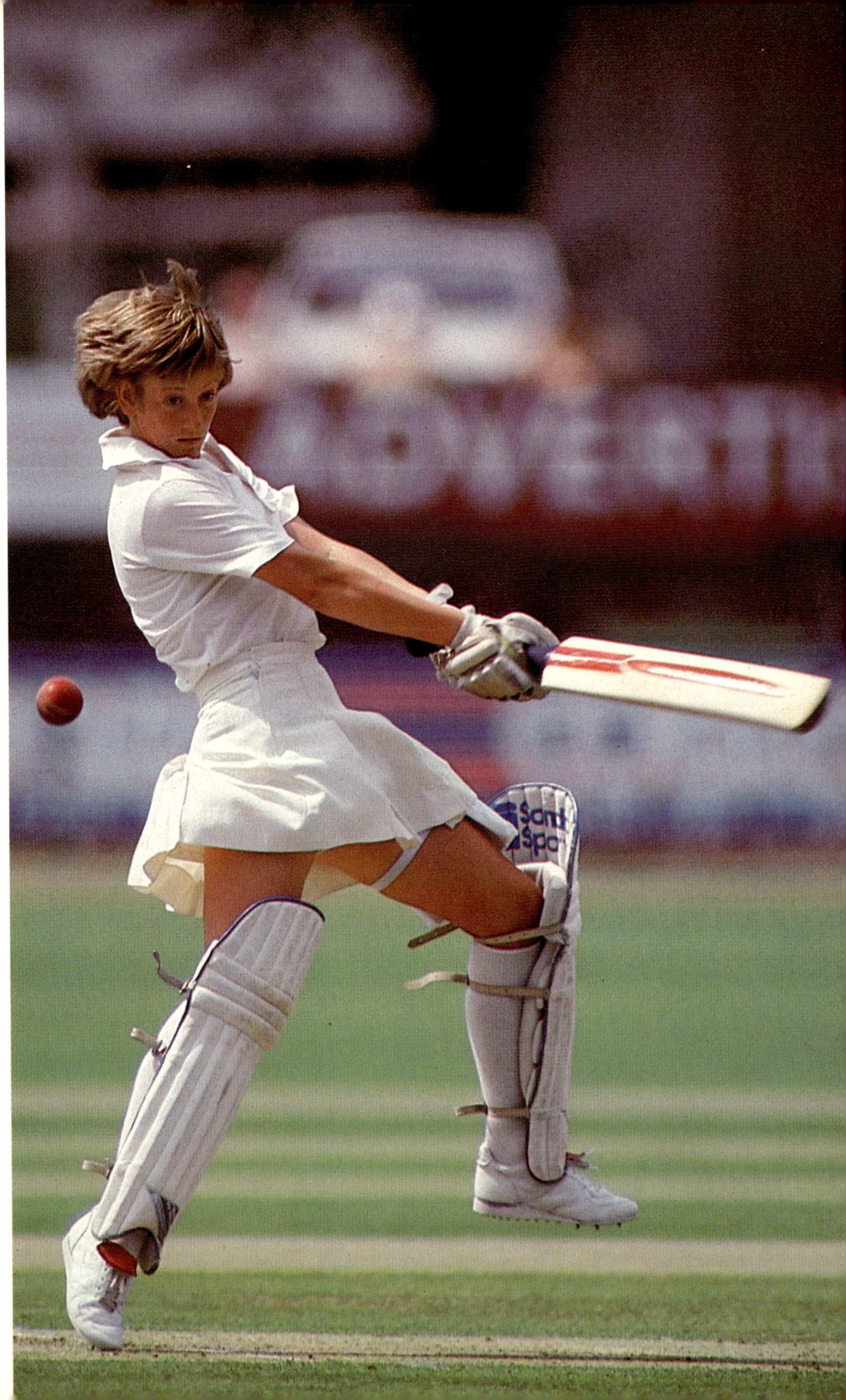

Jeannette Brittain, England and Surrey, third Test, England v New Zealand, Canterbury, July 1984

opposite: *Kapil Dev, Worcestershire and India, lets fly on one leg, Taunton, September 1984*

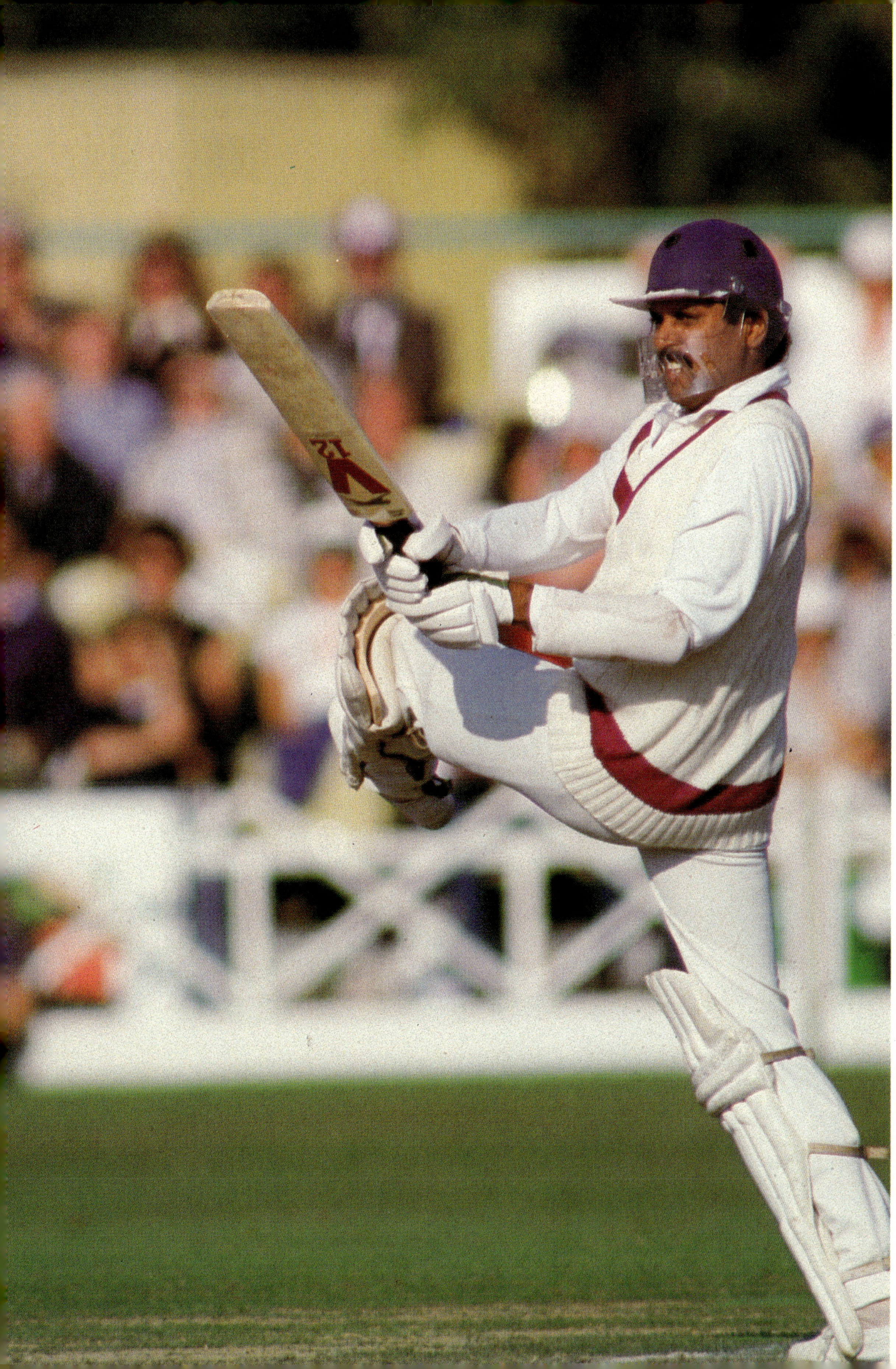

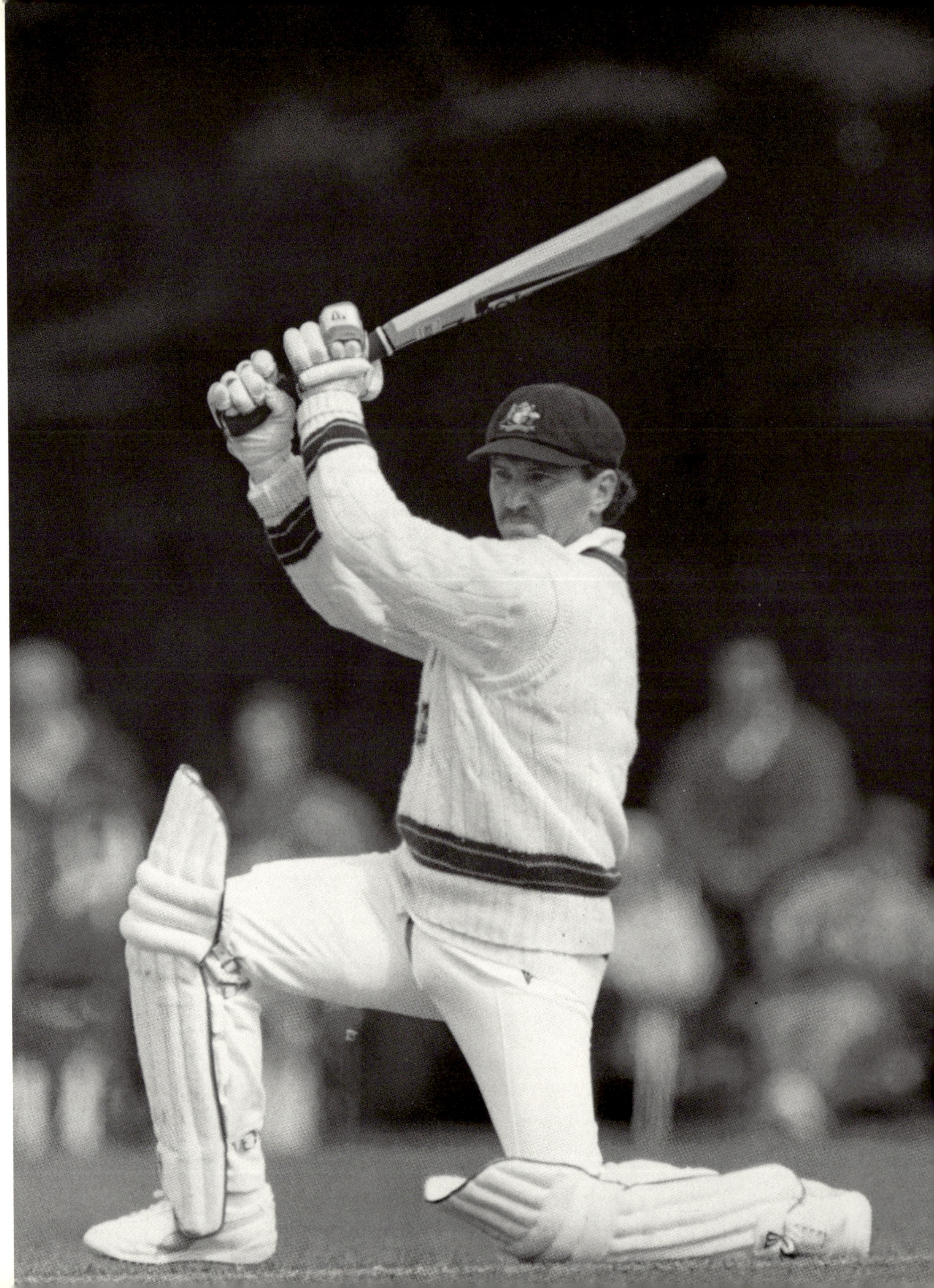

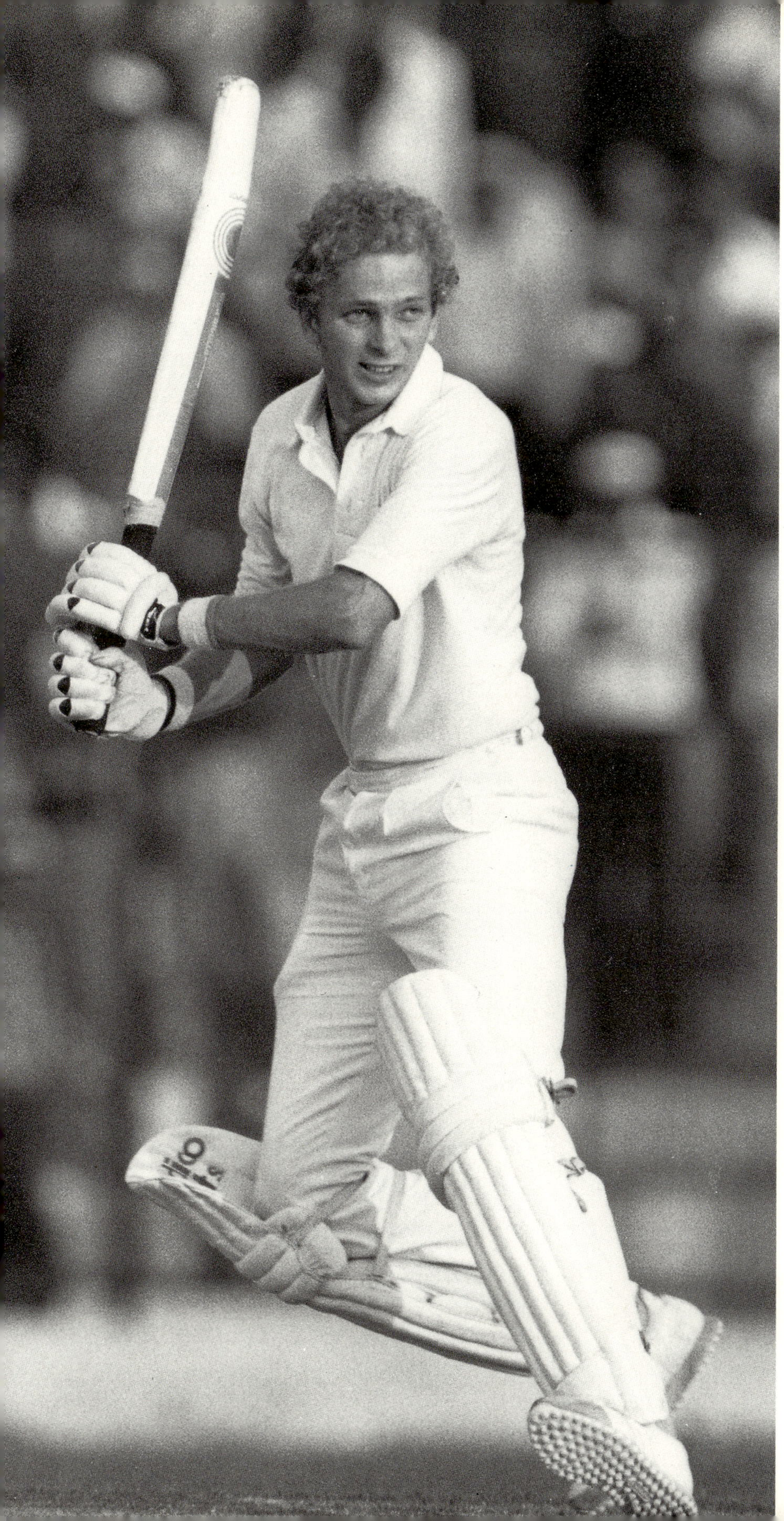

These few pages have been devoted to batsmen or, in the case of Jeannette Brittain (on page 84) – batsperson? She has been England's best batswoman over the past few years, and during the 1985 season averaged over 90. Unfortunately this is just about my only decent shot of her. This is not due to any male chauvinist piggery on my part, but simply because the women's Test matches clash with the men's and I can't be in two places at once.
This spread shows two of the greatest left-handers the world of cricket has ever seen, Allan Border and David Gower. The picture of Gower, because it shows perfect balance, is perhaps the best batting photograph I have yet taken of him.

David Gower, Lavinia, Duchess of Norfolk XI v Australia, Arundel, May 1985

opposite: *Allan Border, also at Arundel, May 1985*

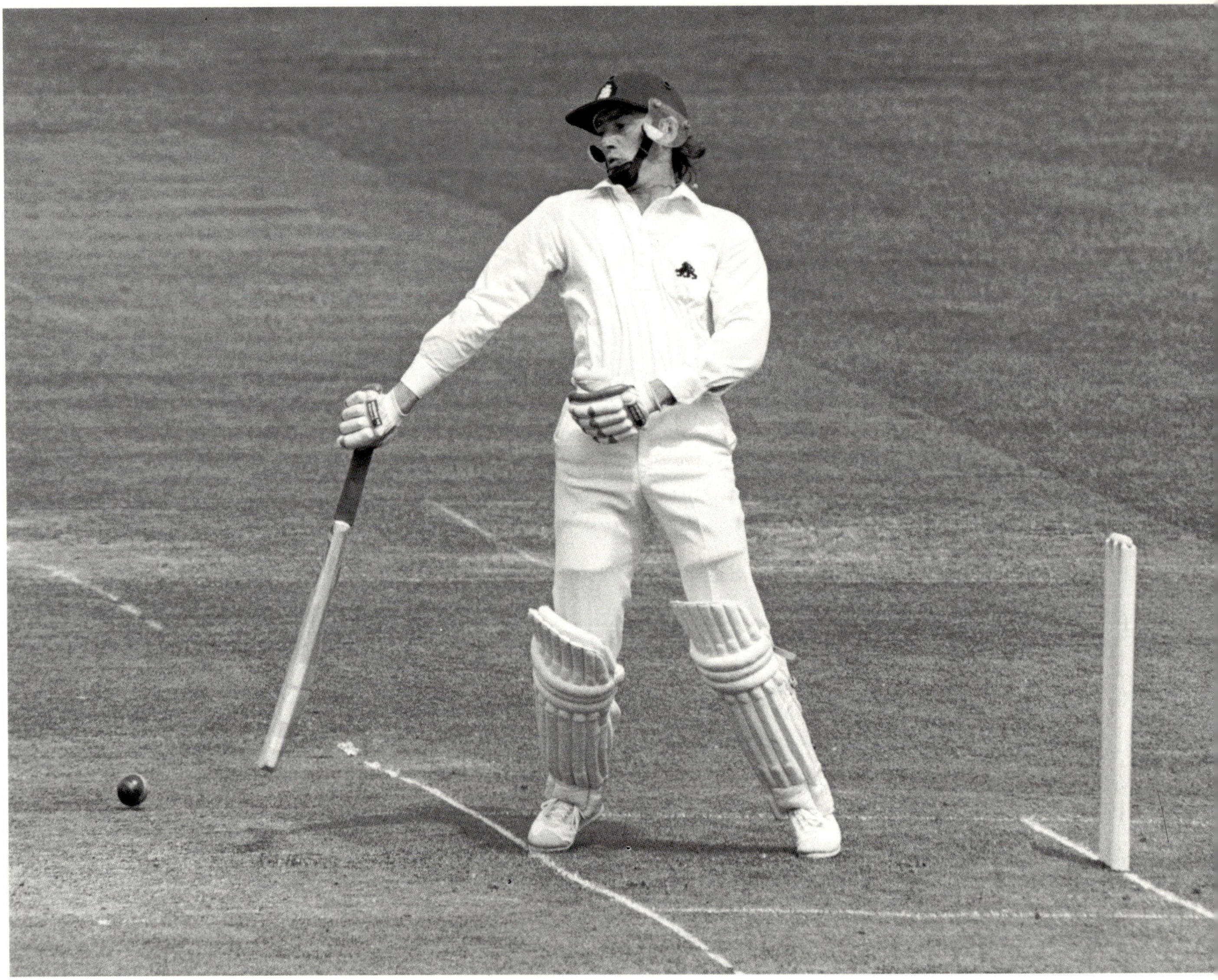

Graeme Fowler demonstrates how to face Joel Garner, one-day international, England v West Indies, Lord's, June 1984

The career life of a professional cricketer can be disturbingly up and down. He doesn't start off as office boy and end up managing director. For sportsmen life is not usually so straightforward, and it hasn't been for Graeme Fowler.

Sailing on the crest of a wave during England's 1984/85 tour in India, he scored a double century in the Madras Test, and by January 1985 he was probably earning in the region of £30,000 a year. However, during the World Championship in March of that year in Australia, his form began to suffer and he was dropped from the England side for the 1985 season. He was even briefly relegated to Lancashire's second XI. Then he had a neck problem which put him in hospital. By the end of the year his annual income had dropped to around £8,000, and yet today – still out of the England side – he may well be a more knowledgeable and even a better cricketer than he ever was.

As with cricket photographers, the public is apt to say of cricketers 'Oh, what a lovely job' – and yet is it? It is a sobering thought that what starts as a hobby at which a young boy excels may later become an almost insupportable pressure, sapping confidence and eroding pleasure.

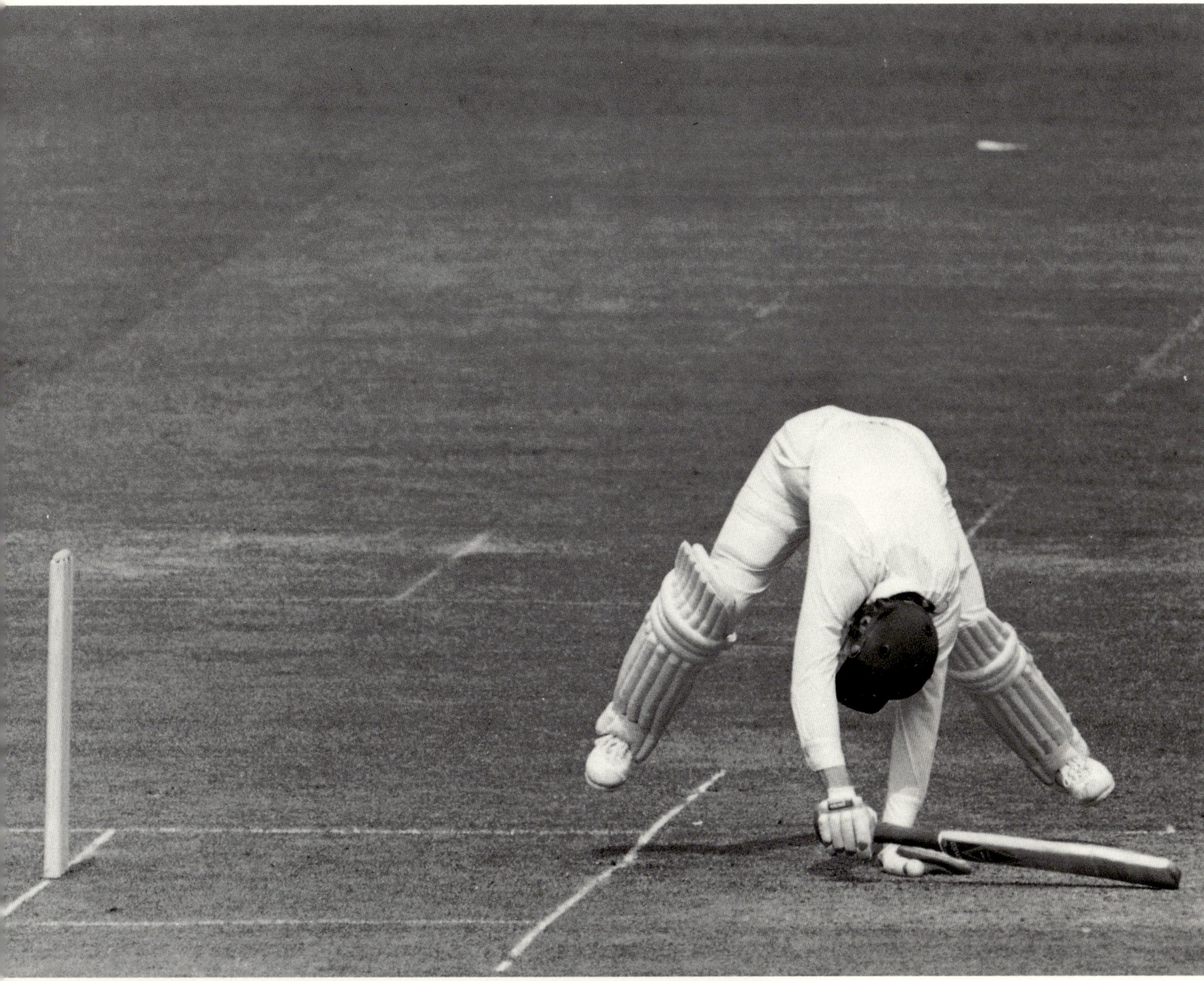

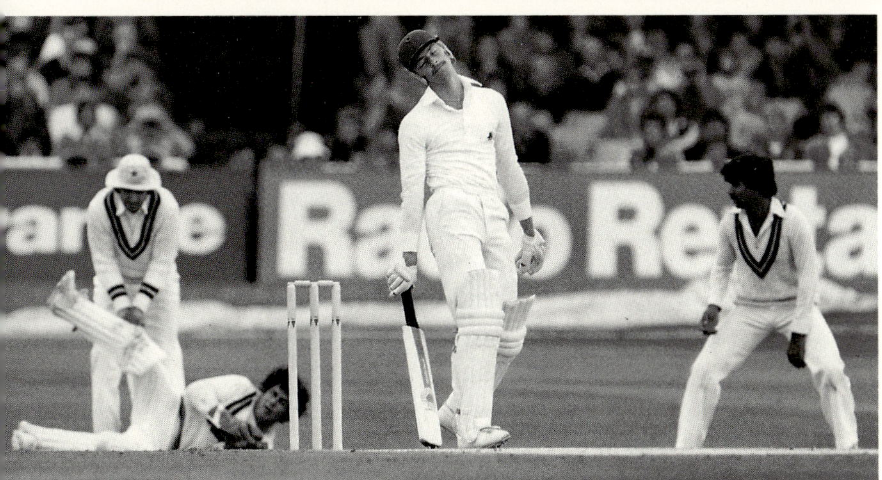

Fowler takes avoiding action against Malcolm Marshall, second Test, England v West Indies, Lord's, June/July 1984

Narrow escape for new boy Graeme Fowler, third Test, England v Pakistan, Headingley, August 1982

Experimentation is part and parcel of the creative process. The first time cricket photographers had to deal with the problems of floodlighting was in Sydney, on 28 November 1978 – a year before this picture was taken. This photograph of Willey was nonetheless a gamble, but having shot night soccer games helped. Using 400 ASA film (pushed 2 stops to 1600 ASA) I shot this picture at F5.6 and a shutter speed of 1/250 sec. This is the slowest speed at which one can 'freeze' the action. The gamble paid off. Willey's action is novel (what he calls the Kangaroo Special) and I'm glad to have preserved it for posterity.

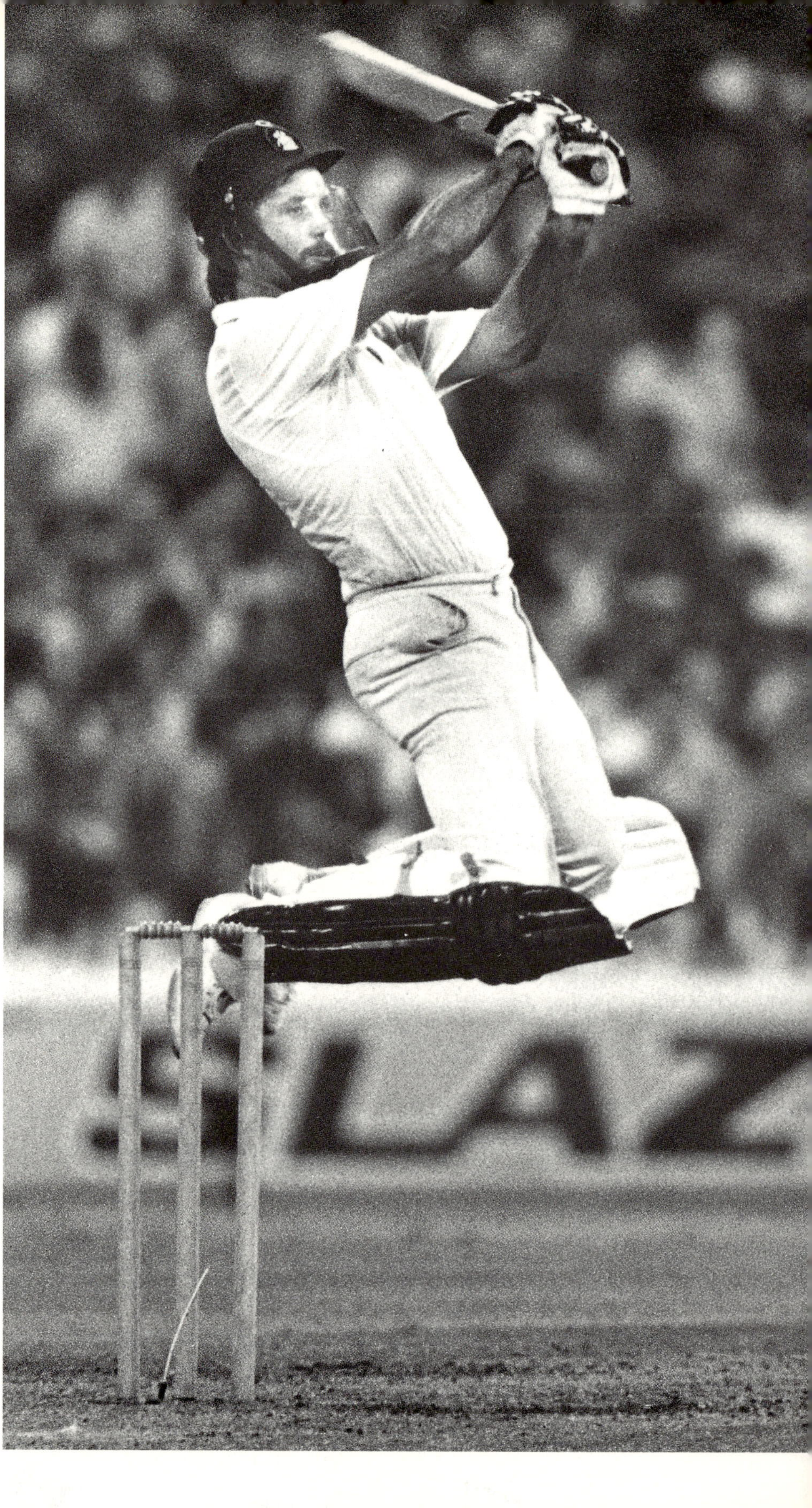

Peter Willey during England's victorious one-day international, Australia v England, in Sydney; note the WSC microphone between the stumps, December 1979

opposite: *Willey in The Parks on a freezing afternoon in Oxford, April 1985*

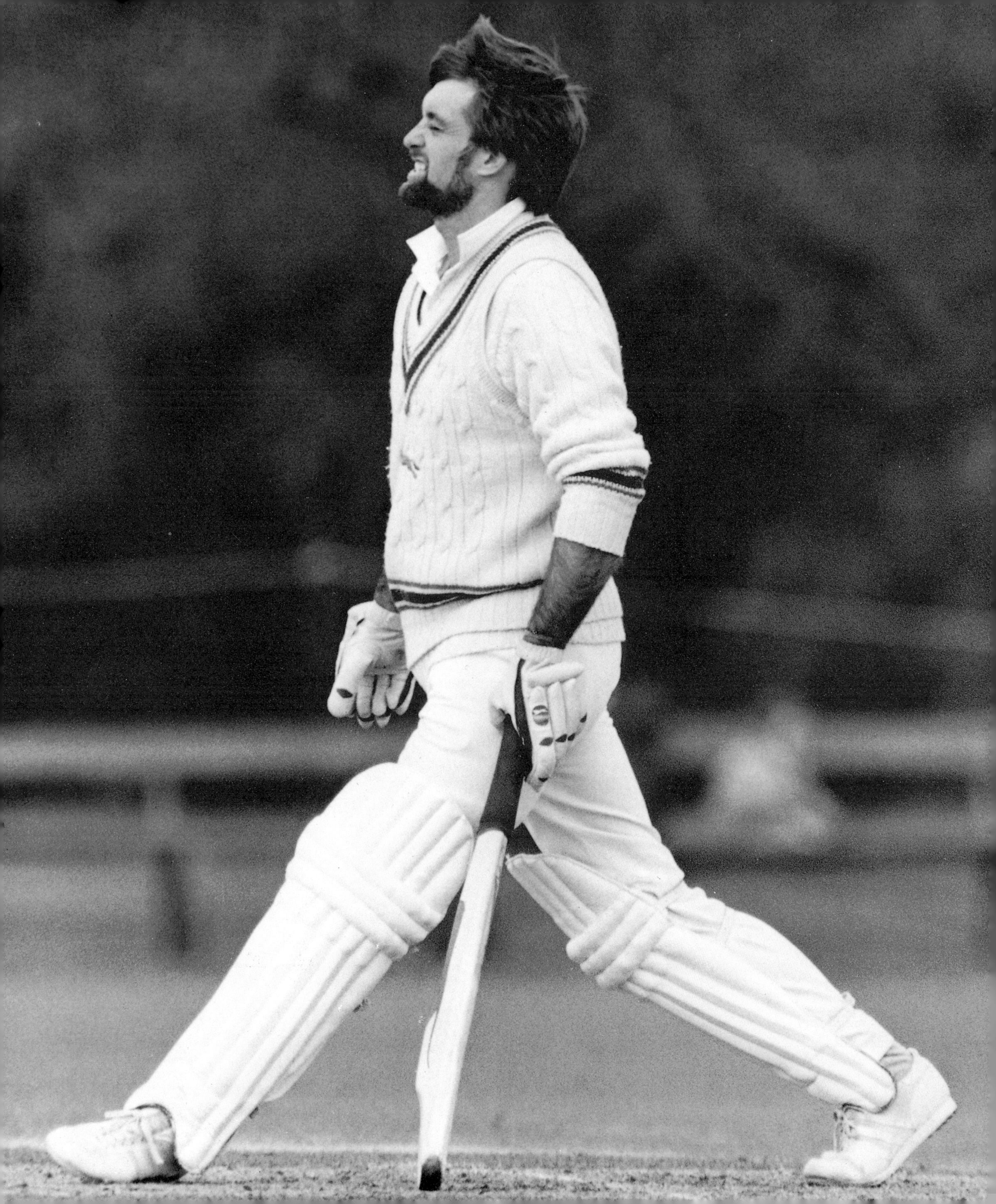

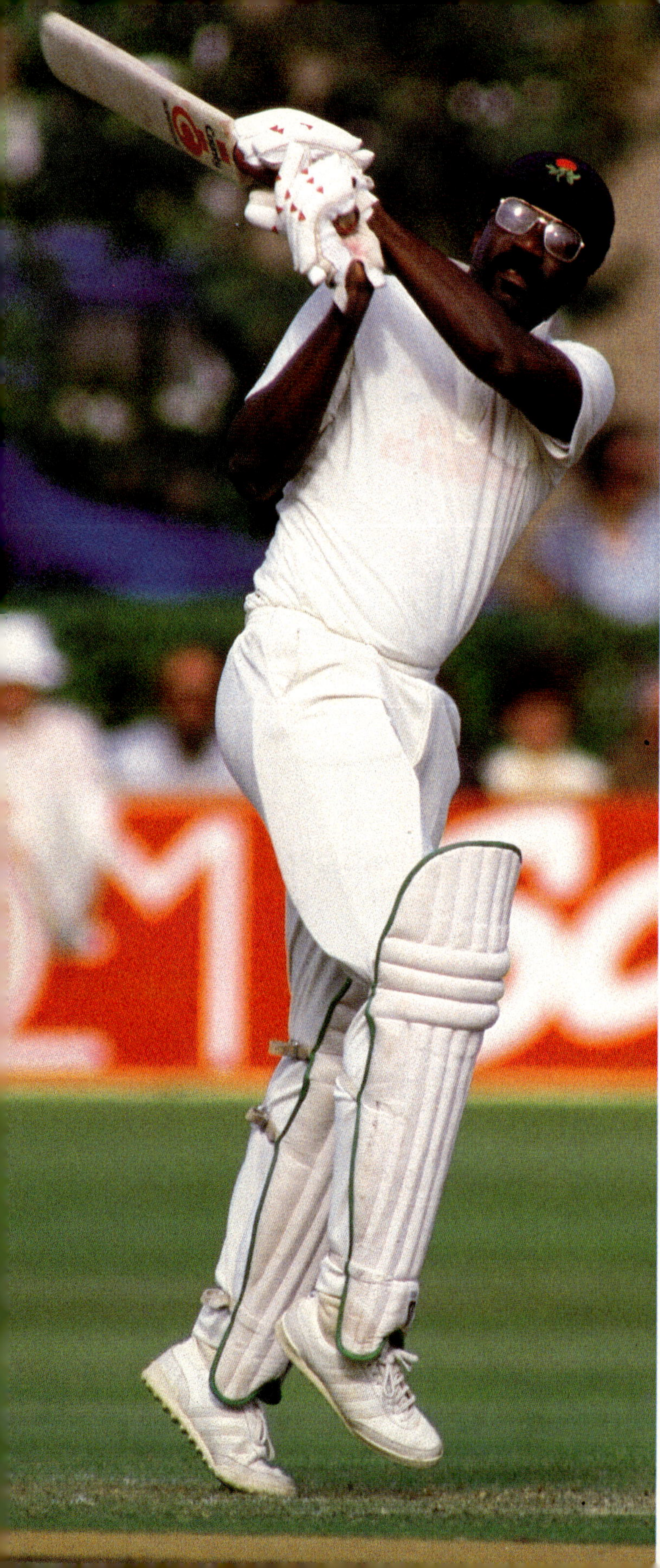

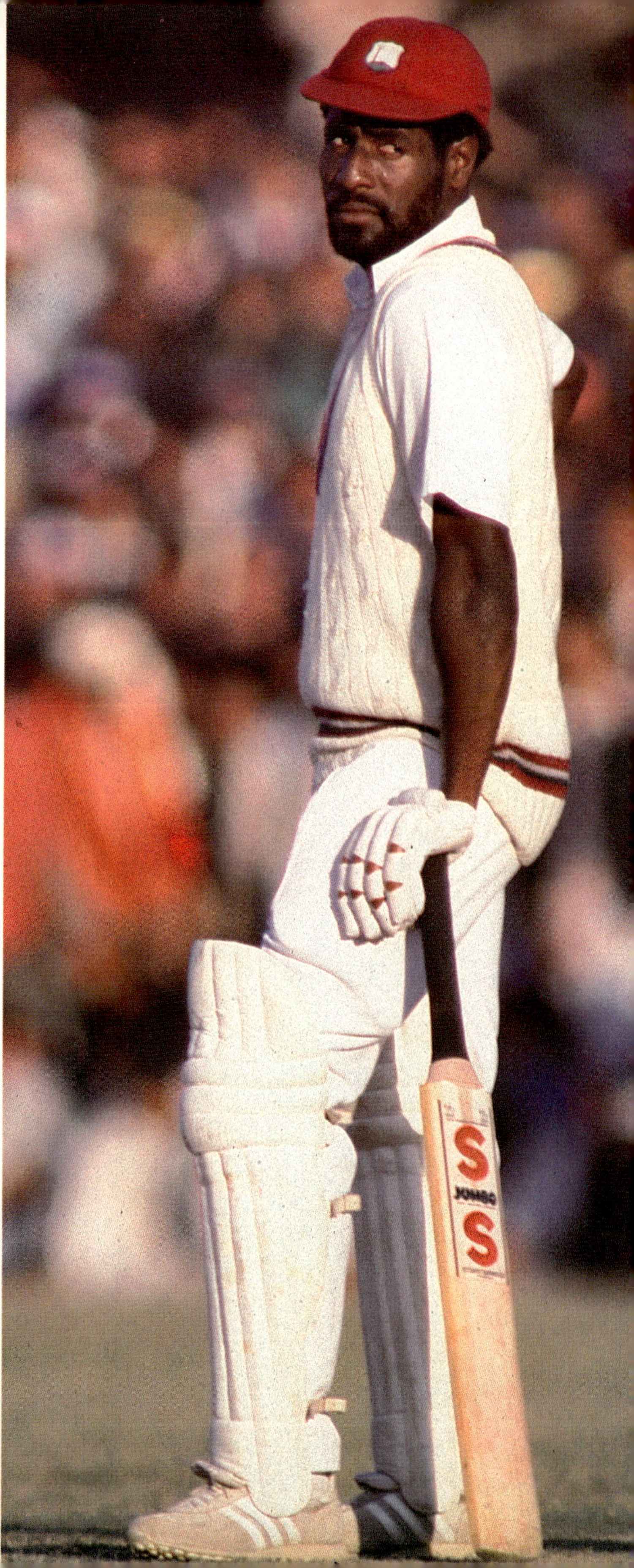

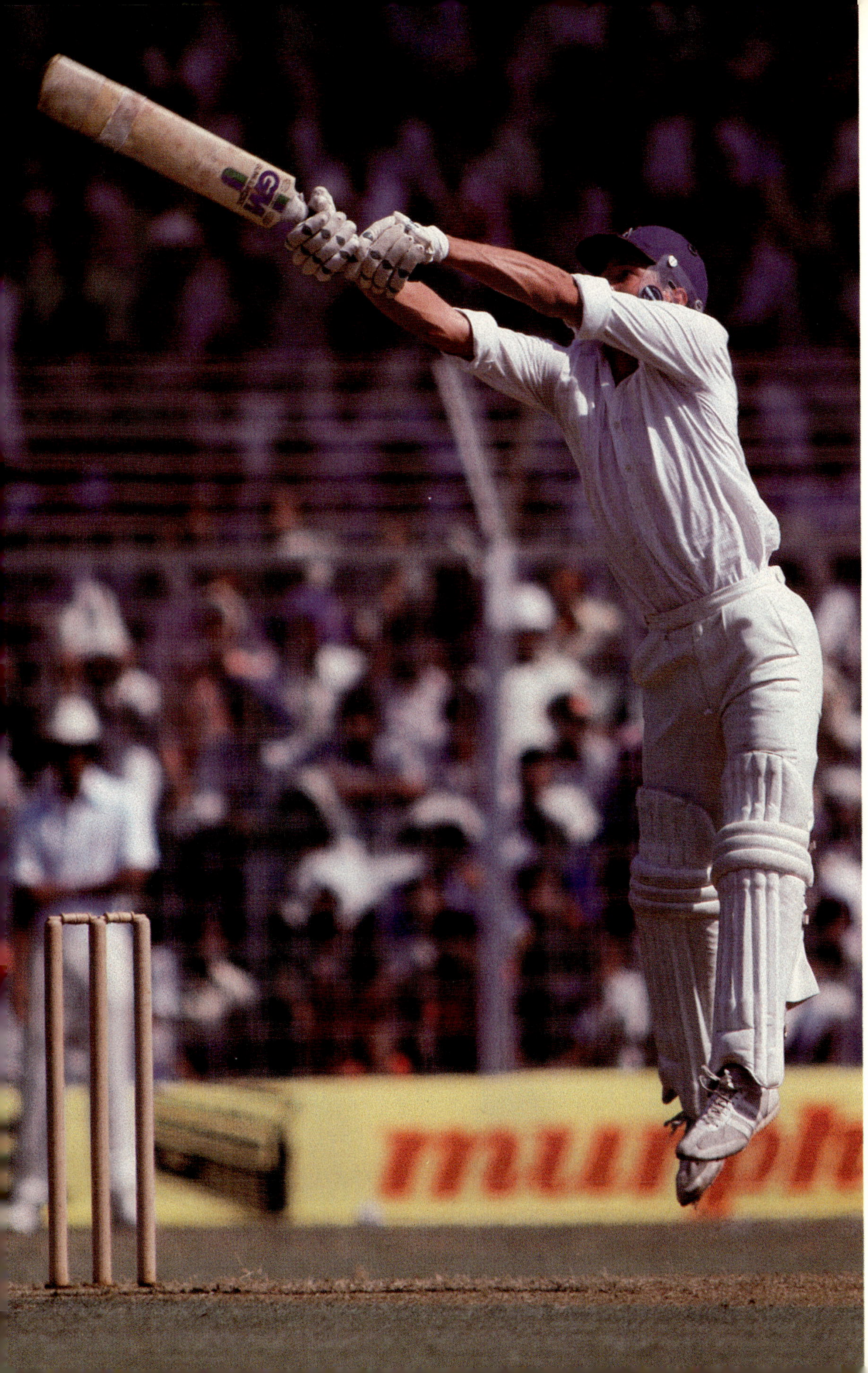

Derek Randall, one-day international, India v England, Bombay, February 1980

opposite, left: *Clive Lloyd, Lancashire and West Indies, Sussex v Lancashire, Hastings, June 1985*

opposite, right: *Viv Richards, one-day international, Pakistan v West Indies, Sialkot, December 1980*

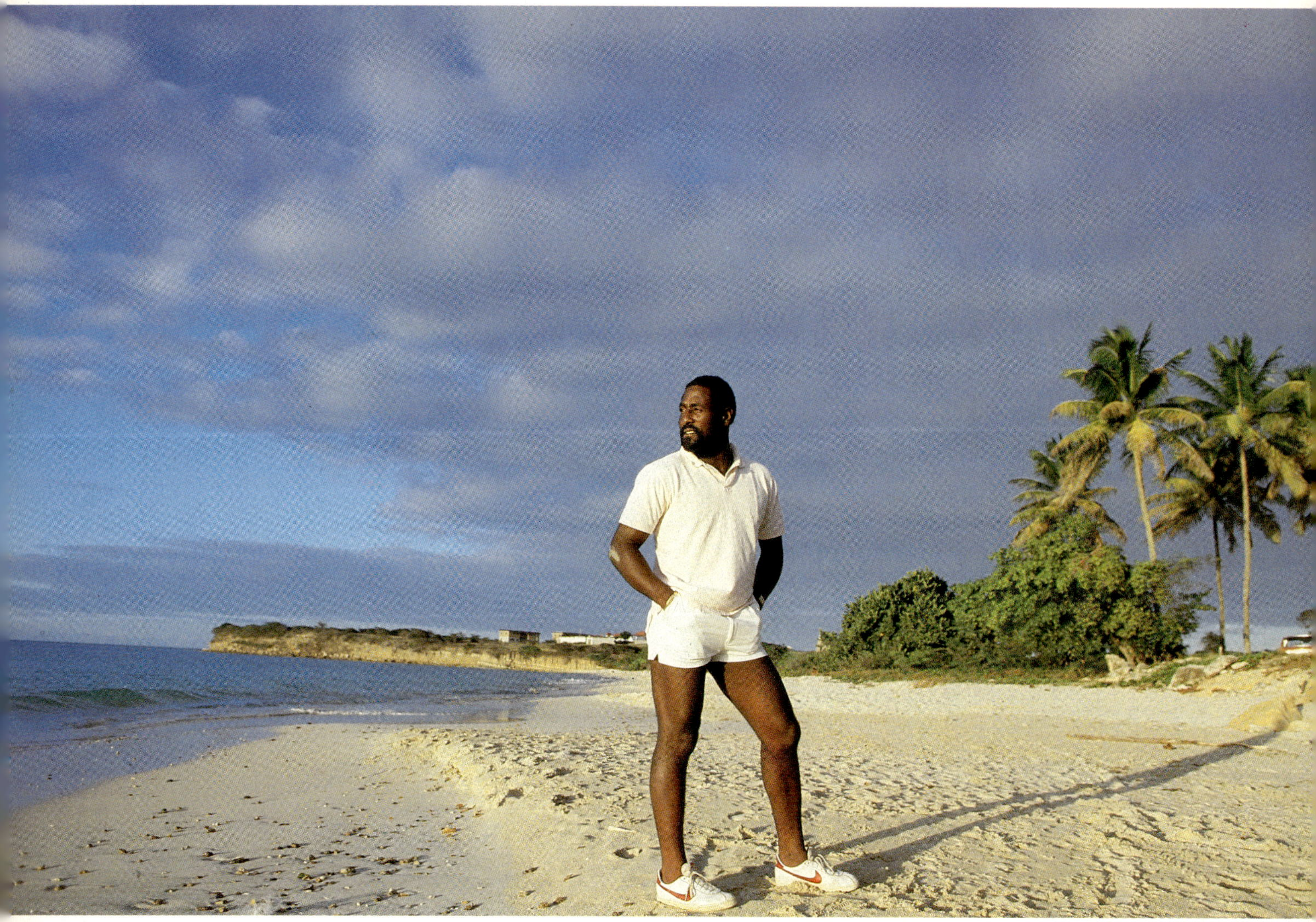

Vivian Richards, captain of the victorious West Indies side that defeated England 5–0 in the early part of 1986, nevertheless found time to relax, Antigua, March 1986

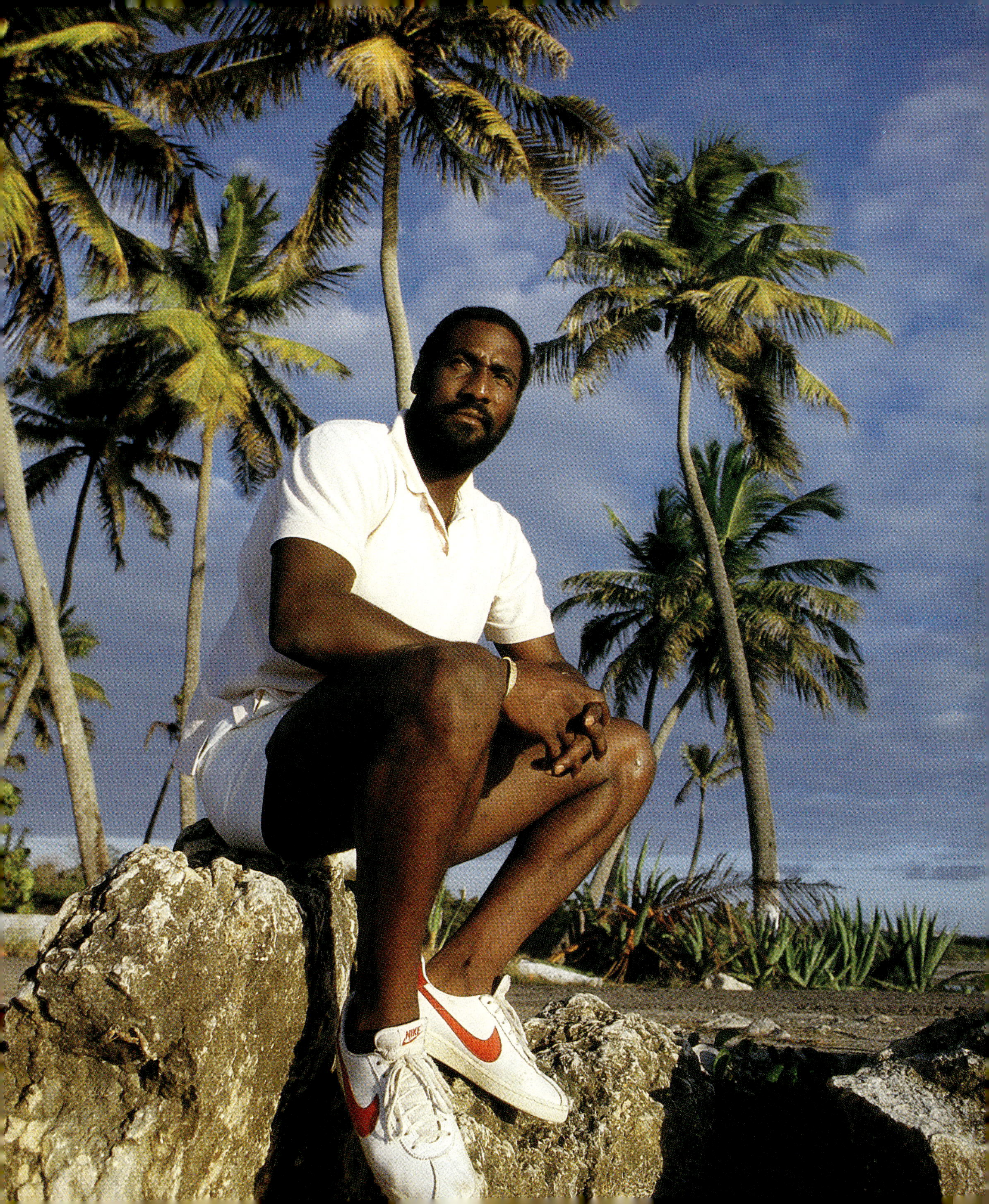
NIKE

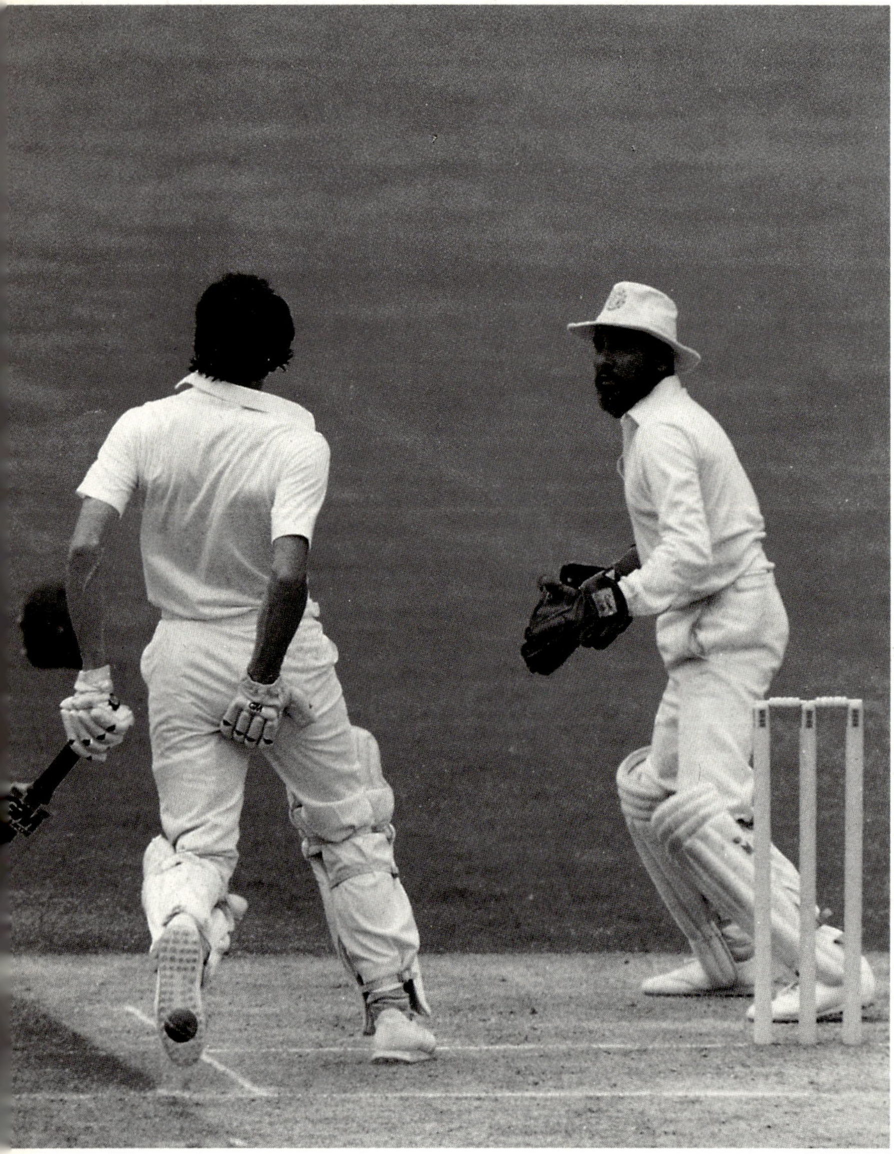

Derek Randall receives a blow on his posterior during the third Test, England v India, the Oval, August 1982

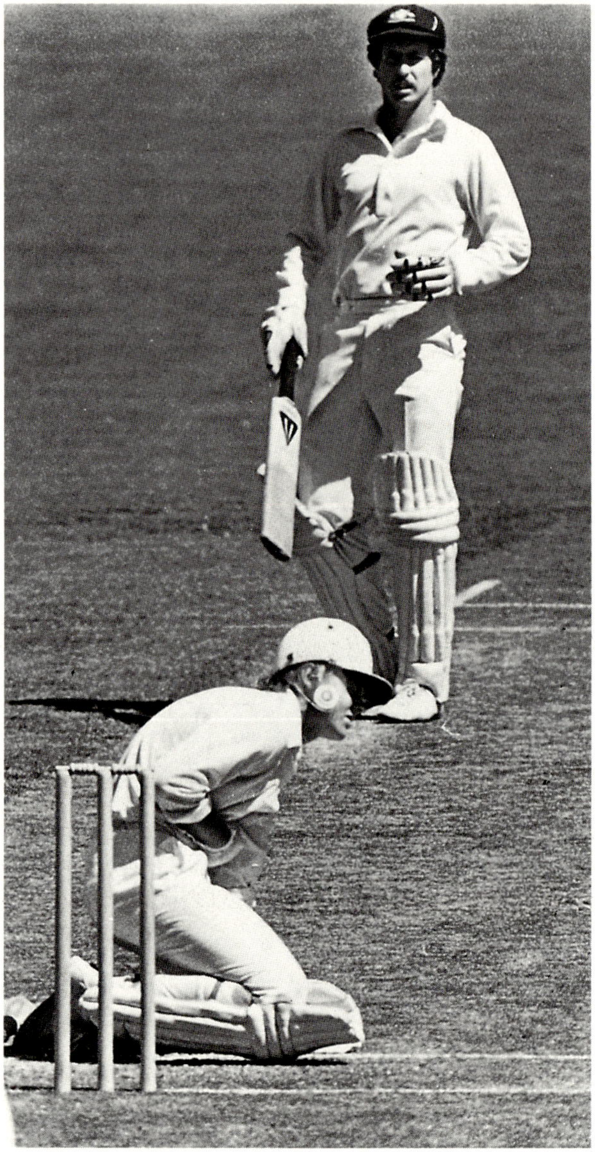

Rick Darling hit on the heart by a ball from Willis during the Ashes series. He was rushed to hospital, fifth Test, Australia v England, Adelaide, January 1979

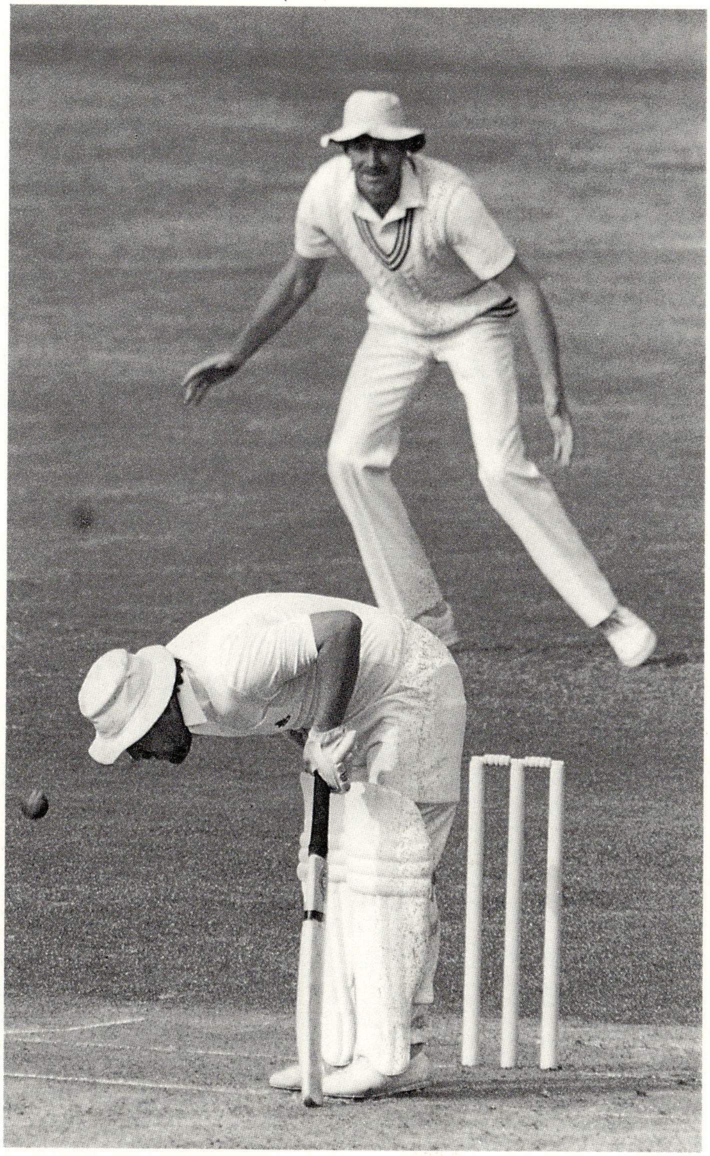

Mike Gatting temporarily halted by a bouncer from Richard Hadlee during his double century, Middlesex v New Zealand, Lord's, August 1983

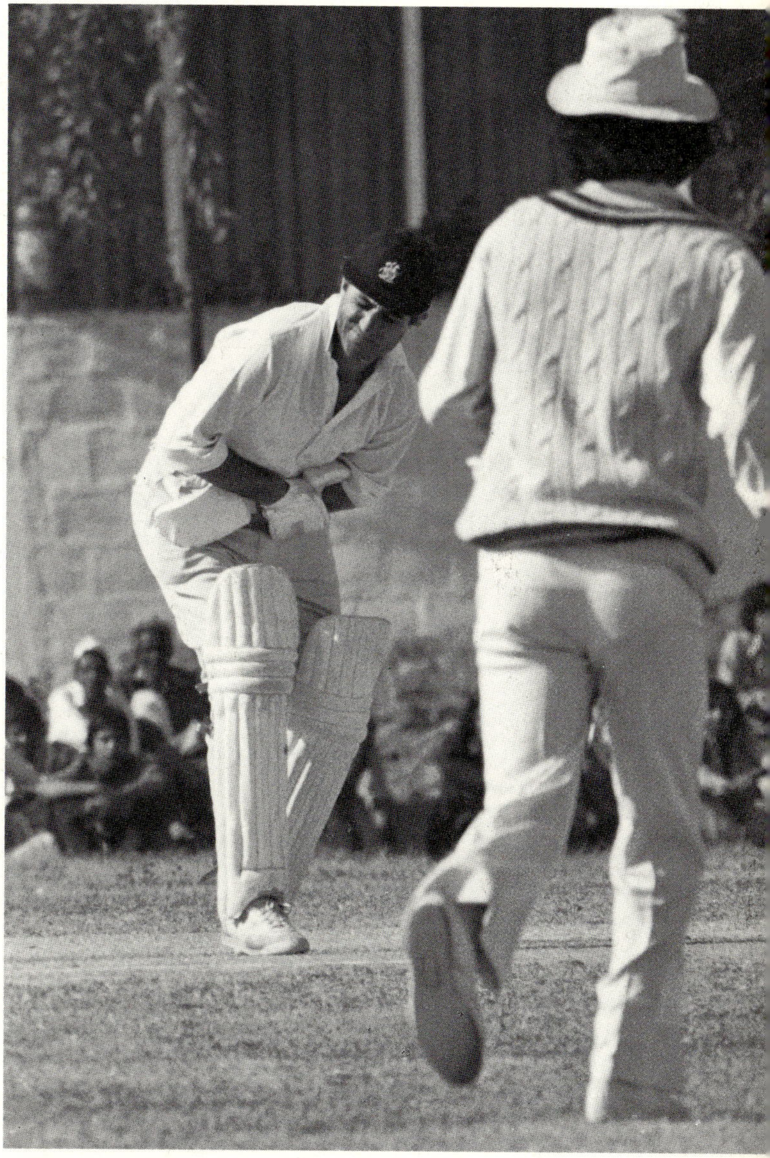

Mike Brearley's arm is broken in a minor match on a particularly bad wicket in Pakistan when the ball suddenly reared up. Brearley returned home and Boycott led England for the first time, Gymkhana Ground, Karachi, January 1978

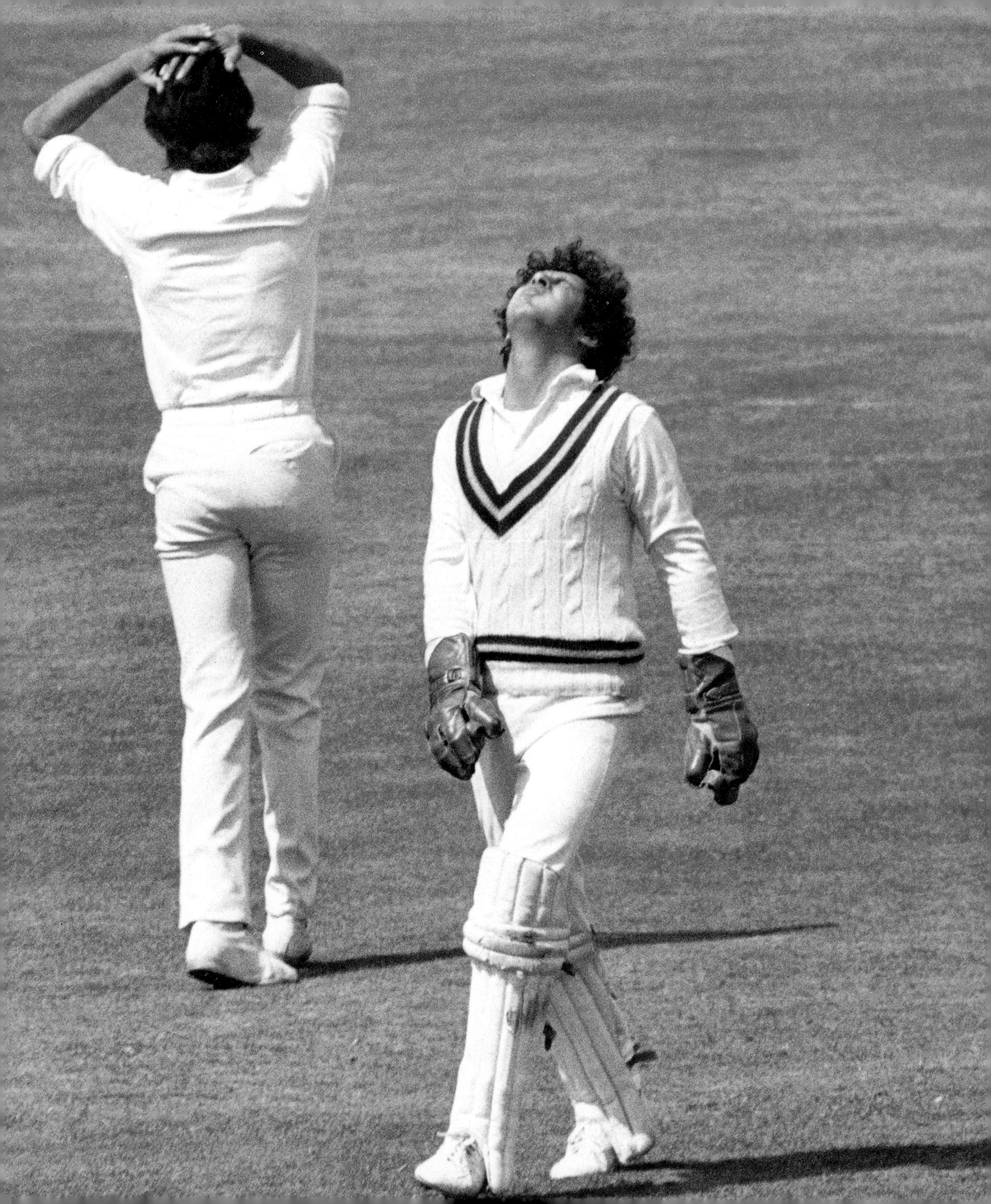

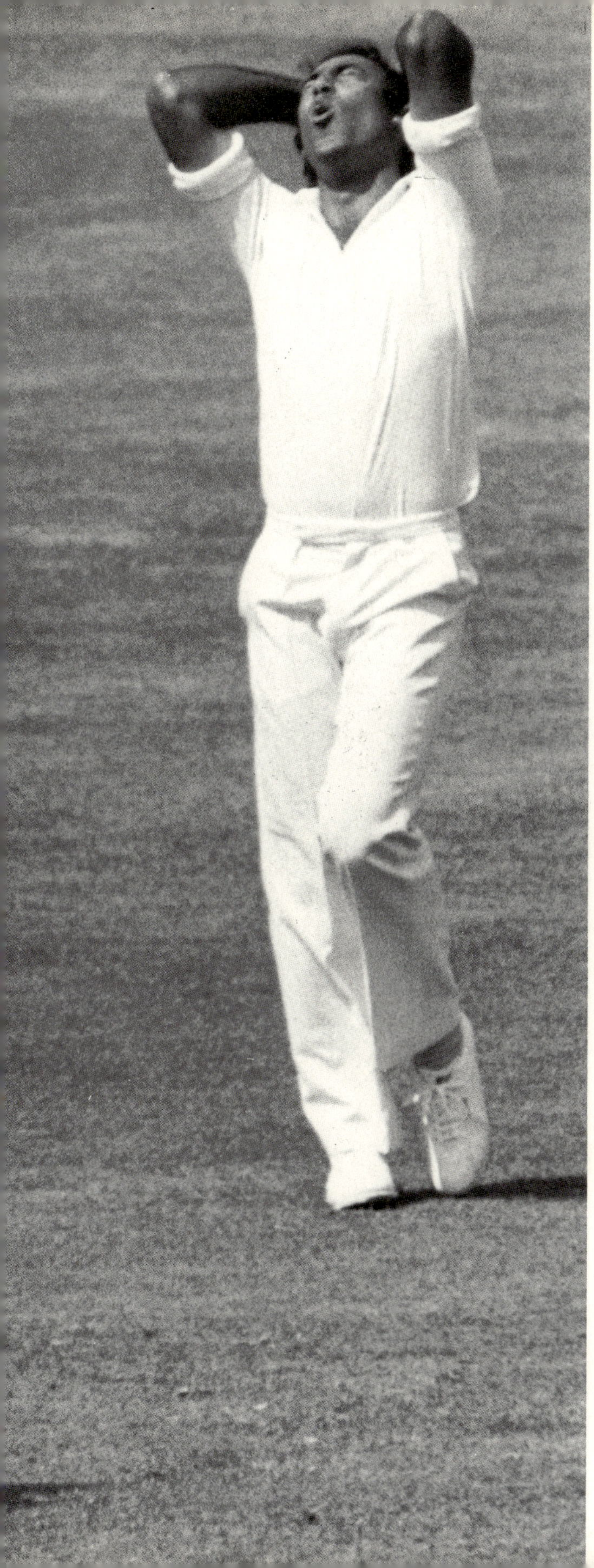

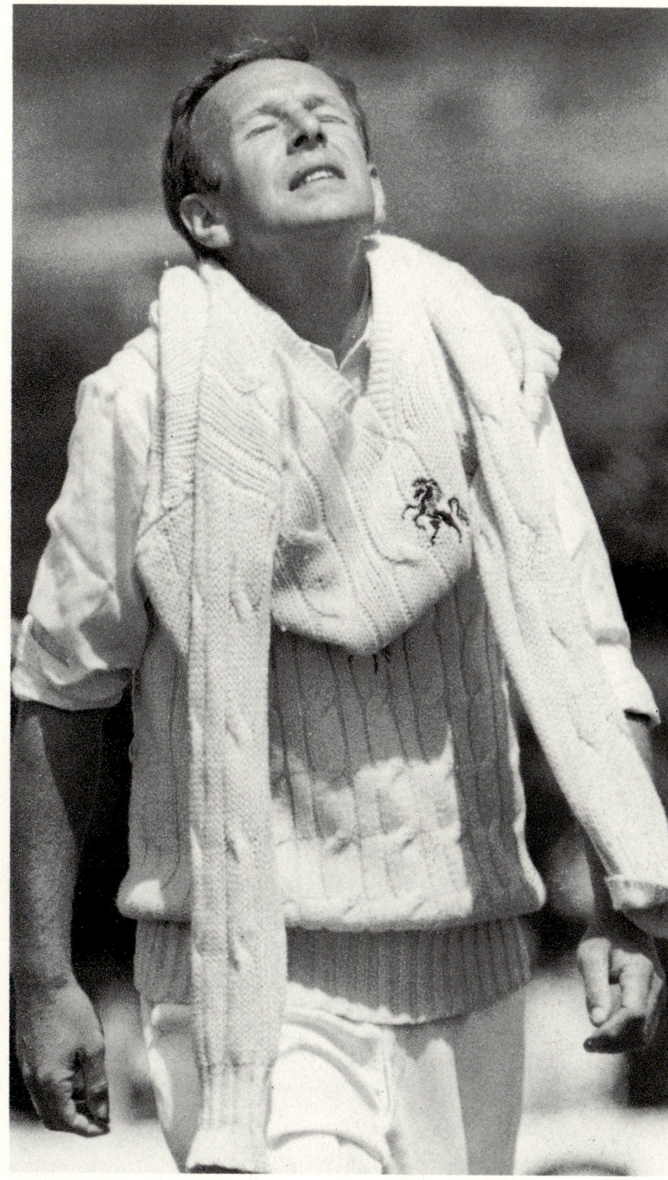

At the beginning of August 1982, Pakistan hadn't won a test against England for twenty-eight years. However, after Mohsin Khan's double century at Lord's in the first innings of the second Test, they scented victory. And when they sought to dismiss the England tailenders, the tension was electric. In the picture I have tried to show the agony of the missed opportunity.

Wasim Bari and slip fielders, second Test, England v Pakistan, Lord's, August 1982

above: *Derek Underwood, also overwrought, May 1985*

One might be forgiven for assuming that Bob Willis's run-up problems have finally got the better of him, but the picture here is of an attempted run-out, not an attempted delivery. It took place during the really close fourth Test in the 1982 Ashes series, in Melbourne. England finally won by three runs. As the tension mounted, it was perhaps not surprising that Willis fell over his own feet, and anything else around, in his excitement. Phil Edmonds (shown opposite), on the other hand, during the 1984/85 tour in India after two years away from Test cricket, sometimes seemed to have no direct communication with his feet at all. Nonetheless, he bowled superbly in the second Test at Delhi and without doubt the England team owed its victory in large part to his relentless accuracy, and his euphoria is obvious.
You will notice that the two pictures of Edmonds are not

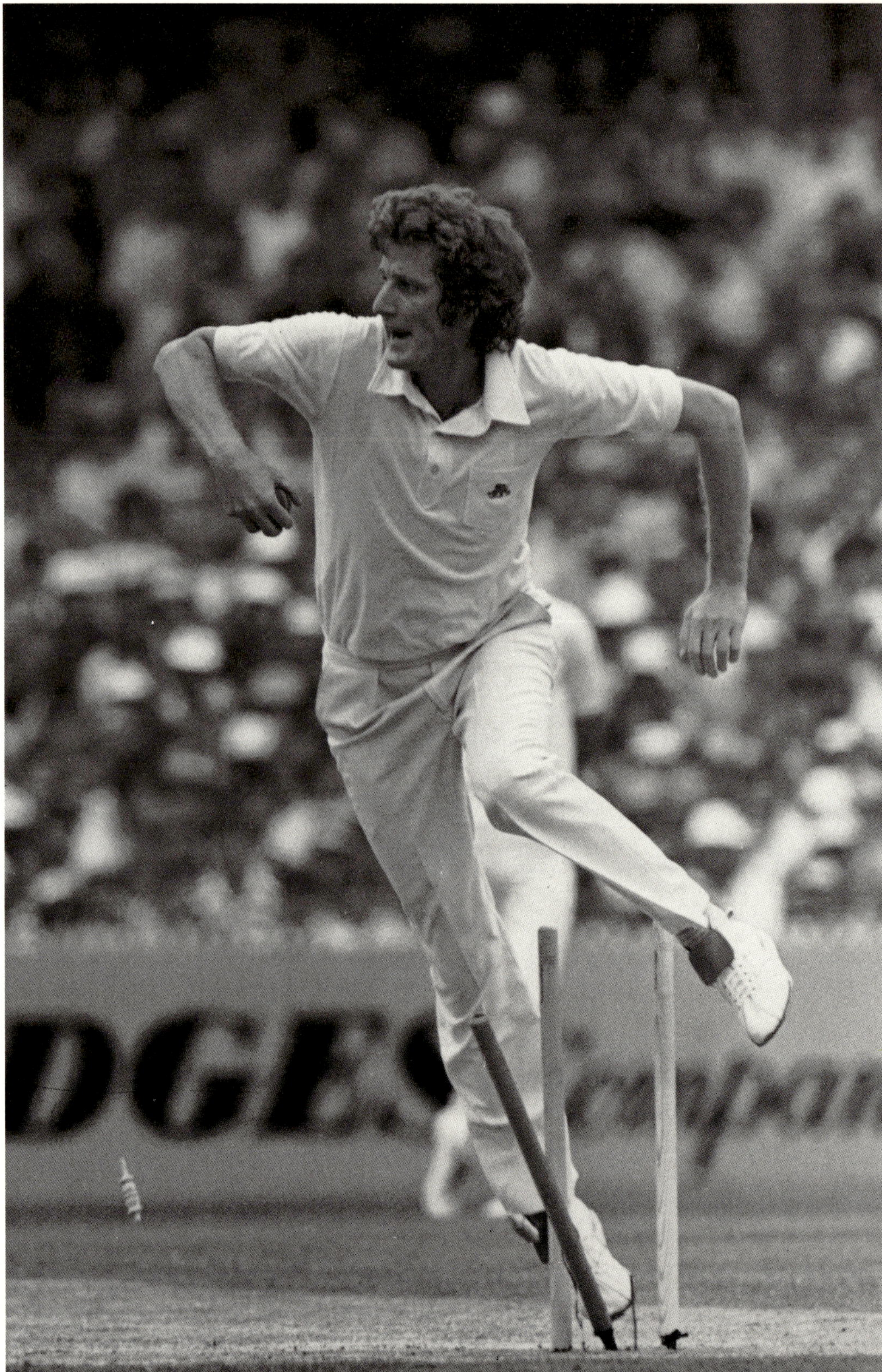

Bob Willis, fourth Test, Australia v England, Melbourne, December 1982

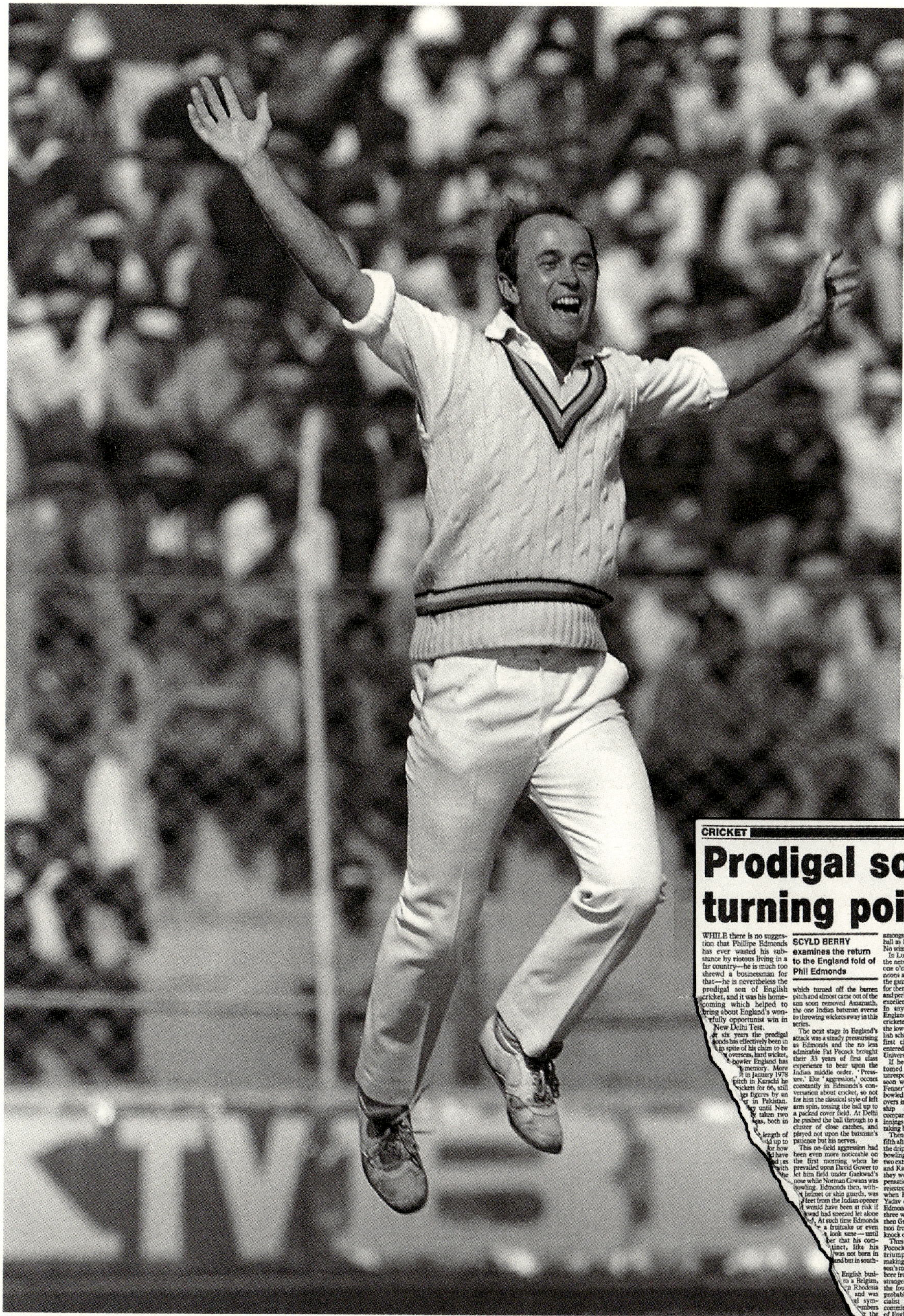

identical. Without motordrive it would not have been possible to capture his exuberance in two shots so close together. The other side of the coin can be seen in the near despair of Derek Underwood, shown on page 99. The picture was taken during a county match, Kent v Middlesex, after Underwood had bowled a particularly disappointing over.

Phil Edmonds, second Test, India v England, Delhi, December 1894

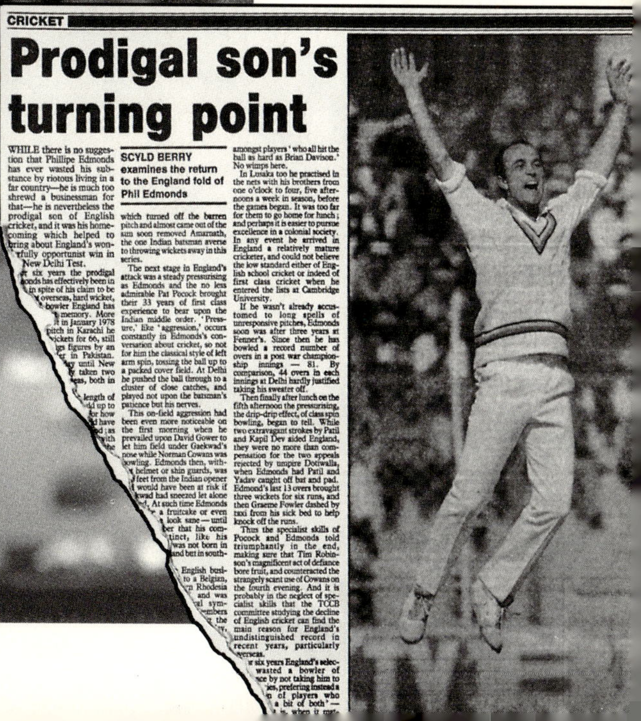

CRICKET

Prodigal son's turning point

SCYLD BERRY examines the return to the England fold of Phil Edmonds

WHILE there is no suggestion that Phillipe Edmonds has ever wasted his substance by riotous living in a far country—he is much too shrewd a businessman for that—he is nevertheless the prodigal son of English cricket, and it was his homecoming which helped to bring about England's won- ...rfully opportunist win in ... New Delhi Test.

...r six years the prodigal ...onds has effectively been in ... in spite of his claim to be ... overseas, hard wicket, ... bowler England has ... memory. More ... in January 1978 ... pitch in Karachi he ... wickets for 66, still ... figures by an ... in Pakistan. ... until New ... taken two ... both in

... length of ... up to ... how ... have ... as ... with ... the

which turned off the barren pitch and almost came out of the sun soon removed Amarnath, the one Indian batsman averse to throwing wickets away in this series.

The next stage in England's attack was a steady pressurising as Edmonds and the no less admirable Pat Pocock brought their 33 years of first class experience to bear upon the Indian middle order. 'Pressure,' like 'aggression,' occurs constantly in Edmonds's conversation about cricket, so not for him the classical style of left arm spin, tossing the ball up to a packed cover field. At Delhi he pushed the ball through to a cluster of close catches, and played not upon the batsman's patience but his nerves.

This on-field aggression had been even more noticeable on the first morning when he prevailed upon David Gower to let him field under Gaekwad's nose while Norman Cowans was bowling. Edmonds then, with... helmet or shin guards, was ... feet from the Indian opener ... would have been at risk if ...kwad had sneezed let alone ... At such time Edmonds ... a fruitcake or even ... look sane — until ... that his com... ...tinct, like his ... was not born in ... and bred in south-

... English busi... to a Belgian, ... Rhodesia ... and was ... sym... members ... the ...

amongst players 'who all hit the ball as hard as Brian Davison.' No wimps here.

In Lusaka too he practised in the nets with his brothers from one o'clock to four, five afternoons a week in season, before the games began. It was too far for them to go home for lunch; and perhaps it is easier to pursue excellence in a colonial society. In any event he arrived in England a relatively mature cricketer, and could not believe the low standard either of English school cricket or indeed of first class cricket when he entered the lists at Cambridge University.

If he wasn't already accustomed to long spells of unresponsive pitches, Edmonds soon was after three years at Fenner's. Since then he has bowled a record number of overs in a post war championship innings — 81. By comparison, 44 overs in each innings at Delhi hardly justified taking his sweater off.

Then finally after lunch on the fifth afternoon the pressurising, the drip-drip effect, of class spin bowling, began to tell. While two extravagant strokes by Patil and Kapil Dev aided England, they were no more than compensation for the two appeals rejected by umpire Dotiwalla, when Edmonds had Patil and Yadav caught off bat and pad. Edmond's last 13 overs brought three wickets for six runs, and then Graeme Fowler dashed by taxi from his sick bed to help knock off the runs.

Thus the specialist skills of Pocock and Edmonds told triumphantly in the end, making sure that Tim Robinson's magnificent act of defiance bore fruit, and counteracted the strangely scant use of Cowans on the fourth evening. And it is probably in the neglect of specialist skills that the TCCB committee studying the decline of English cricket can find the main reason for England's undistinguished record in recent years, particularly overseas.

...r six years England's selec... wasted a bowler of ...ce by not taking him to ...ies, prefering instead a ... of players who ... a bit of both' — ... when it ...

Like it or not, Kerry Packer, initiator of World Series Cricket and aided by Tony Greig, a former England captain, brought cricket in from the dark ages and into the moneywise twentieth century. The first major WSC game was between Australia and the West Indies and took place at the Victoria Football League ground in Melbourne in December 1977. From then on there was no looking back, even though in its first season WSC lost A$3.5 million. The one-day matches attracted huge crowds, but the test matches struggled, despite the enormous amount of publicity.
In January 1978, WSC came into direct conflict with the cricket establishment for the first time. England were in Pakistan, but Mushtaq Mohammed, Zaheer Abbas and Imran Khan were in Australia – 'Packerstanis'! The story then becomes confused. Who authorised their return to Karachi? Whoever it was, just before the third Test in Karachi, there they were in the nets. Everyone objected; the England players were resentful, the Cricket Board was outraged, even members of the original Pakistani test team were uneasy.

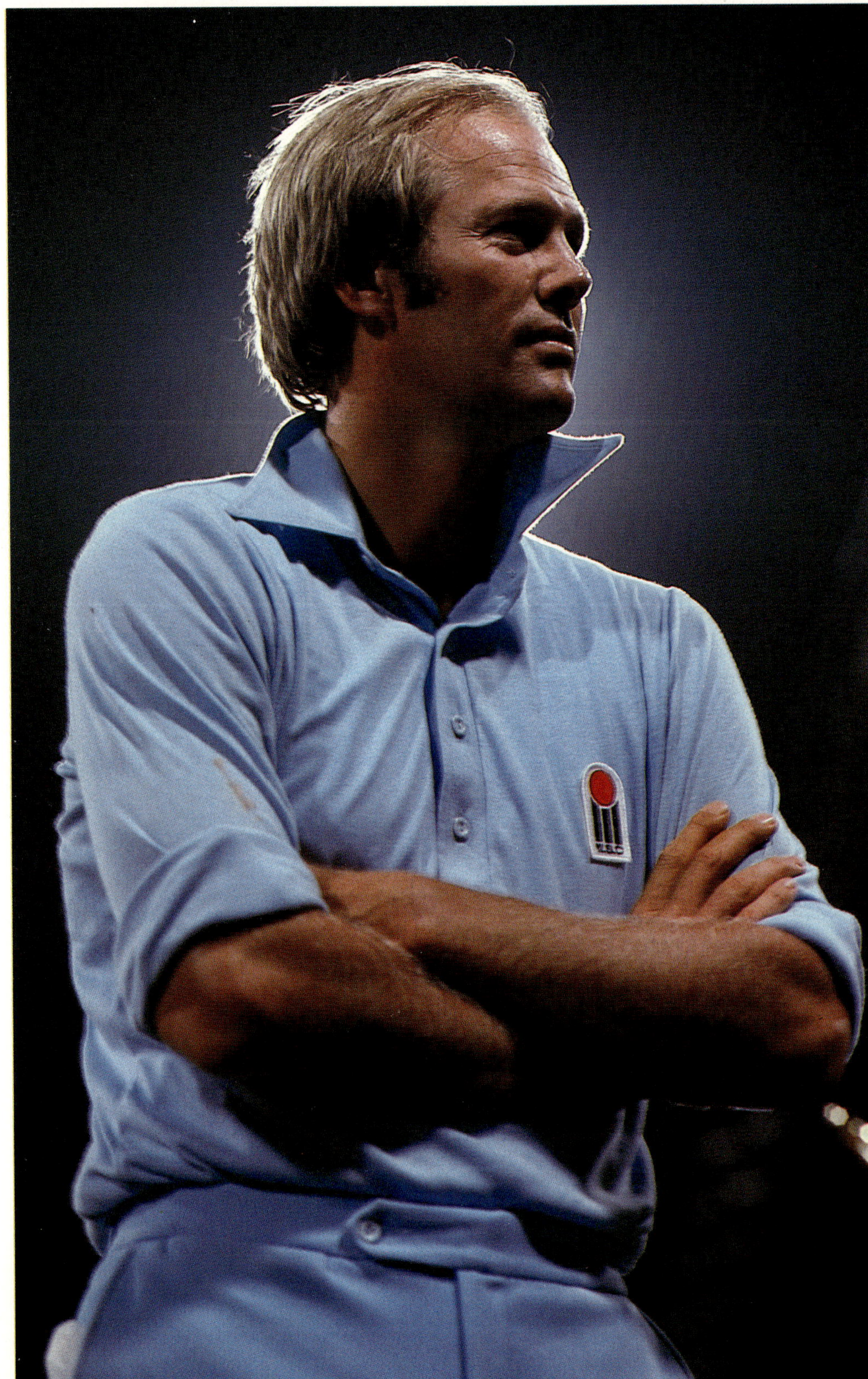

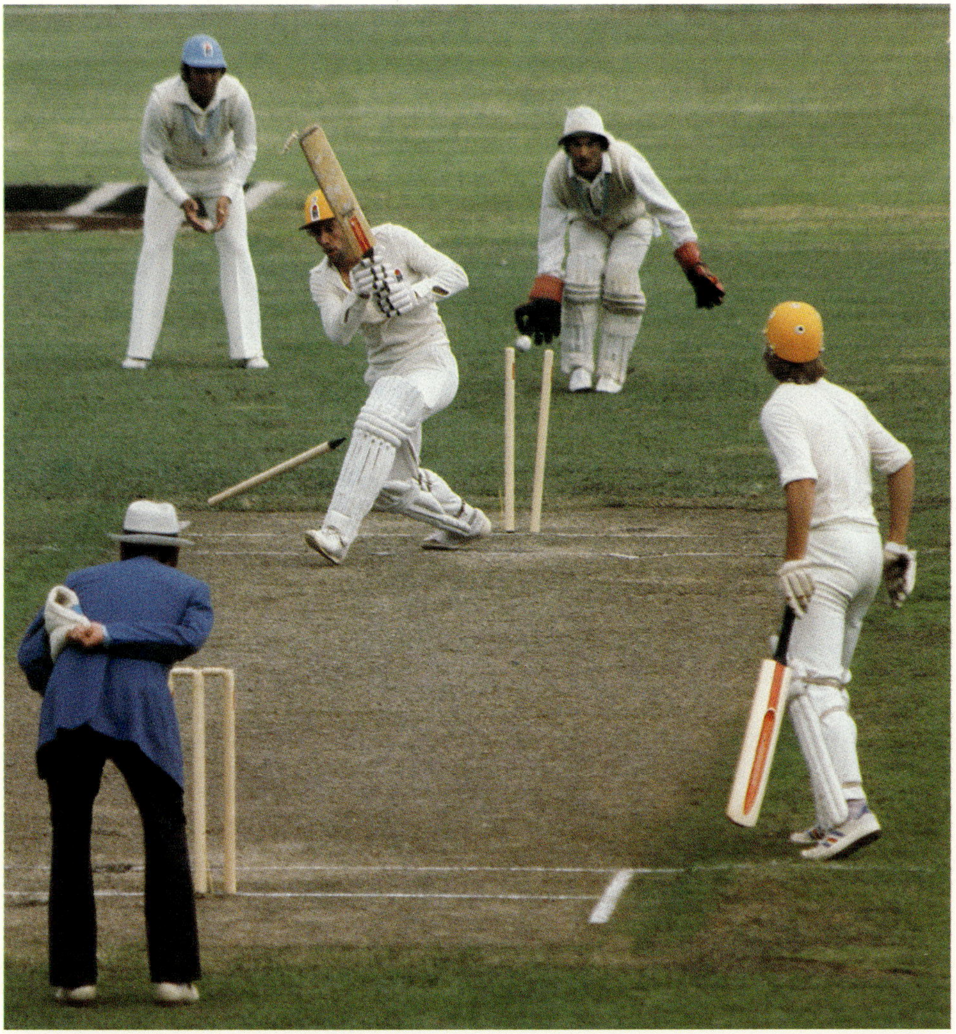

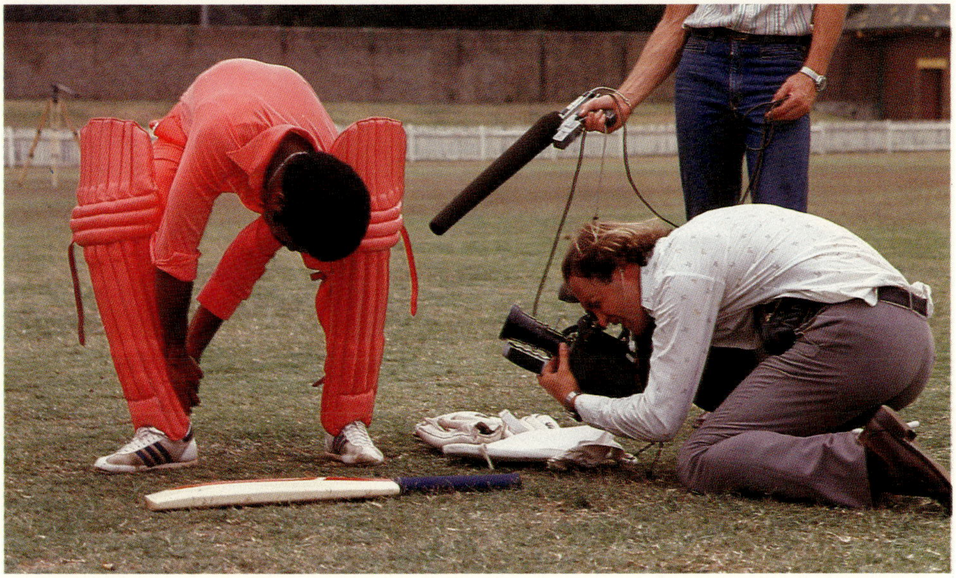

Brearley, his arm in plaster, read out an uncompromising team statement opposing the selection of the Packerites. The Pakistani selectors then capitulated and the tour continued on its somewhat chequered course.

By the end of 1978 the conflict was even more marked. An 'establishment' England touring team was in Australia and the Ashes series competed directly with WSC for spectator support. Oddly enough, it was the Australian Cricket Board which finally resolved the problem. They gave Packer what he wanted. According to a settlement negotiated with PBL Sports Pty Ltd (Packer's organisation), WSC was disbanded on January 31 1980 and PBL was given 'the exclusive right, for a term of ten years, to promote the programme of cricket organised by the Board and to arrange the televising and merchandising of that programme'.

And cricket – and cricketers – has never been quite the same since.

ITN cameraman – the day the West Indians were in the pink, Sydney, 17 January 1979

above: *Ian Chappell and Garth le Roux, Australia v the World in Packer Supertest, Melbourne, January 1979*

opposite: *Tony Greig, after his World XI won the Grand Final Supertest, Melbourne, January 1979*

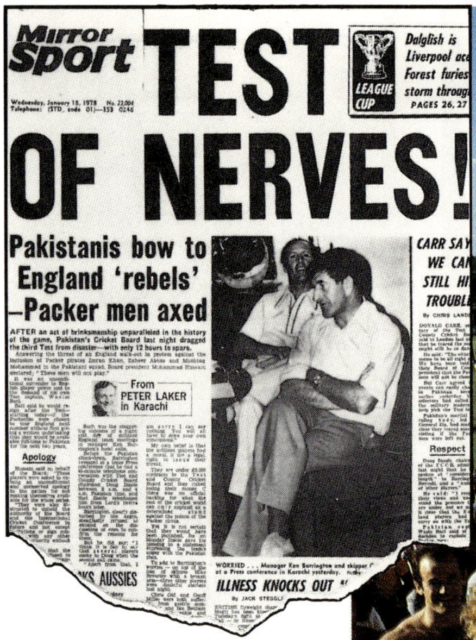

Mirror Sport

Wednesday, January 18, 1978 No. 23,004
Telephone: (STD. code 01)—353 0246

TEST OF NERVES!

LEAGUE CUP

Dalglish is Liverpool ace Forest furies storm through
PAGES 26, 27

Pakistanis bow to England 'rebels' —Packer men axed

From PETER LAKER in Karachi

AFTER an act of brinksmanship unparalleled in the history of the game, Pakistan's Cricket Board last night dragged the third Test from disaster—with only 12 hours to spare.

Answering the threat of an England walk-out in protest against the inclusion of Packer pirates Imran Khan, Zaheer Abbas and Mushtaq Mohammad in the Pakistani squad, Board president Mohammad Hussain declared: "These men will not play."

Apology

WORRIED . . . Manager Ken Barrington and skipper G... at a Press conference in Karachi yesterday.

CARR SAY... WE CAN... STILL HI... TROUBLE

By CHRIS LANDER

Respect

ILLNESS KNOCKS OUT ...

By JACK STEGGLES

...KS AUSSIES

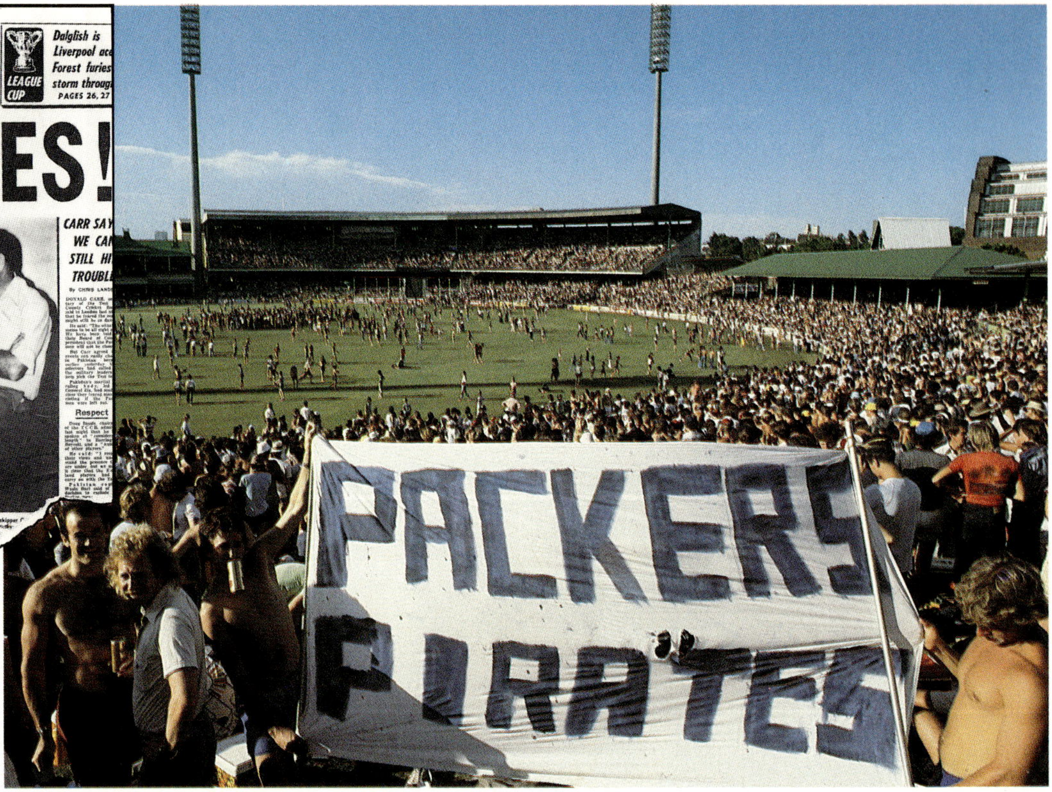

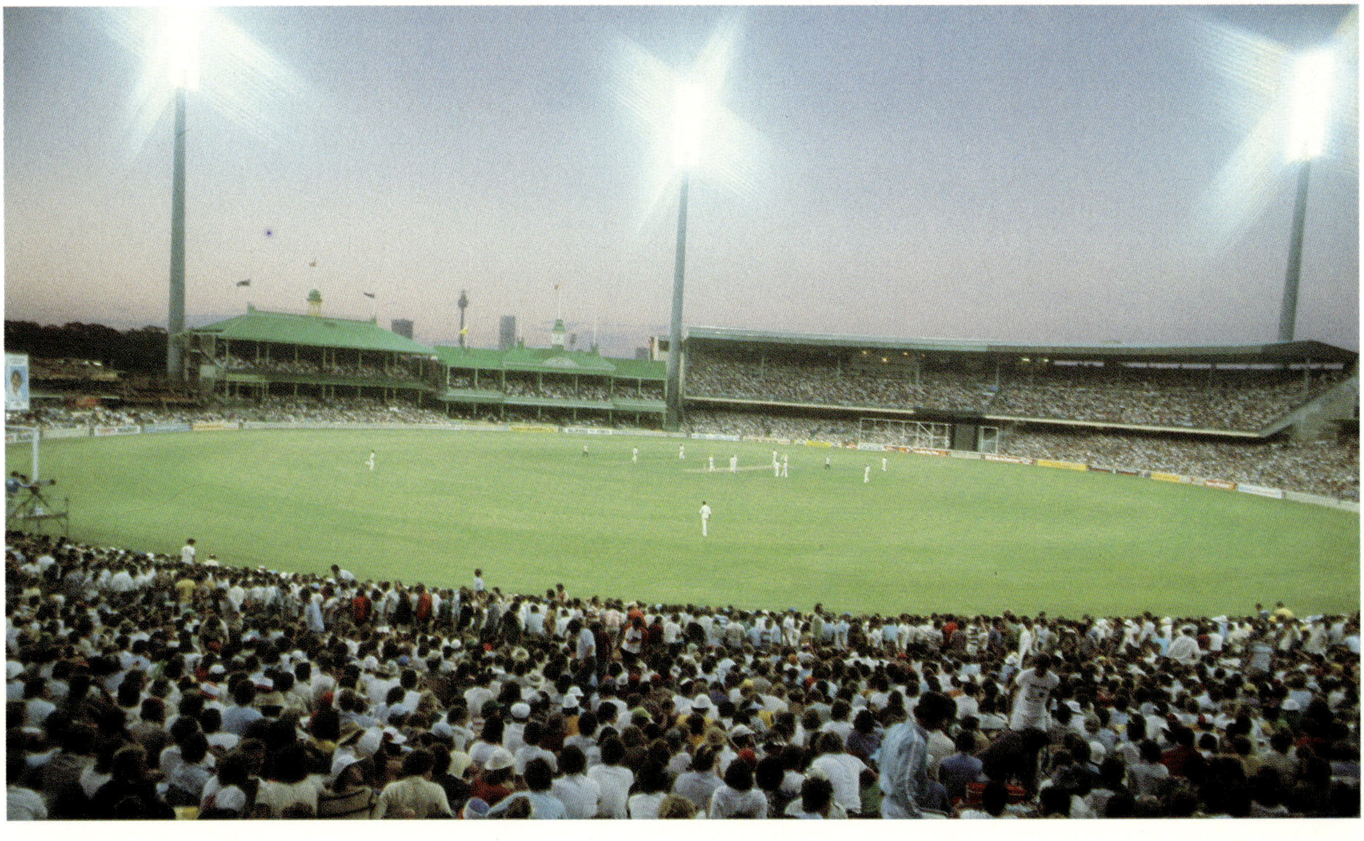

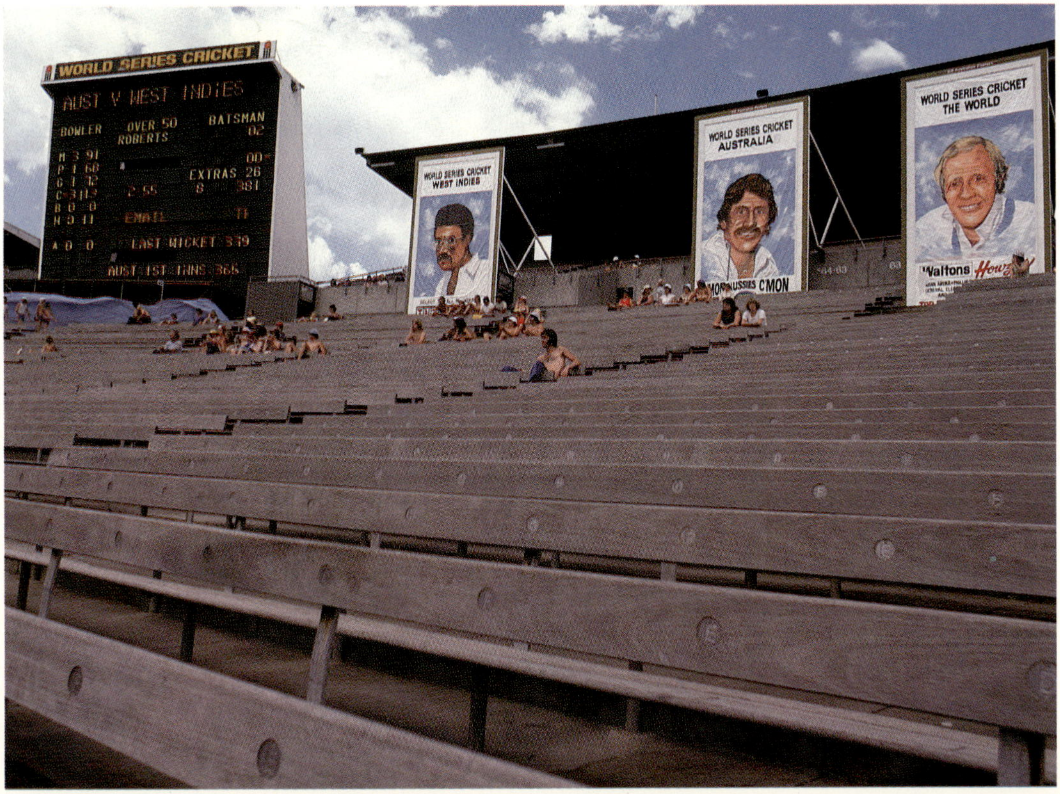

The five-day tests struggled to attract decent crowds, Australia v West Indies, Melbourne, November 1978

below: *Redpath and Knott, Grand Final Supertest, Australia v World XI, Sydney, February 1979*

opposite, above: *Tickets were completely sold out for the first day–night game, but still the crowds poured in, Australia v West Indies, Sydney, 28 November 1978*

opposite, below: *The floodlights go on, Sydney, 28 November 1978*

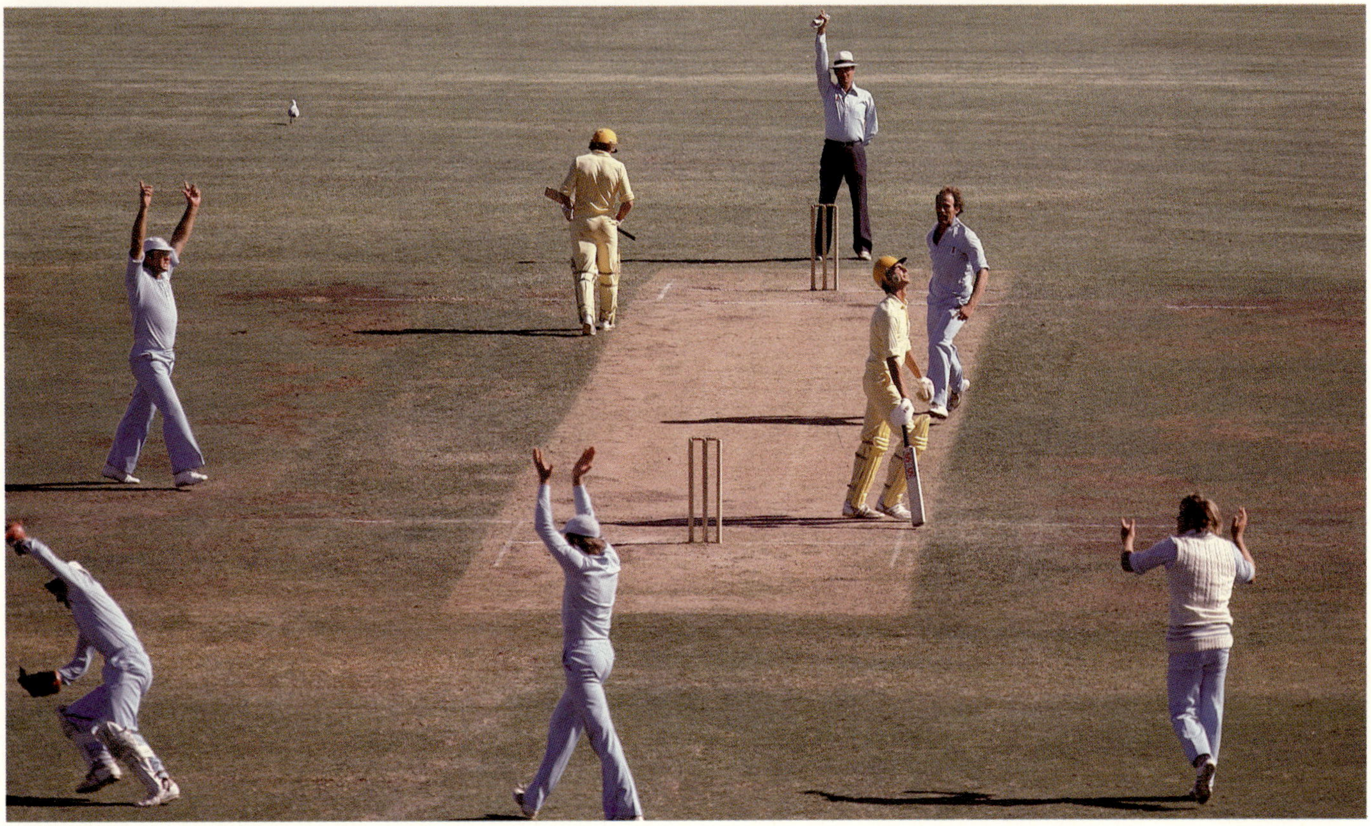

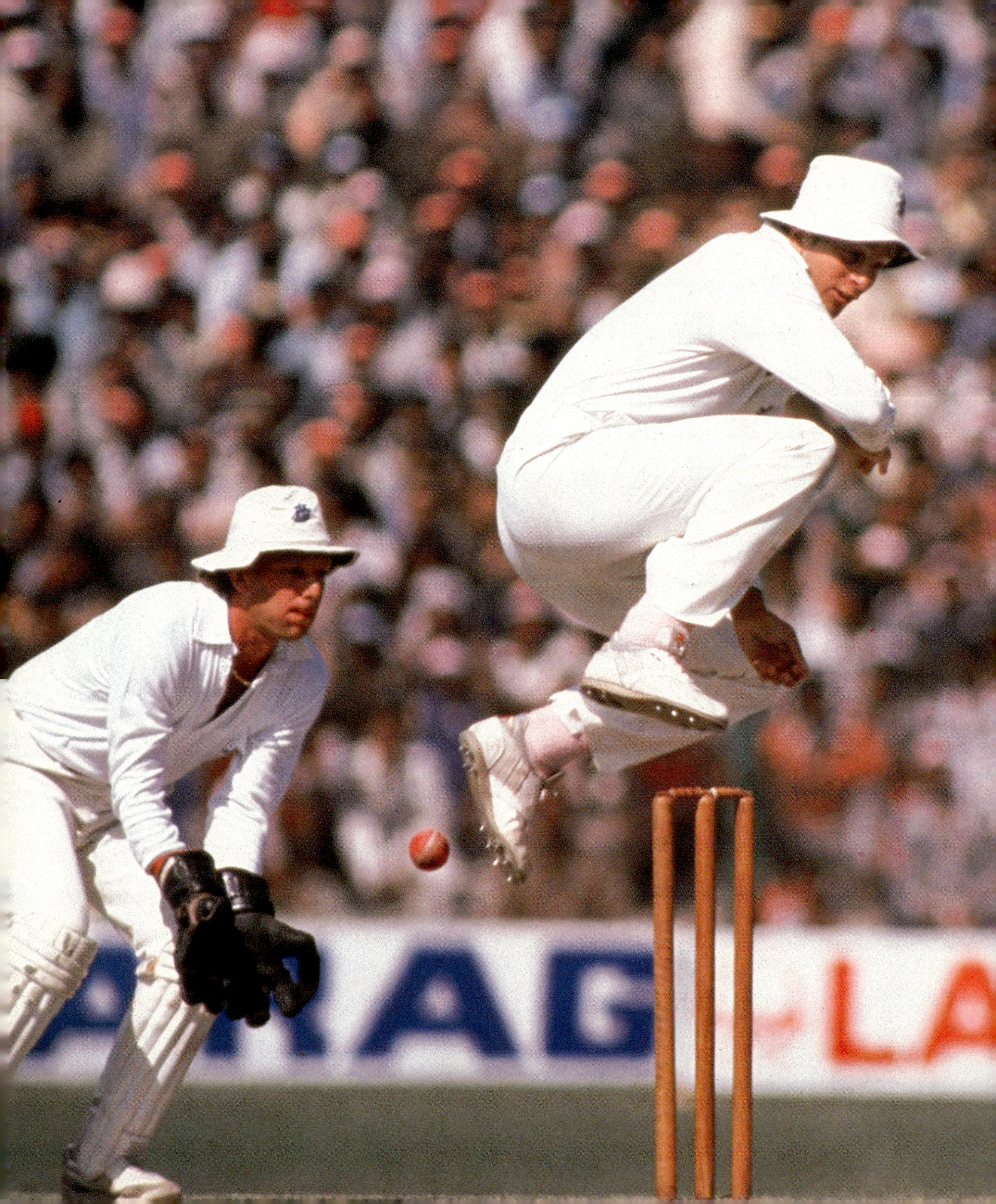
ARAG
LA

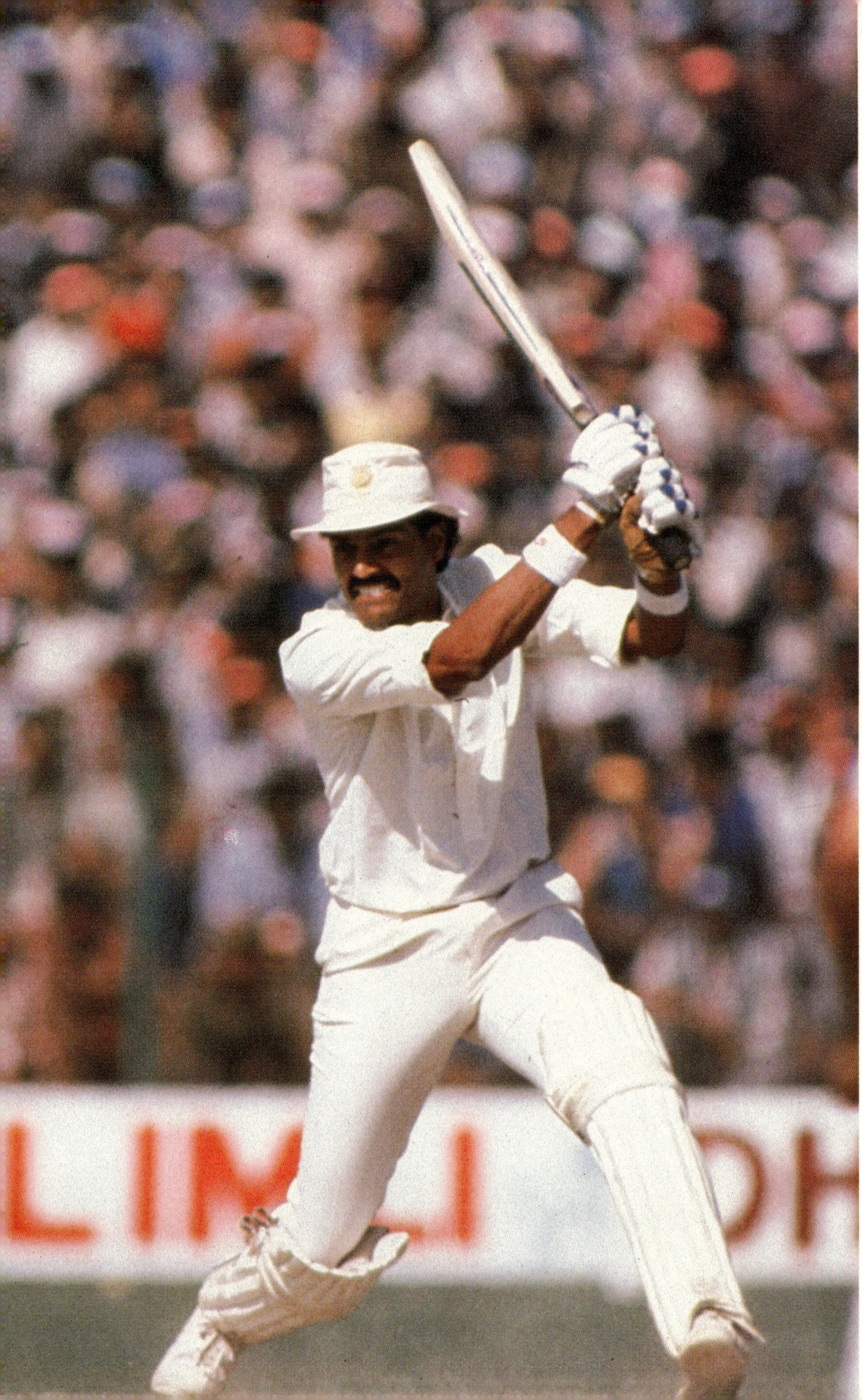

The pictures on this and the next eight pages are grouped together because they are what I like to think of as 'happy accidents'. The accident is not always optical illusion as it is here, sometimes it is simply a freak incident, such as is shown in the pictures on pages 112 and 113. Notice that in the picture of Bob Taylor overleaf, the shadow gives the game away.

David Gower wins the 1500 m hurdles, despite unsportsmanlike distractions from Dilip and Paul Downton, fifth Test, India v England, Kanpur, February 1985

CRICKET

Men to follow Methuselah

SCYLD BERRY speculates on the deputies behind England's stumps

ASSUMING Methuselah never kept wicket against Egypt or the touring Philistines — and if he had it would be reasonable to suppose that the event would be chronicled in the good book ('Wisden,' that is)—then the oldest wicket-keeper to appear in international cricket was England's Herbert Strudwick. He finally tossed in his gloves at the age of 46. At 42, Bob Taylor is as white-haired as any patriarch, but still keeping wicket—and himself—in immaculate trim.

So long as Taylor maintains his form, speculation is idle about a successor. Still, even Taylor will need a deputy on this winter's tour of Fiji, New Zealand and Pakistan. The question is what sort of deputy.

Paul Downton, Roger Tolchard, David Bairstow, Jack Richards and Ian Gould, in that order, have been the apprentices serving the master on England's recent tours, but it is possible that no specialist reserve keeper will be chosen this time. If Bob Willis is captain—which after his much improved leadership in the ...rd's Test is inevitable — ...n be expected to air ... favourite theories: ... a person on ...te one of ... land

game was the only form of county competition, all keepers were more or less in the 'purist' tradition. The oldest remaining practitioners on the circuit—Taylor, Eifion Jones, George Sharp, Alan Knott (if you can classify a genius)—were the last to be brought up before one-day cricket took hold.

Their wicket-keeping comes first; run-making, while important, is secondary. This revised purist tradition continues with Downton, Richards, David East, Bruce French, Bobby Parks, Terry Davies, Trevor Gard and Andy Brassington.

But the demands of one-day cricket have also produced the pragmatists. To them batting, especially in 'one-dayers,' is as much a part of their job as wicket-keeping, and the rough-and-readiness which may be an occasional defect in their keeping is the virtue of their batting. In effect, they are all-rounders: Bairstow, Gould, Tolchard, Geoff Humpage, David Humphries and Chris Maynard are of this school.

However, neither a purist nor pragm... quite suits the ... of England's ... a Richards ...ot going to ... a place in ... not even ... banned ... will chal- ...d batsmen ... so help to ...tandards. ...nd his ... one-

do the job in one-day internationals.

It would seem to me that only one cricketer fills this bill and the requirements of the Willis theory. That is Gloucestershire's opening batsman A. W. Stovold, first name Andy, second by coincidence Willis. This season so far he has scored more runs than any other batsman born in England.

As for wicket-keeping, Stovold kept on and off for Gloucestershire until the end of the 1981 season, when he recorded more stumpings than anyone else. Then he was asked if he would like to concentrate on his batting, to which he agreed because he found the combination too hard on his legs —for a complete season. But he has always kept a pair of gloves in his car since then, just in case.

Stovold's selection would only be a temporary measure, since he could never be considered a successor to Taylor; though he might make the grade as a Test batsman; he has the shots, off the back foot as well as front, and says he has learnt to calm down this season. Should Taylor ever flag, the moment may come after England's tour to select one of the young purists like Downton (who has already played four Tests and put only one glove wrong) or Richards or East or French, all much-of-a-muchness but deserving a trial.

Another consideration is that Stovold's selection for this tour would encourage the others in that part of England and discourage the widespread notion that selectors have their favourite counties. It is 10 years since a cricketer from Gloucestershire, Glamorgan or Worcestershire was capped by England.

The person who might be most encouraged could be the ... wer to the question ... ccessor. ... ll, aged ... the ... m ... d

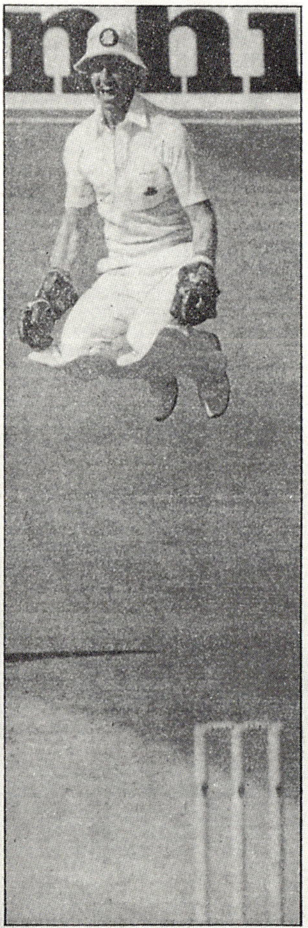
ADRIAN MURRELL

Bob Taylor : Will he ever flag ?

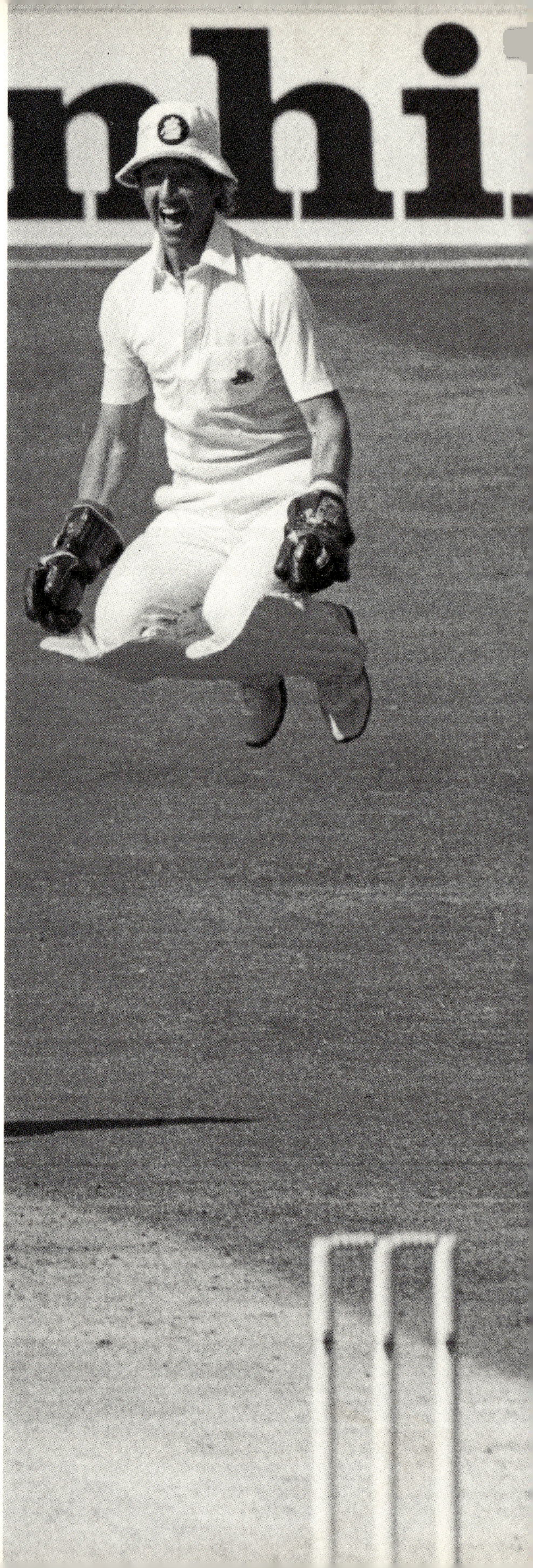

I don't really know why optical illusions please me so much. Perhaps it is because they make me, and the public, and – not to be overlooked – the picture editor, smile.

These new man-made soles are unpredictable, Bob Taylor, second Test, England v New Zealand, Headingley, July 1983

opposite: *Syed Kirmani attempts to distract Rodney Hogg with his new juggling routine, India v Australia, Chelmsford, June 1983*

overleaf, left: *Get off, you're too heavy! Mike Brearley and David Bairstow, Middlesex v Yorkshire, Lord's, May 1980*

overleaf, right: *If you can't run 'em out, knock 'em out, Ian Botham and Rod Marsh, fifth Test, England v Australia, Old Trafford, August 1981*

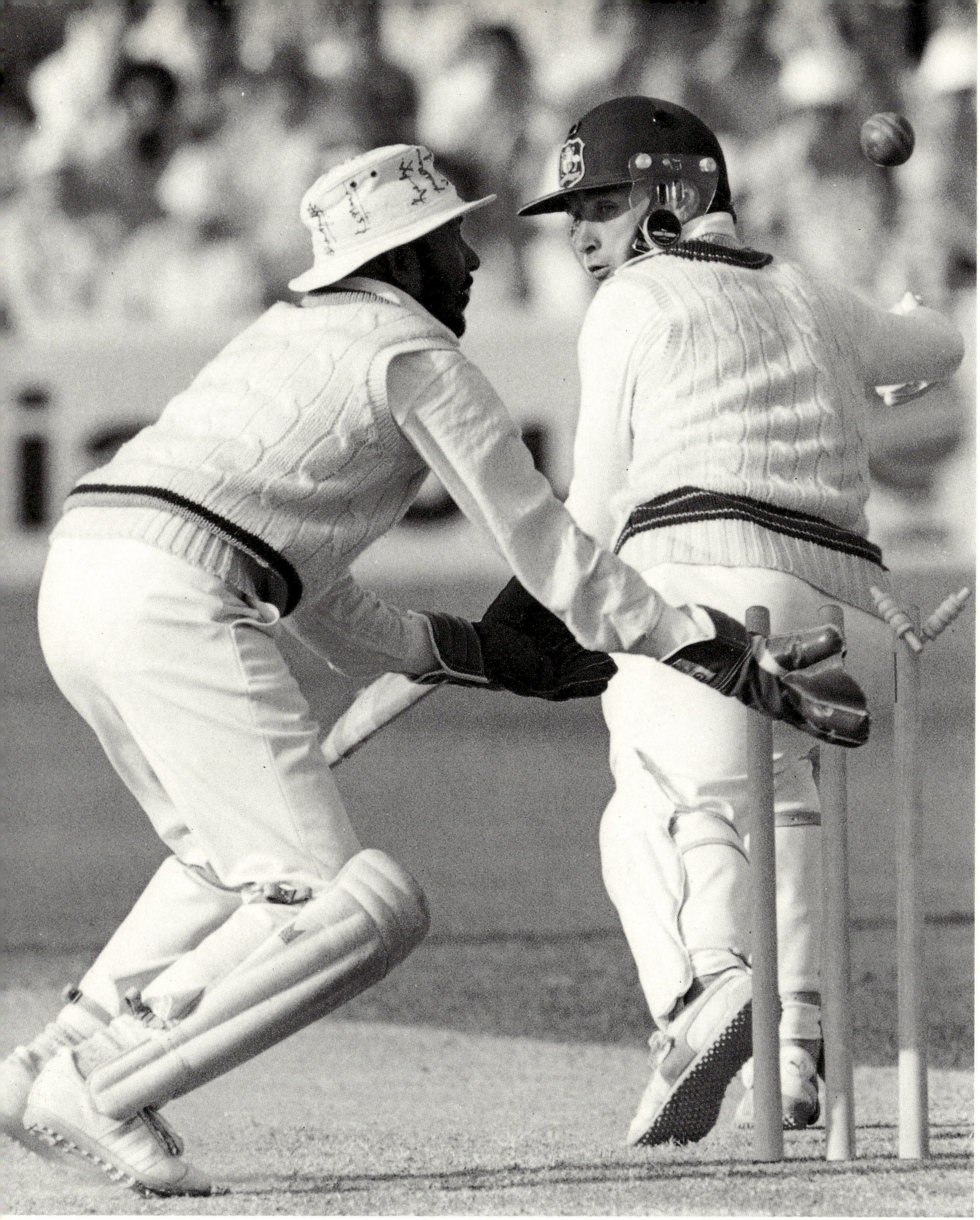

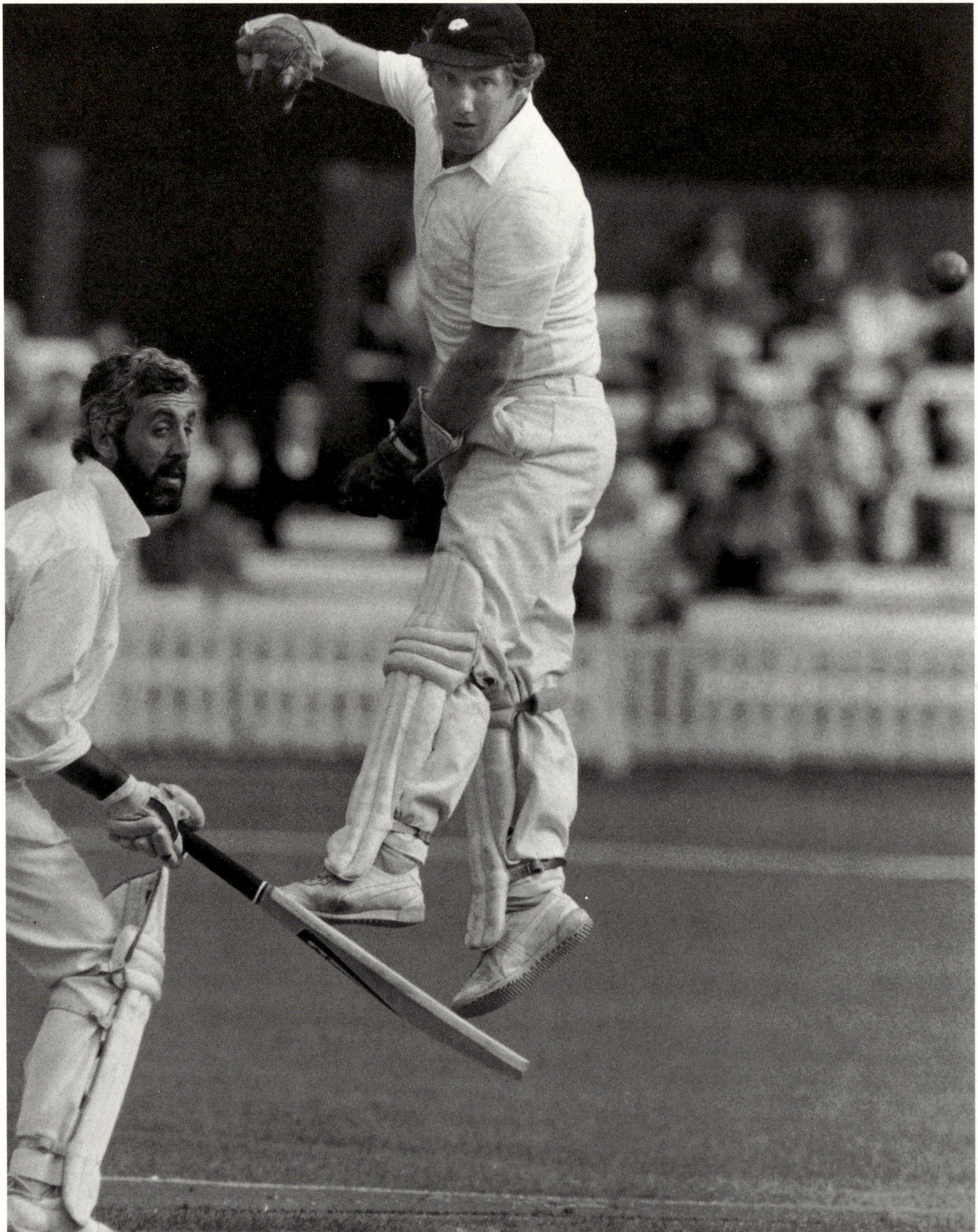

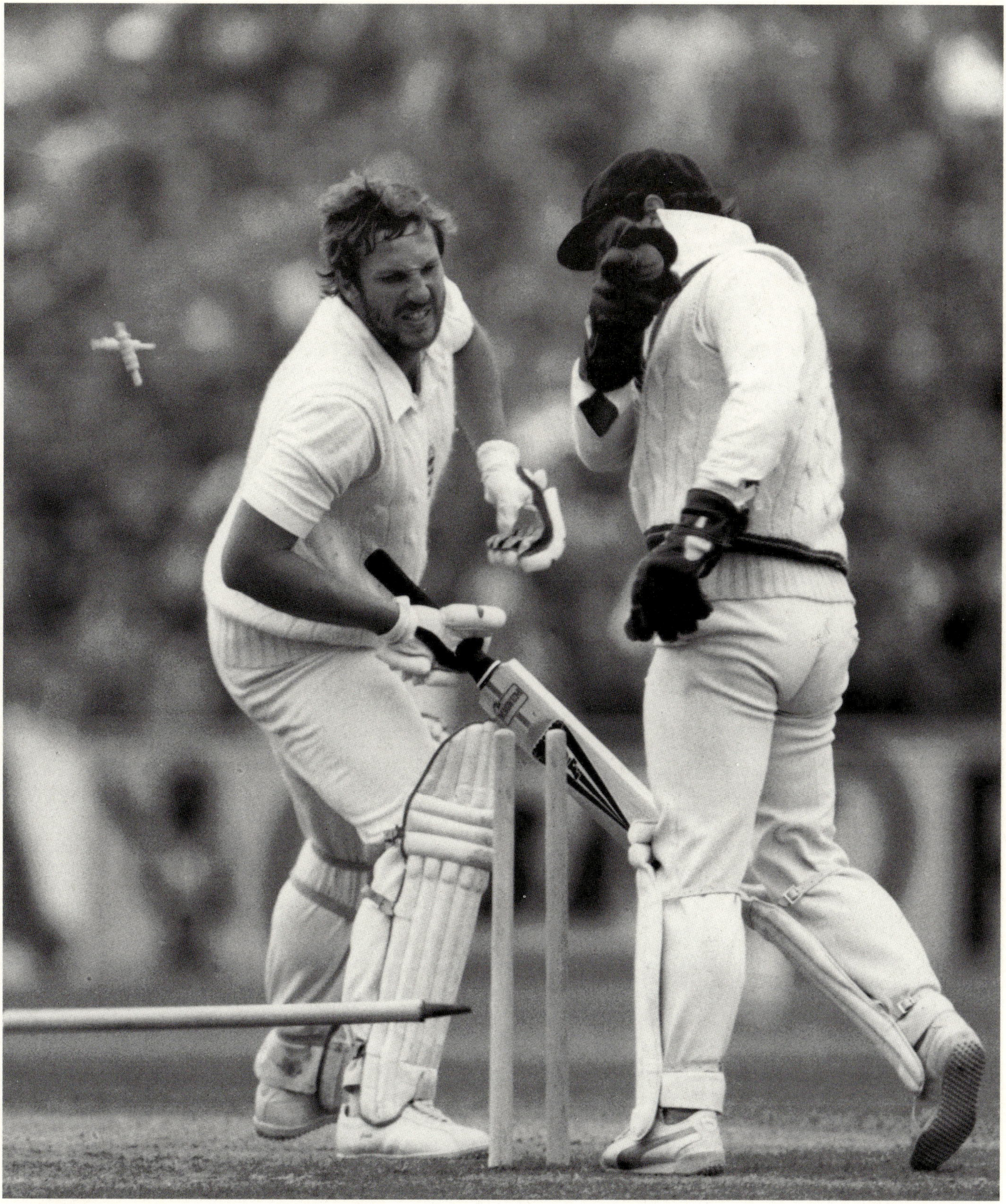

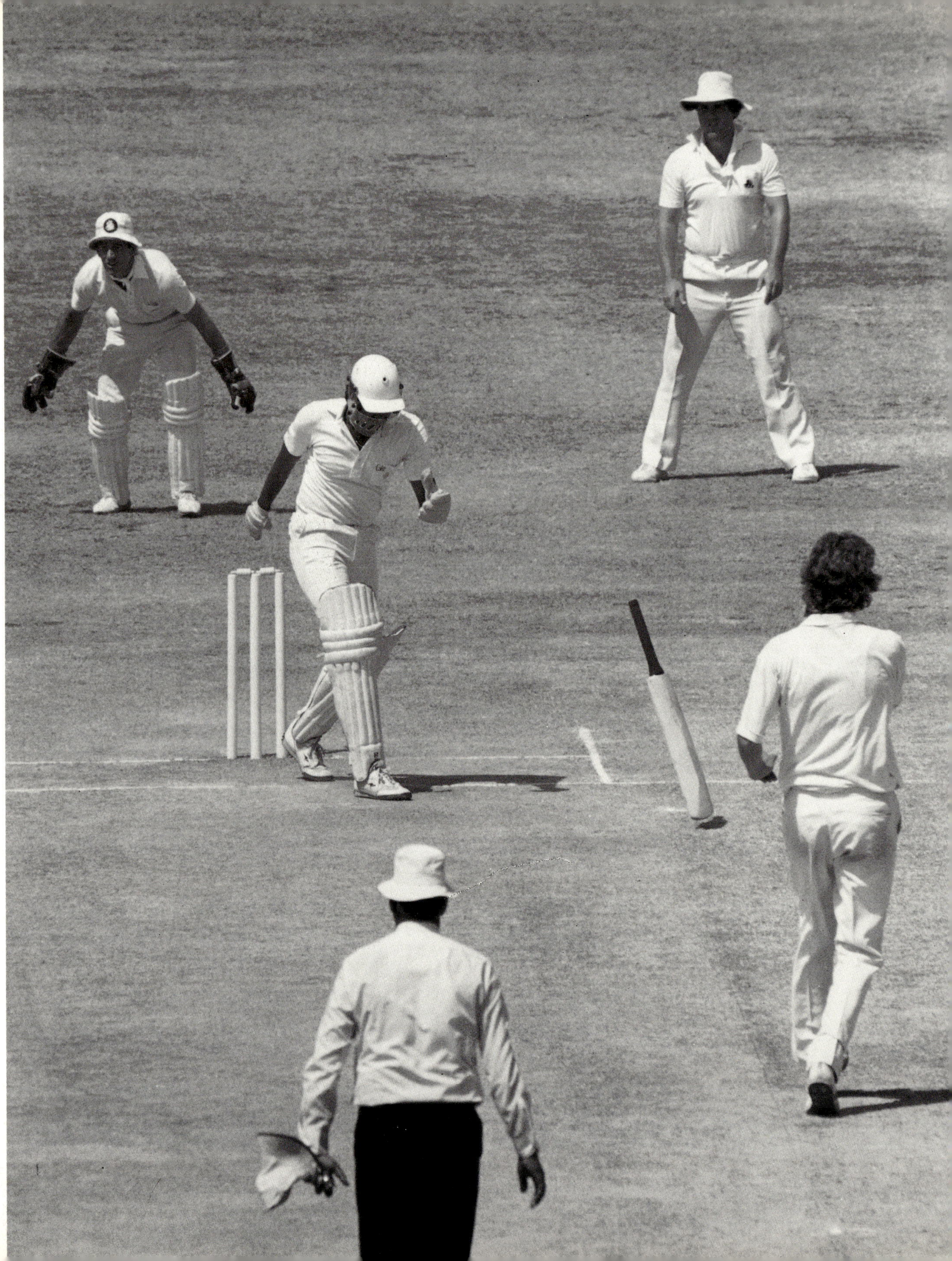

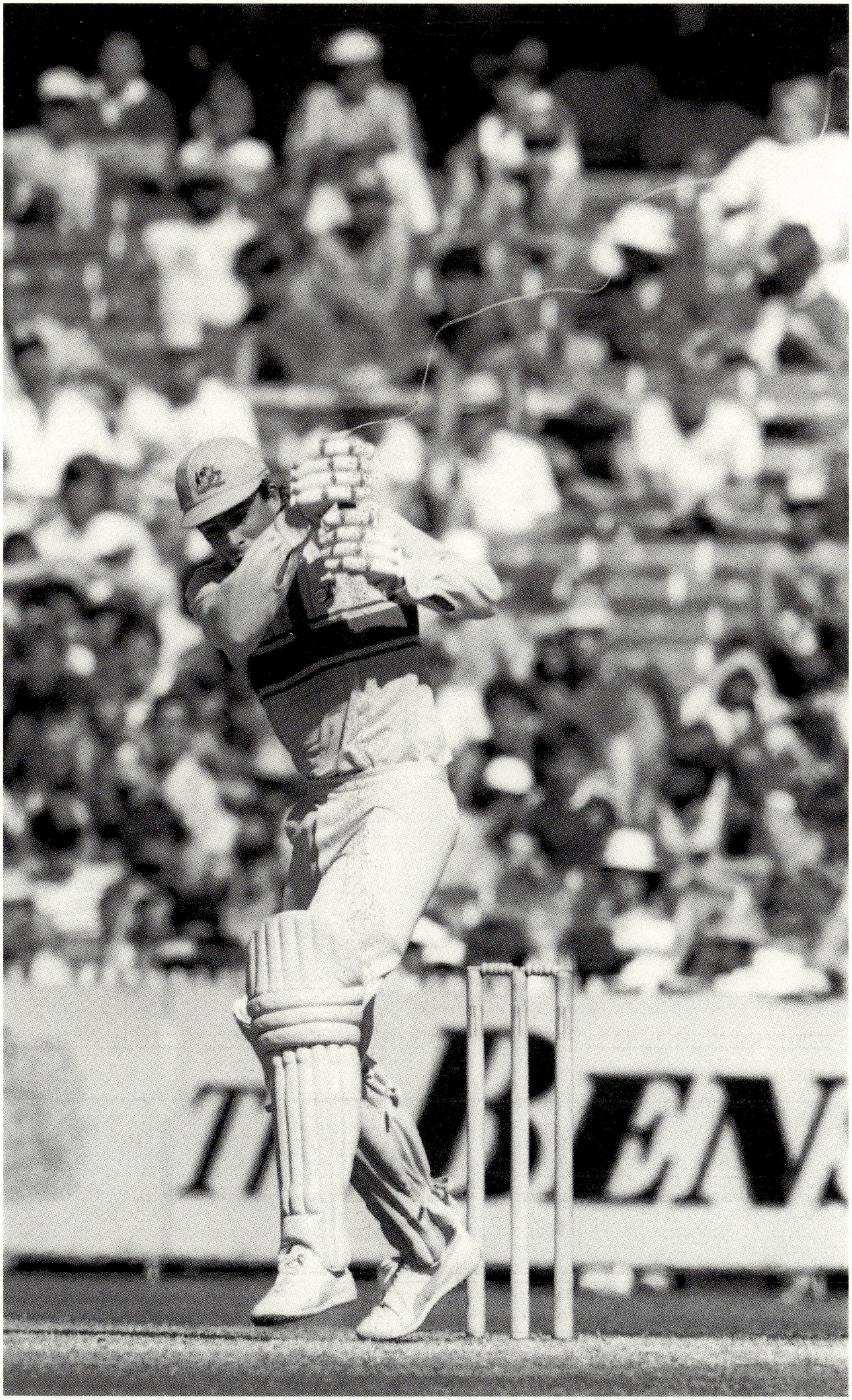

Simon O'Donnell finds looping the loop tricky, World Championship of Cricket, Australia v West Indies, Melbourne, March 1985

below: *In the tea interval he tears up telephone directories. Man of the Match Safraz (final score 90), and Zaheer, third Test, Pakistan v England, Lahore, March 1984*

opposite: *OK, so where's first base? Azeem Hafiz after facing torrid bouncer from Bob Willis, first Test, Pakistan v England, Karachi, March 1984*

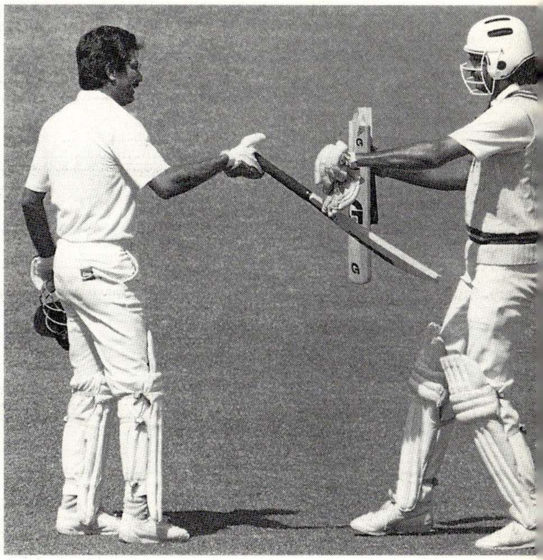

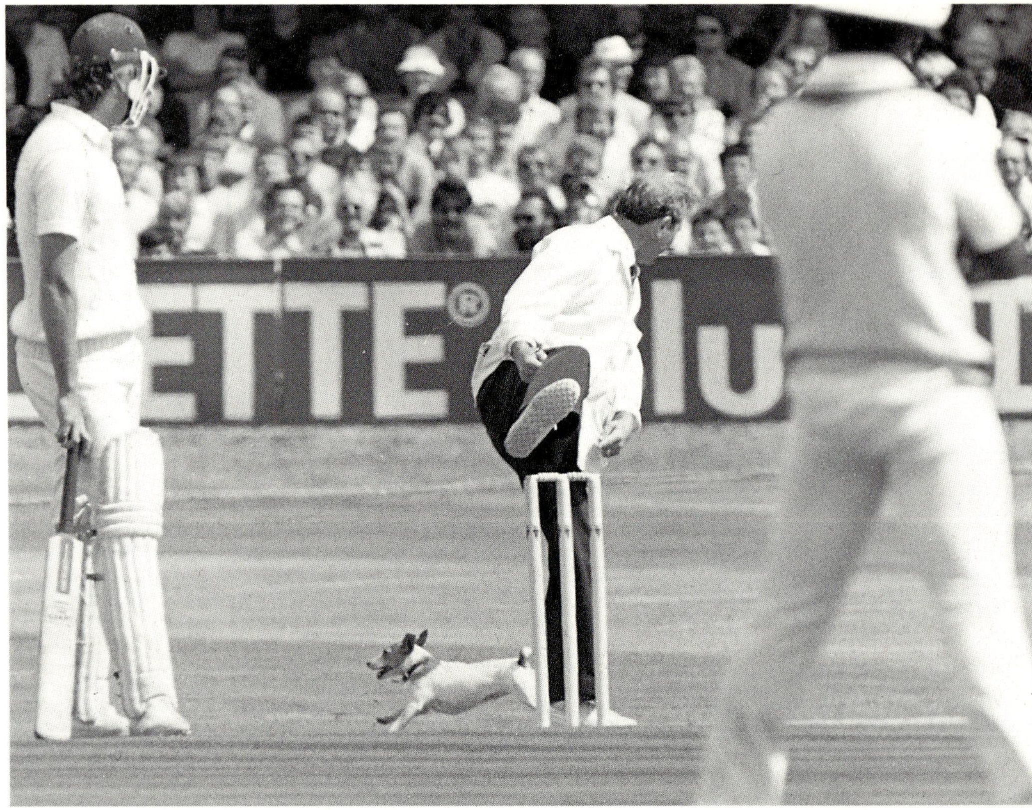

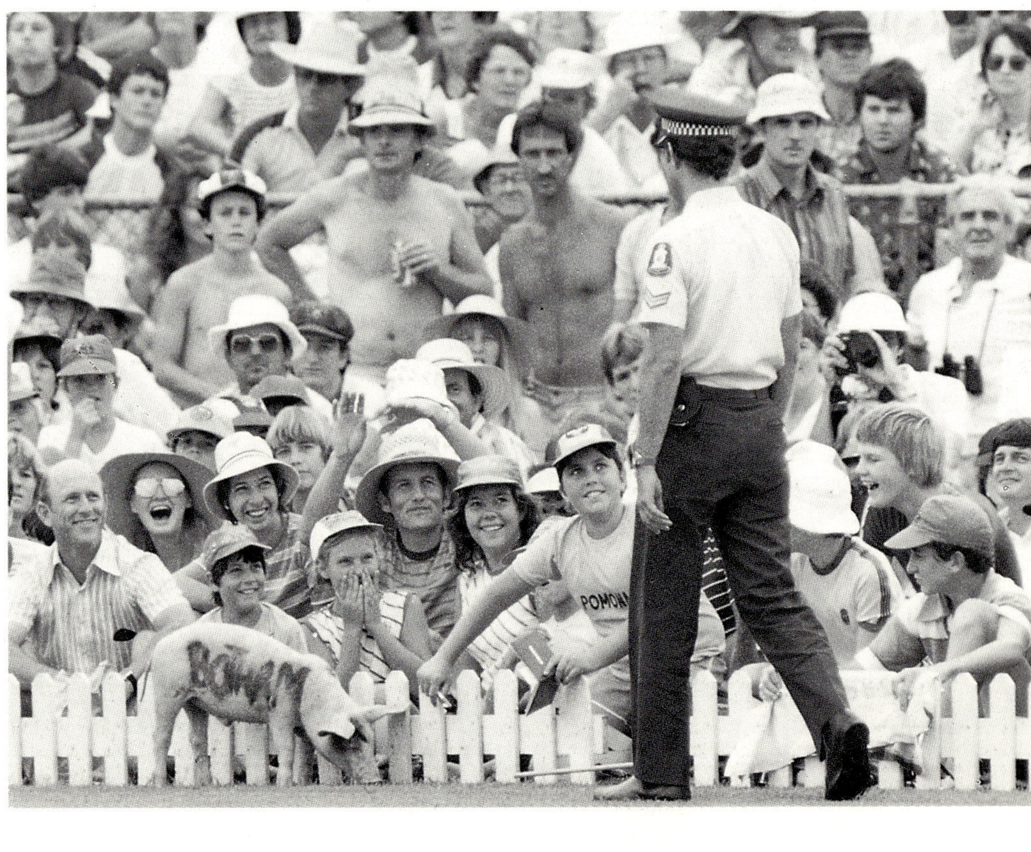

The umpire gives a wrong decision, third Test, England v West Indies, Headingley, July 1984

Botham fan invades pitch – and then eats it, one-day international, New Zealand v England, Brisbane, December 1982

opposite: *Kim Hughes attacked by frenzied seagull, but quick-thinking Colin Croft comes to the rescue, third Test, Australia v West Indies, Adelaide, January 1980*

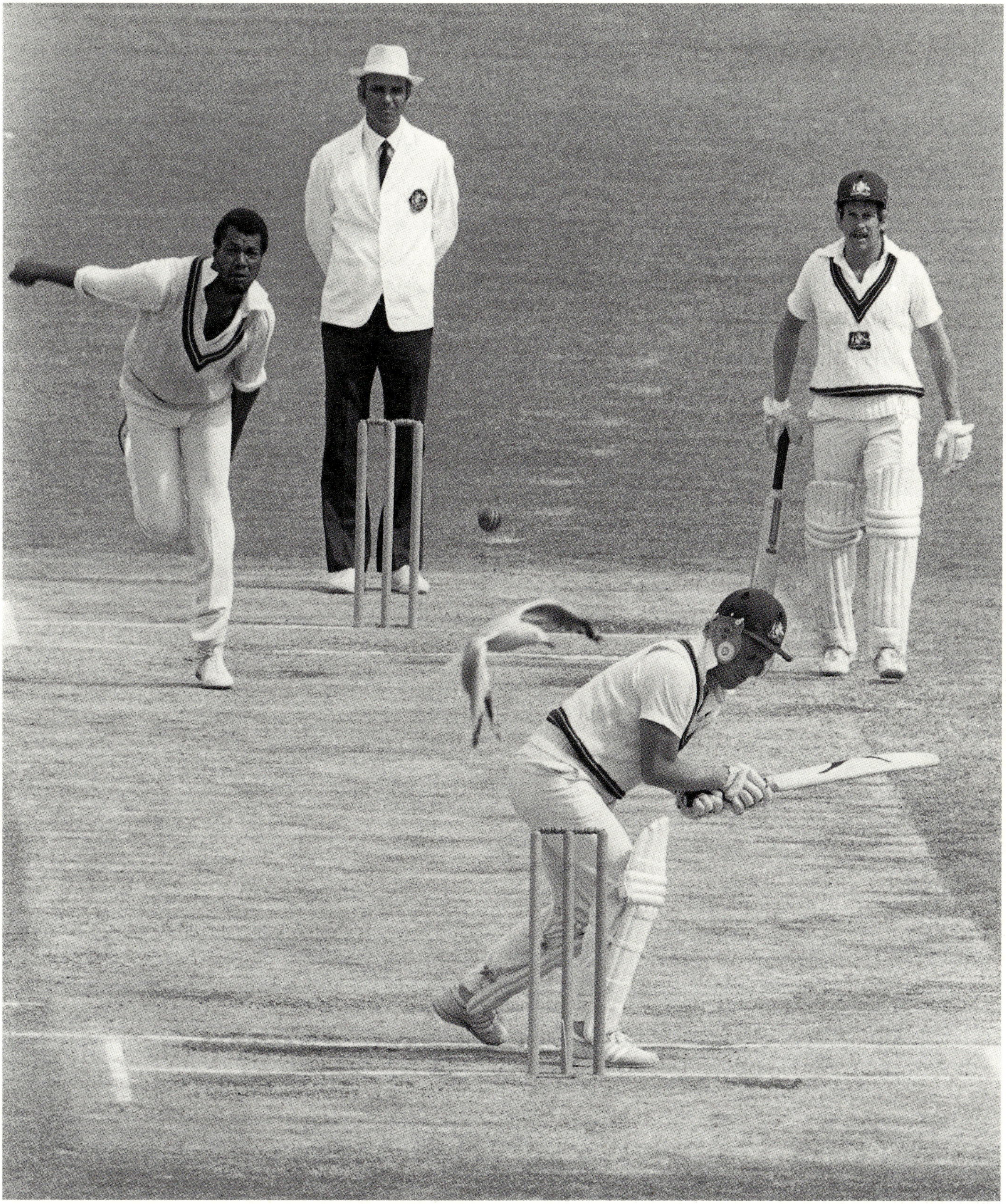

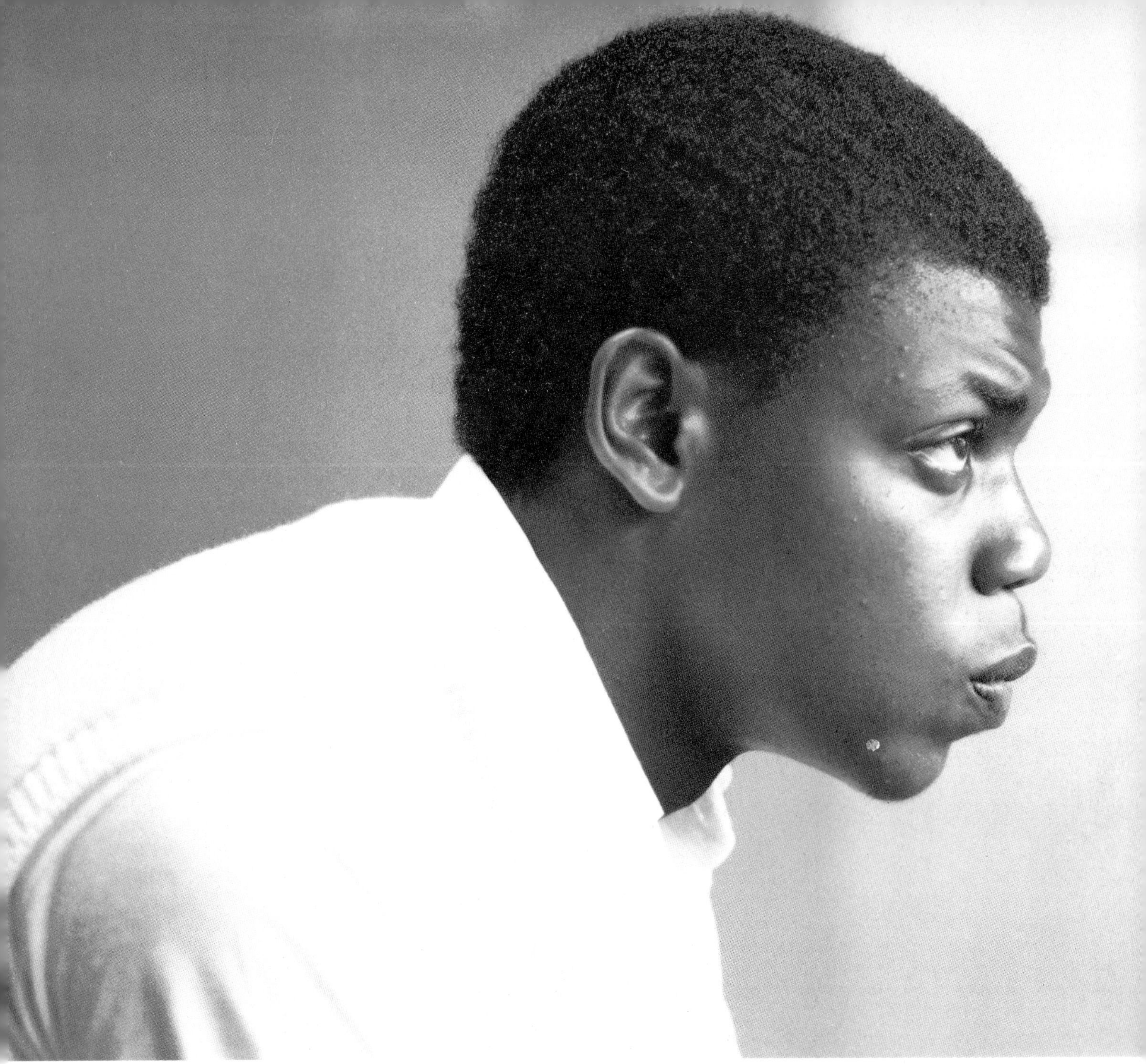

David Lawrence, a favourite portrait, July 1981
opposite: *Syed Kirmani in Kanpur, February 1985*

Although I am a sports photographer and spend my days and now, with the advent of floodlights, sometimes my nights also, taking photographs of cricket, I am most at home with portraiture, happiest when trying to capture in print my understanding of the people I have watched playing. If you are alert and concentrating – and competent – sooner or later you are bound to get any number of action shots, but capturing the elusive personality of a man (or a woman) is far less certain. Nor is portraiture confined to straightforward studies of the subject's head and shoulders. Sometimes the complex messages of 'body language' are more explicit than the face alone would be.

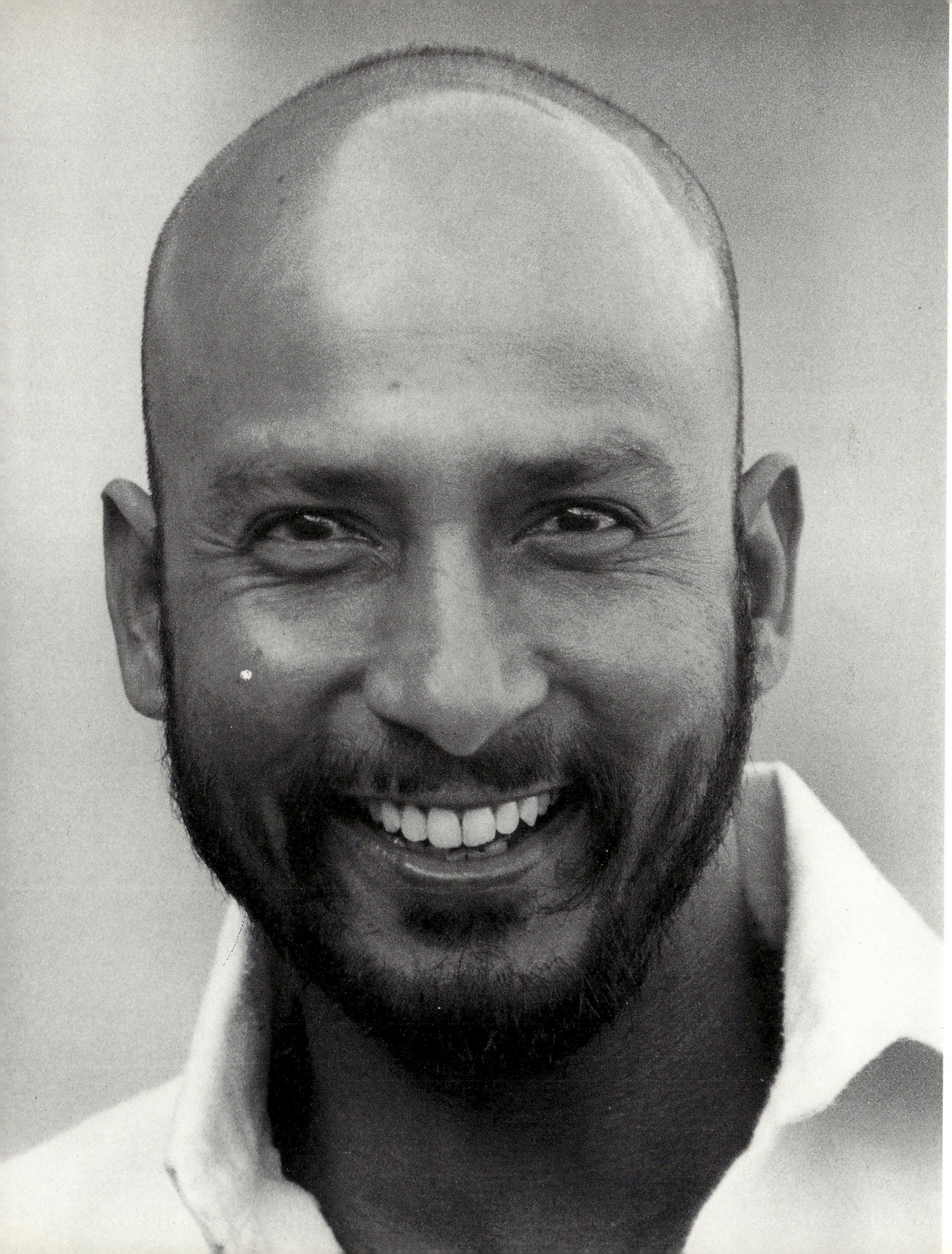

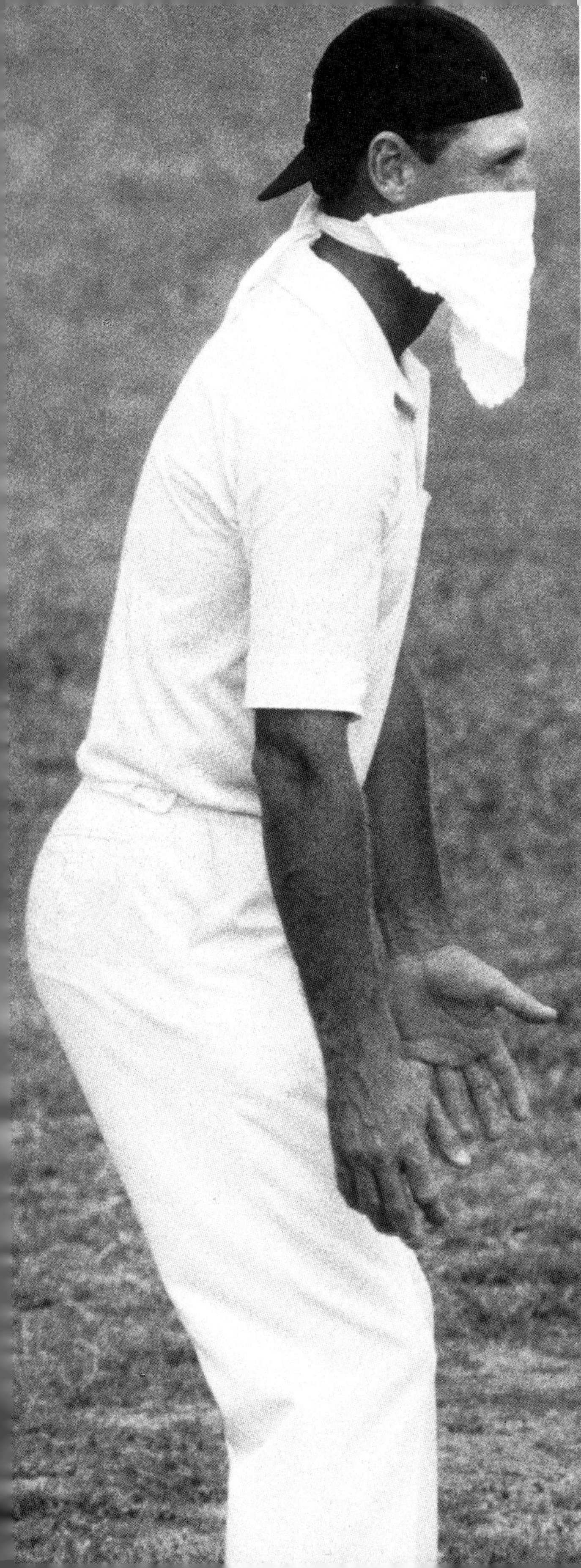

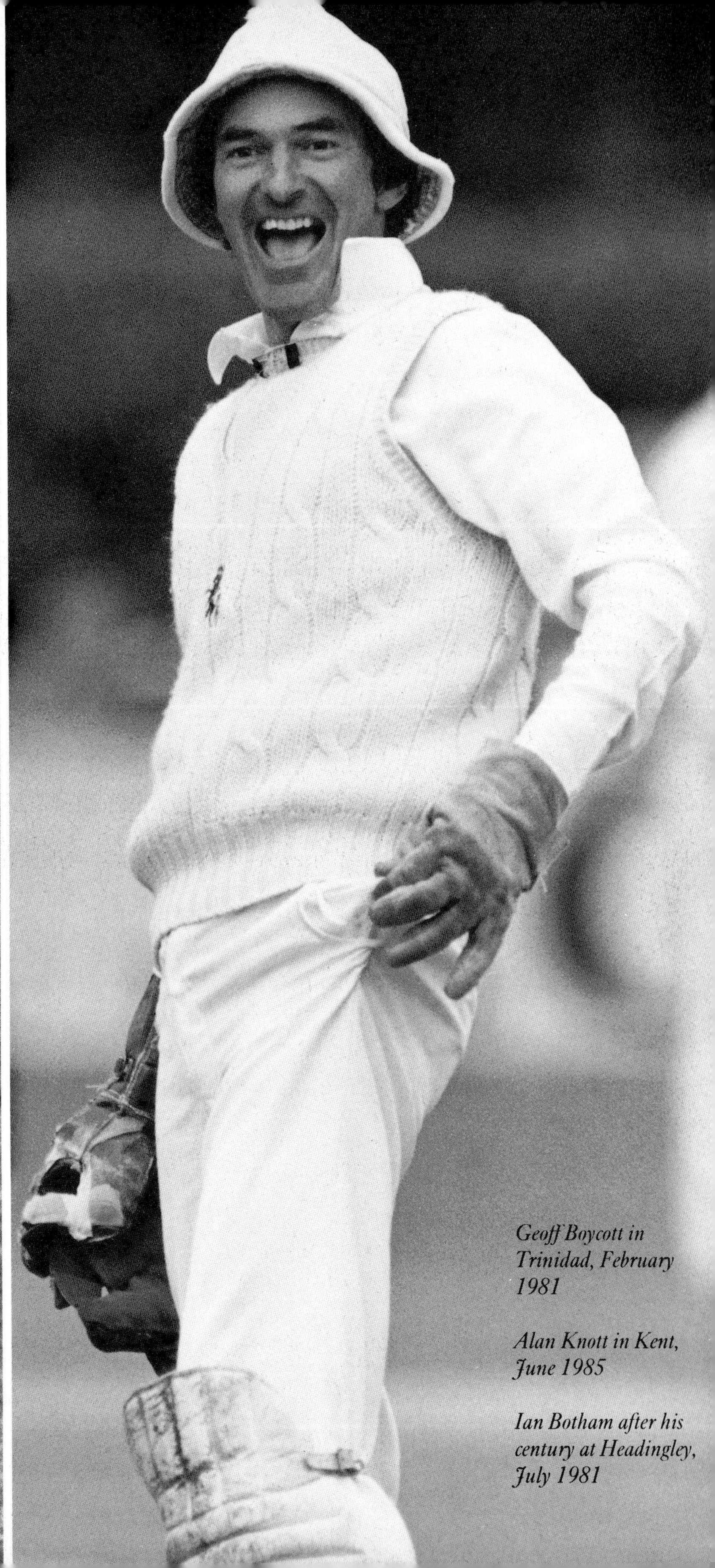

Geoff Boycott in Trinidad, February 1981

Alan Knott in Kent, June 1985

Ian Botham after his century at Headingley, July 1981

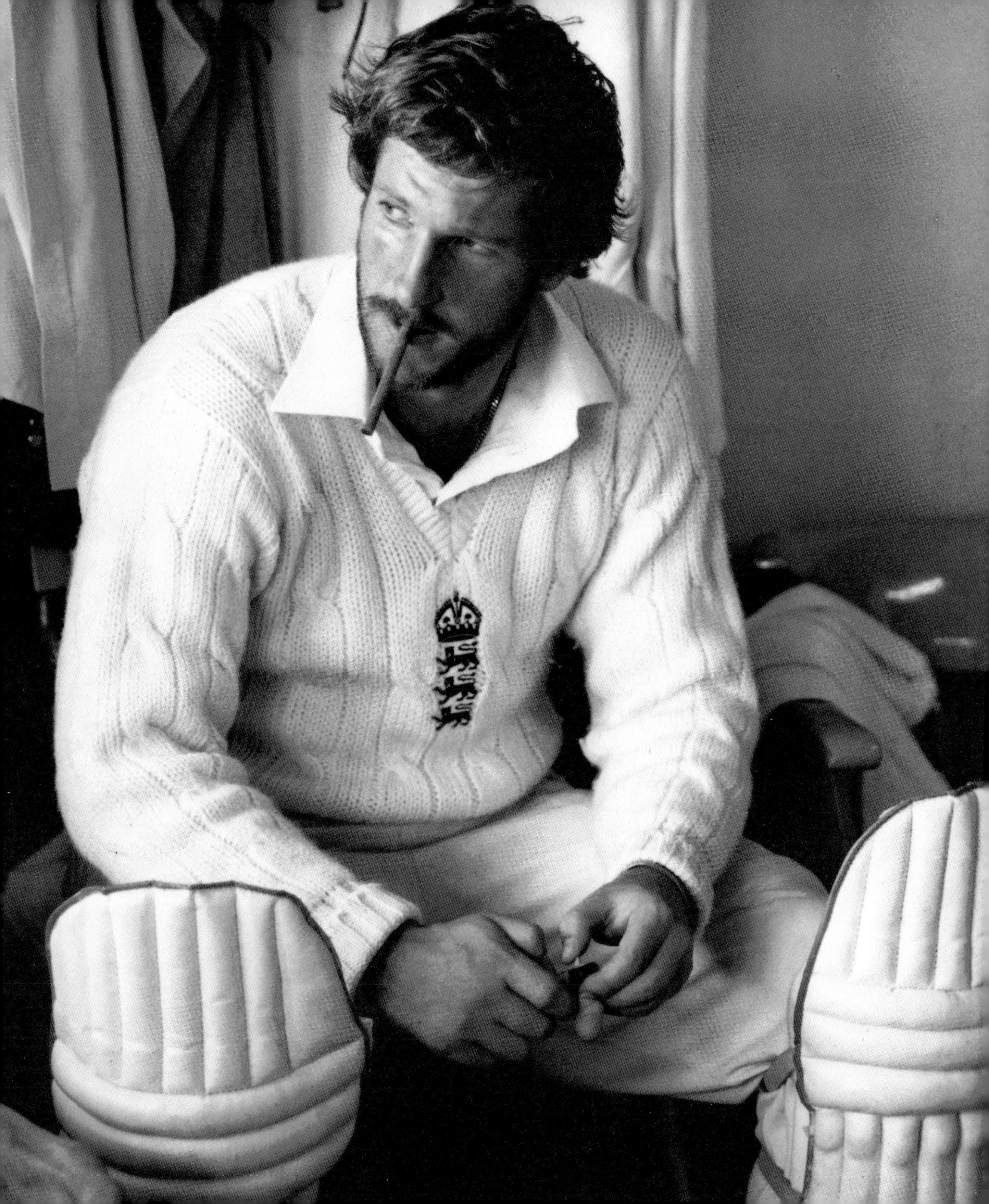

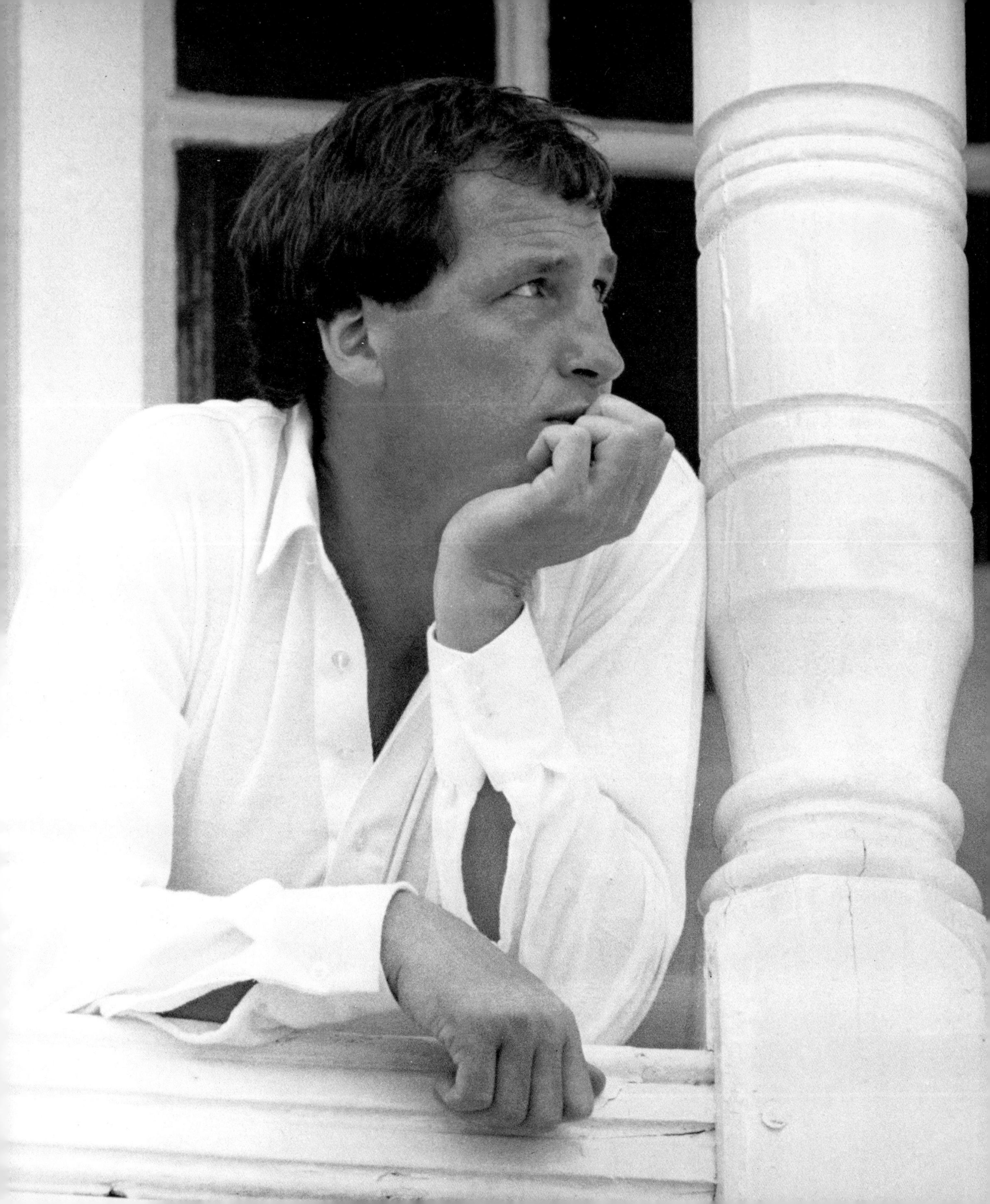

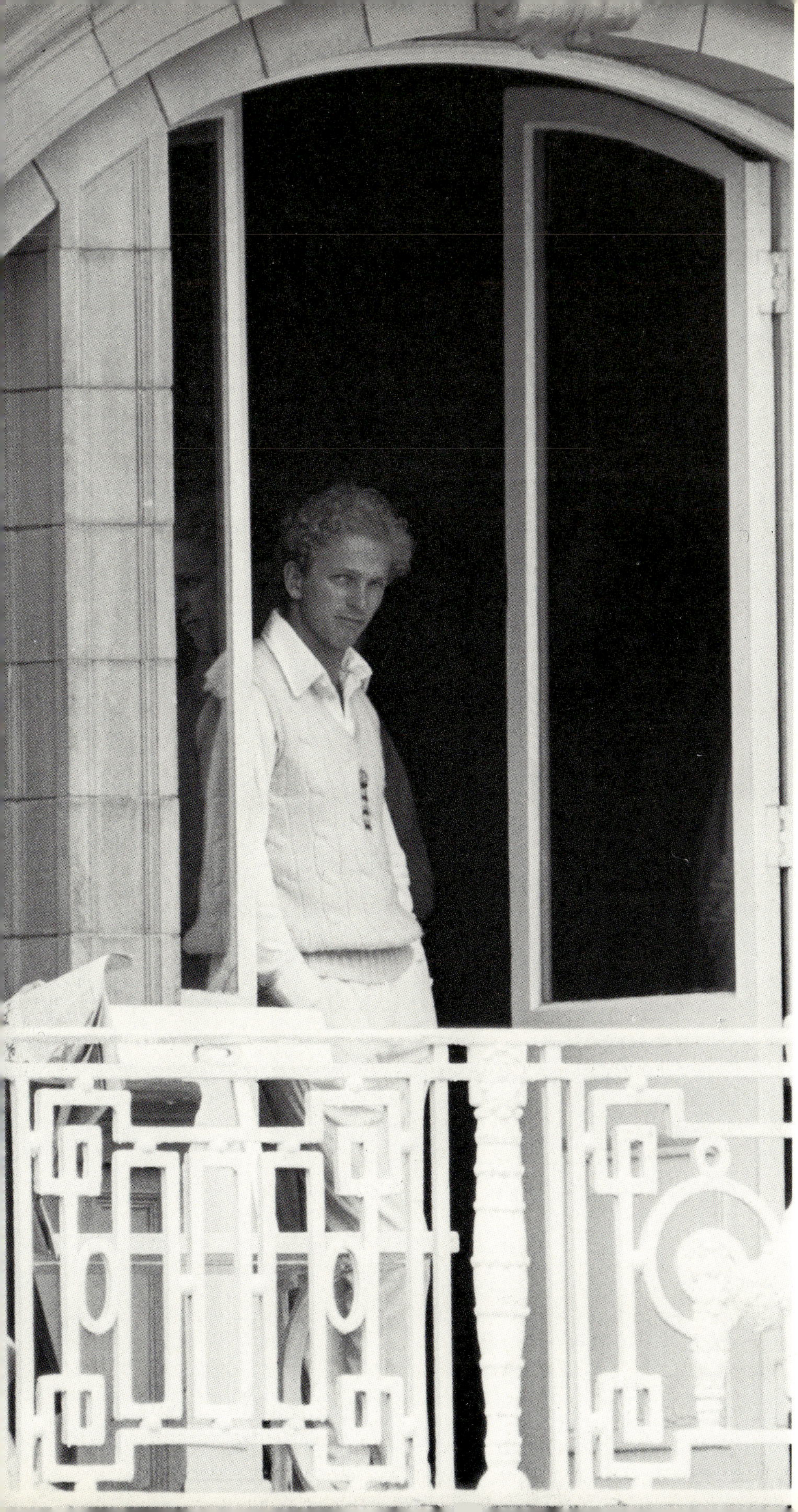

These revealing shots don't just happen to order, you have to watch and wait for them, and above all *recognise* the moment when it occurs. This last applies particularly to the shot of David Gower. For me, this is the definitive picture of the loneliness of the captain who is losing. I took it during the second Test against the West Indies in 1984, after Gower had declared prematurely. (He was the first England captain to lose after declaring since Yardley made the same mistake in 1948.) He then had to watch Gordon Greenidge hammer the English attack, making 214 not out. At that stage Gower could not have known (neither could I) how complete defeat was going to be in that series, yet the pressures already weighing on him as captain are implicit in this study.
On the facing page, John Emburey, who had been banned for three years from Test cricket for taking part in the South African tour in 1982, is also thoughtful. This picture was taken during the three-year ban at a match at Trent Bridge in which Emburey was playing for Middlesex against Nottingham. Maybe it reflects some of his doubts.

David Gower – What have I done? second Test, England v West Indies, Lord's, June 1984

opposite: *A thoughtful 'Embers' at Trent Bridge, July 1984*

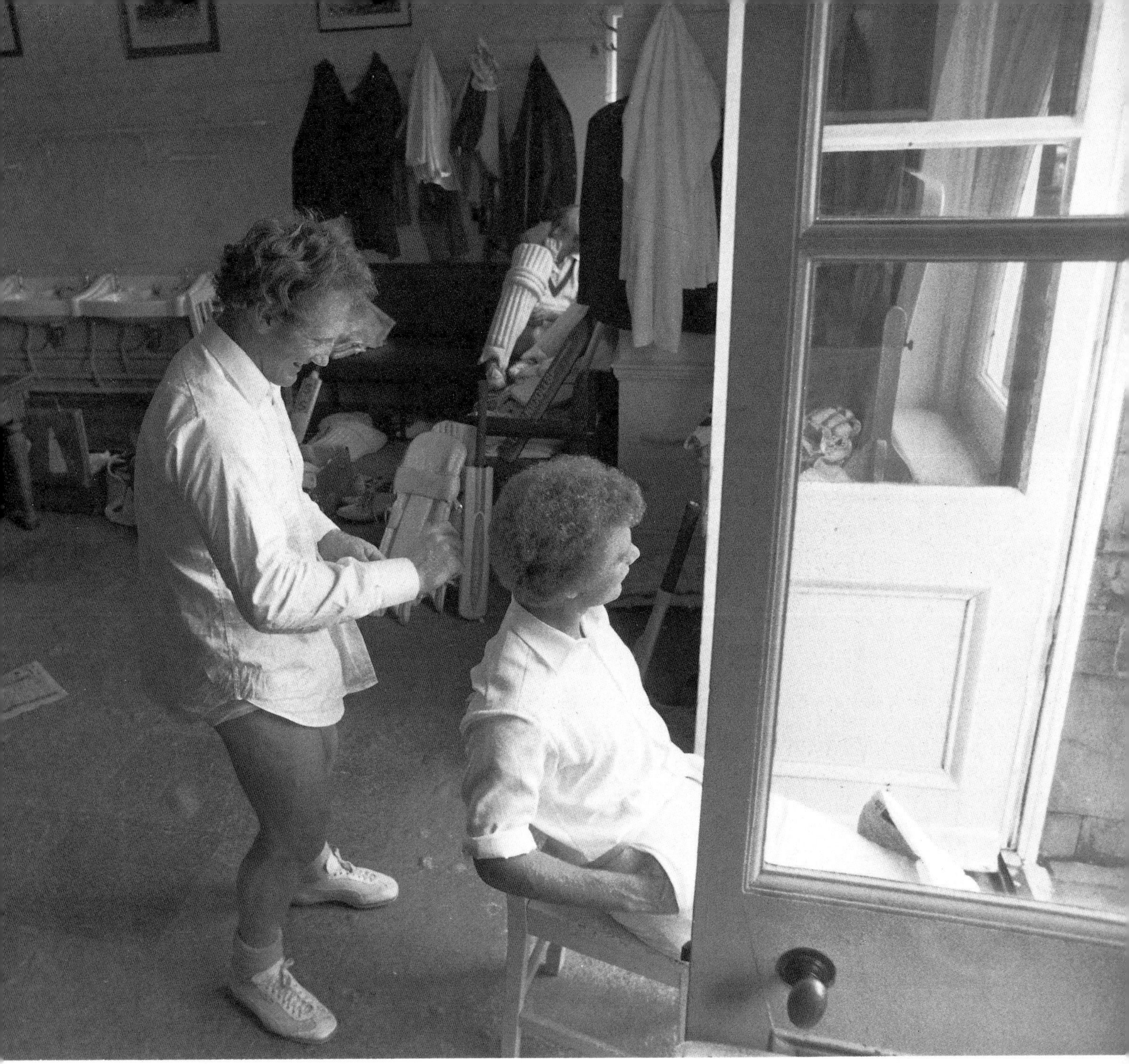

These off-the-field shots are subtly different from portraits, although the dividing line is not clear. They are grouped together here – and perhaps they were taken for this purpose also – to convey the atmosphere of the dressing room rather than the character of the subjects, although that too emerges.

Kevin Sharp having his hair cut by David Bairstow in the dressing room at Lord's, June 1980

opposite, above: *Bill Athey, Gloucestershire (ex-Yorkshire) and England in reflective mood, Lord's, June 1980*

opposite, below: *The young David Lawrence on his debut for Gloucestershire under 19's, July 1981*

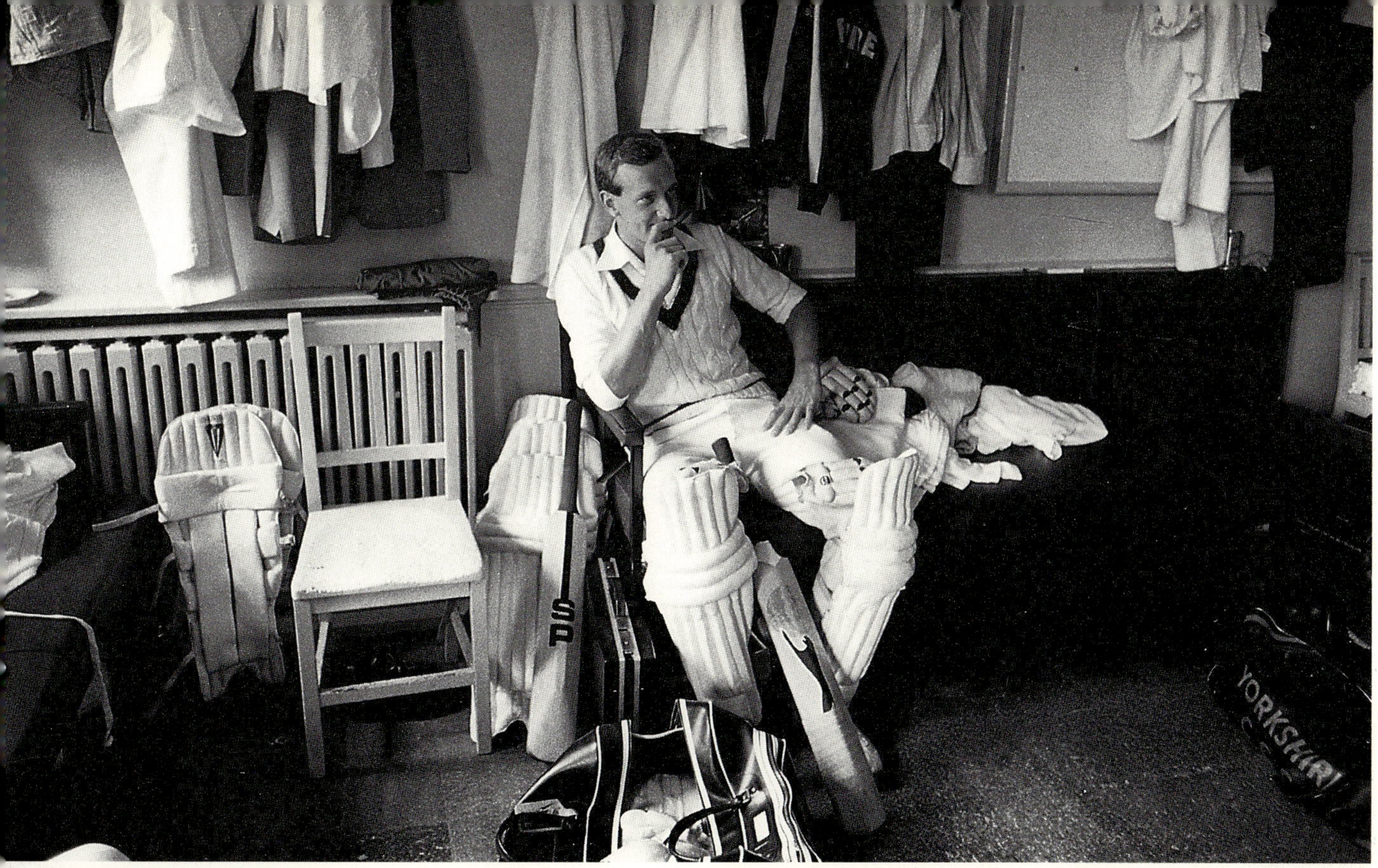

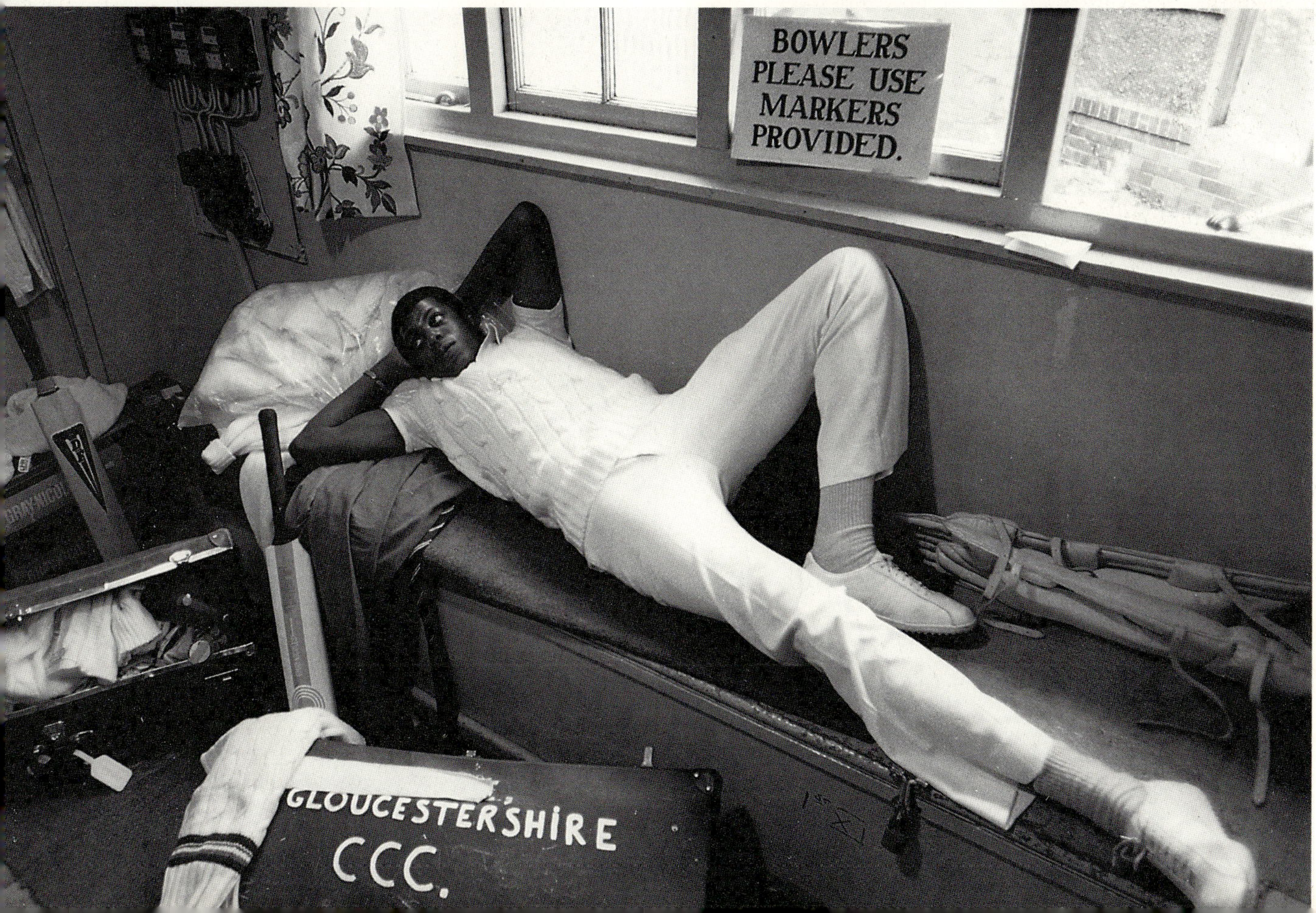
BOWLERS
PLEASE USE
MARKERS
PROVIDED.
GLOUCESTERSHIRE
CCC.

I've shined your shoes,
I've moved your mountains
And marked your cards.
But Eden is burning,
Either brace yourself for Elimination,
Or else your hearts must have the courage
For the changing of the guards.
Bob Dylan 1978

Finally – Bob Willis, a complex character, who changed his name by deedpoll to include Dylan. He is a fanatical Dylan follower and used to listen to his music before a match to help him relax. Although these are all action shots reproduced here, I think they also show something of the man's (as opposed to the cricketer's) inner tension.

opposite, left: *Directing the field* and right: *Bowling during the Pakistan tour in 1984*

Bob Willis receives a Marshall bouncer in the second Test, England v West Indies, Lord's, July 1984

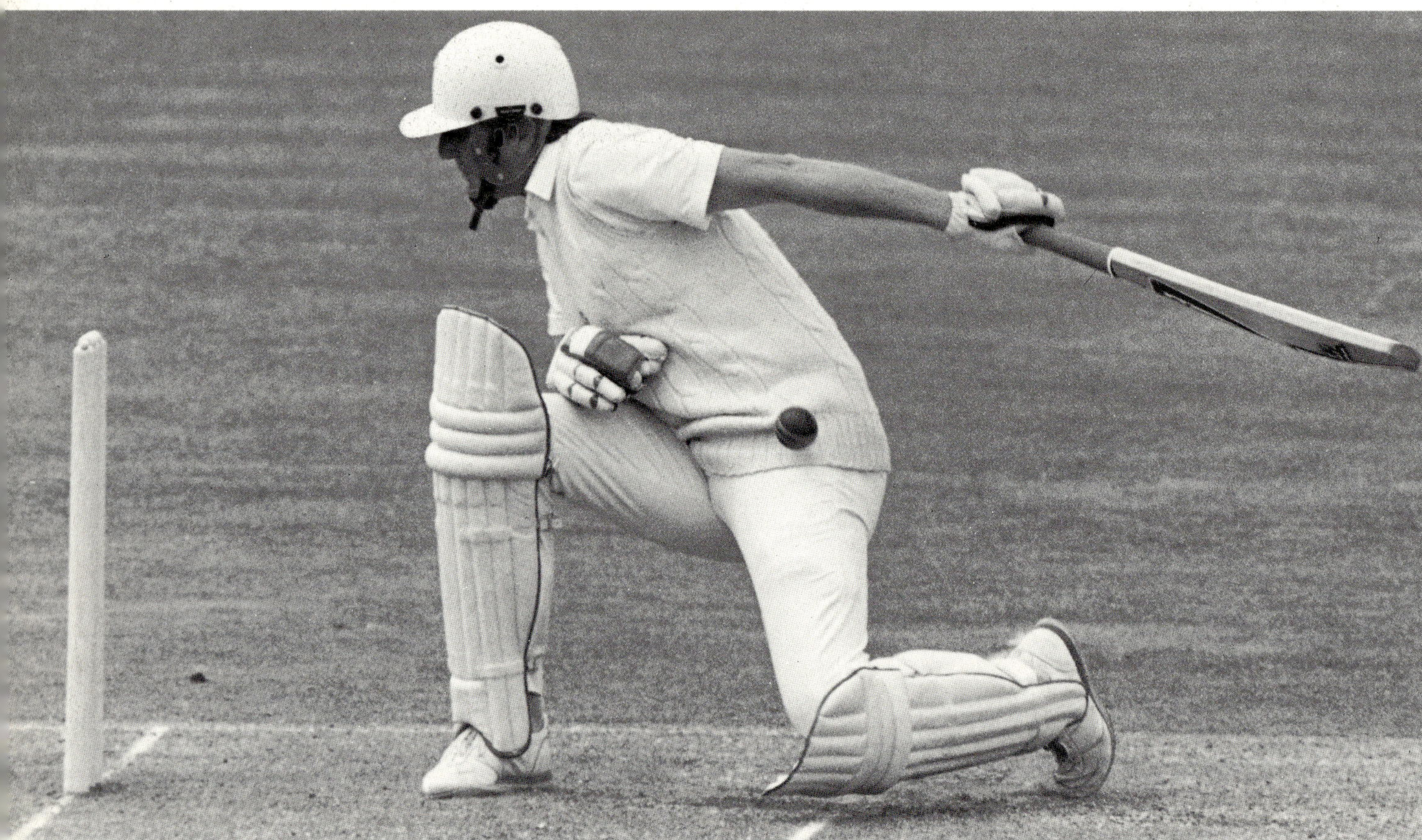

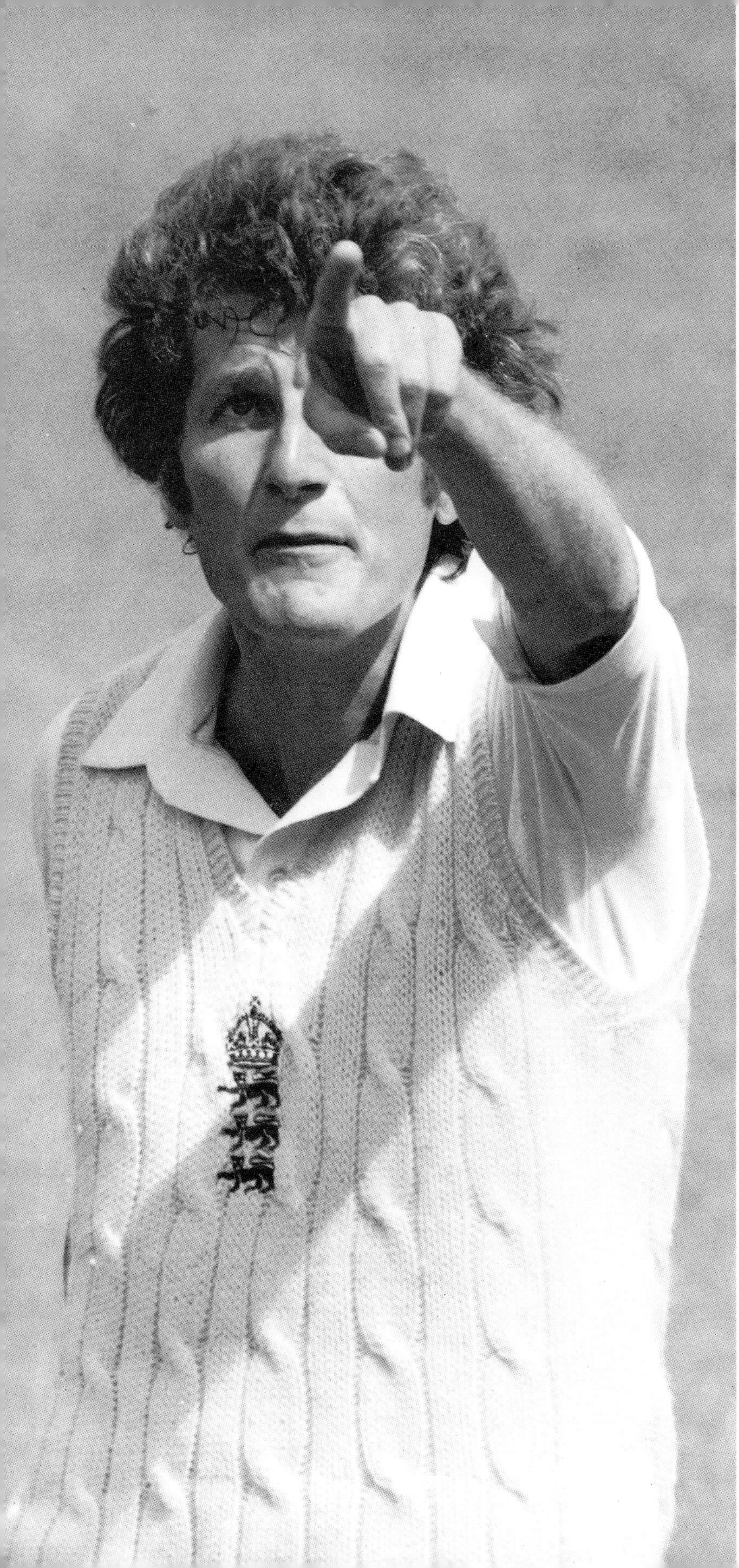

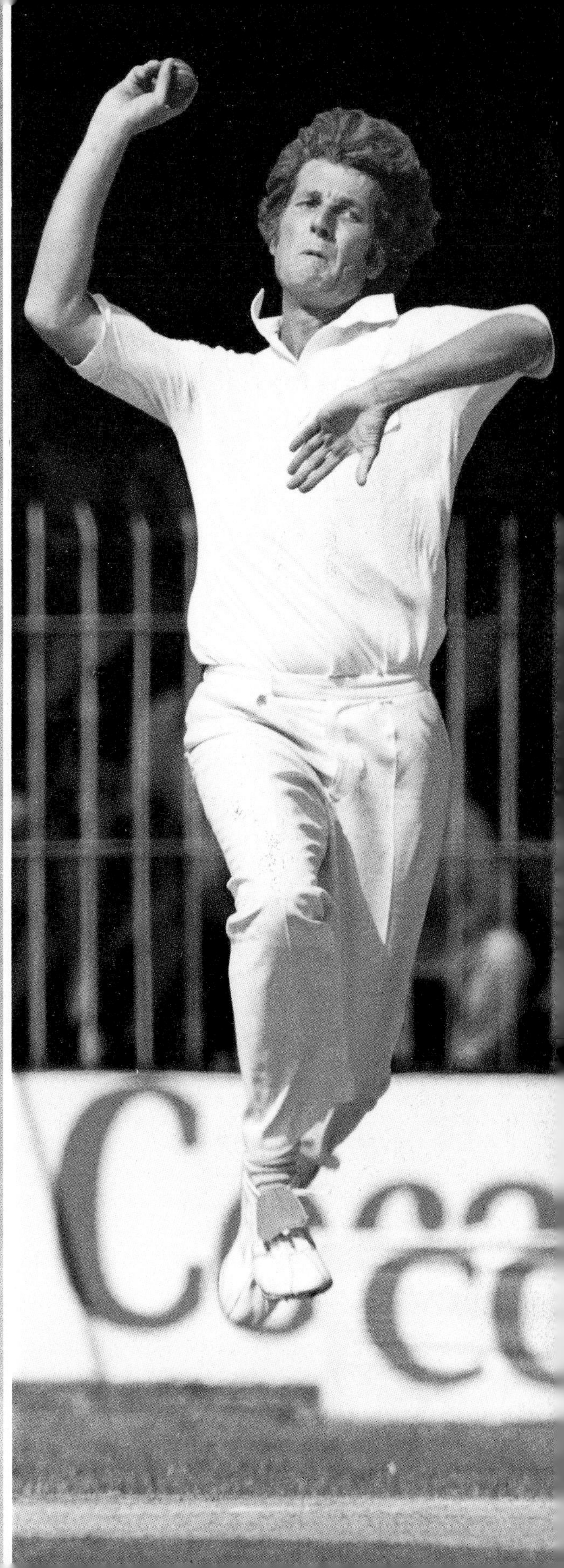

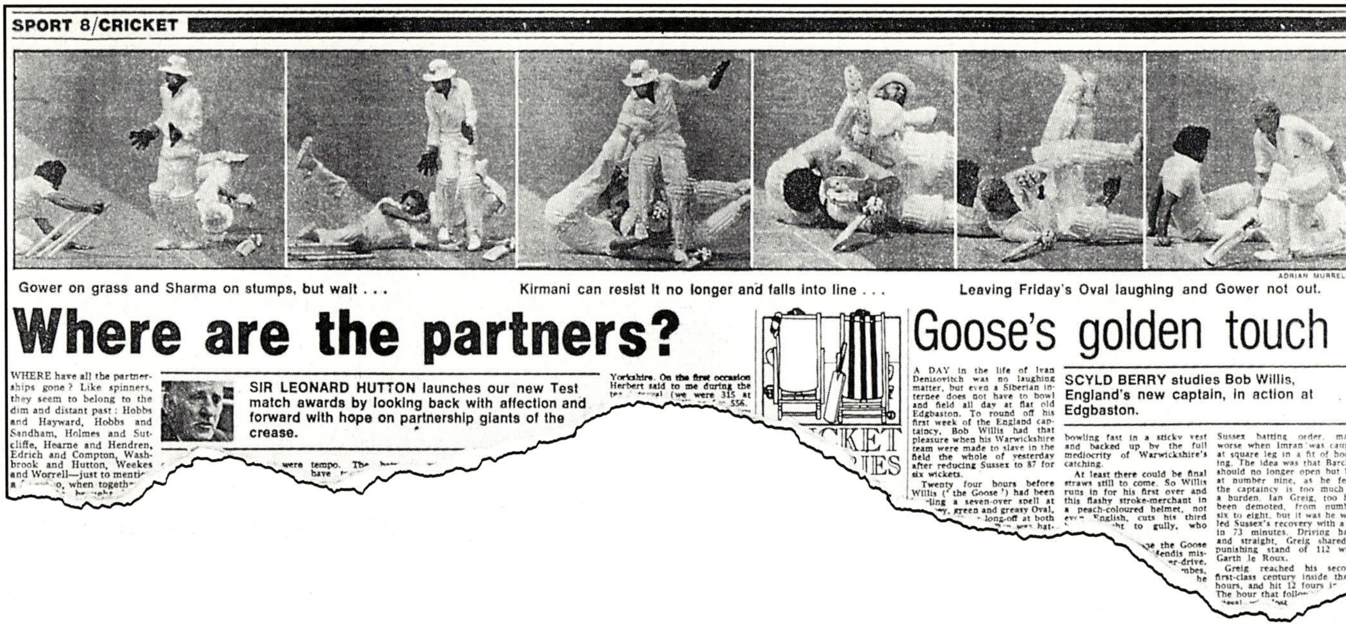

SPORT 8/CRICKET

Gower on grass and Sharma on stumps, but wait . . .

Kirmani can resist it no longer and falls into line . . .

Leaving Friday's Oval laughing and Gower not out.

ADRIAN MURRELL

Where are the partners?

SIR LEONARD HUTTON launches our new Test match awards by looking back with affection and forward with hope on partnership giants of the crease.

WHERE have all the partnerships gone? Like spinners, they seem to belong to the dim and distant past: Hobbs and Hayward, Hobbs and Sandham, Holmes and Sutcliffe, Hearne and Hendren, Edrich and Compton, Washbrook and Hutton, Weekes and Worrell—just to menti[illegible]

Yorkshire. On the first occasion Herbert said to me during the

Goose's golden touch

SCYLD BERRY studies Bob Willis, England's new captain, in action at Edgbaston.

A DAY in the life of Ivan Denisovitch was no laughing matter, but even a Siberian internee does not have to bowl and field all day at flat old Edgbaston. To round off his first week of the England captaincy, Bob Willis had that pleasure when his Warwickshire team were made to slave in the field the whole of yesterday after reducing Sussex to 87 for six wickets.

Twenty four hours before Willis ('the Goose') had been [illegible]ling a seven-over spell at [illegible] green and greasy Oval, [illegible] long-off at both [illegible]

bowling fast in a sticky vest and backed up by the full mediocrity of Warwickshire's catching.

At least there could be final straws still to come. So Willis runs in for his first over and this flashy stroke-merchant in a peach-coloured helmet, not even English, cuts his third [illegible] to gully, who [illegible]

Sussex batting order, made worse when Imran was caught at square leg in a fit of hooking. The idea was that Barclay should no longer open but bat at number nine, as he feels the captaincy is too much of a burden. Ian Greig, too has been demoted, from number six to eight, but it was he who led Sussex's recovery with a 50 in 73 minutes. Driving hard and straight, Greig shared a punishing stand of 112 with Garth le Roux.

Greig reached his second first-class century inside three hours, and hit 12 fours i[illegible] The hour that follo[illegible]

One-day international, England v India, the Oval, June 1982

This sequence was taken one Friday evening at the Oval. Ten or fifteen years ago, it would not have been technically possible but now, with a motor drive, you can shoot up to six or seven frames a second. The *Observer* did not need any picture from me that weekend but, suspecting that I had something good, I processed the film that evening and took the sequence in to the paper on Saturday morning anyway. They were as pleased with it as I was and ran it across the entire page. This is very rare, as newspapers don't usually have the space for a sequence. Again, as with the pictures of Phil Edmonds on page 101, the *Observer's* choice of shots varies slightly from mine.

These shots illustrate a point of which I am becoming increasingly aware: it's not necessarily the most memorable matches which produce the best pictures. That particular match has long been forgotten, in fact what little I do remember of it was quite boring, but the sequence has been used many times and has acquired, if not an immortality, then at least a *life* of its own. This was not my doing – I didn't make Gower and Co fall about like that – but it does reinforce my view that it pays to be alert even when nothing much is happening. For this reason I never go to a game and think: Well, I'll just take a couple of shots and then go home. I always go equipped to take several hundred. Indeed, going to a cricket match for me is like going on safari. I take three cameras – two Nikon F3s and one F2, all with motor drive. One is for black and white, one is for colour and one spare for emergencies. I also take about fifty rolls of film – colour and black and white; eight lenses: from telephoto to wide angle and fish-eye; my tripod and a golfing umbrella. All that's missing is the partridge in a pear tree. And believe me, all that gear is both cumbrous and heavy. The prime prerequisite for a cricket photographer is neither intelligence nor even diligence, but muscle.

People often ask me: How many rolls of film do you take in a day? Well, if the cricket is uneventful, I might take only one roll, but on a good day, I might take up to fifteen. Of those fifteen rolls, one or two single pictures may be used by the *Observer*, and perhaps I'll have around a dozen pictures in the next month's *Cricketer* (but not all from one day's cricket) and the best of the rest will go into our library at All-Sport. They will eventually be used in cricket biographies, in periodicals – such as *Country Life* and the *Illustrated London News*, and in annuals – such as the *Telegraph* and the Benson and Hedges year books. I like to keep our cricket library up to date and well stocked, which means never letting up, even when there is no immediate call for a picture. You never know when the next 'classic' will occur, although – unhappily – I don't expect Sharma, Gower and Kirmani to stage a repeat performance.

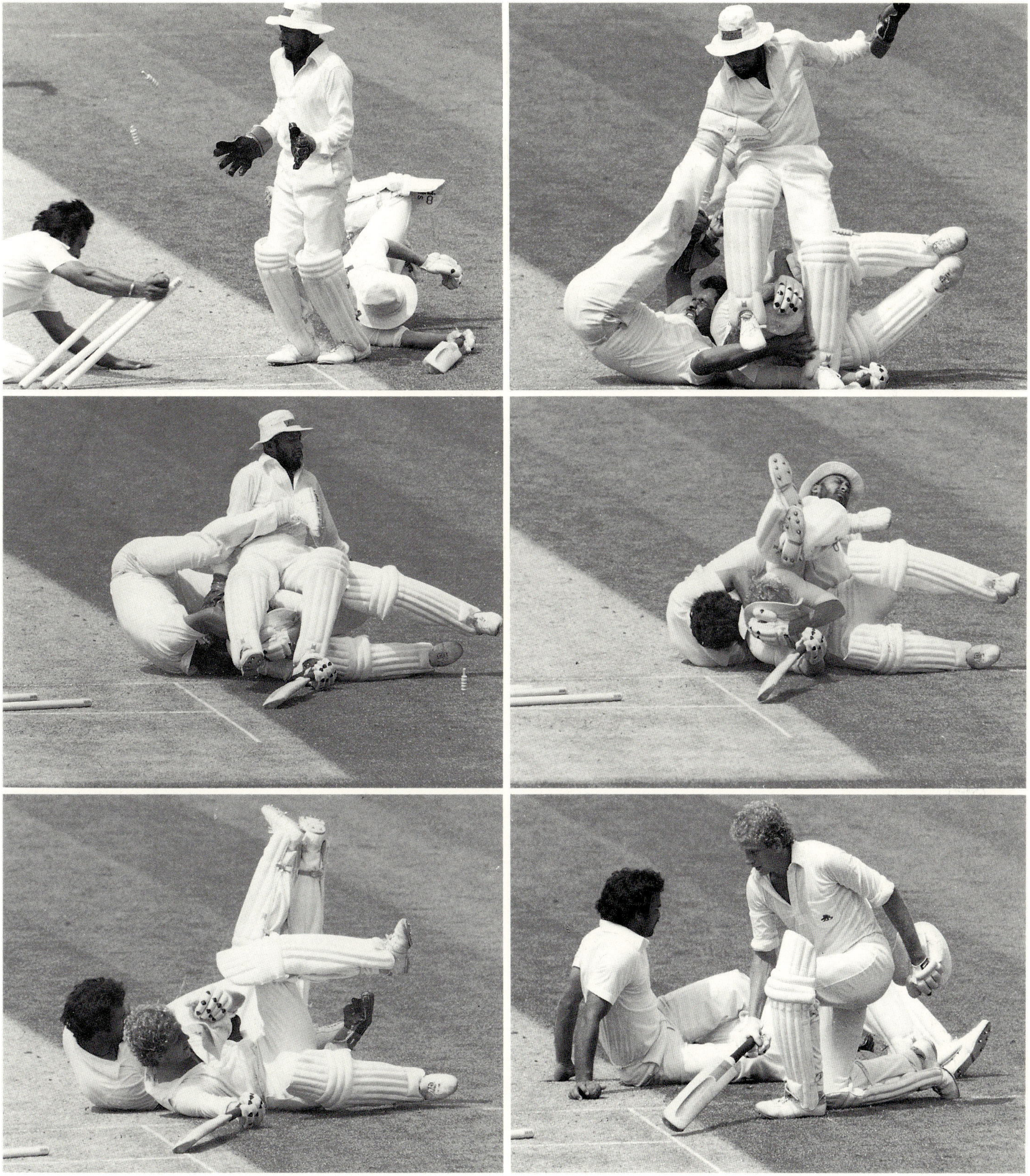

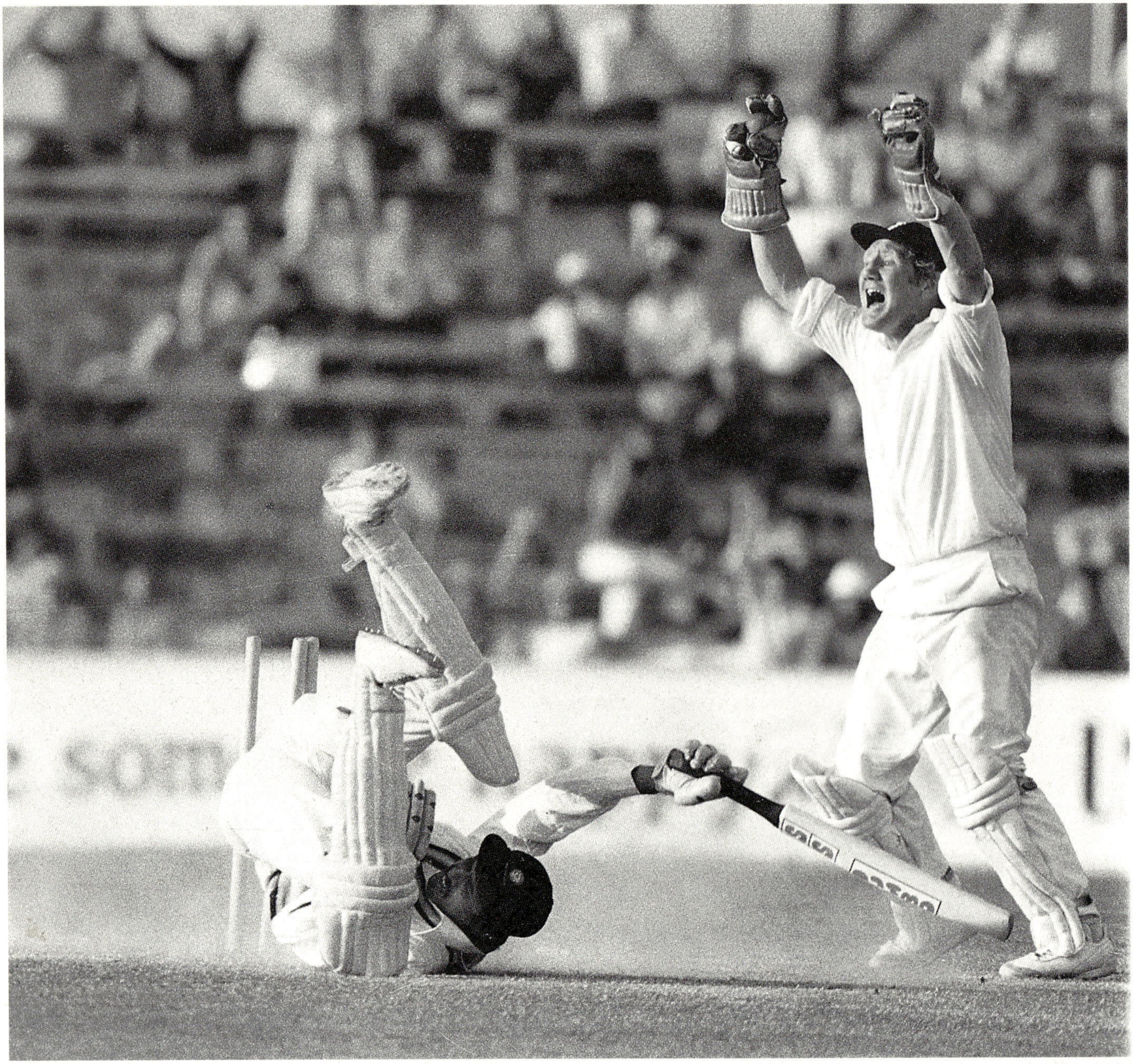

David Bairstow and Venkat during the third Test, England v India, the Oval, September 1979

opposite: *Jeff Dujon, World Series Cup Final, Australia v West Indies, Melbourne, February 1985*

Not everyone can bite the dust with such grace and artistry as David Gower, but they keep right on trying. On this and the following three pages, wicketkeepers are still in the thick of the action (admittedly, on page 131, Wayne Phillips is not actually keeping wicket – batsmen fall about quite a lot too). Although a wicketkeeper obviously *is* so often in the thick of the action, few appreciate the pressure he is under. He has to maintain concentration for up to six hours a day, where one error is frequently costly – but getting it right is glorious.

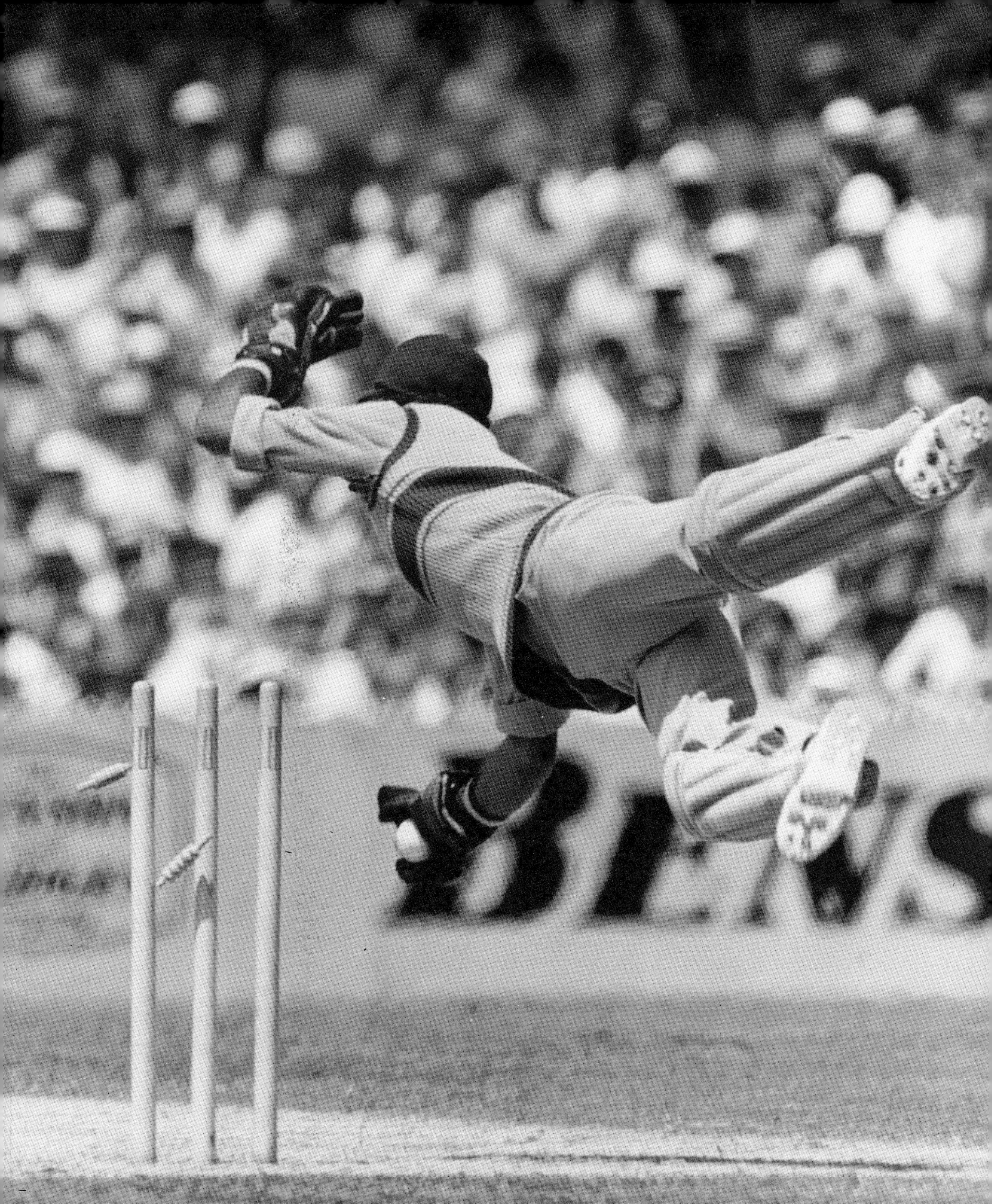

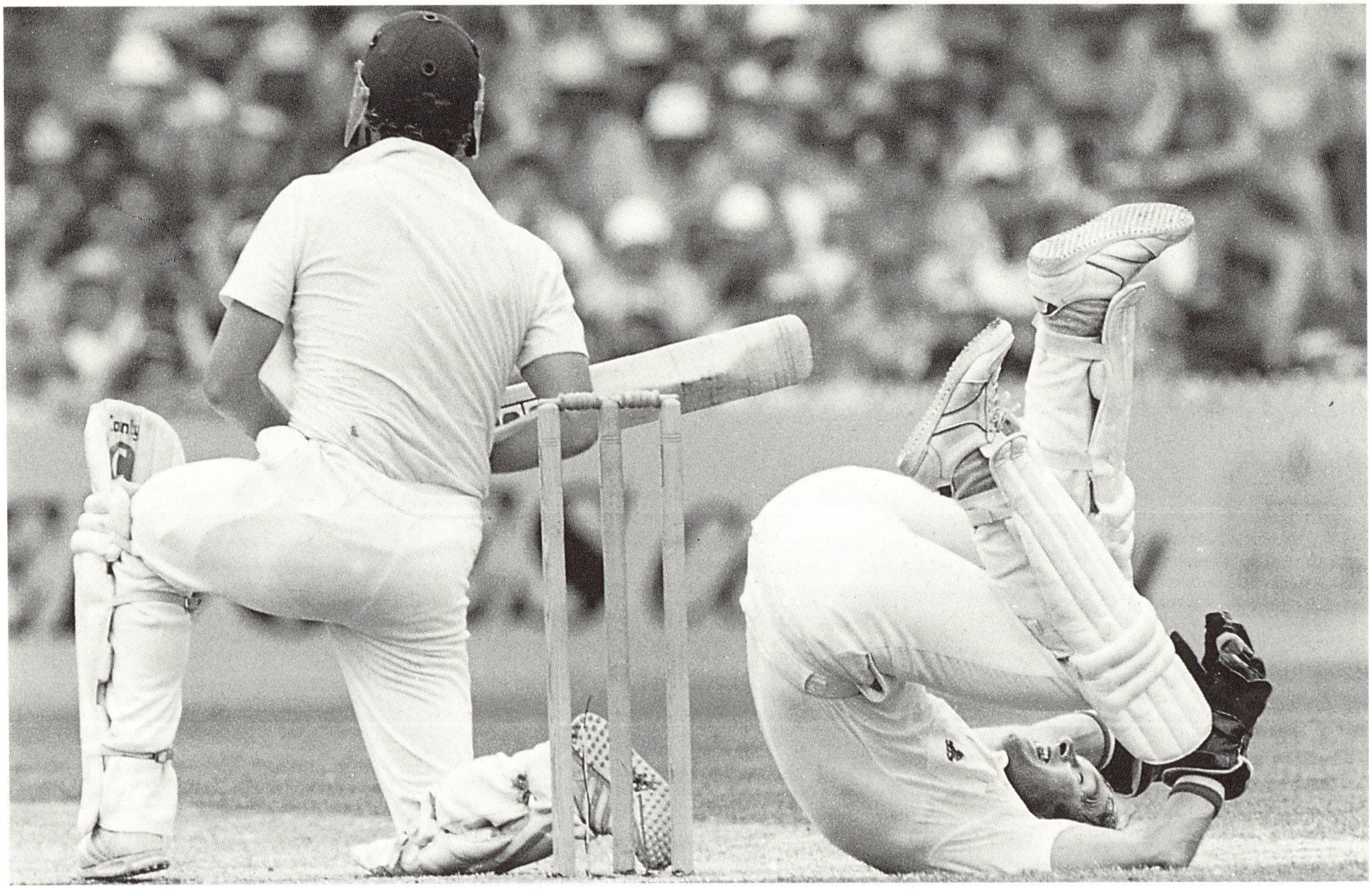

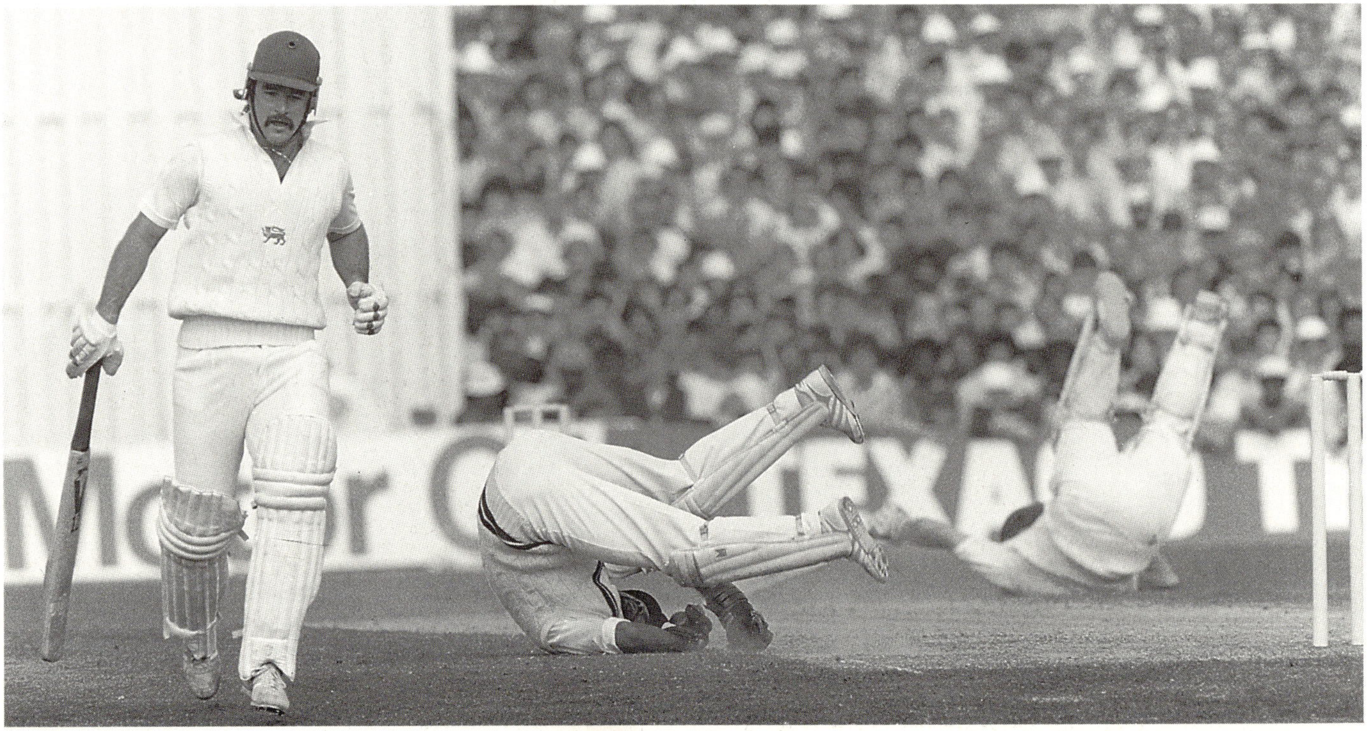

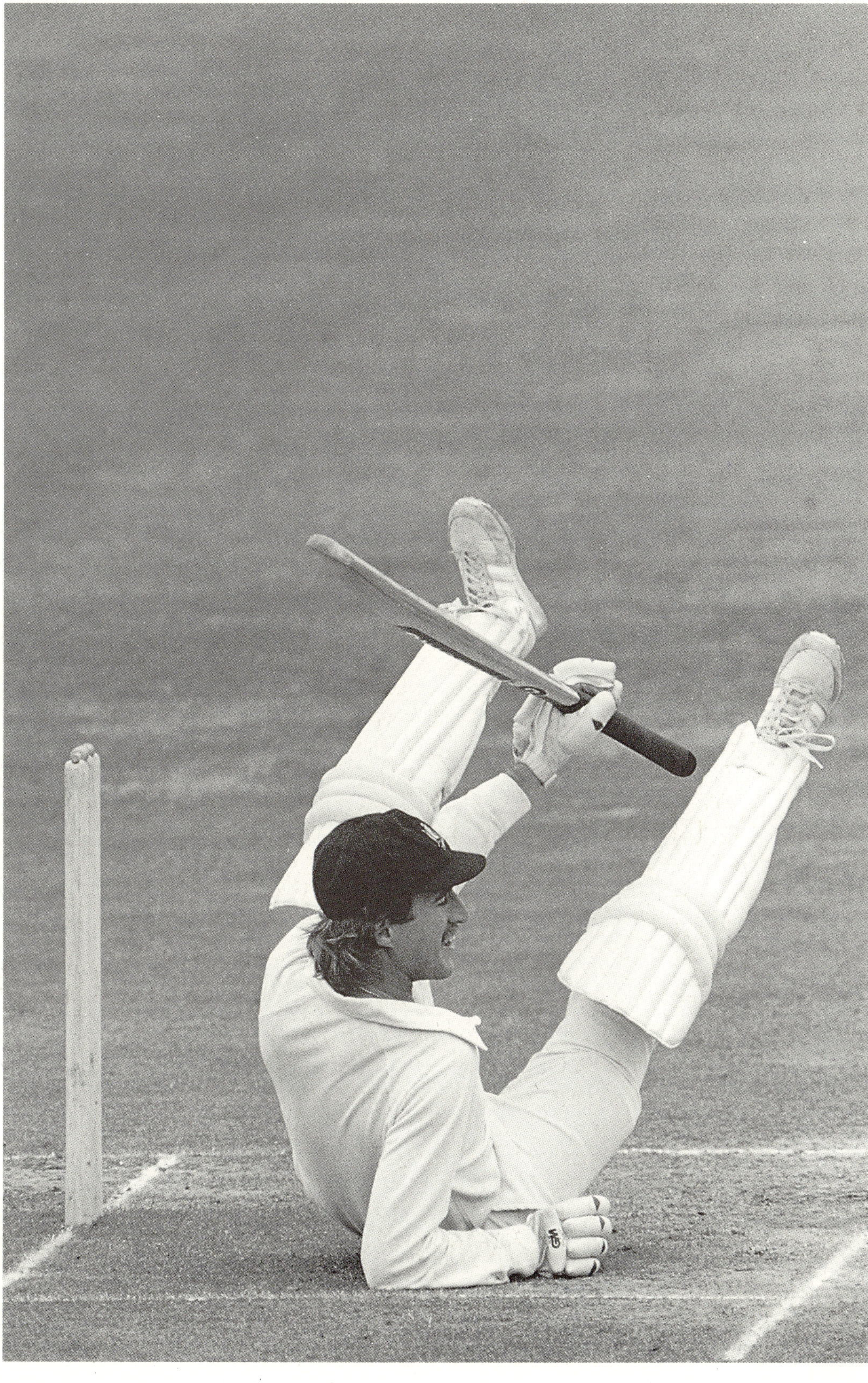

Wayne Phillips, wicket-keeper, Middlesex and Australia, Lord's, August 1985

opposite, above: *Bob Taylor catches Kim Hughes during the fourth Test, Australia v England, Melbourne, December 1982*

opposite, below: *Allan Lamb keeps going regardless, one-day international, England v West Indies, Old Trafford, June 1984*

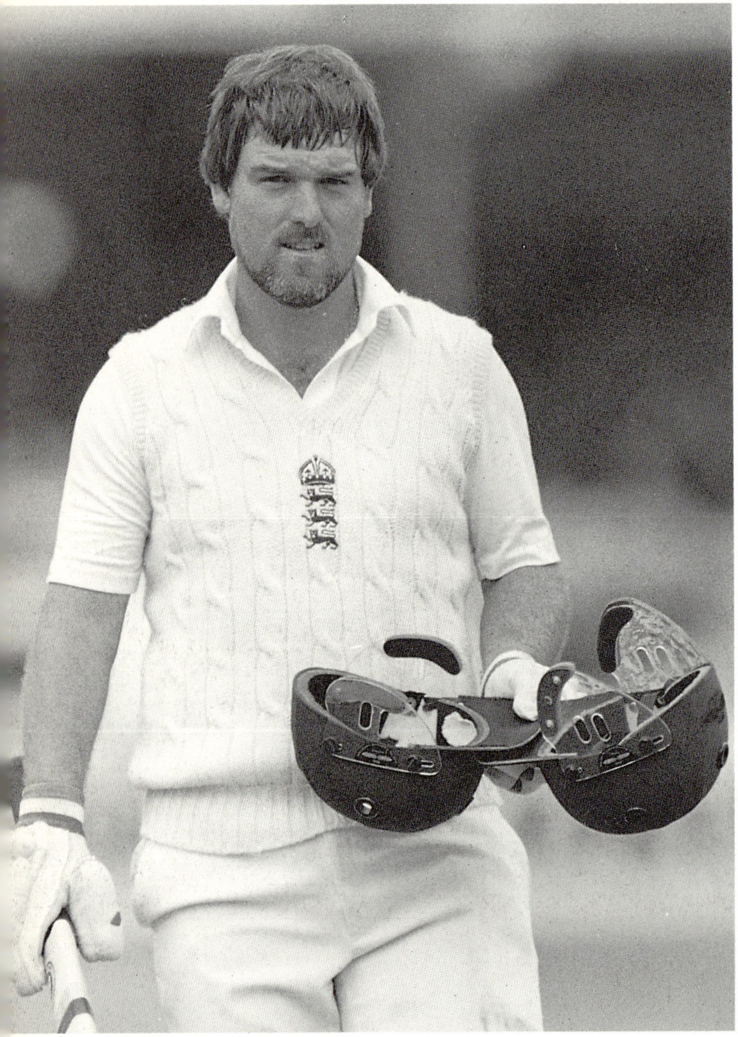

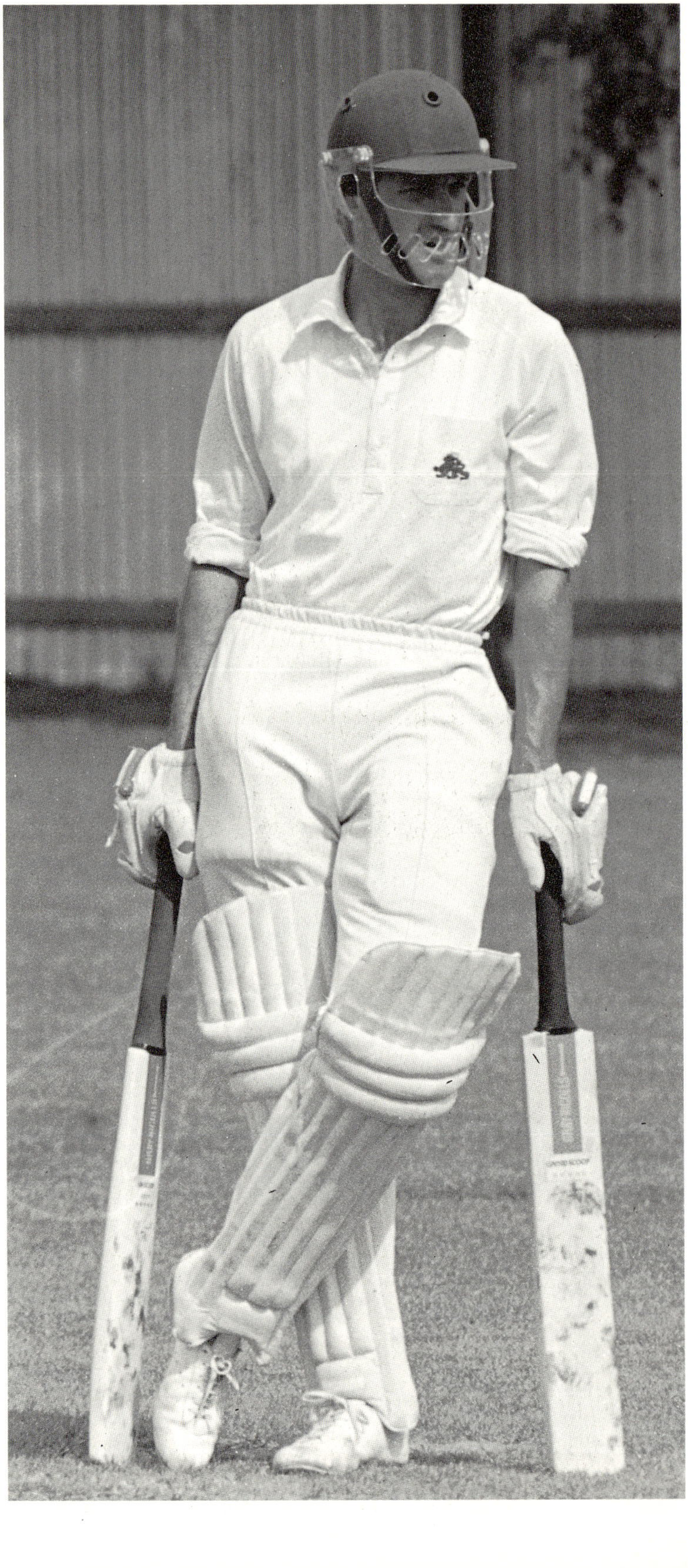

These pictures don't really mean anything special. I just took them because – like Everest – they were there.

Two of a kind –

Two bats – Chris Tavare in the nets before the second Test, New Zealand v England, Christchurch, January 1984

above: *Two hats – Mike Gatting looking for double protection during third Test, England v Australia, Trent Bridge, July 1985*

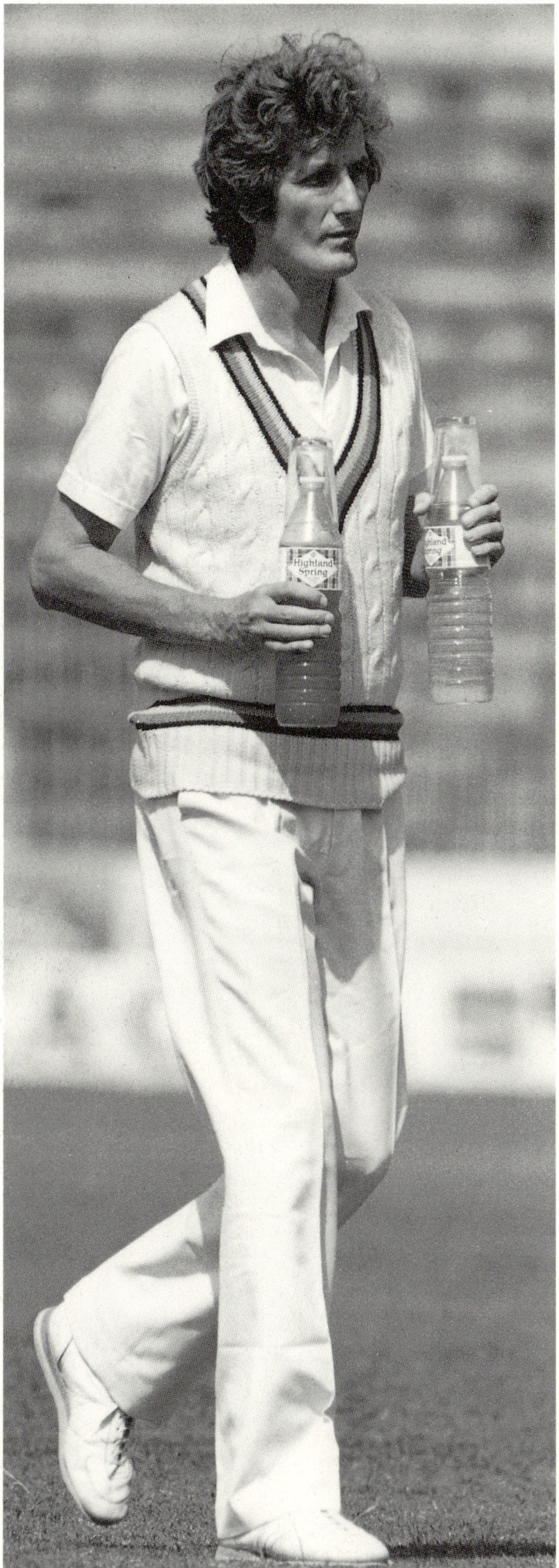

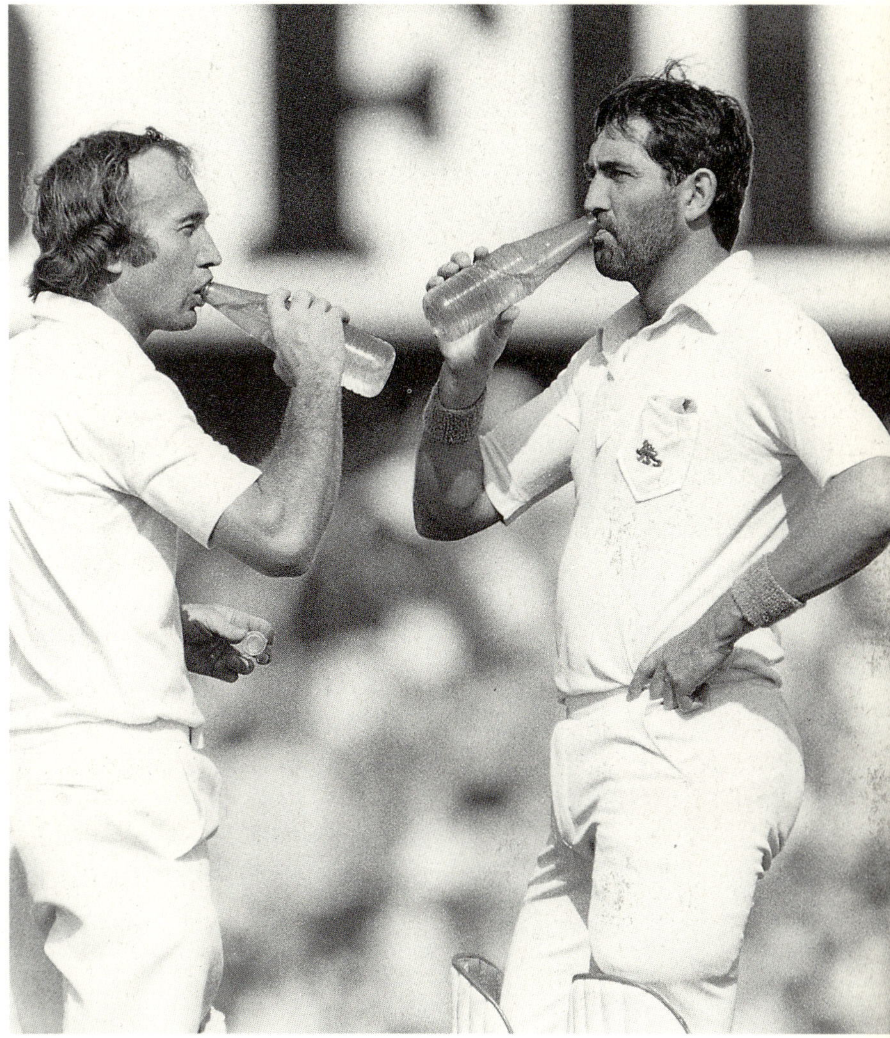

And having taken them, I now rather like the composition the doubling up creates.

Two bottles – Bob Willis, the England captain was ill during the third Test, Pakistan v England, and became the water waiter, Lahore, March 1984

above: *Two thirsty men – Essex and England players, captain Keith Fletcher with Graham Gooch during the fourth Test, India v England, Calcutta, January 1982*

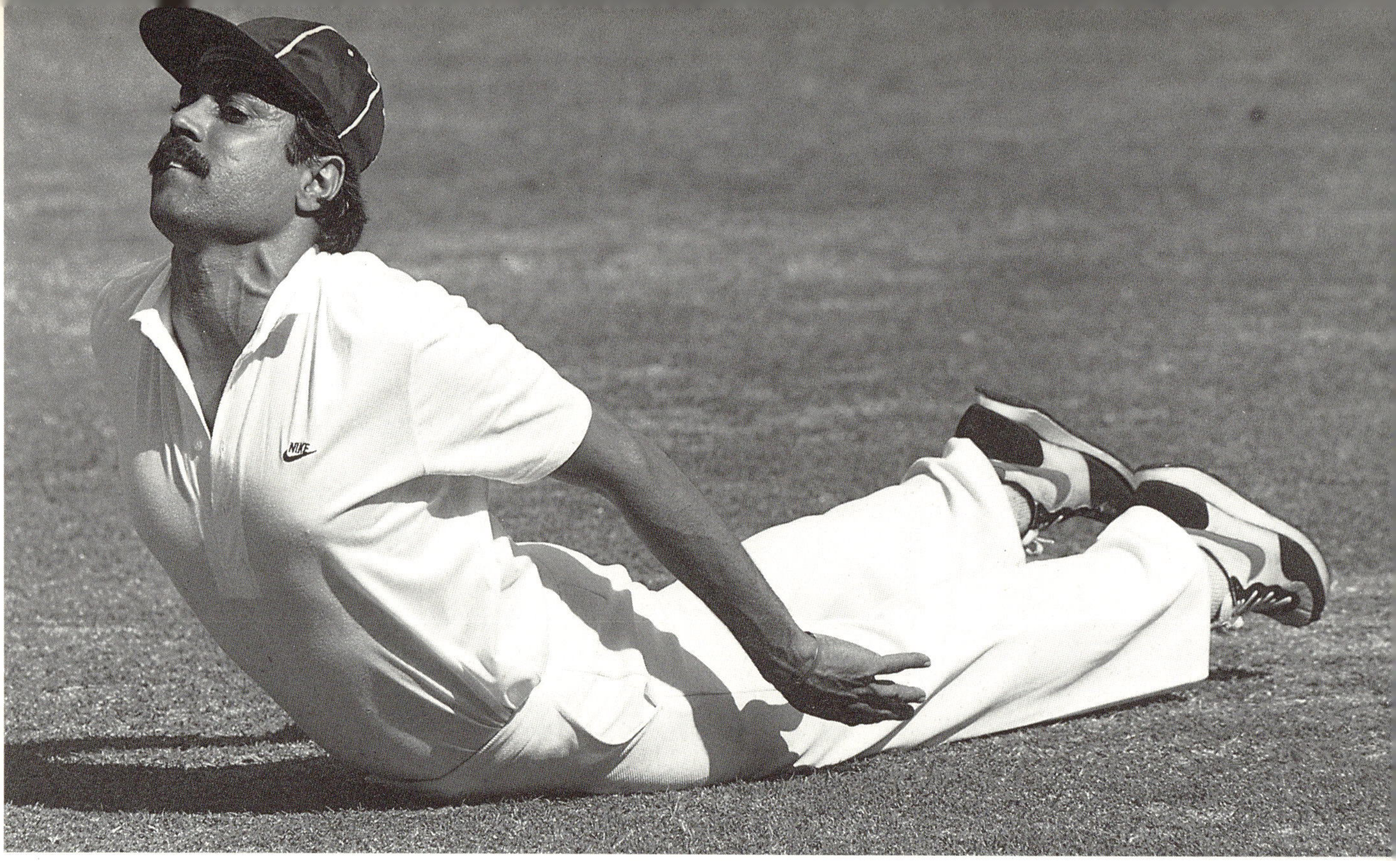
NIKE

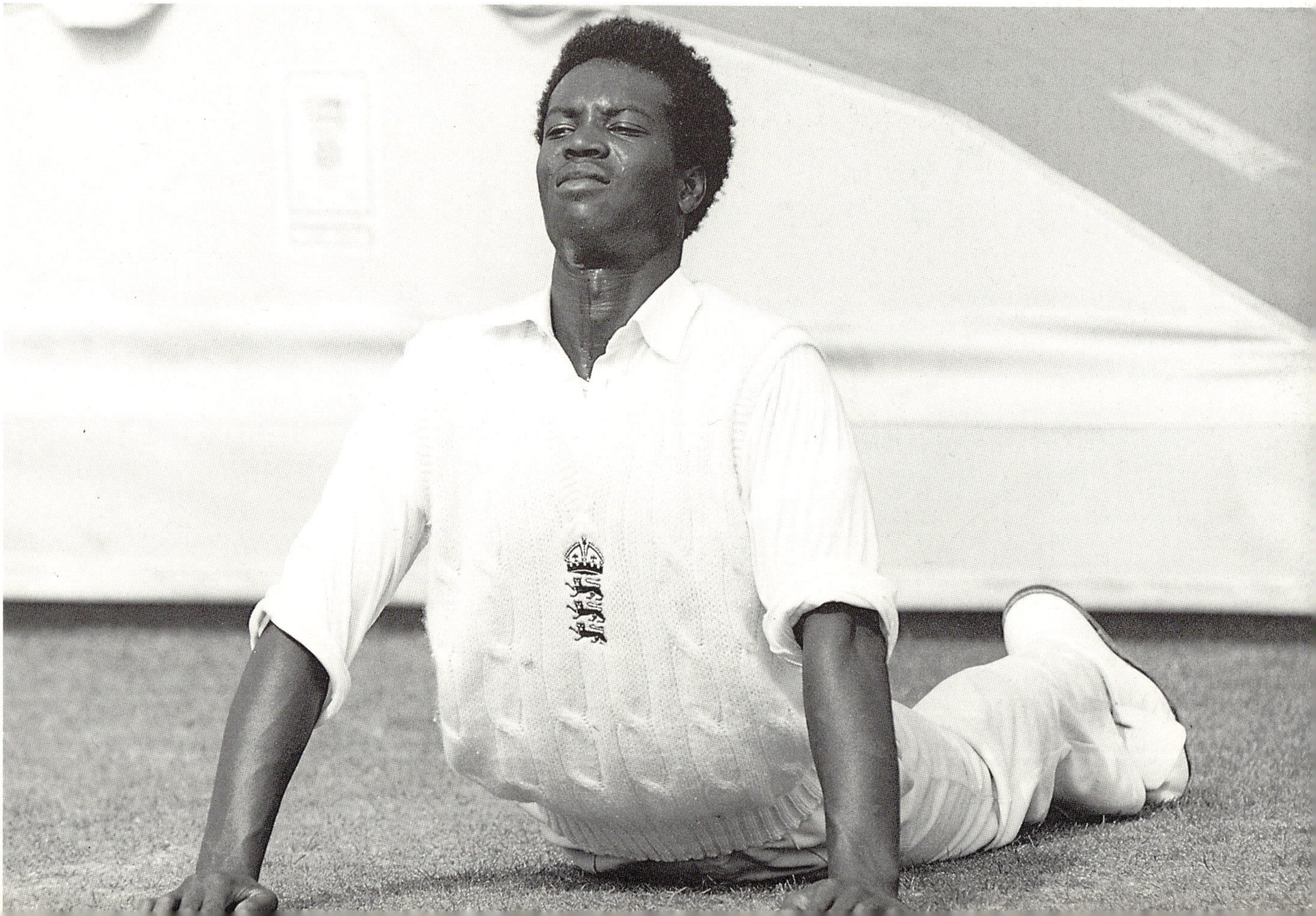

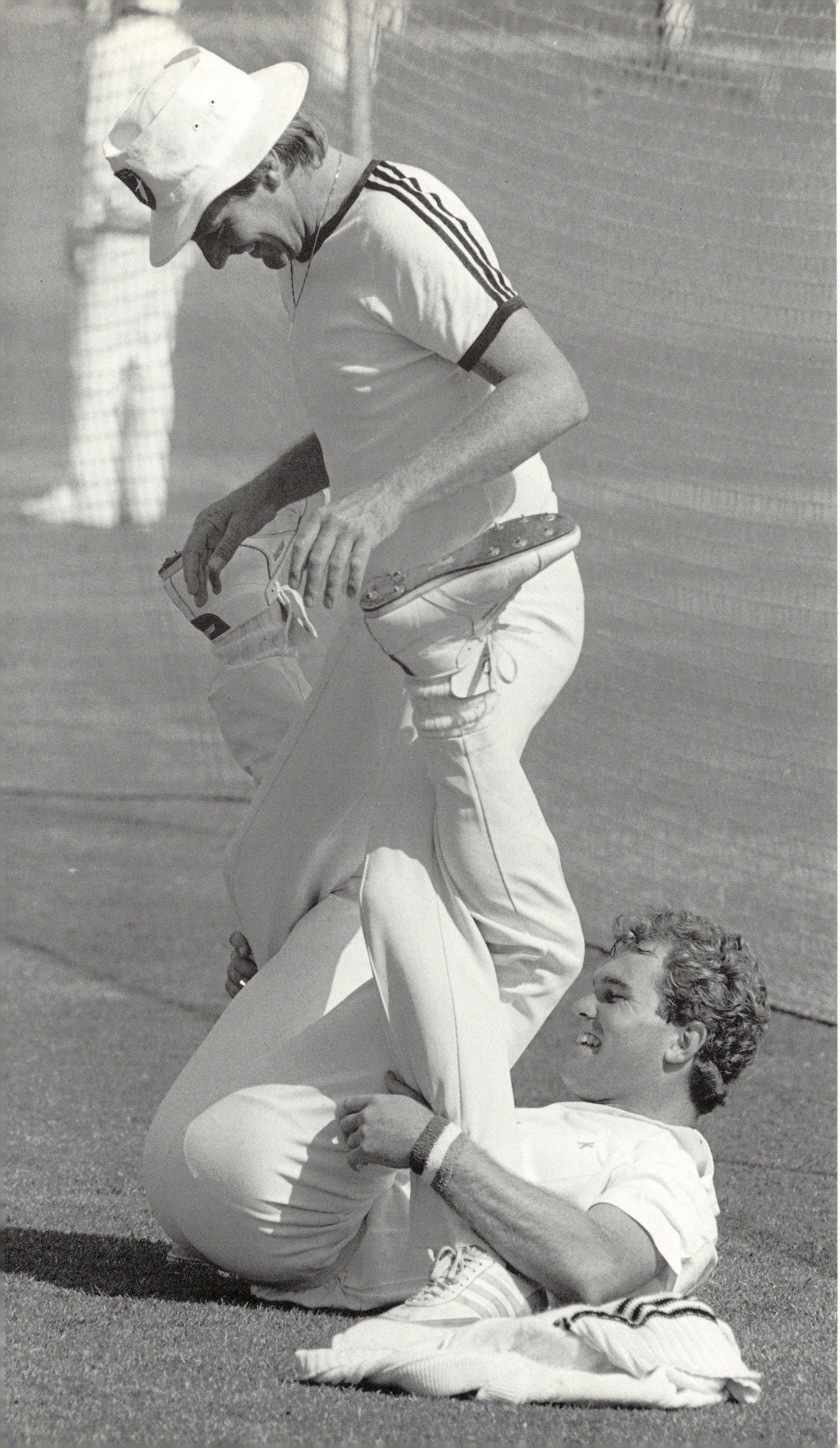

Cricket is no longer a game for 'Gentlemen' and 'Players'; it is for professionals. And professionals must be fit. The attitude regarding this has changed noticeably since I first started photographing cricket and cricketers in 1977, although England still has a long way to go to match the West Indians.

Martin Crowe (on the ground) and Geoff Howarth, Auckland, February 1984

opposite, above: *Kapil Dev, Bombay, December 1985*

opposite, below: *Norman Cowans, Lord's, July 1984*

Behind every story there is another story, and behind every picture there is another picture. Newsmen, photographers, seek out these stories and pictures and what we find is frequently poignant.

The homeless men waiting outside Lord's, hoping to help with the day's clearing up, reveal more of themselves by covering their faces than does the one man who looks at the camera. They are obviously more distressed by their lives than is the Indian sweeper in Calcutta, pictured opposite. There is, however, something profoundly disturbing about the picture of the Indian children making cricket equipment for British manufacturers. They work twelve hours a day in this and other sweat shops like it.

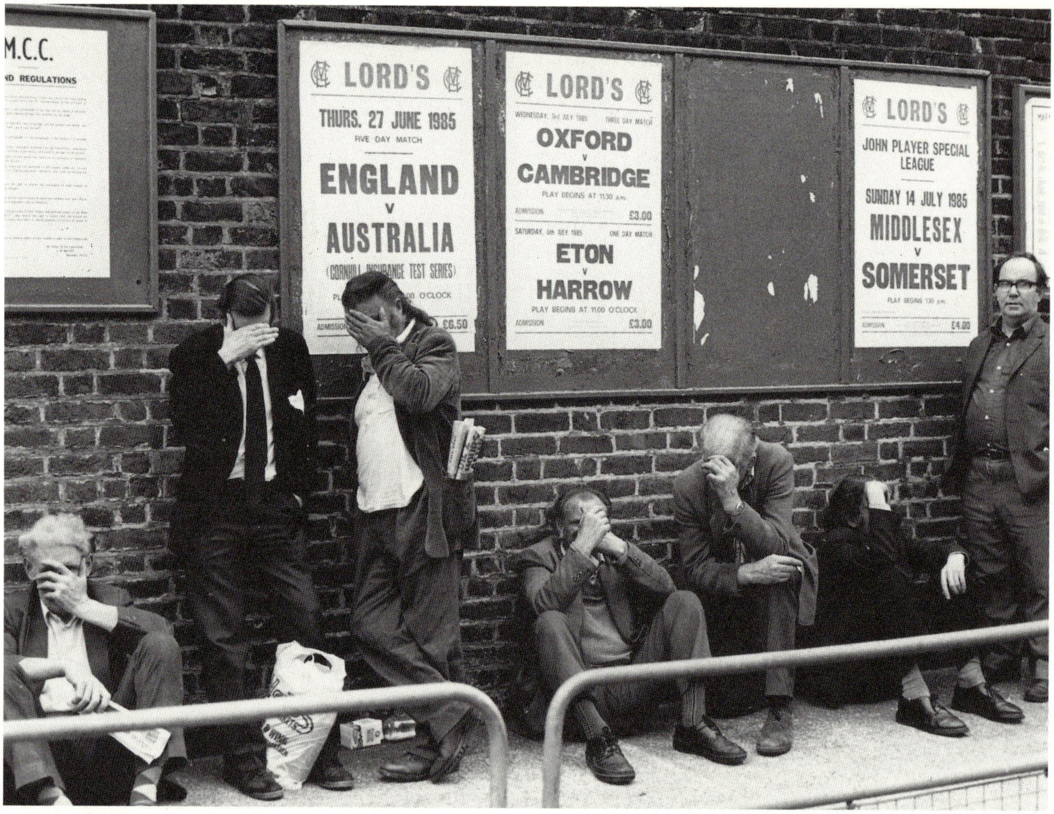

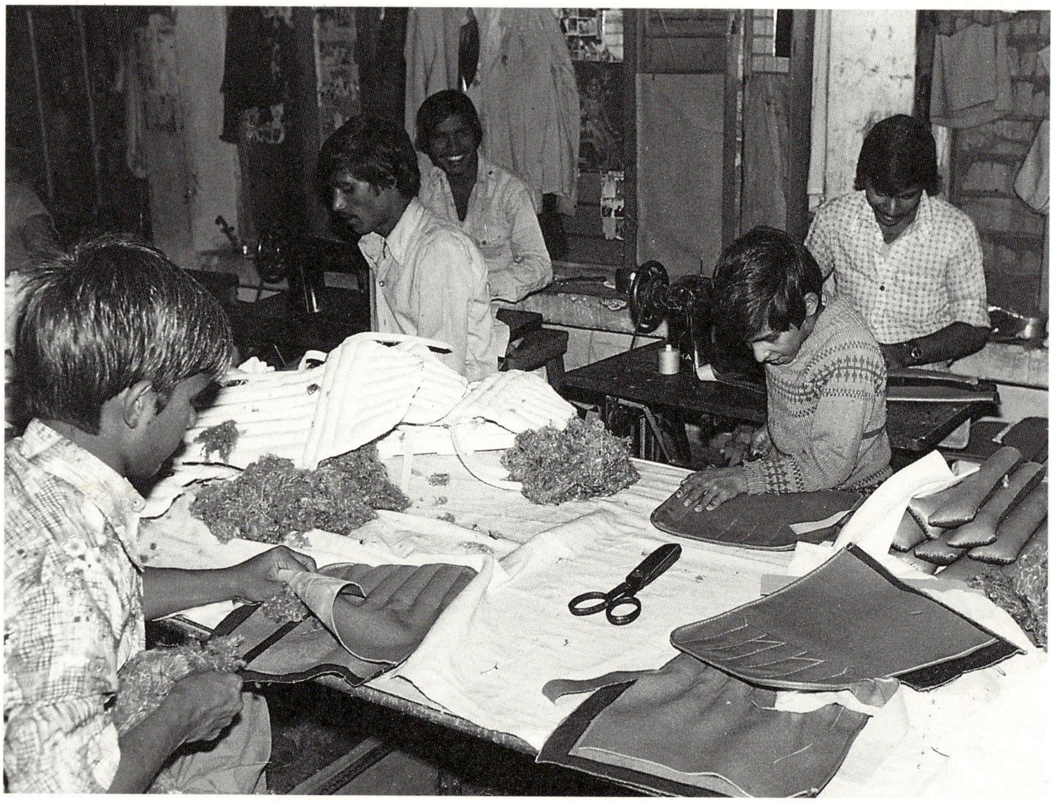

'Made in India', Jullundur, December 1981

above: *Outside the wall, a different world, Lord's, July 1985*

opposite: *The dignity of labour, second Test, India v England, Calcutta, January 1977*

Pitch and toss-up

LIKE THE Queen of the Maypole, John Snagge or the allboys at Wimbledon, a est match groundsman njoys one week in the spot-ight every year. The cameras ome to focus on him when he 22-yard strip of current ational interest is his reation.

Objective people may wonder why such fuss should be made bout a bit of grass, but the ficionado is well aware that he nature and texture of the urf are extremely influential actors in the way a game is layed, and especially a five-day Test. After all, the pitch is fun-amental to any cricket match.

For instance, the Headingley itch last year, the one on which an Botham hit his wonderful 49, was—like a good concubine —st and of

SCYLD BERRY goes to the roots of the groundsman's art

supper goes cold on the table in summer as they remain absorbed until late at night. But much as they have in common, each has his own local problems to contend with.

At Edgbaston for example, Bernard Flack has no say in choosing his Test strip. It is determined by television. The TV cameras have their one special place at Edgaston, and the Test strip has to be in line with that. Flack says he has a better, faster pitch nearby but it cannot be used. This year, February was excessively wet, March too dry: 'and that,' —ding to Flack, 'is the time —pitches are made.' Rol-—tering is still the —achi—

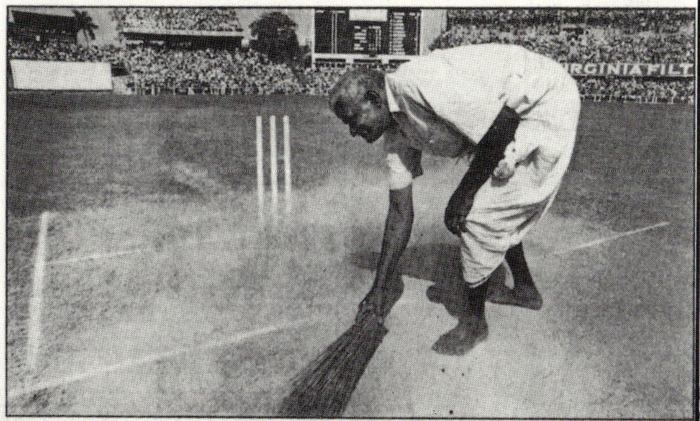

ADRIAN MURPH—

—ch preparation, Indian-style—a time to bend and a time to sweep

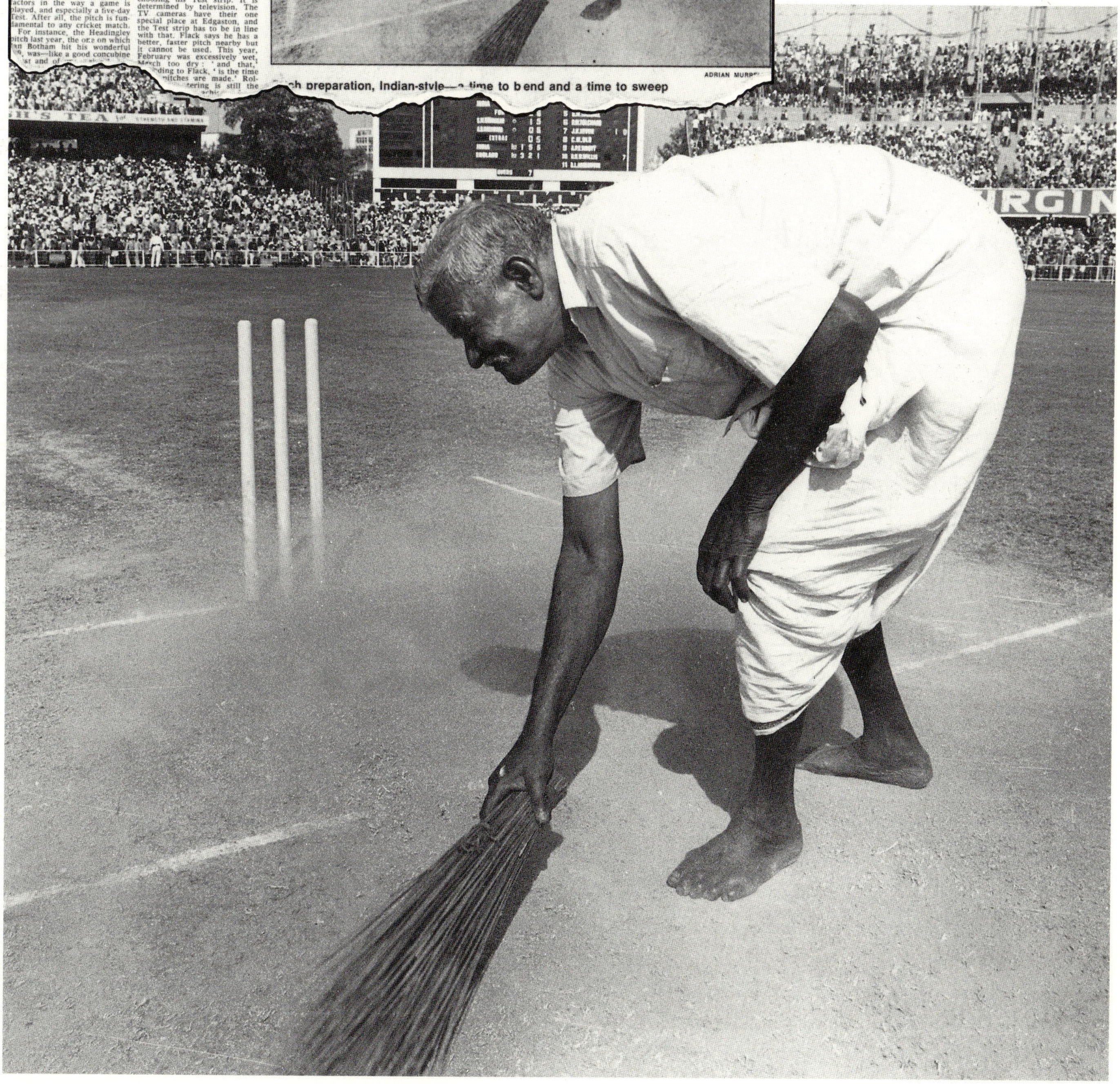

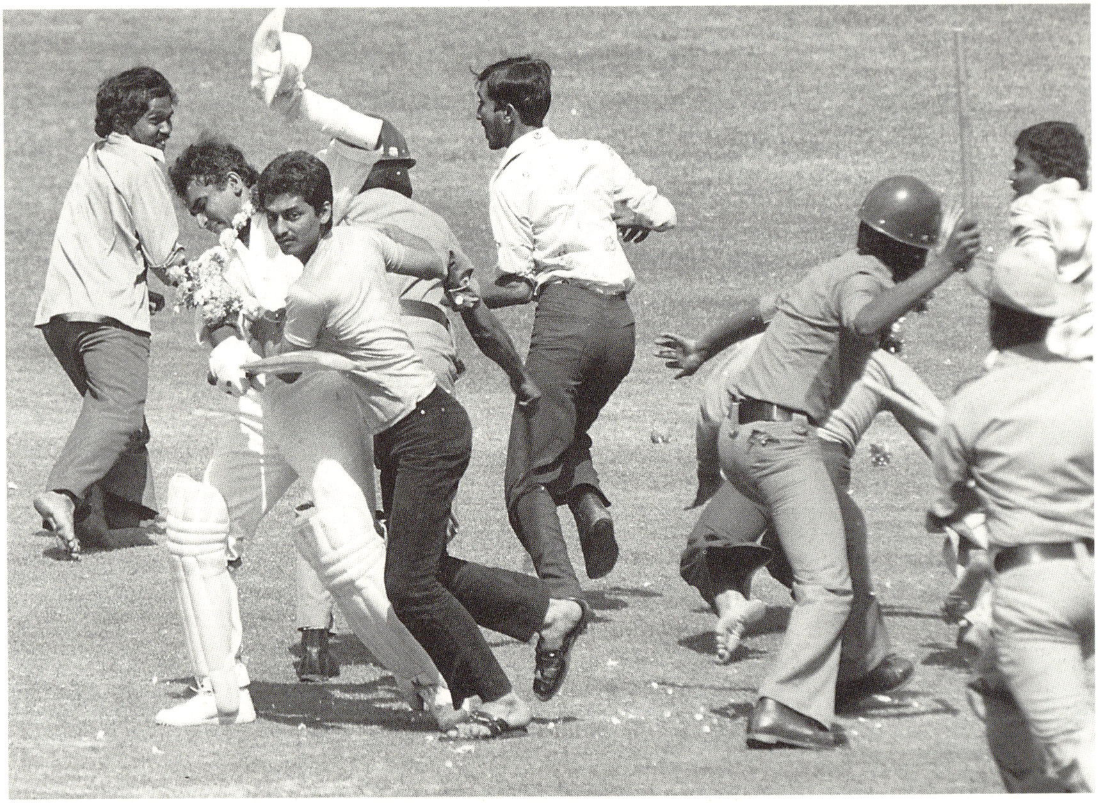

It seems appropriate to close this book with a look at the people who watch cricket. Wherever they are and whoever they are: in Sydney or in Bangalore; in Kingston or at Headingley; it is surely for them the game is played.

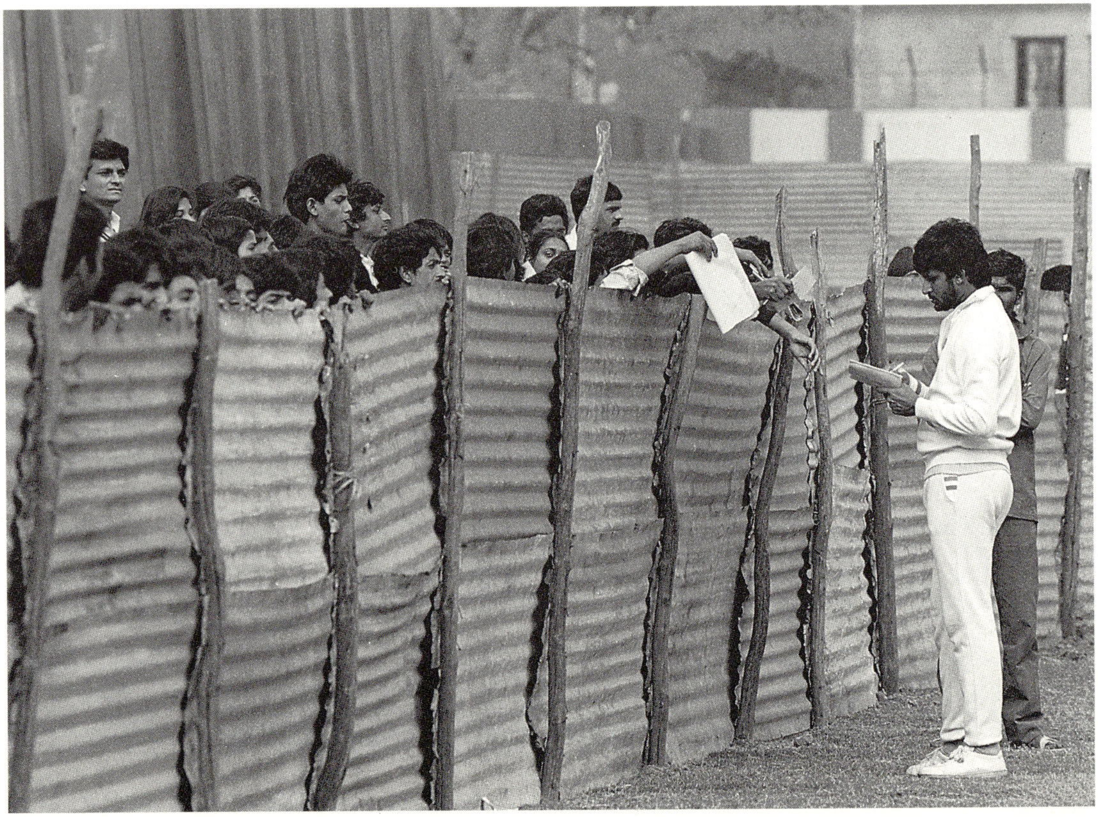

Sandeep Patil signs autographs in Delhi, December 1984

above: *Sunil Gavaskar is feted in Bangalore, December 1981*

opposite, above: *Botham runs for cover after his sensational century, third Test, England v Australia, Headingley, July 1981*

opposite, below: *Allan Lamb signs autographs during a one-day international, Australia v England, Sydney, January 1983*

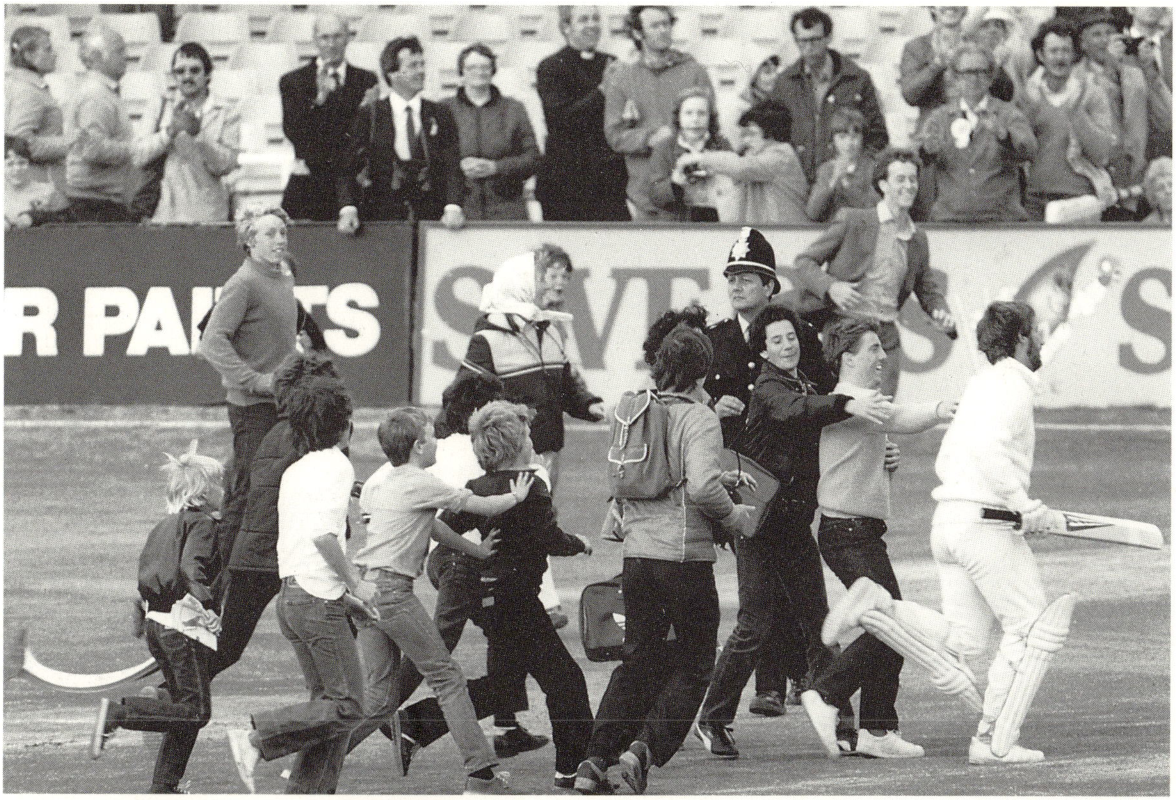

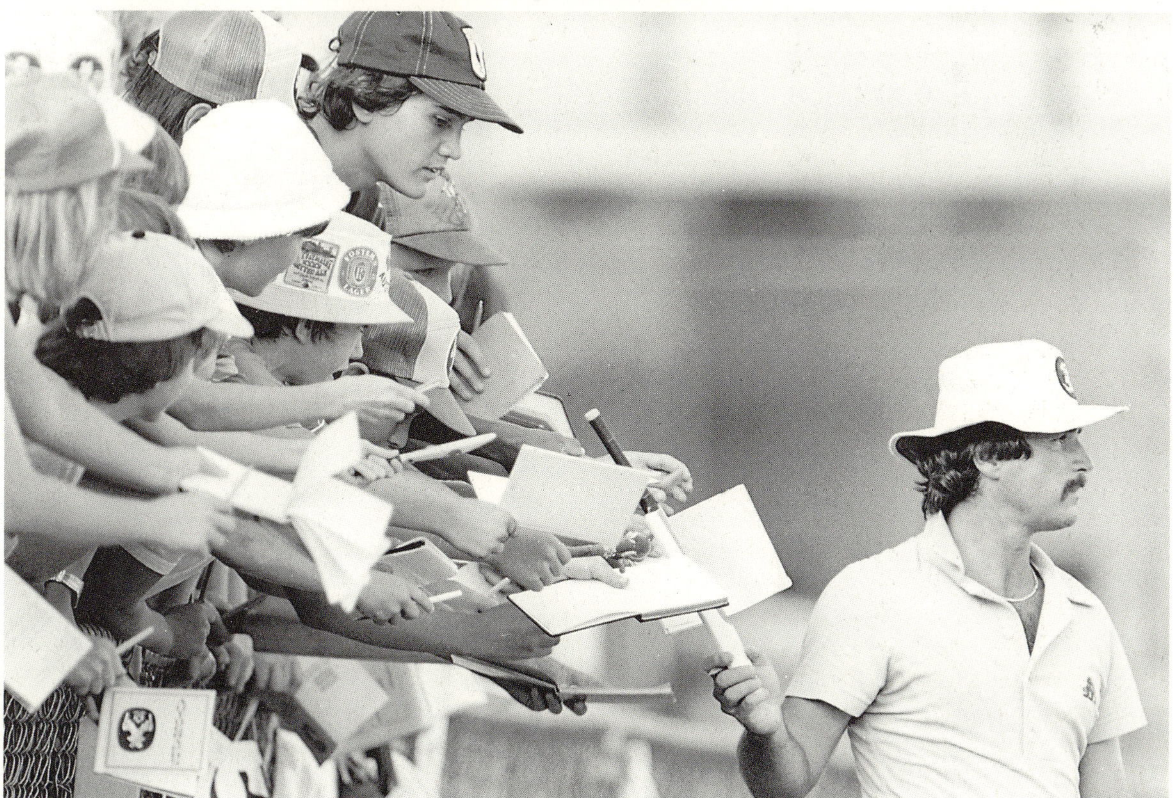

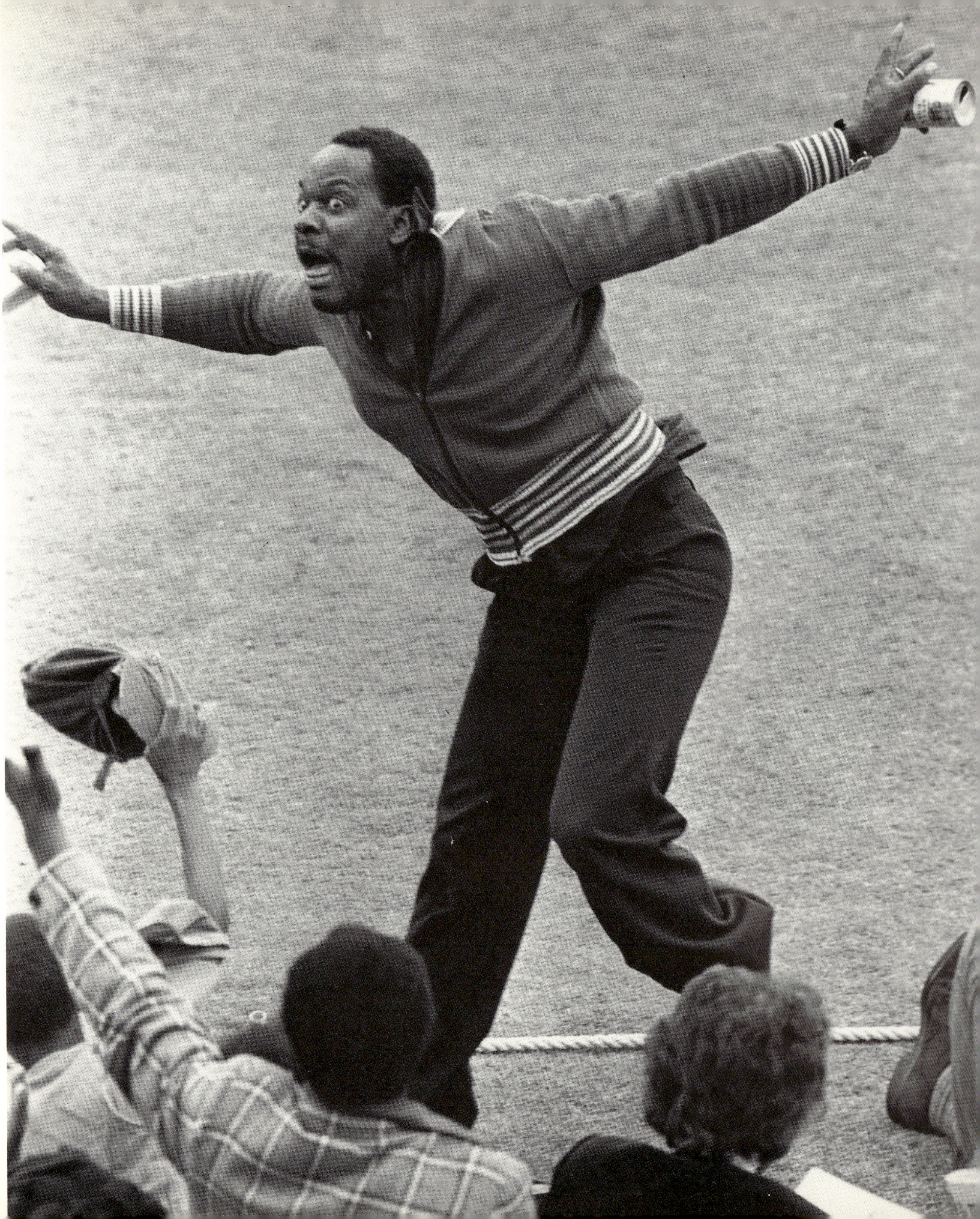

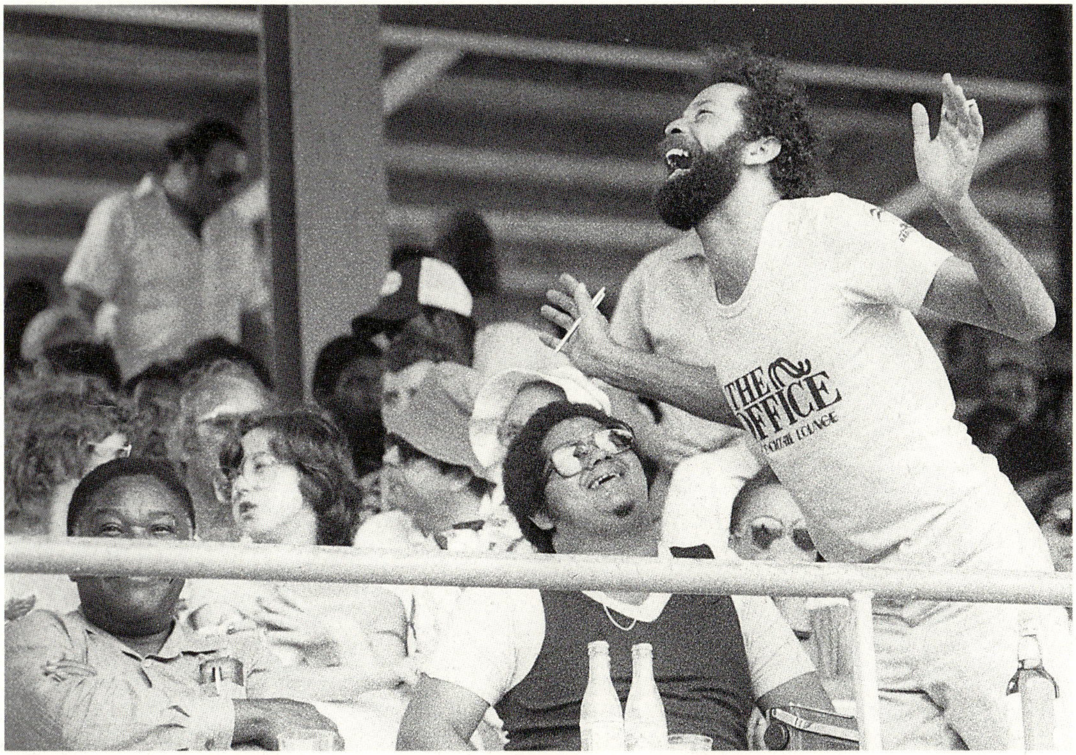

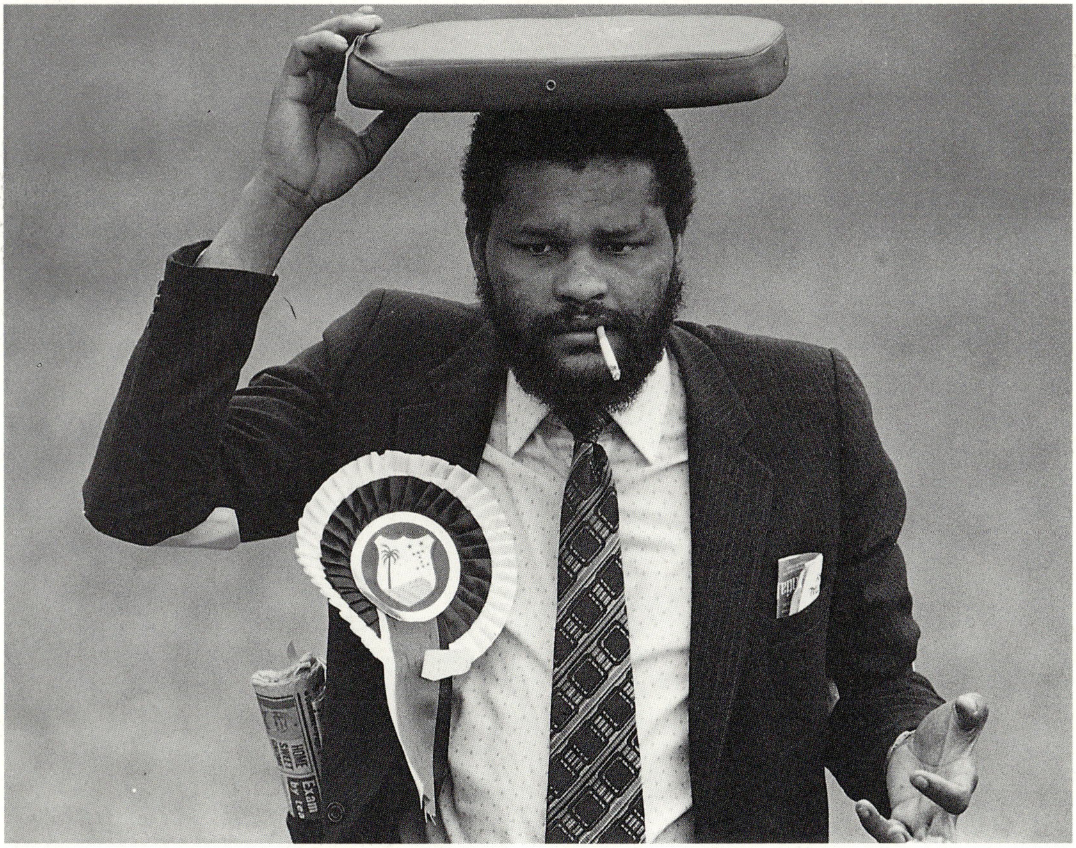

A spectator at the India v West Indies match during the World Cup Final, Lord's, June 1983

above: *The crowd went mad after Holding bowled Boycott in what was considered to be the fastest over in living memory, third Test, West Indies v England, Barbados, March 1981*

opposite: *Crowd entertainment at the World Cup Final, England v West Indies, Lord's, June 1979*

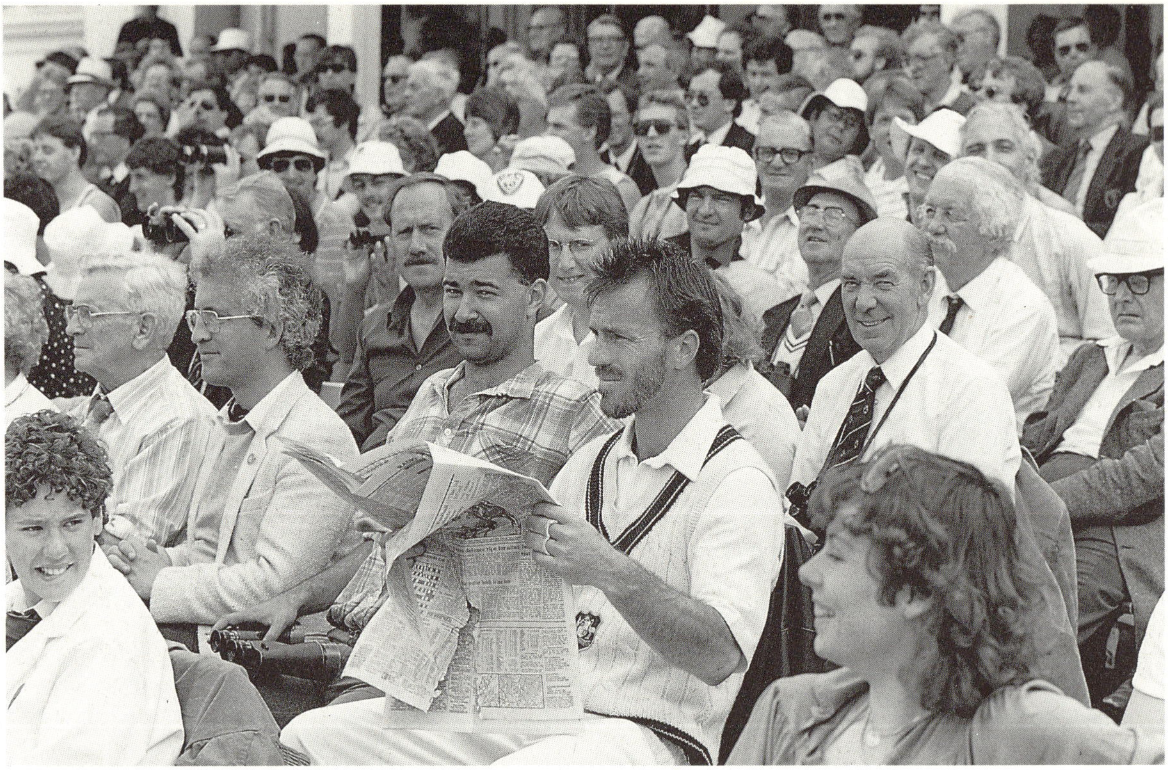

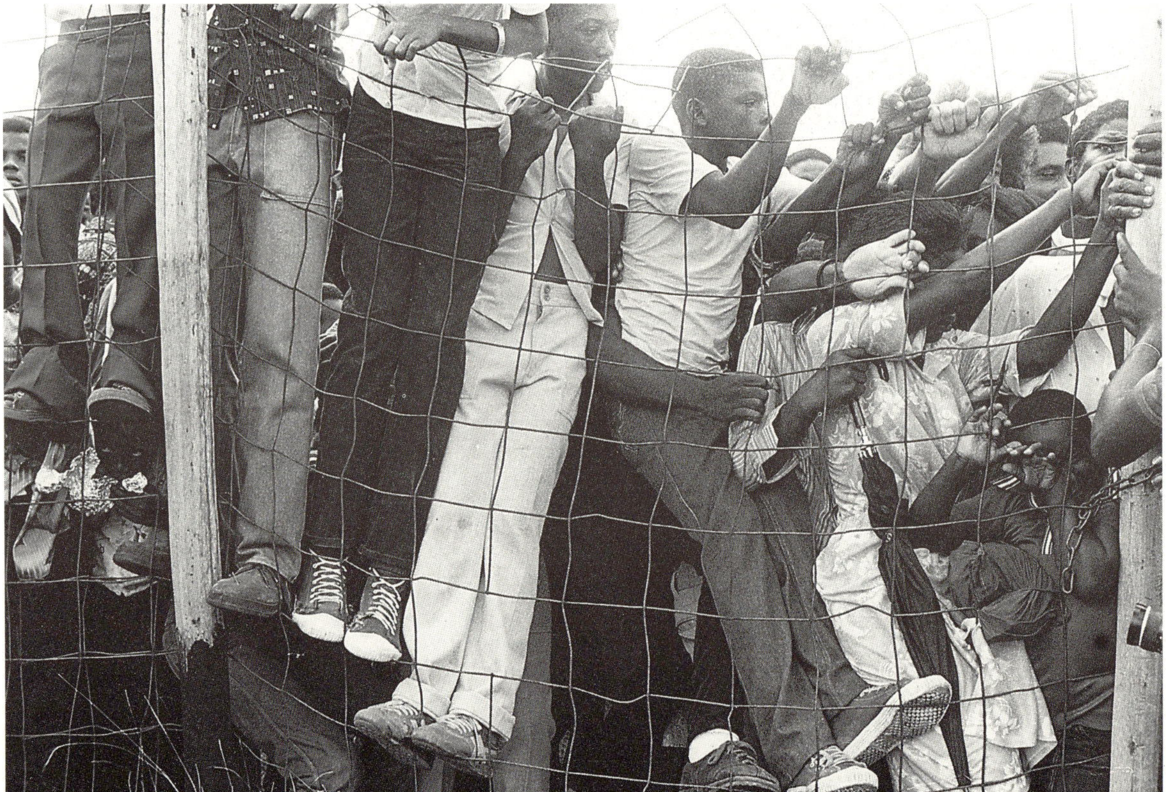

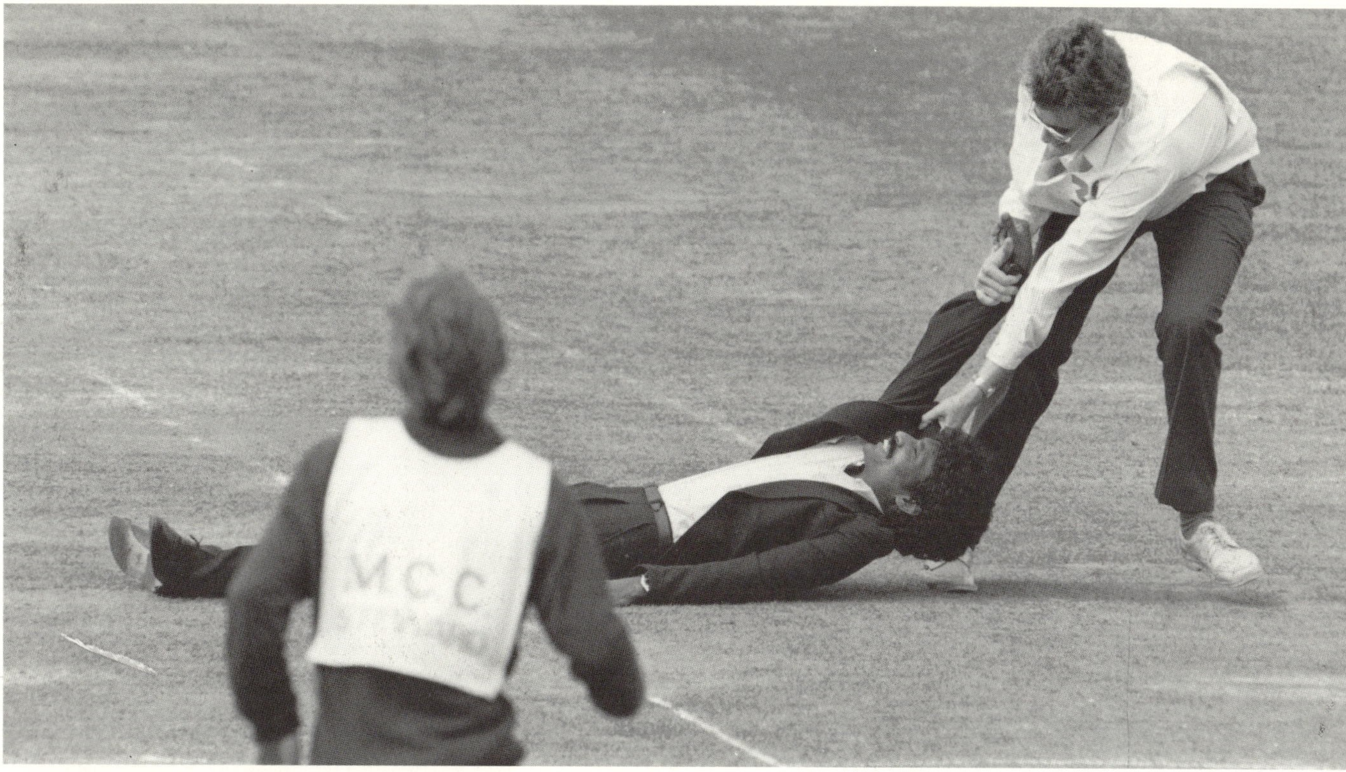

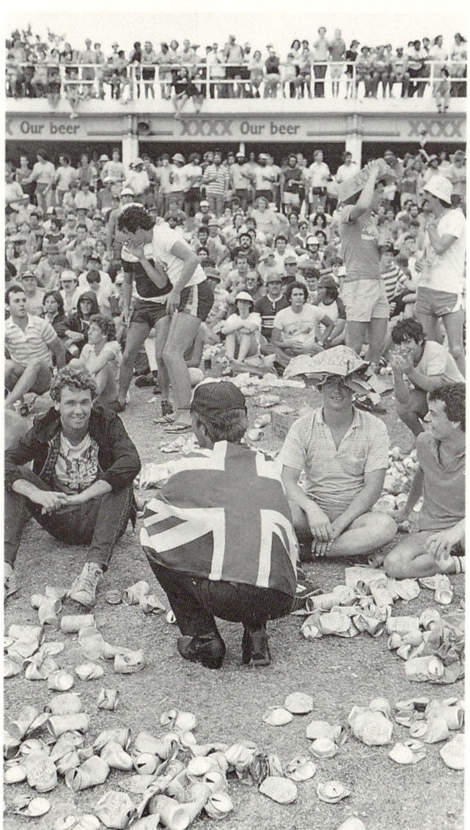

On the 'hill' at Brisbane, second Test, Australia v England, November 1982

above: *Stewards dragging a demonstrator off the pitch, England v Sri Lanka, Lord's, August 1984*

opposite, above: *Greg Matthews reads the* Guardian, *third Test, England v Australia, Trent Bridge, July 1985*

opposite, below: *Behind the barrier, St Vincent, West Indies, March 1981*

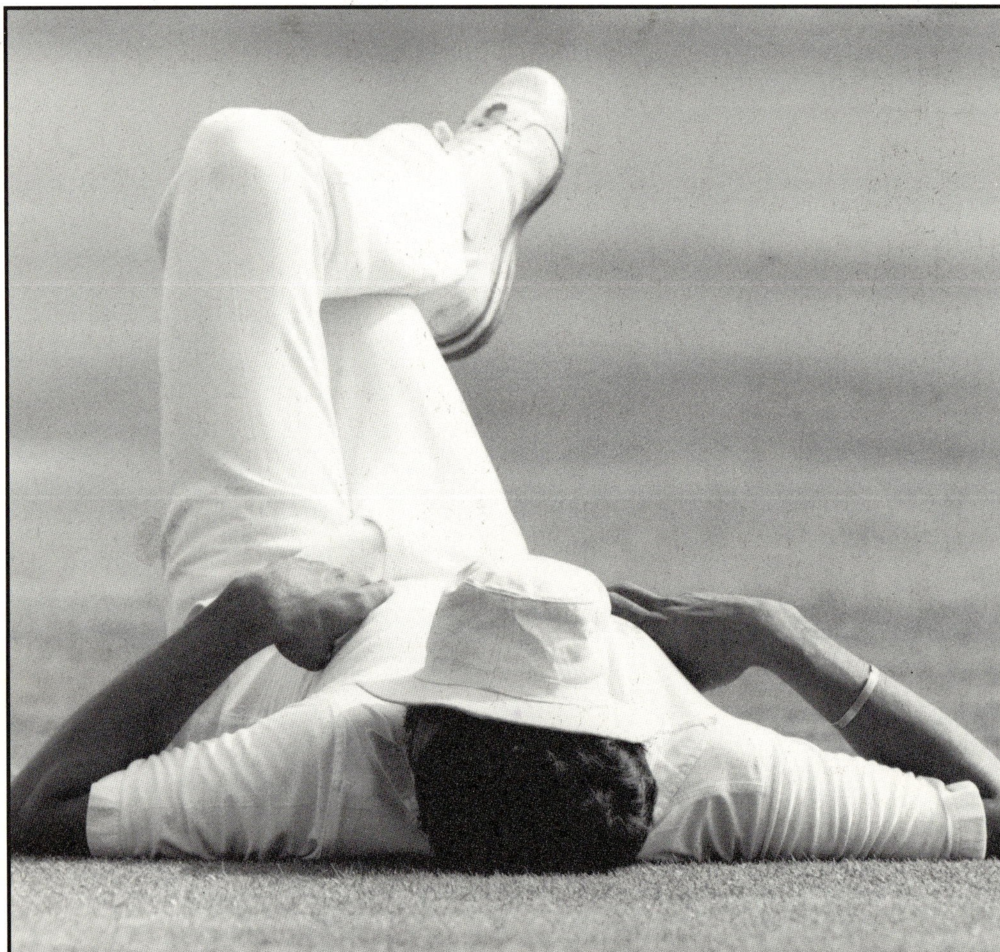

It's still only a game

Kapil Dev at the Oval, June 1982

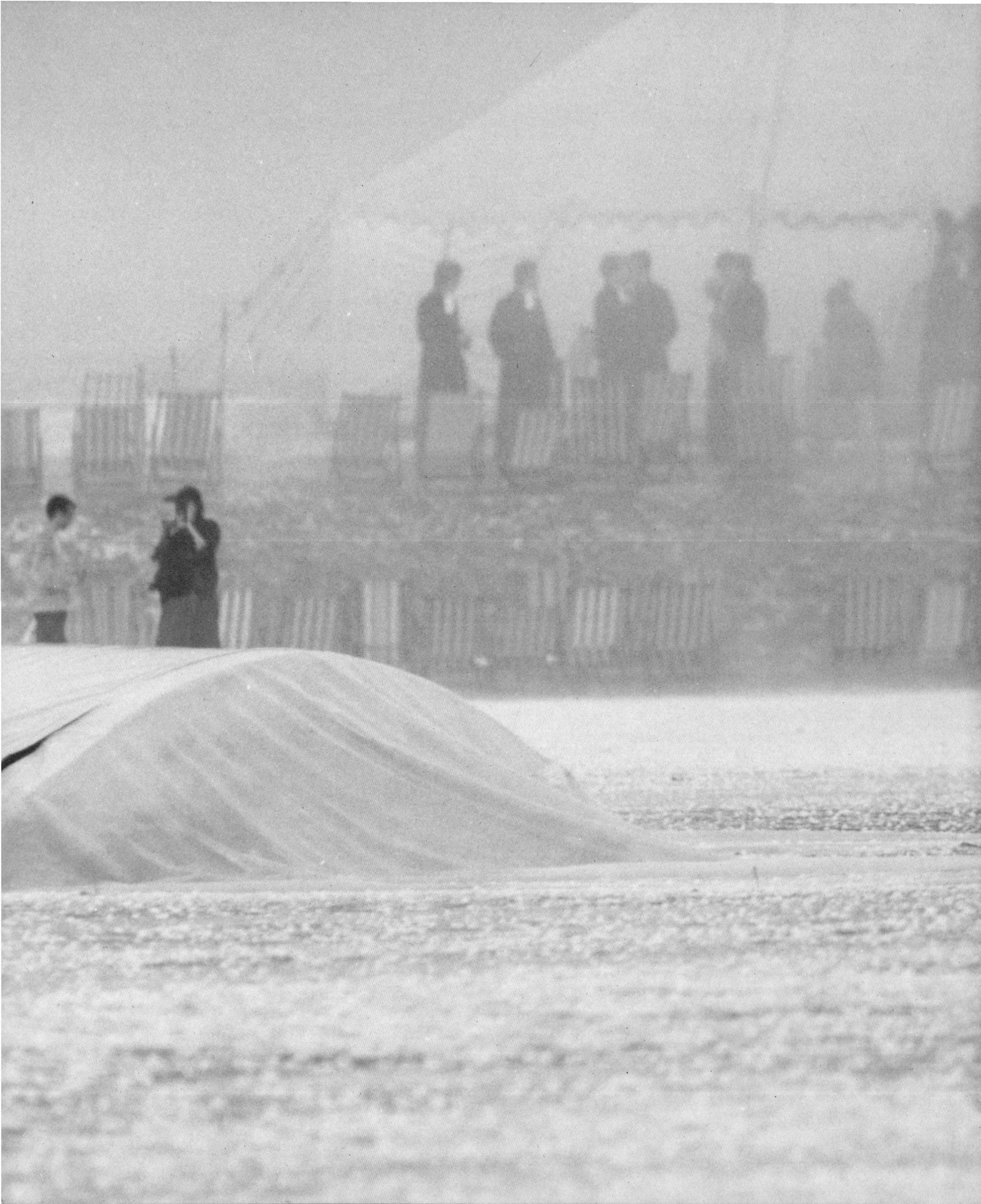